W9-ANV-426

LIBRARY
UNIVERSITY OF NEW HAVEN

STUDENTS, SOCIETY, AND POLITICS IN IMPERIAL GERMANY

STUDENTS, SOCIETY, AND POLITICS IN IMPERIAL GERMANY

The Rise of Academic Illiberalism

·   ·   ·

KONRAD H. JARAUSCH

PRINCETON UNIVERSITY PRESS
PRINCETON, NEW JERSEY

Copyright © 1982 by Princeton University Press

Published by Princeton University Press,
41 William Street, Princeton, New Jersey
In the United Kingdom: Princeton University Press, Guildford, Surrey

All Rights Reserved

Library of Congress Cataloging in Publication Data will be
found on the last printed page of this book

This book has been composed in Linotron Times Roman with Benguiat display

Clothbound editions of Princeton University Press books
are printed on acid-free paper, and binding materials are
chosen for strength and durability

Printed in the United States of America by Princeton
University Press, Princeton, New Jersey

LA
727
J36

Preface

FROM KARL SAND'S ASSASSINATION of the czarist informer August von Kotzebue in 1819 to Ulrike Meinhof's war on affluent authoritarianism in 1968, German students have made headlines with their penchant for left-wing terrorism. Yet their participation in the vigilante murders of Weimar republicans like Walter Rathenau and the Nazi Student League takeover of student government two years before the party's seizure of political power in 1933 indicate that German academic youths have embraced right-wing extremism with equal enthusiasm. From the time of the Humboldtian reforms in the early nineteenth century, outcries about student activism have been accompanied by recurrent complaints about educational inequality, culminating in the controversy over the educational emergency (*Bildungsnotstand*) of the 1960s. Government attempts to broaden the elite basis of higher education by making the university accessible to the underprivileged strata have repeatedly produced academic unemployment and subsequent pressure for protectionist restrictions to prevent the rise of a politically volatile academic proletariat. The recent catchwords of "loyalty checks" for state employment (*Berufsverbot*) and "teacher surplus" (*Lehrerschwemme*) demonstrate that neither the problem of student radicalism nor the issue of educational elitism has been resolved successfully. A historical case study of one crucial phase of the development of activism and inequality should bring their dynamics and interrelationship into clearer focus and thereby add some sense of perspective to the inconclusive policy debates. Such an analysis requires a fresh approach to the history of higher education—not another look down from professorial and administrative heights, but a view up from the objects of education, the students, as they act and react to institutions and ideologies.

The endemic social and political problems of higher education in Central Europe attracted my interest for both personal and scholarly reasons. The conflict between academic elitism and social mobility played itself out in my own home, for my mother descended from generations of scholars and clerics, while my father came from petit bourgeois origins, despite his doctorate from the University of Berlin. The political failure of the neohumanist tradition when confronted with the Third Reich is still evident in his writings on Protestant pedagogy, particularly the articles in the journal *Schule und Evangelium*, which he edited. Whenever I reread his wartime letters from Russia, where he died while fighting for the rights of prisoners of war, I am struck by the question: How could such a humane and cultivated man fall prey to volkish neoconservatism and fail to offer a viable alternative to national socialism? From my own postwar education in the humanist Ernst Moritz Arndt Gymnasium in Krefeld in the Rhineland, I remember a sense of cultural excellence and a feeling of social superiority without much concern for the problems of the modern world or vital democratic commitment. While the student activism of the 1960s dramatized the questions about the relationship of higher education and politics in the United States, my experience as visiting professor at the Universität des Saarlandes underscored that despite the social reforms of the early 1970s, the ideological polarization of German society continues to render the emergence of a liberal academic climate difficult.

Often neglected, the relationship between university, society, and polity makes up one important strand of the German problem. My earlier research on the European response to Adolf Hitler's seizure of power convinced me that literal examination of diplomatic and domestic documents has only limited explanatory power and that one needs to look beneath the surface of politics into the social and ideological forces shaping men and events. During my work on Theobald von Bethmann Hollweg, the most academic of the imperial chancellors, I was astounded by the narrowness of the choices perceived by the ruling elites. The diary of his assistant, Kurt Riezler, vividly demonstrates that even the modernist segment of educated Germans, while more flexible in its political means (liberal imperialism), was incapable of a fundamental critique of the Bismarckian system, for it shared many of the authoritarian prejudices of the traditionalists. Because so many of the key decision makers in government, the bureaucracy, and the Reichstag between 1914 and 1945 were educated in Imperial Germany, one significant clue to the "unspoken assumptions" of these leaders might be found in their last common life experience, their student years at the university. Another important key to their collective behavior might lie in the structural transformation of higher learning, which fundamentally altered the number, demographic selection, social recruitment, and career patterns of German academics after unification in 1871. Thus, the *trahison des clercs* of the cultured during the Weimar Republic and the Third Reich was not only a reaction to the immediate problems of the day, but also a result of the dual social restructuring and political reversal of the educated from the liberal nationalism of the first half of the nineteenth century to the national socialism of the first half of the twentieth century. Because I have explored some of the methodological problems in previous articles and assembled quantitative tools in an earlier volume, the present study attempts to explore the pattern, causes, and consequences of this momentous social transformation and ideological *Tendenzwende*.

Such an inquiry raises the issue of the social conditions and political results of liberal education in general. The German conception of neohumanist cultivation (*Bildung*) is only one version of a wider Western ideal of elite higher education, steeped in the classics and directed toward non-utilitarian goals. Based on industrialization or democratization, reformist demands for the expansion of educational opportunity for the underprivileged posed major social and political problems for every European country in the second half of the nineteenth century. The transition from a liberal phase of competitive opportunities, which in fact camouflages elite recruitment with meritocratic rhetoric, to a social democratic phase of welfare-supported educational mobility for the lower-middle and lower classes has yet to be achieved completely. Moreover, the political content of classical liberal education varies greatly over time and place. In many instances there is little relationship between a cultivated taste and liberal politics; neohumanism does not always mean humaneness. Even where the connection is close, the ideological interpretations of what is to be considered as man's essence differ sharply. Hence, the social and political transformation of liberal education needs to be examined in a series of comparative studies in order to bring the limitations of the nineteenth-century elitist vision of neoclassical training into sharper focus. Although budget-minded administrators consider liberal education less relevant than professional training, published research, or demonstrable service, the German example illustrates the grave dangers of a purely scientific or technical higher education. Instead of leading to resignation in the face of mounting doubts and difficulties, the present crisis should prompt a reexamination of the broader purpose of the humanities and a rededication to those egalitarian and democratic values that are vital to the survival of a free society.

ONLY a few of the many debts incurred in such a long and complex enterprise can be acknowledged publicly. The generous financial support of the Alexander von Humboldt Stiftung, the American Council of Learned Societies, the American Philosophical Society, and the University of Missouri Research Council made various stages of the research possible. The gracious hospitality of the Woodrow Wilson International Center for Scholars in Washington and a Rockefeller Humanities Fellowship facilitated the actual writing. The unselfish help of Herr Waldmann at the Zentrales Staatsarchiv Merseburg, Drs. Trumpp and Buchmann at the Bundesarchiv Coblenz, Dr. Wreden at the Bundesarchiv Aussenstelle Frankfurt, Dipl. Hist. Kossack at the Archive of the Humboldt University, Dr. Schmidt at the University Archive Bonn, Dr. Leist at the University Archive Marburg, and Dr. Angerer of the Institut für Hochschulkunde facilitated the gathering of documentary evidence. The frank criticism of B. vom Brocke, M. Heinemann, H. Kaelble, P. Lundgreen, D. K. Müller, T. Nipperdey, the QUANTUM group, W. Schieder, P. Baumgart, and H.-U. Wehler in Germany and the suggestions of J. Craig, G. Feldmann, T. S. Hamerow, J. F. Harris, A. Heidenheimer, M. Kater, L. Krieger, V. A. Lidtke, C. E. McClelland as well as Lawrence Stone's guidance at the Davis Center in this country improved many portions of the manuscript. I am equally grateful to W. König, H. Schilling, W. Kamphoefner, and T. Baldeh for their technical help. At the risk of straining the reader's credulity with yet another tribute to that exalted but elusive species, the academic wife, I do want to thank Hannelore Louise Flessa-Jarausch for her intellectual, emotional, and physical sustenance in this project. Finally, I hope that when my sons Tino and Peter go to college they may still experience something of *Die alte Burschenherrlichkeit*, which inspired the famous verse:

> *Gaudeamus igitur, iuvenes dum sumus!*
> *Post iucundam iuventutem, post molestam senectutem*
> *Nos habebit humus, nos habebit humus!*

Contents

Preface   v
List of Figures   xi
List of Tables   xii
Glossary   xiii
Abbreviations   xv

One • In the National Spirit   3
    An Academic Mission   6
    Approaches to the Problem   13

Two • The Enrollment Explosion   23
    Dynamics of Expansion   27
    Causes of Growth   32
    Problematic Consequences   49

Three • The Social Transformation   78
    Neohumanist Patterns   81
    Demographic Trends   90
    Social Changes   114
    Faculty Structures   134

Four • The Teaching of Politics   160
    Implications of Cultivation   165
    Ceremonial Speeches   174
    Scholarly Lectures   189
    Political Instruction   206

Five • The Hidden Curriculum   234
    Corporate Subculture   239
    Organizational Developments   262
    Societal Settings   294

Six • The Politics of Academic Youth   333
    Constraints on Activism   336
    Varieties of Nationalism   345
    Student Self-Government   367

Seven · For Kaiser and Reich   393
    Students at War   394
    Sources of Illiberalism   399
    Academic Continuities   416

A Note on Sources   426
Index   431

List of Figures

2.1   Student Enrollment in Imperial Germany   28
2.2   Fields of Study in the Nineteenth Century   29
3.1   Levels of Cultivation in Prussia, 1911   88
3.2   Geographic Distribution of Bonn Students   95
3.3   Religious Denomination of Bonn Students   98
3.4   Type of High School of Bonn Students   101
3.5   Economic Function of Bonn Students   117
3.6   Fathers' Social Class of Bonn Students   128

List of Tables

2-1	Sources of Enrollment Growth	39
2-2	Overcrowding of Academic Fields in Prussia	55
2-3	Prussian Academic Professions, 1852-1907	71
3-1	Matriculation Age of German University Students	92
3-2	Urbanization of Bonn Students	94
3-3	Religion of Prussian Students	97
3-4	Social Origin of School-Reform Petitioners, 1888	105
3-5	Female Students in Prussia, 1896-97	111
3-6	Economic Origins of Prussian Students	118
3-7	Fathers' Generic Professions at Bonn, 1865-1914	124
3-8	Social Origin of Students at Berlin, Bonn, Leipzig, and Tübingen	125
3-9	Most Frequent Fathers' Professions at Bonn	127
3-10	Educational Opportunities in Prussia	130
3-11	Fields of Study at German Universities	136
3-12	Demographic Structure of Bonn Faculties	138
3-13	Social Composition of Bonn Faculties	141
3-14	Father's Profession and Field of Study at Bonn	152
4-1	Social Origins of German University Professors	168
5-1	Local Student Organization Membership at Marburg, Berlin, and Bonn	296
5-2	Number of National Student Organization Chapters	300
5-3	Distribution of Student Organizations in 1914	303
5-4	Membership in National Student Organizations	306
5-5	Demographic Characteristics of Marburg Student Organizations	308
5-6	Social Structure of Marburg Student Associations	312
5-7	Student Body Structure of Bonn and Marburg	315
5-8	Fields of Study of Marburg Student Associations	318
5-9	Careers of Alumni of Student Associations	322
5-10	Corporation Members in the Reichstag, 1903-12	326
6-1	Student Councils at German Universities	382

Glossary

Abitur   final high-school examination
Akademiker   graduate of German-speaking university
Alte Herren   Old Boys of student corporations
Arbeiterunterrichtskurse   workingmen's courses, taught by students
Auslandsstudien   international studies
Beamter   state official
Berechtigung   entitlement to job, education
Besitz   property
Bildung   cultivation
Bürgertum   middle class
Bursch   antiquated term for student
Burschenschaft   national and liberal student organization; member called *Büchsier*
Corps   exclusive, traditional student corporation; member called *Corpsier*
deutschnational   German nationalist
Doktor   doctorate, chief university degree
Ehrengericht   student honor court
Einjähriges   privilege of one-year volunteer (*freiwillige*) military service
Festreden   ceremonial speeches
Freistudenten   independent students, also called *Finken*
Gebildete   cultivated
Gelehrter   scholar
Gymnasium   classical, neohumanist secondary school
Habilitation   qualification for university teaching
Hochschule   institution of higher learning, usually not a university
Immaturi   students without an *Abitur*
Kathedersozialist   academic proponent of social policy
Komment   student custom
Kommers   formal drinking bout
Kommilitone   fellow student
Kränzchen   study circle
Kultur   German notion of culture; often contrasted with civilization
Lebensprinzip   principle of lifelong membership in a corporation
Lehrplan   government teaching plan

Lehr- und Lernfreiheit   freedom of teaching and learning; also *akademische Freiheit*

Lesehalle   student library

Matrikel   matriculation register

Mensur   ritualized mock duel

Mittelstand   (lower) middle class, divided into old (*Alt*) or new (*Neu*)

Mittlere Reife   intermediate maturity certificate (after 6 years)

Oberrealschule   most modern high-school type

Oberlehrer(in)   high-school teacher with academic training

Ordinarius   full professor

Philister   graduated academic, philistine

Politikvorlesung   lecture on politics

Privatdozent   lecturer

Rat   councillor (functional as in *Landrat* or honorary as in *Kommerzienrat*)

Realgymnasium   hybrid traditional and modern secondary school

Rechtsstaat   state characterized by the rule of law

Referendar   probationary legal trainee

Rektor   university president, elected yearly by the *Senat*

satisfaktionsfähig   capable of defending his honor by the sword

Schulkonferenz   school conference

staatsbürgerliche Erziehung   civics, also called *Bürgerkunde*

staatserhaltend   loyal

Staatsexamen   state examination (professional degree)

Stand   estate, later narrowed to profession (*Berufsstand*); hence, *standesgemäss*: socially appropriate

Studentenausschuss   student council, sometimes also called *Studentenschaft*

Technische Hochschule   technical college

Universitätsstatistik   university census

Verbindung   student association; *schlagend*: duelling, *farbentragend*: color-carrying

Verein Deutscher Studenten   anti-Semitic student society, sometimes called *Kyffhäuser-Verband*

Vertreterprinzip   representation principle of free students

Verruf   custom of student ostracism

Volk   cultural or racial people rather than political nation

Vorschriften für die Studierenden   Prussian student regulations

Waffenstudent   duelling student

Wandervogel   life-reform youth movement

Weltpolitik   world policy

Wissenschaft   science or scholarship

Abbreviations

ABl   *Akademische Blätter* (VDSt)

Ac   *Academia* (CV)

AH   *Stenographische Berichte über die Verhandlungen des Preussischen Abgeordnetenhauses*

AHR   *American Historical Review*

AMbl   *Akademische Monatsblätter* (KV)

AMh   *Akademische Monatshefte* (Corps)

AR Akademische Rundschau (Freistudentenschaft)

ATZ   *Akademische Turnerzeitung* (VC)

BA   Bundesarchiv Koblenz

BAF   Bundesarchiv Aussenstelle Frankfurt

BBl   *Burschenschaftliche Blätter* (Burschenschaft)

BSSt   *Badische Schulstatistik*

BUA   Bonn University Archive

BuBü   *Burschenschaftliche Bücherei*

CCA   Corps Convent Archiv

CEH   *Central European History*

CER   *Comparative Education Review*

CSSH   *Comparative Studies in Society and History*

DZA Po   Deutsches Zentralarchiv Potsdam

DH   *Deutsche Historiker*

FBl   *Finkenblätter* (Freistudentenschaft)

FR   *Freistudentische Rundschau* (Freistudentenschaft)

GG   *Geschichte und Gesellschaft*

GWU   *Geschichte in Wissenschaft und Unterricht*

HEQ   *History of Education Quarterly*

HH   *Stenographische Berichte über die Verhandlungen des Preussischen Herrenhauses*

HSR   *Historical Social Research*

HUA   Humboldt University Archive

HUB   Humboldt Universitäts Bibliothek

HZ   Historische Zeitschrift

IASL   *Internationales Archiv für Sozialgeschichte der deutschen Literatur*

IESS   *International Encyclopedia of the Social Sciences*

IHK   Institut für Hochschulkunde (Würzburg)

IZEBF   Informationen zur Erziehungs- und Bildungshistorischen Forschung

JCEA   Journal for Central European Affairs

JCH   Journal of Contemporary History

JMH   Journal of Modern History

JSH   Journal of Social History

KCBl   Kartell-Convent Blätter (Jewish)

KZ   Kyffhäuser Zeitung

KZfSS   Kölner Zeitschrift für Soziologie und Sozialpsychologie

MUA   Marburg University Archive

NAZ   Norddeutsche Allgemeine Zeitung

NBZ   Neue Bonner Zeitung

NPL   Neue Politische Literatur

PrGStA   Preussisches Geheimes Staatsarchiv at Dahlem

PrJhb   Preussische Jahrbücher

PrSt   Preussische Statistik

RHZ   Rheinische Hochschulzeitung (Freistudentenschaft)

SA   Sozialistischer Akademiker (socialist students)

SSH   Social Science History

StdtR   Statistik des deutschen Reiches

VA   Vivat Academia

VJHfZG   Vierteljahrshefte für Zeitgeschichte

VSWG   Vierteljahrschrift für Sozial- und Wirtschaftsgeschichte

WBl   Wingolfsblätter (Wingolf)

ZfP   Zeitschrift für Pädagogik

ZStA Me   Zentrales Staatsarchiv Merseburg

STUDENTS,
SOCIETY, AND
POLITICS IN
IMPERIAL
GERMANY

One

IN THE NATIONAL SPIRIT

BANNERS WAVED, caps flew into the air, sabres gleamed, and a thousand-voiced "Hurrah!" rang through the stately park of Schloss Friedrichsruh. Massive, white-haired, and commanding, Prince Otto von Bismarck stepped to the balustrade to accept the homage of German students on his eightieth birthday. Flanked by the university rectors in their red, violet, and gold gowns, he listened to the oration of A. Bruch, a *Burschenschafter* from Bonn: "On this festive day, when joy resounds from mountain to sea, the German student community deeply feels the holy national duty to present its heartiest congratulations to Your Serene Highness in reverent tribute. The enthusiastic sympathy welling up in our hearts is but a faint echo of our love for Germany's greatest son, of our indelible gratitude and glowing adoration for the brilliant creator and heroic chancellor of our powerfully united empire." In rapt attention, university and technical students alike awaited Bruch's peroration. "Solemnly we vow: German academic youth will bravely seek to maintain and zealously attempt to complete the work to which Your Serene Highness has dedicated the untiring and unselfish efforts of his fruitful life."[1] Waves of thunderous applause from the enthusiastic crowd drowned out the concluding tributes to the Iron Chancellor.

When the tumult subsided, Bismarck began to reply, haltingly at first, then eloquently, inspired by his audience: "I accept your greetings as the pledge of the future, which someone of my age values perhaps even more than the need for recognition. Many of you will be able to act upon the sentiments that your presence reveals far into the new century, while I, long condemned to inactivity, belong to the past. That is a consolation to me, because the German character does not usually disown the enthusiasms

---

[1] W. Siemering, *Die Huldigungsfahrt der deutschen Studentenschaft zum Fürsten Bismarck am 1. April 1895* (Berlin, 1895), pp. 20-40 is the printed prize essay on the homage. See also G. L. Mosse, *The Nationalization of the Masses* (New York, 1975), pp. 75ff. For the sake of brevity, citations are by and large cumulative, with sources listed in order of appearance in the preceding text.

of its youth." More pointedly, he confessed his faith in the political views of the students: "In forty to sixty years you will probably not have exactly the same opinions that you hold today, but the seed that the rule of Kaiser William I has planted in your young hearts will continue to bear fruit, and no matter what form our state institutions will have assumed when you are old, your point of view will still be national-German, because that is what it is today." After general reflections on the difficulty of achieving positive goals in politics, he complimented the universities for "keeping the flame of German unity alive for centuries." Implicitly warning against the adventurism of William II, the exchancellor struck a conservative note: "Let us above all keep what we have before we attempt new tasks." Accepting the cleavages within German society and the need for political struggle, he concluded with a rousing appeal for the preservation of this heritage: "In all conflicts that endanger national unity, there must be a rallying point! This is the empire, not as we might perhaps wish it, but as it exists, the empire and the emperor who embodies it. . . . May those of you who are still alive in the year 1950 join wholeheartedly in the cheer: 'Long live Kaiser and Reich!' " Once again the applause was deafening. Men were not ashamed to weep. In this solemn hour, many vowed to "carry out the words of this magnificent man" and joined in the hymn:

> Our peacemaker on land and sea,
> Smith of the Kaiser's sword,
> Flagbearer for the imperial lord:
> Bismarck, we hail to thee![2]

The patriotic celebration culminated that same evening of 1 April 1895 in a *Kommers* in Hamburg, nourished by streams of beer and encouraged by the well-dressed ladies in the galleries. Speaking for the 5,250 pilgrims, law student Dertz, a member of the Verein Deutscher Studenten of Göttingen, acclaimed the chancellor a true man of the people: "Bismarck represents what our people call heroic and great, what they want to become, their ideal!" After thundering toasts, the customary salute to the fair sex, and the obligatory telegram to the Kaiser, Hamburg burgomaster Mönckeberg defined the political purpose of the assembly: "There is a saying that tomorrow belongs to the young; I want to add: In Germany, he who commands the allegiance of academic youth possesses the future. Therefore, we adults look confidently ahead. We know that German students will forever follow the banner that Prince Bismarck has raised. They will defend the unity, power, honor, and greatness of our fatherland." A new

[2] Siemering, *Huldigungsfahrt*, pp. 21-24, third verse of the prize poem of H. Schmieden. Most translations are my own, but wherever contemporary versions exist, they are used, even if their diction is sometimes awkwardly Victorian.

round of cheers greeted this tribute to academic leadership and national fervor. But stronger words yet came from the philosopher Wilhelm Windelband of the University of Strassburg, the newest bastion of German scholarship, who extolled Bismarck as "the greatest German student of this century, the honorary doctor of numerous faculties, the mightiest teacher of our entire people, a true *praeceptor Germaniae*, the most successful professor of Germanics." Hurling protests against the Catholic, Progressive, and Socialist naysayers of the Reichstag (who had refused to participate in the celebration), he vocalized the unquestioning self-confidence of Wilhelmian academics: "Verily, a nation whose youth can rouse itself for a great man and his manifest ideals—such a people is sure of its future."[3]

This homage to the Iron Chancellor, the largest and most united student demonstration of the Second Empire, was a tangible expression of the pervasive Bismarck cult, which ultimately attracted almost all German academics. It had been launched on the chancellor's seventieth birthday with flaming invocations of a new, anti-Semitic, imperialist, and social-Christian nationalism by the historian Heinrich von Treitschke, the imperial court chaplain, Adolph Stöcker, and the Vereine Deutscher Studenten.[4] Trying to live down their radical past, the Burschenschaften later joined this agitation and honored their former enemy for finally realizing, "albeit in another manner and through other ways, the ideal that the Burschenschaft first put before the people." Basking in this tribute, Bismarck ironically allowed that "the basic difference lies only in the means and not in the goals," and that he merely disliked the Burschenschaft's social tone and not its political philosophy.[5] At the same time, the elitist Corps, which "*der tolle Otto*" had found more congenial during his student years at Göttingen in the 1830s, began to claim the exchancellor as one of their own: "We thank God that Your Serene Highness has sprung from the core of our beautiful national student culture . . . that you have succeeded in unifying the nation and in founding the imperial crown on the *rocher de bronze* of the Hohenzollerns and thereby erected a monument more permanent than any other."[6] The implicitly democratic, uncommitted students

[3] Ibid., pp. 26-33.
[4] For the background of the homages, see H. von Petersdorff, *Die Vereine Deutscher Studenten: Zwölf Jahre akademischer Kämpfe* (Leipzig, 1900, 3rd ed.), pp. 193ff. See also *ABl* 10 (1895), nos. 1-2.
[5] "Von den Alten Herrn," *BBl* 9 (1895): 138-40. For further background, see also O. Oppermann, *Die Burschenschaft Alemannia zu Bonn und ihre Vorläufer* (Bonn, 1925), 2: 1-65.
[6] "Aus dem Leben und Treiben der Alten Herren," *AMh* 12 (1895): 83f. The Old Boys meekly listened to his critique of dissipation ("I would have studied more and made fewer debts, if I had not belonged") as long as the chancellor affirmed: "If I were to go to the university today, I would once again join a Corps; its members stick together more."

were swept along in the floodtide of nationalism, and only the Catholic corporations refused to participate, because it would show "a lack of character of the first order and contradict our tradition." As their opposition was directed only against Bismarck as initiator of the *Kulturkampf*, not against him as the symbol of unification, Catholic organizations reversed themselves and joined the nationalist academic front just before World War I. Only a handful of socialist students continued to stand apart: "Reared in servility and having too quickly abandoned its enthusiasm for liberty, youth, the hope of Germany, sides with the betrayers against the betrayed."[7]

AN ACADEMIC MISSION

The strident self-congratulatory rhetoric of the Bismarck homages was echoed in other Western universities, for academics generally considered themselves special guardians of the national spirit. Despite its classical training, the European cultivated elite at the turn of the century was hardly cosmopolitan, egalitarian, or liberal. Many professors, like the French historian Ernest Lavisse, propagated a fervent nationalism that exceeded simple patriotism and verged on chauvinism. While a socially concerned minority opposed the lure of empire, the majority embraced a cultural or economic imperialism, stressing the *mission civilisatrice* toward the heathens and savages in the colonies. Even American academics tempered their "spirit of service" with a dash of elitism: "The college is not for the majority who carry forward the common labor of the world," said Woodrow Wilson at his inauguration as president of Princeton: "It is for the minority who plan, who conceive, who superintend, who mediate between group and group and must see the wide stage as a whole." Such social superiority was frequently combined with scientific racism, which "proved" the inferiority of Jews and blacks in the firm conviction that "intelligence and temperament are racially determined and unalterable." While anti-Semitism was largely a matter of social tone and rarely as explicit as during the Dreyfus Affair in France, "the superiority of the Anglo-Saxon" or other whites over lesser breeds was rarely questioned in cultivated circles. Thus, the political temper of the educated was generally conservative in national issues and paternalistic toward students, exceptions like the radical circles at the Ecole Normale notwithstanding. Though

---

[7] Renner, "Cartellverband und Bismarckhuldigung," *Ac* 9 (1895): 243-44, and 27 (1914), no. 3. Quote from the *Sozialistische Akademiker*, in F. Schulze and P. Ssymank, *Das deutsche Studententum* (Munich, 1932, 4th ed.), pp. 366-67. For the anglicization of such terms as *Festschrift*, see *Webster's Third New International Dictionary of the English Language, Unabridged* (Springfield, Mass., 1968). More specialized German terms, such as *Bildung*, are italicized at their first appearance and explained in the glossary.

universally praised, the principle of academic freedom was threatened by "reactionary and visionless" boards of trustees in the United States, challenged by centralized bureaucratic control in France, and undermined by clubbish snobbery and vested interests in Britain. Although the party politics of the cultivated varied widely, the political attitudes of higher learning at the turn of the century were hardly devoted solely to "the discovery and the promulgation of truth."[8]

In this general academic desertion of liberalism, German higher education constitutes a particularly illustrative case because of its scientific leadership around 1900 and the drastic political consequences that followed. While the nobility was preoccupied with patrimonial and dynastic concerns, the commercial middle class championed local and regional enterprises, and the small-town burghers could hardly see farther than their parish steeple, the educated jettisoned cosmopolitanism in favor of the new gospel of nationalism and became spokesmen for the unification of the cultural *Volk* into a political nation. Prussian historians from Treitschke to Friedrich Meinecke never tired of recounting how valiantly academics had fought against Napoleon in the Wars of Liberation, how steadfastly the Burschenschaft had struggled against Restoration after 1819, how gallantly the professorial parliament had crossed swords with the European powers during the Revolution of 1848, and how dramatically the Progressives had wrestled with the crown during the constitutional conflict. Although individual instances (such as the role of the Lützow free corps) were undoubtedly exaggerated, this *kleindeutsch* version of history correctly emphasized that despite all religious, regional, and ideological differences, the educated had rallied more emphatically around the national standard than any other group.[9] But the belated and incomplete nature of the German unification from above gave a peculiarly insecure and impatient

[8] S. T. Gershman, "Ernest Lavisse and the Uses of Nationalism: 1870-1914" (dissertation, University of Missouri, 1979); L. R. Vesey, *The Emergence of the American University* (Chicago, 1965), 279ff.; R. Hofstadter and W. Smith, *American Higher Education: A Documentary History* (Chicago, 1961) 2: 684-95, 854, 883-92; T. F. Gosset, *Race: The History of an Idea in America* (Dallas, 1963), pp. 253-338; R. J. Smith, "L'Atmosphère politique à l'École Normale Supérieure à la fin du XIXe siècle," *Revue d'histoire moderne et contemporaine* 20 (1973): 248-68; A. Prost, *L'Enseignement en France 1800-1967* (Paris, 1968), pp. 223ff.; M. Sanderson, ed., *The Universities in the Nineteenth Century* (London, 1975), pp. 145, 187, 232; and A. J. Engel, "From Clergyman to Don: The Rise of the Academic Profession in Nineteenth-Century Oxford" (dissertation, Princeton University, 1975). Since an explicit treatment would have swelled the size even further, the comparative perspective must remain largely implicit in this study.

[9] The exaggeration of the role of the academics began with the Borussian historians of Treitschke's stripe and maintained itself in the textbooks until the ninth edition of Gebhardt's *Handbuch der deutschen Geschichte* (Stuttgart, 1970), edited by H. Grundmann, 3: 55-59, 107-13, 132-39, 167-75. See also G. G. Iggers, *Deutsche Geschichtswissenschaft: Eine Kritik der traditionellen Geschichtsauffassung von Herder bis zur Gegenwart* (Munich, 1971).

flavor to the academics' perception of their national mission, in contrast to the self-assured chauvinism of the educated in other European countries. While it would be accepting their own exaggerated sense of self-importance at face value to consider the "German mandarins" responsible for all important decisions, the academics were quite significant in defining the climate within which crucial policies were determined and implemented.[10]

Implicit in their claim to custody of the national shrine was the elite status of university graduates (collectively known as *Akademiker*), which had been achieved in the early nineteenth century during the transition from an estate (birth) to a class (wealth) society. By substituting cultivation for lineage, the academics challenged the nobles for control of the Prussian bureaucracy, for educational qualification made for a more efficient leadership criterion in an industrializing society than inherited privilege. Although the graduates of the neohumanist secondary school (*Gymnasium*) were also considered cultivated (*Gebildete*), the university alumni formed the core of the educated middle class, the *Bildungsbürgertum*, setting the cultural and political tone of this social stratum, for the Gymnasium teachers were trained at the university. The particular sequence of German modernization—bureaucracy preceding industry, parliamentary government, or unity—gave the educated the political lead in the struggle between middle class and aristocracy; only in the middle decades of the nineteenth century was this leadership shared by the commercial and industrial middle class.[11] Even if the process of their professionalization is still somewhat indistinct, many university graduates in law, medicine, and college teaching (as well as some divines) attained an elevated social position, either through the borrowed nimbus of the bureaucracy or through the substitution of scholarly learning for religious revelation in a secularizing society. In principle egalitarian (open to anyone of sufficient ability), the educated class formed, in practice, a stratum that sought to perpetuate itself by turning its cultivation into a guarded possession, ostensibly based on merit.

---

[10] H. Plessner, *Die verspätete Nation: Über die politische Verführbarkeit des bürgerlichen Geistes* (Dillingen, 1959); F. K. Ringer, *The Decline of the German Mandarins* (Cambridge, Mass., 1969). For Max Weber's distinction between German *Akademiker* and Chinese mandarins, see H. H. Gerth and C. Wright Mills, *From Max Weber: Essays in Sociology* (New York, 1958), pp. 240-44, 426-44.

[11] H. Gerth, *Die sozialgeschichtliche Lage der bürgerlichen Intelligenz um die Wende des 18. Jahrhunderts* (dissertation, Frankfurt, 1935); H. Holborn, "German Idealism in the Light of Social History," in *Germany and Europe* (Garden City, 1971), pp. 1-31; and L. O'Boyle, "Klassische Bildung und soziale Struktur in Deutschland zwischen 1800 und 1848," *HZ* 207 (1968): 584-608.

Although the Akademiker have been generally neglected by social historians, they did play a special role in Central Europe, because they formed a more cohesive social type than the educated in the West.[12]

The ideal that animated the educated was the notion of cultivation (as *Bildung* is imperfectly rendered) rather than the companion concept of scholarship (as *Wissenschaft* might be translated). For Wilhelm von Humboldt, the true aim of man was "the highest and most harmonious development of his physical and mental faculties"; cultivation was not a means to a better life but an end in itself, an unfolding of the personality to its full potential. A curious blend of individualism, idealism, and neohumanism, Bildung postulated "improvement of our inner selves" as the path toward true humanity and focused on cultural rather than political progress. It could be achieved by steeping oneself in scholarship (*Bildung durch Wissenschaft*), imbuing it with a pedagogical purpose and linking cultivation to institutions of higher learning rather than to circles or salons of like-minded intellectuals.[13] Initially this ideal had "liberal and humane" overtones, for it sought "to enable the individual to make use of his freedom" and thereby throw off the shackles of estate society (codified for the last time in the Prussian Code of 1794) by postulating all men as at least potentially equal. Instead of enlarging man's practical capacities and encyclopedic knowledge in the manner of the Enlightenment, Bildung intended to refine the human soul through an appreciation of the texts and artifacts of Rome or, preferably, Greece. Although in the genre of the *Bildungsroman* this notion achieved a quasi-mystical hold on German thought, the concept suffered from internal contradictions: humanism versus humaneness, elitism versus egalitarianism, classicism versus modernism, privatism versus political responsibility. These conflicts were further aggravated by bureaucratic institutionalization and repressive administration after the fall of the Prussian reformers. Even if during the course of the century it became romanticized, diluted, and externalized, cultivation continued to dominate the rhetoric and practice of higher education sufficiently to imbue German academics with a distinctive cultural style.[14]

[12] K. H. Jarausch, "Die Neuhumanistische Universität und die bürgerliche Gesellschaft, 1800-1860," *Darstellungen und Quellen zur Geschichte der deutschen Einheitsbewegung im 19. und 20. Jahrhundert* 11 (1980): 11-58. See also F. K. Ringer, "The German Academic Community, 1871-1914," *IASL* 3 (1978): 108-29.

[13] K. H. Jarausch, "*Menschenbildung* as Bourgeois Ideal: The Social Role of the Neohumanist Prussian University" (unpublished paper, Princeton University, 1971); and W. H. Bruford, *The German Tradition of Self-Cultivation: 'Bildung' from Humboldt to Thomas Mann* (New York, 1975).

[14] R. Vierhaus, "Bildung," in W. Conze, ed., *Geschichtliche Grundbegriffe* (Stuttgart, 1972), pp. 508-51; and Fritz Ringer's essay review on Bruford's *The German Tradition of Self-Cultivation* in *CEH* 11 (1978): 107-13.

The institution that molded successive student generations into Aka-demiker, sharing a broad similarity in social background and a related ethos of Bildung, was the German university. Half a century after the Prussian reforms, it was approaching the zenith of its international scientific reputation, demonstrated by the number of foreign students and by the most sincere form of flattery, imitation abroad.[15] Although the twenty institutions differed widely in size, religious composition, and regional tradition, the *peregrinatio academica* of students and the practice of com-petitive hiring of faculty had created something like a national system of higher education even before the country was politically unified. Justly famous for developing the modern research imperative, based on the ad-vancement of philology and the expansion of natural science and medicine, the university provided the majority of students with training for specific professions, such as clergyman, lawyer, doctor, and Gymnasium teacher. When Prince Metternich tried to restrict public discussion during the Res-toration era, universities offered an important refuge for political debate and thereby facilitated the growth of German liberalism and nationalism far beyond the restricted membership of the Burschenschaft. Through the dreaded state examinations (administered by a committee largely made up of professors), the university controlled entry into the liberal professions and government service, which were linked to higher education by the rigid standards for qualification (*Berechtigungen*) that entitled specific de-grees to particular jobs.[16] Through general or liberal education it influenced the collective mentality of the Akademiker, since the university was the last shared institution of their lifetime. Although formally somewhat intrac-table, informally the university proved a quick conductor of new intellectual fashions and trends, such as the debate over socialism in the 1880s and the discussion of imperialism in the 1890s. Even if the university was as often a battleground as an influential force, the triple task of advancing scholarship, training professionals, and liberally educating the elite made it the central cultural institution of nineteenth-century Germany.[17]

[15] Because of the lack of comprehensive university historiography, the standard work is still Friedrich Paulsen, *Geschichte des gelehrten Unterrichts* (Berlin, 1921), 3rd expanded edition by R. Lehmann, especially vol. 2. See also W. Lexis, ed., *Die deutschen Uni-versitäten* (Berlin, 1893), 2 vols.

[16] R. Meyer, "Das Berechtigungswesen in seiner Bedeutung für Schule und Gesellschaft im 19. Jahrhundert," *Zeitschrift für die gesamte Staatswissenschaft* 12 (1968): 763-76 and A. J. Heidenheimer, "Education and Social Security Entitlements in Europe and America," in A. Heidenheimer and P. Flora, eds., *The Development of Welfare States in Europe and America* (New Brunswick, N.J., 1981), pp. 269ff.

[17] F. Schnabel, *Deutsche Geschichte im Neunzehnten Jahrhundert* (Freiburg, 1929-1936), especially vols. 1, *Die Grundlagen*, 408-57; 3, *Erfahrungswissenschaften und Technik*, 239ff.; and 4, *Die religiösen Kräfte*.

The general political outlook of the cultivated, fostered by neohumanist higher education, was an academic version of the liberalism of the middle class, called *Bildungsliberalismus*. Reflected in the advertising slogan of a popular library—"Cultivation makes free"—this attitude stressed the essential congruity between social progress, personal freedom, individual ability, national unity, and cultural enlightenment. Thus, academic liberalism was not a narrow commitment to a single party but rather a broad liberality of spirit, spanning the political spectrum from reforming conservatism and liberal Catholicism to constitutionalism or republicanism (with a few intellectuals even advocating social liberalism), all united in tolerance and openness to change, while disagreeing about actual political means. Even if the triumph of liberalism in Central Europe was never complete, from the prerevolutionary agitation to the constitutional conflict and the campaign for unification, its slogans and demands dominated the political agenda in the German Confederation and its member states, marking the peak of its relative influence. While Bildungsliberalismus never reached all academics (many of whom remained particularist, Protestant orthodox, or bureaucratically conservative), the most prominent spokesmen of the educated elites were liberals, and within the liberal movement academics played a larger part than in Western Europe, for the commercial-industrial bourgeoisie was less developed.[18] Although many professors quietly pursued Wissenschaft, their most celebrated representatives, like the Göttingen Seven, were liberal teachers, so much so that the revolutionary national assembly in Frankfurt was often derided as a "professors' parliament." Despite their declining political involvement, the professors' influence, through former pupils in the bureaucracy, remained considerable. The often forgotten university reform conferences during and immediately after the 1848 revolution testify to the strength of this Bildungsliberalismus among the faculty, even if bureaucratic reaction combined with the self-interest of full professors to prevent lasting changes. Among the students, the confused initial enthusiasm of the Burschenschaft (1815-19) and the revolutionary dabbling (around 1830) are better known than the liberal and democratic *Progress* agitation of the 1840s, which spilled over into the Corps and dominated the campus not only during the revolution itself but in its ideological aftereffects until the 1860s. Thus, in the

[18] L. Krieger, *The German Idea of Freedom: History of a Political Tradition* (Chicago, 1957); J. J. Sheehan, *German Liberalism in the Nineteenth Century* (Chicago, 1978), pp. 14-28, 40-48, 80-90; and R. S. Elkar, *Junges Deutschland in polemischem Zeitalter: Das schleswig-holsteinische Bildungsbürgertum in der ersten Hälfte des 19. Jahrhunderts* (Düsseldorf, 1979).

middle of the nineteenth century many German academics, though still politically divided, shared a broadly liberal mentality.[19]

Since by the time of the Weimar Republic the majority of the politically conscious Gebildete had become antidemocratic if not neoconservative, the crucial ideological reversal of academics occurred during the Second Empire. At the same time, the universities (first the students and then the professors) experienced a profound social transformation. Although enrollments continued to grow into the 1920s before stabilizing in the 1930s, the critical quantum jump in student numbers occurred after 1870, when small colleges became modern mass universities with all their problems: Berlin enrolled over 9,000 students on the eve of the First World War.[20] As the stagnation of the 1840s to 1860s had made the universities more exclusive, while the broadening of recruitment during the 1920s was undone by the restrictions of the Third Reich, the central social mutation of the student body also took place in the Second Reich.[21] While repressive administration had already begun to neutralize the liberal impulses implicit in neohumanist cultivation, after 1870 the inner erosion of Bildung hastened the deliberalization of professorial instruction and strengthened authoritarian patterns in academic thinking.[22] In contrast to the first decades of the nineteenth century, the political tone of student subculture shifted from left-wing to right-wing nationalism, thereby transferring the allegiance of the majority of adult academic professionals from various forms of liberal to a spectrum of antiliberal movements.[23] Thus, many of the answers to the riddle of how the liberal nationalist students of the Vormärz could become the vanguard of national socialism a century later must be sought in the complex relationship between higher education, society, and politics in the Second Empire. This obvious but hitherto ignored observation raises

[19] W. Jens, *Eine deutsche Universität: 500 Jahre Tübinger Gelehrtenrepublik* (Munich, 1977), pp. 236ff., 268ff.; E. J. Hahn, "The Junior Faculty in 'Revolt': Reform Plans for Berlin University in 1848," *AHR* 82 (1977): 875-95; K. Griewank, *Deutsche Studenten und Universitäten in der Revolution von 1848* (Weimar, 1949); and the rich evidence from the Bonn and Heidelberg university archives, cited in K. H. Jarausch, "The Sources of German Student Unrest, 1815-1848," in L. Stone, *The University in Society* (Princeton, 1974), 2: 533-69. For the continuation of professorial and student liberalism after the revolution, see below, Chapters 4 to 6.

[20] K. H. Jarausch, "Frequenz und Struktur: Zur Sozialgeschichte der Studenten im Kaiserreich," in P. Baumgart, ed., *Bildungspolitik in Preussen zur Zeit des Kaiserreichs* (Stuttgart, 1980), pp. 119-49.

[21] K. H. Jarausch, "The Social Transformation of the University: The Case of Prussia, 1865-1914," *JSH* 12 (1979): 609-36.

[22] K. H. Jarausch, "Studenten, Gesellschaft und Politik im Kaiserreich," *IZEBF* 3 (1976): 61-90.

[23] K. H. Jarausch, "Liberal Education as Illiberal Socialization: The Case of Students in Imperial Germany," *JMH* 50 (1978): 609-30.

a host of perplexing questions: What forces within or without the university account for the transformation? When did the crucial shifts take place? Who brought the changes about or benefited from them? Who opposed the reversal? What were the alternatives? Why did they fail?

APPROACHES TO THE PROBLEM

Despite a great number of relevant titles, the extant literature has little to say about the relationship between academic youth, society, and politics between 1870 and 1914.[24] Although the protest movement of the Burschenschaft and the Fascist activism of Weimar students[25] have often been analyzed, since Paul Ssymank's work half a century ago hardly anything has been written about the student generations in-between.[26] The jubilee history syndrome, institutional particularism, professorial hagiography, and the lack of theory of most *Festschriften* have hampered the growth of university history in Germany; it has hardly surpassed the standard set by Friedrich Paulsen before World War I.[27] However, the recent social problems of higher education have produced more sophisticated studies on the topics of enrollment growth and unemployment[28] as well as on the issues of educational opportunity[29] and academic elitism. These works are beginning to transcend national limitations with a comparative perspec-

[24] W. Ermann and E. Horn, *Bibliographie der deutschen Universitäten* (Leipzig, 1904-1905); H. Hassinger, ed., *Bibliographie zur Universitätsgeschichte* (Munich, 1975). See also L. Petry, "Deutsche Forschungen nach dem zweiten Weltkrieg zur Geschichte der Universitäten," *VSWG* 46 (1959): 145-203.

[25] For instance, R. R. Lutz, "Fathers and Sons in the Vienna Revolution of 1848," *JCEA* 22 (1962): 161ff. and K. H. Wegert, "The Genesis of Youthful Radicalism: Hesse-Nassau, 1806-19," *CEH* 10 (1977): 183-205; M. H. Kater, *Studentenschaft und Rechtsradikalismus in Deutschland 1918-1933* (Hamburg, 1975); M. S. Steinberg, *Sabres and Brown Shirts: The German Students' Path to National Socialism 1918-1935* (Chicago, 1977).

[26] F. Schulze and P. Ssymank, *Das deutschen Studententum von den ältesten Zeiten bis zur Gegenwart* (Munich, 1932). While Schulze was a Prussian liberal, Ssymank, an erstwhile member of the Freistudentenschaft, instituted the first library collection on university and student history at Göttingen (now at the IHK in Würzburg). P. Krause, *"O alte Burschenherrlichkeit:" Die Studenten und ihr Brauchtum* (Graz, 1979) is a colorful coffee-table book.

[27] See n. 15 above as well as C. E. McClelland, "A Step forward in the Study of Universities," *Minerva* 14 (1976): 150-61; and P. Lundgreen, "Quantifizierung in der Sozialgeschichte der Bildung," *VSWG* 63 (1976): 433ff.

[28] R. Riese, *Die Hochschule auf dem Wege zum wissenschaftlichen Grossbetrieb: Die Universität Heidelberg und das badische Hochschulwesen 1860-1914* (Stuttgart, 1977); D. K. Müller, *Sozialstruktur und Schulsystem: Aspekte zum Strukturwandel des Schulwesens im 19. Jahrhundert* (Göttingen, 1977); and H.-G. Herrlitz and H. Titze, "Überfüllung als bildungspolitische Strategie: Zur administrativen Steuerung der Lehrerarbeitslosigkeit in Preussen 1870-1914," *Die deutsche Schule* 68 (1976): 348-70.

[29] R. Dahrendorf, *Society and Democracy in Germany* (Garden City, N. Y., 1967), pp. 71-74, 99-106. See also pp. 142-150.

tive.[30] The political polarization of the universities in the late 1960s on both sides of the Atlantic prompted fresh looks at professorial politics, reconsiderations of the concept of cultivation, and analyses of the general relationship between state, society, and university.[31] But aside from some work on academic politics or the nontenured faculty,[32] students have been almost completely neglected.[33] Thus, the general historiography on the structural problems of the empire and the growing literature on the history of education have demanded an investigation of the social and ideological development of universities, students, and academics but have so far failed to provide it. Studies of modernization subordinate the educated to the nobility, the entrepreneurs, the lower middle class, or the workers;[34] while the political reversal of the cultivated is often mentioned, it is rarely, if ever, confronted specifically.[35] Monographs on the composition and careers of the educated usually center on the bureaucracy rather than on its educational background.[36] Because of the disciplinary limitation of educationists to primary and secondary schooling, there has been little carryover from the new social history of education[37] to the study of higher

[30] W. Zorn, "Hochschule und Höhere Schule in der deutschen Sozialgeschichte der Neuzeit," in K. Repgen and S. Skalweit, eds., *Spiegel der Geschichte* (Münster, 1964), pp. 321-39; F. Ringer, *Education and Society in Modern Europe* (Bloomington, Indiana, 1979); and H. Kaelble, "Educational Opportunities and Government Policies in Europe in the Period of Industrialization," in *The Development of Welfare States in Europe and America*, pp. 239-68.

[31] F. K. Ringer, *The Decline of the German Mandarins*, pp. 81ff.; H. Tompert, *Lebensformen und Denkweisen der akademischen Welt Heidelbergs im Wilhelminischen Zeitalter* (Lübeck, 1969); J. E. Craig, "A Mission for German Learning: The University of Strasbourg and Alsatian Society, 1870-1918" (dissertation, Stanford University, 1973); W. H. Bruford, *The German Tradition of Self-Cultivation*; and C. E. McClelland, *State, Society and University in Germany, 1700-1914* (Cambridge, 1979).

[32] R. vom Bruch, *Wissenschaft, Politik und öffentliche Meinung: Gelehrtenpolitik im Wilhelminischen Deutschland* (Husum, 1980); A. Busch, *Die Geschichte der Privatdozenten* (Stuttgart, 1959); K.-D. Bock, *Strukturgeschichte der Assistentur: Personalgefüge, Wert- und Zielvorstellungen in der deutschen Universität des 19. und 20. Jahrhunderts* (Düsseldorf, 1972).

[33] M. Studier, "Der Corpsstudent als Idealbild der Wilhelminischen Ära: Untersuchungen zum Zeitgeist 1888 bis 1914" (dissertation, Erlangen, 1965); C. Helfer and M. Rassem, eds., *Student und Hochschule im 19. Jahrhundert* (Göttingen, 1975).

[34] H.-U. Wehler, *Das deutsche Kaiserreich* (Göttingen, 1973) and the subsequent controversy. See also his essay, *Modernisierungstheorie und Geschichte* (Göttingen, 1975) and A. J. Mayer, "The Lower Middle Class as Historical Problem," *JMH* 47 (1975): 409-36.

[35] Such as the works by L. Krieger, G. L. Mosse, F. Stern, and W. Mommsen. See also the exception of K. Vondung, ed., *Das wilhelminische Bildungsbürgertum: Zur Sozialgeschichte seiner Ideen* (Göttingen, 1976).

[36] H.-J. Henning, *Das Westdeutsche Bürgertum in der Epoche der Hochindustrialisierung 1860-1914* (Wiesbaden, 1972), vol. 1, *Das Bildungsbürgertum in den preussischen Westprovinzen*. For the general state of the art, see W. Zorn, ed., *Handbuch der deutschen Wirtschafts- und Sozialgeschichte* (Stuttgart, 1976), vol. 2.

[37] J. E. Talbott, "The History of Education," *Daedalus* 100 (1971): 133-50, and the

learning.[38] Important contributions on Wilhelm von Humboldt, the reform of the Gymnasium, and the emergence of the *Abitur* as a mandatory graduation examination are as sharply circumscribed as studies of teachers.[39] Despite the plethora of material on this as on any German topic, the present analysis is, therefore, forced to break fresh historiographical ground.

As students arouse the most interest when they revolt, the methodological approaches linking them with society and polity tend to center around sociological, psychological, or historical explanations of dissent. The generational crisis argument, which places youth rebellion within the wider context of modernization,[40] is plagued by immense problems of defining a "historical generation"[41] and requires a series of subsidiary notions to establish the actual causal links that sometimes run across age groups and divide cohorts.[42] Discovered in the late nineteenth century by educators, psychologists, and literati, the concept of adolescence focuses on the high school rather than the college years and does not particularly illuminate quiescent periods of maturation.[43] The interesting effort to trace the development of youth as an age group and as a concept throughout the last two centuries fails to explain analytically the differences between activism and conformity.[44] Unfortunately, the historical and social science ap-

---

literature under "Bildung etc." in H.-U. Wehler, *Bibliographie zur modernen deutschen Sozialgeschichte* (Göttingen, 1976), pp. 196-203.

[38] P. Lundgreen, "Historische Bildungsforschung," in F. Rürup, ed., *Historische Sozialwissenschaft* (Göttingen, 1977), pp. 96-125; and L. O'Boyle, "Education and Social Structure: The Humanist Tradition Reexamined," *IASL* 1 (1976): 246ff.

[39] C. Menze, *Die Bildungsreform Wilhelm von Humboldts* (Hanover, 1975); K.-E. Jeismann, *Das preussische Gymnasium in Staat und Gesellschaft* (Stuttgart, 1974); H. G. Herrlitz, *Studium als Standesprivileg: Die Entstehung des Maturitätsproblems im 18. Jahrhundert* (Frankfurt, 1973); M. Heinemann, *Schule im Vorfeld der Verwaltung* (Göttingen, 1974); F. Meyer, *Schule der Untertanen: Lehrer und Politik in Preussen 1848-1900* (Hamburg, 1976); and James C. Albisetti, "Kaiser, Classicists and Moderns: Secondary School Reform in Imperial Germany" (dissertation, Yale University, 1976).

[40] S. N. Eisenstadt, *From Generation to Generation: Age Groups and Social Structure* (New York, 1966); and L. S. Feuer, *The Conflict of Generations: The Character and Significance of Student Movements* (New York, 1969).

[41] A. Esler, *The Youth Revolution: The Conflict of Generations in Modern History* (Lexington, 1974); A. B. Spitzer, "The Historical Problem of Generations," *AHR* 78 (1973): 1353-85; and Hans Jaeger, "Generationen in der Geschichte: Überlegungen zu einer umstrittenen Konzeption," *GG* 3 (1977): 429-52.

[42] R. Flacks, "Social and Cultural Meanings of Student Revolt," in E. E. Sampson and H. A. Korn, *Student Activism and Protest* (San Francisco, 1970), 117ff.; the articles in the special issue on "Generations in Conflict" of the *JCH* 5 (1970), vol. 1; and S. M. Lipset, *Rebellion in the University* (Boston, 1972).

[43] Erik H. Erikson, "Reflections on the Dissent of Contemporary Youth," *Daedalus* 99 (1970): 154-76; and P. Loewenberg, "The Psychohistorical Origins of the Nazi Youth Cohort," *AHR* 76 (1971): 1457-1502.

[44] J. R. Gillis, *Youth and History: Tradition and Change in European Age Relations 1770-Present* (New York, 1974); and K. H. Jarausch, "Restoring Youth to its Own History," *HEQ* 14 (1975): 445-56.

proaches are hardly more useful in illuminating the transformation of students in Imperial Germany. Although it provides a helpful taxonomy of the industries of education, research, graduate training, problem solving, and cultural consciousness, Parsonian functionalism abstracts recent American patterns and postulates as proven those connections between educational processes and social changes which have yet to be investigated empirically.[45] Historians of science concerned with the "institutional sociology of scholarly activity" are preoccupied with the emergence of the modern "research imperative" and have little to say about social selection and liberal education at the university.[46] Similarly, the historical economists are more interested in the contributions of educational investment to industrialization than what happens to students,[47] and macrosociological schemata of educational modernization, focused on growth, socialization, and mobility, identify important problem areas without establishing their sequence and relationship contextually.[48] "Rather than by evolving a grand strategy and then trying it out on the empirical data," a historian ought, according to Lawrence Stone, to proceed "by adopting a series of tactical approaches to specific problems" in order to produce middle-level generalizations, more firmly grounded in past evidence.[49]

One way of developing a systematic, interdisciplinary, and comparative framework might be to isolate the dominant historical questions and to use whatever methodology seems particularly suited for their analysis, as long as the parts finally add up to a comprehensive whole.

1. Since the most striking aspect of German higher education after 1870 was the enrollment explosion, any analysis must begin with an investigation of its reasons, dynamics, and consequences. An important aspect of social mobilization, the expansion of higher learning raises not only the problem of its relationship to social change in general but also a number of specific difficulties in assessing the relative importance of economic or ideological factors.[50]

[45] T. Parsons and G. Platt, *The American University* (Cambridge, Mass., 1973).

[46] J. Ben-David, *The Scientist's Role in Society* (Englewood Cliffs, N.J., 1971); F. Pfetsch, *Zur Entwicklung der Wissenschaftspolitik in Deutschland 1750-1914* (Berlin, 1974); and S. R. Turner, "The Prussian Professoriate and the Research Imperative, 1760-1848" (dissertation, Princeton University, 1972).

[47] P. Lundgreen, *Bildung und Wirtschaftswachstum im Industrialisierungsprozess des 19. Jahrhunderts* (Berlin, 1973); and "Educational Expansion and Economic Growth in Nineteenth Century Germany: A Quantitative Study," in L. Stone, ed., *Schooling and Society* (Baltimore, 1976), pp. 20-66.

[48] P. Flora, *Modernisierungsforschung: Zur empirischen Analyse gesellschaftlicher Entwicklung* (Opladen, 1974) attempts a comparison of basic numerical indicators of educational development.

[49] L. Stone, introduction to *The University in Society* (Princeton, 1974). See also J. Rury, "Elements of a 'New' Comparative History of Education," *CER* 21 (1977): 342-51.

[50] W. Rüegg, "Bildungssoziologische Ansätze für die Erforschung des Bildungswesens

2. Because the most dramatic consequence of the educational expansion was the transformation of the social background of the student body, the origins, sequence, and results of this phenomenon ought to be probed as well. Even if Christopher Jencks argues, perhaps somewhat exaggeratedly, that "differences between schools have rather trivial long term effects" and that the "most important determinant [of academic achievement is] family background," the debate about educational inequality poses stimulating questions about the social role of higher education.[51]

3. While the Prussian government controlled the goals of higher learning through ministerial edicts and professorial appointments, the political content of the formal curriculum at individual universities ought to be analyzed to determine how much of the reversal of academic mentality was the result of regular instruction. Although somewhat unspecific, the notion of "political culture" suggests the importance of cultivation in the political orientation of academics.[52]

4. As the beliefs of the students were equally, if not more, shaped by corporate character training, the hidden curriculum of subculture should be investigated for its stated aims as well as its unstated effects. Despite the difficulty of defining it and applying it on the university level, Emile Durkheim's concept of political socialization might aid in analyzing the official and unofficial shaping of ideology.[53]

5. Because much of politics is learned through personal experience, the theory as well as practice of student politics must be probed in order to resolve the paradox of progressive means and regressive ends. Even if the radical "social control" approach of Clarence Karier tends to overemphasize the stabilizing function of education, its critical light might help penetrate the fog of adult or youthful academic rhetoric.[54]

6. Finally, the collective attitudes and characteristics of students, professors, and graduates ought to be scrutinized in order to uncover how the

---

im 19. Jahrhundert," in Rüegg and O. Neuloh, eds., *Zur soziologischen Theorie und Analyse des 19. Jahrhunderts* (Göttingen, 1971), pp. 34-41; and "Bildung und Gesellschaft im 19. Jahrhundert," in H. Steffens, ed., *Bildung und Gesellschaft* (Göttingen, 1972), pp. 28-40.

[51] C. Jencks, *Inequality: A Reassessment of the Effect of Family and Schooling in America* (New York, 1972); see also H. Preisert, *Soziale Lage und Bildungschancen in Deutschland* (Munich, 1967) as well as the documentary volumes of the *Hochschul-Informations-System*.

[52] L. W. Pye, "Political Culture," *IESS* 12 (1968): 218-25; and G. A. Almond and S. Verba, *The Civic Culture: Political Attitudes and Democracy in Five Nations* (Boston, 1965).

[53] F. I. Greenstein, "Socialization," *IESS* 14 (1968): 551-55; J. R. Ahrens, *Zur Sozialisationssituation von Studenten* (Hamburg, 1972); A. Deichsel et al., *Politische Sozialisation von Studenten* (Stuttgart, 1974); and A. W. Astin, *Four Critical Years* (San Francisco, 1977).

[54] B. Franklin, "Education for Social Control." *HEQ* 14 (1974): 131-36 discusses Karier et al.; and H. Titze, *Die Politisierung der Erziehung: Untersuchungen über die soziale und politische Funktion der Erziehung von der Aufklärung bis zum Hochkapitalismus* (Frankfurt, 1973).

"unspoken assumptions" of an important part of the German elite informed their decisions in crises from 1914 to 1933.[55]
Instead of fastening on a single cause, this multifaceted approach tries to pursue the interplay of social structures and the political mentalities of the educated while balancing unity and diversity in order to do justice both to the nationalist majority and the progressive minority.

To escape burial in an avalanche of documentation set off by Teutonic bibliomania, the historian has to sink carefully selected shafts to reconstruct the subterranean features of the landscape. Unfortunately, the bombings of the Second World War left deep craters in the mountain of sources, which distort the terrain and make mining intellectually hazardous. A combination of quantitative and qualitative methods seems preferable, striving for statistical precision wherever possible, but structuring questions and interpretations through traditional documentary and literary analysis as well.[56] To blend the specific with the general, it seems useful to proceed on three levels simultaneously. Individual university case studies offer the detailed concreteness to resolve specific problems. The considerable institutional differences nevertheless also require an examination of statewide policy, for which Prussia, dominant member of the German Empire, appears most suitable. Finally, regional characteristics are brought into greater relief by comparing them to national patterns and interpretations in the literature.

Because of the bureaucratic nature of the academic job market, the enrollment explosion is studied through government measures, public debates, and printed statistics. The social transformation of the student body is analyzed through the example of the second largest Prussian university, whose matriculation registers are the most detailed, the Rheinische Friedrich-Wilhelms-Universität at Bonn, which is contrasted with five other institutions for the first two-thirds of the century. Prussian student policy is examined on a statewide basis, while the formal curriculum is also investigated at Bonn, but because of the greater national prominence of the professors and the existence of a more politicized university atmosphere, it is at the same time studied at the largest and internationally most famous German university, the Friedrich-Wilhelms-Universität in Berlin.

[55] J. Joll, *1914: The Unspoken Assumptions* (London, 1969). The fourfold approach of this study deals directly ("political socialization" and "social differentiation") and indirectly ("professional qualification" and "cultural orientation") with all the topical areas of Lundgreen's historical educational sociology in *Sozialgeschichte der deutschen Schule im Überblick* (Göttingen, 1980) 1: 9-11.
[56] K. H. Jarausch, "Möglichkeiten und Probleme der Quantifizierung in der Geschichtswissenschaft," in his *Quantifizierung in der Geschichtswissenschaft* (Düsseldorf, 1976); and "Promises and Problems of Quantitative Research in Central European History," *CEH* 11 (1978): 279-90. See also H. Graff, " 'The New Math,' Quantification, the 'New' History, and the History of Education," *Urban Education* 11 (1977): 403-40.

While student politics were also particularly explosive in the German capital and therefore need to be probed there, traditional student subculture, more typical of the informal curriculum, is scrutinized at the middle-sized Prussian Philipps-Universität at Marburg as well as through the archives, journals, and pamphlets of the larger student corporations. Finally, the problems and responses of Wilhelmian academics are viewed through the rich incidental literature of the Institut für Hochschulkunde in Würzburg. Although vexing, because of its lack of symmetry and frequent shifts of locale, this combination of methods and case studies allows a broader approach to the question and, it is hoped, yields a more firmly based and comprehensive interpretation.[57]

ALTHOUGH golden memories of the "most beautiful years of my life" seem a fairly universal phenomenon, the "student experience" in Central Europe embodies it in heightened form. Perhaps the "indescribable charm of Old Heidelberg" has something to do with the ritualistic description of college years in academic autobiographies and with the popular success of the literary genre of the *Studentenroman*.[58] Certainly the social freedom of student life as an escape from parental authority and a moratorium before the professional regimentation of adulthood (the *Philisterium*) contributed to the retrospective romanticization of the *Burschenzeit*.[59] Probably the pervasiveness of organized subculture, in Meinecke's words "the poetry of the old Germanic corporate instinct," reinforced the view of university study as personal license and brought the Old Boys back year after year to celebrate the founding of their corporation.[60] Beyond the drinking and duelling, the student experience served as a central stage in the formation of an individual *Weltanschauung*, a basic outlook on society and polity. The loafing of the first few semesters was often accompanied by an avid browsing in contemporary literature and by a sampling of different lectures by famous professors without regard to professional training but with much attention to general cultivation. Eberhard Gothein describes the

[57] For a more detailed discussion of the problems posed by the incompleteness of documentation, see "A Note on Sources."

[58] L. Heffter, *Beglückte Rückschau auf neun Jahrzehnte: Ein Professorenleben* (Freiburg, 1952), pp. 33ff.; R. Kleissel, "Der deutsche Studentenroman von der Romantik bis zum Ausbruch des Weltkrieges" (dissertation, Vienna, 1932). Some of the best-known authors were O. Bierbaum, W. Bloem, H. Conradi, and O. Meding (pseud. G. Samarow).

[59] J. Habermas et al., *Student und Politik* (Neuwied, 1961); K. Keniston, *Young Radicals: Notes on Committed Youth* (New York, 1968). For the sexual component of this romanticism, see also Jarausch, "Students, Sex and Politics in Imperial Germany," forthcoming in *JCH* 17 (1982).

[60] F. Meinecke, *Erlebtes 1862-1919* (Stuttgart, 1964), pp. 57ff. ("to dedicate one's heart to a common cause and to clothe it with a tightly-woven dress of external forms and customs"). For a recent example of this Old Boy reflex, see Verein Alter Bonner Franken, ed., *Frankonia Dir gehör ich: Ein Buch der Bonner Franken, 1845-1970* (Bonn, 1970), pp. 52ff.

heady effect of intellectual freedom on a recent high-school graduate: "I felt like an amphibian creature on land which breathes through its lungs for the first time and throws off its gills."[61] Although often an indigestible smorgasbord of conflicting dishes, this ideological fare exposed the student to the leading intellects and theories of the day as well as to some remnants of the neohumanist heritage, thereby providing a smattering of Bildung in the classical sense. In contrast to "this double life," career preparation entered largely as an afterthought during the last semesters, through cramming before the inevitable final examination, and seems not to have held a very central place in student perspective, except for those poor enough to have to depend on their performance alone. For a minority, a gradual self-dedication to Wissenschaft seems to have grown out of such curricular freedom, especially when inspired by an outstanding personality, such as Heinrich von Treitschke.[62]

According to the recollections of the Akademiker, their student experience had not only personal and professional, but also social and political, impact. One of the first attitudes the young "knight of the spirit" acquired was "the arrogance of an independent *Bildungsbürger* [cultivated middle class] vis-à-vis the laborious *Interessenbürger* [working middle class]" which divided the German bourgeoisie and created a deep gap between cultured elite and uncultured masses. Nevertheless, even within the realm of the intellect, there were profound social differences: "Through bearing, facial expression and gestures, a few elegantly dressed young individuals distinguished themselves from the mass of uncultivated, if not to say proletarian [students] in Berlin." Only a minority of the privileged recognized consciously the moral obligation to "do something" charitable about their less fortunate comrades (*Kommilitonen*) as well as about the glaring social injustices ("the social question") outside university walls.[63] The political complement to this educational arrogance (*Bildungsdünkel*) was naiveté and lack of interest. Few individuals arrived at the university, as did Theodor Heuss, with already awakened political consciousness, eager to gather intellectual ammunition for their preexisting commitment. The vast apolitical majority would have agreed with professor of medicine Alfred Hoche: "We students had little interest in politics. . . . Bismarck

[61] M.-L. Gothein, *Eberhard Gothein, ein Lebensbild: Seinen Briefen nacherzählt* (Stuttgart, 1931); see also E. Ermatinger, *Richte des Lebens: Geschichte einer Jugend* (Frauenfeld, 1943).

[62] Meinecke, *Erlebtes*, p. 57. See also the cautionary literature on the dangers of college, such as C. Müller, *Der tugend- und lasterhafte Student von 1890* (Leipzig, 1890) and H. Teutsch, *Der brave Student* (Ravensburg, 1899).

[63] T. Heuss, *Vorspiele des Lebens: Jugenderinnerungen* (Tübingen, 1953), critical phrase from the progressive T. Barth. L. Curtius, *Deutsche und Antike Welt: Lebenserinnerungen* (Stuttgart, 1950), pp. 70ff. See also the literature on "Student und Soziale Frage" in the IHK Würzburg, F 1730-64.

ran things, and that was enough." Nevertheless, under the influence of dynamic scholars such as the famed liberal economist Lujo von Brentano, many "began their German political thinking" during their university years; even if few emancipated themselves from the previous influences of Gymnasium and family (like Gustav Radbruch, who moved toward socialism through reading critical social literature), they at least formalized and rationalized their political outlook.[64] The leading authority on German students in the last decade of the century, Theobald Ziegler, enunciated the official position of the Prussian state: "Students should not yet want to engage in practical politics" but rather prepare for their citizenship tasks by "acquiring political convictions" through study. Naturally these should be based "on a true and warm patriotism, without which . . . I cannot imagine a German student."[65]

Such outbursts of nationalism created the widespread cliché of academic illiberalism outside Germany, even if within the present Federal Republic such an assertion would still be rejected as "putting our grandfathers on trial."[66] Nevertheless, in contrast to stereotypical Anglo-Saxon views, the association between universities and right-wing politics in Central Europe was neither inevitable nor necessarily permanent, as the evidence of Vormärz liberal nationalism and the present-day Marxist radicalism of German youths amply demonstrates.[67] Moreover, many contemporary students in other Western countries were hardly less nationalist, elitist, and illiberal. Perhaps the underlying fear of past revolutionary and future Socialist activism made imperial academic rhetoric so strident. It may be that this recollection and anticipation inspired Otto von Bismarck to reiterate to student deputation after deputation: "Hold fast to the national spirit . . . ! What is it that sustains the German official? The university and the army, indeed, two imponderables, which nonetheless exert a weighty influence."[68] Nevertheless, academic illiberalism was not inevitable, and one ought to investigate how it came about. To succeed, however, such an inquiry must proceed by small, simple steps: How many students were

[64] A. Hoche, *Jahresringe: Innenansicht eines Menschenlebens* (Munich, 1936), pp. 81ff.; Curtius, *Lebenserinnerungen*, pp. 70ff.; G. Radbruch, *Der innere Weg: Aufriss meines Lebens* (Göttingen, 1951), p. 22. Meinecke, *Erlebtes*, pp. 57ff. ("I felt quite close to the national idealism" of the Kyffhäuser students).

[65] T. Ziegler, *Der deutsche Student am Ende des 19. Jahrhunderts* (Stuttgart, 1895), pp. 117-30.

[66] F. Lilge, *The Abuse of Learning: The Failure of the German University* (New York, 1948); T. Nipperdey, "Wehlers 'Kaiserreich.' Eine kritische Auseinandersetzung," *GG* 1 (1975): 539-60.

[67] See note 24 and L. Becker, *Hitler's Children: The Story of the Baader-Meinhof Terrorist Gang* (Philadelphia, 1977).

[68] Oppermann, *Alemannia* 2: 1ff. For a plea for a social historical approach, see also R. J. Evans, "Introduction: Wilhelm II's Germany and the Historians," *Society and Politics in Wilhelmine Germany* (London, 1978), pp. 11-39.

there in Imperial Germany? From what social strata were they recruited? What values and attitudes did formal instruction try to teach them? What social ideas dominated the hidden curriculum of student subculture? What ideological forces controlled imperial student politics? How did academics respond to the sociopolitical problems of their age? The questions are endless. Perhaps the answers will shed some light on the Akademiker's subsequent collective behavior.

Two

THE ENROLLMENT EXPLOSION

"WHAT A MARVELOUS DEVELOPMENT!" exclaimed Rector Adolph Wagner, reflecting on the growth of the University of Berlin during its first three-quarters of a century. "The incredible expansion, advancement, and specialization of research and teaching [following unification in 1871] have made our university both a national center of higher education and a veritable world institution beyond any other German or European university." The primary cause of this "astounding increase" in teaching staff, research institutes, and university budgets was the unprecedented enrollment expansion during the Second Empire.[1] For the individual institution such as Bonn, the ever-accelerating influx of students was a source of profound satisfaction: "The flag waving over our building indicates that one of you is the four-thousandth student to be admitted to the Rheinische Friedrich-Wilhelms-Universität." Rector Philipp Zorn welcomed matriculating students on 7 May 1910: "When the university opened its doors in 1818, only forty-seven students found their way here. . . . It took sixty years until the first thousand was reached. Twenty-three years later, in the summer semester of 1899 and the winter semester of 1901, the figure of two thousand was surpassed. [Six] years later the number three thousand, and five years after that four thousand, was reached." Extending from the largest metropolitan to the smallest provincial institution among Germany's twenty-one universities, this enrollment explosion provided manifest proof of the national renown as well as international prestige of imperial academics: "Countless times full and joyous hearts have sounded the call: *Vivat, crescat, floreat alma mater bonensis*. You see, this wish has now come true."[2]

---

[1] Adolph Wagner, *Die Entwicklung der Universität Berlin 1810-1896* (Berlin, 1896), oration for the seventy-fifth anniversary of its founding.

[2] *Chronik der Rheinischen Friedrich-Wilhelms-Universität zu Bonn*, vols. 25 (1889-1900), 31 (1905-1906), and 36 (1910-1911).

The dramatic growth of the student body also created unforeseen problems: "You will understand that this joy is mixed with some forebodings. First, a concern for you[r future]," said the Bonn rector in his enrollment address: "What shall become of the thousands upon thousands who irresistibly crowd into the universities and the liberal professions? Their struggle for existence will become ever more difficult. The fear that an academic proletariat could arise which would have to fight its way through life even harder than an unskilled worker haunts me time and again." Unrestrained expansion also produced threatening consequences for the institutions themselves: "We can be anxious as well for the universities and their development when we see with what elemental force the throng of students grows. Both the number of teachers and the facilities of the institutes no longer suffice to imbue those masses either with necessary professional knowledge or with true education." Impersonality in teaching, deterioration of secondary preparation, enrollment of women, and primacy of careerism over cultivation or scholarship rendered "the fulfillment of the most important academic tasks more arduous" and endangered "the pursuit of Wissenschaft, the essence of the German university." The expansion of student numbers therefore created new challenges: "The spread of the thirst for knowledge and scholarship and the desire of ever-lower social strata to enter the universities . . . is a splendid phenomenon; but in order to turn it into a blessing, we must try more conscientiously than ever to cultivate not only the mind but also character and judgment."[3]

By the turn of the century, perceptive professors began to realize that quantitative growth had led to qualitative changes. In 1890 the venerable Theodor Mommsen had coined the term *Grosswissenschaft* as a scientific counterpart to big government and big industry. Six years later Adolph Wagner saw "in the great natural science institutes a capitalist parallel to large-scale factory enterprise." In 1905 the theologian Adolf von Harnack combined the emergence of collaborative research with the enrollment explosion into the concept *Grossbetrieb der Wissenschaft*, signaling the arrival of the mass research university.[4]

As historians have largely taken the inevitability of the enrollment expansion for granted, they have disagreed less about its causes than about its consequences, such as academic unemployment. Some argue that "in comparison to the growth of primary schooling the development in sec-

---

[3] *Chronik*, 36: 22ff. and O. Wenig, *Verzeichnis der Professoren und Dozenten der Rheinischen Friedrich-Wilhelms-Universität zu Bonn 1918-1968* (Bonn, 1968).

[4] Theodor Mommsen, "Antwort an Harnack, 3. Juli 1890," *Reden und Aufsätze* (Berlin, 1905), pp. 209f.; A. Wagner, *Die Entwicklung*; A. von Harnack, "Vom Grossbetrieb der Wissenschaft," *PrJhb* 119 (1905): 193-201; F. Eulenburg, *Der akademische Nachwuchs* (Leipzig, 1908) talks about "the character of modern large enterprise."

ondary and tertiary education was much less impressive" or that "the access percentages fell just short of doubling between 1870 and the First World War," indicating that the system expanded only slowly. Others are more impressed with the dynamism of enrollments after unification compared to earlier decline or stagnation and conclude: "The actual quantum jump in student numbers already took place in the Empire."[5] But there has been little systematic discussion about the determinants of the diffusion of schooling on any level. Lists of somewhat incommensurate factors such as the political aims of the state in creating citizens, the importance of ethnocultural or religious attitudes, the impact of the bureaucratic self-interest of school officials, the investment in human capital to improve productivity, and the Marxist "qualification of labor" thesis still predominate.[6] Because of the obvious social costs of the contemporary surplus of educated men, there has been considerably more debate among economists and educationists about the ambivalent results of educational expansion. Defining his central concept as "qualification crisis," which denotes "the reduction in the market value of primary- and secondary-school certificates for access to higher education and for employment or mobility within the economic system," Detlev Müller, in a controversial model, analyzes the relation of population growth to education, the development of secondary-school types, the structure of the entitlement system (linking education and jobs), the overcrowding of the legal profession, and state expenditures for education.[7] This sometimes desultory, sometimes heated debate raises three questions about the enrollment increase: What was the extent and pattern of educational growth? What were the causes of the proliferation of student numbers? What were its institutional and social consequences?

Attempts to explain the enrollment dynamics of the second half of the nineteenth and early decades of the twentieth centuries have centered loosely around modernization paradigms. Despite the presentist Anglo-American bias of most such theories, the undeniable parallelism between general

[5] P. Flora, *Modernisierungsforschung* (Opladen, 1974), pp. 143ff.; F. Ringer, *Education and Society in Modern Europe* (Bloomington, Indiana, 1979), pp. 61-69, and K. H. Jarausch, "Frequenz und Struktur," *Bildungspolitik* (Stuttgart, 1980), pp. 122-32.

[6] David B. Tyack, "Ways of Seeing: An Essay on the History of Compulsory Schooling," *Harvard Educational Review* 46 (1976): 355-89 and the session on "The Determinants of the Diffusion of Schooling" with papers by M. J. Maynes, J. E. Craig, and D. Tyack at the Social Science History Association meeting in Columbus, Ohio, November 4, 1978.

[7] D. K. Müller et al., "Modellentwicklung zur Analyse von Krisenphasen im Verhältnis von Schulsystem und staatlichem Beschäftigungssystem: Materialien und Interpretationsansätze zur Situation in Preussen während der zweiten Hälfte des neunzehnten Jahrhunderts," *ZfP* 14. *Beiheft* (Weinheim, 1977): 37-77 and the session on "Academic Unemployment" with papers by W. L. Hansen, D. K. Müller, B. Zymek, and John Haag at the 1978 SSHA meeting in Columbus, Ohio.

social evolution and specific educational growth might provide a useful starting point, if timing, speed, and extent of the expansion could be systematically related to broader societal changes.[8] Unfortunately, such causative connections are more often posited than proven. It is easier to assert that "in all innovation crises [of Western history] the question of Bildung arises as a central existential problem of society" than to specify the nature of the relationship.[9] For certain aspects, such as the connection between education and economic growth, some useful concepts exist. C. Arnold Anderson suggests four categories of causes that warrant further investigation (cost of schooling, expected or perceived returns, anticipated noneconomic benefits, and total resources within the subpopulation available for schooling), although they are neither completely quantifiable nor all-inclusive.[10] On a somewhat broader front, a comparison of developments in England, Germany, and Russia with American patterns yields a catalogue of questions that define at least the outlines of the overall development: What was the role of direct institutional changes in the enrollment explosion? Was the increase in student numbers due to the foundation of new universities, the lowering of admissions barriers for modern-high-school graduates, the emergence of a compensatory sector of less prestigious institutions, the introduction of new curricula, or the transformation of financial aid? What was the importance of indirect, long-range social developments for educational growth? What was the relative significance of population increases, economic growth, social prestige, state policy, or cultural trends such as neoclassicism or scientism? A similar list of queries could and should be drawn up regarding the effects of the growth of higher education on rationalization, social mobility, economic growth, secondary schooling, and so on.[11] While the coincidence between "modernization" and educational expansion in the West is too striking to be merely accidental, the complexity of the interrelationship requires a series of intervening investigations, based upon an inductive historical rather than an deductive theoretical approach.

[8] H.-U. Wehler, *Modernisierungstheorie und Geschichte* (Göttingen, 1975) and W. Conze, ed., *Modernisierung und nationale Gesellschaft im ausgehenden 18. und 19. Jahrhundert* (Berlin, 1979).

[9] W. Rüegg, "Bildungssoziologische Ansätze für die Erforschung des Bildungswesens im 19. Jahrhundert," *Zur soziologischen Theorie* (Göttingen, 1971), pp. 34-41.

[10] C. Arnold Anderson and M. J. Bowman, "Education and Economic Modernization in Historical Perspective," in L. Stone, ed., *Schooling and Society* (Baltimore, 1976), pp. 3-19.

[11] K. H. Jarausch, "Higher Education and Social Change, 1860-1930," as well as the expansion chapters by R. Lowe on England, P. Alston on Russia, C. Burke on America, and H. Titze, "Enrollment Expansion and Academic Overcrowding in Germany," in *The Transformation of Higher Learning, 1860-1930* (Stuttgart, 1982).

DYNAMICS OF EXPANSION

"No matter how much more important and successful other ways of looking at [university] conditions might be," the Prussian statistician Wilhelm Dieterici argued in 1836, "in a certain sense, in a certain perspective, it is interesting to see in numbers what can be seen in numbers."[12] Because of their drastic fluctuations, student enrollments in nineteenth-century German universities are a case in point. During the Napoleonic Wars the number of German students (figure 2.1) sank to a low exceeded only during the Thirty Years War and the Reformation. In the following one and one-half decades (up to 1830), student numbers multiplied from an estimated 5,500 to over 16,000, a relative increase of about 2.62 times (from around 20 to 52.5 per 100,000 German inhabitants). However, the peak reached in the postwar boom could not be maintained, and in the middle of the nineteenth century enrollments stabilized for one entire generation around 12,000 to 13,000 until the late 1860s, when a second, even more spectacular, wave of growth began. In comparison with the increasing population, student numbers actually decreased over one-third until the Wars of Unification. While Protestant and, to a lesser degree, Catholic theologians and lawyers, the frontrunners of the 1820s expansion, contracted most dramatically in the 1830s and 1840s, students of medicine also declined until the late 1840s before beginning a slow climb, while students of philosophy (least affected by the boom) gradually grew throughout the period (figure 2.2). The renewed popularity of law in the 1850s reversed the overall decline, but only in the 1860s did the expansion of the philosophical and medical faculties sufficiently counteract the contraction of the others to initiate another expansion. While during the low point of the Napoleonic Wars the average size of the surviving institutions hovered around 300, hardly exceeding that of a small medieval college, by 1830 the then twenty universities had grown to an average enrollment of 800, only to decrease to somewhat over 600 for the next generation. Thus, during the first three-quarters of the nineteenth century, German institutions of higher learning reversed the long-range decline of the eighteenth century, weathered the Napoleonic crisis, witnessed a spectacular period of neohumanist expansion, but did not succeed in initiating sustained educational growth.[13]

---

[12] Wilhelm Dieterici, *Geschichtliche und statistische Nachrichten über die Universitäten im preussischen Staate* (Berlin, 1836), pp. 4f.; and L. Stone, "The Size and Composition of the Oxford Student Body 1580-1909," in *The University in Society* (Princeton, 1974), 1: 3ff., calling "major changes in the size of the student body" the "structural pivot around which the history of the university has been built."

[13] Franz Eulenburg, *Die Frequenz der deutschen Universitäten von ihrer Gründung bis zur Gegenwart* (Leipzig, 1904), pp. 250ff. and C. E. McClelland, *State, Society and University* (Cambridge, 1980), pp. 116-17, 156-59, 187-88, 198-200. See also W. Frijhoff,

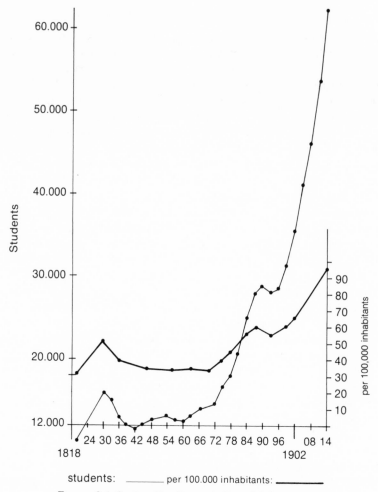

FIGURE 2.1 Student Enrollment in Imperial Germany

What were the causes of these dramatic fluctuations in attendance? The low of 1800-1810 was undoubtedly related to the closing of over a dozen marginal institutions (such as once flourishing Duisburg, which had shrunk to an average of thirty-eight students during the last decade of its existence) and to the military conscription, political and administrative chaos, and economic insecurity of the Napoleonic campaigns. Moreover, during the century of the Enlightenment, which preferred encyclopedic, practical, and

"Surplus ou deficit? Hypothèses sur le nombre des étudiants en Allemagne à l'époque moderne (1576-1815)," *Francia* 7 (1970), 173-218.

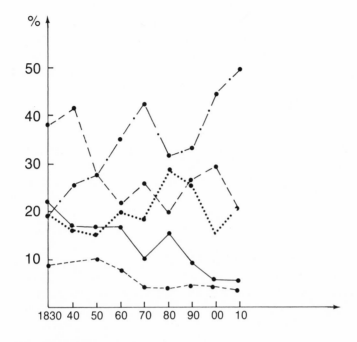

Prot. Theology: ●————●
Cath. Theology: ●- - - - - ●
Law: ●— — —●
Medicine: ●·········●
Philosophy: ●— · —●

FIGURE 2.2 Fields of Study in the Nineteenth Century

aristocratic forms of higher education outside of traditional institutions, university study had become less attractive. Contemporaries like Johannes Hoffmann explained the boom after the restoration of peace as a result of "the progress of higher intellectual culture," while Dieterici viewed it as a consequence of "the increasing demand for judges and officials caused by advancing population and civilization." Writing during the second growth wave of the 1880s, the economist Johannes Conrad echoed these themes by referring to "the resurgence of national spirit," the "pursuit of general culture," and a "revival of religion." More specifically, he added that "the extensive foundation of schools necessitated a supply of teachers," and the laxity of enrollment procedures allowed the admission of students who had not properly graduated from the Gymnasium.[14]

[14] J. G. Hoffmann, "Übersicht der auf den sämmtlichen Universitäten des Preussischen

The initial expansion was largely precipitated by a deficit of about 15,000 graduates caused by the Napoleonic upheavals, while the gradual spread of secondary education produced a larger pool of potential students, and the post-Napoleonic agrarian and commerical depression made bureaucratic careers more attractive. The continuation of enrollment growth into the early 1830s is probably related to the increased prestige of university education following Wilhelm von Humboldt's neohumanist reforms, to the formalization of prerequisites for admission into state service, and to the expansion of government positions. Moreover, the new universities succeeded in attracting greater numbers of students (Berlin had two thousand by 1830), and the previously propaedeutic philosophical faculty rose to respectability and thereby increased its share of university enrollment. In contrast, the subsequent stagnation of the 1840s to 1860s resulted from "an oversupply of the cultivated," from repeated official warnings that "on the whole *more* are studying than are clearly needed for immediate appointments," and from restrictive cultural policy. While bureaucratic positions grew only slowly after the 1820s, the resurgence of business life and the beginnings of industrialization offered nonacademic career alternatives. Most important, the Prussian Abitur Edict of 1834 created the notorious university monopoly for graduates of the Gymnasium, restricted *immaturi* and auditors (down from one-third to one-tenth of Berlin students), and thereby reduced the supply of incoming students. Moreover, expenses such as matriculation fees increased, and the great intellectual impetus of the reform era was stifled by the repression of Metternichean reaction.[15] These causes demonstrate that enrollments do not simply expand automatically with the population but fluctuate according to changing circumstances (thereby curiously paralleling the growth curve of book publishing).

In the 1860s student numbers slowly began to rise again, surpassing 13,000 in 1863-64 but, because of the German Wars of Unification, reaching 14,000 only in 1871-72. With the onset of the depression in 1873 the stream turned into a veritable torrent, swelling to 28,820 in 1889-90. However, the increase had been so rapid that a pause followed, with the tide ebbing to 27,321 in 1893-94. Once growth resumed in 1896-97, the expansion continued unabated toward a new high of 60,748 in the summer

---

Staats vom Sommersemester 1820 bis zum Wintersemester 1839-40 Studirenden: Mit Bemerkungen über das Verhältnis derselben zu den Bedürfnissen der Zeit," in his *Sammlung kleiner Schriften Staatswirthschaftlichen Inhalts* (Berlin, 1843), pp. 187ff.; Dieterici, "Geschichtliche," pp. 109ff.; Johannes Conrad, *German Universities During the Last Fifty Years* (Glasgow, 1885), pp. 19-27.

[15] Konrad H. Jarausch, "Die Neuhumanistische Universität und die bürgerliche Gesellschaft 1800-1870," *Darstellungen und Quellen* 11 (1980): 11-58; U. Preuss, "Bildung und Bürokratie," *Der Staat* 14 (1975): 370-95; J. Cobb, "The Forgotten Reforms: Non-Prussian Universities 1797-1817" (dissertation, University of Wisconsin, 1980); and, problematically, Elkar, *Junges Deutschland*, pp. 46-80.

semester of 1914. (More generous figures put the peak over 63,000.) In contrast to the stagnation of the previous generation, enrollments literally exploded after the creation of the Second Reich, increasing 4.6 times between 1870-71 and 1914 (or 4.15 times between the quinquennia 1865-66 to 1869-70 and 1910-11 to 1914), a staggering increase for contemporaries used to counting students in hundreds. The momentum carried over into the Weimar Republic, where it peaked at 87,315 in 1921, owing to the backlog of students registered but not actually studying during World War I. Numbers returned to the prewar level in 1925-26 before once more swelling to 103,912 at the height of the Great Depression. During the Third Reich enrollments were drastically cut back below the level of the empire, and not until the new expansion of the 1950s and 1960s were these absolute and relative figures exceeded permanently. This massive influx into the universities raised the proportion of students per 100,000 of the population from 32.4 in 1870-71 (it hovered around 34 in the 1860s) to 93.7 (or 96 if one takes the higher figure) in 1914, a 2.9 fold increase over population growth! Similarly, compared with the twenty-to-twenty-three-year-old age cohort, university enrollments rose about three times during Imperial Germany from 0.5 to 1.5 percent, indicating that student numbers increased considerably faster than their age group. As this startling absolute growth in enrollments meant a substantial increase in relative university attendance, the decisive takeoff in the expansion of higher education occurred during the Second Empire.[16]

This "rapid increase in the number of our students, about which all circles and journals, regardless of political persuasion, complain at present [1886]" made itself felt at every institutional level. Average university attendance climbed from somewhat over 600 in 1870 to close to 3,000 in the last prewar years, with Berlin approaching 10,000, Munich and Leipzig surpassing 5,000, Bonn exceeding 4,000, and even lowly Rostock, which hitherto eked out a marginal existence, closing in on 1,000 students. Individual faculties shared in the expansion but to different degrees. Protestant theologians nearly doubled (from 2,346 to 4,621); Catholic theologians increased only 1.5 times (from 1,170 to 1,768) to which one might add the approximately 1,000 students in episcopal clerical seminaries; law students multiplied more strongly, 3.2 times (from 3,168 to 10,119); while medical enrollments swelled most of all, about 7 times (from 2,541 to 17,698); and students of philosophy expanded almost as strongly, 5.6 times (from 4,486 to 25,027), and thereby constituted the largest faculty. At the

[16] Königliches Statistisches Bureau, *Preussische Statistik*, vol. 102 (Berlin, 1890), edited by Dr. Petersilie and containing the *Universitätsstatistik* for 1886-87 in loose sequence until vol. 236 (Berlin, 1913), containing the *Universitätsstatistik* for 1911-1912. In contrast to Fritz K. Ringer, *Education and Society*, pp. 53ff., and 61ff.

same time, students in the technical universities (*Technische Hochschulen*), which achieved full equality with their older sisters in 1900, grew from 2,929 to 12,458, while representing a constant 17 percent of pupils in higher education; students in the commercial academies (*Handelshochschulen*), which did not achieve formal parity with the other universities until after the war, increased from 118 in 1898-99 to 2,695 in the summer of 1914; hence, including students of the various other institutions (such as the mining academy, veterinary school, etc.), enrollment in higher education burgeoned from 17,857 to over 76,792 on the eve of the war, a 4.3 fold increase.[17]

Although international comparisons are fraught with dangers (chief of which is the problem of defining comparable institutions of higher learning), two developments stand out concerning students and their respective age cohort (twenty-to-twenty-four-year-olds): In all European countries "a vast seismic shift" doubled university attendance five decades before the First World War, except for backwaters like Portugal and Romania, where there was little or no development; aside from Switzerland (10.0), Scotland (1.8), and Austria (1.7), Germany showed the highest absolute enrollment per age cohort (1.3) and, aside from Hungary (2.66), the greatest relative growth (2.6). Thus, although these figures reflect a general trend of educational mobilization in the second half of the nineteenth century, they confirm the preliminary impression that "Germány would continue to have far more students at that level, both in numbers and in proportion of the entire student generation, than any other European state."[18]

Causes of Growth

"The striking increase in university attendance in the last decade" provoked a lively debate among contemporaries about its causes. Prince Otto von Bismarck was one of many concerned: "What shall become of all the educated pupils? Look at Russia." In 1882 the *Politische Wochenschrift* editorialized about "the overproduction of university graduates," which in some cases assumed "frightening dimensions," and warned of the

---

[17] H. von Petersdorff, "Der Zudrang zu den Deutschen Hochschulen," *ABl* 4 (1888-89): 3-4; R. Riese, *Die Hochschule auf dem Wege zum wissenschaftlichen Grossbetrieb* (Stuttgart, 1977), pp. 19-61; and R. Locke, "The End of the Practical Man: Higher Education and the Institutionalization of Entrepreneurial Performance in France, Germany and Great Britain, 1880-1940" (book manuscript, Univ. of Hawaii, 1980).

[18] H. Kaelble, "Educational Opportunities and Government Policies," in *The Development of Welfare States* (New Brunswick, 1981), pp. 239-68; and P. V. Meyers, *The Modernization of Education in Nineteenth Century Europe* (St. Louis, 1977), p. 11.

danger of a "scholarly proletariat."[19] In his classic statistical inquiry into "German university study during the last fifty years," the Halle economist Johannes Conrad regarded "the extraordinary increase" as "springing only in the very smallest degree from any higher ideal aim of the time, and just as little from any greater interest in science and theology." He rather pointed to three more material reasons:

> The first of these is the social position held by university-bred men in Germany. For the sake of this, pecuniary advantages are willingly sacrificed, and although not a new influence, it still prepared the way for the increased attendance. The second is the universal spread of classical culture. This is caused by increasing demand for the means of preparing for the official posts, and it is favoured by the wide spread of the higher educational institutions, which can now be attended at relatively small cost even by the less wealthy classes. The third factor is the commercial depression, which has now lasted longer than at almost any period in the time under our consideration, and that, too, when wealth and consequently the wants of life have materially increased. Artisans and tradespeople are anxious for even the smallest posts, which secure them regular employment and a steady if not a large income. There are hundreds of candidates from all classes for an advertised situation such as porter or clerk; and at present the farmer, the small trader, the artisan has no inclination to put his son into his own precarious occupation, but prefers to send him to the university.[20]

To produce a solid statistical base for government decisions, Privy Councillor Friedrich Althoff suggested the inauguration of a periodic university census "illustrating even to the average person of limited intelligence the great dangers that flow from an overproduction of the academically educated." In the introduction to the first volume on 1886-87, the editor, Albert Petersilie, nevertheless argued that the exceptional growth ought not to be seen in only a negative light: "The rush to the institutions of higher learning could and should not be prevented; that would run counter to the goal of cultural progress for our people and would ultimately lead

[19] Marginal note by Otto von Bismarck on letter of Stoelle to Bismarck, 15 November 1881, petitioning the chancellor to raise the *Progymnasium* at Schlawe to a full Gymnasium; "Überproduktion an studierten Leuten," *Politische Wochenschrift*, September 16, 1882, both in DZA Po, Rkz 2181. The term *academic proletariat*, coined originally by W. H. Riehl, dominated the subsequent discussion. See *Die bürgerliche Gesellschaft*, 6th ed. (Stuttgart, 1861), pp. 285ff.

[20] Johannes Conrad, *Das Universitätsstudium in Deutschland während der letzten fünfzig Jahre* (Jena, 1884), citations from the English translation: *German Universities during the Last Fifty Years* (Glasgow, 1885), p. 26, containing a series of appendices on the structure of the German educational system, not found in the original.

to a diminution of the significance of the universities for our national development.''[21] While the Prussian statistical bureau eschewed causal interpretation, partisans of educational reform placed the blame "solely and alone [on] the organization of secondary education and the entitlements connected with it," in short, the university monopoly of the Gymnasium. In his authoritative work on the development of German university enrollment since the Middle Ages, the Leipzig statistician Franz Eulenburg took a more detached view of the negative correlation between university attendance and business cycles and argued that the expansion after 1870 was largely the result of "changed societal circumstances," such as the increasing demand for the educated.[22]

Surprisingly enough, contemporary analysts tended to slight the most obvious cause of all, the increase in the German population. Would not the growth from 40,089,000 to 64,926,000 inhabitants during the Second Empire alone produce a sizable increase in the student body of institutions of higher learning? Plausible though it may seem that a 62 percent demographic expansion should lead to a corresponding university boom, the connection is more tenuous in fact, for greater population density sometimes also means greater job efficiency and therefore less increase in academically trained personnel. More important, the entire eighteenth century, during which Central European population grew steadily, witnessed a startling decline in student enrollment (about one fourth), while the 61 percent population growth in the half century after 1817 contributed to the boom of the 1820s, but failed in the subsequent decades to sustain student growth. Unless social habits change (and encourage a higher proportion of a cohort to enroll), demographic growth appears a *necessary* but *not a sufficient* precondition for a rise in student enrollments. It is necessary, because as long as the proportion of an age group attending college does not change, only a larger birth cohort will produce more potential students. It is insufficient, because universities require a considerable degree of preceding secondary education for admission, which tends to dampen the effects of population shifts.[23]

The chief institution of secondary education which funneled its graduates (*Abiturienten*) into higher education was the neohumanist Gymnasium.

---

[21] Gossler to Rottenburg, January 16, 1886, detailing the policy of the Prussian Ministry of Culture toward the "overproduction" of academics, DZA Po, Rkz 2182; *PrSt*, 102 (for 1886-87). See also A. Sachse, *Friedrich Althoff und sein Werk* (Berlin, 1928), p. 168.

[22] E. Kuntzemüller, *Die Überfüllung der gelehrten Fächer* (Berlin, 1889) and F. Eulenburg, *Die Frequenz*, pp. 250-58.

[23] Wolfgang Köllmann, "Bevölkerungsgeschichte 1800-1970," in W. Zorn, *Handbuch der Deutschen Wirtschafts- und Sozialgeschichte*, 2: 9-50; and Walther G. Hoffmann, *Das Wachstum der deutschen Wirtschaft seit der Mitte des 19. Jahrhunderts* (Berlin, 1965), pp. 171ff. Unfortunately there are no demographic figures for individual social strata, which would reveal the population at risk.

Centered around the classics (Latin and Greek) and including some training in mathematics and the natural sciences, this German high school served on the one hand as a kind of comprehensive school in its lower grades and as a well-nigh exclusive university preparatory school in its higher grades. In contrast to the universities, the number of Gymnasia as well as pupils increased steadily from the 1820s, beginning with about 50 schools with 13,767 pupils and growing to about 133 schools with 38,681 scholars in 1858-59, an average annual increase of 7.8 percent. Since by 1870-71 there were already 205 institutions with 59,031 pupils, the high-school pool of potential freshmen was expanding rapidly while student enrollment was still stagnating, indicating that a considerable proportion of high-school graduates entered business or government careers directly after the Abitur (in 1873 as many as 27.1 percent). Thus, a part of the enrollment boom in higher education after 1870 was simply a result of Abiturienten switching to the university; in 1879, only 13 percent did not enter college.[24] However, during the empire the number of institutions grew only to 346 (another 68.78 percent) while pupils increased to 101,745, a further 72.3 percent, and fell considerably short of student growth between 1870-71 and 1914. Since fewer Gymnasium pupils dropped out than in midcentury, the number of graduates increased much faster than the general Gymnasium enrollment, transforming the high school even more into a college preparatory institution, raising the proportion of graduates from 4.24 percent to 6.41 percent of enrollment. Thus the 159 percent increase in Abiturienten indicates that quite a considerable part of the university expansion must have come from the Gymnasium. Among Bonn students, 254 of 275 matriculants between 1865 and 1875 were Gymnasium graduates, and 882.5 of 1,213 new enrollees between 1905 and 1914 had neohumanist training. If there were an estimated 6,852.8 (91.75 percent) *Gymnasialabiturienten* studying at Prussian universities between 1866-67 and 1870-71, while in 1911-12 there were 16,711 (69 percent), then 2.34 of the fourfold increase was due to an expansion of their number, while the remaining increase would have to be explained by other factors. Johannes Conrad correctly concluded in 1906: "It follows, therefore, that the Gymnasia themselves are to a large part the problem and thereby also the cause of the rush to university study."[25]

Another important source of new students were the modern high schools

[24] Conrad, *German Universities*, pp. 215ff.; and P. Lundgreen, "Educational Expansion and Economic Growth in Nineteenth Century Germany: A Quantitative Study," in L. Stone, *Schooling and Society*, pp. 20-66. See also F. Paulsen, *Geschichte des gelehrten Unterrichts*, 3rd ed. (Berlin, 1921), 2: 238-637.

[25] Conrad, "Einige Ergebnisse der deutschen Universitätsstatistik," *Jahrbücher für Nationalökonomie und Statistik* 32 (1906): 433-92; Detlev K. Müller, *Sozialstruktur und Schulsystem* (Göttingen, 1977), pp. 45ff.; *PrSt*, 236: 108ff.

which obtained the right of university matriculation for their graduates during the Second Empire after a long and bitter struggle. The older and more prestigious of the two, the *Realgymnasium*, survived Humboldt's animus against practical secondary education (demanded by the commercial and industrial middle class) by becoming an imitation Gymnasium (without Greek and with less Latin but with more modern languages and natural sciences) instead of providing a realistic alternative to neohumanist cultivation. Supported largely by municipalities rather than by the state, the *Realschule I. Ordnung* (organized in 1859 and renamed Realgymnasium in 1882) fought a lengthy battle for admission of its Abiturienten to university study. Granted in 1870 by Minister of Culture Heinrich von Mühler for the philosophical faculty, permission to enroll was limited by his successor, Adalbert Falk, to modern languages and natural sciences in 1879, almost rolled back entirely in the school conference of 1890 owing to concern about academic unemployment, before full matriculation privileges were finally granted in 1900 (subject to certain subsidiary Latin tests in law and medicine).[26] Enrollment figures reflect this checkered development. Between 1870 and 1914 the total number of institutions and pupils grew from 76 to 187 and from 22,964 to 55,094, respectively, and thereby multiplied about twice as rapidly as the Gymnasium. But from the second half of the 1870s to 1899, enrollments actually contracted from 28,091 to 20,682, before they burgeoned again with the advent of full admission to the university. Over the whole period the proportion of *Realgymnasiasten* to *Gymnasiasten* rose from 37 percent to 54 percent, while the number of Abiturienten increased even more, from 384.3 to 2,542.3, of which initially none, and in the last prewar decade well over half, entered the university. In Bonn there were practically no graduates of modern high schools before 1875, but they amounted to 6.5 percent in 1880-85 (declining to 4.9 percent by 1890-95) and 15 percent in the last prewar years, while in Prussia their number had increased to 14.33 percent by 1911-12. If over one-seventh of German students in 1914 were Realgymnasialabiturienten, then another 46 percent of the enrollment growth after 1870-71 must be attributed to their admission to the university.[27]

Partly as complement, partly as competition, a second type of modern high school developed in Germany during the Empire: the *Oberrealschule*.

---

[26] Paulsen, *Geschichte*, pp. 544-76; Müller, *Sozialstruktur*, pp. 190-218. See also A. Petersilie, *Das öffentliche Unterrichtswesen im Deutschen Reiche* (Leipzig, 1897), 2: 268ff. and Albisetti, "Kaiser, Classicists and Moderns" (dissertation, Yale University, 1976), chapters 2-5.

[27] Müller, "Modellentwicklung," pp. 57ff.; Conrad, *German Universities*, pp. 222ff.; and "Ergebnisse," pp. 444f.; *PrSt*, 236: 109f. Initially the Realgymnasiasten comprised 13.1 percent, and, by the last prewar years, 23.44 percent of all Prussian high-school graduates.

Reflecting more directly the wishes of the urban bourgeoisie, this high school taught neither Greek nor Latin, but more French, English, and especially mathematics and natural sciences than its two more philological competitors. Restricted to a six-year course in 1859, this type developed out of older *Gewerbeschulen*, which were directed toward those practical pursuits demanded by a commercial and artisan clientele. During 1879-82 it was recognized by Minister of Culture Gustav von Gossler as providing general cultivation (*allgemeinbildende Schule*), renamed Oberrealschule, and expanded to a nine-year course. The school conference of 1890 made it into the model preparatory institution for higher technical education, and in 1900 (with appropriate supplementary courses in Latin and other subjects), admitted its graduates to full university study as well. Despite its lack of neohumanist subjects, the Oberrealschule had to assume the institutional trappings of the other two types of high school and in many ways appeared a copy of the Realgymnasium to its pupils. Expanding from three to 111 institutions as well as from 1,705 to 44,591 pupils between 1879 and 1914, this modern high school witnessed the most spectacular expansion of the Second Empire. From 5.15 percent compared to Gymnasium enrollment in 1882-83, the Oberrealschule grew to 43.82 percent within the next generation, while its Abiturienten multiplied from about 13 in the early 1870s to an average of 1,731 in the last prewar years, rising from .44 of the total Prussian high-school graduates in that period to a substantial 17.31 percent, of which almost half went to the university. In Bonn there were practically no Oberrealschüler among the students until the second half of the 1890s, but by 1910-14 they had grown to 8.1 percent of the student body, while in Prussia they comprised 9.99 percent of all students by 1911-12. If one-tenth of German students were graduates of these most modern high schools by 1914, another 32 percent of the enrollment growth of the German universities in the Second Empire must be attributed to them.[28]

Searching for other sources of the enrollment boom, Conrad could still write in 1906 that women "play no significant role at all in our figures," for "in Prussia they are not yet allowed to matriculate." But within the decade, the situation had changed dramatically. Admitted as auditors to Prussian universities in 1896-97 after a protracted struggle, female students finally won the right to enroll in 1908. By 1914, 6.9 percent of the Bonn students and 7.44 percent of the Prussian Kommilitonen were women. If one breaks down the 300 percent Prussian increase, another 29.7 percent

[28] Paulsen, *Geschichte*, pp. 591-617, 715-67; Müller, *Sozialstruktur*, pp. 219-43 and "Modellentwicklung," pp. 57ff.; Conrad, "Ergebnisse," pp. 442ff.; *PrSt*, 236: 109f.

of the student body after 1870-71 derives from female enrollment.[29] Although by the beginning of the Second Empire 5.16 percent of the students already came from outside of Germany, the renown of Central European institutions increased the proportion of foreign students by 1905-06 to 8.7 percent. Even if the xenophobic agitation of the right reduced the attractiveness of studying in Germany somewhat in the last prewar decade, on the eve of the war 8.2 percent of Prussian students were foreigners. If one once again takes the Prussian figure as typical, another 25.9 percent of the growth in student numbers after 1870-71 stemmed from the influx of foreigners in succeeding decades. The final cause of the rise in student numbers is largely artificial, for it results from an increase in the length of study. Although the evidence of Prussian statistics is somewhat contradictory on this point (the 1886-87 to 1911-12 comparison reveals that Protestant theologians, lawyers, and doctors spent an average of .36 semesters more, while students in the philosophical faculty finished .23 semesters more quickly), Franz Eulenburg claims that over the entire period of the empire the average length of university study increased approximately 10 to 15 percent per student. This makes numbers look larger without creating additional students, for those studying spent more time at the university and were therefore counted more often.[30]

Although the listing of categories of new students in table 2-1 does not add up to a causal model, it does suggest some hypotheses about the relative importance of different trends, about their temporal sequence, and about the role of state policy in the extension of higher education. Since two-fifths of the new enrollment derived from an expansion of the Gymnasium graduates, much of the growth of German universities stemmed from traditional sources. But the one-fourth of new students entering as Abiturienten from the more modern high schools indicate that the expansion beyond population growth was spurred by the modernization of secondary education, broadening access at least numerically. The additional increases caused by the admission of women and the slight rise in the attendance of foreign students can be measured precisely, whereas the impact of the prolongation of study can only be estimated. The initial growth phase of the 1870s was produced through an expansion of Gymnasium and Realgymnasium enrollment, with the former carrying the boom into the 1880s, while the latter dropped off after 1875. The pause of the early 1890s is

[29] Conrad, "Ergebnisse," pp. 439f.; Paulsen, *Geschichte*, pp. 774ff.; Preussisches Statistisches Bureau, ed., *Statistisches Jahrbuch für den Freistaat Preussen* 19 (Berlin, 1923): 303ff.

[30] Conrad, *German Universities*, pp. 45ff.; *Statistisches Jahrbuch* 19: 303ff.; *PrSt*, 236: 113ff.; Eulenburg, *Frequenz*, pp. 250ff.

TABLE 2-1
Sources of Enrollment Growth

	Number of Students in 1870-71	Number of Students in 1914	Increase over 1870-71, in percent	Share of Growth, in percent
Germany	13,206	60,748	360	
Prussia	7,469	29,781	299	100
		(1911/2)		
Gymnasium graduates	(est.) 6,853	16,711	144	44.72
Realgymnasium graduates	5	3,470	69,300	15.53
Oberrealschule graduates	none	2,420		10.84
		(1914)		
Women	none	2,217		9.94
Foreign students	500	2,434	386.4	8.66
Prolongation of study				10.31

NOTE: Because of the incompleteness of prewar German statistics, Prussian figures have been used for calculating rates of increase. The relative contribution to growth represents the percentage of 1911-12 students in a given category beyond its 1870-71 base of the Prussian 1913-14 number minus its 1870-71 counterpart. Since the women and foreign students figures are for 1914 rather than 1911-12, the share of Gymnasium, Realgymnasium and Oberrealschule graduates is slightly underweighted. For the sources of this table, such as *PrSt*, vol. 236, see notes 24-30.

largely a consequence of the stagnation of attendance and graduation from these two high-school types: the final growth phase of the late 1890s was at first once again carried by the Gymnasium, then after 1900 also by the Abiturienten of the modern high schools, and eventually (after 1908) also by women. Hence, instead of one sustained enrollment tide, there are a number of separate waves, cresting on top of each other and flowing into different fields of study, which produce the impressive overall growth. Although Prussian policy facilitated the foundation of new Gymnasia, eventually permitted the enrollment of new kinds of students in the universities, and financed the concomitant institutional expansion, the state apparently acted more in response to social needs (vocalized by local and statewide pressure groups) than as a conscious promoter of expansion for its own sake.[31]

While the increase and diversification of secondary school graduates provided a growing source of students, the enrollment explosion stemmed more fundamentally from aspects of modernization, such as economic growth and bureaucratization. Since a macroeconomic approach, especially when dealing with long-range time-series correlation, is likely to yield tautologies (indicating that both the economy and higher education grew at similar rates, without defining the interrelationship), a microeconomic analysis appears more promising. Focusing on individual decisions, this "human capital" and to a lesser extent "consumption good" orientation can be supplemented by a collective analysis of the changing demand for academic labor caused by increasing bureaucratization in the private and public sectors. Although the incompleteness of the historical evidence prohibits precise mathematical calculations, the sources available indicate trend directions and therefore suggest some additional causes of the expansion of higher education.[32]

In contrast to Anglo-Saxon practice, direct *costs* for studying at a German university traditionally have been modest. Johannes Conrad calculated for 1882-83 that the state regularly contributed 72 percent of the university budget, whereas student fees amounted to only 9.3 percent. In a report to the minister of culture, Friedrich Althoff stated in 1890 that only 10 Mk per semester were levied as matriculation fee (supplemented by another 5 Mk for medical students for experimental materials and an additional 10 Mk for laboratory expenses). The average honorarium in the theological and philosophical faculties was 60 Mk per semester for private courses (80 Mk for the lawyers and 120 Mk for the doctors), but a poor student could largely subsist on public lectures. Thus, the average annual tuition per student rose from 67 Mk in 1873 to 169 Mk in 1911 in Prussia. Complementing the low costs, considerable financial aid was available. In 1886-87, 37 percent of Prussian students were supported at an average of 152 Mk per semester, a proportion that was reduced during 1890-91 to 30 percent and fell by 1911-12 to 20 percent because enrollment growth outstripped available funds. Total remission of matriculation fees was relatively rare (less than 10 percent). More frequent was the postponement of payment of lecture fees (*Stundung*), an option used by between two-thirds and one-half of students receiving assistance. About half the needy

[31] See also F. K. Ringer, *Education and Society*, pp. 62ff. His assertion that university enrollment per age group not quite doubled in the empire is contradicted by the data in his table 1.5, on which it is based. See also C. E. McClelland, *State, Society and University*, pp. 239ff. and R. Riese, *Hochschule*, pp. 19ff. for less systematic attempts.

[32] C. A. Anderson, "Education and Economic Modernization in Persepctive," pp. 3-19 as well as the other literature indicated there.

students also had direct stipends of around 180 Mk per semester, while one-fifth were supported through free lunches (*Freitische*) worth some 70 Mk per semester. Although there were relatively few large fellowships, there was substantial financial support (most for theologians and least for law students) as supplement for those who could only partially pay the costs of university study.[33]

Johannes Conrad correctly pointed out that "the main burden for the parents lies in the maintenance of the students, and in a very large number of cases this is already heavy enough." Estimates vary greatly over time and place (higher during the later years of the empire and in large cities such as Berlin) and depend on the social aspiration of the student, some subsisting by work-study, others complaining if they did not get a check (*Wechsel*) of 300 Mk per month in order to keep up with their fashionable friends in the Corps. Most writers agree that it took at least the average wage of an unskilled laborer to study at the university, in other words, about 50 Mk per month or (including fees) about 500 Mk per semester. Althoff argued that in Germany total annual expenses could hardly exceed 1,400 Mk, while at Oxford and Cambridge they were reported to be between 5,000 and 6,000 Mk. Hence, the proletariat was well-nigh totally excluded, and even for the lower middle class the burden was so great that it could only be borne for an exceptionally gifted son. The largest economic barriers, however, were not out-of-pocket costs, but rather foregone earnings, first through the high-school years up to nineteen (at a time when a youth could start an apprenticeship at fourteen), then through the university (an additional four years), and finally during the unsalaried probationary period before state employment after the degree had been received. Although amounts vary with the putative job of the nonstudent, thousands of marks in lost income were clearly involved; if one assumes eight years of study, military service, and probation at an average pay of 75 Mk per month for an Abiturient, the loss would amount to 7,200 Mk. Thus, although the direct expenses were modest, the indirect costs proved a major obstacle to higher education in Central Europe. While both tended to increase slowly, middle-class incomes rose gradually, making foregone earnings a less important consideration.[34]

[33] J. Conrad, "Einige Ergebnisse," pp. 487f. calculated the average fee as 18.5 Mk per semester in 1891-94; F. Althoff memorandum about overcrowding, 31 March 1890, ZStA Me, Rep 92, AI, No 100; P. Lundgreen, "Educational Expansion and Economic Growth," pp. 20-66; and *PrSt* 236: 73ff.; W. Lexis, "Übersicht der gegenwärtigen Organisation der deutschen Universitäten," in his *Die Universitäten im Deutschen Reich* (Berlin, 1904), pp. 45f. puts the fee per weekly hour at 5 Mk.

[34] J. Conrad, *German Universities*, pp. 270ff.; Althoff memorandum, March 31, 1890, ZStA Me, Rep 92, AI, No 100; Schulze-Ssymank, *Das deutsche Studententum*, p. 432; and pamphlet literature on student poverty, IHK, F 1775-97.

The expected or perceived *returns* of university study, on the other hand, promised substantial earnings or occupational advantages and therefore exerted a powerful pull toward higher education. In 1899, Hugo Gruber analyzed the prospects of the academic professions in monetary terms. Perhaps as an echo of the biblical injunction to poverty, Protestant theologians fared least well, starting with 1,800 Mk annually (aside from free housing) and rising to a peak of 4,800 Mk after twenty-five years (supplemented in the larger cities by additional housing subventions and other perquisites). In contrast, law school graduates in the Prussian judicial service began at 3,000 Mk, increasing to 6,600 Mk annually, while the starting salary in higher administration (such as the railroad service) was 4,200 Mk and went to 7,200 Mk, and the popular career of *Landrat* began at 3,600 Mk and peaked at 6,600 Mk annually. Since medical doctors earned their living as free professionals exposed to the vicissitudes of competition, there were no fixed starting salaries or, indeed, earnings limits. In general, the hospital assistants began at 2,100 Mk, while the *Medizinalräte* in government service initially received 4,200 Mk and reached 7,200 Mk. Few physicians in private practice (like the independent lawyers) earned less than the starting salary of the clergy; most probably did as least as well as the equivalent officials; some received annual incomes of well over 10,000 Mk, above what anyone but a Prussian cabinet member could obtain in the public sector.

Because of the great diversity of subjects included, prospects for graduates of the philosophical faculty were even more difficult to assess. While the remuneration of probationary teachers ranged from 1,700 to 2,100 Mk, *Oberlehrer* at the Gymnasium began at an annual salary of 2,700 Mk and could rise to 5,100 Mk, which might be supplemented by another 900 Mk for exceptional service. High-school teachers at private institutions, on the other hand, were less well paid. Chemists in private industry generally started around 1,200 Mk annually, and journalists received equally low initial salaries, which made state employment for liberal arts graduates more attractive than free-lance work. On the other hand, the highest level of the professions reached incomes that fell well short of peak business earnings of 10,000 Mk annually. The lower third of college graduates was economically not much better off than members of the lower middle class (such as artisans, peasants, and shopkeepers), while the middling third was located in the prosperous middle class, and only the top third reached into the elites. Thus, the financial rewards of university study in Imperial Germany were attractive but hardly more so than careers in commerce or industry. However, two elements encouraged academic pursuits: increased security, such as the pension system, and the greater job satisfaction of following a "higher calling."[35]

Perhaps even more important than the anticipated economic rewards were the intangible benefits of superior social status. While the prestige of the Gebildete in the early nineteenth century derived from such complex causes as the nimbus of the Prussian state official and the substitution of secular scholarship for religious authority, after 1870 a popular conception had arisen that "humanity truly begins with classical Bildung." Friedrich Paulsen reflected with concern: "We are so used to this phrase that we no longer feel what an affront it must be for those who have not passed through the Gymnasium" as if they were some kind of inferior beings. Oblivious to the higher ideals contained in the concept of cultivation, most contemporaries saw it as "knowledge of all intellectual and historical developments both past and present, or at least having once been exposed to them, so that one does not have to blunder when they come up in conversation, but can talk like one of the cognoscenti." Institutionalized in a rigorous nine-year course in the Gymnasium, such liberal education used the classics as a device of social discrimination: "Hence, Latin and Greek appear as a kind of uniform, which demonstrates to the masses their distance from the academics and maintains their respect." Especially when modified with the adjective *akademische*, denoting university study, Bildung marked a form of social superiority in Imperial Germany, which became more exclusive the harder it was to obtain. The statistician Johannes Conrad agreed: "A second cause of the disproportionate rush to the universities and especially to official careers lies in the deplorable class antagonisms, which are sharper in Germany than in any other civilized country." Bildung not only set the cultivated off from the masses but also separated them from the industrial and commercial bourgeoisie through a distinctive cultural style. Hence, enrollment boomed also because of "the medieval remnants of class antagonisms, the educational arrogance of our better social strata, the lack of understanding for the importance of our entrepreneurs and their high intellectual achievements, which are as unfamiliar to our academics as to our workers."[36]

A final economic determinant of educational expansion is the ability of

[35] H. Gruber, *Welche Aussichten bieten die akademischen Berufe?* (Berlin, 1899), pp. 5-69; W. Hoffmann, *Das Wachstum der Deutschen Wirtschaft*, pp. 470f.; E. G. Spencer, "Between Capital and Labor: Supervisory Personnel in Ruhr Heavy Industry before 1914," *JSH* 9 (1975): 178-92; and "Businessmen, Bureaucrats, and Social Control in the Ruhr 1896-1914," in H.-U. Wehler, ed., *Sozialgeschichte Heute: Festschrift für Hans Rosenberg* (Göttingen, 1974), pp. 452-66.

[36] F. Paulsen, *Geschichte des gelehrten Unterrichts*, 2: 682-92; J. Conrad, "Einige Ergebnisse," pp. 484-92.

a population *to pay* for higher learning. While some observers, like J. G. Hoffmann, argued that "the increase in wealth" led to a rise in student numbers, others, like Johannes Conrad, believed: "Economic depression leads youth rather to the secure career of public service or to the professions with academic Bildung."[37] Recent research has emphasized economic growth over the business cycle since the economist Walter Hoffmann established a correlation coefficient of $r = .958$ between industrial production per capita and student proportion of the 18-25-year-old population between 1850 and 1913. This relationship between university attendance and GNP for the empire has been reaffirmed, but the connection between enrollment at the Technische Hochschulen and economic expansion appears much weaker (at $r = .266$ between 1860 and 1886 and at $r = .646$ between 1887 and 1913). Although the impressive coincidence in growth curves seems at first to suggest a strong causative relationship, it is largely a statistical artifact. While the net social product grew 50 percent between 1850 and 1870, student numbers increased only 7.1 percent, indicating that for the enrollment stagnation in the middle of the nineteenth century the association is much weaker. Second, a closer look at Hoffmann's scatter diagram reveals that the curve moves in wavelike fashion and the high final correlation is a result of the mutual canceling of substantial short-run fluctuations around the regression line. Hence, the lag of enrollment during the boom period of the fifties and sixties and the spurt during the onset of the depression demonstrate that the contemporary observers were not totally mistaken in seeing a short-term negative covariation. The 1890s present a more contradictory picture, for the enrollment slump started before the last recession began, and only after 1900 did the underlying momentum of growth appear as a simultaneous economic and academic boom. Finally, although industrial production and net domestic product are useful indicators of the overall economic climate, the ability to pay depends more directly on public and private resources generated through taxation and personal income. Certainly public expenditure for universities rose from 6,770,000 Mk in 1873 to 23,435,000 Mk in 1911 (increasing 3.5 times) and thereby facilitated the institutional expansion that accommodated larger student numbers. But equally important is the average annual income per capita, which grew 56 percent between 1850 and 1870 without producing a corresponding growth in student numbers and increased 154 percent in the empire while university enrollment more than trebled per capita. Thus, one is inclined to conclude that economic growth (like population increase)

[37] J. G. Hoffmann, "Übersicht der auf den sämmtlichen Universitäten des Preussischen Staats vom Sommersemester 1820 bis zum Wintersemester 1839-40 Studierenden," in *Sammlung kleiner Schriften*, pp. 187ff.; J. Conrad, "Allgemeine Statistik der deutschen Universitäten," in W. Lexis, ed., *Die Deutschen Universitäten* (Berlin, 1893), 1: 116f.

is a long-term necessary but insufficient cause; that business cycles can but do not necessarily possess a short-term negative association with student enrollment; and that a rise in incomes down the social scale was more directly responsible than a rise in industrial production for decisions to study.[38]

One additional impetus for educational expansion which appears only tangentially in the above discussion is the increased demand for trained academics caused by the spread of bureaucratization. Though building on older foundations in Central Europe, it reached new heights during the Second Empire. In contrast to the limited role of officialdom in Anglo-Saxon countries, Otto Hintze described its pervasiveness in 1911:

> The professions of judge and administrative official and, closely con-
> nected with them, the career of officer form the core; but beyond that,
> in a broader social sense, the bureaucratic estate also includes the
> clergy, not only the Protestant men of the cloth, who are at least
> partly in state employ, but also the Catholic priests. . . . And the
> clerics are followed by the different levels of the teaching profession
> in universities, Gymnasia, and primary schools; further come the
> numerous groups of technical officials in public enterprises such as
> the postal service and the railroads. At present constitutional law
> considers the officials of the cities, counties, and provinces as mediate
> *Beamte* similar to immediate government employees. And finally, in
> the background, we must consider the great army of private officials
> in whom the public has recently taken a great interest.

In Germany the definition of public official extended beyond administrative, judicial, and military officers to include clergymen (the state collected church taxes and therefore paid clerics), teachers (there was little
private education), and employees of public enterprises such as the postal
and railroad services. Thus, the process of bureaucratization did not stop
with the creation of a new federal and state administration after the Wars
of Unification but spread to city and communal self-government, which
grew rapidly in the wake of urbanization. Moreover, official behavior
patterns and privileges were so envied that an ever-growing number of
white-collar employees (*Angestellte*) tried to achieve the status of *Privatbeamte*, which, in cases such as banking, were hardly distinguishable from
their state counterparts. According to W. G. Hoffmann, there were 352,000

---

[38] W. G. Hoffmann, "Erziehungs- und Forschungsausgaben im wirtschaftlichen Wachs-
tumsprozess," in G. Hess, ed., *Eine Freundesgabe der Wissenschaft für E.H. Vits* (Frankfurt,
1963), pp. 101-33; *Das Wachstum*, pp. 454f., 492ff.; R. Riese, *Die Hochschule auf dem
Wege*, pp. 49-53; and P. Lundgreen, "Education and Economic Growth," pp. 38f. Lundgreen's essay is an interesting attempt to analyze the impact of educational investment on
economic growth.

public officials (excluding officers) in the territory of the empire by 1852, 539,500 by 1871, and 2,046,000 by 1913 (including postal and railroad employees). When controlled for population growth, government employees grew from 2 percent to 6.18 percent of males, a trebling over sixty years beyond demographic increase! Hintze estimates another 1.8 million Privatbeamte in the private sector by 1907, indicating that the demand for Akademiker, which occupied the top one-seventh to one-fifth of these positions, spilled over from government into private industry.[39]

Although there is some reciprocity between faculties of study, career prospects in individual fields governed the demand for university graduates in largely unchecked liberal-capitalistic market cycles. "The shortage of candidates for the clerical office, which was undoubtedly felt at the beginning of the seventies" and amounted to about one-third of all new appointments, improved the possibilities for advancement sufficiently to draw more students into Protestant theology. After the surplus of the late eighties, low salaries, the expansion of schools, the limitation of scholarships, and the general secular climate combined by 1906 to create another "deficit of at least 800-900" students, which produced a sharp enrollment spurt in the last half-decade before the war.[40] In the case of Catholic theologians, politics, in the guise of the Kulturkampf, reinforced other barriers such as the expense and secularism of the Gymnasia, the poverty of priests, and the introduction of compulsory military service. Prince Bismarck's struggle with the Church drastically reduced the number of students of theology at the university, and his suspension of the seminaries dried up this alternate source, so by 1884 Conrad predicted: "The clergy must shortly die out . . . unless there is a speedy change for the better." The slowness of the recovery produced a strong relative growth in the 1890s and a continued absolute increase in Catholic theologians until 1910, when a new equilibrium was reached. In the case of law students, expectations of opportunities consistently outstripped any calculable increases in real demand. Government warnings against the surfeit of the 1850s produced a deficit in the 1860s, and Conrad hypothesized, "even at the beginning of the seventies the required number was not reached." This perceived demand led to a doubling of Prussian law students in the 1870s,

[39] Otto Hintze, "Der Beamtenstand," in G. Oestreich, ed., *Otto Hintze: Soziologie und Geschichte* (Göttingen, 1964), pp. 66-125; W. Hoffmann, *Wachstum*, pp. 204ff.; and J. Kocka, "Bildung, soziale Schichtung und soziale Mobilität im Deutschen Kaiserreich am Beispiel der gewerblich-technischen Ausbildung," in B. J. Wendt et al., eds., *Industrielle Gesellschaft und politisches System* (Bonn, 1978), pp. 297-313.

[40] Titze, "Enrollment Expansion"; Conrad, *German Universities*, pp. 81ff.; W. Lexis, "Denkschrift über die dem Bedarf Preussens entsprechende Normalzahl der Studierenden der verschiedenen Fakultäten," 2nd ed. (1891, printed as manuscript), ZStA Me, Rep 92, AI, No 92; Conrad, "Einige Ergebnisse," pp. 452-56.

which leveled out in the 1880s until overproduction had moderated some-what, followed by a renewed expansion in the 1890s. The hope of openings incident to the introduction of the new national civil code (*Bürgerliches Gesetzbuch*) continued to attract students until 1910, when the supply was "twice as high" as necessary for official positions.[41]

In contrast, the number of openings in medicine could grow more freely, for they depended upon general prosperity and social custom. The gradual elimination of surgeons after 1852 and the opening of medical practice in 1869 to free competition led to a steady growth of students until 1872, followed by a brief decline and a resumption of the increase in the 1880s. "As yet, at any rate . . . there is no overcrowding in the medical faculty," Conrad observed in 1884, and the skeptical Lexis predicted that the deficit would disappear only with the class of 1890. Until 1903-04 the number of medical students once again contracted precipitously owing to over-supply hysteria, which reduced the rate of doctors per 100,000 from 182.1 to 100.1, in turn creating the image of a new deficit in comparison with Western Europe and with the level of prosperity. In response, medical students more than trebled until 1914, reaching a new high of 262 per 100,000. Because of the heterogeneity of the philosophical faculty, which included political and rural economy, forestry, pharmacy, dentistry, and other subjects, the demand for its graduates is even more difficult to analyze, although a growing proportion of students enrolled in the phil-ological-scientific core subjects. A steady growth in the number of new Gymnasia and Realgymnasia and a shift of emphasis to modern languages and natural sciences created a demand for high-school teachers, which led to a spectacular growth in the number of philosophical students until the early 1880s, when deteriorating employment conditions halted further ex-pansion and forced some absolute contraction in the first half of the 1890s. The slow response of the cultural bureaucracy, the anticipated deficit after 1900, as well as fluctuating prospects for agronomists and pharmacists triggered a new student avalanche in the second half of the 1890s, which fell upon the universities until the last prewar years, when the impetus was finally spent.[42]

Widely publicized in student periodicals, statements by professional organizations, ministerial announcements in the Prussian Landtag, and press debates, the professional prospects of individual faculties therefore influenced enrollment patterns decisively, albeit to different degrees at various times. While all subjects except medicine grew in the 1870s, first

[41] Conrad, *German Universities*, pp. 114ff., 124ff.; Lexis, "Denkschrift," parts III-IV; Conrad, "Einige Ergebnisse," pp. 456-65.

[42] Conrad, *German Universities*, pp. 141ff., 154ff.; Lexis, "Denkschrift," parts V-VIII; Conrad, "Einige Ergebnisse," pp. 465-74.

law (1881), then philosophy (1884), theology (1887), and finally medicine (1890) outran the demand and paused in the early-to-mid-1890s. Law and philosophy resumed their growth, eventually leveling off, while Protestant theology and medicine climbed once more until 1914. The interdependence between the faculties of law and medicine as well as theology and philosophy needs to be explored further in terms of underlying social characteristics. Although the varying degrees of state employment for different fields render exact demand calculations hazardous, contemporaries did make choices based not on hard evidence but on their general impression of career prospects, however much these assessments lagged behind actual developments.

In the final analysis, the process of mobilization of higher education was both more simple and complex than current theories on the determinants of educational expansion suggest.[43] Inside the university neither educational philosophy nor institutional structure changed sufficiently to account for the remarkable increase in attendance. Only the lifting of statutory restrictions against modern-high-school graduates and women played an important part. Outside the alma mater the average annual population increase of 1.42 percent, especially when channeled through expanded secondary schools, enlarged the pool of potential matriculants. The 2.03 percent average annual economic growth per capita, which increased the individual and collective ability to pay for additional schooling, provided another impulse for rising enrollments. Yet another spur to expansion stemmed from the ongoing process of bureaucratization which fueled the demand for highly qualified labor in government and in the general economy, thereby promising greater returns on investment in education. However, the requirements of an "emergent, hierarchically ordered, rationally administered factory system" related more directly to the growth of the Technische Hochschulen than the universities, since only such subjects as chemistry, economics, and perhaps law led to immediate industrial rewards. Contemporaries already emphasized the importance of aspirations for social mobility (or fears of status loss) as powerful motives for university study. Finally, the stimulus of the neohumanist tradition, which prized higher learning for cultural and personal reasons, was more important than "integration with a national and political culture." Acting together, these only partially quantifiable factors led to individual choices in favor of longer schooling and to collective political decisions to finance the growth

[43] J. E. Craig and N. Spear, "The Diffusion of Schooling in Nineteenth-Century Europe: Toward a Model," paper presented at the Third SSHA meeting in Columbus, Ohio, November 1978. Only the final "normative integration" hypothesis seems inappropriate for higher education. See also Stone, "Size and Composition," pp. 6-12.

of institutions of secondary and higher education. As similar patterns of expansion occurred in most Western countries during the last decades of the nineteenth and the first decades of the twentieth century, the enrollment explosion seems one of those fundamental social transformations characteristic of modernization in general. Once set in motion, educational expansion fed upon itself, for institutional growth created demand that led to more growth until it encountered social limits that time and again checked its further course.[44]

PROBLEMATIC CONSEQUENCES

The direct result of the enrollment explosion was the emergence of the modern mass university. Many contemporaries, like Ulrich von Wilamowitz-Moellendorff, viewed the institutional expansion positively as part of "Germany's rise to world power, not only in the political realm but also through the undeniable achievements of German labor of hand and mind." Indeed, there was much to celebrate. New, ostentatious university buildings were springing up everywhere, and their dedications were celebrated with much pomp and circumstance. Similarly, chairs were established at all institutions at a surprising rate, multiplying the total teaching staff in Germany from around 1,200 in the 1860s to well over 3,860 after 1907. Moreover, seminars (in the humanities) and research institutes (in the natural sciences) proliferated so rapidly during the empire that their costs almost surpassed personnel expenditures by 1913. Although some were founded in the early part of the nineteenth century, well over two-thirds of these auxiliary institutions came into being after 1870. At the same time, scholarly discoveries in philology, science, and medicine increased year by year "as in no other country in the world." Imperial academics had reason to boast, especially since many agreed with Gustav Roethe that "German liberty and the spirit of Prussian discipline are happily wed." New buildings, institutes, career opportunities, research discoveries, academic freedom—no wonder many professors believed "German

---

[44] A. Rienhardt, *Das Universitätsstudium der Württemberger seit der Reichsgründung* (Tübingen, 1918), pp. 3-4 lists factors somewhat haphazardly. See more recently R. Riese, *Die Hochschule*, pp. 13-61; F. K. Ringer, *Education and Society*, pp. 64f.; and C. E. McClelland, *State, Society and University*, pp. 257f.; P. Flora, *Indikatoren der Modernisierung: Ein historisches Datenhandbuch* (Opladen, 1975), pp. 57-174. In 1905 the Berlin professor O. Hertwig attributed the astounding enrollment expansion to compulsory schooling; the draft (more specifically the Einjährige privilege); the spread of newspapers; and the fact that "the respect for scholarship has risen the more the usefulness of its discoveries could be recognized"; see O. Hertwig, *Das Bildungsbedürfnis und seine Befriedigung durch die deutschen Universitäten* (Berlin, 1905).

scholarship has gained a place of honor at home and abroad" and transmitted some of this Wilhelmian booster mentality to their students.[45]

In contrast, observers like Wilhelm Kahl called for "turning from the external back to the internal" values of the university, which they felt endangered by the all-too-rapid growth. In 1913 the historian Karl Lamprecht warned, in his rectoral address at Leipzig: "The dangers that exist or threaten today primarily come from the dislocations of the extraordinary enrollment increases which the German universities have experienced since the foundation of the empire." The most obvious problem was "the overcrowding of the lecture halls. No German university has added to its teaching personnel as quickly as to the mass of students." Indeed, the teacher-student ratio declined from around 1 : 9 before 1870 to 1 : 14 by 1905. "The increase in the number of full professors remained far behind the rising enrollment. As a consequence, auxiliary staff such as extraordinary professors and Privatdozenten were used in a way unknown before," so that nontenured teachers provided the majority of instruction after 1900. In some subjects, like medicine and philosophy, the lower ranks far outnumbered the *Ordinarien*, or full professors. This shift, which increased the distance between the lowly student and the exalted full professor, also made the irregular staff more essential to the functioning of the university. The lack of adequate remuneration or self-government rights within the university community therefore led to the emergence of a reform movement of the untenured *Nichtordinarien* in the last years before the war.[46]

A related problem, "the intensification and specialization of scholarly research in all areas during the last generation," threatened to break up the hallowed "unity of teaching and research." Lamprecht called for the foundation of interdisciplinary centers, "which, despite increased division of labor, provide the necessary synthesis of efforts without which further specialization threatens to undermine culture." Although the creation of special institutes served the needs of researchers, the distance between advanced scholars and beginning students widened with every succeeding cohort, for many of the new creations, such as the Kaiser-Wilhelm Institute, were simply added on to the existing system without the necessary inte-

[45] U. von Wilamowitz-Moellendorff, *Neujahr 1900: Rede zur Feier des Jahrhundertwechsels* (Berlin, 1900); G. Roethe, "Deutsche Freiheit," in E. Schmidt, *Jahrhundertfeier der königlichen Friedrich-Wilhelms-Universität zu Berlin* (Berlin, 1911); H. Diels, *Internationale Aufgaben der Universität* (Berlin, 1906). See also P. Lundgreen, "Differentiation in German Higher Education, 1860-1930," forthcoming in *The Transformation of Higher Learning* (Stuttgart, 1982).

[46] W. Kahl, *Geschichtliches und Grundsätzliches über Universitätsreform* (Berlin, 1909); K. Lamprecht, "Die Zukunft der Universität Leipzig," *AR* 14 (1912-13): 5-16; Franz Eulenburg, *Der akademische Nachwuchs: Eine Untersuchung über die Lage und Aufgaben der Extraordinarien und Privatdozenten* (Leipzig, 1908); and K.-D. Bock, *Strukturgeschichte der Assistentur*, chapter 2.

gration of teaching. Other professors worried about "those elements which lack the preparation" for university study in terms of motivation, secondary education, or wealth and "in the interest of teaching vehemently protested against this decline into intellectual mediocrity." As many believed that "*scholarly* cultivation can only be won where there is real Wissenschaft . . . and Bildung through scholarship only where tradition is a living force," the arrival of new kinds of students as well as the bloating of the universities seemed to endanger scholarly standards and the very mission of the university itself. Finally, the increasing state control, which defined the university "primarily as an institution for the training of public officials," began to undercut that freedom of teaching and learning which seemed essential to higher education.[47]

How did students react to this transformation of their alma mater? Although always ready to help celebrate new milestones of institutional development, many were disturbed by the deterioration of their "college experience." On the practical level, the enrollment explosion led to a constant overcrowding of lectures, laboratories, and seminars, which brought about new restrictions (entrance tests for seminars) and a worsening of the teaching and learning climate. On the theoretical level, more critical minds recognized that the university had become "an institution that breeds specialists" and provided less effective liberal education and professional training. "It could easily inspire the freshman for ideal goals; instead it makes him skeptical, estranges him, and gives him stones rather than bread." According to academic memoirs, disappointment with the formal curriculum prompted many to seek solace in student life, in corporate subculture, an impression that seems borne out by the repeated complaints about the increase of loafing (*Bummeln*) during the empire. To counteract alienation from professors and at the same time to escape the facelessness of *Vermassung*, students joined corporations and associations in droves. Their journals expressed resentment against the admission of graduates of modern high schools and women. Spearheaded by the *Alldeutsche Blätter*, the student periodicals of the right unleashed a well-orchestrated campaign against "foreigners in German Hochschulen," which spilled over into the Prussian Landtag after 1900. On the other end of the political spectrum, the *Freistudenten* mounted a vociferous campaign for university reform: "It must instead become a school for life, which on the basis of his subject enables the individual to comprehend present-day culture in its entirety." Concretely they demanded "the development of richer teaching methods

---

[47] Lamprecht, "Zukunft," pp. 13ff.; F. Pfetsch, *Zur Entwicklung der Wissenschaftspolitik in Deutschland 1750-1914* (Berlin, 1974); M. Rubner, *Unsere Ziele für die Zukunft* (Berlin, 1910); E. Zeller, *Über akademisches Lehren und Lernen* (Berlin, 1879); and E. Spranger, *Wandlungen im Wesen der Universität seit 100 Jahren* (Leipzig, 1913).

in order to shape the character of academic youth" as well as "the introduction of cultural science" in order to restore cultivation to its central place in university education.[48]

An even more important consequence of the enrollment explosion was the overcrowding of fields of study and of the related academic professions. In response to current academic unemployment, Detlev Müller argues that the "qualification crisis" of the 1880s resulted in:

1. The disciplining of socially privileged groups through school and university qualifications, thereby stabilizing the power of capital and bureaucracy;

2. The radical limitation of social mobility through institutionalized and internalized barriers (entrance and transfer requirements of secondary schools; motivation blocks against social ascent among parents and pupils); and

3. The realization and legitimation of a socially selective system of school types (i.e., a class school system).

The sweeping assertion that this excess of educated men fixed the basic structure of the German educational system for the last century has drawn fire from a number of critics. Some have especially attacked the second thesis and countered: "The structural change of secondary education signified not a limitation but, on the contrary, an expansion of motivation for socially mobile strata." Others have taken issue with the underlying assumption that "the unemployment problem for 'academics' in Imperial Germany was created and manipulated to insure the stability of the social order and to frustrate social" mobility and did not result from natural processes.[49] Because both the facts and interpretations of the "qualification crisis" are in dispute, a number of questions need to be answered: Was unemployment real or contrived? How did the public and the government react to it? What were its sociopsychological effects?

Overcrowding first attracted concern in the early 1880s for political

[48] "Die Ausländer an deutschen Hochschulen," *AMh* 18 (1901): 136-37; H. Danneberger, *Der Streit um die Universitäten: Reform an Haupt und Gliedern!* (Munich, 1913); H. Kühnert and H. Kranold, *Wege zur Universitätsreform* (Munich, 1913) and *Neue Beiträge zur Hochschulreform* (Munich, 1913); Schulze-Ssymank, *Das Deutsche Studententum*, pp. 418ff.; P. Ssymank, "Die moderne Studenschaft, ihre Gruppierungen und Ziele," *AR* 15 (1913-14), no. 1.

[49] D. K. Müller, *Sozialstrukur und Schulsystem*, pp. 274-97 and "Qualifikationskrise und Schulreform," *ZfP* 14. *Beiheft* (Weinheim, 1977): 13-35; U. Herrmann and G. Friedrich, "Qualifikationskrise und Schulreform—Berechtigungswesen, Überfüllungsdiskussion und Lehrerschwemme," ibid., pp. 309-25; P. Lundgreen, "Die Bildungschancen beim Übergang von der 'Gesamtschule' zum Schulsystem der Klassengesellschaft im 19. Jahrhundert," *ZfP* 24 (1978): 101-15; and Charles E. McClelland's comments on a session on "Academic Unemployment" at the Social Science History Association meeting in Columbus, Ohio, November 1978.

reasons. In two marginal notes Prince Bismarck wondered about what would become of all the pupils in the Gymnasia:

> For the state this accumulation of learned schools is a mistake that sooner or later will avenge itself by producing a much greater number of discontented climbers who, on the basis of their *gelehrte Bildung*, will make demands that the state will be unable to fulfill entirely. Already now I have seen in the region [of Pomerania] that sons of wealthy peasants are physically and psychologically lost to farming through their parents' ill-fated decision to send them to grammar schools and provide only unusable recruits for scholarship. Russian nihilism was primarily created by a foolish educational system which had led many more people onto the path of higher cultivation than government service or the other studied professions could absorb, who therefore cannot find any employment appropriate to their effort and resulting self-confidence.

In March 1882, Gossler, the Prussian minister of culture, raised "a most significant and far-reaching question" in the Landtag: "Is there an overproduction of the educated, and can the state take measures in order to employ the Gebildete suitably?" Two years later a broader public became aware of academic overcrowding through the publication of Johannes Conrad's pioneering work on the German universities: "The fact we specially aimed at establishing, and which is generally known and recognized, was the enormous increase in the attendance at the universities of recent years." The Halle economist argued: "In our time such a disproportion [between supply and demand] has arisen almost all over, and that rapidly, too." He recommended that "the authorities have first and foremost to discontinue their partial and artificial fostering of the learned schools."[50]

Such alarmist warnings were picked up in the general press, reprinted with cautionary editorials in the student journals, and even found their way into the *Norddeutsche Allgemeine Zeitung*, which wrote in January 1886: "The need of employment for the cultivated classes is great." Bismarck continued to be concerned:

> The surplus of lawyers is known from the daily press. The overproduction of doctors is already reaching a threatening level. The number of teachers of modern languages, mathematics, and natural sciences, not less that of chemists, surpasses the demand by far. Even

---

[50] Stoelle to Bismarck, 15 November 1881 (with marginal note of the chancellor); Bismarck memorandum, 25 November 1881, DZA Po, Rkz 2181; Gossler speech in *AH* (1882): 930; and Johannes Conrad, *Das Universitätsstudium in Deutschland*, pp. 278-86.

Protestant theologians have multiplied so rapidly that in at most ten years they will lack appropriate employment.

Minister Gossler requested the publication of university enrollment figures in an official *Universitätsstatistik* intended to "characterize the unhealthiness of our development, especially [caused by] the rush of the sons of property owners, artisans, lower officials, and primary teachers into secondary education and universities." On the basis of this material the ministry authorized Professor Wilhelm Lexis to write a "memorandum on the normal number of students of different faculties corresponding with Prussia's need" in order to provide a scholarly basis for political decisions. The experience of student radicalism before 1848 and the contemporary Russian agitation led many to believe that "the opposition, from simple Progressives down to Socialists and Communists, derives its most dangerous support from educated circles" and that academic unemployment posed a grave danger for state and society.[51]

Although the perception of overcrowding produced important consequences in its own right, contemporaries argued endlessly about the reality of academic unemployment. While many newspapers merely echoed the warnings implicit in Lexis's first *Denkschrift*, other statisticians claimed that his "calculations were quite uncertain." The royal statistical bureau pointed out a number of factual errors, university curators criticized specific assumptions about the philosophical faculty, and some journals questioned the entire thrust of any attempt to compare "a certain annual need for personnel" with the number of students necessary to fill it. Since there was "a difference between studying with the firm purpose of a government job or going to college in general," the *Nationalzeitung* argued: "One needs to remember that with growing prosperity more and more young people gain academic cultivation without expecting to live from it." Attempting to incorporate as many of the suggestions as possible, Lexis penned a second, more definitive version of his memorandum in 1891, which defined "a field as overcrowded when the time of preparation or waiting [before state employment] extends beyond the norm; the insufficiency of supply shows itself in the shortening of the waiting period or by its total disappearance." He calculated demand as the total number of positions divided by the mortality rate, plus annual new foundations, while he figured the supply as the number of Prussian students in a subject divided

[51] *NAZ*, 14 January 1886; Gossler to Rottenburg, 16 January 1886 with extensive Bismarck marginalia, DZA Po, Rkz 2182; correspondence Althoff-Lexis, 30 August 1888 in ZStA Me, Rep 76 Va, Sekt 1 Tit XIII, No 10, vol. 1, "Der Bedarf an Studierenden"; BUA, C20: W. Lexis, "Denkschrift über die dem Bedarf Preussens entsprechende Normalzahl der Studierenden der verschiedenen Fakultäten" (Göttingen, 1889, printed as manuscript); Bismarck to Gossler, 7 March 1889, DZA Po, Rkz 2183.

by the length of study plus a varying percentage for dropouts, failure, deaths, and so forth (table 2-2). On the basis of 9,090 pastoral positions, he derived an annual need for 350 new ordinations, which meant a demand for 1,260 students of Protestant theology. Adjusting for attrition during the course of study produced an estimate of 1,520 as the "normal number" for the next two decades. Compared with that figure the 1870s showed a deficit until 1881, which was made up in 1886-87 by the subsequent surplus. Thus, Lexis called it "an incontestable fact that since 1883 or 1884 a slowly increasing overcrowding of the Protestant theological faculty has developed." Although the waiting time before appointments grew only from 1889 on and church officials consulted did not yet consider the situation critical, Lexis concluded, in anticipation of even greater surpluses in the future: "It can only appear desirable for the decline in the student number to continue." In contrast, proof of unemployment for Catholic theologians proved impossible. Of the 8,738 positions, 330 were currently unfilled, for the surplus of the early 1870s had given way to an enormous deficit when the episcopal seminaries were closed during the Kulturkampf. Even their reopening in 1886 could not immediately remedy the situation, so it was likely that there would be around 260 students too few well into the 1890s.[52]

TABLE 2-2

Overcrowding of Academic Fields in Prussia

Field	Positions 1890	Annual Demand	Normal Number	Actual Number 1880	1885	1890	Difference 1880	1885	1890
Protestant Theology	9,090	350	1,520	1,330	2,605	2,651	+70	+1,285	+1,131
Catholic Theology	8,738	?	820	349	590	656	−520	−270	−164
Law	10,887	475	2,080	3,103	2,411	3,090	+1,023	+331	+1,010
Medicine	11,009	550	3,225	2,826	4,596	5,212	−339	+1,368	+1,987
Pharmacy	2,640	152	380			634			+254
Dentistry (ca.)	1,200	100	300			250			−50
Philology	4,317	222	1,220	2,952	2,323	1,299	+1,732	+1,103	+79
Mathematics	2,159	82	480	1,915	1,591	573	+1,435	+1,111	+93

NOTE: On the basis of Lexis's revised memorandum, the annual demand for each field was estimated and translated into a normal number of students needed to supply it. Actual enrollments for the 1880s were then compared with this putative *Normalzahl* in order to establish the relative magnitude and trend of overcrowding for each faculty (or subspecialty). For the sources of this table, see notes 53ff.

[52] Conrad to Althoff, 23 May 1889, ZStA Me, Rep 92, Nachlass Althoff, AI, No 92; memorandum of the Königliche Statistische Bureau, July 3, 1889, ZStA Me, Rep 76 Va,

For the law faculty prospects looked rather grim. There were about 7,048 Prussian positions in the judicial and administrative services, another 520 jobs with local government, places for 3,069 lawyers and notary publics, and for another 250 (and this is the most hazardous part of the computation) in banks and industry, which produced an annual demand of about 475 new law graduates. Even at a 25 percent dropout rate and a "normal number" of 2,080, the deficit of the 1860s was quickly filled in the 1870s, and already by 1881 a surplus of over 1,000 students crowded legal lectures, leading to a drop during the mid-1880s but another oversupply of 1,000 students by 1890. "The fact of an increasingly serious overcrowding of the law faculty cannot be denied," Lexis argued, calling for a sizable reduction in enrollment: "Otherwise there is a danger that segments of this crucial profession will become proletarianized or that numerous lives will be ruined." The rise of the failure quota in state examinations, the tightening of admission regulations for government service, and the extension of the probationary period before state appointment indicate that from 1875 to 1890 the excess of law graduates was a stark reality. For the medical faculty calculations became even more difficult, for the overwhelming majority of the doctors were free professionals, and judgments about oversupply depended upon what level of medical care was considered adequate or desirable. The 11,009 Prussian doctors meant (assuming growth with the population, but not beyond it) an annual replacement need of 550 physicians. With a "standard number" of 3,225 (owing to the longer period of study), the deficit of the 1870s disappeared by 1885-86, so graduates of the second half of the 1880s found increasingly stiffer competition. But even Lexis admitted, "one cannot objectively speak of an overcrowding of the medical profession according to social need" and warned that this point might be reached with 5,000 medical students and 800 new doctors annually in the near future.[53]

Lexis's attempt to arrive at reliable figures for the philosophical faculty proved even more hazardous because of the large number of chemists enrolling in the natural sciences, the sizable proportion of *immaturi* attending to further their general education, and the presence of agronomists (in Bonn) and auditors. Assuming 4,676 regular positions at 264 Gymnasia,

Sekt 1 Tit XIII, No 10, vol. 1; Gandtner to Gossler, 6 December 1889, BUA, C20; "Die Überfüllung der Berufe," *Nationalzeitung*, 18 August 1889. The reports of the individual ministries and Reich agencies are in Schwartzkoppen to Gossler, 29 November 1889, while Lexis's rebuttal to Althoff was sent on 24 March 1890, all in ZStA Me, Rep 76 Va, Sekt 1 Tit XIII, No 10, vol. 1. A copy of the revised version of the Denkschrift of 1891 is in the Althoff papers, No 92.

[53] "Denkschrift über die dem Bedarf Preussens entsprechende Normalzahl" 2. Bearbeitung (Berlin, 1891, printed as manuscript). Because of the lack of relevant figures, it is unclear how academic emigration or immigration affected the job market for university graduates.

88 Realgymnasia, and 11 Oberrealschulen by 1889-90 and another 850 posts in administration, private and girls' schools as well as technical schools, another 500 places for professors, 150 for natural scientists in museums, and another 300 for librarians, Lexis calculated the annual need at 222 philologists and 82 mathematicians-scientists. Since in 1885-86, 422 of the former and in 1882-83, 221 of the latter passed state examinations, he concluded that the deficit of the 1870s had been filled by the early 1880s, which increased the normal waiting period for appointment by two to three years and added another four to five years of teaching as poorly paid *Hilfslehrer* before regular appointment. Because of the many sources of error, Lexis carefully estimated the "normal number" at 1,220 students of philosophy and 480 natural scientists and indicated that the surplus of 92.8 percent in the former and 173 percent in the latter during 1881-82 was already declining by the end of the decade to 9.3 percent of the former and 25.8 percent of the latter. "The reaction against the overcrowding has been far more vigorous in these subjects than in the others," even if it had created a dangerous excess of industrial chemists. In response to public criticism, Lexis amplified his calculations in a private letter to Althoff in February 1892, admitting that the ratio of candidates to teachers was favorable until 1880, but maintaining "the balance was lost" between 1880 and 1885. Of the 5,207 candidates during the 1880s who had passed their examinations, at best 3,100 had found regular employment, indicating that even under the most favorable assumptions 600 young teachers were still unemployed. "Against their will and without their personal fault they were deflected from their chosen path as a consequence of the overcrowding of their field." Thus, although Lexis probably exaggerated the oversupply of Protestant theologians and the dangers among doctors, his figures indicate considerable academic unemployment and underemployment for lawyers and teachers. "In every case the existence of these displaced [professionals] must be declared a social and economic evil."[54]

After a series of articles in the *Münchener Allgemeine Zeitung* in 1887 on "the current danger of an academic proletariat," the surplus of educated men became the focus of general concern. Other newspapers printed scare pieces on "university study and scholarly proletariat," warning against the dire consequences of a "pathologically heightened desire for academic cultivation." Student journals of all persuasions joined the chorus of complaints about "the overcrowding of academic study" and regularly published specific information on such topics as "the prospects of legal study in Germany." A series of pamphlets also addressed the problem of "the

[54] Ibid. A. Schönfliess, "Die Überfüllung im höheren Lehrfach. Bemerkungen zu der Lexis'schen Denkschrift," *PrJhb* 69 (1892): 192-206; Lexis to Althoff, 18 February 1892, ZStA Me, Rep 76 Va, Sekt 1 Tit XIII, No 10, vol. 2.

excess of men in the scholarly professions."[55] Because of anti-Semitic, traditionalist, and Catholic outcries, the Prussian minister of culture faced a Conservative challenge in the Landtag in 1889. Deputy Count Hans von Kanitz conjured up "a grave social danger" in the overcrowding and threatened to slash university funding if nothing were done to stem the flood of potential malcontents. Although the Center party leader, Ludwig Windthorst, and National Liberal deputy Robert Friedberg rejected budget cutting as unsuitable, they maintained, "all the world agrees that in general too many people go to the university." In response, Gossler was forced to ask: "How many academic students do the Prussian people need to fill those positions—and I don't want to be misunderstood here—which one counts among the so-called governing classes?" In the debate on high-school reform, he stated: "More important than the problem of how to organize the Realgymnasia is the question, How can I hold back the rush to the universities? That is for me the most important issue of all." Ironically, the government-inspired specter of academic unemployment had come back to haunt the Prussian Ministry of Culture.[56]

Gossler faced two alternatives: he could seek to alleviate individual hardships by persuading his ministerial colleagues to create temporary positions for the excess; or he could counsel restricting the influx of new students in order to restore the balance between supply and demand. Although the number of badly paid Hilfslehrer doubled through the nineties, the Prussian government by and large chose various restrictive measures, arguing: "One can entertain the greatest benevolence towards the candidates; but auxiliary teachers will nevertheless have to admit that the waiting period without remuneration and bad pay constitute the best deterrent to the excessive and dangerous overcrowding of the fields of study that lead to a teaching position." Defending his policies against Bismarck's dis-

[55] J. Conrad, "Die Gefahr eines gelehrten.Proletariats in der Gegenwart," *Münchener Allgemeine Zeitung*, 1887, nos. 2-4; *Westfälischer Merkur*, 17 September 1889; "Universitätsstudium und Gelehrtenproletariat," *Schlesische Zeitung*, 7 September 1890; "Die Überfüllung des akademischen Studiums," *BBl* 1 (1886-87): 52ff.; "Die Aussichten der Juristen in Preussen," *Ac* 5 (1892): 226f.; O. Kuntzemüller, *Die Überfüllung der gelehrten Fächer: Deren Ursachen und Mittel zur Abhilfe* (Berlin, 1889) and other brochures under "Universitätsreformen" in the IHK catalogue.

[56] H. von Petersdorff, "Der Zudrang zu den Deutschen Hochschulen," *ABl* 4 (1889): 3-4; W. R., "Die Gefahr eines gebildeten Proletariats in der Gegenwart," *AMh* 3 (1886-87): 332-35; "Die Aussichten im höheren Lehrfache in Preussen," *Ac* 4 (1891): 28-30; Landtag debates on the budget of the Ministry of Culture, 7 March 1888, 33. session, cols. 897ff., 908ff., and *AH*, vol. 342, cols. 764ff., 844ff.; Gossler announced a restrictionist program: "The creation of a correct relationship between institutions of higher education and the number of inhabitants, a decrease in schools, an increase in the difficulty of new foundations, a preference for schools without Latin with shorter instruction, especially to the detriment of the . . . higher Gymnasia, moreover an expansion of the Lehrpläne, an improvement of the teaching methods, and an attempt to find a caesura after the Untersekunda," i.e., the form entitling graduates to the privilege of one-year military service.

pleasure, Gossler argued in January 1886 that he had already undertaken positive measures to stem the tide:

> 1. The reform of the *Lehrpläne* for secondary institutions [in 1882] set itself the great task of determining the school type which, according to my opinion . . . suffices for the educational needs of our middle class and should absorb all those elements which overcrowd our Gymnasia much to their detriment—the so-called higher *Bürgerschule* with six forms [the later Oberrealschule with the privilege of one-year military service].

Unfortunately, Bismarck's grumbling that "these produce too many half-educated" had proven correct, and the siphoning off did not occur. But the continued overcrowding

> 2. gave me until now the courage to resist the steadily increasing campaign of the Realgymnasia for admission to the study of medicine and eventually to the study of jurisprudence. I am convinced that if this sluice gate were opened a powerful new torrent would inundate the universities.

There was one other potential remedy:

> 3. The oversupply of the academically cultivated and high-school seniors can also be prevented by refusing the applications of the smaller and middling towns to expand their incomplete institutions with seven forms [the *Progymnasia*] into full institutions with nine forms.[57]

Since individual cities like Schöneberg were still trying to upgrade their institutions, the Prussian Ministry of State had to settle the issue in January 1889. Gossler explained the predicament: "Together with a number of other influences, the great victory of 1870-71 transformed the educational ideal and produced a universal demand for the founding of new Gymnasia beyond any need, even in the smallest towns." Since the early 1880s he had therefore been working to: dissolve weak institutions; postpone new foundations; and favor the higher Bürgerschulen, which prepared pupils directly for commercial pursuits. Nevertheless, the Schöneberg Gymnasium was approved in late October 1889 because parental pressure proved stronger than political fear, especially when, as the minister of finance

[57] See Rottenburg to Gossler, 15 January 1886 for Bismarck's phobia of "half-educated people"; Gossler to Rottenburg, 16 January 1886 for a spirited defense of his policies, DZA Po, Rkz 2182. See also Lexis to Althoff, 18 February 1892, ZStA Me, Rep 76 Va, Sekt 1 Tit XIII, No 10, vol. 2 for the argument *not* to hire more temporary teachers. Also see Herrlitz and Titze, "Überfüllung als bildungspolitische Strategie," 348ff. for its implementation.

pointed out, such new institutions served the sons of officers and public officials.[58]

As this attempt to restrict the growth of Gymnasia only reduced the annual increase from four to two in the 1880s and 1890s, the efforts of the Prussian Ministry of Culture concentrated on the dual goal of denying graduates of the Realgymnasium access to the university and on deflecting educational aspirations into technical or commercial training through a new school type, the Oberrealschule. While two articles in the *NAZ* suggested such a strategy, a report to the emperor on "considerations about the need for secondary-school reform" stated flatly: "A main problem lies in the excess number of university preparatory institutions and in the artificial inducement to attend them which our present system exerts." Echoing the Iron Chancellor's concern, the *Immediatbericht* stressed: "The consequence of this is the overcrowding of all academic subjects and the production of an educated proletariat dangerous to the state." To keep out "undesirable elements," tuition should be raised and "the number of commercial and technical schools" should be increased. Because of these fears, at the school conference of 1890 the cards were stacked against the proponents of equality for the Realgymnasium. Both the emperor and Minister Gossler made explicit references to "the great overproduction of Gebildete" and suggested as a radical cure "classical Gymnasia with humanist cultivation, a second kind of school with practical education, but no Realgymnasia." The conference therefore decided to leave the Gymnasium's monopoly of university access untouched, to deflect pressures for reform into a new nine-year institution without Latin (the Oberrealschule, whose graduates were allowed to study at technical universities), and to dissolve Realgymnasia wherever possible.[59]

Not content with these measures, Bismarck pressed for direct restrictions at the university level. Since graduates with debts were most likely to "sympathize with those elements fighting against the existing political and social order," the Iron Chancellor suggested a reexamination of financial aid and college costs. Although convinced that "the present spirit of academic youth hardly leaves anything to be desired in terms of patriotic warmth and dedication," Gossler nevertheless agreed to try "making en-

[58] ZStA Me, Rep 90a, B III 2b, No 6, vols. 100-101 (1888-89) of the *Staatsministerialsitzungsprotokolle*, sessions of 8 October 1888 and 2 January 1889. For the specific surrounding correspondence, such as Rottenburg to Boetticher, 30 December 1888 and the note of 23 October 1889, see DZA Po, Rkz 2183.

[59] "Statistisches zur Frage der Schulreform," *NAZ*, 25 and 26 January 1889; Bismarck to Lucanus, 8 March 1890 and *Immediatbericht*, 16 March 1890 in DZA Po, Rkz 2183a. See also DZA Po, Rkz 2190 (*Reform des höheren Unterrichtswesens*); Ministerium der geistlichen, Unterrichts- und Medizinalangelegenheiten, ed., *Verhandlungen über Fragen des höheren Unterrichts, Berlin 4. bis 17. Dezember 1890* (Berlin, 1891); and James C. Albisetti, "Kaiser, Classicists and Moderns," 156ff.

trance into the university somewhat more difficult'' by raising various fees. On his own accord, he added that ''the present management of stipends'' contributed to the overcrowding, for too many scholarships were subdivided into amounts of less than 50 Mk and thereby enticed ''many poor students to the university who would do much better to choose some kind of [practical] occupation.'' Bismarck assented and also suggested abolishing the ancient custom of Stundung, the deferment of lecture fees until after graduation. Although the member states of the empire agreed that ''it is necessary to reduce overproduction [and] restrict studies to the level of real need by keeping out undesirable elements,'' university rectors pointed out that these measures would be difficult to implement, for Stundung involved the remuneration of individual professors, and the consolidation of stipends failed to touch on all those scholarships in private trusts. As long as not too many poor students would be excluded, general fees could be raised moderately, and more specific institute, seminar, and experimental fees could safely be increased. Saxon minister von Gerber countered that deferment of payment was ''managed with such a benevolent consideration of individual means that it cannot produce an embittered and hostile attitude towards the state,'' goading Bismarck to the outburst: ''All the more easily can it be inflamed! [Deferment] is an increased inducement for studying; [hostility comes] not *from it*, but from the overcrowding of the subject!'' Warning of ''a considerable setback'' in theology and philology, a memorandum of the University of Leipzig argued: ''It would correspond as little to the spirit of the German universities as to the intention of the noble donors if academic study appeared as the privilege of the well-to-do.'' Because of the lack of cooperation from the larger states, Prussia alone raised general and special student fees, consolidated government scholarships, and tightened regulations governing Stundung.[60]

What effect did the government campaign against overcrowding have on the influx of new students into the universities? Repeated in the Landtag, the daily press, and student periodicals, the slogan *"es studieren zu viele!"* proved such a deterrent that in 1891-92 only 2,900 of 4,400 Prussian Abiturienten chose to go to college, and over one-third elected to enter a profession directly. The slowdown in Gymnasium expansion, uncertainty about the Realgymnasium, and the smaller birth cohort of 1870-71 produced a slight dip in high-school graduates in 1889-90 (followed by a

---

[60] Bismarck to Gossler, 7 March 1889; Gossler to Bismarck, 27 March 1889; Bismarck to Gossler, 18 April 1889; Bismarck to the ministers of culture of the federal states, 19 April 1889; Gerber (Saxony) to Bismarck, 29 April 1889; Bismarck to Gerber, 6 May 1889; all in DZA Po, Rkz 2183. See also F. Althoff memorandum 31 March 1890; Sarwey to Bismarck, 27 April 1889; Gerber to Bismarck, 29 April 1889; Memorandum of the Senate of the University of Leipzig, 3 July 1889, in ZStA Me, Rep 92, AI, No 100. See also *PrSt*, 236: 150-61. For Althoff's role, see Sachse, *Friedrich Althoff*, pp. 218-19.

return to steady growth after 1892-93) but did not arrest the increase in the pool of potential students. The fee increases, scholarship consolidation (from 164 Mk to 184 Mk), and deferment reduction also decreased the proportion of students with some kind of support from 37.18 percent to 30.96 percent, and thereby discouraged poorer students. But most effective was the repetition of individual horror stories of failed careers, suicides, and dire poverty, which were supported by figures for the unpaid waiting periods, which rose up to 8.4 years in 1898-99 for Prussian state teachers and 6 years for private instructors in 1894-95. As a consequence, only 708 Abiturienten wanted to study theology in 1902-03 (compared to 1,013 in 1887-88); 611, medicine in 1900-1901 (compared with 1,135 in 1880-81); 160, philology in 1892-93 (compared with 745 in 1880-81); and 79, mathematics in 1890-91 (compared with 270 in 1880-81). Law students alone were not to be dissuaded by such dismal prospects and increased their numbers from a low of 540 in 1882-83 to a peak of 1,483 in 1904-1905.[61]

The prognostications of gloom were increasingly challenged both on statistical and conceptual grounds after 1892. In the prestigious *Preussische Jahrbücher*, the pedagogue A. Schönfliess attacked the accuracy of Lexis's calculations for teachers, while Richard Bünger presented his own analysis of "Prussia's demand for Abiturienten." Even the daily press warned that restrictive overreaction might create "a deficit of properly educated leaders in the future." Attempting to calculate the number of cultivated men whom Prussia would need and not the number who could find an appropriate position, Bünger came up with a Normalzahl of 2,810 and concluded: "In the foreseeable future there is no surplus of high-school graduates." Looking at the situation in the academic professions, during the early 1890s he admitted an oversupply of 200 to 300 theologians (which he thought desirable), considered the increase of medical doctors no problem, and predicted that the present excess of around 900 teacher candidates would be used up by 1896. Only for the lawyers did he see a lasting problem of 1,200 to 1,900 too many *Assessoren*. "Hence, I conclude practically that if successful, the present attempt of the educational administration to limit schools with a nine-year course must have disastrous consequences for the life of our society." Although others criticized these

---

[61] The topic of academic overcrowding became a staple in the debates of the budget of the Ministry of Culture, usually in early March of each year. See *AH*, vol. 342; "Die Kultusdebatte im preussischen Abgeordnetenhaus," *AMh* 5 (1888-89): 368ff.; *Vossische Zeitung*, 23 November 1898; "Ein Vorschlag zur Reform der Berufswahl in den 'gelehrten Ständen,' " *Academische Revue*, July 1897; "Es studieren zu viele," *ATZ* 9 (1894): 298-302; figures from Herrlitz and Titze, "Überfüllung als bildungspolitische Strategie," appendix, pp. 365ff. The proportion of students with deferred fees was reduced from 25 percent in 1886-87 to 11 percent by 1911-12.

computations as overly optimistic, Lexis admitted to Althoff: "There should be no more reason for further warnings against entering the teaching career, but we need have no fears about filling the demand during the next two decades."[62] Adopted by the partisans of the modern schools, this line of reasoning undercut the overcrowding hysteria in conservative circles. Together with the reestablishment of equilibrium through government measures (in all areas but law), this more optimistic assessment of the growing need for educated manpower in a rapidly developing economy, which was at last coming out of the great depression into the great prewar boom, set off even more rapid enrollment growth in the second half of the 1890s.

Although the psychology and rhetoric of overcrowding remained an academic staple, the Prussian government largely disassociated itself from educational protectionism after 1900. In preliminary deliberations the dynamic minister of finance, Johannes von Miquel, voted against the admission of modern high-school graduates: "It would probably lead to a considerable increase in the already greatly overcrowded subjects of medicine and jurisprudence." But the minister of culture, Konrad von Studt, countered the Deutsche Ärztevereinsbund's claim that there were already far too many doctors by pointing out that "the likely increase in obstacles, such as the length of study, the difficulty of the examinations as well as the introduction of an internship year at the least cancel out" the effect of the reforms. The issue of academic unemployment was conspicuously absent from the final debate of the Prussian Ministry of State on the question of university admission of modern-high-school graduates. Studt's advice that "the entitlement monopoly has become harmful for the Gymnasia themselves" prevailed, for their excessive pupil load could then be deflected into the modern-high-school types. Hence in contrast to the *Schulkonferenz* of 1890, the meeting of 1900 recommended equality of all high schools for university preparation as long as modern graduates acquired those additional linguistic tools (like Latin) necessary for law and philology in special remedial courses at the universities.[63] When the overcrowding

[62] See note 54; Richard Bünger, "Der Bedarf Preussens an Abiturienten," *PrJhb* 73 (1893): 52-84; A. Kannegiesser, "Der Bedarf Preussens an Kandidaten des höheren Lehramts," *PrJhb* 74 (1893): 167-73; "Die Regelung des Zustroms zu den höheren Berufen," *Nationalzeitung*, 27 April 1894; W. Lexis to Althoff, 23 November 1893; the Ministry of Culture refused as too costly a suggestion by Schönfliess to publish a regular supply and demand statistic (Ehlmann memorandum, 21 April 1897 in ZStA Me, Rep 76 Va, Sekt 1 Tit XIII, No 10, vol. 2).

[63] Miquel votum, 30 December 1898 in ZStA Me, Rep 76 Va, Sekt 1 Tit XIII, No 10, vol. 2; Studt countervotum, 25 January 1900; minister of justice, votum 30 March 1890; Löbker to Bülow, 10 May 1900, and other correspondence in DZA Po, Rkz 2200. For the sessions of the Prussian Ministry of State on 7 March and 3 April 1900, see ZStA Me, Rep 90a, B III 2b No 6, vol. 140. See also Albisetti, "Kaiser, Classicists and Moderns," pp. 185ff. and protocol of Prussian Ministry of State session, 23 February 1901, DZA Po, Rkz 2200.

slogan surfaced again in the debate about female access to higher education, it proved equally ineffective in preventing the Prussian decision to permit women to enroll as regular students in 1908.

Despite a theologian and teacher deficit, the renewal of expansion prompted Johannes Conrad to resume his warnings against the "quite striking and frightening increase" of students in 1906. Firmly established in academic folklore, the impression of an "excessive popularity of higher studies" dominated the debate until the second wave of growth produced such masses of graduates that reality once more caught up with ideology. "The golden time in which almost every candidate was immediately employed is over and prospects are deteriorating," observed *Academia* in 1910. The number of Prussian law probationers (over 7,500) exceeded available starting positions considerably (by over 2,300), while the 3,847 teaching hopefuls in the empire in 1913-14 were enough to supply the demand for the next seven and a half years. In spite of growing criticism in the Landtag by Center party deputy Johannes Bell, by Free Conservative deputy Oktavio von Zedlitz und Neukirch, and by Progressive party deputy Richard Eickhoff, Minister of Culture August von Trott zu Solz stubbornly maintained: "It is simply impossible for the government to take measures that can succeed in damming the excessive tide flowing into higher education." The Prussian ministry refused to act on the clamor of the educated elite because of a changed perception which accepted growth and publicly declared it the responsibility of private individuals to cope with its consequences. The experience of the deficit of qualified professionals in all careers except law around 1900, which resulted from the restrictive overreaction to the overcrowding of the 1880s, led to a shift from direct measures to prevent growth in student numbers to an adoption of indirect strategies for maintaining elite privileges in an era of mass competition. Bureaucratic attitudes changed from prohibition to sham meritocracy.[64]

When the government would no longer act, educated circles found a new scapegoat—foreign students. Although in 1905-06 only some 8.7 percent of German university students hailed from abroad, 21.1 percent of the students at the Technische Hochschulen, almost half of them Russians, came from beyond the Reich's borders. Two-thirds of these were

---

[64] J. Conrad, "Einige Ergebnisse," pp. 433-92; R. Bünger, "Die Lage des höheren Lehrerstandes in Preussen," *PrJhb* 100 (1900): 452-80; "Die Überfüllung der akademischen Berufe," *BBl* 21 (1906-07): 62f. and "Was ist gegen den zu grossen Zudrang zu den höheren Studien zu tun?" *BBl* 21 (1906-07): 167f.; "Die Beschäftigungsaussichten für die Kandidaten des höheren Lehramts in den verschiedenen preussischen Provinzen," *Ac* 23 (1910): 427f. and W. Montag, "Die Philologenaussichten in Preussen," *Ac* 26 (1913-14): 488-90; *AH*, vols. 544, 554, 569, and 598, especially the speech of Minister of Culture Trott zu Solz on 4 May 1914. The files on "the demand for students," etc. in the ministry simply run out around 1900.

Jewish, for they were virtually denied higher education at home through minimal quotas. From 1901 on pressure groups like the Verein Deutscher Ingenieure began to call for protectionist measures such as raising entrance requirements and increasing fees so that "in case of overcrowding the needs of our own students can be met first." Picked up by the academic press and by Conservative Landtag deputies (1904), this campaign led to a formal resolution by the Alldeutsche Verband in 1905, which hoped to capitalize on the insecurity of the academics to foster its pan-German program. The agitation revolved around charges of "hindering [our] students in the pursuit of their studies" by taking laboratory places away; it exploited anxieties about "trash and Jews" by arguing that they were inadequately prepared; it fastened upon traditional academic fears that "openly revolutionary movements such as anarchists and socialists misuse German hospitality"; and finally, it played upon the threat of international economic competition: "It would be stupid for us to supply [foreigners] with the weapons, i.e., the training of those leaders, with which they intend to defeat us in battle." Eventually the xenophobic right realized, in Professor Paul Samassa's words: "There are 'desirable' as well as 'undesirable' foreigners and that potential measures must uniquely or at least predominantly be directed against the latter." Ethnic Germans outside the Reich—Dutch, Scandinavians, Anglo-Saxons—were welcome, while "Russian Jews" loomed as the primary enemy. In "such a modern, national task," the practical challenge was to exclude the latter without discouraging the former.[65]

Although by and large favoring the *nobile officium* of German *Kultur-mission* and therefore liberality, the government was somewhat divided in its response to this protectionist pressure. With astute opportunism, Chancellor Bernhard von Bülow noted in July 1902:

> We must keep the male and female Polish students out. For the Russians, the story is different as long as they do not openly embrace anarchism. What the enclosed letter says about the positive influence of the presence of foreigners at our universities on our international position is generally accurate.

For reasons of cultural imperialism as well as out of genuine conviction,

---

[65] Conrad, "Ergebnisse," pp. 438f.; "Die Ausländer an den deutschen Hochschulen," *AMh* 18 (1901): 136-37; debate on the *Ausländerfrage*, 12 April 1904 (with Althoff defending liberal admissions), *AH*, vol. 470; "Die Ausländerfrage an den deutschen Hochschulen," *ABl* 19 (1904): 41-43 by P. B.; W. La Baume, "Das Studium der Ausländer an deutschen Hochschulen," *BBl* 19 (1904-1905): 225-28. See also the pamphlet of the Pan-German League by K. Heusing, *Die Ausländerfrage an den deutschen Hochschulen* (Munich, 1905) versus J. Heilbronner, "Die Ausländerfrage an den deutschen Hochschulen und die Stellung des K.C.," *KCBl* 3 (1913-14): 120-34.

Privy Councillor Friedrich Althoff was a committed internationalist and did not mind saying so. A number of liberal pamphlets (as well as articles in the press of the Freistudentenschaft) viewed the attendance of "foreign students at German institutions [as] an ethical duty" and warned that "a closing or a restricting of foreign access to German universities would reduce our influence abroad and strengthen the spiritual and physical forces of our enemies." Thus, Minister of Culture Studt argued in the Ministry of State in December 1905 for a discriminating stance. "Foreigners who, like the British . . . prove useful friends of German ways" ought to be admitted, but "the influx of Russian Jews ought to be curtailed if possible." Prussian procedures already kept the number of foreigners lower than in the other German states, and the rectors of the universities unanimously opposed a general policy of restriction. Thus, "the entrance requirements for Russians [might] be tightened," and fees might be increased. "The political surveillance of Russians and especially Jews was careful and thorough." In the Landtag Studt tried to steer a similar middle course, opposing Karl von Arnim-Züsedom's Conservative tirades by invoking "the reputation of German scholarship and of the German name abroad" against any too obvious forms of educational protectionism, while at the same time emphasizing: "We cannot tolerate the harming of [German students] through the competition of foreigners."[66]

Gradually the concerned institutions adopted not a *numerus clausus* of fixed quotas but a set of specific entrance requirements such as university admission in a foreigner's own country, higher matriculation, lecture and institute fees, and German priority in laboratory places. Sometimes this policy of bureaucratic obstruction misfired. In the spring of 1911 a brilliant Russian student of physics named Dimitri Dubrowsky was denied admission to Berlin University because he could not prove to a subordinate police official's satisfaction that he possessed sufficient means of support, although his father was an estate owner and a high Russian bureaucrat; he also refused to join the reactionary student association sponsored by the Russian embassy, although he was totally apolitical. When his dream of studying with Max Planck was crushed, he despaired and committed suicide. In the Landtag Karl Liebknecht called the unfortunate youth "a victim of the Prussian police and university administration" and charged: "The existing conditions for the admission of foreigners are highly hu-

[66] Bülow memorandum, 20 July 1902, DZA Po, Rkz 2185; for Althoff's internationalism, see Sachse, *Althoff*, pp. 309-17; F. Siegmund-Schulze, *Ausländische Studenten auf deutschen Universitäten: Eine Gewissenspflicht der deutschen Christenheit* (n.p., n.d.); E. Boninger, *Das Studium von Ausländern auf deutschen Hochschulen* (Düsseldorf, 1913); protocol of session of the Prussian Ministry of State, 20 December 1905, DZA Po, Rkz 2186, pointing out that Russian students amounted to only 195 of 2,872 at the Berlin TH, or less than 10 percent. See debate in the Prussian Landtag, 10 April 1907, *AH*, vol. 505.

miliating, and the relationship between university and police is as undignified as it could be." As all parties on the center and right rose in the government's defense, Minister of Culture Trott zu Solz's explanation of the necessity of controlling subversive elements and of protecting local tradesmen against defaulting debtors was accepted, despite liberal and foreign denunciations of such "narrow-minded chauvinism."

When a year later medical students at the University of Halle went on strike to protest the excessive number of foreigners in their faculty (27 percent), the government faced a more difficult dilemma. As the left immediately pointed out in the Landtag, the student strikes were unprecedented in Prussian history, while the ends of reducing competition of foreign students struck nationalist opinion as thoroughly laudatory. Conservative deputy Count von Osten-Warnitz presented a list of demands that had been endorsed at Berlin University as well and called for a high-school graduation certificate, official proof of good character, a German language test before beginning the practical course, a state examination before practicing medicine, the doubling of fees, and the abolition of lecture fee deferment for non-Germans. Despite the combined criticism of the right (against his lack of decisive action) and of the left (against "the reactionary, anti-Semitic movement"), Trott zu Solz clung to his intermediate position: "I believe we have to continue to welcome foreigners at our universities. . . . But naturally this hospitality cannot go so far that our own students and institutions suffer from it." Thus, the ministry tightened up admission standards (such as the science prerequisite for medicine) while rejecting any blanket exclusion of foreigners and thereby prevented any further increase in the proportion of alien students in the last prewar years.[67]

Because of the two waves of overcrowding in the Second Empire, the educated gradually abandoned liberal and moved towards statist solutions of such academic problems as the "impairment of teaching by a lowering of [academic] standards." A memorandum of the philosophical faculty of Göttingen brought this concern about an "extraordinary deterioration of instruction" before the Prussian upper house. A petition by the rector of the University of Münster, Dr. Busz, called for the establishment of a commission of inquiry into "the undeniable difficulties and dangers" in order "to find a remedy for them." The "enthusiastic welcome" of the Bonn faculties for this proposal reveals the depth of professorial discontent with "the heterogeneity of students of both sexes," even if the outbreak

[67] For the Dubrowsky case, see especially *AH*, 24 May 1911, vol. 558; 28 March 1912, vol. 569; and 4 April 1913, vol. 569. For the various measures, see the protocols of the university and rector conferences, 1898ff. in ZStA Me, Rep 92, AI, No 29 and Schmidt-Ott, C 21. Polish deputy Korfanty claimed that there had been hundreds of xenophobic resolutions and that Polish students (though Prussian citizens) were equally required to prove their solvency and political reliability.

of World War I postponed any concrete action.[68] Instead of perceiving the presence of students with modern secondary training as a challenge to develop more timely teaching methods, as advocated by Ernst Bernheim, the majority sought to exclude "unsuitable," "undesirable" or "uncalled-for elements [from] our universities, which for a great number of reasons, be it their education, their talent, or the means of their parents, do not at all belong in the ranks of academic citizens and had better learn a craft, become a merchant, or tend the crops on their fields at home." Because talented lower-class individuals could not play the "social role associated with authority," National-Liberal Reichstag deputy Herrmann Paasche put it even more bluntly: "Studying costs money, a great deal of money: whoever does not have it and can't get any decently ought not go to the university!" Resentment against "the aspirations of the lower orders" was so pervasive that it inspired a genre of cautionary essays on *Studentenelend*, which painted the sufferings and temptations of poor students in lurid colors: "There is only one way to avoid such misery," one all-too-typical article argued. "That is to warn all segments of the population against destining their sons for higher education if they do not possess the necessary means for helping the young academic enter professional life."[69]

Another reason for this restrictive response to the enrollment explosion was the fear of "a decline of the academic professions" due to overcrowding. Theologians complained that the estate of the clergy was "sick, quite sick" because of waning public respect, bad pay (the lowest among academics), and regimentation of conscience by ecclesiastical bureaucracy. Law graduates pointed to the ever-lengthening probationary period before state appointment, to the decreasing chances for advancement, and the increasing competition among lawyers, driving many into near poverty. Doctors warned of "the declining economic position of the medical profession" due to the struggle for public patronage, to higher mortality among physicians, and to lack of old-age pensions. Teachers decried lengthening waiting periods before public employment (*Hungerkandidaten*), inequality

<hr />

[68] A. W. Hofmann, *Die Frage der Teilung der philologischen Fakultät* (Berlin, 1880) represents a typical view: "The idealism of academic study . . . recedes the more the classical soil of our higher cultivation is eliminated from the preparation for matriculation." Göttingen memorandum on "Die Vorbildung zum Studium in der philosophischen Fakultät," *AR* 15 (1913-14), no. 10; Busz petition and discussion, *HH*, 25 May 1914, cols. 543ff., 548-55; votes by the rectors of the various faculties, 9 June 1914 in BUA, A16 1, III, vol. 2.

[69] E. Bernheim, *Das Persönliche im akademischen Unterricht und die unverhältnismässige Frequenz unserer Universitäten* (Leipzig, 1912); *ABl* 4 (1889-90): 3f.; *AMh* 7 (1890): 286f. ("these ever more numerous parasites of our institutions of higher education"); Paasche speech reprinted in *AMh* 4 (1887): 306f.; *AMh* 3 (1886-87): 332-35; Franz Malvus, *Das heutige Studium und das Studentenproletariat* (Berlin, 1889); H. L., "Berliner Studentenelend," *BBl* 24 (1910-11): 262ff.; H. Paalzow, "Reiche und Arme Studenten," *ABl* 17 (1902-03): 185ff.; letter to the *AMh* about overcrowding, 6 (1889), no. 7.

of salaries with other officials, and increasing numbers of dropouts pushed into journalism or other economically insecure existences. Because there was more likelihood of government action if their complaints had a political dimension, academics quickly embraced the slogan of the "academic proletariat." Max Kempener argued in a typical pamphlet: "Proletarians of intellectual labor are much more dangerous enemies of the existing order," for "their cultivation predestines them to be officers of the working class." True in surprisingly few instances, the equation between academic unemployment and political radicalism served as a justification for protectionist demands: "At all costs a dam must be erected against the flooding of the academic professions." Amenable to anti-Semitic and xenophobic currents, this campaign joined other restrictionist efforts in the wake of the depression of the 1870s and sold itself as "a spiritual struggle against the masses," using the special national mission of the academics as cover for social exclusivity.[70] Instead of welcoming greater competition within the liberal professions as a spur to improved religious, legal, medical, and educational services, many Imperial German academics saw it as a threat to their cultural standards, social prestige, economic security, and political conformity.[71] They clamored for direct restrictions to deflect the ambition of the masses from their own prerogatives and, when those failed to stem the tide, for indirect measures, such as an enlargement of the *Mittelschulen* without formal entitlement to university study.

The above evidence indicates that the stimulating hypotheses regarding the "qualification crisis" require substantial modification. Instead of conspiratorial manipulation of overcrowding by the government, the Bildungsbürgertum itself generated much of the concern about the excess of educated men, for it thought largely in static statist categories rather than in terms of a growing economy and changing society capable of employing increasing numbers of university graduates. The frequent complaints about "the strange desire of parents in lower classes to raise their children above their own sphere" must have had some basis in fact, and growing student

[70] G. Baumgärtner, "Der Niedergang der akademischen Berufe," *AR* 13 (1910): 30-34; Müller, "Zu dem Aufsatze: Warnung vor dem Studium der Medizin," *BBl* 15 (1900-01): 29f.; F. Hertel, "Die Aussichten der preussischen Juristen," *Ac* 20 (1907-08): 219-21; W. H. Becker, "Warnung vor dem Studium der Medizin," *BBl* 15 (1900-01): 8-11; W. Montag, "Die Philologenaussichten in Preussen," *Ac* 26 (1913-14): 488-90; for further articles, see ZStA Me, Rep 92, AI, No 92; M. Kempener, *Studententum und Proletarier* (Berlin, 1895²); E. Preuss, "Verbindung des Offizierskorps mit dem Geiste der Universität," *Deutscher Volkswart* (1913), no. 1.

[71] Only the pamphlets of the champions of the Realgymnasium argued the benefits of free competition between the graduates of different high schools, such as O. Kuntzemüller, *Die Überfüllung der gelehrten Fächer: Deren Ursachen und Mittel zur Abhülfe* (Berlin, 1889); O. Perthes, *Die Mitschuld unseres höheren Schulwesens an der Überfüllung in den gelehrten Ständen* (Gotha, 1889); and H. Matztat, *Die Überfüllung der gelehrten Fächer und die Schulreformfrage* (Berlin, 1889).

numbers indeed meant an influx of "undesirable elements" rather than a hardening of social barriers. Finally, the thesis of the erection of "a socially selective system of school types" departs from an overly optimistic view of the early-nineteenth-century Gymnasium as a comprehensive school and describes the decisions of the school conference of 1890 better than those of 1900, where the Prussian government opted for a degree of equality. Instead, the academic unemployment of the 1890s and 1910s resulted from a badly steered process of educational mobilization which was taking place in other Western societies as well. Since in the 1880s higher education expanded faster than the demand for academic personnel, some overcrowding was inevitable. Rather than immediately providing jobs for excess graduates, the Prussian government opted for a triple policy of limiting numbers of new students (school conference of 1890), of discouraging economically pressed parents from sending their children to college, and of not increasing permanent positions. When this approach created a pause in enrollment growth followed by new demand, the Prussian administration reversed its stand, yielded formal equality in entitlement to the graduates of modern high schools, abandoned enforcement of the Gossler package, and began hiring again in greater numbers. This was not an option for egalitarianism but rather a policy of co-optation of the upwardly mobile lower middle class by admitting the *Mittelstand* into the lower prestige professions of clergyman and teacher while informally reserving the higher careers in civil service and medicine for the elites. Ironically, the combination of actual overcrowding and of real government concessions to mobility created a perception of an "academic proletariat," which contributed to the abandonment of economic liberalism by the educated, although actual employment grew impressively in the long run.[72]

A last result of the enrollment explosion was the expansion of the academic professions and, thereby, an increase in the number of the educated within the elite and the population at large (table 2-3). According to the 1852 census, there were approximately 34,857 academic professionals in the Prussian work force (amounting to .642 percent), whereas by the 1907 census they had grown to approximately 135,537 (amounting to 1.156 percent). Hence, in the intervening fifty-five years college graduates almost doubled beyond population growth, and with 1914 as end point, the increase is even greater. Similarly, within the elite the most numerous professions in the 1850s had been commercial and agrarian, followed by clerical. Although by 1907 merchants were still the largest

<hr/>

[72] D. K. Müller, "Qualification Crisis and School Reform," paper delivered at the SSHA meeting in Columbus, Ohio, October 1978; quote from "Universitätsstudium und Gelehrtenproletariat,"*Schlesische Zeitung*, 7 September 1890; Jarausch, "Frequenz und Struktur," pp. 146-49, and Titze, "Enrollment Expansion."

TABLE 2-3
Prussian Academic Professions 1852–1907

	1852		1907
Bildung			
	7,461	officials	22,808
	11,850	clergymen	25,877
	652	professors	1,960
	1,882	teachers	19,788
	5,000	officers	20,472
Professionals			
	1,586 (1860)	lawyers	8,672 (1910)
	4,919	doctors	30,000
	<u>1,507</u>	apothecaries	<u>5,960</u>
	34,857 of 5,430,156		135,537 of 11,718,431
	male workers		male workers
	= .642%		= 1.156%
			or 3.89 times increase
Besitz			
	14,692	agrarians	22,099
		(over 600 Morgen	
		in 1852)	
	2,000	industrialists	17,000
		(over 50 employees	
		in 1858)	
	25,285	commerical	59,029
		(10% of owners)	
	41,977 of 5,430,156		98,128 of 11,718,431
	male workers		male workers
	= .773%		= .837%
			or 2.34 times increase

NOTE: On the basis of Prussian census figures the number of professionals is compared in the middle of the nineteenth and the beginning of the twentieth century. This juxtaposition permits calculating the weight of the educated or propertied stratum as proportion of the male workforce and thereby the estimation of absolute as well as relative growth indices. It also suggests the shifting importance of different professions within each larger group, even if the classification of the Besitz category must necessarily remain tentative. For the sources of the tables, see note 73.

group, doctors had outstripped clergymen, and public officials were over-taking them as well (if one includes the about 19,000 communal officials in Prussia), while entrepreneurs were now beginning to outnumber estate owners, if one counts smaller industrialists. While college graduates mul-tiplied, at times more quickly than available jobs (and therefore had to take positions not formally identifiable in the census data as requiring university training), the doubling beyond population growth of the liberal professions must be considered an important index of the beginning expansion of the upper reaches of the tertiary sector in the economy. Although together with wives and an estimated two children per household the Akademiker comprised only 0.828 percent of the Prussian population in the 1850s, fifty-five years later they had multiplied to 2.313 percent and therefore played a larger social role. The Abiturienten figures point in the same direction of more than doubling (2.37 times) in comparison with the population at large between the founding quinquennium and the last prewar years of the Second Empire, while those who attained the *mittlere Reife*, the bottom level of the cultivated, grew only 1.89 times. Thus, the enrollment explosion after 1870 necessitated (at times grudgingly) an increase in bureaucratic careers for graduates (3.38 times), an even greater multiplication of the free professions (5.57 times!), and a numerically untraceable spread of academics into business.[73] The expansion of higher education therefore led to an important change within economy and society, namely the professionalization of the careers of graduates as well as to the academization of the elites in general.

IN THE FINAL ANALYSIS the Central European enrollment explosion was only one dramatic instance of the general process of educational mobilization in the West. In Great Britain students in higher education grew from around 5,500 to 28,000 in the half-century between 1860 and 1910, while in Russia they increased even more astoundingly from about 7,000 to over 110,000. Although the rise continued (and in some cases accelerated) into the 1920s and 1930s, before halting on a higher plateau, the expansion of the second half of the nineteenth century initiated the numerical transition from the small college to the mass university. This process fundamentally altered not only size but also institutional structure, social composition, graduates' career patterns, and the content of research and teaching. Explanations of the spread of primary, secondary, or tertiary schooling have either invoked modernization as a catch-all or fastened on some particular aspect, such as the growth of communication, as explanation for the whole. Nevertheless, the precise nature of the postulated relationship remains elusive. A retreat into scholarly obfuscation seems tempting: "The interdependence between independent and dependent variable [such as eco-

---

[73] Preussisches Statistisches Bureau, *Tabellen und amtliche Nachrichten über den Preussischen Staat für das Jahr 1849*, vols. 2-5 (Berlin, 1851-55); *StdtR* (Berlin, 1909), vol. 202; H. Kaelble, "Sozialer Aufstieg in Deutschland 1850-1914," in Jarausch, *Quantifizierung*, pp. 279ff. The Abiturienten figures are from Müller, "Modellentwicklung," pp. 63ff. See also Henning, *Bildungsbürgertum*, pp. 483ff. and Vondung, *Wilhelminisches Bildungsbürgertum*, pp. 20-33.

nomic development and higher education] is, however, neither necessarily given for all periods nor is it monocausal and direct." Put more plainly, there seems to be some connection between modernization and expansion of higher education, but its links are implicit and indistinct. The British example points toward successful industrialization with a relatively low level of neoclassical higher schooling. The German case demonstrates the pivotal role of neohumanist bureaucracies in economic development, which then sponsored technical higher education and more technological industrialization. And the Russian experience shows the significance of rapid expansion of first university and then institute higher education for Westernization on the political and economic fronts. The comparative perspective therefore suggests the relative autonomy of the mobilization of higher education and economic growth as well as substantial differences in their interrelation in various national contexts.[74]

Precisely what social changes grouped under the problematic heading of "modernization" contributed to educational expansion? Although hardly a sufficient explanation (as the stagnation of the 1840s to 1860s indicates), one necessary cause seems to be population growth, if it widens the pool of potential students through increased secondary schooling. A second general reason appears to be economic development adding to overall societal wealth and individual prosperity, which can be transferred into education, even if German university enrollment appears to have been countercyclical until the end of the depression in the 1890s (in contrast to the technical college enrollment). A third large area of determinants of expansion relates to the processes of bureaucratization and professionalization (commonly called the emergence of the tertiary sector), which raises the demand for trained personnel. Although the level of educational qualification can fluctuate with the immediate supply of applicants, in the long run both government and industry required ever higher degrees of graduation certificates (and thereby devalued them). Finally, a cultural tradition of viewing higher education as an end in itself and as a hallmark of social attainment gave significant impetus to enrollment growth, even if the content of such "cultivation" may not have been functionally related to modernization (i.e., the anti-industrial bias of Bildung). Breaking down the perception of a stable supply of graduates meeting a fixed demand for

[74] P. Flora, *Indikatoren der Modernisierung*, pp. 57-174 and B. R. Mitchell, *European Historical Statistics, 1750-1970* (New York, 1975), pp. 771ff. Since the aggregate figures disagree, neither time series seems definitive. See F. Pfetsch, *Zur Entwicklung der Wissenschaftspolitik in Deutschland* (Berlin, 1974), pp. 173-81 for the quote. R. R. Locke, "Industrialisierung und Erziehungssystem in Frankreich und Deutschland vor dem 1. Weltkrieg," *HZ* 225 (1977): 265-96. See also R. Lowe, "The Growth of Higher Education in England," and P. Alston, "The Dynamics of Expansion: Russia," in *The Transformation of Higher Learning* (Stuttgart, 1982).

academics, the interplay of these forces created a growth syndrome in which the participants (educational bureaucracies, institutions, professors, and even alumni) developed a vested interest in further expansion. This dynamic operated until it reached the limit imposed by population size, expendable wealth, available jobs (judged socially suitable), and the weakening of the value of cultivation in competition with other goals. Although some of these aspects involve modernization, it is tautological to view enrollment expansion as a simple result of that diffuse phenomenon rather than stressing its conditional and contradictory relationship to some of its subprocesses and its relative autonomy in others.[75]

Although bureaucratic control over all levels of education increased during the Second Empire, the role of the state in the enrollment explosion was muted and indirect. The imperial, state, and local governments provided around 95 percent of the jobs for theologians, 70 percent of the positions for law graduates, 15 percent of the employment for doctors, and 66 percent of the career openings for alumni of the philosophical faculty (teachers, not chemists). Although restrictive during Robert von Puttkamer's tenure as minister of interior, the overall thrust of state personnel policy was toward expansion slightly faster than population growth, for when one avenue was closed (such as the freeze in judicial appointments in the early nineties), others (such as local government positions) opened. The Prussian Ministry of Culture controlled entitlements and formal admission criteria for different types of Abiturienten to the universities or Technische Hochschulen. But despite the resistance of the neohumanist party and the opposition of many academics, the government did yield formal equality to the technical colleges, modern high schools, and women around the turn of the century. Finally, the Landtag and also the government had authority over educational funding, necessary for institutional expansion. Public pressure and bureaucratic self-interest combined to produce a 13.8 fold increase in total educational expenditure between 1864 and 1911, most of which went to primary schooling, while higher education's share multiplied only 4.2 times and sank from almost 6 percent to less than 4 percent of total expenditures. Thus, overall budget growth also contributed

---

[75] For examples of the dangers of an unreflected use of the concept of modernization, see G. Goldmann, *The German Political System* (Boston, 1974) and R. Anchor, *Germany Confronts Modernization: German Culture and Society, 1790-1890* (Lexington, Ky., 1972). See also L. Stone, "The Size and Composition of the Oxford Student Body, 1850-1909," pp. 3-110. In the German example, the internal institutional factors (restrictive regulations, space, teaching methods, curriculum, financial support) seem to have been less significant, for they changed largely in response to enrollment growth instead of preceding it. Similarly, "changes in the ease of communication" seem to have made little difference, since the *peregrinatio academica* was well established earlier and student bodies became more localized after 1870.

to the enrollment boom.[76] But nowhere in the files of the Prussian Ministry of Culture are there any traces of a conscious, long-range decision favoring enrollment growth for universities. The attendance increase rather resulted from individual private decisions to enter higher education for the sake of potential economic, social, and cultural rewards, risking failure as in law because of the high gains for those who did succeed. In this social process the Prussian and other state governments acted as expediter or occasionally as brake. Because of the government's negative experience in the 1890s, Prussian Minister of Culture Trott zu Solz eventually turned over responsibility for steering university enrollments to private individuals. Government policy contributed significantly to the enrollment explosion, but it responded to public demand rather than initiating the process itself.

The social results of the enrollment explosion involve societal change in an equally ambiguous manner. The criterion of inclusiveness has been suggested as one measurement: "An *inclusive* system [of higher education] is one that schools a relatively large proportion of the population or of the relevant age group." By comparing either all freshmen with their average matriculation year cohort or, more practicably in the German context, by relating total university attendance to its appropriate age group, one can calculate an index figure to trace developments over time and in different countries.[77] After subtracting women students, a male cohort-based index of the nineteen-to-twenty-three-year-olds shows a 2.3 fold increase for all students in higher education (from 1.24 to just under 2.9 percent) and a slightly larger rise of 2.34 for university students (from .964 to 2.26 percent) between 1869 and 1914. Because of the stagnation of the 1840s to 1860s, during which secondary education expanded vigorously, higher education outstripped the growth of Abiturienten in Prussia after 1870, which rose only 1.78 times (from 1.58 in 1869-71 to 2.82 percent in 1912-14 of all males nineteen years old). Whatever the causes and consequences of this expansion, the inclusiveness of German higher education increased significantly during the Second Empire. Some observers applauded this

[76] W. Heinemann, "Dezentralisation—Die politische Problematik der Ansätze zur Reform der preussischen Unterrichtsverwaltung vor 1914," *Bildung und Erziehung* 28 (1975): 416-35 and McClelland, *State, Society and University in Germany*, pp. 300ff. For calculations, see W. Lexis, "Denkschrift," rev. 1891 version. Funding figures from P. Lundgreen, "Educational Expansion and Economic Growth," pp. 20-66.

[77] F. K. Ringer, *Education and Society*, pp. 22ff. Based on a comparison between nineteen-year-olds and Abiturienten, Ringer calculated a 50 percent rise from .8 to 1.2, based on twenty-to-twenty-three-year-old university students, he computed an increase of 2.5 to 3 times from .5 or .6 (with technical colleges) to 1.4 (without women) or 1.5 (with females and THs). H. Kaeble arrived at a 2.6 time multiplication using a broader range of twenty-to-twenty-four-year-olds; see his "Educational Opportunities and Government Policies," pp. 239-68. However, both refer to the entire age cohort, including females, although until after 1900 higher education was a male prerogative, and thereby somewhat distort the pattern.

"phenomenon, which we perhaps ought to consider the most beautiful and ideal [development] of our time." In the Prussian Landtag the Socialist deputy Liebknecht pictured the desire for university study as proof of the most high-minded thirst for knowledge: "This rush to higher education is basically a wonderful event, typical of the immense upward striving of our present time, which has reached the broadest masses of the population, who do not want to be content any longer simply to toil in the depths, but long for the heights of culture." In international perspective only some smaller nations like Hungary rivaled the speed of German educational expansion, while Switzerland, Austria, Scotland, and Sweden alone exceeded the level of inclusiveness reached. Hence, among the major European nations, Germany enrolled more students per age group than France, England, and Russia.[78]

Contemporary academics observed the emergence of Grosswissenschaft with a mixture of nostalgic regret at the loss of innocence and self-satisfied pride in modern scholarly accomplishments. The great ancient historian Theodor Mommsen reflected in a memorial speech on Leibniz in 1895: "Indeed, Wissenschaft progresses inexorably and majestically; but in comparison to this gigantic edifice the individual worker appears ever smaller." The fragmentation of knowledge into more and more specialties had become "an indispensable and effective surrogate, but [it is] neither necessarily healthy nor absolutely encouraging." Despite increased funding from public and private sources, despite the general progress of humanity and extension of civilization, Mommsen sensed that something was being lost. "The deep inner relationship between scholarship and the state, upon which Prussia's greatness and Germany's world position also rest, no longer exists as it did before." With the rise of the specialist, Wissenschaft was losing its effect as Bildung and therefore also its public influence. Many German academics shared Mommsen's ambivalence about the expansion of higher education. Although proud of the progress of their own institution, they worried about declining academic standards and stubbornly clung to "maintaining the maturity certificate of the Gymnasium" as precondition for university study. While deploring the introduction of "unsuitable elements" as a threat to the liberal professions, many German Akademiker uncritically accepted Bismarck's argument that academic un-

---

[78] Since most high-school graduates were nineteen years old , it seemed preferable to use this year both for a comparison with the Abiturienten and as the beginning of the student age span. The average time of study fluctuated somewhere between four and five years, making most graduates twenty-three years old, even if further time elapsed before the taking of the various state examinations (*PrSt*, 236: 108). Quote from Karl Liebknecht, *AH* (25 April 1910), vol. 554.

employment necessarily led to political radicalism.[79] Some of the specific research accomplishments (in medicine, the darling of the age) and some of the physical manifestations of progress (such as new university buildings) filled the hearts of Wilhelmian academics with fierce pride in the *Weltgeltung der deutschen Wissenschaft*. But at the same time a considerable number perceived a scholarly, social, and political threat which put them on the defensive and made them instinctively pull to the political right. While they favored growth and specialization (because of the expanding career opportunities they provided), as a group the cultivated viewed educational modernization with deep-seated ambivalence.

[79] Theodor Mommsen, "Das Verhältnis der Wissenschaft zum Staat: Ansprache zum Leibnitzschen Gedächtnistage, 4. Juli 1895," *Reden und Aufsätze* (Berlin, 1905), pp. 196-98; Landsberg to Schultz, 23 June 1914; Ritschl to Schultz, 27 June 1914; Sarre to Schultz, 22 June 1914 in BUA, A16, III, vol. 2. Bismarck to Gossler, 7 March 1889 DZA Po, Rkz 2183. See also Jarausch, "Liberal Education," *JMH* 50 (1978): 609-30.

Three

THE SOCIAL TRANSFORMATION

AN ESSENTIAL ELEMENT in the self-image of the neohumanist university was the liberal notion of cultivation according to individual talent rather than social station. In his introduction to the official German volumes for the Chicago World Exhibition of 1893, Friedrich Paulsen stated with much satisfaction: "As regards the ranks of society from which proceed the possessors of academic culture, we may say that they come from all classes of society. In the Gymnasium and the university we find the sons of peasants and mechanics by the side of the sons of the aristocrats of birth and wealth." In its own view, the imperial university fulfilled an important function of meritocratic selection and social integration. "On the whole the principle prevails: Whoever has gained the right of academic citizenship has thereby the privilege of treatment of an equal—a privilege which in case of need, he may demand sword in hand, since nobody may refuse satisfaction on the score of his birth." In contrast to Western Europe, where university access was restricted to a narrower circle by the expense of public schools or lycée preparation, German academics prided themselves on their social diversity. "It is thus that we speak of the democratic character of the German university, inasmuch as it excludes nobody by reason of his birth and makes equals of all its members."[1]

Critical contemporaries, however, challenged this idyllic picture. Socialist deputies called "higher education a right reserved for the propertied class but not for the great mass of the people," and Karl Liebknecht thundered in the Prussian Landtag: "University education is only a question of available money [Geldsackfrage]!" For him, the composition of the student body proved that the implicit egalitarianism of the Prussian reformers around Wilhelm von Humboldt was not being realized in practice: "The students generally come from the so-called higher class of the population." Even if heroic individuals could overcome all obstacles through

[1] Friedrich Paulsen, *The German Universities: Their Character and Historical Development* (New York, 1895), pp. 110-25.

exceptional exertions, "for the great mass, the average, matters are such that they come only from certain social strata, more or less from the same circles as the professors. The great costs of studying and the long probationary period make it thus; the state has erected an enormous barrier against the lower orders' thirst for knowledge."[2] The liberal sociologist Max Weber similarly argued that although income determined social class and political authority conferred power, educational attainment decisively influenced social status in Central Europe:

> In contrast to the class-forming element of property and economic function, differences in "cultivation" are today without doubt the most important estate-making distinction. Especially in Germany [this is true], where almost all privileged positions within or without government service are not only tied to a qualification of technical knowledge but also to [the criterion] of "general education" and the whole school and university system is put at its service. All our examination diplomas also certify this important status property.[3]

As the basic facts about the social origin of German students are still in dispute, there can be no agreement on their interpretation. Dependent upon statistics gathered by contemporaries, the traditional view emphasizes the high self-recruitment of "the academically cultivated circles." Some stress "the lack of change in this picture until the First World War," while others point to "the increase in broad middle-class representation in the student body."[4] The new social historians seek to resolve this contradiction by comparisons with other European countries. While musing that "the

[2] Deputy Ströbel in the Prussian Landtag, 27 April 1910, *AH*, vol. 544. See also his statement on 27 April 1909, *AH*, vol. 525: "For the higher officials academic education is required. But it is likely to be only a means of keeping the nonpropertied classes out, a way to keep the lower orders from reaching the higher positions." Compare K. Liebknecht in Prussian Landtag, 25 April and 13 June 1910, *AH*, vol. 544. His speeches are the most stringent and intelligent critique of German higher education in the prewar quinquennium.

[3] Max Weber, "Wahlrecht und Demokratie in Deutschland," in his *Gesammelte politische Schriften* (Leipzig, 1920), pp. 297f. See also his comments: "In Germany, such a [liberal] education, until recently and almost exclusively, was a prerequisite for the official career leading to positions of command in civil and military administration. At the same time this *humanist* education has stamped the pupils who were to be prepared for such careers as belonging socially to the *cultured* status group. In Germany however—and this is a very important difference between China and the Occident—rational and specialist expert training has been added to, and in part has displaced, this educational status qualification" (H. H. Gerth and C. W. Mills, eds., *From Max Weber: Essays in Sociology* [New York, 1958], p. 427).

[4] W. Zorn, "Hochschule und höhere Schule in der deutschen Sozialgeschichte der Neuzeit," *Spiegel der Geschichte* (Münster, 1964), pp. 321-39 and H. Mitgau, "Soziale Herkunft der deutschen Studenten bis 1900," in H. Roessler, ed., *Universität und Gelehrtenstand 1400-1800* (Limburg, 1970), pp. 233-68. This traditional view also informs W. Conze, "Sozialgeschichte 1850-1918," in *Handbuch der deutschen Wirtschafts- und Sozialgeschichte*, 2: 670-80.

real surprise . . . is that German higher education was socially as progressive as it was," Fritz Ringer stresses the decline of academic self-recruitment, suggests that "some of the ground thus vacated was taken up by the lower officials and teachers," and concludes that "the economic middle and lower middle classes strengthened their representation at the universities" in the last two prewar decades. On the other hand, Hartmut Kaelble argues: "There are indications that this is the final stage of a long-term process of growing exclusiveness of higher education in Europe." It was only around 1900 that "the traditional economic and educational elites became less visible. . . . Students from the rising economic elite of businessmen increased. Furthermore, higher education became somewhat more open for sons of the petite bourgeoisie and parts of the lower white-collar employees." On the basis of "commercial-technical training," Jürgen Kocka counters these interpretations of partial mobility by stressing that German higher education "contributed to producing and perpetuating a *degree* of social inequality which was neither caused nor demanded by economic development, and in the late empire even collided with the imperatives of business."[5] These imaginative hypotheses raise a number of crucial issues about the recruitment of German students throughout the nineteenth century: Did the social background of the cultivated narrow or broaden? Which of the nonacademic strata became the primary milieu for higher education, the grande or the petite bourgeoisie? What were the societal consequences of the transformation of the student body?

Recent efforts to analyze social access to the university center on the debate about educational opportunity. Since quantitative studies of cognitive achievement have shown that student success is "related more to what students bring to school than what schools do to them," social reforms tend to discount the liberal myth of education according to ability by exposing drastic social inequalities in schooling. In the German context Ralf Dahrendorf emphasizes that in universities "we encounter three great categories of German society in ever diminishing proportions: children from the country, children from working-class families, and girls. A fourth group, Roman Catholics, must be added to these under certain conditions." According to the critics, the causes for this underrepresentation are to be found less in formal restrictions than in "a complex pattern" of invisible obstacles. "They range from the financial preconditions of education to the availability of schools, from the mentalities of social strata that are hostile to education—such as the absence of a sense of deferred gratification—to aspects of school and university life that discriminate against

[5] F. K. Ringer, *Education and Society* (Bloomington, Indiana, 1979), pp. 10ff.; Hartmut Kaelble, "Educational Opportunities and Government Policies" *Welfare States* (New Brunswick, N.J., 1981); and J. Kocka, "Bildung, soziale Schichtung und soziale Mobilität im Deutschen Kaiserreich," *Industrielle Gesellschaft* (Bonn, 1978), pp. 297-313.

certain groups.'' From the French perspective Pierre Bourdieu adds the notion of *privilège culturel*, arguing that ''school culture is class culture,'' which ''for [the underprivileged] represents a conquest at great cost; for the others a heritage which offers both ease of command and its temptations.'' The result of a system of higher education built upon such disparities, while putatively egalitarian, seems to be ''the transformation of privilege into merit'' which internalizes inequality and renders it thereby even more unassailable.[6]

The reformist politics and social science methodology of the educational inequality approach nevertheless create a number of problems. The categories of the imperial aggregate statistics severely limit secondary analysis, whereas self-generated figures permit the testing of older views as well as the elaboration of fresh hypotheses. As many studies include a relatively short time span which freezes patterns, a longer period can uncover the direction and strength of incremental changes. Because discrimination usually involves more than one disparity between students and the general population, clusters of disadvantage can be discovered only with multidimensional indices. As contemporary matrices of stratification presuppose postindustrial structures, scales designed to measure mobility ought to take into account the self-perception of historical actors and seek to reconcile the different perspectives of political power, economic class, and social status. Finally, the effect of changes in student recruitment on the composition of the educated social stratum should not be taken for granted but investigated through a study of the impact of professionalization on fields of study. Although consciousness is not simply determined by class position, the transformation of demographic structure, social recruitment, and professional preference of students in the empire contributed not only to a changing teaching and learning climate but also to a reversal of student politics which fundamentally affected academic mentality.[7]

NEOHUMANIST PATTERNS

The stratum from which most German students were drawn and to which they returned after graduation was the Bildungsbürgertum. Set off from the nobility by their birth and separated from the commercial middle class

[6] As examples of the vast literature, see only C. Jencks, *Inequality: A Reassessment of the Effect of Family and Schooling in America* (New York, 1972); R. Dahrendorf, *Society and Democracy in Germany* (Garden City, 1967), especially pp. 71-74, 100-107; and Pierre Bourdieu and J. C. Passeron, *Les Héritiers: Les étudiants et la culture* (Paris, 1966).

[7] In contrast to R. Riese, *Die Hochschule auf dem Wege zum wissenschaftlichen Grossbetrieb* (Stuttgart, 1977), pp. 43f., it must be emphasized that a quantitative analysis of the matriculation registers is not only possible, but represents the only means of checking the accuracy of current interpretations and of proposing new hypotheses. For another warning against reductionism, see P. Lundgreen, ''Historische Bildungsforschung,'' *Historische Sozialwissenschaft* (Göttingen, 1977), pp. 96-125.

by their cultivation, these educated formed a more cohesive and self-conscious group than other college graduates of Western Europe. As leaders of the transition from estate to class society, the university-trained were recognized by the Prussian Code of 1794 (ALR) as *Eximierte* citizens, exempted from the draft, freed from many taxes, endowed with a special judicial code of honor, and permitted marriage with the aristocracy. These privileges stemmed from a unique combination of three interdependent developments. The absolutist state's need for trained officials gradually led to the introduction of meritocratic examinations for entrance into the higher bureaucracy. Instead of inherited title or wealth, university study (especially of law) became the preferred avenue toward state appointment. At the same time, the culmination of German idealism in neohumanism provided the academically cultivated (*akademisch gebildete*) university graduates with a particular Weltanschauung, justifying their leadership in the general struggle for social and political emancipation. Finally, the professionalization of the careers of medical doctors (disestablishment of surgeons in 1859) and of Gymnasium teachers (with the introduction of the state examination *pro facultate docendi* in 1810) created for university graduates a series of career monopolies in the liberal professions. While the dissolution of the scholarly estate (*Gelehrtenstand*) began in the eighteenth century and took decades to complete, the enrollment boom of the 1820s and 1830s produced sufficient academics to form a new stratum, the Bildungsbürgertum, justified through individual achievement rather than through collective legacy.[8]

Contemporaries viewed the rise of academics in the first half of the nineteenth century with somewhat mixed emotions. While liberals welcomed the spread of higher learning, radicals deplored that "everywhere in cities, towns, even villages, two classes are sharply separated from each other, one cultured and one uncultured." In contrast to other countries, "a special concept has arisen defining as *gebildet* a person who has gone to a Latin school and a university, was fortunate enough to pass his state examination, and then either earned a living from his learning or, preferably, if he had enough means, pursued his chosen path of scholarship until the end of his life." On the other hand, "those are called *ungebildet* who have only gone to middle schools, have been taught more in the exact sciences, and later figure in the body politic as artisans and peasants."

[8] H. Gerth, *Die sozialgeschichtliche Lage der bürgerlichen Intelligenz um die Wende des 18. Jahrhunderts* (dissertation, Frankfurt, 1935); H. Holborn, "Der deutsche Idealismus in sozialgeschichtlicher Beleuchtung," *HZ* 174 (1952): 359-84; R. Koselleck, *Preussen zwischen Reform und Revolution: Allgemeines Landrecht, Verwaltung und soziale Bewegung von 1791 bis 1848* (Stuttgart, 1967); L. O'Boyle, "Klassische Bildung und soziale Struktur in Deutschland zwischen 1800 und 1848," *HZ* 207 (1968): 584-608; and U. Preuss, "Bildung und Bürokratie," pp. 370-95.

Either in the traditional caste spirit or as bearers "of higher knowledge, intended for the people, but far above them," the cultivated acted as a superior stratum, challenging the birth prerogative of the aristocracy.[9]

Much of the leadership aspiration of the cultivated derived from the social aims of the Prussian reformers, which Wilhelm von Humboldt expressed in idealist rhetoric. In contrast to the estate system of training, in which each individual received the teaching "proper" to his calling, the neohumanists aimed at *allgemeine Menschenbildung*, the all-around development of the free individual personality, which would transform passive subjects into responsible citizens. "There surely is some knowledge that everyone must have and beyond that a certain cultivation of mind and character that nobody can do without," Humboldt argued. "Everyone is only a good artisan, merchant, soldier or businessman, if as such and without regard for his special calling he is a good, decent and, according to his station, enlightened human being and citizen." Hence, in principle the reformers championed the comprehensive school (*Einheitsschule*), which everyone could attend according to need, and not a hierarchy of specialized school types. "Therefore [our] goal is to equip the different levels of schools in such a way that every subject of Your Royal Highness is educated in them as moral man and good citizen, according to his means, and that no one receives instruction so that it will be unnecessary and sterile for the rest of his life." Even if the reformers recognized distinctions in estate and profession, their three-tiered system of primary school, Gymnasium, and university would build "on one and the same foundation" and therefore enable "everyone, even the poorest, to receive complete human cultivation." This social egalitarianism was coupled with a political liberalism that aimed at encouraging every citizen "to educate himself," thereby setting the nation free from the excessive tutelage of the absolutist state.[10]

Although attractive, this neohumanist vision was somewhat subverted in implementation because restoration bureaucrats used Humboldt's measures to extend state control over the educational system. In practice, the

[9] L. Freihardt, "Gelehrte und Bürger," *Akademische Zeitschrift* (1845), no. 3, 29-32; no. 4, 45-49; no. 5, 61-86; no. 7, 94-98; and H., "Über das Verhältnis der Studenten zu den andern Ständen," *Zeitschrift für Deutschlands Hochschulen* (1844), no. 6, pp. 53-55. These progressive students urged that the false barriers between academics and other *Bürger* be broken down. For the entire complex, see also S. Turner, "Social Mobility and the Traditional Professions in Prussia, 1770-1848," and "On the Origins of the *Bildungsbürgertum* in Prussia" (unpublished papers, Fredericton, N.B., 1979).

[10] A. Leitzmann, ed., *Wilhelm von Humboldts Gesammelte Schriften* (Berlin, 1903ff.), 10: 81ff., 100ff., 205ff. See also B. Gebhardt, *Wilhelm von Humboldt als Staatsmann* (Stuttgart, 1899); S. Kaehler, *Wilhelm von Humboldt und der Staat* (Munich, 1927); H.-J. Heydorn, "Wilhelm von Humboldt," in his *Studien zur Sozialgeschichte und Philosophie der Bildung* (Munich, 1973), 2: 57-84; and Paul Sweet, *Wilhelm von Humboldt: A Biography* (Columbus, 1980), especially vol. 2.

establishment of the Gymnasium as a comprehensive school led to the curtailment of the flourishing Bürgerschule, the urban middle school, responsive to the needs and aspirations of the commercial and artisan middle class. Finally, the principle of educational equality foundered on the rock of cultural elitism and bureaucratic entitlement, which made education one of the fundamental divides of German society. True cultivation could only be obtained through a scholarly acquaintance with the classics, begun at the Gymnasium and brought to fruition at the university. Johann Gottlieb Fichte could speak rhapsodically of the "future scholars from whose midst the offices of the state are likely to be filled" as a new "nobility given to them by God's grace through exceptional talent and earned through its appropriate development." Inveighing against the "general mass of the commercial and dumbly hedonistic bourgeoisie" and deprecating the philistine *Spiessbürgertum* of the stagnant towns, the philosopher claimed, "there is no higher estate [than the scholarly one], and whoever is not educated scientifically is plebeian." The dynamic liberalism of the reformers, directed against the static hierarchies of estate society, implied impatience with the limited horizon of the commercial bourgeoisie and patronizing superiority over the masses who were to be enlightened. The leading apologist for the Humboldtian tradition, Eduard von Spranger, unwittingly revealed the fundamental ambivalence of neohumanist social aims by calling for "an aristocracy of pure humanity."[11]

The social limitations of the neohumanist university become apparent in the demographic composition of the student body during the first half of the nineteenth century. The formalization of secondary education contributed to increasing the median age of matriculating students from 17.96 (in 1787) to 20.54 (in 1837), a two-and-a-half-year extension which rendered higher education more time-consuming and expensive and made for longer dependence of youth. Though not formally barred, students from the countryside were drastically underrepresented (only half as many as the general population came from villages), while agricultural towns and small cities were the typical academic milieu (47 percent) and larger cities became important after midcentury. Similarly, Catholic students (20 percent) were represented less than in the general population (34 percent), whereas Protestants studied more frequently (70 percent of students compared to 65 percent of the population), and Jews were overrepresented even more dramatically, producing almost 10 percent of the students from

[11] J. G. Fichte, *Deduzierter Plan einer zu Berlin zu errichtenden Höheren Lehranstalt, die in gehöriger Verbindung mit einer Akademie der Wissenschaften stehe* (Berlin, 1817); and E. Spranger, *Wilhelm von Humboldt und die Reform des Bildungswesens* (Berlin, 1910), pp. 99ff. See also K.-E. Jeismann, *Das preussische Gymnasium in Staat und Gesellschaft*, pp. 295-334 and C. Menze, *Die Bildungsreform Wilhelm von Humboldts*, especially pp. 121-37.

1.3 percent of the inhabitants. Resulting from the less urban, less educated, and less wealthy structure of German Catholicism and from the Jewish drive to escape the ghetto through education (the only alternative to commerce), this skewed distribution led to the popular identification of cultivation with a secularized Protestantism that characterized the entire Bildungsbürgertum. The filter that increasingly strained out heterogenous social elements was the neohumanist Gymnasium, which, with the *Abitur-Reglement* of 1834, obtained a monopoly of university access and therefore practically eliminated alternative forms of preparation such as the modern Bürgerschule (the later modern high-school types), private tutoring, and the completion of secondary schooling in the philosophical faculty (the medieval pattern). Since it usually lost much of its artisan-peasant clientele after the seventh grade (*Quarta*) and its commercial-industrial pupils after the tenth grade (*Untersekunda*), the Gymnasium provided its coveted graduation certificate for those who possessed the necessary motivation or means to reach a university. While presiding over classical and romantic salons, women were completely excluded from the universities. Although the enrollment boom of the 1820s increased the diversity of the student body somewhat, the academic recession of the 1840s to 1860s once again reinforced the male, urban, Protestant, and neohumanist traits of the cultivated as a group.[12]

The inertia of estate society which the reformers sought to overcome is especially evident in the social origins of German students before 1870. In the economic-functional categories of Prussian statistics, the most startling development was a decline of sons of government employees from three-fifths to less than two-fifths, partially counterbalanced by an increase in children from free professional backgrounds (who rose from 6 to 16 percent). Contrary to expectation, students from agricultural homes increased from 7 to over 12 percent, while sons of industrialists and artisans similarly climbed from about 5 percent to over 11 percent. Although children from commercial families rose to over 17 percent during the enrollment boom, their share dropped slightly afterwards, while domestic servants virtually disappeared altogether. The overwhelming importance of government in Central Europe, the relatively late onset of industrialization, and the continuation of agrarian wealth limited the diversification

---

[12] This profile represents the results of a quantitative analysis of a ten-year sample of the published matriculation registers of the universities: Tübingen (1777-1817); Göttingen (1797-1837); Erlangen (1798-1843); Kiel (1827-1865); and Heidelberg (1800-1867). See K. H. Jarausch, "Die neuhumanistische Universität und die bürgerliche Gesellschaft 1800-1860," *Darstellungen und Quellen* 11 (1981), pp. 11-58 for details of sources, methodology, and conclusions. See M. Kraul, "Untersuchungen zur sozialen Struktur der Schülerschaft des preussischen Gymnasiums im Vormärz," *Bildung und Erziehung* 29 (1976): 509-19; *StdtR* 2: especially pp. 172ff. (*Anleitung zur Ausfüllung der Zählformulare*).

of academic backgrounds to the noncultivated upper and middle classes. Similarly, the proportion of noble students (18 percent around 1800), highest at the fashionable universities of Göttingen and Heidelberg, declined only gradually during the enrollment boom, recovered once more during the stagnation, and decreased to under 10 percent only in the 1860s. Thus, the German nobility seems not to have been as anti-intellectual as the stereotype of the Prussian Junker suggests and sought to reinforce its traditional hold on the bureaucracy by educational certificates.[13]

In social terms derived from contemporary statisticians the Bildungsbürgertum produced almost half of the non-noble students, indicating an astounding degree of self-recruitment and perpetuation by the academics. The often newly wealthy commercial and industrial *Besitzbürgertum* hardly accounted for 15 percent of the student body, which indicates a psychological and social barrier within the middle class, since this group possessed the financial means for higher education but did not send many of its sons to college before 1870. In contrast, the lower middle class was the second largest parent group (with one-fifth), for university study represented an important path of social mobility (which was still chosen by sons of artisans and tradesmen more often than by children of lower officials and teachers). Finally, the lower classes were practically excluded from higher education, constituting only 1 percent. Although the dominance of the educated lessened during the enrollment boom, when more children of the lower middle class (*Kleinbürgertum*) gained access to the university, in the subsequent stagnation their preponderance was restored, while the propertied middle class also became more numerous. In contrast to the relatively open Gymnasium, which derived two-fifths of its pupils from the lower middle class and almost 3 percent from the lower class, the neohumanist university was more elitist. In comparison with the entire population, the Bildungsbürgertum showed a startling propensity for higher education (around 70 times overrepresented), followed by the nobility (around 35 times), the Besitzbürgertum (around 6 times), while the lower middle class (around .6 times) was underrepresented, and the proletariat nearly totally barred (at .01 times), not to speak of the poor and unemployed. In the first two-thirds of the nineteenth century, almost 60 percent of the student body at German universities stemmed from the top 5 percent of the population, while the middle third produced one-fifth of the students, and the lower three-fifths of the population were denied access except in rare individual

---

[13] C. E. McClelland, "The Aristocracy and University Reform in Eighteenth-Century Germany," pp. 146-73, and H. Reif, *Westfälischer Adel: Vom Herrschaftsstand zur regionalen Elite* (Göttingen, 1979), pp. 357-70.

cases.[14] The reversal of the expansion of the 1820s once more froze the educated stratum in its self-recruited, government-employed, and limited-access pattern, characteristic of the traditional elite university.

The dynamic effects of neohumanist ideas and industrial progress are nevertheless visible in the development and social structure of the individual faculties of study. During the first three-quarters of the nineteenth century, the German university developed from an almost exclusive training ground for clerical and legal state officials into a somewhat broader center of cultivation and medical or philosophical scholarship. Students of theology, while religiously homogeneous, tended to come from the countryside or small towns and were generally older than the rest. Only rarely were they noble or propertied, but instead were recruited from academic families (the Protestant parsonage) and (in the Catholic case, almost exclusively) from the older and newer segments of the lower middle class. In contrast, law students were more privileged, for they were the youngest, most Protestant, and moderately urban group. Four-fifths of noble sons preferred jurisprudence, and academic and propertied children thronged into legal lecture halls as well. With 80 percent of upper- and upper-middle-class students, it was by far the most exclusive faculty. Enrolling the oldest pupils, and more Catholics and Jews from small to large urban areas, medicine, although still restrictive, attracted more students from the lower middle class to make up for its lack of aristocrats. With the least orthodox secondary education, students in philosophy were diverse in age, more Protestant and Jewish than Catholic, and also the most urban. Although there were few nobles and the proportion of the commercial-industrial bourgeoisie was only strong in Berlin, this faculty was the actual social melting pot of the university, for it contained the highest percentage of pupils from nonacademic homes. For sons of academics, university study was largely a matter of professional self-perpetuation (165 of 343 sons of pastors at Göttingen studied theology); for the nobles and propertied, it generally meant securing their status not with birth or wealth but with training in law and medicine; and for the lower middle classes, it was a question of rising to the stratum of the cultivated through theology or philosophy.[15]

---

[14] For comparative figures on Halle and Berlin, see J. Conrad, *German Universities*, pp. 57-70 and M. Lenz, *Geschichte der königlichen Friedrich-Wilhelms-Universität zu Berlin* (Halle, 1910), vol. 4. The index of representation is based on Preussisches Statistisches Bureau, *Tabellen und amtliche Nachrichten* (1849), vols. 4-6. See also M. Kraul, *Gymnasium und Gesellschaft im Vormärz* (Göttingen, 1980), pp. 150-53; and Elkar, *Junges Deutschland*, pp. 81-102.

[15] W. Dieterici, *Geschichtliche und statistische Nachrichten*, pp. 138ff. A. Neher, *Die katholische und evangelische Geistlichkeit Württembergs 1813-1904* (Regensburg, 1904), pp. 62ff.; W. Bleek, *Von der Kameralausbildung zum Juristenprivileg* (Berlin, 1972); C. Marx, *Die Entwicklung des ärtzlichen Standes seit den ersten Dezennien des 19. Jahrhunderts*

This pattern of composition, origin, and study shaped the social, cultural, and political world of the Bildungsbürgertum. Formal institutionalized "cultivation" determined the degree of prestige within the educated stratum, beginning with "academic" (university) attendance and descending through higher technical training (during the empire engineers gradually achieved formal but not social equality) and the Gymnasium Abitur as prerequisite for being gebildet (with lesser prestige for the modern school types). A marginal group were those with the certificate of intermediate maturity (*mittlere Reife*), also known as the *Einjährig Freiwillige*, who obtained the privilege of one-year military service as preparation for reserve officer status (figure 3.1). Although intellectuals with individual success as artists and poets might be included among the cultivated, academics were suspicious of the lack of educational credentials and bohemian social mores of the intelligentsia. The academically cultivated were members of "good society" in the small and middling cities, the proverbial German "home towns" of the early nineteenth century. They possessed the privileges of marriage (*connubium*) and intercourse (*commercium*) with the nobility and dominated the voluntary associations that organized local

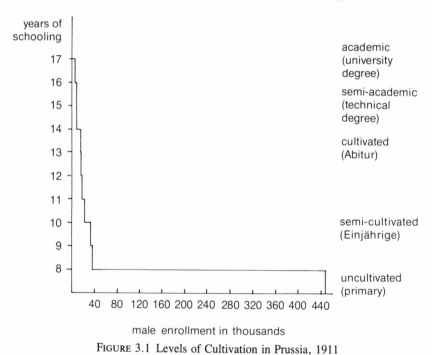

FIGURE 3.1 Levels of Cultivation in Prussia, 1911

(Berlin, 1907); and E. Brand, *Die Entwicklung des Gymnasiallehrerstandes in Bayern 1773-1904* (Munich, 1904), pp. 19-88.

social affairs, such as the Harmonie or the Casino. As members of their own professional associations (such as the Ärzteverband) and sometimes as alumni of their student corporations, the educated set the general social tone of much urban life because their higher calling conferred superiority over the commercial middle class, who followed material pursuits. Lawyers, doctors, or Gymnasium teachers tended to belong to the leading circle (*Stammtisch*), while merchants were included only on the basis of some additional distinction, such as public service as burgomaster.[16]

Although split according to employment into state officials and free professionals, most academics were engaged in serving the exalted and somewhat mystical Central European notion of Kultur. Official cultural institutions such as church, higher school, court, and hospital were controlled by the educated, while private (or municipal) enterprises such as theaters, museums, orchestras, and newspapers were also largely directed by university graduates. Although their symbiosis with creative intellectuals was sometimes uneasy, the academics were also the leading consumers of art, music, and literature and influenced informal cultural life through salons, circles, and discussion groups. Relics of neohumanist learning combined with elements of recently enshrined German classics and strains of romantic sentimentality to produce the Biedermaier version of middle-class (*gutbürgerliche*) life-style, characteristic of cultivated homes well into the present century. Vacillating between loyalty to state or dynasty and aspirations for freedom, in politics the Bildungsbürgertum became the primary champion of the national and liberal movement up to 1870. As local notables (*Honoratioren*) and self-appointed opinion leaders, the cultivated dominated bureaucratic politics as well as the emerging national associations and political parties and therefore constituted the overwhelming majority of the members of the 1848 parliaments. Although divided in a multitude of ways according to religion, region, or tradition, the educated were the foremost supporters of the tenuous reconciliation of power and culture in the ideal of the rule of law (*Rechtsstaat*). Even if strictly speaking it comprised less than 1 percent of the population in 1852, the Bildungsbürgertum nevertheless constituted a crucial stratum within the German upper and middle class which determined much of its social habits, cultural goals, and political actions.[17]

[16] Ernest K. Bramsted, *Aristocracy and the Middle-Classes in Germany: Social Types in German Literature 1830-1900* (Chicago, 1964); and the memoir literature cited in H. Tompert, *Lebensformen und Denkweisen der akademischen Welt Heidelbergs* (Lübeck, 1969), pp. 36-46.

[17] L. Beutin, "Das Bürgertum als Gesellschaftsstand im 19. Jahrhundert," *Blätter für Landesgeschichte* 90 (1953): 135-62; W. Mommsen, *Grösse und Versagen des deutschen Bürgertums* (Stuttgart, 1949); H. Henning, *Das Bildungsbürgertum* (Wiesbaden, 1972), pp. 214ff., 373ff., and 474ff., and K. Vondung, "Zur Lage der Gebildeten in der wilhelminischen Zeit," in *Wilhelmisches Bildungsbürgertum* (Göttingen, 1976), pp. 20-33.

DEMOGRAPHIC TRENDS

Beginning with the Wars of Unification (1864-71), changes in the composition of the student body fundamentally transformed the structure of this educated middle class. Contemporary statistics (and secondary analyses based upon them) reveal contradictory outlines of development. Hence, the historian faces a dual problem of sources of information and criteria of measurement. Because the student census forms used by the Prussian Statistical Bureau were destroyed, the only escape from the categorical prison of previously published figures is a fresh empirical case study. Since the Berlin records fell victim to the Second World War, the present study will analyze a systematic 10 percent sample, comprising 6,510 students, of the matriculation registers of the University of Bonn, the second largest Prussian institution.[18] The beginning of the enrollment explosion in 1865 serves as the starting point (with the decade of the 1840s as comparative background), while the First World War, during which few male students attended classes, constitutes the end of the time series. The matriculation registers contain the date and inscription number, the semester of study, the estate, name, and thereby also sex of the student, age, birthplace, present residence, father's profession, religious affiliation, names of previous universities attended, place and type of secondary education, and the faculty of studies. They are a fairly accurate record, because it was in the financial interest of the university (for collecting direct student fees and indirect government subsidies) to enter anyone actually using institutional facilities.[19]

When analyzed according to the criteria of the educational inequality debate, this demographic data allows a diversified approach to the question of social transformation. *Age structure*, indicated through the median age of matriculation, sheds interesting light on the increase in institutionalized schooling and the growing dependence of youth. *Geographic distribution*, construed as the degree of regionalism, urbanization, and internal migra-

---

[18] R. S. Schofield, "Sampling in Historical Research," in E. A. Wrigley, ed., *Nineteenth Century Society* (Cambridge, 1972), pp. 146-92. The physical bulk of the matriculation register volumes and the lack of running numbers in Bonn made random sampling impossible. To have sufficient entries for each decade and for each subgroup (e.g., female students), a systematic 10 percent sample offered the best practical alternative. When the distributions of the sample for 1890-95 were compared with the patterns of the entire year of 1893, the differences were so slight that confidence in the results must be considered high.

[19] BUA, Matrikel der Rheinischen Friedrich-Wilhelms-Universität (MS Bonn, 1840-1850, 1865-1914), first series. See also ibid., A 16, 1, vols. 2-3 (*Immatrikulationen*) and MUA, 305a, 1950/9, no. 623 for the government regulations. For a vivid description of the actual enrollment process, see J. M. Hart, *German Universities: A Narrative of Personal Experience* (New York, 1874), pp. 36ff. See also W. Ebel, ed., *Die Matrikel der Georg-August Universität zu Göttingen, 1837-1900* (Hildesheim, 1974), 2 vols., which I am currently analyzing in a control study.

tion, serves as a telling indicator of spatial access to higher education. *Religious toleration*, shown by the diversity of religious affiliations, is a vital measure of cultural discrimination. *Segmentation*, viewed as the degree of tracking between classical and modern secondary schools, aids in tracing the institutional diversification of university preparation. Finally, *sexual equality*, evident in the proportion of females in the student body, is an important index of the structure of educational opportunity. Combined, these five measures reveal typical clusters of privilege or deprivation and capture some of the complexities of the process of change, through comparisons between the Bonn case study, Prussian universities, and the general population.[20]

Imperial statisticians worried that "a great number of students come to the university only at a relatively advanced age and that a not inconsiderable portion remains there quite long." Indeed, the upward shift in age structure of the student body was striking, for the median age at enrollment in Bonn rose from 20.22 in 1840 to 21.54 in 1910 (table 3-1). The primary reason for the three-and-a-half year increase in the entering age of German students during the entire nineteenth century was the formalization of secondary education as a nine-year course even if the proportion of twenty-year-olds (and above) among the Abiturienten tended to decrease somewhat, from 56.2 in 1859-63 to 43.5 in 1899-1905. A second important cause was the prolongation of university study in all disciplines, which increased the proportion of upperclassmen registering in Bonn from 33.3 percent in 1840 to 58.7 percent in 1910. (Their median age was 22.03 years, compared with 20.28 years for freshmen.) Less significant was "the rendering of military service before enrollment," since three-fourths of the Prussian students postponed their military duty until after graduation. Moreover, the growth in *immaturi* and foreign students, as well as in auditors already practicing a profession, also contributed to the aging of the student body.[21]

The influx of socially heterogeneous elements during the enrollment explosion pushed up the students' entrance age, since the speed of completion of educational requirements is a clue to social affinity to schooling. Hence, foreigners (21.71), villagers (21.72), Catholics (21.39), students with irregular secondary education (22.28), females (22.60), as well as

[20] See note 4; L. Stone, "Size and Composition of the Oxford Student Body," pp. 16ff.; F. Ringer, *Education and Society*, pp. 22ff.; and K. Jarausch, "The Social Transformation of the University," *JSH* 12 (1979), 609-31.

[21] A. Rienhardt, *Das Universitätsstudium der Württemberger*, p. 42; F. Paulsen, *German Universities*, pp. 177ff.; J. Conrad, *German Universities*, p. 36; "Einige Ergebnisse," pp. 445f.; F. Eulenburg, *Die Entwicklung der Universität Leipzig in den letzten hundert Jahren* (Leipzig, 1909), p. 201 (shows a decrease of students under twenty from 54.3 percent in 1859-63 to 34.2 percent by 1904-08); and *PrSt*, 236: 108ff. The median is a more useful measure of central tendency for student age, since a few adults in their forties tend to throw off the mean, while the mode fails to register shifts under one year.

TABLE 3-1
Matriculation Age of German University Students

	Bonn	Erlangen	Heidelberg	Kiel	Tübingen	Median Age	Number of Cases
1776					17.98	*17.98*	73
1787					17.96	*17.96*	67
1797		19.17			17.89	*18.62*	174
1807		19.43			18.60	*18.88*	156
1817		19.86	19.42		19.86	*19.48*	451
1827		20.05	20.05	20.70		*20.17*	697
1837		20.60	20.46	20.70		*20.54*	562
1840–49	20.27		20.30	20.54		*20.30*	1060
1857			20.04	20.27		*20.05*	577
1865–69	20.86		20.14	21.56		*20.52*	861
1870–74	20.60					*20.60*	275
1875–79	21.06					*21.06*	327
1880–84	21.10					*21.10*	410
1885–89	21.43					*21.43*	438
1890–94	21.38					*21.38*	469
1895–99	21.22					*21.22*	646
1900–04	21.34					*21.34*	796
1905–09	21.46					*21.46*	1115
1910–14	21.54					*21.54*	1305

NOTE: In order to gain the perspective of the entire nineteenth century, figures from an earlier pilot study were added to the Bonn data. Since matriculants contain both first-time students and older transfers from different universities, the above time series is not comparable to freshmen data from other countries. For the sources of this table, see notes 12, 19, and 21.

agrarian (21.78), industrial (21.38), and old-middle-class (21.45) students exceeded the average of 21.25. On the other hand, North Germans (21.02) or East Elbians (21.07), urban students (21.01), Protestants (21.09), Jews (21.04), and new-middle-class (20.96) offspring had easier access to higher education and therefore reached comparative levels of accomplishment earlier. The increase in matriculation age in the second half of the nineteenth century led to an "excessive prolongation of school life," which in turn produced the later entry into professional careers deplored by many contemporaries. This lengthening period of dependence created some of those generational tensions portrayed in "youth literature" and motivated the campaign of the Freistudentenschaft for less restrictive student laws in the last prewar years.[22] But the arrival of older students also reflected the slow diversification of milieus which broke down the mold of neohumanist self-recruitment.

Despite the campaign against foreign students, contemporaries paid little attention to the shifting patterns of *geographic distribution*, for statisticians lacked the technical means to measure the urbanization of the student body.[23] At first glance, rural underrepresentation continued during the empire, but a second look reveals that the urbanization of the general population reduced the overrepresentation of metropolitan students and made the entire student body somewhat more like the population at large (table 3-2). Instead of becoming more cosmopolitan, the students of Bonn University became more provincial, with the proportion of Rhinelanders rising from 45.3 percent in 1840 to 71.9 percent by 1910 (figure 3.2). Although the percentage of foreign students grew from around 5 percent to about 8 percent at all German universities and at least Berlin became less of a local institution, the increase of Saxon students at Leipzig from 22.7 percent in 1869-73 to 37.9 percent in 1904-09 indicates that there may be a turning point in modernization after which the student body becomes less cosmopolitan and urbane.[24]

The reasons for this paradox lie in the same cause, the extraordinarily rapid population growth of the Rhine-Ruhr area (99 percent) from 1870 to 1910, which exceeded the average demographic increase in the German Empire by two-fifths. Attracted by the coal mines and steel factories of the Ruhr basin, a wave of internal migration swelled the population in this industrial core of the Rhineland and made it the most urbanized region of Central Europe. While only one-fifth of the students changed their residence between birth and enrollment in the 1840s, over one-third had done so by

[22] The chi-squares of contingency tables were generally high, but for brevity's sake only the most important cross-tabulations have been summarized in the text. For replication and secondary analysis, the data set has been deposited in the West German Federal Archives (Bundesarchiv) at Coblenz. See J. R. Gillis, *Youth and History*, pp. 95ff. and S. Fishman, "Suicide, Sex and the Discovery of the German Adolescent," *HEQ* 10 (1970): 170-88. See also Schulze-Ssymank, *Das deutsche Studententum*, pp. 428ff. and J. Conrad, *German Universities*, pp. 226-28.

[23] Conrad, *German Universities*, pp. 38-51 treats only foreign students and the question of provincial representation. A. Petersilie in the *Universitätsstatistik*, vol. 236, presents elaborate tables on *Die Heimat der Studierenden* according to citizenship and even calculates a provincial index of participation, but fails to inquire into urbanization. A. Rienhardt (*Das Universitätsstudium der Württemberger*, p. 49) notes the need for such an investigation but refuses to undertake it for practical reasons.

[24] F. Lenz, *Friedrich-Wilhelms-Universität*, 4: 519; F. Eulenburg, *Leipzig*, pp. 196-99. Table 3-2 and figure 3.2 are based on an analysis of the students' birthplaces according to population (the figures are taken from the 1855, 1874, 1895, and 1910 editions of *Ritters Geographisch-statistisches Lexicon*); state and province; and a comparison with the parents' current place of residence.

TABLE 3-2

Urbanization of Bonn Students

	Under 2,000	5,000	Town Size 20,000	100,000	Over 100,000
1870					
Percent of Prussian population	63.9	12.4	11.2	7.7	4.8
Percent of students	37.2	17.3	14.8	19.1	11.5
Index of representation	.582	1.395	1.321	2.48	2.40
1890					
Percent of Prussian population	53.0	11.9	13.2	9.8	12.1
Percent of students	29.8	10.1	19.0	16.3	24.7
Index of representation	.562	.848	1.439	1.663	2.04
1910					
Percent of Prussian population	40.0	11.3	14.1	13.3	21.3
Percent of students	21.7	10.8	16.4	19.5	31.6
Index of representation	.542	.955	1.163	1.466	1.483

NOTE: The categories (village, rural town, provincial city, large city, and metropolis) follow standard Prussian census practice. To calculate an index of representation for a given town size in the student body, the percentage of students born in one such unit was divided by the population percentage residing there. Values under 1 indicate underrepresentation, while values over 1 indicate overrepresentation. For the sources of this table, see note 24.

the 1890s. Other demographic developments contributed to the dual outcome. The increase of Jewish students (who were more urban), of graduates of modern high schools (who came from the larger cities), of women (who were more metropolitan), of sons of industrial and commercial families (who were from medium to large cities), and of the offspring of the Besitzbürgertum (and the rentiers who preferred larger towns) contributed to urbanization. The presence of beginning students, of Catholics, of Gymnasium graduates, of industrial-commercial parents (who were overrepresented in the Rhine-Ruhr area), of non-nobles, of free professionals, and especially of the sons of the old middle class made the student body more provincial with each succeeding decade.[25] If the Bonn pattern is indicative of the entire empire, the universities of the last prewar years were still as

[25] For a convenient summary, see W. Köllmann, "Bevölkerungsgeschichte 1800-1970," in W. Zorn, Handbuch, 2: 9-50; H. Kellenbenz, "Wirtschafts- und Sozialentwicklung der nördlichen Rheinlande seit 1815," in F. Petri and G. Droege, eds., Rheinische Geschichte (Düsseldorf, 1979), 3: 71-112; and D. Crew, "Definitions of Modernity: Social Mobility in a German Town, 1880-1901," JSH 7 (1973): 51-74.

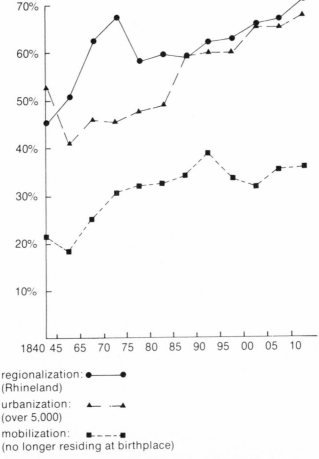

regionalization: ●———●
(Rhineland)

urbanization: ▲— ·—▲
(over 5,000)

mobilization: ■————■
(no longer residing at birthplace)

FIGURE 3.2 Geographic Distribution of Bonn Students

inaccessible as ever for rural children, but the advantage of metropolitan youths decreased and more students came from the institution's home province than ever before. The shift from the quiet rural town with its church steeple horizon to the raw and bustling industrial city of over 100,000 as typical home environment left many German academics with a nostalgic longing for the wholeness of a lost world and a fundamental ambivalence about the problems and temptations of the modern megalopolis.

Because it combines cultural values with social position and political outlook, the criterion of *religious toleration* reveals the persistence of privilege and the increase in diversity in the student body of the imperial university. The Prussian denominational pattern in the quarter century before World War I shows a significant (and continuing) overrepresentation of Protestant students, a substantial (but decreasing) underrepresentation of Catholic Kommilitonen, and an astounding (but declining) disproportion of Jewish pupils in higher education (table 3-3). Despite some early differences, local Bonn distributions demonstrate a similar transformation from the Protestant Prussian Bildungsbürgertum to the Catholic Rhenish industrial bourgeoisie and Jewish commercial middle class. In the 1860s the German Wars of Unification prevented Protestants from outside the Rhineland from attending, while the Old Catholics' schism after the Vatican Council of 1870 (which asserted papal infallibility and the virgin birth) led the Cologne archbishop to prohibit the study of Catholic theology at Bonn, for the faculty had joined the schismatics (figure 3.3). Protestant students had easier access to the universities, for they were mostly cosmopolitan, mobile, modern educated, female, and came from noble, government-employed, elite, higher official, and new-lower-middle-class families. In contrast, Catholics were more local, rooted, recent high-school graduates, neohumanist, male, and stemmed from bourgeois, agrarian, industrial, commercial, nonelite, and old-middle-class homes. Because of their greater social distance from schooling, they had to be more conformist to get into the university. Finally, Jewish students combined the advantages of wealth, mobility, modernity, previous study, and cosmopolitanism with such disadvantages as commercialism, bourgeois origin, and propertied and old-middle-class backgrounds which forced them into conventional secondary schooling.[26] The spread of higher education to the Catholic minority therefore contributed to the social diversification of the student body.

The reasons for the disproportion among confessions were intensely debated. In 1856 the politician and academic Georg von Hertling made "the dissolution of the Holy Roman Empire and secularization" responsible for the Catholic educational deficit, but contemporary statisticians argued that "economic reasons more than confession determined the decision to study." The subsequent discussion isolated as causes:

1. The "lack of parity" in the appointment to higher public offices, evident in the glaring underrepresentation of Catholic professors at German universities;

2. "The celibacy" of the Catholic clergy, in contrast with the Protestant

---

[26] *PrSt*, vols. 102-236; *Badische Schulstatistik: Die Hochschulen* (Karlsruhe, 1926); see also the volume on *Katholische Theologie* in the series *Bonner Gelehrte: Beiträge zur Geschichte der Wissenschaften in Bonn* (Bonn, 1968); W. Ruppel, *Über die Berufswahl der Abiturienten Preussens in den Jahren 1875-1890*, pp. 14ff. for the relation between confession and profession.

TABLE 3-3
Religion of Prussian Students

	1886/87				1902/03				1911/12			
	Percent of Population	Percent Students	College Affinity	Representation Index	Percent of Population	Percent Students	College Affinity	Representation Index	Percent of Population	Percent Students	College Affinity	Representation Index
Protestant	64.24	69.84	9.04	1.09	62.75	65.62	8.38	1.05	61.47	66.43	13.19	1.08
Catholic	34.15	20.12	4.89	.58	35.65	26.65	6.62	.75	36.56	27.52	9.19	.75
Jewish	1.29	9.58	61.20	7.43	1.12	7.41	55.58	6.62	1.03	5.60	66.22	5.44
Other	.32	.46		1.43	.48	.32	5.24	.67	.94	.45	5.77	.48

NOTE: On the basis of Prussian statistics the religious distribution of students is compared to the general population, while the desire for higher education ("college affinity") is based on the number of students per 10,000 males of each denomination. For the calculation of the index of representation, see note for table 3-2. For the sources of this table, see note 26.

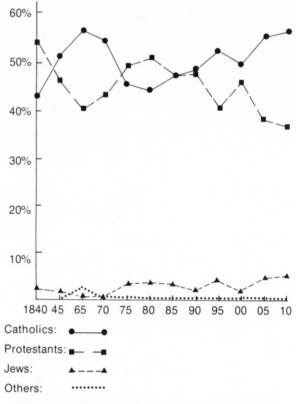

Catholics: ●——●

Protestants: ■— —■

Jews: ▲ – – –▲

Others: ••••••••

FIGURE 3.3 Religious Denomination of Bonn Students

pastors, whose sons made up 7 percent of the Prussian student body in the late 1880s;

3. The differences in "domicile" between the confessions, for in the 1890s, 82 percent of the Jews, 40 percent of the Protestants, but only 31 percent of the Catholics lived in cities and therefore had direct access to secondary education;

4. The unequal "distribution of wealth," which consigned a disproportionate share of Catholics to the lower Prussian tax brackets and meant that in the late 1880s only 13.3 percent Protestants but 22.4 percent Catholics and 24 percent Jews deferred their lecture fees in law, medicine, and philosophy;

5. Finally, "the German Catholics' distrust of public high schools," deriving from the Kulturkampf of the 1870s, the antimodernist stance of the Church, and the suspicion of the climate of Wissenschaft at the uni-

versities, "where they saw so many enemies of their Christian faith."[27] In contrast, the "century-old exclusion from owning land and making goods as well as discrimination in public life" did not discourage, but rather propelled Jewish intellectuals into the universities at an extraordinary rate. Referring generally to "the peculiar character of Judaism," Gentile statisticians sought to explain this thirst for cultivation by "their natural desire to keep their offspring in the higher classes . . . 'the strong ambition to enter professions that bring renown through academic education, and a personal strength of will, restlessness, and energy in pursuit of any goal."[28]

The differing social settings and cultural traditions of the denominations led to contradictory ideological responses to higher education. Liberal and orthodox Protestants viewed cultivation as identical with their own faith and claimed Bildung as their natural prerogative. At the quadri-centennial of his birth, Luther was presented as "a fighter for truth for conscience's sake." The Berlin rector Hugo Kleinert claimed: "There is no area in the whole wide field of German Wissenschaft worth its name which does not actually or potentially share in Luther's spirit and bear the stamp he placed upon German culture." Defensive about the contradictions between Church dogma and the principle of free inquiry, Catholics, on the other hand, argued for the compatability between faith and scholarship in numerous articles, speeches, and books such as *Das Prinzip des Katholizismus und die Wissenschaft*. To overcome popular mistrust of a higher education controlled by Protestants and infused with the dangerous spirit of the Reformation, Catholic academics launched a wide-ranging campaign for equality: "The continuation of the present state . . . of [im]parity would mean the moral and material degradation of the Catholic population. To bring about a change in this regard is the noblest and most pressing task." Repeated in countless public meetings, these arguments and improving socioeconomic conditions slowly led to an increase of Catholic pupils in the Gymnasia and universities, even if the deficit in the modern high schools and technical colleges continued.[29]

[27] Hertling cited in "Der deutsche Katholizismus und die Wissenschaft," AMBl 9 (1896-97): 247-51; L. Cron, *Glaubensbekenntnis und höheres Studium* (Heidelberg, 1900); and Fliegen, "Der Anteil der deutschen Katholiken am akademischen Studium," *Ac* 10 (1898-99): 121-24. See also R. J. Ross, *Beleaguered Tower: The Dilemma of Political Catholicism in Wilhelmine Germany* (Notre Dame, 1976), pp. 1-32.

[28] Rienhardt, *Universitätsstudium der Württemberger*, pp. 44-48; and M. Richarz, *Der Eintritt der Juden in die akademischen Berufe* (Tübingen, 1974). The Jewish case proves that "confession and economic situation" alone are not a sufficient explanation for the differential desire to study, but that cultivation as social value can motivate efforts to overcome discrimination.

[29] P. Kleinert, *Luthers Verhältnis zur Wissenschaft und ihrer Lehre* (Berlin, 1883); G. von Hertling, *Das Prinzip des Katholizismus und die Wissenschaft* (Freiburg, 1899); J. P. Bachem, *Die Parität in Preussen* (Cologne, 1897). See also Dr. Grauert, "Katholizismus und Wissenschaft," *Ac* 8 (1896-97), no. 7; "Das Prinzip des Katholizismus in der Wissenschaft,"

Because of greater formal and informal discrimination in other areas, the Jewish minority viewed higher education as an important avenue of emancipation from the ghetto toward the free professions of law and medicine, which were not officially barred, like the Officer Corps. The relative meritocracy of secondary and higher education promised sufficient rewards for achievement to make the development of individual talent worth the sacrifice, but the price of admission was cultural assimilation into academic Germany, and the cost of professional success (obtaining a full professorship) often was as high as complete amalgamation by conversion. Confronted with increasing numbers of Catholic and Jewish students as professional competitors, the Protestant Bildungsbürgertum reacted with Catholic baiting (the *Hochschulstreit* of 1904-05) and overt or covert anti-Semitism (the foundation of the Vereine Deutscher Studenten in the 1880s and the foreign student, or, anti-Russian and anti-Jewish, agitation of the 1900s).[30] Thus, the slow increase in religious diversity among German academics sharpened confessional conflicts and, given the fear of unemployment, poisoned academic politics.

Although it apparently involved merely a pragmatic choice of suitable preparation for a given field of study, the criterion of *segmentation*, based on the curricular content of secondary education, involved another set of social and ideological cleavages. Instead of a pyramid, Johannes Conrad preferred to "compare the students to a column that rests on a base of its own," indicating that German high schools were rigorously separated from each other, with the neohumanist Gymnasium intended to prepare for the university, the Realschulen at best for the technical colleges, and the Bürgerschulen for practical commercial pursuits. Whereas in the 1860s around 95 percent of Prussian students received a neohumanist secondary education prior to matriculation, less than 70 percent were prepared in that traditional manner in the last quinquennium before the First World War (figure 3.4). In contrast, the Realgymnasium, a "hybrid seeking to cultivate both the ancient and the modern and satisfying neither," raised its share

Ac 12 (1900-01), no. 4; and Dr. Huckert, "Zu dem Mangel an katholischen Kandidaten für das höhere Lehrfach in Preussen," *AMbl* 10 (1897-98); "Die Parität in Preussen. Eine Denkschrift 1897," *AMbl* 10 (1897-98); "Katholische Wissenschaft," *AMbl* 9 (1896-97): "All attempts to explain this intellectual inferiority of German Catholics are of no use; only action can help."

[30] There is no study of Jewish students in Imperial Germany. For the general background, see F. Gilbert, "Bismarckian Society's Image of the Jew," *Leo Baeck Memorial Lecture*, 22 (New York, 1978), and P. Gay, "Encounter with Modernism: German Jews in Wilhelmian Culture," in his *Freud, Jews and Other Germans* (New York, 1978), pp. 93-168. See also S. Weissenberg, "Die russisch-jüdischen Studenten an den deutschen Universitäten," *Zeitschrift für Demographie und Statistik der Juden* 10 (1914): 60-62; W. Angress, "Prussia's Army and the Jewish Reserve Officer Controversy before World War I," *Yearbook of the Leo Baeck Institute* 12 (1972): 19-42; and N. Schafferdt's forthcoming dissertation.

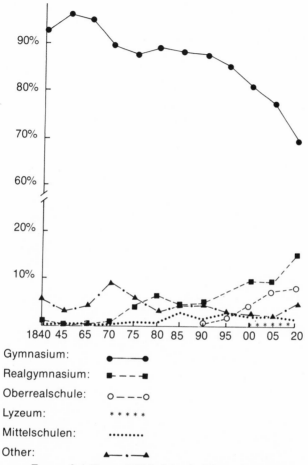

FIGURE 3.4 Type of High School of Bonn Students

from practically nil in 1870 to almost 15 percent by 1914. The Oberreal-schule, which attempted "by quite another way, by modern languages namely and mathematics and science, at providing a complete higher culture," progressed from virtually nothing in 1890 to over 8 percent by the last prewar years, and the *Lyzeum*, a Realgymnasium for girls, made its tentative appearance after 1900.

Already in 1904, Wilhelm Ruppel wondered that "in proportion to their share of the population, circles with higher education provide most graduates of the Gymnasium and to a lesser degree also of the Realgymnasium and Oberrealschule," indicating that different social strata preferred distinctive school types, given a viable alternative. The somewhat traditional elements (rural, Catholic, male, noble, agrarian, governmental, educated, bureaucratic, peasant, and lower official) favored neoclassicism, whereas the more modern segments (urban, mobile, Protestant or Jewish, female, bourgeois, commercial-industrial, propertied, salaried, and artisan) championed realistic forms of preparation. Although the requirement of a nine-year course did "suffice to keep out the entirely unsuitable element," the admission of the graduates of modern high schools allowed those strata already entrenched in the universities greater freedom of choice in secondary schooling, while permitting other groups (like the commercial-industrial occupations) easier access to higher education.[31]

The universities played an important role in the "school war" over classical or modern secondary preparation, albeit by formulating the rationale for both camps rather than by setting actual policy. In the empire the ideological hold of the Humboldtian tradition was still so strong that prominent medical scientists like Rudolf Virchow accepted the neohumanist goals of "general scholarly and ethical cultivation along with mastery over one's special field." For most academics, the "spirit of humanity" was to be found "in classical antiquity [which] is for all of us a spiritual home, to which we like to return from our different professional tasks." The majority of professors and students agreed with the judgment of the *Akademische Monatshefte*: "Though we do not deny the defects of our Gymnasia, we cannot consider the limitation or abolition of humanistic Bildung justified."[32] Numerous faculty memoranda argued that the Gymnasium provided superior "general cultivation of mind and heart"; that only training in the classical languages developed the capacity for "scholarly reasoning"; that the heroic art and politics of Greece and Rome instilled "the idealist spirit in our officialdom, which excells that of any other country"; and that an abandonment of unity and quality of secondary schooling would threaten a "throwback to barbarism." In contrast, they attacked the Realgymnasium as "heterogeneous and internally unfinished" and as conveying a dangerous half-education (*Halbbildung*), which lacked the mental discipline and philological methodology for scholarship and did

[31] J. Conrad, *German Universities*, pp. 217-39; A. Rienhardt, *Universitätsstudium der Württemberger*, pp. 40ff.; *PrSt* 236: 108-11; *BSSt*, pp. 120-23; W. Ruppel, *Berufswahl der Abiturienten*, pp. 25ff.; F. Paulsen, *German Universities*, pp. 176-77. For a more recent quantitative study confirming a similar association between stratum and type of high school, see D. Müller, *Sozialstruktur und Schulsystem*, pp. 517-48 and Albisetti, "Kaiser, Classicists and Moderns," chapters 6-9.

[32] R. von Virchow, *Lernen und Forschen* (Berlin, 1892); E. von Curtius, *Über das Priestertum bei den Hellenen* (Berlin, 1878) and his many other ceremonial speeches such as *Athen und Eleusis* (Berlin, 1884): "Everything that comes from Athens is not a dead leaf for the herbarium of history, but a fresh twig and a blossom. . . . It touches us in such a human way, like news from our own home." "Realschule und Gymnasium," *AMh* 5 (1889); 304f.

not provide that general acquaintance with the classics necessary for successful university study. Speaking for the philosophical faculty of the University of Halle, Professor Zacher phrased his objections tellingly: "As praiseworthy and exemplary as many North American virtues are, such as 'go on' or 'go through,' so may the good Lord in all His mercy preserve us from sinking down into Americanism, toward which the government equalization of modern and humanist teaching or the equation of the principles of usefulness and ideality would be a first step." Put even more bluntly, the majority of German academics believed: "The Gymnasium cultivates, but the Realgymnasium trains."[33]

In contrast, the protagonists of realistic education could look to a minority of natural scientists, professors of modern languages, medical scholars, and economists in the law faculties for support. To the botanist Carl Gerhardt it was undeniable that "we live in the age of natural sciences. It is the duty of every cultivated man not to close his eyes to the forces that have changed the living conditions of human society." Modern science, technology, industrial economy, and international trade seemed to demand "concessions in preparation," such as more stress on natural sciences and living languages. As drawing these branches of knowledge into the Gymnasium would "make it succeed neither in the one nor in the other," only a more modern school like the Realgymnasium could satisfy these new educational needs. This change would free traditional institutions from many pupils "who are only ballast," because they were forced to attend them in order to prepare for the university. Many educational reformers sincerely believed that modern languages and mathematics could make "Realgymnasia equivalent nurseries of general scholarly cultivation," which would provide a different but equally effective version of mental training and cultural polish. The partisans of realistic schooling were highly critical of the philological drudgery of Gymnasium teaching, of the overburdening of pupils with grammatical exercises, and of the subtle social prejudice: "Classical education . . . alienates its pupils from economic activity through its ideal of the cultivated life and its almost exclusive training in abstract reasoning." Invoking the "direction of the Zeitgeist" as authority, reformers complained: "We can no longer permit the schools to ignore the great works of our century by Bunsen, Helmholtz, Siemens, Faraday, and Darwin!" Progressive opinion therefore saw clas-

[33] For a systematic analysis of the content of the faculty memoranda of 1876 and 1878 see Gandtner to Falk, 4 November 1878, ZStA Me, Rep 76 Va, Sekt 1, Tit VIII, No 12, vol. 3; for specific examples, see Beseler to Falk, 20 June 1876 and 28 June 1878, ibid. For the internal faculty discussions, see also BUA, A16, 1, vols. 2-3; Zacher memorandum, 10 August 1878; and petition of the Ärztevereine, ZStA Me, Rep 76 Va, Sekt 1, Tit VIII, No 12, vol. 3. See also Paulsen, *Geschichte des gelehrten Unterrichts*, pp. 558-611 for more detail on curricula.

sicism as an impediment to "the practical, the present-minded" leadership training necessary for German *Weltpolitik*.[34]

Many of these ideological differences, expressed in such pretentious rhetoric, rested on tangible social grounds. In the neohumanist camp the primary fear of philologists was the probable status loss for the cultured stratum (*gelehrte Stände*) within the imperial elite. Reflecting on a massive petition of doctors' associations, Minister of Culture Falk summarized: "It can be called the *communis opinio* of the profession that the admission of modern-high-school graduates to medical examinations would bring grave harm to medical science and practice as well as to the entire condition of the medical estate." Physicians' fears centered on the loss of a "unified and uniform education of the cultivated strata," on "the establishment of a depressed and subordinate relationship of medical students toward other faculties," on "the diminution of the respect and social position of the medical profession," and on the "reintroduction of a dualism within medical practice through different kinds of education." Law professors had similar reservations: "Their chief objections . . . are not against the ability of Realabiturienten for university study; but in private conversation they oppose an enlarged influx from the lower classes of the population, which would further overcrowd as well as depress the social and cultural niveau." This educational conflict was therefore also a social struggle between clergymen, lawyers, doctors, and Gymnasium teachers, securely established as the cultivated, and those societal groups who clamored for admission to the same privileges. Among the 22,203 signatories of the petition of the executive committee of the Deutsche Schulreformverein, only 24.09 percent were educated officials (in contrast to the majority of the Gymnasium party), while 27 percent were free professionals, and the largest group were the propertied, with 37.84 percent who consistently preferred modern to classical secondary education. Professors at the technical colleges almost rivaled their colleagues at the regular universities, architects were more numerous than clergymen, doctors far exceeded lawyers, while merchants, engineers, teachers (mostly from the Realschulen), and factory owners outnumbered all others (table 3-4). Although disputed in the realm of educational philosophy, the issue of university admission for graduates of modern high schools was, in the words of Prussian Minister Studt, essentially "a question of social prestige [*eine Dignitätsfrage*]."[35]

---

[34] C. Gerhardt, *Heilkunde und Pflanzenkunde* (Berlin, 1888); R. von Virchow, *Lernen und Forschen* (Berlin, 1892); Conrad to Studt, 27 March 1900, ZStA Me, Rep 76 Va, Sekt 1, Tit VIII, No 12, vol. 4; Adickes to Studt (lawyers' petition from Frankfurt), 25 June 1898, ibid.; Rudolf Rabe, conclusion of his article series "Erziehung der Deutschen zum nationalen Egoismus," in *BBl* 14 (1899-1900): 169-72.

[35] Falk votum, 19 April 1897, ZStA Me, Rep 76 Va, Sekt 1, Tit VIII, No 12, vol. 3; petition of the Deutsche Ärztevereine, 1879, ibid.; J. Conrad to Studt, 27 March 1900,

TABLE 3-4

Social Origins of School-Reform Petitioners, 1888

Educated Officials		*Free Professionals*	
State officials (legal)	762	Doctors	1,473
State officials (technical)	697	Apothecaries	477
Local officials	230	Lawyers	433
Clergymen	289	Scholars	445
University professors	299	Engineers	2,443
Technical professors	242	Architects	328
Gymnasium teachers	291	Artists	289
Modern teachers	2,002	Booksellers	231
Foresters	189		6,119
Officers	348		= 27.56%
	5,349		
	= 24.09%	*Old Middle Class*	
		Businessmen	898
Propertied			= 4.04%
Estate owners	692		
Factory owners	2,050	*New Middle Class*	
Merchants	4,069	Middling state officials	1,118
Burgomasters	643	Lower state officials	318
Privatiers	422		1,436
Rentiers	525		= 6.4%
	8,401		
	= 37.84%		

NOTE: For the categories of this table, see pages 120-25. Officers are included as higher officials, not because of their education. Booksellers could also be grouped among the propertied, but contained a considerable number of former academics. Privatiers are men without specific profession, living on their wealth. It is significant that officials considered this social information relevant enough to tabulate it rudimentarily. For the sources of this table, see note 35.

Because of this division within their own ranks, university professors succeeded only in postponing the parity of modern secondary schooling when the general political climate made the Prussian Ministry of Culture responsive to their fears. The majority of the universities rejected any concessions in their memoranda of 1869, while only Göttingen favored

ibid., vol. 4; Protocol of the session of the Prussian Ministry of State, 8 October 1888 with the petition of the Geschäftsausschuss des deutschen Schulreformvereins, 30 September 1888 in DZA Po, Rkz 2183; Studt votum to the Prussian Ministry of State, 25 January 1900, DZA Po, Rkz 2200. Already in 1896 Friedrich Paulsen uncovered the social dimension of the debate: "The exclusion from the medical and legal faculty rests only on arbitrariness and prejudice, along with which arrogance and caste spirit also are likely to play their role: for the teaching estate the lesser [students] are still good enough; in contrast, the most noble estate may only recruit itself from the most prestigious school" (*Geschichte des gelehrten Unterrichts*, p. 573).

general admission of realists (and Marburg, Königsberg, and Greifswald voted for limiting them to certain philosophical subjects). Nevertheless, Minister Mühler decided in 1870, "Realschulen of the first order shall be entitled to enroll [in the philosophical faculty] those pupils who have gained a regular high-school certificate." Beginning with objections to the new Strassburg University statute, the howl of protest from the neohumanist professors against the "illegality" of this procedure was so persistent (in two additional rounds of consultation in 1876 and 1878) that Mühler's successor, Falk, wrote his Saxon colleague Gerber that he "could not recognize the need for the admission of realistic graduates to university study" in other disciplines. As even the scientists were only willing to admit that "modern graduates were superior to those of the Gymnasium at the beginning of their studies . . . but were, after several semesters, consistently outdistanced by them," Falk again restricted the enrollment permission to mathematics, natural sciences, and modern languages, where a minority of professors was willing to support reform.[36] When the philologists of the University of Berlin in 1880 continued their objections ("our fears have not been allayed"), the rectors of the Realschulen in 1881 petitioned for further concessions. In pamphlets, newspaper articles, and debates in the Prussian House, the reformers sought to create a ground swell for change, while a slowly decreasing majority of traditionalists defended the neohumanist heritage:

> The undersigned professors and instructors of the University of Bonn declare that they consider the preparation of students in all scholarly subjects on the basis of the humanist Gymnasium with Greek language and literature unquestionably desirable. They fear grave dangers for the universities and the cultural level of our people if the educational community of the students is undermined beyond its already reduced state.[37]

[36] For a systematic listing of the memoranda of 1869, 1876, 1878, see the tabulation by councillor Göppert, 2 February 1882, ZStA Me, Rep 76 Va, Sekt 1, Tit VIII, No 12, vol. 4; Mühler circular, 7 December 1870, in ZStA, Rep 76 Va, Sekt 1, Tit VIII, No 3, vol. 7; and protest of Bonn philosophical faculty, 21 January 1871 in BUA, A16, 2, vol. 1; Schaefer to Falk (Strassburg), 13 January 1872, ibid., No 1, vol. 1 and Craig, "Mission for German Learning," pp. 155ff.; Falk to Gerber, 16 July 1878, ZStA Me, Rep 76 Va, Sekt 1, Tit VIII, No 12, vol. 3; votum by Lipschitz (Bonn mathematician), 29 April 1876, ibid. See also Müller, *Sozialstruktur und Schulsystem*, pp. 209-14, 236-43.

[37] Memorandum of the Berlin philosophical faculty, 8 March 1880; petition of the directors of the Realschulen to Gossler, 22 October 1881, protesting against A. W. Hofmann, *Die Frage der Teilung der philosophischen Fakultät* (Berlin, 1880), in ZStA Me, Rep 76 Va, Sekt 1, Tit VIII, No 12, vol. 4; petition of fifty-three Bonn professors, 28 November 1890, initiated by J. Bona-Meyer and the votes of individual faculty members like Prof. Nissen: "I too received, on the 18th of November, a request from the ministry to work for 'the speedy formulation and publication of a declaration of the Bonn professors for the humanist Gymnasium similar to that of Leipzig' " (BUA, A16, 2, vol. 1).

Although even the Prussian army argued for rectifying "the great mistake in our educational system," the school conference of 1890 produced no reform because of the Kaiser's last-minute desertion of the Realgymnasium. Under the sway of the unemployment and overcrowding anxiety, it decided: "In the future only two kinds of high schools should be kept, Gymnasia with both ancient languages and schools without Latin, such as the Oberrealschule." The complete lack of classical training made the latter type a conduit for the surplus of secondary pupils to the technical colleges and the modern subjects in the philosophical faculty while alleviating future demands for general university admission. This clever deflection, enshrined in the Lehrpläne of 1892, failed to quiet the agitation in the universities, the government, and the general public: "The entire technical world strives not to lag behind the lawyers and other academically cultivated, not even in the demands for general cultivation," the Prussian minister for public works argued in the cabinet. On the other hand, "the concerned specialists' fear of allowing entry to elements who stand on a lower social and cultural level and thereby detract from the entire group" militated against further concessions. When more and more professors of the sciences and modern languages as well as doctors began to accept the inevitable, the stoutest resistance came from the lawyers, who called "knowledge of the Greek language indispensable for true cultivation" and inveighed against "lowering the intellectual level of future lawyers and jurisprudence." But the reformers considered "Greek of only little value for the study of law and not the only path towards cultivation . . . [but] the modern languages of higher importance for today's jurists" and submitted that legal practice derived little benefit from classical training.[38]

The deadlock was finally broken when even partisans of neohumanism like Wilamowitz-Moellendorff became convinced that with equality the Gymnasium would prepare even more exclusively for the three higher faculties: "Success will prove that . . . not out of compulsion but out of free choice of the people, the Gymnasium shall become even more the school of the ruling classes and the circles from which they derive." After the admission of *Realgymnasialabiturienten* to the study of medicine had been conceded in the ministry, the argument that "the respect and position

[38] Herrfurth to Bismarck, 4 March 1890 and other correspondence in DZA Po, Rkz 2183a; Gossler to Caprivi, 23 January 1891, ibid., Rkz 2199; Zedlitz to Caprivi, 12 January 1892 ("Denkschrift über die geschichtliche Entwicklung der Revision der Lehrpläne und Prüfungsordnungen für höhere Schulen, sowie Gesichtspunkte für die vorgenommenen Änderungen"), ibid., Rkz 2190. Discussion of the Prussian Ministry of State, 22 February 1891; 1 March 1891; Gossler to Caprivi, 23 January 1891, DZA Po, Rkz 2199, leading to minor concessions to the graduates of the Oberrealschule in terms of entering the technical public service. Councillor Wille, "Auszüge aus den Gutachten," regarding admission to the legal faculty and the role of Greek, 11 March 1901, ZStA Me, Rep 76 Va, Sekt 1, Tit VIII, No 12, vol. 4.

of the medical estate would be depressed through a one-sided lowering of preparation requirements'' eventually overcame the resistance of the legal traditionalists like Minister of Finance Miquel, as long as indirect barriers such as more demanding examinations blunted the effects of open admissions. When Althoff persuaded the Kaiser to follow his own impulses, the school conference of 1900 took the plunge: "Regarding entitlements, the Gymnasium, Realgymnasium, and Oberrealschule must be considered equal in their education for general intellectual cultivation.'' Grumbling from the legal and philosophical faculties about this fundamental departure in educational philosophy and structure succeeded in preserving only the inviolability of theological studies. Moreover, a supplementary directive warned prospective law students: "It will be their own responsibility to acquire the necessary linguistic and technical tools for a thorough understanding of the sources of Roman law.'' Although universities therefore introduced remedial Latin courses, Conrad was right in predicting: "This concerns only a small percentage. The lengthy and expensive legal career keeps out the less well off anyway.''[39]

In the long run the reform of 1900 turned out to be a typical Wilhelmian compromise. By allowing access, it created a channel of social mobility for the graduates of modern high schools into the less prestigious subjects, turning them into defenders of the social and political system by offering them a share of power. It thereby rescued the Gymnasium from further invasion by the propertied and plebeian hordes and reconfirmed its status as chief university preparatory school. Moreover, it maintained subtle starting advantages for classical graduates in the core professions of law and medicine, for Abiturienten of the Oberrealschule were admitted to the state examinations only after a long battle. Although considered far-reaching and progressive abroad, the achievement of equality for modern preparation largely transferred the external tensions between Bildung and Besitz or between government and economy into internal strains within the educated elite. Not surprisingly, students were ignored during the entire struggle, and professors provided more rhetoric than decisions. Parliamentary institutions like the Prussian Landtag played virtually no role in

---

[39] Memorandum by Wilamowitz-Moellendorff, 26 March 1900; memorandum by Schmoller, 22 April 1900, ZStA Me, Rep 76 Va, Sekt 1, Tit VIII, No 12, vol. 4. Bosse to Ministry of State, 9 December 1898, DZA Po, Rkz 2199; Tirpitz votum, 5 January 1899, and Miquel votum, 30 December 1898, ibid.; Studt circular, 25 January 1900; Prussian Ministry of State debate, 7 March 1900; Prussian Ministry of State debate, 3 April 1900; Löbker to Bülow, 10 May 1900; Studt, 15 January 1901; Prussian Ministry of State session of 23 February 1901 (Studt: "In the last analysis the elimination of its admission monopoly involves the rescue of the humanist Gymnasium itself") and implementation orders, all in DZA Po, Rkz 2200. Althoff circular, 5 April 1902, BUA, A16, 1, vol. 2; and Conrad to Studt, 27 March 1900, ZStA Me, Rep 76 Va, Sekt 1, Tit VIII, No 12, vol. 4, and "Die soziale Bedeutung der Schulreform um 1900," *BBl* 19 (1905-06): 204-205.

the reform conflict. It was fought in the educational bureaucracy as *Politikbefragung* by inviting the comments of experts and interest groups, for it involved the makeup of the bearers of state power, the Prussian officials. The granting of university access to graduates of modern high schools reduced formal segmentation somewhat, but the retention of the Latin requirement (*Grosse Latinum* of nine years) for the higher faculties contributed to its informal perpetuation. Hence, both the elitist ("legitimation of class-school system") and the egalitarian (moderate increase in mobility) interpretations of the reform are equally correct. The Wilhelmian elites apparently realized that partial equality was the best defense for continued privilege.[40]

The final criterion, *sexual equality*, measured by the proportion of female students, also reveals a limited and controversial process of transformation. While several South German states were somewhat more liberal, the political elites of Prussia and of smaller North German states resisted concessions to the women's movement for fear of undermining the "divinely willed dependency" of females in the home and society. Admitted as auditors in the 1890s, women nevertheless flocked to the universities, and by 1905-06 1,669 of the 5,842 auditors among German students were female. Although they did not account for even 1 percent of all students by 1907, once the Prussian barrier fell in 1908, their proportion increased rapidly to 7.44 percent on the eve of the First World War, while in Bonn it rose from .1 percent in 1900 to 6.7 percent in the years between 1910 and 1914. Because of its pioneering role, the first generation of female academics was in almost ail attributes distinct from its male counterpart. On the average, women were older, for they reached the universities later owing to considerable formal and informal obstacles. They were more cosmopolitan, urban, and mobile than their male colleagues. Moreover, females were more Protestant and especially more Jewish than the student body at large. In contrast to men, their secondary training was more modern (Realgymnasium and Lyzeum) and more incomplete (with about one-third *immaturi*), for girls' academic secondary schools were not organized until the turn of the century. Finally, women students came more from the commercial and governmental sectors of the economy, from more elitist backgrounds, and from more college-educated families than the rest. "In the early stage of female study, the decision to acquire academic cultivation

---

[40] P. Cauer, "Der Sinn der neuesten Schulreform," *PrJhb* 105 (1901): 19-38. The classic account is F. Paulsen, *Geschichte des gelehrten Unterrichts*, pp. 715ff. Cf. the contrasting views of D. K. Müller, *Sozialstruktur und Schulsystem*, pp. 274ff.; C. Albisetti, "Kaiser, Classicists and Moderns," pp. 185ff.; E. Heydorn, "Zur Bildungsgeschichte des deutschen Imperialismus," in his *Studien zur Sozialgeschichte der Bildung*, 2: 179-238; and C. Führ, "Die preussischen Schulkonferenzen von 1890 und 1900. Ihre bildungspolitische Rolle und bildungsgeschichtliche Bewertung," *Bildungspolitik in Preussen*, pp. 189-223.

presupposed a home receptive to cultural achievements and capable of bearing the cost, considering the limited possibilities for preparation and the low prospects for employment." Only a social elite that prized higher education and possessed the necessary means encouraged its daughters to enter upon the arduous path of university study before World War I. Hence, although the beginning of female higher education in Imperial Germany diversified the student body sexually, the elitist character of the first generation of women students did little to further the social opening of the university (table 3-5).[41]

Because it involved both philosophical ideals of womanhood and material considerations of male self-interest, the struggle for female admission to university studies was protracted and bitter. As early as May 1871 the senate of the University of Königsberg petitioned the Ministry of Culture to admit women to medical lectures, for both Catholic nuns and Protestant deaconesses traditionally played important healing roles. Mühler answered drily that such reform would "require express statutory revision, for which I see no reason in the present situation," and reiterated a few months later that he "could not permit" such a course. Rebuffed, female activists organized in various pressure groups during the 1870s and bombarded the Ministry of Culture with numerous individual requests for exceptions. Although he restated his general objections against female admissions, Liberal Minister of Culture Falk yielded somewhat in May 1878: "The admission of women to university lectures can take place only quite exceptionally and under special circumstances which must be investigated in each case." As individual universities were to rule on all requests before seeking ministerial approval, some progressive faculties began to admit a trickle of women as auditors in the 1880s. This limited concession whetted the appetite of the women's movement, which began to agitate in the Reichstag, the Landtag, and the press, arguing that female matriculation was a financial necessity for future teachers, a basic human right, a practical proposition, and a necessary consequence of improved secondary education. Male opposition centered on the overcrowding of the academic professions, on the defeminization of women, and most tangibly on their inadequate university preparation in the *höhere Töchterschulen*, designed for "the education of the heart and soul appropriate for women" rather than for academic cultivation. Hence, the emancipation movement petitioned the Prussian Landtag in 1892 "that women be permitted to take the Abitur examination of a Gymnasium or a Realgymnasium." Unable to

---

[41] F. Paulsen, *Geschichte des gelehrten Unterrichts*, pp. 774-82; A. Sachse, *Althoff*, pp. 340-54; *PrSt* 236: 111, 124, and 150; *Statistisches Jahrbuch des Freistaats Preussen* 19 (Berlin, 1923): 303; *BSSt*, pp. 124-26; A. Rienhardt, *Universitätsstudium der Württemberger*, p. 18; and J. Conrad, "Einige Ergebnisse," p. 439.

TABLE 3-5
Female Students in Prussia, 1896–97

1. Admitted as Auditors		5. Family Status	
Berlin	95	single	183
Bonn	16	married	23
Breslau	35	widowed	3
Göttingen	40	divorced	1
Greifswald	5	6. Purpose of Study	
Halle	10	general cultivation	160
Kiel	12	Oberlehrerin examination	40
Königsberg	0	doctorate of philosophy	5
Marburg	10	medical examination	5
Münster	0	legal teacher examination	1
Total	223	7. Subject of Study	
2. Age		natural sciences and mathematics	20
under 20	14	history and philosophy	28
20 to 30	93	modern languages	65
above 30	87	ancient languages	5
3. Citizenship		art history and literature	76
German	132	economics	6
West European	8	theology	3
Russian	14	medicine	9
American	53	law	1
4. Religion		8. Estate of Father	
Protestant	158	academic profession	71
Catholic	11	officer	11
Jewish	29	estate owner	23
other	3	merchant, industrialist	63
		rentier	13
		artisan	2
		middling/lower official	19

NOTE: Compiled by Althoff's collaborator, Dr. Schmidt, this survey reflects the differing admission practices of individual universities before permission to audit became general. Especially intriguing is category 6, which indicates goals of study, usually unavailable. For the source of this table, see note 42.

overcome the resistance of the conservative faction in the Prussian cabinet, the Ministry of Culture preferred to eliminate the objection of inadequate secondary schooling before pressing the issue and therefore permitted the establishment of "Gymnasium-like courses" under the direction of Helene Lange in Berlin, which produced the first ten *Abiturientinnen* in 1896. The majority of professors still "emphatically opposed allowing women to study at the same universities as men for practical reasons and in the interest of morality," but the influx of a "great number of female auditors belonging to the best circles" made formal exclusion ever more intolerable.[42]

To bring the legal situation into conformity with reality, Minister of Culture Bosse agreed, in March 1899, "in the interest of bureaucratic simplification, to drop the requirement of ministerial consent for each individual and to have university rectors grant permission for female auditing of lectures in the same manner as for male auditors." When, on the basis of progressive Southwest German opinion, the Bundesrat in the same year voted to admit women to the medical doctorate, Halle students protested that clinical cases could no longer be demonstrated thoroughly enough, auditors lacked background, and patients were embarrassed. But the ministry countered similar complaints of traditionalist deputies by inspiring an article in the *Norddeutsche Allgemeine Zeitung* which claimed that "no violations of academic conduct due to coeducation have come to light" despite the presence of 414 female auditors. Not content with half a loaf, 42 women students from six German universities petitioned "to permit them and others similarly qualified regular matriculation in Prussian universities . . . on the basis of their graduation examination, taken in the presence of a state commissar." Because of the fundamental opposition of many professors, the threat to "character and spirit of the university," the probability of a strong increase in enrollment, and the "differences in preparation," nine rectors in 1904 cautioned "emphatically against the matriculation of women in the Prussian universities." Although prominent scholars like Virchow and Lexis as well as the head of the university section of the Prussian Ministry, Friedrich Althoff, supported reform, the obstinate resistance of Minister Georg von Rheinbaben, Count Arthur von Posadowsky, and Beseler in the Prussian cabinet in April 1905 torpedoed Minister Studt's rescript and postponed action for three more years.[43]

[42] Königsberg Senate to Mühler, 15 May 1871; Mühler reply, 5 June 1871; petition by deaconess B. Fertig, 6 November 1871; Mühler reply, 30 November 1871; Falk decree, 6 May 1878; Falk to Ministry of State, 25 October 1881; petition by the Deutsche Frauenverein Reform, 30 March 1892 to Prussian Lower House; petition of M. Cauer to Prussian Lower House, 5 January 1892 and subsequent discussions, all in ZStA Me, Rep 76 Va, Sekt 1, Tit VIII, No 8, vol. 1. Rector Stradonitz to academic Senate, 5 March 1892; Minister Zedlitz inquiry, 1 March 1892; Senate to Zedlitz, 3 May 1892, all in BUA, A16, No 1, vol. 2. Dr. Schmidt, "Gehorsamste Notiz über die gegenwärtige Lage des Frauenstudiums in Preussen," 21 January 1897, ZStA Me, Rep 92, AI, No 101. See G. Bäumer, "Entwicklung und Stand des Frauenstudiums und der höheren Frauenberufe," *Die Frau* 19 (1911), nos. 8-9 and L. Boehm, "Von den Anfängen des akademischen Frauenstudiums in Deutschland," *Historisches Jahrbuch* 77 (1958): 298-317.

[43] Bosse decree, 10 March 1899; protest of the Halle medical students 10 March 1899; draft notice for *NAZ* January 1900 in ZStA Me, Rep 76 Va, Sekt 1, Tit VIII, No 8, vol. 8. Petition of forty-two students to Bosse, 3 February 1902 with ministerial request for memorandum, BUA, A16, No 1, vol. 2. Petition of rectors of nine Prussian universities, 6 March 1904; Virchow to Studt, 29 April 1905; Lexis to Studt, 12 June 1905; Althoff/Studt draft decree for admission, 8 May 1905 in ZStA Me, Rep 76 Va, Sekt 1, Tit VIII, No 8, vol.

To prepare such a "fundamental departure from the traditional standpoint," the Ministry of Culture, supported by Empress Auguste Victoria, energetically pushed for the reform of girls' secondary education. By combining the common introductory course of the Frankfurt *Reformgymnasium* with a choice of finishing stages (Realgymnasium, teacher training, or practical education), Althoff established a new category of high school, called Lyzeum, with Abitur entitlement. Petitions from such groups as the Verband Studierender Frauen Deutschlands continued to argue the inconsistency of denying women with Abitur formal enrollment privileges. At the same time 160 professors from the universities of Bonn and Breslau called for the "admission of female high-school graduates to matriculation" in order to "remedy the injustice . . . of their unequal treatment," to catch up with more progressive states, and to capitalize on "positive experiences" with female students preparing for the high-school teacher's examination. Wearing down the conservatives in the Prussian cabinet with the argument that "the present situation, considered provisional, cannot be maintained in the long run," the new minister of culture, Holle, pointed out that auditing prerequisites left the door open for badly prepared Russian girls, who could be excluded by regularizing matriculation and that further resistance would arouse "the displeasure of the leftist parties . . . which needs to be avoided" during the tenuous Liberal-Conservative coalition of the Bülow bloc. Over the continued resistance of the hard-liners, the Prussian Ministry of State, in the spring of 1908, finally adopted the reform, since Holle stressed that permission to study did not mean admission to professional practice of law and theology: "Especially, the question which professions are to be opened to them and which shall stay closed remains untouched." After forty years of acrimonious struggle, women were allowed to enroll as regular students in Prussian universities in the fall semester of 1908-09, an important emancipatory step toward their becoming academic teachers and doctors. In the future they could carry on the campaign for acceptance as professors, divines, and lawyers with the aid of Prussian university degrees. Ironically, this partial victory, like demographic diversification in general, increased tensions among academics as a group.[44]

---

11. Session of Prussian Ministry of State, 13 April 1905, ZStA Me, Rep 90, BIII, 2b, No 6, vol. 150. See also MUA 905a, 1950/9, No 626, H. Schmelzle, "Die 'Frauenfrage'," *AMbl* 8 (1896): 171-77, 239-41, and J. Albisetti, "Helene Lange and the Dilemmas of Equal Educational Opportunity for German Girls, 1887-1908," paper at the Missouri History Conference, Columbia, Mo., March 1981.

[44] A. Sachse, *Althoff*, pp. 340ff.; petition of the nineteen Bonn female students with Abitur to the rector, 20 May 1906; draft petition of the Bonn Senate to Studt, 29 June 1906; draft petition of Bonn Senate to Studt, 18 December 1907 in BUA, A16, No 1, vol. 3; further draft decrees, vota, etc. of the Ministry of Culture; petition of the Verband Studierender Frauen Deutschlands, 3 March 1907; petition of 160 Bonn and Breslau professors, March

SOCIAL CHANGES

Since it confronts the question of egalitarianism or elitism directly, the criterion of *progressiveness*, based on the social origin of the pupils, is the most important indicator of the transformation of the imperial student body. Unfortunately, the nature of the sources makes this aspect also quite difficult to assess. The aggregate figures of older statisticians are resistant to secondary analysis, while the ambiguity of the students' characterization of their fathers' professions in the matriculation register renders the compilation of new tables hazardous. These obstacles can be overcome by continual comparisons between published and original statistics, cross-references between individual institutional and general Prussian patterns, and by repeated checking against clusters of demographic variables. More formidable are the conceptual difficulties posed by conflicting ideologies, which manifest themselves in competing stratification schemata. The leading social thinker of Imperial Germany, Max Weber, offers one way out of this quandary in his threefold approach, which represents contemporary self-perceptions. For him the first fundamental aspect of societal organization is political power:

> With the triumph of *formalist* juristic rationalism, the legal type of dominion appeared in the Occident at the side of transmitted types of domination. Bureaucratic rule was not and is not the only variety of legal authority, but it is the purest. The modern state and municipal official, the modern Catholic priest and chaplain, the officials and employees of modern banks and of large capitalist enterprises represent . . . the most important types of this structure of domination.

A second basic set of social hierarchies derives from economic class:

> By "class situation," in contrast, we shall understand the opportunities to gain sustenance and income that are primarily determined by typical, *economically* relevant situations; property of a certain kind, or acquired skill in the execution of services that are in demand, is decisive for income opportunities. "Class situation" also comprises the ensuing general and typical living conditions.

The third crucial element of societal differentiation is social status:

1907; negative votes of Beseler, 29 February 1907 and of Rheinbaben, 3 March 1907; votum by the new minister of culture, Holle, 16 January 1908, all in ZStA Me, Rep 76 Va, Sekt 1, Tit VIII, No 8, vol. 11. Session of Prussian Ministry of State, 14 February 1908, ZStA Me, Rep 90a, BIII, 2b, No 6, vol. 156; Holle draft decree, 12 July 1908; Holle Immediatbericht to William II, 12 July 1908 and further implementation orders in ZStA Me, Rep 76 Va, Sekt 1, Tit VIII, No 8, vol. 12. For the polemics, see also IHK, E, No 973ff. (Frauenstudium) and R. J. Evans, *The Feminist Movement in Germany, 1894-1933* (Beverly Hills, 1976).

We understand by "status" situation the probability of certain social groups' receiving positive or negative social *honor*. The chances of attaining social honor are primarily determined by differences in the *styles of life* of these groups, hence chiefly by differences of *education*. . . . Secondarily, social honor very frequently and typically is associated with the respective stratum's legally guaranteed and monopolized claim to sovereign rights or to income and profit opportunities of a certain kind.

Power, wealth, and prestige therefore need to be considered separately in order to gain a three-dimensional perspective on the question: Did educational opportunity increase or decrease in Imperial Germany?[45]

As there were still too few professional politicians to appear in any numbers among student fathers, the definition of political power needs to be broadened to include bureaucratic and economic forms of authority. Weber described the close connection between higher education and public influence in the Second Reich: "The 'cultivated' personality formed the educational ideal, which was stamped by the structure of domination and by the social condition for membership in the ruling stratum." Aside from bureaucratic rank, power over others stemmed from the inherited prestige of landowning and from the acquired industrial or commercial *imperium*. Although in Bonn the localization of the student body around 1870 reduced the proportion of sons of the higher bureaucracy from one-fifth to one-tenth, they did not decline further with the enrollment expansion, but rather rebounded to about 14 percent. At the same time, the share of the landed and economic leaders doubled from around 8 percent to 15 percent during the empire, thereby changing the balance of groups within the ruling classes, but reestablishing their proportion in the student body at about one-third. Part of this elitist stability resulted from contradictory demographic developments, for decreases in cosmopolitanism and Protestantism were cancelled out through rises in urbanity and feminism and thereby did not change the hold of the governing strata in the long run. The faster growth of the industrial-commercial elite compensated for the slower expansion of the higher reaches of the bureaucracy, although landed families

---

[45] W. Hubbard and K. H. Jarausch, "Occupation and Social Structure in Modern Central Europe: Some Reflections on Coding Professions," *Quantum-Information* (1979), no. 11, pp. 10-19; Max Weber, *Wirtschaft und Gesellschaft* (Tübingen, 1922), pp. 631-40 and "Die Wirtschaftsethik der Weltreligionen," *Gesammelte Aufsätze zur Religionssoziologie* (Tübingen, 1922-23), 1: 260-68, translated and excerpted by Gerth and Mills, *From Max Weber*, pp. 180-95 and 295-301. For concise introductions to the immense stratification literature, see J. Kocka, "Theorien in der Sozial- und Gesellschaftsgeschichte: Vorschläge zur historischen Schichtungsanalyse," *GG* 1 (1975): 9-42 and H. Kaelble, *Historische Mobilitätsforschung: Westeuropa und USA im 19. und 20. Jahrhundert* (Wiesbaden, 1978), pp. 73-106.

continued to be numerous. For many academics the equation of students as future "leaders of the nation" with the "so-called ruling classes" was both natural and desirable. Others, like Friedrich Paulsen, worried that "of late years a narrowing of the recruiting district for the learned professions" had begun, which excluded industrial workers and agricultural laborers. "This is the dark side of the development that has brought about the state of affairs in which academic training gives one a place in the ruling class!" Nevertheless, both conservatives and liberals agreed on the leadership mission of academics, although the former preferred inherited, and the latter acquired, privilege. Hence, most students aspired if not to political then at least to bureaucratic authority. Only a few even understood Karl Liebknecht's warning against those "who want to make the university into a whore of the ruling classes."[46]

Although in Marxist perspective "the cultivated do not form an economic class in the same sense as the bourgeoisie or the proletariat," their relationship to "the forces of production" nevertheless is an important aspect of their societal position. Unfortunately, the categories of the Prussian statisticians, established with the professional census of 1849, indicate class position only indirectly by analyzing economic function; they divide the population into 6 sectors, 23 subdivisions, and 153 generic professions. The coding instructions of the census of 1882 define as category A all pursuits relating to "agriculture, stock raising, gardening, forestry, hunting, and fishing"; as B, "mining and metallurgy, industry and building"; as C, "commerce and transport"; as D, "domestic service (including personal servants), and varying wage labor"; as E, "military, court, and local public officials, clergymen, and the so-called free professions"; and conclude with F as "without occupation or without indication of occupation," such as rentiers, welfare cases, students, the institutionally confined, etc.[47] In Bonn, the agrarian sector declined slowly but continuously

[46] Gerth and Mills, *From Max Weber*, pp. 240-44; members of the bureaucratic elite were defined as having the rank of *Rat* or above, while members of the economic elite were harder to determine; for the sake of consistency, all *Gutsbesitzer*, *Industrielle*, and *Grosskaufleute* were included, whereas among free professionals, only lawyers and doctors with honorary rank (such as *Justizrat*, *Sanitätsrat*) were considered. Nevertheless, this definition is still considerably more restrictive than *PrSt*, 236: 147. Gossler to Prussian Landtag, 4 March 1889, *AH*, vol. 342; Paulsen, *German Universities*, pp. 119ff.; Liebknecht to Prussian Landtag, 13 June 1910, *AH*, vol. 545. For a recent summary of the elite literature, see H. Kaelble, *Historische Mobilitätsforschung*, pp. 136-153.

[47] "Die Sozialdemokratie und die Schichten der Studierten," *BBl* 9 (1897-98): 269-77, based on a speech by W. Heine. Preussisches Statistisches Bureau, *Tabellen und amtliche Nachrichten*, 1849, vols. 4-6; *StdR*, 1 (Berlin, 1884), *Berufsstatistik nach der allgemeinen Berufszählung vom 5. Juni 1882*, 1: 172ff. For an attempt to transform these functional categories into classes, see T. Geiger, *Die soziale Schichtung des deutschen Volkes* (Stuttgart, 1932), largely a failure. Since the "self-employed," "supervisory and accounting personnel," and "other assistants" produced, because of its preindustrial bias, no meaningful

from over 20 to barely above 10 percent; the industrial sector rose from less than one-tenth to over one-seventh; the commercial sector grew from around 10 percent over 2.5 fold; servants were practically excluded; the governmental sector contracted from over one-half to two-fifths, while the unclassified group remained relatively stable (figure 3.5). In general terms, the Prussian pattern is remarkably similar (table 3-6). Only the growth in industry and the decline in government preceded the 1886-87 figures. Except for the "no profession" category, all segments expanded their participation relative to the population (thereby underscoring the increase in inclusiveness). But characteristic differences of access remained between

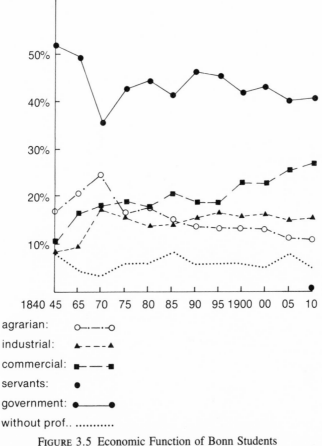

agrarian: o—·—·—o

industrial: ▲ – – – ▲

commercial: ■— — ■

servants: ●

government: ●———●

without prof.. ....

FIGURE 3.5 Economic Function of Bonn Students

results in the present analysis, it was deleted. See also H. Reinke, "The Analysis of Change and Persistence in German Society: The German Census of Occupations as a New Data Base," in J. Clubb and E. Scheuch, eds., *Historical Social Research* (Stuttgart, 1980), pp. 501-12.

TABLE 3-6
Economic Origins of Prussian Students

Sector	Among Students						In the Population per 100,000 of Profession		
	1886/87		1899/1900		1911/12		1886/87	1899/1900	1911/12
	No.	Percent	No.	Percent	No.	Percent			
Agriculture (A)	1788	14.1	1767	11.9	2519	10.4	14.0	14.2	21.2
Industry (B)	2363	18.7	2643	17.8	4203	17.35	22.8	19.4	23.0
Commerce (C)	2813	22.27	3808	25.7	6338	26.17	98.3	97.6	116.2
Domestic service (D)	15	0.11	19	0.12	32	0.13	1.0	1.3	2.0
Government (E)	4408	34.90	5210	34.59	8588	35.46	321.8	288.5	394.9
Without profession (F)	1244	9.8	1441	9.73	2538	10.47	92.0	67.6	71.8

NOTE: Based on Prussian census categories, these figures portray the changing economic background of students and the varying propensity of different sectors to study. For the source of this table, see note 48. Calculated with the German census figures of 1882, 1895, and 1907, the index of representation for students is:

	1882	1895	1907
A	.331	.332	.360
B	.53	.46	.40
C	2.33	2.23	1.95
D	.06	.07	.10
E	7.1	6.3	6.4
F	1.85	1.50	1.20

the various economic groups. The propensity to study was greatest for sons of clergymen (968.1), followed by teachers (737), state officials (383.8), and doctors (362.3), but in turn the entire public sector showed more desire for education than the commercial part (116) or the rentiers (72), while agriculture and industry seemed equally removed from academe, as did servants.[48]

The changes in the economic background of the student body were caused "not by the universities and even less by the students, but by the entire economic and social order of our society." One clue is the proportion of fathers with higher education. While few estate owners and peasants had been to college (7.37 percent), the higher echelons of the forest service (28 percent) were educated there. Similarly, among industrial parents, few manufacturers had studied, although 18.22 percent of the miners were engineers, 84.98 percent of the chemists had been trained at a university, 32.53 percent of the builders had attended a school of architecture, and 25.58 percent of the artists had been instructed at an art academy. Only an average of 2.68 percent of fathers in the commercial field had received higher education, whereas 17.54 percent of the officers, 35.54 percent of the state officials, 90.48 percent of the clergymen, 26.25 percent of the teachers, 94.18 percent of the doctors, 55.26 percent of the writers and scholars, and 35.44 percent of the actors were academically cultivated, while 16 percent of the rentiers had also been to college. Parents with university backgrounds account for the high desire for study in the governmental or free professional sector and in selected outside professional groups (such as chemists). But the growth in students from a commercial background derived from the general economic transformation, typical of the second stage of industrialization, in which agriculture declined from 51.5 percent to 35.5 percent of all persons employed, while industry expanded from 27 percent to 37.8 percent, the commercial sector advanced from 7.1 percent to 15 percent (showing the strongest relative increase), and government progressed from 5.5 percent to 7.6 percent. But why should students from industrial homes increase less rapidly than those from the service sector of government and commerce? One explanation might lie in their regional origin, which shows that industrial and artisan parents were more numerous in the Ruhr districts, where there were more modern high schools, and in rural areas (Aachen and Trier), where there were fewer Gymnasia. Moreover, as Badensian figures reveal, industrial families generally preferred to send their sons to the Technische Hochschulen, if

---

[48] *PrSt*, 236: 136-50; for the professional census figures for 1882, 1895, and 1907, see *StdtR*, vols. 2, 111, and 211, whereas a set of interpolated numbers for the in-between years can be found in W. Hoffmann, *Das Wachstum der deutschen Wirtschaft* (Berlin, 1965), pp. 188-206.

they let them go to college at all, for classical cultivation rarely helped their economic pursuits. As a result of the transformation of the economy, the Prussian academic elite became less agrarian and also less governmental, slightly more industrial, and considerably more commercial. Although this breaking down of the internal barrier between the educated and economic strata unified the grande bourgeoisie, it also added to the already prevalent Standesdünkel of the students a "new kind of arrogance, based on wealth."[49]

The third element of stratification, social status of the student's parents, is the most controversial. As the application of such contemporary sociological categories as "upper, upper middle, lower middle . . ." to late-nineteenth-century structures might produce misleading results, it is preferable to develop a historical approach to status hierarchy. Whether seen as "an institution, or a political theory, or a system of social differentiation," the ancient notion of estate (*Stand*) was such an important "ingredient of the cultural system that [it] touched everyday lives and shaped attitudes and behavior" even after Central European industrialization. Because the particle *von* of the German language divides the nobility clearly from the lower estates (however they might be subdivided in turn), one useful but often neglected approach is a comparison between the aristocracy and the commoners. While in the 1840s around 13 percent of the Bonn students still were noblemen, by 1910 only 2 percent stemmed from the *Adel*, so the proportion of nobles in the student body declined both relatively and (somewhat less so) absolutely. This drying up of noble enrollment is startling, especially when considering the continued prominence of the aristocracy in the Prussian military, the higher bureaucracy, and court society. Demographic characteristics do not fully explain the decrease, for noble scholars were younger, more East Elbian, more rural or metropolitan, more mobile, more Protestant, more upperclassmen, more classically educated, and more male than their bourgeois counterparts, thereby combining attributes of modernity and backwardness. While they were more elitist than the commoners, aristocratic students came primarily from agrarian and governmental sectors of the economy and were frequently sons of landed proprietors and rentiers or high officials (state, judicial, and military). The declining fortunes of estate agriculture after the collapse of grain prices in the 1870s threatened the solvency of many aristocratic families, while the slow expansion of higher bureaucratic positions limited enrollment of sons of government officials. Although the attraction of higher

---

[49] See above; "Die Gleichheit der Studenten," *BBl* 17 (1903-04): 232-34; *BSSt, Die Hochschulen* (Karlsruhe, 1912) allows a comparison between two universities and one technical college. See also G. A. Ritter and J. Kocka, eds., *Deutsche Sozialgeschichte* (Munich, 1974), vol. 2 for impressionistic evidence.

education appears to have increased, if anything, Westphalian nobles seem to have sent fewer of their younger sons to the university, since other alternatives (Officer Corps, forestry academies, or agricultural schools) became increasingly available. Ironically, the German university became more bourgeois just when contemporaries like Weber began to criticize the "social aristocratic tendency of our time" among the cultivated and when student subculture in the duelling corporations was becoming more neofeudal![50]

With its dissolution into numerous professions (*Berufsstände*), the estate system became an occupationally stratified hierarchy in the second half of the eighteenth century. When trying to reconstruct the ranking of different professions, one first needs to consider the self-perceptions of individuals and groups which are often systematized by contemporary social statisticians and appear frequently in literary evidence. Second, in order to make recombinations possible, it is necessary to look at the entire range of hundreds of occupational designations, then to reduce them systematically to dozens of generic professions (such as *Volksschullehrer, Hauptschullehrer, Armenschullehrer, Dorfschullehrer* to *teacher*) and only as a last step to establish a few social strata. Third, to escape from logical contradictions, it is crucial to test these larger status groups against such supplementary variables as income or education, for societal space is multidimensional, and social position therefore usually depends upon a cluster of demographic attributes.[51]

This threefold approach produces a six-strata scheme, which, though developed in a pilot study of 7,500 German students for the first half, is particularly appropriate for the second half of the nineteenth century. Since cultivated self-recruitment was most important to contemporary statisticians, they grouped all those occupations that overwhelmingly demanded academic preparation into the Bildungsbürgertum (the cultivated middle class), which can be divided by predominant employment into educated officials (such as privy councillors) or free professionals (such as lawyers).

---

[50] R. Berdahl, "The Concept of Stand as a Reflection of Social Change in Germany before 1848," paper read at the 1976 American Historical Association meeting in Washington; and K. H. Jarausch's comment, "Contemporary and Historical Perceptions of Social Order in 19th-Century Germany." See also H. Rosenberg, "Die Pseudodemokratisierung der Rittergutsbesitzerklasse," in his *Probleme der deutschen Sozialgeschichte* (Frankfurt, 1969); L. Cecil, "The Creation of Nobles in Prussia, 1871-1918," *AHR* 75 (1970): 757-95; F. Stern's chapter on the Junkers in D. Spring, ed., *European Landed Elites in the Nineteenth Century* (Baltimore, 1978); and Reif, *Westfälischer Adel* (Göttingen, 1979), pp. 357-60.

[51] W. A. Armstrong, "The Use of Information about Occupation," in E. A. Wrigley, ed., *Nineteenth Century*, pp. 191-310; M. B. Katz, "Occupational Classification in History," *Journal of Interdisciplinary History* 3 (1973): 63-99; W. H. Hubbard and K. H. Jarausch, "Occupation and Social Structure in Modern Central Europe," pp. 10-19. M. Kraul's ALR-based five-strata matrix appears more appropriate for the early than the later nineteenth century. *Gymnasium*, pp. 70-72.

Because the other distinction of the grande bourgeoisie rested on property, either rural or urban, or on leading economic position, the different aspects of wealth were grouped together in contemporary parlance as Besitzbürgertum, be it agrarian, industrial, or commercial. In contrast, the petite bourgeoisie was divided, according to Schmoller, into a traditional and new sector, the *Alte Mittelstand*, comprising the preindustrial peasants, artisans, or small traders, and the *Neue Mittelstand*, including the more modern service elements such as nonacademic officials, white-collar workers, and lower-school teachers. Like the differentiation between bureaucrats and professionals, this distinction permits an analysis of changes within broader strata, which is often neglected in mobility studies. Because of their scant representation, the heterogeneous elements of the lower classes were combined into just one stratum, a mélange of skilled and unskilled workers, agricultural laborers, domestic servants, and so forth. Although classification of bureaucratic ranks is easier than discrimination among merchants, this matrix meshes the three status hierarchies of countryside, industrial/commercial city, and government, combines economic wealth with educational prestige, and permits the integration of the findings of the nineteenth-century statisticians into the new results.[52]

The basic outlines of the transformation of social recruitment during the Second Empire appear in the case study of Bonn as well as in the older statistics for Berlin, Leipzig, and Würtemberg (tables 3-7, 3-8, 3-9). Despite the inherent bias of this sample, which includes three of the four largest German universities and only one (Tübingen) of the smaller ones, and the crudeness of the categories, which lack subdivisions within Bildung and Mittelstand, some major trends seem incontrovertible. First, everywhere "the secure core of students, the sons of the educated classes" declined drastically, sinking in Prussia to 22.07 percent by 1911-12 despite some absolute increase in number. Because of this halving of the academic share, "a growing proportion of students undoubtedly recruits itself from the nonacademic classes," which made the university's task of educating

[52] Lenz, *Berlin* (4: 521) knows only educated, propertied, and lower middle class; Conrad, *Germany Universities* (pp. 57ff.) subdivides into sixteen professional groups that are neither strata (too many) nor generic professions (too few); Eulenburg, *Leipzig* (pp. 204ff.) adds three more to Conrad's categories but condenses them again into three basic strata. *PrSt*, 102: 132ff. obviates the problem by starting with the A-F economic census subdivisions and supplementing them with twenty professional groups built upon Conrad. Cron, *Glaubensbekenntnis* (pp. 46ff.) similarly uses eighteen generic occupations; while the *BSSt* (pp. 74ff.) dissolves them into thirty professions and once again employs A-F census groups. Jarausch, "Neuhumanistische Universität," sorted the original professions alphabetically, reduced them to around forty-five generic professions, and developed the six strata matrix. See also G. von Schmoller, "Was verstehen wir unter dem Mittelstand? Hat er im 19. Jahrhundert zu- oder abgenommen?" *Verhandlungen des 8. Evangelisch-sozialen Kongresses 1897* (1897), pp. 155ff.

them into cultured patterns more difficult. Second, the propertied bourgeoisie, "which had become the social equal of cultivated circles owing to the economic and professional transformation of big industry and commerce," grew into the strongest parent stratum in the 1890s, almost doubling its proportion from one-fifth to two-fifths. This influx of wealthy students contributed a plutocratic tone to the educated elite in the Second Empire. "It is incontestable that the overwhelming majority of the students derives from quite specific strata of 'better society,' especially from academic families, and that the most numerous classes account for only a diminutive proportion." Nevertheless, in the final prewar expansion "this monopolization of Bildung by Besitz" declined again somewhat to between one-third and one-fifth (Prussian figures for 1911-12).[53]

Third, "the preponderant proportion of the students who do not come from academically educated fathers stems from the petite bourgeoisie, especially from the smaller and middling cities." Although the lower middle class helped carry the initial enrollment growth (figure 3.6), in the recession of the 1890s "those without means [were] gradually eliminated and the student body show[ed] a socially aristocratic tendency," reducing the share of the Mittelstand to less than one-third. When "the rise of the middling and lower strata" (or rather of the "comparatively well-to-do among them") resumed in the second part of the boom, the Kleinbürgertum became the strongest parent stratum. Though it did not quite increase so much in Berlin, Bonn, Leipzig, and Tübingen, the lower middle class accounted for half of the students in Prussia during the last prewar years. "Enterprising artisans or small businessmen were able to gather fortunes, sufficient to allow their sons to study, but insufficient to permit them to inherit the business as an industrialist or large merchant. These people use the university as a ladder to ascend into higher society," one contemporary observer mused. "Other reasons contribute to a lesser degree. For instance, the occupation of elementary school teacher is strangely desirous of mobility." Finally, the marginal representation of the lower classes contracted even further to a minuscule .01 percent before making somewhat of a comeback after the turn of the century, indicating that the barrier between the Kleinbürgertum and the proletariat was as insuperable as ever. Socialist critics were fond of citing this fact as "drastic proof that

[53] Jarausch, "Social Transformation," pp. 620-28; P. Ernst, "Das gebildete Proletariat in Deutschland," *SA* 2 (1896): 232-38; Conrad, "Einige Ergebnisse," pp. 446ff.; H. Potthoff, "Die Gleichheit der Studenten," *BBl* 18 (1903-04): 232-34; S. Katzenstein, "Die Akademiker in der Sozialdemokratie," *SA* 2 (1896): 729-36. For the limits of secondary analysis of published statistics, see Riese, *Hochschule*, pp. 40-48; Ringer, *Education and Society*, pp. 81-104; and Jarausch, "Frequenz und Struktur," pp. 122-49.

TABLE 3-7
Fathers' Generic Professions at Bonn, 1865-1914

Bildungsbürgertum (Educated)					
Higher Officials			Professionals		
	No.	Percent		No.	Percent
State	186	2.9	Lawyer	104	1.6
Local	108	1.6	Doctor	218	3.3
Court	27	.4	Apothecary	90	1.4
Legal	197	3.0	Scholar	5	.1
Church	251	3.8	Engineer	50	.8
Medical	75	1.2	Artist	36	.6
Education	287	4.4	Writer	5	.1
Military	99	1.5	Journalist	7	.1
Forestry	21	.3	Other	27	.4
	1,251	19.2		542	8.3

Besitzbürgertum (Propertied)		
	No.	Percent
Landed property	348	5.3
Patrician	8	.1
Industrialist	342	5.3
Merchant	282	4.3
Transport	38	.6
Salaried	126	1.9
Rentier	379	5.8
Financial	28	.4
Other	38	.6
	1,589	24.4

Mittelstand (Lower Middle Class)					
Alt (Old)			Neu (New)		
	No.	Percent		No.	Percent
Farmer	525	8.1	Subaltern state official	161	2.5
Administrator	31	.5	Subaltern local official	74	1.1
Artisan	441	8.8	Subaltern post/rail official	186	2.9
Trader	861	13.2	Subaltern legal official	69	1.1
Traffic	123	1.9	Subaltern church official	33	.4
Foreman	46	.7	Subaltern teacher	420	6.5
Bourgeois	6	.1	Subaltern military	9	.1
Other	5	.1	White collar	85	1.3
	2,038	31.3	Other	5	.1
				1,132	17.4

TABLE 3-7 (*cont.*)

Proletariat (Lower Class)

	No.	Percent
Farm laborer	2	.0
Servant	4	.1
Skilled labor	29	.4
Unskilled	1	.0
Soldier	1	.0
Unemployed	9	.1
Other	2	.0
	48	.7
No information	10	.2

NOTE: Table 3-7 presents the comparative frequency of fathers' occupations at Bonn and thereby also the coding scheme. Higher officials represent ranks with preponderant academic training (or equivalent: officers). Professionals do the same, although they include the graduates of technical colleges and a few artists, writers, or journalists who considered themselves also cultivated. Propertied comprise estate owners, industrialists, large merchants, managers, and rentiers (some of whom are probably government pensioners). The old lower middle class is made up of the middling and lower reaches of the same economic pursuits, while the new lower middle class contains the nonacademic officials and white-collar workers. For the sources of tables 3-7 to 3-9, see notes 51f.

TABLE 3-8

Social Origin of Students at Berlin, Bonn, Leipzig, and Tübingen

	Bildung		Besitz		Mittelstand		(Bonn Only) Lower		
	No.	Percent	No.	Percent	No.	Percent	No.	Percent	Totals
1860s	870.2	41.7	477.6	22.86	733	35.13	6	.43	2,086.3
1870s	1,229.8	33.6	1,151.2	31.4	1,245	34.0	1	.1	3,660
1880s	1,861.6	32.2	2,044	35.4	1,870.2	32.3	2	.1	5,776
1890s	2,145.2	31.1	2,619	38.0	2,068	30.0	6	.25	6,889
1900s	2,828.8	31.3	3,278	36.3	2,841	31.4	19	.28	9,033.9
1910s	3,192.8	29.5	3,877.2	35.8	3,757.4	34.7	24	.69	10,827

NOTE: Table 3-8 combines the figures from Lenz, Eulenburg, and Rienhardt with the results of the Bonn case study. As the Berlin data are highly aggregated, broader categories were used.

higher scholarly education and the professions connected with it are the monopolies of the propertied classes." Within the larger strata, changes are somewhat harder to pin down. Although in Bonn the old lower middle class continued to outnumber the new lower middle class by almost two to one, in Prussia as a whole the latter overtook the former by 1911-12

(29.9 percent to 27.9 percent), corresponding to the growth of white-collar professions in the economy and the lower reaches of the bureaucracy. Within the educated elite, the preponderance of state officials over free professionals (above four-fifths) lessened toward the latter part of the nineteenth century (to two-thirds), but seems to have halted at this point without shifting further in favor of the *freie Berufe*.[54]

Because this pattern remained basically unchanged until the middle of this century, a crucial if limited transformation of the German student body did occur in the Second Empire. Although "it may on the whole be said to be the custom for people who have had a university education themselves to give their sons in turn such an education," the evidence of the generic professions casts some doubt on Conrad's corresponding assertion: "When an increase in the attendance at the universities takes place, it is to be attributed to a recruiting from the lower classes, and in this recruiting the subordinate officials, elementary teachers, etc. supply the main contingent." Higher bureaucrats as a stratum declined because the proportion of church, judicial, and state officials decreased precipitously (from 25.2 to 9.2 percent) while only the sons of professors and Gymnasium teachers increased. Numerous during the initial phase of the boom, the free professions (sons of doctors, lawyers, and apothecaries) shared this selective contraction, except for engineers, who grew consistently after 1890. In contrast, the advance of the propertied was initially propelled by rentiers and landed proprietors, who peaked in 1875-80 at 8.6 and 7.9 percent, respectively, and was continued by the commercial and industrial occupations, who grew until 1885 or 1900 before levelling off on a new plateau. The most numerous parent group, tradesmen of the old lower middle class, reflect the two-pronged growth, with their first peak at 1880 (15.1 percent) and another high at 1905 (16.1 percent), while the second largest occupation, farmers, peaked already in 1865 (18.3) only to decline thereafter; artisans (11.5 percent) followed the same pattern. Among the new middle class the sons of elementary school teachers participated in the initial boom (1875-85 at 7 percent) as did the lower state officials (high in 1885 with 4.1 percent), while postal and railroad officials continued the increase until 1900 (4.8 percent), and white-collar employees remained surprisingly weak in Bonn while growing elsewhere. Among the lower classes only skilled

---

[54] The questions about the changes between the 1840s and 1860s and the shifts within social classes cannot yet be answered, because Bonn, owing to its Rhenish and Catholic (more commercial, artisan, and agricultural) character, differs markedly from the general Prussian pattern. See also "Was wir wollen," *SA* (1895): 3f.: "Does the student belong to this natural class of opposition? Not at all. He is no propertyless worker; he owns in his education the most modern tool of profit, his capital, and he has mostly come from the circles of oppression and has grown up in their views."

TABLE 3-9
Most Frequent Fathers' Professions at Bonn

1840s	Percent	1905–14	Percent
1. farmers	8.5	1. small traders	15.6
2. small traders	8.2	2. *teachers*	6.75
3. CLERGYMEN	7.35	3. farmers	6.4
4. landed proprietors	6.9	4. *industrialists*	6.25
5. artisans	6.3	5. artisans	5.75
6. LEGAL OFFICIALS	6.3	6. rentiers	5.65
7. rentiers	6.25	7. big merchants	4.75
8. LOCAL OFFICIALS	6.0	8. landed proprietors	4.75
9. STATE OFFICIALS	5.5	9. *professors*	4.75
10. big merchants	4.0	10. *postal/rail officials*	3.5

NOTE: Occupations that disappeared from the top 10 after 1840 are in SMALL CAPITALS, whereas those that entered after 1905 are *italicized*.

laborers showed some slight gains. Hence, the changes within the component professions indicate that the decline in the proportion of academic students was not universal, that the plutocratization of the student body was only temporary, and that the advance of the lower middle classes stemmed from increases in both commercial and bureaucratic occupations. Albert Rienhardt concluded, largely correctly: "The strata without higher education [in] industry, trade, business, agriculture, the middling officials, and teachers increasingly participate in the intellectual culture of Württemberg."[55]

The reasons for this structural transformation become more transparent when examined in light of the general social changes of the Second Empire. The declining self-recruitment of the educated was largely due to the enrollment explosion and the population transition. "At a time, however, when the number of students has grown faster than the population, as is at present the case, it . . . must be that new circles participate in the training at the universities." As most capable sons of officials and professionals are likely to have gone to college before 1880, while academic families were beginning to decline in size, the expansion had to draw on other sources until the new graduates had sons (and later daughters) of their own who might enroll in higher education. Hence, "people in the higher walks of business now send more students to the universities than

[55] In contrast to W. Conze, "Bildung und Erziehung," in W. Zorn, ed., *Handbuch*, 2: 676; J. Conrad, *German Universities*, pp. 62-65; Rienhardt, *Württemberg*, pp. 17-24.

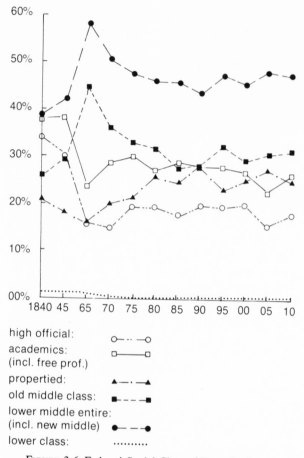

high official: ○— ·· —○
academics: □————□
(incl. free prof.)
propertied: ▲—·—▲
old middle class: ■----■
lower middle entire:
(incl. new middle)   ●— —●
lower class: ··········

FIGURE 3.6 Fathers' Social Class of Bonn Students

formerly." The logical alternative group was the propertied bourgeoisie, which after the postwar boom of the early 1870s (*Gründerjahre*) possessed the necessary means to finance a university education, especially for children who proved inept at commerce or could not inherit. "It will no doubt be regarded as only natural and desirable that the sons of men who have grown rich in business should not follow the example of their fathers. . . . They may be expected rather to aim at a position in life which generally gives solid rank and a certain influence, but in which it is scarcely possible to make a fortune." While the academics handed down their own professions to their sons, the wealthy saw higher education as status insurance through cultural means.[56]

[56] W. Köllmann, "Zur Bevölkerungsentwicklung der Neuzeit," in K. H. Jarausch, *Quan-*

In contrast, it took longer for the lower middle class to benefit from the spread of prosperity and to use higher education as an avenue of social mobility. Professor Petersilie welcomed this phenomenon as *aufsteigende Klassenbewegung*: "This is primarily the increase in those who by origin belong to the middling and lower strata and strive upward through higher education. Since mobility is one of the social concerns of our time, this change is of the greatest importance for the fruitful development of our national strength." The adaptation of artisans and peasants to high industrialization was more successful than has often been assumed; small shopkeepers probably experienced their heyday before 1914, for large department stores and chains only controlled a tiny proportion of the market (2.2 percent). The gradual growth of the new lower middle class resulted from the expansion of the service sector of the economy. On the one hand students responded to the opportunities among new professions (chemists, physicists) or among upper management (bureaucratization of industry), while on the other hand parents considered social mobility easier through education than through an expansion of their own enterprise, such as the transformation of an artisan shop into a small factory. One index of this increasing pressure from below is the reversal of ratios among Prussian students from the Bildungsbürgertum and the Neue Mittelstand between 1886-87 and 1911-12 (245 : 209 versus 214 : 275). Theoretically, German academics applauded this change: "It is no doubt very important that these classes and occupations be represented in our academic life. It is from them that the educated have to recruit and to reinvigorate their frequently diminished physical force." But they often decried its practical consequences, such as "deficient liberal training" or an "insufficient amount of social polish." Finally, the continued exclusion of the lower orders demonstrates the limits of mobility in Imperial Germany, which made it impossible for sons of the proletariat to rise into the lower middle class through education. "The cultivated man still thinks he belongs to another social class, and it is too much to ask him to feel solidarity with a worker."[57]

Did industrialization increase or decrease social equality at the university? Because the neohumanist reform of higher learning preceded industrial development in Germany, the relationship between industrialization and educational opportunity in nineteenth-century Central Europe is indistinct. The *pauperes*, or non-fee-paying students from the lower classes, already

---

tifizierung in der Geschichtswissenschaft, pp. 304-15. For a different argument, see J. E. Craig, "Higher Education and Mobility in Germany, 1850-1930," *Transformation of Higher Learning* (1982).

[57] *PrSt*, 236: 136ff; Conrad, *German Universities*, pp. 66ff.; Ernst, "Gebildetes Proletariat," p. 238. See also H. Kaelble, "Sozialer Aufstieg in Deutschland, 1850-1914," revised version in Jarausch, *Quantifizierung*, pp. 279-304; and P. Lundgreen, *Sozialgeschichte der deutschen Schule*, pp. 100-118.

had decreased during the aristocratic eighteenth century. After 1800, in periods of enrollment growth there seems to have been some expansion of access for the lower middle class; conversely, during contractions of student numbers the character of the student body appears to have become more elitist. Thus, the boom of the 1820s marked an influx of students from the Kleinbürgertum, reduced by the stagnation of the 1850s, before it reemerged with the expansion of the 1870s, only to be reversed once more in the pause of the 1890s until finally triumphing after 1900. In comparison with the general population, the elite and the upper middle class were still vastly overrepresented. Fragmentary evidence from Baden, however, also indicates that the resurgence of academic parents in mid-century was eventually checked by the increase of the old middle class during the following decades and that the plutocratization of the turn of the century was stopped by the new middle class (table 3-10). To the emerging Mittelstand orientation of the Prussian government, it was heartening to see that "proportionally the most students come from this middling social stratum. That is an enormously important result for the consideration of social mobility, which demonstrates a slow and gradual upward movement." Hence, contemporary fears of "the actual exclusion of all who do not belong to the more prosperous classes of society from the university

TABLE 3-10
Educational Opportunities in Prussia

Class	German Population 1895 (million families)	Prussian Students 1911–12	Index of Representation
Upper	.26	33.2%	132.8
Grossbürgertum	2.75	45.5%	16.5
Kleinbürgertum	3.75	21.2%	5.6
Lower	5.75	.18%	.03

NOTE: In order to overcome the crucial difficulty of transforming Prussian economic sectors into class categories, G. Schmoller's estimates, based on the census of 1895, were used. He subdivides the population into "aristocratic and propertied" families ("greater landowners and entrepreneurs, higher officials, doctors, artists, and rentiers"), "upper Mittelstand" families ("middling landowners and industrialists, most higher officials, many members of the liberal professions"), "lower Mittelstand" families ("peasants, artisans, petty traders, subaltern officials, foremen, better-paid laborers"), and "those whom we call the lower classes" ("chiefly wage laborers, but also many lower officials, poorer artisans, and small peasants"). Prussian statisticians followed a generally similar scheme in their 1911–12 compilation, but were somewhat more generous in their definition of the "higher strata," which exaggerates the impression of inequality. For the sources of this table, see note 58.

and the learned professions" were exaggerated. The arrival of women and more students with local, Catholic, modern secondary, and nonacademic backgrounds represented a significant broadening of the "class-oriented school system," but this influx of *homines novi* into the ranks of the cultivated tended to legitimize the continuation of their privileges in the long run.[58]

The transformation of student origins led to an increased stratification of student society at the university. The contemporary sociologist Franz Eulenburg characterized the emerging groups in 1909:

1. The well-to-do and those who traditionally go to college because their social position requires it. They mostly study law and natural sciences and change universities often.

2. The moderately prosperous, who receive a check with which they can just manage to live. The fact that they must later earn their keep gives them the opportunity to let themselves go a bit at present. . . . That is probably the majority.

3. The proletarians. . . . In general they are composed of our previous third stratum [of lower middle class. . . . It is the group] that must get ahead, because without college it lacks any existential security.

A quantitative survey of student income at the University of Prague in 1910 confirms this triple division into "a small group with excessive means, a greater group with sufficient funds, and a regrettably high percentage of students who must struggle along poorly, even wretchedly." Prussian financial aid figures indicate that "the number of students from the economically weaker strata considerably surpasses one-fifth," for already 19.1 percent of all students were supported through deferment of fees (on the basis of a certificate of poverty), received an average stipend of 182.24 Mk, or were granted a free lunch of 72.24 Mk per semester in 1911-12. If one considers a monthly allowance of 120-140 Mk adequate in the last prewar decade, it "is no empty slogan to speak of a 'student proletariat,' " for "the financial situation of a large proportion of the students equals that of the lower wage earners." At the other extreme, Theobald Ziegler felt compelled to admonish his academic audience: "I consider flaunting and showiness, luxury and opulence unnatural and undignified for students; to

[58] H. Kaelble, *Historische Mobilitätsforschung*, pp. 73-93; Cron, *Glaubensbekenntnis*, pp. 46ff. and *BSSt*, pp. 74ff., 168ff., 270ff. reveal the usual decrease of the Bildungsbürgertum from 31.7 percent to 21.6 percent between 1870 and 1905, but the inclusion of the matriculants of the Technische Hochschule Karlsruhe as well as the absence of interpretable figures for the last prewar decade render any other conclusions hazardous. Petersilie in *PrSt*, 236: 147ff.; Schmoller, "Was verstehen wir unter dem Mittelstand?" pp. 155ff; Paulsen, *German Universities*, pp. 124f. See also Müller, *Sozialstruktur und Schulsystem*, pp. 287-97 and J. Kocka, "Bildung, soziale Schichtung und soziale Mobilität," pp. 297-313.

me it appears a dangerous sign of internal and external decadence that this spirit of ostentation has spread among you."[59]

Although differences between rich and poor had perhaps been greater in earlier centuries, imperial academics were more troubled by the contradiction: "For the well-to-do scholar, university life is a time of youthful exuberance and overflowing *joie de vivre*. . . . For the impoverished student it is a period of sorrow and self-denial; this involuntary resignation often leaves a feeling of bitterness in his heart." Many students considered college a "necessary passage in order to obtain certain offices, suitable for their privileged extraction," and spent their time and money not on scholarship, but on " 'noble' passions" such as drinking, gambling, and duelling. But a sizable number of their comrades faced "a cruel struggle for existence," forced "to get on and hunger through in the most miserable manner" by living in wretched quarters, doing without food, and "being exploited by demeaning payment for student work," such as an occasional free meal for private lessons. Although the majority probably belonged to neither extreme, the increase of wealth for the elite and the concurrent influx of students from lower-middle-class families heightened social tensions within the student body. While the rich looked down upon the poor because of their lack of breeding, the latter resented their shameful poverty and polemicized against "the sharp contradictions between pitiful need and wild extravagance allowed a small number of capitalist sons by the present legal and economic order, while down below hundreds have to limit themselves to bare necessities, despite public and private charity." Thus, the purpose of study varied drastically among differing student strata. Some were intent on passing the time pleasantly; others were bent on acquiring the necessary cultural polish for a profession; and yet others prepared for a state examination as quickly as possible in order to earn a living. As "even modest and informal student life" required money, only wealthy students could enter duelling corporations. The moderately well-off could indulge in less formal associations, while the poor were forced "to stay alone." The social transformation fundamentally altered the college experience for academic youth in the empire.[60]

[59] F. Eulenburg, "Über die soziale Auslese der Studierenden," transcript of public lecture at the Ninth Congress of the Freistudentschaft, Weimar, 3 June 1909, in BA Koblenz, R. 129, no. 429; W. Winkler, *Die soziale Lage der deutschen Hochschulstudentenschaft in Prag* (Vienna, 1912); P. Roth, "Das studentische Proletariat," *AR* 1 (1912-13): 242-47; F. Elsass, *Die Studentische Wohnungsfrage in Vergangenheit und Gegenwart* (Berlin, 1914), especially pp. 16-24; and T. Ziegler, *Der deutsche Student am Ende des 19. Jahrhunderts* (Stuttgart, 1895), pp. 70-85.

[60] H. Paalzow, "Reiche und Arme Studenten," *ABl* 17 (1902): 185-87; Eric Montanus (pseud.), "Geistige Arbeit und privilegierte Lebensstellung," *SA* 2 (1896): 642-48; Elsass, *Wohnungsfrage*, pp. 22ff.; Roth, "Studentisches Proletariat," pp. 232ff.; Ziegler, *Der deutsche Student*, pp. 72-74; Ddf., "Die soziale Lage des Akademikers," *SA* 1 (1895): 233-36. See

Finally, the broadening of student origins also changed the position of the Akademiker as a stratum within imperial society. Shared imperium (authority of office), common service in the reserve officer corps as Einjährige, and the adoption of a neofeudal notion of academic honor led to a rapprochement between aristocracy and educated bourgeoisie. Since long probationary periods and low starting salaries forced "the members of the educated estates to look for rich brides," connubium and as a result also commercium brought academics closer to the propertied upper and middle class. Although internal tensions continued, the Wilhelmian decades witnessed that social amalgamation of the triad of birth, wealth, and education into the imperial elite which blended feudal social forms with bourgeois property and academic culture.[61] Nevertheless, Paulsen's collaborator Rudolf Lehmann was also correct in calling "the democratization of cultivation one of the most striking features of this epoch." While university professors became more involved in "the political and social movement" of the last prewar decades, "the number of doctors, Oberlehrer, and lawyers has grown in response to social need and thereby the stratum that links higher education with practical life has become even broader." In this lowering of internal barriers between the worlds of culture and commerce, "the practical professions like industrialists, chemists, apothecaries, and others have contributed to bridging the gap between scholarship and business." For the middle layer of the Bildungsbürgertum the influx of more urban, Catholic, modern-secondary, and female students helped to reduce social isolation and integrated the educated into the broader middle class. Concessions to the "widely spreading thirst for culture of the German people" encountered their limits when they threatened the reputation and status (Standesehre) of traditional or newly admitted possessors of academic culture. Although Paulsen's fears of "the elimination of the impecunious classes" were somewhat exaggerated, increases in university fees, maintenance of the Latin requirement, and subtle social prejudice against the "sons of poor and uncultivated parents" kept most lower-middle-class and virtually all working-class children out of higher education. The failure of the elementary school teachers' campaign for university training demonstrates that the price of the partial opening of higher education was the continued exclusion of the masses. Hence, Socialist critics claimed without too much hyperbole: "It is . . . disgusting that the privileged professions are more concerned with maintaining their

---

also a wealth of cautionary pieces such as "Bettelstudenten," *BBl* 21 (1907): 207f.; H. L., "Berliner Studentenelend," *Aus Kirche und Welt*, 1911, pp. 61-62; and W. Bastiné, *50 Mark Monatswechsel!* (Berlin, 1914).

[61] F. Paulsen, *Geschichte des gelehrten Unterrichts*, 2: 686ff.; Ernst, "Gebildetes Proletariat," 236; Sk., "Das Kleinbürgertum und seine Beziehungen zur 'Intelligenz,' " *SA* 1 (1895): 85-90.

estate prerogatives than with the uncompromising pursuit of scientific truth when it threatens to require social reforms."[62]

FACULTY STRUCTURES

The social transformation of higher learning becomes even more apparent when changing student characteristics and backgrounds are linked to shifting career choices of university graduates. Although professional directories and the like provide sufficient information, the prohibitive costs of quantitative career-line analysis limit the present discussion to the demographic makeup and social composition of the different faculties of study, anticipating later occupations. Family tradition, fee expenses, cultural attitudes, and individual aptitude go far to explain student preferences; but in a more fundamental way the social structure of a field of study depended upon the process of professionalization and the resulting distribution of educational entitlements. Although expressed in the language of estate society, the rise of the academic professions in Central Europe (the creation of *Berufsstände*) involved the same transition from a guild-apprenticeship system to a professional association-academic examination structure as elsewhere in the West. But in Germany the intervention of the state was more decisive in setting up meritocratic testing, beginning in the seventeenth century for theology, in 1725 for medicine, in 1737 for law, and finally in 1810 for secondary teaching. Moreover, the role of education was more important in the homogenization of university preparation (the growth of the Gymnasium monopoly between 1788 and 1834) and the academization of the first *Staatsexamen*, which gradually became the preserve of university professors rather than practicing professionals. Every academic occupation jealously guarded entrance requirements to university study (*Universitätsberechtigung*) as well as prerequisites for admission to state examinations (*Berufsberechtigung*), because "testing certificates are like a passport demanded for entrance into a foreign country. Once inside, it is never asked for again."[63] The impact of higher learning on profes-

[62] R. Lehmann, "Die Reform der höheren Schulen zu Beginn des 20. Jahrhunderts," in Paulsen, *Gelehrter Unterricht*, 2: 715ff.; E. Montanus, "Geistige Arbeit und privilegierte Lebensstellung," pp. 642ff. See also H. Henning, *Das Bildungsbürgertum in den Preussischen Westprovinzen*, pp. 483-91 and K. Vondung, "Zur Lage der Gebildeten in der wilhelminischen Zeit," in his *Das wilhelminische Bildungsbürgertum*, pp. 20-33.

[63] L. Wiese quoted by W. Lexis, "Die Berechtigung zum Studium der Rechtswissenschaft," in his *Die Reform des höheren Schulwesens in Preussen* (Halle, 1902), pp. 99-110. See also D. Rüschemeyer, "Professionalisierung. Theoretische Probleme für die vergleichende Geschichtsforschung," *GG* 6 (1980): 311-25; C. E. McClelland, "Professionalization and German Higher Education," in *The Transformation of Higher Learning* (1982); and R. Graf von Westphalen, *Akademisches Privileg und demokratischer Staat* (Stuttgart, 1980), pp. 90-132.

sionalization raises several crucial questions: How did the curriculum shape theoretical competence and practical skill? How did examinations determine the pattern of professional credentialling? How did admission and costs govern the social selection of future professionals?

The oldest, but by 1914 also the smallest, field of study was theology, split along confessional lines into seventeen Protestant and eight Catholic faculties (table 3-11). The former institutions "were supervised and directed by the state with the purpose of preparing future clergymen of the evangelical churches and therefore serving their needs but in a manner independent of the organism of the church." For professors and students, this position of "theology as university Wissenschaft" produced a triple tension between scholarship, training of ministers, and religious faith. But despite "the irreligious and anticlerical spirit of the times," the prestige of Protestant theology in the homeland of the Lutheran Reformation and its establishment as an academic profession before 1800 continued to attract youths to the spiritual calling. Practical reasons also helped. Formally requiring only an academic triennium, it was the quickest university course, and "some, yes many, choose this faculty because it is the cheapest." Lecture fees were lowest and "a great number of stipends were available," supporting over half of the theology students in one way or another, making it the most heavily subsidized faculty. Despite the prerequisites of a Gymnasium Abitur, academic demands were not overly high, for much of the teaching was directed toward practical (homiletic and catechetic) exercises rather than scholarly seminars, which "gained in importance" in the last prewar decades. Only a small number who wanted to devote themselves "to an academic career . . . or to a thorough study of theological problems" prepared for the licentiate degree, a medieval counterpart to the doctorate in other disciplines. "Most students . . . seek the conclusion of their studies in the prescribed examinations for church office." Established by Julius von Massow in 1799, the first, *pro licentia conconandi*, was an academic test of philosophical and theological knowledge, administered by a commission of full professors, while the second, *pro ministerio*, was a practical examination of teaching and preaching ability, administered by the provincial consistory. Although few failed these state examinations, only a minority gained "an independent theological understanding and judgment," while the majority achieved merely an uneven command of the subject and a "quite superficial relationship to theological scholarship." The practical probationary period between the first and second state examinations spent at a regional seminary (*Predigerseminar*) was usually no longer than a year or two, and most candidates found speedy employment once they had passed the final hurdle. But the "insufficiency of salaries of most of the pastors" provided inadequate material rewards, and in urban

TABLE 3-11
Fields of Study at German Universities

Year(s)	Protestant Theology	Catholic Theology	Law	Medicine	Philosophy Total	Philosophy Humanities	Philosophy Sciences	Together
1865–66	2,346	1,170	3,168	2,541	4,486	2,763	750	13,710
1870–71	1,957	891	2,886	2,870	4,602	3,135	1,204	13,206
1875–78	1,562	735	4,490	3,316	6,387	3,565	1,710	16,490
1880–81	2,350	650	5,229	4,098	8,882	4,615	2,815	21,209
1885–86	4,438	1,080	4,840	7,644	8,994	4,218	2,820	26,996
1890–91	4,332	1,250	6,678	8,552	7,809	2,947	2,298	28,621
1895–96	2,948	1,497	7,670	7,757	8,685	2,978	2,821	28,557
1900–1901	2,325	1,627	9,726	7,205	12,856	4,769	4,796	33,733
1905–1906	2,141	1,739	11,828	5,865	19,448	7,438	5,444	41,158
1910–11	2,422	1,797	10,777	10,638	27,736	12,585	7,276	53,364
1914	4,621	1,768	10,119	17,608	25,027			59,143
Totals	31,442	14,204	77,411	78,094	134,912			336,187

NOTE: On the basis of Prussian statistics student numbers are compared for different faculties. Philosophy is broken into humanities and sciences, but does not add up, since practical subjects like agriculture were included in the totals. Philosophical subtotals for the first year are based on Conrad's figures for 1866–70 and for the second year on his numbers for 1871–75. For the sources of this table, see notes 64ff.

settings clergymen ranked lower than the other liberal professions. "Serious struggles and grave inner conflicts" were built into this course of study, which had to reconcile clerical orthodoxy with academic freedom and therefore fluctuated drastically in student popularity.[64]

The demographic and social structure of Protestant theological students reflects these academic requirements and professional prospects. Because of their relatively short course, these students were generally among the youngest. Since most parsonages were located in villages, they were also the most rural (42.3 percent), although in Bonn they tended to come from outside the Rhineland and to be more mobile than the average. Because of the importance of classical languages in theological training, students showed a high proportion of Gymnasium graduates (94.5 percent) and a remarkable completion of the high-school degree as well. Lingering sexual prejudice derived from the priesthood meant that in Prussia there were only four female students of theology in 1913-14, while in Bonn there were none. The deteriorating social prestige of the ministry made for a minuscule presence of nobility and a low percentage from the ruling classes (13.5 percent). Only the governmental sector of the economy (60.3 percent) was overrepresented among parents, while agrarian, industrial, and commercial families were clearly reluctant to send their sons into the ministry. In terms of social class, the Bonn sample shows a typical polarization among children of educated officials (32.7 percent) and sons of the new middle class (25.2 percent), which resulted from the self-recruitment of clergymen (about one-fourth) and the attraction of a church career for the offspring of nonacademic teachers (about one-eighth), although tradesmen, farmers, and artisans also showed some inclination in this direction. The faculty of Protestant theology, one of the most ancient academic subjects, reveals a curious mixture of academic self-perpetuation and lower-middle-class mobility into the liberal professions. Originally intended to serve poor parsons with many children, the availability of financial aid and the shortness of study led to a decrease of career inheritance, an increase in enrollment from the new middle class, and a renewed influx of academics when its popularity dropped. Hence, the Protestant clergy strengthened its

[64] D. G. Kawerau, "Evangelische-Theologische Fakultät," in W. Lexis, ed., *Die Universitäten im Deutschen Reich* (Berlin, 1904), pp. 61-76; C.F.A. Dillmann, *Über Theologie als Universitätswissenschaft* (Berlin, 1875); W. Jensinghaus, *Quo tendimus? Ein Wort an Theologen und andere Studierende* (Leipzig, 1907); J. Conrad, *German Universities*, pp. 94ff., 291ff.; "Einige Ergebnisse," p. 471, and *PrSt*, 236: 78ff. See also G. Graus, *Der Mangel an Theologen und der wissenschaftliche Wert des theologischen Studiums* (Berlin, 1876); anonymous, *Die Unzulänglichkeit des theologischen Studiums der Gegenwart* (Leipzig, 1886); and A. Harnack, *Die Aufgabe der theologischen Fakultäten und die allgemeine Religionsgeschichte* (Giessen, 1901).

platform role of drawing in upwardly mobile students while sending their children on into even more exclusive careers (table 3-12).[65]

Although similar in purpose, the Catholic theological faculty differed in several respects, for it represented a minority confession in all but the South German states. For instance, the uneasy coexistence of scholarship and faith among the evangelical ministers contrasted with absolute Church control over Wissenschaft among Catholic priests. Only half of the clerics were trained in state university faculties, while the rest of the students

TABLE 3-12
Demographic Structure of Bonn Faculties

	Protestant Theology	Catholic Theology	Law	Medicine	Philosophy	Other	Total
Median age	21.57	21.14	20.95	21.52	21.25	21.87	21.25
Geographic origin in percent							
Rhineland	48.8	90.0	64.4	65.7	66.2	48.3	64.6
Prussia	85.0	96.5	90.4	89.3	79.1	80.8	86.5
rural	54.1	50.0	34.4	41.2	35.6	48.1	40.1
immobile	60.8	77.1	67.7	68.8	62.6	67.8	66.7
Religion in percent							
Protestant	100	0	41.1	36.2	47.7	51.7	43.3
Catholic	0	100	53.5	54.3	49.4	44.9	52.5
Jewish	0	0	4.8	8.6	1.9	2.0	3.5
Secondary education in percent							
Gymnasium	94.5	98.2	90.7	88.3	68.4	61.2	82.0
Realgymnasium and Oberrealschule	1.5	1.2	7.8	8.5	19.3	23.0	11.8
Abitur	95.5	89.8	98.4	97.3	80.4	22.3	83.3
freshmen	26.4	78.1	32.5	40.9	47.5	75.3	46.9
Percent female	0	0	0	1.9	5.2	1.1	1.7

NOTE: For the categories of this table, see pages 90-113. The arts faculty is subdivided into academic (philosophy) and applied (other) subjects. Rural means village and small town under 5,000 inhabitants. Immobile indicates no geographical mobility between the students' birth and enrollment. Freshmen are those who have not previously studied at another university. These summary tables 3-10 to 3-12 are based upon the Bonn case study, notes 19f.

[65] PrSt, 236: 112ff.; Conrad, *German Universities*, pp. 67ff.; and A. Neher, *Die katholische und evangelische Geistlichkeit Württembergs, 1813-1904* (Regensburg, 1904). For problems of published statistics, see also R. Riese, *Hochschule*, pp. 47f. and F. Ringer, *Education and Society*, pp. 301-10.

were instructed under close episcopal supervision in lycées or seminaries. While the "dual task of preparing the clergy of the diocese in which the university is located and of practically cultivating theological . . . specialists" recalled Protestant practice, the archbishop had a larger voice in faculty appointments and in assuring doctrinal orthodoxy. At the university Catholic students completed the customary triennium, starting with a philosophical year and then proceeding to theological studies, but they faced semestral tests and closer personal scrutiny. While the graduating examination *pro introitu* (administered largely by university professors) and the licentiate, doctorate, and Habilitation degrees resembled Protestant usage, the academic freedom of Catholic theological students was considerably more circumscribed. The seven mostly Bavarian lycées (enrolling another one-fourth) occupied "a middle position" between university faculties and episcopal seminaries, as they provided "an organic connection with a philosophical faculty" and thereby offered somewhat broader education without pretention to scholarship. The seven largely Prussian episcopal seminaries, which trained the final one-fourth of Catholic priests, lacked facilities for liberal education, and even Catholic academics complained about "disadvantages such as their isolation, their lack of intellectual contact with secular cultivation, their modest teaching apparatus and scholarly institutes." After completing a three-year course, a Catholic student had to enroll for one and one-half years of practical instruction in a *Priesterseminar* and could be ordained only after another general examination. Therefore, the training of Catholic clergy was less academic, more regimented, and cheaper (university quarters housed three-fifths of all students and seminaries even more). As a consequence, the pay for chaplains and priests was considerably less than that of Protestant ministers, and Catholic men of the cloth ranked lower in social prestige than their evangelical counterparts.[66]

This less demanding curriculum also made Catholic theologians the most traditional and least academic in social composition. Despite the short duration of study, they were consistently the oldest group in the Prussian student body, indicating their greater social distance from higher education. Similarly, in Bonn they were the most local (with 90 percent coming from the Rhineland), the most immobile (with over three-quarters not having

---

[66] Albert Ehrhard, "Katholische-Theologische Fakultät," in *Die Universitäten im Deutschen Reich*, pp. 77-101; Conrad, *German Universities*, pp. 106-24, citing Droste: "The bare incomes of the assistants of the clergy [the chaplains] are, unless in special circumstances, everywhere so small that only in a few cases do they reach the wage of a common laborer or farm servant, to say nothing of rising higher." See also the attack of Count P. von Hoensbroech, *Die Katholisch-theologischen Fakultäten im Organismus der Preussischen Staatsuniversitäten* (Leipzig, 1907) and the response of the Catholic student journals *Academia* and *Akademische Monatsblätter*.

moved between birth and matriculation), and also one of the most rural (38.4 percent) of student cohorts. They were quite conventional in their secondary education, with over 98 percent attending the Gymnasium and obtaining an Abitur, and therefore also produced a higher proportion of freshmen (78 percent) than any other faculty. Thus, their share of elite parents (under one-tenth) was the lowest, and they came more from the agrarian and small industrial sectors of the economy; among 602 Catholic theologians at Bonn, there were only three noblemen. But in contrast to the 36.3 percent academic self-recruitment of Prussian Protestants, only 3.8 percent of Catholic clergymen came from university-educated families! Apologists argued: "A solemn negation of the caste spirit is engraved on the portal of the Church, if only for the reason that the Catholic minister has no son whom he wants to raise in society at all costs." But critics claimed: "The celibacy of the clergy wastes a capital of intelligence, for its talents are not inherited but blotted out." The primary parent stratum for the priesthood was the old middle class (with 58 percent!), followed by the new middle class (18.1 percent) and the lower class (4.2 percent) because one-fifth of the Catholic theologians came from peasant families, and another one-fifth from artisan homes, while less than one-tenth derived from nonacademic teachers and tradesmen, respectively. The Catholic theological faculty proved socially more accessible than any other field of higher study. This nonacademic, neohumanist, lower-middle-class, and impoverished background made Catholic theologians a prime target for social mobility, but limited social ascent to the individual involved. Because of their academic and social marginality within the Akademiker, many adopted a reverse pride: "Owing to his origin, education, and environment, a Catholic priest possesses a certain gift for lessening societal conflicts and for working towards reconciliation and mediation."[67] Although some Catholic theologians rivaled their Protestant colleagues in culture, most remained closer "to the people" in mental outlook and habits of life (table 3-13).

The second and for a long time largest faculty, jurisprudence, offers a secular counterpoint to the decline of divinity. Represented at all twenty-one German universities (after its establishment at Münster in 1902), the study of law continued to be popular throughout the nineteenth century, because it led to a prestigious profession codified in the examination edicts of 1755 to 1817. "Most pupils of legal instruction devote themselves to the study of law with the intention of entering public service . . . either

---

[67] Petersilie, *PrSt*, 236: 112ff.; Conrad, *German Universities*, 106ff.; X. Hartmann, *Die zeitliche, örtliche und soziale Herkunft der Geistlichen der Diözese Augsburg von der Säkularisation bis zur Gegenwart 1804-1917* (Augsburg, 1918), especially 59ff.; and A. Neher, *Die katholische und evangelische Geistlichkeit*, pp. 3-72.

TABLE 3-13
Social Composition of Bonn Faculties
(Percent)

	Protestant Theology	Catholic Theology	Law	Medicine	Philosophy	Other	Total
Elite	13.5	9.8	41.6	29.7	24.5	27.7	29.1
Economic function							
agrarian	11.0	24.6	10.6	10.7	11.1	23.6	13.8
industrial	10.2	28.1	12.4	15.4	15.9	13.5	15.1
commercial	16.0	17.0	23.3	28.3	22.6	19.7	22.3
governmental	60.3	26.0	46.9	39.0	44.4	35.5	42.6
no profession	2.5	4.2	6.8	6.7	5.8	7.3	6.1
Estate							
nobles	1.0	.5	7.3	1.1	2.2	3.2	3.6
Academic parents	36.0	3.8	32.6	27.7	20.5	22.5	25.0
Social class							
high official	32.7	5.3	26.2	15.2	17.7	11.7	19.1
professional	2.5	3.0	9.6	14.5	7.6	6.6	8.3
bourgeois	15.5	10.6	28.8	24.1	22.4	31.4	24.5
old middle class	23.9	58.6	23.5	35.7	31.1	31.8	31.4
new middle class	25.2	18.1	11.7	10.4	20.3	17.9	15.9
lower class	.2	4.2	.2	.2	.9	.2	.7

NOTE: For the categories of this table, see pages 114-34. The percentages for academic parents are not only for Bonn but apply to all Prussian students between 1886 and 1911.

in the form of state and communal office or in the guise of legal practice.'' Repeated calls for ''the introduction of some degree of scholarly cultivation'' demonstrate that the principal task of the law faculty was practical professional training. Originally demanding the Abitur of the Gymnasium, in 1902 legal studies were opened to the graduates of modern high schools, provided that they acquired the necessary language skills. In theory, the required academic triennium was divided, after the introduction of the German Civil Code (BGB) in 1900, into private and public sections. In practice, *Lernfreiheit* permitted extended study and deviation from the recommended sequence, which began with systematic-historical lectures on the bases of law and then proceeded to obligatory practical exercises. Rudolf Gneist complained: ''About one-third really study. . . . The second third can at best be considered semistudents. . . . The last third only studies in name.'' Either by attendance at lectures (the famous *Kollegheft*) or by the services of a crammer (*Einpauker*), the student prepared for the first state examination, administered by a commission of professors and practitioners, which tested "the positive knowledge of the candidate, his insight into the essence and historical development of legal custom, and the necessary general legal and political cultivation [*rechts- und staatswissenschaftliche Bildung*] essential for his profession." After the successful completion of the *erste* Staatsexamen, the *Referendar*, if he chose a judicial career, was apprenticed for four years at various courts and lawyers' offices; if he opted for administrative service, he was transferred to local or district government after his initial year at the courts.[68]

The "great" state examination for admission to *Assessor* rank, administered by the judicial or administrative commission, had rather a "more practical character." In addition to general legal knowledge, it required "an actual paper based on litigation files" and the presentation of "two legal cases according to their documents." Only a small minority of students with scholarly interests or with a desire for a business or private career went further and pursued the legal doctorate "as public proof of academic accomplishment . . . despite its not inconsiderable costs." Inspired by a number of "symptoms of the deficiency of the present system," such as "the laziness of the students, their lack of attendance at lectures, and the ever more flourishing cramming system," critics in and out of academe unleashed "a flood of different proposals for reform." Castigating "the inadequacy of teaching," "the disinterest of the students" or "their lack of motivation," these suggestions agreed only on the need for a four-year course and perhaps on the advisability of an intermediate examination. Because of the cheapness of probationary law clerks, the entrenched bureaucracy and the professional organizations succeeded in subverting all substantive reform efforts during the empire, even if they were advanced with great passion in the Reichstag and the Prussian Landtag. Compared to the study of theology, legal training required "a considerably greater number of years" before state appointment. Moreover, it was unquestionably quite "costly, as even after the university course is finished the study must be prosecuted for several years without receipt of income." The low degree of financial aid (only for 12.1 percent of the students) and the requirement of "proof of *standesgemässe* support for five years" made the legal career much more socially exclusive than the ministry. "The

[68] H. Titze, "Die juristische Fakultät," in *Die Universitäten im Deutschen Reich*, pp. 102-21; G. Cohn, "Über die akademische Vorbildung für den höheren Verwaltungsdienst in Preussen," in Verein für Sozialpolitik, ed., *Die Vorbildung zum höheren Verwaltungsdienst in den deutschen Staaten, Oesterreich und Frankreich* (Leipzig, 1887); J. Kohler, "Das bürgerliche Gesetzbuch und das Rechtstudium," in Lexis, *Universitäten*, pp. 122-26; R. Gneist, *Aphorismen zur Reform des Rechtsstudiums in Preussen* (Berlin, 1887); "Gesetz über die juristischen Prüfungen und die Vorbereitung zum höheren Justizdienste. Vom 6. Mai 1869," in *Die Vorschriften über die Ausbildung der Juristen in Preussen*, 5th ed. (Berlin, 1913), pp. 14-18.

legal faculty offers the best prospects to the ambitious and to the higher classes of society," Johannes Conrad observed. "The less-moneyed classes are repelled from it by barriers that comparatively few are, without special favoring circumstances, able to surmount."[69]

The notorious legal monopoly (*Justizmonopol*) of higher public service and the penetration of lawyers into leading business positions contributed to an elitist self-image for jurists: "It is a matter of keeping the intellectual leadership of political and social life in the hands of an officialdom, which, through its honor and character, its striving and knowing, appears uniquely qualified to solve the great tasks of state and society." Even if academic reality fell short of this claim, the social composition of the law faculty seemed to confirm it. In Bonn and largely also in Prussia, law students were younger than their counterparts. Although they studied preponderantly in their home state, they came from more urban settings (small to large cities) than other students. During the course of the empire the predominance of Protestants lessened somewhat, Catholics began to approach their normal level, but Jewish students increased to 9.5 percent of the Prussian total, thereby exceeding their general share. Although four-fifths were still prepared at the Gymnasium, a larger proportion than among theologians was trained at modern high schools, and over two-thirds of the Bonn matriculants were upperclassmen who had previously studied elsewhere. Not surprisingly, law was virtually a male prerogative (women comprised .6 percent in 1913-14). Moreover, with over two-fifths of its students from elite families (divided fairly evenly between government and business), law was the most exclusive faculty by far. In terms of economic function, Bonn lawyers primarily stemmed from commercial, governmental, and rentier backgrounds. Matriculating 158 of the 236 noble students, the legal faculty also contained the highest proportion of aristocratic youths (7.3 percent). Academic self-recruitment (with around one-third) was second only to Protestant theology. As around two-fifths of the sons of educated officials, professionals, and propertied bourgeoisie enrolled in jurisprudence, two-thirds of law students derived from upper-middle-class families, the highest share in the student body. Because the largest number of law students came from merchant, industrialist, rentier, and landed backgrounds, while over one-half of the sons of officials with legal training

[69] "Allgemeine Verfügung vom 17. Juni 1913—betreffend die Vorschriften über die juristischen Prüfungen und die Vorbereitung zum höheren Justizdienste," in *Vorschriften*, pp. 19-58; Titze, "juristische Fakultät," pp. 119ff.; H. Gerland, *Die Reform des juristischen Studiums* (Bonn, 1911), pp. 20-39 provides an excellent bibliographic essay on the reform discussion; Anonymous, *Wie studiert man Jurisprudenz?* (Leipzig, 1884); J. Conrad, *German Universities*, pp. 67f. See also E. Nasse, "Die Universitätsstudien der preussischen Verwaltungsbeamten und die Gesetze vom 9. Mai 1869 und 11. März 1879," in *Vorbildung*, pp. 169-84; and H. Werner, *Studium und Prüfung des Juristen* (Berlin, 1914).

chose their father's faculty, jurisprudence facilitated the fusion of the aristocratic, wealthy, and cultivated segments into one elite. Perhaps this privileged origin made law students more impervious to neohumanist ideals of cultivation and scholarship than others. Reformers never tired of complaining: "The scholarly sense of our legal Kommilitonen is dead, and even if there may be many exceptions, the great mass has fallen into intellectual philistinism even before it leaves the academic world."[70]

Surpassing law numerically during the last prewar years, the study of medicine (at twenty German universities except Münster) was the last to come into its own among the "higher" faculties. Because of the introduction of a mandatory state examination in 1825, the closing of the surgical schools and the demotion of surgeons in 1852, and the opening of medical practice to free competition in 1869, medical faculties at the universities played a larger role in the professionalization of medicine than theologians controlled by the church or lawyers dominated by the government in the professionalization of their callings. Even before university trained physicians could demonstrate a higher cure rate than folk healers or apprenticed surgeons, academic doctors, because of their superior education, succeeded in establishing their dominance over such competing groups with the help of the state bureaucracy. Despite the greater insecurity which such liberty entailed, the four-fifths of medical graduates not employed by the government (or the military) had great pride: "The doctor is a free and independent man." So that physicians "not be boors [Banausen] and take their place among the cultivated of the nation," medical faculties "introduced the student to the subject on a broad and scientific basis, educated him through clinics and institutes, serving the medical needs of actual practitioners, and kept the physician, approved at the end of his practical year, aways abreast of progressing scholarship through continuing education." Because of the principle that "medicine is in equal measure a scientific and a technical profession," Gymnasium preparation was required until the turn of the century, when modern-high-school graduates were admitted "with the proviso that the candidate possess the linguistic understanding of medical terms."[71]

[70] W. Bleek, Von der Kameralausbildung zum Juristenprivileg (Berlin, 1972), pp. 163-93; H. Ortloff, Die Reform des Studiums der Rechts- und Staatswissenschaften (Berlin, 1887), p. iii; PrSt, 236: 112ff.; Conrad, German Universities, pp. 124-41; L. Goldschmidt, Rechtstudium und Prüfungsordung (Stuttgart, 1887). See also H. Dernburg, Die Reform der Juristischen Studienordnung (Berlin, 1886): "If the Beamtenstand, as the most justified form of spiritual aristocracy, the elite of the cultured and propertied, is to maintain leadership in our social our social and economic life . . . then it has to try to accomplish the best in character and cultivation."

[71] F. Müller, Wie studiert man Medizin? (Munich, 1912); A. Wassermann, "Die medizinische Fakultät," in Die Universitäten im Deutschen Reich, pp. 127-58. See also A. Fick, Über die Vorbildung zum Studium der Medizin (Berlin, 1883); and B. Kern, Humanistische Bildung und ärtzlicher Beruf (Berlin, 1913). See also C. Huerkamp, "Ärzte und Professionalisierung in Deutschland," GG 6 (1980): 349-82.

The imperial reform of 1901 extended the length of study before admission to the medical state examination to ten semesters, thereby making it the longest and, because of numerous laboratory fees, the most expensive course of study. In contrast to the latitude of the legal curriculum, students faced a tightly regulated *Studienplan*, beginning with "general natural scientific and theoretical subjects" for the first five semesters, followed by an exam (*Zwischenprüfung*), and a second period of usually five semesters, "presenting the actual technical subjects." After attending general lectures, participating in practical clinical exercises, and completing a year of internship, a medical candidate would finally be admitted to the Staatsexamen covering seven areas from pathology to hygiene, for such training was still "designed for the needs of the general medical practitioner." The reform also stipulated that the ancient title of *Doktor* could be obtained only *after* the state examination, and though no longer necessary for practice, the medical doctorate became the symbolic conclusion of university study, "for the admission to many positions in public life is dependent upon its successful acquisition." Even university professors had to admit that "given the present teaching methods of the German medical faculties, demands upon the students are quite great." They could only console themselves with the excellence of their resources and their mission of "maintaining the highest good which exists in life: human health." Increasing costs, length of study, and academic standards raised the self-esteem of imperial physicians: "With better training and the elimination of the admission struggle we can hope that the medical man will finally receive his deserved position in national life," which was explicitly modeled after the image of law.[72]

Exacting academic standards and the aura of medicine as the freest of the liberal professions attracted a somewhat mixed student clientele. "The study of medicine is prosecuted from love of the subject and, less than others, from subordinate motives," Conrad surmised in the 1880s. "It is to be assumed, therefore, that all classes will be represented." Because of the actual course length of twelve to thirteen semesters, medical students were the second oldest after Catholic theologians. Even if they were also largely regional (with more Westphalians than average) and immobile, future physicians came from urban backgrounds, ranging from rural towns to large cities. In Bonn, and more so in Prussia, Catholic students began to exceed their average and Protestants were underrepresented. But more

---

[72] Wassermann, "medizinische Fakultät," pp. 127ff.; Christoph Marx, *Die Entwicklung des ärztlichen Standes seit den ersten Dezennien des 19. Jahrhunderts* (Berlin, 1907), pp. 17ff.; M. Hoffmann, *Neueste Satzungen und Bestimmungen für die Erlangung eines Doktorgrades bei den Fakultäten der deutschen Universitäten* (Leipzig, 1897); Rumpf, *Medizinische Fakultäten, medizinische Akademien und praktischer Arzt* (Bonn, 1905). See also G. Mann and R. Winau, eds., *Medizin, Naturwissenschaft, Technik und das zweite Kaiserreich* (Göttingen, 1977).

important, Jewish students comprised 14.52 percent of Prussian medical students, an enormous overrepresentation, given their slightly over 1 percent proportion of the male population. Although almost four-fifths still graduated from the Gymnasium, the share of modern-high-school pupils increased rapidly in the last prewar years, while three-fifths had already previously studied at another university. Medical studies were more open to women than the first two faculties and enrolled 6.02 percent female students (390) in Prussia by 1913-14. After law, medicine had the second highest proportion of elite parents, with three-fifths coming more from industrial and commercial (also rentier) sectors of the economy than from government. But since there were virtually no nobles (ten in Bonn) and the share of academic families was lower (about one-fourth in Prussia), the study of medicine appealed to modern groups within the upper strata. The class origin of future physicians reveals a curious mixture of free professional (14.5 percent) and old middle class (35.7 percent) preponderance, based on the desire of traders, doctors, artisans, rentiers, industrialists, and merchants to have their children become physicians. Thus, despite the medical profession's campaign to rival lawyers in exclusivity, the composition of the medical student body reveals greater diversity. The length of study and its higher expense was partially counterbalanced by more liberal financial aid (for 27 percent of Prussian students). But the greater economic insecurity of the career deterred many academic parents, rendering their share the smallest after Catholic theology. Except for the self-perpetuation of physicians (be they free professionals, medical officials, or professors of medicine), the medical faculty therefore attracted the children of the middling commercial and industrial families with sufficient means to afford such costly training and thereby integrated them into the academic class. "The very wealthy are not represented in this faculty, as neither, for the reasons given above, are the very poor."[73]

The largest field of study at all twenty-one German universities was the newly prestigious philosophical faculty. Raised from its preparatory status as *Artistenfakultät* by the neohumanist reforms, "the philosophical faculty currently comprises all the numerous independent scientific subjects . . . which do not already belong to another faculty." The "extraordinarily great expansion of its scope" from humanities into natural sciences, early social sciences, and such diverse fields as pharmacy, dentistry, and agriculture led to an "increasing difference of views" and its division into

[73] Conrad, *German Universities*, pp. 68f., 141-54, 309-11; *PrSt*, 236: 112ff.; Wassermann, "medizinische Fakultät," pp. 127ff. with appendixes on female medical students and on dentistry. The desire for parity with law is especially evident in the resistance of the doctors to the admission of modern-high-school graduates "only on condition that the other faculties, especially the legal one, open their doors as well." See also R. Spree, "The Impact of the Professionalization of Physicians on Social Change in Germany," *HSR* 15 (1980): 24-39.

"philosophical" and "scientific" faculties at Tübingen (1862) and other South German institutions. This fragmentation heightened the tension between "general cultivation of the spirit," practical "training for future teachers," and the ultimate aim of scholarship. Increasing specialization of Wissenschaft and the professional demands of the state examination commissions in teaching, chemistry, and pharmacy eroded the philosophical unity of liberal education and transformed this mammoth faculty (*Riesenfakultät*) into a series of discrete subject areas, clustered around a seminar or an institute. As academic philosophy during the empire abandoned its claim "of teaching a positive Weltanschauung," students obtained only some grounding in scholarly methods and the historical development of philosophical discourse. Because there was "no plan of study and no compulsory lecture," a student in the humanities and sciences had to structure his own program. The only guidance was the distinction between introductory lectures (four hours weekly with the goal of "systematic presentation of material"), proseminars (with the aim "of pointing the student toward his own scholarly reading") as well as specialized lectures (of two hours) and regular seminars (directed toward "leading the student to an independent approach to scientific tasks"). While the seminar, with its library, provided the focus for teaching and scholarship in the philological-historical subjects, research and instruction in the natural sciences took place "in the institute, equipped with all necessary [experimental] apparatus and led by a director."[74]

In theory, it was "a sign of a correct course of study that an examination so to speak takes itself," but in practice, the changing Prussian state examination regulations for teachers determined the academic curriculum in the philosophical faculty. The reorganization of the *examen pro facultate docendi* in 1866 (valid for half of the empire) demanded a Gymnasium Abitur, three years of study at the university, and "a year of practical (and practically unpaid) work" in a high school. In terms of "general culture" it "required a knowledge of the basic laws of logic and of the main points of empirical psychology" and an acquaintance with the history of philosophy and the methods of pedagogy in order to demonstrate "some power of independent thought." Certificates for the four special branches—philology and history, mathematics and science, religion and Hebrew, and modern languages—were divided into three levels, authorizing the can-

[74] W. Lexis, "Philosophische Fakultät: Vorbemerkung," in his *Universitäten*, pp. 159-62, together with numerous articles on specialized subjects by scholars like R. Lehmann, "Philosophie, Psychologie, Pädagogik," pp. 163-71; F. Leo, "Klassische Philologie," pp. 172-78; and F. Frech, "Mineralogie, Geologie, Paläontologie,"pp. 274-79, to mention only a few. See also A. Petersilie, *Das öffentliche Unterrichtswesen im Deutschen Reiche* (Leipzig, 1897), vol. 3: *Verfassungsmässige Organisation des öffentlichen Unterrichts*, pp. 445-55.

didate to teach in the lower, middle, or higher grades of the Gymnasium. However, the fundamental revision of 1887 and the codification of 1898 largely jettisoned humanistic cultivation in favor of greater mastery of a particular subject matter. Reducing the culture requirement to the reading of one major philosophical treatise, it divided teaching certification into a higher and lower level, limited the time for writing a scholarly thesis to eight weeks, and defined two major and one minor areas of competence. In 1890 practical preparation was subdivided into a seminar year "designed to acquaint the candidate . . . with the tasks of psychology and pedagogy and their application to secondary schools" and into a probationary year "serving primarily as independent proof of the teaching expertise acquired at the seminar."

This tightening of academic standards in response to the overcrowding of the 1890s, which threatened to devalue degrees, is also evident in the imperial reform of doctoral requirements in 1901. "In order to preserve the historic scholarly and social importance of the *Doktorgrad* of the German philosophical and natural scientific faculties," the Prussian government persuaded the other German states to institute standard minimal requirements, such as oral examinations, a printed dissertation that was "scientifically noteworthy," graduation from a nine-year high school, and completion of a three-year course at the university. Especially in those subjects, like chemistry, for which there was no general state examination, the receipt of the doctoral degree served as "proof of suitable training" for employment in commerce and industry. Nevertheless, lower costs and quicker completion of studies gave the philosophical faculty a less exclusive image in the eyes of contemporaries: "The students of philosophy, like those of theology hitherto, can count not only upon immediately receiving an appointment with an income attached to it, but, during their whole university course, also have far more copious support to look to from bursaries of all kinds; they have, besides, opportunities of making a little by private teaching. It is no wonder then, if the less-moneyed classes confine themselves mainly to the latter faculties."[75]

The intellectual and occupational diversity of the philosophical faculty attracted students from a greater variety of backgrounds than any other

---

[75] W. Lexis, "Zur Reform der Doktorpromotion," 30 May 1898 and ministerial records in ZStA Me, Rep 92, Schmidt-Ott, ALVI, 7. Leo, "Klassische Philologie," pp. 172ff.; appendix, "On the Training and Examination for the Prussian Higher-School Service," in Conrad, *German Universities*, pp. 312-18; Petersilie, *Verfassungsmässige Organisation*, pp. 318-22 for the 1890 reorganization of the practical year; Lexis, "Philosophische Fakultät," and F. Klein, "Mathematik, Physik, Astronomie," in *Universitäten*, pp. 159-62, 242-73; and Conrad, *German Universities*, pp. 67f. See also H. Titze, "Die soziale und geistige Umbildung des preussischen Oberlehrerstandes von 1870 bis 1914," *ZfP, Beiheft*, no. 14 (Weinheim, 1977), pp. 107-28.

field. As well over two-thirds were aspiring to a career in secondary teaching (with two out of three choosing the humanities over the sciences), these future Oberlehrer form a coherent group. When the tightening of academic standards extended the length of study beyond ten semesters, the median age of the teachers became almost exactly the average of the student body. Because of the one-fifth share of non-Prussians and foreigners at Bonn, philosophy students came predominantly from urban backgrounds and proved more mobile than the rest. Protestants were slightly over-represented, while Catholics approached and eventually exceeded their share; but Jewish students, at 4.4 percent, chose philosophy less often than law or medicine. While two-fifths of the philologists still prepared at the Gymnasium, only slightly more than one-half of the scientists received classical training. Graduates of modern high schools flocked into this faculty, and as many as one-fifth of the students had yet to complete their high-school degree. As by the last prewar years, 10 percent of Prussian philosophy majors were female, three-quarters of all female students grav-itated toward this faculty because of the demand for Oberlehrerinnen at the expanding girls' secondary schools. Since philosophy had retained some of its prestige as a general subject, it attracted an average share of the elite and a fairly even distribution of economic sectors, with the industrial, commercial, and governmental sectors slightly overrepresented. However, the number of noblemen (2.2 percent) was small, and more important, only one-fifth of the parents were academically trained themselves, the lowest proportion outside of Catholic theology. The upper-middle strata fell short of the norm, while the new middle class (teachers 9.7 percent, postal and rail officials 3.7 percent) as well as workers were represented beyond their usual levels, and the old middle class made a fairly strong showing. Although in some respects philosophical students reflected the central tendency of the student body at large, future teachers were more urban, modern educated, more nonacademic, and therefore more lower middle class than students of law and medicine. Since secularization and low pay made a theological career unattractive, while the expansion of secondary education created openings in the teaching profession, the phil-osophical faculty became the crucial channel of mobility from the petite bourgeoisie into the Bildungsbürgertum during the empire.[76]

The remaining third of the philosophical faculty comprised students of

[76] *PrSt*, 236: 106ff.; Conrad, *German Universities*, pp. 154-68; Titze, "soziale und geistige Umbildung," pp. 107ff. For comparative data on the "extraordinary influx" of the Klein-bürgertum, see also Rienhardt, *Universitätsstudium*, pp. 26f. See also O. Wallach, "Chemie," in Lexis, *Universitäten*, pp. 267-70 and L. Burchardt, "Professionalisierung oder Berufs-konstruktion?" *GG* 6 (1980), pp. 326-48. Many chemists did go into high-school teaching, although the "preponderant majority" completed the doctoral degree in order to work in industry.

those incomplete liberal professions which, on the basis of lower admissions standards, required some academic training and therefore conferred less powerful entitlements. Chief among them (two-fifths) was scientific agriculture, pursued by large-scale farmers, while the paramedical occupations of pharmacist, attracting especially sons of apothecaries, and dentistry, favored by those who could not afford regular medicine, drew somewhat less than one-fifth each. While the mittlere Reife certificate (six years of a nine-year high school) sufficed for admission, some previous practical experience (such as a formal apprenticeship in pharmacy) was necessary. But these courses of study could be completed in about half the regular time (three or four semesters). As a result of this marginal academic status (all protestations of "scholarly training" notwithstanding), students in the nonteaching part of the philosophical faculty were older (21.87 years median age at admission to Bonn), more rural, but also less Rhenish than their counterparts. On the Rhine as well as in Prussia as a whole, Protestants were overrepresented and Jews even rarer than among prospective Oberlehrer. Only three-fifths had still attended a Gymnasium at some time, while well over a third had been prepared at modern high schools, and three-fourths were freshmen when matriculating. Female students were also scarcer, amounting only to 3.3 percent in Germany in the last prewar years. Because of this more traditional and rural character, the elite proportion was somewhat higher than among other philosophy students (27.6 percent), and the economic sectors of agriculture and rentiers were overrepresented. The number of noblemen was smaller than expected (around 3 percent), but 22.5 percent of the students came from academic families, as these fields often offered a second chance for high-school dropouts. The propertied bourgeoisie was considerably stronger than average, while the old and especially the new middle class were also numerous, for landed families (16.7 percent), farmers (12.0), tradesmen (10.8), rentiers (6.9), artisans (5.6), and teachers (5.3) made up the bulk of this group. Although objections against "subjects that are not quite homogeneous with those that originally constituted the faculty" were unable to eliminate these peripheral fields from philosophy, their students, though not markedly different in social origin, could not escape inferior status at the university because of their less stringent secondary education, their quicker completion of studies, and the lack of prestigious state examinations.[77] Hence,

---

[77] PrSt, 236: 98ff. Conrad, German Universities, pp. 169-75 and 316-19 (on pharmacy); A. Wassermann, "medizinische Fakultät," in Universitäten, p. 157 (appendix on dentistry); and Th. von der Goltz, "Landwirtschaft," ibid., pp. 290-300. Since Prussian statiticans included cameralism in the figures for agriculture in the philosophical faculty, this survival of the eighteenth-century "sciences of the state" (and forerunner of the twentieth-century social sciences) is included in this section, even if at some universities it constituted an

they kept to themselves and contributed little to the intellectual atmosphere, social life, or political culture of the university.

The above evidence suggests that different social groups (denominations, professions, and so on) pursued distinctive academic strategies. Contemporaries speculated that the choice of a given faculty was influenced by "its relation to the profession of the father, the social position of the parent, the inclination for a specific calling, the financial means of a family, etc." For sons of academics, inheritance of the paternal profession was most desirable, since over two-fifths of the officials' and lawyers' children who studied turned to law, about two-fifths of the doctors' offspring went into medicine, and almost that many students from academic teachers' homes followed in the footsteps of their fathers (table 3-14). As many Akademiker had limited financial means but possessed enough cultural resources to facilitate their children's education, the choice of parental profession or a closely related career (one-fifth of the clergymen's sons at the university went into teaching, or one-third of the doctors' offspring enrolled in law) was virtually a necessity. For the nonacademic groups within the upper and middle classes who could afford to finance the more costly legal and medical studies, the selection of a faculty was largely a matter of turning wealth into security via bureaucratic entitlement. Thus, almost one-half of the industrialists, two-fifths of the landed proprietors and rentiers, and one-third of the merchants sent their sons to study jurisprudence. Either agriculture (for the agrarians) or teaching was a second choice, while medicine usually was only a third preference, and theology was shunned by the entire Grossbürgertum. For the old-middle-class occupations the prime motive was social mobility into the academic professions, with the choice of faculty largely dependent upon the family's wealth. While over one-fourth of farmers and artisans entered Catholic theology (and somewhat less the philosophical faculty), tradesmen (who were more well-to-do) preferred law (with well over one-third) to teaching (less than one-fourth). Similarly, the new middle class of nonacademic officials and teachers strove to reach the higher social realm of its bureaucratic superiors, but it chose according to the proximity of a given career to the occupation of the father, even if this resolve required considerable financial sacrifice. Thus, the children of government employees still selected jurisprudence (28.6 percent) over philosophy (26.9 percent), while the offspring of primary teachers preferred a higher version of their parental profession (the Oberlehrer career, with 36.3 percent) over all others. Finally, for the few workers' sons there was little or no choice at all but to turn where financial

independent minifaculty and at others it was attached to law. See also W. Lexis, "Staatswissenschaften," in his *Universitäten*, pp. 219-24.

TABLE 3-14
Father's Profession and Field of Study at Bonn

Student's Field		Clergy	Lawyer	Doctor	Academic Teacher	Officer	Engineer /Other	Landed Property	Entrepreneur	Commerce
Protestant	(no.)	105	17	5	12	1	4	6	7	24
Theology	(row) %	26	4.7	1.2	3.0	.2	1.0	1.5	1.7	5.9
	(col.) %	41.8	2.7	1.7	3.1	.8	3.2	1.7	2.0	7.5
Catholic	(no.)	0	20	11	12	0	4	15	11	12
Theology	(row) %	0	3.4	1.9	2.0	0	.6	2.5	1.8	2.0
	(col.) %	0	3.2	3.2	3.8	0	3.2	4.3	3.2	3.7
Law	(no.)	48	399	100	128	68	38	142	154	106
	(row) %	2.2	18.3	4.6	5.9	4.1	1.7	6.5	7.0	4.9
	(col.) %	19.1	64.3	34.2	33.5	56.5	30.4	40.8	45.0	33.1
Medicine	(no.)	24	59	112	43	5	16	33	51	48
	(row) %	2.7	6.8	12.9	4.9	.6	.8	3.8	5.9	5.5
	(col.) %	9.6	9.5	38.4	11.2	4.2	12.9	9.5	14.8	15
Philosophy	(no.)	56	77	46	142	30	44	52	73	79
	(row) %	3.6	4.9	2.9	9.0	1.9	2.8	3.3	4.7	5.0
	(col.) %	22.3	12.4	17.7	37.1	25	35.3	14.9	21.3	24.7
Other	(no.)	18	49	18	46	16	19	100	44	51
	(row) %	2.0	5.5	2.0	5.2	1.8	2.1	11.3	5.0	5.7
	(col.) %	7.2	7.9	6.2	12.0	13.3	15.2	28.7	12.8	15.9
TOTAL	(no.)	251	621	292	382	120	125	348	342	320
	(row) %	3.9	9.6	4.5	5.9	1.8	1.9	5.3	5.3	4.9

aid could be obtained; over one-half chose Catholic theology and about one-third philosophy.[78] Although individuals could and did break out of these patterns when strongly attracted to a particular profession, the general choice of faculty (and thereby career) was determined by a strong set of social relations, based on inheritance, prestige, aspiration, and affinity of parental occupation with a given field.

The connection between academic requirements and social composition of individual faculties was largely governed by a system of formal enti-

[78] A. Rienhardt, *Universitätsstudium*, pp. 33-40; *PrSt*, 236: 137ff. indicates a declining theological self-recruitment and an increasing philosophical (teaching) inheritance. See also J. Conrad, *German Universities*, pp. 57-70.

Salaried	Rentier	Financial /Other	Farmer	Artisan	Tradesman	Other Old Middle Class	Subaltern Official	Teacher	White Collar /Other New Middle Class	Laborer	Total
11	12	2	34	21	34	7	37	58	6	1	401
2.7	3.0	.5	8.4	5.2	8.4	1.7	9.1	14.3	1.5	.2	
8.7	3.2	2.7	6.8	4.8	3.4	7.9	7.5	13.0	7.3	2.0	6.2
6	17	3	130	128	74	20	39	59	11	25	601
1.0	2.8	.5	21.7	21.4	12.4	3.3	6.2	9.7	1.8	4.2	
4.8	4.5	4.0	24.7	29.0	7.5	22.7	8.0	13.3	11.6	52.0	9.2
49	150	25	84	59	356	12	140	80	35	4	2177
2.2	6.9	1.1	3.8	2.7	16.3	.6	6.4	3.7	1.6	.2	
38.9	39.6	33.8	16.0	13.3	36.2	13.6	28.6	18.0	36.8	8.4	33.5
12	55	10	57	60	183	10	41	38	11	2	869
1.4	6.3	1.1	6.6	5.7	21.0	1.1	4.7	4.4	1.3	.2	
9.5	14.5	13.5	10.9	13.6	18.6	11.4	8.4	8.6	13.6	4.2	13.6
37	84	24	113	120	226	27	132	161	24	14	1561
2.4	5.4	1.5	7.2	7.7	14.5	1.7	8.5	10.3	1.5	.9	
28.4	22.2	32.4	21.5	27.1	23	30.7	26.9	36.3	25.3	29.2	24.6
11	61	10	107	54	110	12	101	47	12	2	884
1.2	6.9	1.1	12.1	6.1	12.4	1.3	11.4	5.3	1.3	.2	
8.7	16.1	13.5	19.8	12.1	11.2	13.6	20.6	10.6	12.6	4.2	13.6
26	379	74	525	442	983	88	490	443	95	48	6498
1.9	5.8	1.1	8.1	6.9	15.1	1.3	7.5	6.8	1.3	.7	

NOTE: The professions listed are the more numerous entries in table 3-7. Strata do not total 100 percent as some of the minor occupations were omitted. To illuminate the academic strategies of professions as well as the social composition of different faculties, both column and row percentages were included.

tlements, highly developed in Central Europe. Pondering the emergence of "rational, specialized and expert testing," Max Weber described the effect of the *Berechtigungswesen*:

> Above all, the development is greatly furthered by the social prestige of the educational certificates acquired through such specialized examinations. This is all the more the case as the educational patent is turned to economic advantage. Today, the certificate of education becomes what the test for ancestors has been in the past, at least where the nobility has remained powerful: a prerequisite for equality of birth, a qualification for canonship and for state office.

By the end of the nineteenth century the process of bureaucratization had created a hierarchy of occupations, corresponding closely to a system of school qualifications, which linked education with the job market. Vastly simplified, the system consisted of five levels, separated by differences in earning, prestige, and cultural style, which were most distinctive on the top and on the bottom:

Schooling:	1. little	2. Volksschule	3. Einjährige	4. Abitur	5. university study
Rank:	none	simple	middle	elevated	higher public service
Job:	unskilled	skilled	white-collar	supervisory	professional and managerial

Perhaps one ought to visualize this structure as a series of successively higher thresholds, limiting access with each upward step while guaranteeing an ever more rewarding form of state employment for each level reached. As advancement above one's entrance category through superior job performance became harder and harder, the entitlement to additional education which a graduation certificate from a classical or modern secondary school conferred grew increasingly important.[79]

The top of the schooling-rank-job staircase was occupied by university graduates. Through state examinations they controlled the ministry, dominated higher government service and the practice of law, maintained exclusive rights over the occupation of physician, and eliminated all competition for teaching in the higher schools and universities. As appointment by and large proceeded by seniority, passing an examination became more important than doing well, thereby favoring economic staying power over intellectual attainment. According to Max Weber, the stakes were so high because educational "certificates support their holders' claim for intermarriages with notable families . . . claims to be admitted into the circles that adhere to 'codes of honor,' claims for a 'respectable' remuneration rather than remuneration for work done, claims for assured advancement and old-age insurance, and above all, claims to monopolize socially and economically advantageous positions." Legally established through the examination requirements (*Prüfungsordnungen*), specifying (before 1900) graduation from the Gymnasium and requiring six or more semesters of university study, this entitlement system was severely strained by the increasing number of university graduates during the Second Empire. The

---

[79] Max Weber, *Wirtschaft und Gesellschaft*, part 3, pp. 650-78; W. Lexis, "Die Berechtigung zum Universitätsstudium im allgemeinen," in his *Reform des höheren Schulwesens*, pp. 61-74; R. Meyer, "Das Berechtigungswesen in seiner Bedeutung für Schule und Gesellschaft im 19. Jahrhundert," *Zeitschrift für gesamte Staatswissenschaft* 124 (1968): 763ff.; D. K. Müller, *Sozialstruktur und Schulsystem*, pp. 65-84; and Westfalen, *Akademisches Privileg*, p. 150.

"desire for restricting the supply for these positions" led to increasing academic standards and rising certification requirements for specific jobs, which in turn devalued those *Zeugnisse* already obtained and necessitated further education. On the other hand, the "excess of educated men" made nonmeritocratic criteria among a pool of applicants (such as family background or Corps membership) more significant for success. As "the bureaucratization of capitalism, with its demand for expertly trained technicians, clerks, etc.," introduced an entitlement gradation into many business careers, the educational hierarchy of the Berechtigungswesen stamped German social and economic life beyond functional justification. Through its peculiar use of testing, this system reconciled the liberal insistence on meritocratic advancement with the conservative demand for ascriptive status security. It allowed the Akademiker to use education in order to perpetuate themselves in leading positions while legitimating their prestige by drawing in students from the economic elite and, to an extent, from the lower middle class.[80]

DID THE student body of the Imperial German university become more egalitarian or more elitist? There is little doubt that "the two decades before the First World War may in fact be regarded as a turning point in the history of the German social structure and of the German university as well." Only the extent and direction of this transformation are still vigorously disputed.[81] The demographic evidence examined above suggests an extension of the length of schooling, a lessening of urban overrepresentation, an increase in toleration for Catholics, a reluctant modernization of university preparation, and an even more grudging extension of sexual equality after 1870. While the rise in age is somewhat ambivalent, the other four criteria point toward a gradual but limited increase in the diversity of backgrounds. A similar comparison of students' social origins over the nineteenth century reveals an initial decrease of elite representation, a series of functional economic changes away from agriculture toward industry,

[80] M. Weber, "The 'Rationalization' of Education and Training," in Gerth and Mills, *From Max Weber*, pp. 240-44; S. Turner, "On the Origins of the *Bildungsbürgertum* in Prussia," pp. 15ff.; and Kocka, "Bildung, soziale Schichtung und soziale Mobilität," pp. 297ff. See also H. Perkin, "Professionalization and English Society since 1880" (manuscript, Princeton University, 1980); and A. J. LaVopa, "The Emergence of the Idea of Profession," paper read at the 1980 Western Association of German Studies meeting.

[81] F. Ringer, *Education and Society*, pp. 93-104; D. Müller, *Sozialstruktur und Schulsystem*, pp. 287-97; and H. Kaelble, *Historische Mobilitätsforschung*, pp. 73-79. Although the categorical prison of secondary statistics prevents Ringer from going beyond economic functional analysis, Müller's data focus on secondary education (where the Gymnasium might have become more homogenous with modern high schools siphoning off bourgeois and petit bourgeois elements), whereas Kaelble's comparative figures suggest the hypothesis of a contraction of opportunities with industrialization without specifying its duration and extent. Cf. K. H. Jarausch, "The Social Transformation," pp. 609-31.

commerce, and government, a drying up of nobility enrollment, a precipitous decline of academic self-recruitment, a temporary plutocratization of academe, and finally a partial opening of the university for children of the lower middle class, shifting from traditional to white-collar occupations. Although industrialization probably reduced petit-bourgeois access in the academic recessions of the 1840s and 1890s, during the last prewar decades students recruited themselves more broadly from nonacademic and kleinbürgerliche homes. A final contrast between pre-1848 and Wilhelmian career choices (as evident in faculties of study) indicates the continued social dominance of law and medicine over theology or philosophy in terms of exclusiveness. But it also shows some improvement of access to the higher faculties for outsiders and the replacement of preaching by teaching as the primary channel of mobility. Although the pattern of change varied in speed and extent among Western nations, the German data as well as the comparative evidence suggest that the enrollment explosion and resultant institutional diversification led to a transition from the traditional elite to a modern middle-class university.[82]

Despite the impressive Mittelstand figures of the last prewar years, the social opening of the bourgeois university was limited. By 1905, 54.2 percent of all Badensian students stemmed from the Kleinbürgertum, while in 1911-12 almost 60 percent of Prussian enrollment came from the petite bourgeoisie, and in 1914 nearly 58 percent of Bavarian university pupils derived from the lower middle class. In terms of Dahrendorf's four underprivileged groups, there were proportionally fewer students from the countryside than ever before, Catholics had made some gains but remained underrepresented, women were still a small minority (less than one-tenth), and the children of the working class continued to be virtually excluded from higher education. Even though the old and new lower middle class succeeded in undermining the academic and plutocratic elitism typical of bureaucratization and industrialization, Bildung remained a privilege of the few, jealously guarded against the aspirations of the many. After 1900 academic strategy turned from formal exclusion to partial co-optation of previously disenfranchised groups (such as modern-high-school graduates) in order to legitimate selection as meritocratic and thereby defend it more effectively against further reform. Rural, modern, female, and lower-middle-class students primarily matriculated in the mass faculty of philosophy (and to a lesser degree theology), while the higher academic pursuits of

[82] H. Perkin, "The Pattern of Social Transformation: England," and D. R. Brower, "Social Stratification in Russian Higher Education, 1855-1930," in *The Transformation of Higher Learning* (1982). See also R. Angelo, "The Students at the University of Pennsylvania and the Temple College of Philadelphia 1873-1906: Some Notes on Schooling, Class and Social Mobility in the Late Nineteenth Century," *HEQ* 19 (1979): 179-205 and n. 5.

law and medicine, leading to government service and the liberal professions, remained largely reserved for the cultivated or propertied elites. When members of disadvantaged groups graduated from the university, they faced even greater difficulties because positions, such as for Catholic high-school teachers, were harder to find. The flood of "new students" raised the importance of informal tests of ideological conformity, social suitability, and financial solvency through membership in a duelling corporation, a reserve officer's patent, or appropriate maintenance during the unsalaried probationary period. Although the neofeudal notion of honor came to serve as a shorthand, discriminating among academics beyond their formal qualifications, some restrictions even found their way into official documents, such as the Prussian *Prüfungsordnung* for the judiciary of 1913. While paragraph 24, section b permitted rejection "if a candidate appears undignified for higher judicial service," paragraph 25 instructed the "*Oberlandesgerichtspräsident*" to deny an application if more referendaries . . . cannot be trained in the district," which suggests preference for local applicants.[83] Although the educated gradually lost their caste, or "mandarin," character, the concept and reality of the Akademiker broadened only slowly in Imperial Germany.

Collectively, the Bildungsbürgertum, "formed by the group status symbol" of cultivation, reached its apogee in the Second Reich. Defined by their academic training, self-recruitment, in-group behavior, social prestige, and secularized Protestantism, the educated were the cultural elite of German society and occupied the leading bureaucratic, liberal, and teaching professions. The enrollment explosion had increased their absolute and relative size, making them comparable to the economic elite. Although the pay of Prussian officials was generally miserly, the entitlement system provided legal protection against competition, while government pensions offered social security. Therefore, meritocratic recruitment worked so well in practice that between one-half (before 1890) and one-third of all higher officials in the western Prussian provinces stemmed from academic backgrounds (with another one-fifth to one-third from the bourgeoisie) while only 3 percent of nonacademic bureaucrats came from cultivated families (with another 1.3 percent from propertied homes). The exclusiveness of the free professionals from the same areas (with two-thirds coming from the upper middle classes) also demonstrates the growing integration of Bildung and Besitz in terms of origin, *connubium* (necessary to make up for meager salaries), and *commercium* (broadly defined as social inter-

[83] *BSSt*, pp. 64ff., 168ff. and 270ff.; *PrSt*, 236: 136ff.; *Zeitschrift des bayerischen statistischen Landesamts* 55 (1923): 115ff. W. Montag, "Die Oberlehreraussichten in Preussen," *Ac* 26 (1913): 448-50. "Prüfungsordung vom 17. Juni 1913," in *Die Vorschriften über die Ausbildung der Juristen*, pp. 40f.

course). Although still overshadowed by military and court society, the prestige of the academics, derived from the imperium of the state (from sharing its authority), outshone the reputation of the newly rich commercial and industrial leaders if one can believe Theodor Fontane. Moreover, both educated officials and free professionals were animated by a common ethos, which, dominated by the neo-Kantian conception of duty, formed a cohesive life ideal focused on a shared notion of honorable service. Even if direct political participation decreased from the levels of the unification and constitutionalization movement before 1870, the Bildungsbürgertum dominated the *Ersatz* politics of the bureaucracy, led the patriotic societies, and provided articulate spokesmen for economic and ideological interest groups. The academics' indirect influence through public opinion and direct political power through state office were, therefore, considerable: "They form a generally homogeneous stratum in which all influential or controlling circles take part."[84] Hence, in the empire the cultivated proudly saw themselves as an aristocracy of merit.

In many respects "the social-aristocratic tendency, which in the last generation has so remarkably emerged in our national life," was a result of the very success of the Bildungsbürgertum. While in the pre-1848 period the rising educated middle class favored universalist aims in order to gain allies in its liberal struggle against the nobility, after 1870, with the achievement of unity, constitution, free trade, and the rule of law, it began to exhibit more exclusionist strains. The perceptive Friedrich Paulsen understood the dynamics behind this great reversal: "The middle class, which one hundred years ago raised the banner of freedom and equality against the privileged, has in the meantime changed fronts. Fused with the old nobility into a generally homogenous group, the class of the 'cultivated and propertied' now strives to defend itself against the masses pressing upward from below. This effort is visible in all areas, in politics, society, and in the school."[85] By legally requiring ever-rising educational qualifications for higher careers, it tried to secure its position and attempted to pass its acquired capital of culture to its children in order to maintain their ascendancy. While shifting its gaze from the nobility to "the masses" as the principal adversary, the Bildungsbürgertum became disunited, for

---

[84] Vondung, "Zur Lage der Gebildeten in der wilhelminischen Zeit," in his *Wilhelminisches Bildungsbürgertum*, pp. 20ff.; J. Henning, *Das Bildungsbürgertum in den preussischen Westprovinzen*, pp. 214ff., 373ff., 474ff. for the comparative figures. F. Paulsen, *German Universities*, pp. 110f.

[85] F. Paulsen, *Geschichte des gelehrten Unterrichts* 2: 573, 686ff.; Bleek, *Juristenprivileg*, pp. 44ff. For the political implications, see also Jarausch, "Social Transformation," pp. 628-31. The imaginative reconsideration of the German middle class by D. Blackbourn and G. Eley, *Mythen deutscher Geschichtsschreibung* (Frankfurt, 1980), does not take the Bildungsbürgertum sufficiently into account.

enrollment growth and social opening internally stratified university graduates into three distinct groups: The successful alumni of law (as *Räte* in the bureaucracy) and medicine as well as a minority of leading theologians and professors coalesced with the landed aristocracy and propertied middle class into the imperial elite. A minority of less astute lawyers, doctors, and the bulk of the clergy and high-school teachers (such as the Oberlehrer) formed a contented, but only locally influential middle group, viewing itself as solid middle class, poorer than most merchants and businessmen, but culturally superior to them. Finally, the failures from the higher faculties (like *Winkeladvokat, Armenarzt*) and a considerable part of the poor clergy and private-high-school teachers as well as marginal journalists and many industrial chemists constituted a lower-middle-class segment of university educated struggling against a descent into the "academic proletariat." Although bitter conflicts within the triad of birth, wealth, and education continued, in a crisis the three elements of the elite tended to pull together in the name of a common interest—the preservation of the political system and the social status quo. Because of the overriding role of the state in their employment, the middle group of academics could always be counted upon by a chancellor like Bethmann Hollweg to defend the empire against subversion (*Umsturz*) at home and encirclement abroad, despite disagreement on specific policies. Social and political conformity was at a premium as well for the proletarianized members of the Bildungsbürgertum, because only through exclusivist arrogance and demonstrative loyalty (*staatserhaltende Gesinnung*) could they protect their membership among the cultivated against the pressure from the Socialist proletarian masses. While the social transformation somewhat widened access to German higher education, it also increased pressures for social defensiveness and political conformity.

Four

THE TEACHING OF POLITICS

DURING "the great and eventful time" of the Franco-Prussian War, Rector Carl Bruns welcomed students to the University of Berlin: "How the success [of Sedan] has surpassed our boldest hopes and expectations!" For many academics the key to the German victory lay not only in military might but also in spiritual force: "The idea that founded our university has twice conquered France, once in youthful enthusiasm and now in manly maturity." Castigating the "frivolous hubris and immeasurable conceit" of the Gallic claim to fight against barbarism, Bruns turned it on its head: "*Therefore Germany's victory is the victory of civilization . . . of freedom . . . as well as of peace and tranquillity in Europe.*" To thunderous applause, the Berlin rector drew a sober moral for his students: "The deep and lasting source [of our greatness] lies in the power of our spirit, our cultivation, our scholarship. Whoever fights for this and in his quiet study risks his health in order to achieve victories of the mind with weapons of scholarship does not contribute any less to the glory of our fatherland than he who sacrifices his life on the field of battle." For German academics cultivation was not only an intellectual endeavor but also a deeply serious task with important political implications. During the war, Rector Emil DuBois-Reymond bluntly defined the national mission inherent in Wissenschaft: "Housed across from the royal palace, the University of Berlin is, according to its founding charter, the spiritual bodyguard of the House of Hohenzollern." Only a few academics escaped this infectious enthusiasm and, like Friedrich Nietzsche, warned against "the strange degeneration which shall erode the core of a culture, if the state is allowed to believe it dominates it, uses it for political ends, and employs it against foreign powers and . . . the 'truly German' spirit."[1]

---

[1] C. G. Bruns, *Deutschlands Sieg über Frankreich* (Berlin, 1870); E. H. DuBois-Reymond, *Über den deutschen Krieg* (Berlin, 1870); and F. Nietzsche, "Über die Zukunft unserer Bildungsanstalten," in G. Colli and M. Montinari, *Nietzsches Werke: Kritische Gesamtausgabe* (Berlin, 1973), vol. 2, pt. 3, 133-244. Nietzsche objected to the dual "trend

The notion that defined the relationship between cultivation and politics for nineteenth-century German academics was the idea of the *Kulturstaat*. Seeking to animate the mechanistic absolutist state with a cultural soul, J. G. Fichte coined the term: "There is no kind of Bildung which does not, strictly speaking, emanate from the state and which is not compelled to strive to return to it." Although aware of the tension between politics and scholarship, the neohumanist reformers around Wilhelm von Humboldt made the government the institutional guardian of cultivation by charging it with material support and administrative control of higher education. Because "all human value, all spiritual reality derives solely from the state," Friedrich Wilhelm von Hegel deified the synthesis of power and spirit as "the Kulturstaat, the self-representation of culture as state." Although this identity between political and cultural ends was more easily postulated than practiced, the theory of the culture state appealed to all segments of the Bildungsbürgertum in and out of bureaucratic office, for it ennobled public service and justified the claim of the educated to political leadership.[2] "Long awaited and shunned, the happy marriage of Prussia's genius to the German soul" in 1871 reinforced the fusion of the contradictory realms of state and culture and provided academics with a standard for measuring (and transforming) political reality. "The attempt had to be made to fit the university into the organism of the state in such a way that it would become the nursery of true higher cultivation, harmoniously uniting intelligence and morality, ideal striving and practical ability, scholarly aspiration and patriotic spirit." Like the leading university historian Max Lenz, most of the cultivated considered higher learning and the Second Empire eminently compatible: "Since Prussia's power sprang from Reformation soil, since the spirit of true freedom, of drinking directly from the fount of knowledge, found a home in the state of Frederick the Great, the monarchy did and still does allow full liberty to the pursuit of truth, regardless of its consequences." Only a few outsiders like Robert Michels dared question the legitimacy of the union between Weimar and Potsdam: "During the entire century from Rotteck to Naumann, German scholars

---

toward broadening Bildung and . . . toward diminishing and weakening it. According to the former, cultivation is to be carried into ever wider circles, and according to the latter, Bildung is to give up its highest claims to autonomy and to subject itself to the service of another sphere, i.e., the state."

[2] Although the idea of the Kulturstaat lacks a central formulation and a single overriding spokesman, it permeates the writings of the neohumanist reformers as well as the Festreden of academic speakers throughout the nineteenth century. For brief introductions, see F. Schnabel, *Deutsche Geschichte im 19. Jahrhundert* (Freiburg, 1926) 1: 296-99 and 2: 12-19; and M. Lenz, *Friedrich-Wilhelms-Universität zu Berlin* (Halle, 1910) 2: 372ff. See also H. Schelsky, *Einsamkeit und Freiheit: Idee und Gestalt der deutschen Universität*, 2nd ed. (Düsseldorf, 1971), pp. 102-15, and R. S. Turner, "On the Origins of the Bildungsbürgertum," pp. 40-45.

have, by the sweat of their brow, tried to combine the natural antitheses of democracy and military monarchy into a higher theoretical whole. Hand in hand with this honest idealism went their attempt to defeudalize the monarchy, if possible; that is, to replace the aristocratic guardians of the throne with academics."[3]

In contrast to the paeans of contemporary self-praise, historians have evaluated the political implications of cultivation in Imperial Germany more critically. The most recent summary of Anglo-Saxon scholarship berates the majority of nineteenth-century professors for tending "to conform to official opinion, as expressed by government agencies and to lend their authority to the support of government policies that appeared to more objective minds to be dangerous and irrational." Many West German historians of the last decade also view "the school as administrative instrument of state rule" and decry the "conformity pressure" of the universities, which on the whole served "as bulwarks of the status quo" instead of as agents of sociopolitical modernization. More outspoken yet, East German scholars complain that "the education of the students and the political attitude of the faculty fell more and more under a Prusso-German nationalist spell." Hence, "the Wilhelmian-Prussian state and particularly the Fascist regime greatly subjected scholarship to their inhuman policies. That is especially true of the social sciences, which were demoted to apologetics of the capitalist system and could be abused to prepare and justify the war and exploitation of German imperialism."[4]

A few important voices have dissented from this chorus of condemnation. Although conceding that the "ideas of 1871" contributed to the "nationalization of German science" in the empire, Theodor Schieder concludes: "One can almost say that along with the guarantees of the Rechtsstaat against arbitrary administrative acts and along with local and communal self-government, academic freedom belonged to the free areas

---

[3] M. Lenz, *Bismarck* (Berlin, 1899), a commemorative oration for the chancellor's death, attempting to rehabilitate the contribution of the national-liberal movement of the academics. C. G. Bruns, *Hohenzollern, Preussen, Deutschland* (Berlin, 1871); C. T. Weierstrass, *Über das Universitätswesen in Deutschland* (Berlin, 1874); and R. Michels, *Zur Soziologie des Parteiwesens in der modernen Demokratie* (Leipzig, 1925), pp. 10f. For a similar critique from the right, see J. Langbehn, *Rembrandt als Erzieher*, 35th ed. (Leipzig, 1891), pp. 162-64.

[4] G. A. Craig, *Germany 1866-1945* (New York, 1978), pp. 180-223, summarizing most notably F. Ringer's *The Decline of the German Mandarins*; C. Berg, *Die Okkupation der Schule: Eine Studie zur Aufhellung gegenwärtiger Schulprobleme an der Volksschule Preussens, 1872-1900* (Heidelberg, 1973); as well as "Schulpolitik als Verwaltungspolitik: Die Schule als Herrschaftsinstrument staatlicher Verwaltung," *Vierteljahrsschrift für wissenschaftliche Pädagogik* 51 (1975): 211-36; and H. U. Wehler, *Das deutschen Kaiserreich* (Göttingen, 1973), chapter 4. E. R. Berthold et al., eds., *Die Humboldt-Universität: Gestern-Heute-Morgen* (Berlin, 1960) and Der Rektor, ed., *Die Humboldt Universität zu Berlin* (Berlin, 1976).

[*Freiräume*] in the otherwise largely authoritarian-bureaucratic Reich.'' Rejecting the "radical cliché of the repressive empire," Thomas Nipperdey argues that "partial truth writ large becomes untruth." Aside from an "underestimation of mobility," he criticizes "the overestimation of conservative institutions and mentalities" and deplores the lack of attention to "countervailing tendencies in the development of youthful bourgeois-academic attitudes." There were "fundamental changes, spilling over into the political realm" which "cannot be explained with an analysis concentrating on the maintenance of a political system." This clash of opinions raises two basic questions: How did the universities turn from "centers of liberal-progressive ideas and research into cadre schools of imperialism?" And what was the political thrust not of "decrees, declamations and declarations of intent," but rather of the "actual teaching" of students in Germany?[5]

In methodological terms, the debate about the politics of cultivation implicitly or explicitly centers on the concept of political culture. Developed for systematic comparisons of political ideals and operative norms between various countries, it is commonly defined as "the set of attitudes, beliefs and sentiments which give order and meaning to a political process and which provide the underlying assumptions and rules that govern behavior in the political system." Less explicit than ideology but more specific and durable than attitude, this notion deals with rational and emotional orientations toward politics shared by members of a group. As it "assumes that each individual must in his own historical context learn and incorporate into his own personality the knowledge and feelings about the politics of his people and community," political culture emphasizes the crucial significance of political education. While a number of agents and influences compete in shaping such collective outlooks, for the highly educated segment of society the university plays a crucial role in the explicit formulation of political views by challenging family sentiments or school truths and transforming them into a more conscious Weltanschauung. Although it is sometimes diffuse and redundant, the concept of political culture raises a number of issues about the role of cultivation at imperial German universities: Did Bildung convey a cohesive set of values and

---

[5] T. Schieder, "Kultur, Wissenschaft und Wissenschaftspolitik im Deutschen Kaiserreich," in *Medizin, Naturwissenschaft, Technik*, pp. 9-34; T. Nipperdey, review of Christa Berg's *Okkupation der Schule, HZ* 225 (1977): 194-96, and his "Wehlers 'Kaiserreich': Eine kritische Auseinandersetzung," *GG* 1 (1975): 539-60. For the questions, see W. Fläschendräger and M. Straube, *Die Entwicklung der Universitäten, Hochschulen und Akademien im Spiegel der hochschulgeschichtlichen Forschungen, 1960-1969* (Berlin, 1970). For an overview, see L. Boehm, "Das akademische Bildungswesen in seiner organisatorischen Entwicklung, 1800-1920," in M. Spindler, ed., *Handbuch für bayerische Geschichte* (Munich, 1975), vol. 4, pt. 2, 991-1033.

were they congruent with those of the wider polity? What attitudes did academic culture instill about politics in general, about power, authority, nationality, or society? How successful were professors in transmitting orientations to particular issues, such as parliamentarism or imperialism, and what information or political skills did they communicate to enable their students to assume public leadership?[6] Answering these questions requires abandoning the illusion of the scientific objectivity of higher learning. In the belief that they could pursue eternal truth and at the same time cultivate students politically, imperial academics either subscribed to the ideal of *Bildung durch Wissenschaft* or embraced the "duty to awaken and strengthen the feeling of national and civic responsibility."[7]

The analysis of the political component of university teaching necessitates a fresh approach and new evidence. To establish the framework of political cultivation, one ought to begin by examining governmental aims and professorial opinions. To determine which "image of man, social attitudes, and basic political values" professors sought to transmit to the pupils, one might look at the ceremonial speeches delivered by leading professors to commemorate: the Kaiser's birthday (22 March for William I and 27 January for William II); the anniversary of the founding of the university (3 August in Berlin and Bonn); the beginning of the new academic year in October; and other special occasions, such as the quadricentennial of Luther's birth in 1883. Many of these Festreden celebrated the university as the place that "makes [youth] capable of independently serving the fatherland."[8] To assess the general political thrust of cultivation, one should analyze regular lectures in those disciplines, such as law, economics, and history, where politics was an essential part of the argument. To grasp the specific political message of teaching one must also scrutinize the *Politikvorlesung*, which explicitly intended to impart basic factual information and strengthen the loyalty of future state officials. This progressively narrower focus on the shaping of political consciousness of youth finally requires an investigation of the movement for civic edu-

[6] L. W. Pye, "Political Culture," *IESS* 12: 218-25; G. A. Almond and S. Verba, *The Civic Culture: Political Attitudes and Democracy in Five Nations* (Boston, 1965); L. W. Pye and S. B. Verba, *Political Culture and Political Development* (Princeton, 1965). For a more recent historical application, see also R. Chickering, *Imperial Germany and a World Without War* (Princeton, 1975), pp. 26-37.

[7] B. Litzmann, *Im Alten Deutschland: Erinnerungen eines Sechzigjährigen* (Berlin, 1923), p. 340. For a different approach see also R. vom Bruch, *Wissenschaft, Politik und öffentliche Meinung. Gelehrtenpolitik im Wilhelminischen Deutschland* (Husum, 1980), pp. 414-23.

[8] W. König, "Politische Komponenten von Forschung und Lehre an der Universität Bonn im Kaiserreich 1871-1918" (unpublished paper, Saarbrücken, 1976), a pilot study supported by the Thyssen Stiftung. The present discussion builds on its conceptual framework and compares the Bonn results with a second case study of the University of Berlin. See also E. Curtius, *Festrede am Geburtstage S.M. des Königs im Namen der Friedrich-Wilhelms-Universität am 22. März 1870* (Berlin, 1870).

cation and the campaign for world political training during the last prewar years. Professors like Berthold Litzmann were convinced of the significance of educating the younger generation to become "politically aware and upright personalities." Moreover, they believed that "words of this kind do not fail to make an impression upon receptive young minds and . . . that between students and myself something more than a formal relationship gradually developed."[9]

IMPLICATIONS OF CULTIVATION

The implementation of the rhetorical goals of German higher education, which "bound the sphere of freedom to the power of the state," suffered from a fundamental tension between Bildung and *Ausbildung*, cultivation or professional training. The 1817 statutes of the University of Berlin aiming toward "the completion of general scientific cultivation" represent the view of Bildung durch Wissenschaft which "grew out of the same spiritual soil as liberal political ideology." But as the neo-Humboldtian historian Eduard Spranger remarked, the university was "primarily considered by the state as an institution for training public officials" and therefore had to impart not only skills but also a loyal outlook. Despite his famous claim of "replacing with spiritual forces what has been lost in physical" might after the defeat of Napoleon, Fredrick William III was more interested in "piety, thorough scholarship, and morality." In the same vein, Minister of Culture Altenstein considered

the universities institutions of cultivation and education and nothing else. Thus, the teachers are to be held responsible for moral, religious, and intellectual Bildung, as required by political training for citizenship, and they are to have the means for it. Pupils however must unconditionally dedicate and subject themselves to these ends. The universities are not states within the state. . . . The governments are masters of the institutes and should only consider them according to their purpose. And everything that does not necessarily relate to higher education as such, but involves general political conditions, should be completely excluded.

[9] The most famous of these political lectures is the historian Treitschke's *Politik*. For the choice of the three disciplines, see below and König, "Politische Komponenten," pp. 1-7. Litzmann, *Im alten Deutschland*, p. 340; H. Hüffer, *Lebenserinnerungen*, edited by E. Sieper, 2nd ed. (Berlin, 1914), pp. 352f. Ringer (*Decline of the German Mandarins*, pp. 81-199) focuses on professorial politics (in the philosophical faculty) but not their influence on students. Despite some overlap, the framework, Festreden, scholarly lectures, and *Politikvorlesung* were examined individually in order to convey the texture of each layer of evidence and to build successively on every substudy.

The constitution of the University of Bonn (1827) therefore stressed patriotic attitude formation over cultivation or scientific research. It defined the university as ''a state institute, charged with the propagation of morality and religiousness of youth as well as the full scope and highest possible perfection of scholarly cultivation, for which the learned schools are supposed to provide the foundation.'' In contrast to ''advancing and widening science itself''

> all teachers are to lead the students entrusted to their care to that level of ethical-religious training and to that degree of theoretical and practical knowledge as well as to confirm them in those loyal and good attitudes and tendencies that make them capable of entering into the service of the church and state, as well as every profession that demands higher scholarly cultivation. Therefore, the university must become a purposefully organized nursery of thoroughly and broadly trained and prepared servants of state and church.

Nevertheless, the spirit that animated Bildung before 1848 and 1871 among politically interested professors and students was by and large liberal.[10]

After 1870 political cultivation vacillated between positivist covert and patriotic overt indoctrination, owing to the growing professorial commitment to scholarship as research and the hardening insistence of Prussian officials on professional training. On the one hand, the conflict between governmental and neohumanist perceptions of the goals of higher education continued to smolder. The Mühler draft of paragraph 146 of the school law (*Unterrichtsgesetz*) talked about ''propagation of Wissenschaft and scholarly training of future servants of state and church,'' while the more liberal Falk version of paragraph 250 hearkened back to ''teaching and advancement of scholarship in its entirety.'' On the other hand, the political demands on cultivation increased with the resolution that ''there should be founded in Strassburg a German university of the first rank, a respectable cultural home for the German intellect and a guardian of the German scientific method.'' The Germanizing mission of the new imperial university required great faith in the political effectiveness of Bildung to undo the harm of ''French dilettantism and scientific superficiality.'' One means would be the foundation of ''a chair of German history, particularly in order to instruct the numerous prospective Protestant clergymen and Gymnasium teachers who will be educated there and will become the repre-

---

[10] M. Lenz, *Freiheit und Macht im Lichte der Entwicklung unserer Universität* (Berlin, 1911); and *Friedrich-Wilhelms-Universität*, 1: 384ff.; E. Spranger, *Wandlungen im Wesen der Universität seit hundert Jahren* (Leipzig, 1913); and quotes from Fredrick William III and Altenstein in K. T. Schäfer, *Verfassungsgeschichte der Universität Bonn 1818 bis 1960* (Bonn, 1968), pp. 83ff., 448ff.

sentatives of Germanness in the province.'' Prince Bismarck formulated the government view more clearly than others:

Our universities deserve praise, for during a time of imperial decline, they were the bearers of the idea of national unity and took care to perpetuate it in German youth. True to these traditions they shall help defend the new empire against the dangers threatening its unified existence from the interest politics of factions and the enmity of the parties of revolution.

The fundamental agreement of the bureaucrats and professors on "recognizing the existing as rational and exposing the machinations of political adventurers and unpatriotic egotists so that they cannot withstand the judgment of the German people" tended to break down over the means of influencing students. While the Prussian state time and again resorted to direct political control (lex Arons), academics still clung to the neohumanist faith that "the university does better for itself or its charges and serves the public life of the nation more constructively, the more steadfastly it concentrates its efforts on the pursuit of Wissenschaft."[11]

The implementation of patriotic education at the university was primarily the task of the professor. Conceived of as "a kind of double being, at once scholar and teacher," he sought "not to produce pupils who follow direction, but [create] free men, who, independent of fashion or party, and ennobled through scholarship, dedicate themselves to the fatherland with mature intelligence and integrity." As a secular priesthood claiming to speak objectively, however, the professoriate could only transmit political attitudes filtered by its own social origin and professional recruitment. In contrast to the students, two-thirds of the professors who finished their second dissertation (the Habilitation) before 1890 still came from academic homes, while in the last prewar decades around one-half stemmed from cultivated families (table 4-1). Hence, they reflected the views of the Bildungsbürgertum more clearly than their increasingly heterogeneous pupils. Because an increase in plutocratic backgrounds compensated for declining self-recruitment, in the first half of the empire the faculty became even more elitist and only opened ever so slightly in the last prewar years.

[11] *Unterrichtsgesetz* drafts in ZStA Me, Rep 92, Falk, No 1k and in BUA, Kuratorium C12; F. V. Roggenbach, "Report Concerning the Reorganization of the University of Strassburg," cited in John E. Craig, "A Mission for German Learning: The University of Strasbourg and Alsatian Society, 1870-1918" (dissertation, Stanford University, 1973), 142ff.; Bismarck to Richard, 26 August 1887, DZA Po, Rkz 2195; and Paul Kleinert, *Vom Anteil der Universität an der Vorbildung fürs öffentliche Leben* (Berlin, 1885). For an opposite view, see also Paul de Lagarde, *Deutsche Schriften*, 4th ed. (Göttingen, 1903), pp. 168, 179, 188-208.

TABLE 4-1
Social Origins of German University Professors

Social Class			Full Professors		Other Professors,
		Habilitation Before 1859	Habilitation Before 1889	Habilitation Before 1919	Habilitation Before 1919
Educated Officials	no.	369	591	1118	301
	%	48.9	46.2	37.1	31.8
Free Professionals	no.	117	237	431	158
	%	15.5	18.6	14.3	16.7
Total Educated	%	64.4	65.0	51.4	48.5
Propertied	no.	40	112	483	178
	%	5.3	8.8	16.0	18.8
Total Upper Middle Class	%	69.7	73.8	67.4	67.3
Old Middle Class	no.	134	223	657	221
	%	17.8	17.5	21.8	23.4
New Middle Class	no.	77	98	293	84
	%	10.2	7.6	9.7	8.6
Proletariat	no.	12	12	30	3
	%	2.2	.9	1.0	.3
Sample as Proportion of All Professors	%	56.9	52.5	71.9	63.5

NOTE: For the social categories, see pages 120-25. Habilitation means the completion of the second dissertation and the admission to university lectureship. Full professors indicate *Ordinarien*, whereas other professors comprise *Extraordinarien* and instructors down to *Privatdozenten*. For the sources of this table and the results of a 1907 nontenured faculty survey, see notes 12 and 13.

The considerable expense of the unsalaried lectureship meant that sons of the old middle class increased slightly and continued to outnumber the offspring of the new middle class, while proletarians were exceedingly rare. As the composition of the professors lagged one generation behind the makeup of the students, "their position has become more exalted and therefore the distance to the students greater."[12] Although making for

[12] T. Ziegler, *Der deutsche Student* (Stuttgart, 1895), pp. 202f.; H. Pohl, *P. Zorn als Forscher, Lehrer und Politiker* (Tübingen, 1928), p. 24; E. Curtius, *Wissenschaft, Kunst und Handwerk* (Berlin, 1881); table 4-1 based on C. von Ferber, *Die Entwicklung des Lehrkörpers der deutschen Universitäten und Hochschulen, 1864-1954* (Göttingen, 1956), pp. 172-84; Paulsen, *Die deutschen Universitäten* (Berlin, 1902), pp. 230-36. See also

intense scientific competition, the Privatdozent system of professorial recruitment contributed further pressures toward political conformity. "Advancement regularly involves three major steps: one enters the academic
career as Privatdozent; after a shorter or longer period of years, the person
who has distinguished himself by scholarly achievement and proven himself
as a lecturer is promoted to extraordinary professor and finally [he] reaches
the last stage, a regular chair." Although both a free profession open to
merit and a complete career (in contrast to British fellowships), professorial
rank depended upon so many other factors beyond scientific merit that
with the swelling of Privatdozenten numbers in the empire any racial,
social, or political unconventionality made ultimate success more difficult.
Thus, social selection and professional recruitment implicitly limited the
spectrum of divergent views offered to students in Imperial Germany.[13]

A more direct self-constraint was, paradoxically, the theory of academic
freedom.[14] Countless speeches, pamphlets, and monographs claimed it as
a customary right: "The freedom of teaching is the pride of the German
university." Nowhere else was there such a "center of free thought, unfettered by any dogma, and unlimited by any norms other than reason
itself." The conception of untrammeled "liberty of thinking, researching,
and teaching, the jealously guarded palladium of the unwritten constitution
of the German people," provided an unending challenge for personal
political cultivation:

> May the individual, in consequence of these studies and works, go
> in one or the other direction, may he become liberal or conservative,
> reactionary or progressive, orthodox or libertine: for us it is essential
> that he not do whatever he wants from youthful custom, unclear mood,

---

Ringer, *German Mandarins* (Cambridge, 1969), pp. 34ff; Riese, *Hochschule* (Stuttgart,
1977), pp. 94ff., and McClelland, *State, Society and University* (Cambridge, 1980), pp.
258-80.

[13] Paulsen, *Die deutschen Universitäten*, pp. 222ff.; F. Eulenburg, *Der 'akademische
Nachwuchs'* (Leipzig, 1908), pp. 11ff., based upon a 1907 survey of nontenured faculty
with around 2,200 personnel cards:

	Bildung	*Freie Berufe*		*Besitz*	*Alter Mittelstand*	*Neuer Mittelstand*	*(Total Mittel.)*	*No. D.*
No.	888	92	(980)	704	173	164	(338)	167
Percent	40.6	4.2	(44.8)	32.0	7.8	7.6	(15.4)	7.6

See also A. Busch, *Die Geschichte des Privatdozenten* (Stuttgart, 1959), and K. D. Bock,
Strukturgeschichte der Assistentur (Düsseldorf, 1972). See also I. Schorsch, "The Religious
Parameters of Wissenschaft: Jewish Academics at Prussian Universities," *Leo Baeck Institute
Yearbook* 15 (1980): 3-19.

[14] For the external radiation, see R. H. Samuel and R. H. Thomas, *Education and Society
in Modern Germany* (London, 1949), pp. 113ff.; and R. Hofstadter and W. Metzger, *The
Development of Academic Freedom in the United States* (New York, 1955), pp. 383-407.

traditional obedience but that he [choose] his future life out of scholarly consideration, critical thinking, and independent resolve.[15]

Although the famous physicist Helmholtz could boast in 1878, "at this moment the most extreme conclusions of materialist metaphysics, the boldest speculations on Darwin's theory of evolution can be heard as freely at the German universities as the most radical glorification of papal infallibility," he had to admit that academic freedom was limited by taste ("disparaging of motives, vilification of the personal traits of an opponent") and by law ("incitement to the committing of a legally forbidden action"). To such warnings against license, Paulsen added: "As the [theologian] requires a constructive attitude towards religion and church, so the [social scientist] needs a positive relationship to people and state for his position." Thus, it would be "an excess of tolerance" for the state to permit propaganda against its own foundations by a public official sworn to loyalty. "As long as Social Democracy confesses such attitudes, as long as it is an ideological enemy of the government, hostile to this regime and the state in general, it will be impossible to lecture on political science according to its principles in state institutions." Nevertheless, in the liberal mind, "the exclusion of subversive doctrines from the university lectern . . . is of course not at the same time a prohibition against criticism of existing state institutions and social conditions." As a consequence of trying to defend academic freedom by insisting on its necessary limitations, the majority of German academics agreed: "Scholars cannot and shall not be in politics." While many believed "Theory makes one incompetent for politics, and politics spoils one for theory," they nevertheless thought the "formation of a philosophical view of state and law necessary, and politicians not well advised to disregard them."[16] Not neo-Platonic philosopher-kings but neo-Kantian philosophical commentators were the political ideal of the German professoriate in the empire.

In practice, academic freedom often failed to live up to its lofty theory.

[15] For a listing of some of the literature, see "Lehrfreiheit," IHK, E 176-213. F. Paulsen, *Die deutschen Universitäten*, pp. 286-335; H. von Sybel, *Die deutschen Universitäten, ihre Leistungen, ihre Bedürfnisse* (Bonn, 1874). W. Kahl, *Bekenntnisgebundenheit und Lehrfreiheit* (Berlin, 1897). See also G. Kaufmann, *Die Lehrfreiheit an den Deutschen Universitäten im neunzehnten Jahrhundert* (Leipzig, 1898); and M. Lenz, *Freiheit und Macht im Lichte der Entwicklung unserer Universität* (Berlin, 1911).

[16] See Paulsen, *Die deutschen Universitäten*, pp. 292ff. for an argument limiting academic freedom toward church and state but insisting on uncurbed philosophical criticism. H. von Helmholtz, *Über die akademische Freiheit der deutschen Universitäten* (Berlin, 1878); and W. Waldeyer, *Über Aufgaben und Stellung unserer Universitäten seit der Neugrüdung des deutschen Reiches* (Berlin, 1898). German academics were fond of citing foreign observers like Stanley Hall to support their argument that "the German university is today the freest spot on earth" (*The Pedagogical Seminary* 1 [1891]: 7ff.).

On the basis of ample personal experience, the sociologist Max Weber commented caustically: "If the state . . . conceives of the influence that it enjoys . . . as a means of attaining a certain politcal obedience among university students, instead of looking upon it as an assumption of cultural responsibility," then scholarship was hardly any better off than under church control:

> The fact is that the alleged academic freedom is obviously bound up with the espousal of certain views which are politically acceptable in court circles and in salons, and furthermore with the manifestation of a certain minimum of conformity with ecclesiastical opinion, or at least a facsimile thereof. *"Freedom of scholarship" exists in Germany within the limits of political and ecclesiastical acceptability.* Outside these limits there is none. Perhaps this is inseparably bound up with the dynastic character of our system of government.

In the relative liberty of the Southwest, Weber took the Prussian "Althoff system" to task for conformity in appointments, for dismissals of professors who protested publicly against the political system, and for not even respecting the sanctity of the lecture hall. Was this criticism exaggerated and unjust? Clearly, in contrast to the overt police repression of the Carlsbad Decrees and the *Zentraluntersuchungskommission* of the Vormärz, imperial academics had much greater freedom. But as Bismarck pointedly reminded Gossler, one of the central customary rights of self-government of the faculties, the *Vorschlagsrecht*, existed only at the sufferance of the ministry: "Governmental authority to fill positions without consultation of the faculty threatens to become obsolete if it is not applied more frequently. Theoretically and legally it is the rule, but today it is already treated as an exception." The Iron Chancellor professed to be especially concerned about "the danger of ossification" through professorial co-optation. "The need to prevent this and to organize the regeneration of faculties, not in the interest of their members but according to the requirements of society and population, will make it the duty of the government not to give up its legally justified influence but to exercise it as much as possible." Although the minister of culture refused to recognize it as a statutory privilege, "some cooperation of the faculties in the renewal of the professoriate has developed, or is rather being claimed. It is this consultation, usual in all of Germany, which is often called the 'university's right of proposal.' " Although Gossler was more sensitive to the necessity of professorial independence, he also viewed universities "not without a certain political interest" and applauded the defeat of the progressive Virchow by the conservative Gerhardt in the Berlin rectorate election of 1888.[17]

Several cases demonstrate how the governmental power of appointment (and remuneration) was used to exclude unacceptable political views in the Second Reich. When in 1890 the Halle medical *Extraordinarius* Ernst Kohlschütter was considered for promotion to full professor, the strictly conservative curator, Wilhelm Schrader, advised against it, because of

> political considerations which according to my opinion totally exclude the advancement of Kohlschütter into a paid government position. Indeed, the same has always been an active member of the progressive, or *Deutschfreisinnige*, party. During the recent runoff Reichstag election in the city of Halle and the Saale district, he recommended a measure to the members of his party which led them to support the Social Democratic candidate and which, according to the judgment of respected and knowledgeable men, actually contributed to the latter's election.

As the ministry followed this advice and failed to promote Kohlschütter thereafter, in spite of respectable scholarly accomplishments, it seems that even left-wing liberal (i.e., democratic) political activity was sometimes considered unacceptable. A second, more famous instance was the disciplinary expulsion of the Jewish Socialist Privatdozent of physics Leo Arons from Berlin University over the protests of the philosophical faculty. As Bosse explained to his colleagues in the Prussian cabinet: "In the present case it is not a matter of scientific teaching ability, but a question of whether a declared member of the Social Democratic party can be left in a public teaching position or in a bureaucratic office." Not only did the Prussian government "say no to this query, but even if, as the faculty maintains, the man in question did not propagandize in favor of socialism in his physics lectures, [the minister of culture] considered being a public official incompatible with membership in the Social Democratic party." Because Arons, as a nonsalaried lecturer, was technically not a government official (*Beamter*), the Prussian government was forced, with much specious logic, to pass a special ad hominem law through the Landtag establishing disciplinary controls over Privatdozenten. As a final example, the pacifist

---

[17] E. Shils, ed., *Max Weber: On Universities* (Chicago, 1973) reprints Weber's polemical newspaper articles on academic freedom from 1908 on. Although he applauded Althoff's "often brilliant selections," he opposed the "morally debilitating effect" of government control. Bismarck to Gossler, 11 August 1884; Gossler reply of 19 August 1884 (concerning the case of Dr. Schweniger, an extraordinary professor of the medical faculty); and "Politischer Tagesbericht," *NAZ*, 15 September 1884, all in DZA Po, Rkz 2195. See also B. vom Brocke, "Hochschul- und Wissenschaftspolitik in Preussen und im Deutschen Kaiserreich, 1882-1907: das 'System Althoff'," *Bildungspolitik* (Stuttgart, 1980), pp. 9-118.

jurist Walter Schücking of Marburg was reprimanded and ejected from the lucrative state examination commission after denouncing as "a monument of shame" the seizure of Polish landholdings in the wake of the Expropriation Law. Although greater damage was done by the covert discrimination against unruly spirits like Kohlschütter and Schücking, the luster of *Lehrfreiheit* was more tarnished by the overt dismissal of Arons against the wishes of his university and the entire left.[18]

While the censorship was "quite voluntarily" exercised by the faculties themselves, professors' careers could also be furthered in order to propagate certain kinds of political views among the students. One of the better known incidents involved the appointment of the twenty-six-year-old Martin Spahn, son of a well-known Center party leader, to a Catholic chair of history at the University of Strassburg in total disregard of faculty recommendations. Stadtholder Alexander von Hohenlohe-Langenburg supported the plan "so that the religious views [of the four-fifths Catholic population] will be better represented than" by the eighty-three Protestant, eleven Catholic, fifteen Jewish, and two unaffiliated professors (not counting Protestant theologians). It was not Spahn's somewhat uncertain scholarly promise but the fact that he was known as "firmly patriotically minded and not ultramontane" which recommended him. Not even Theodor Mommsen's famous philippic ("a feeling of degradation is spreading through university circles" for "confessionalism is the mortal enemy of the university") could stop the Prussian government from pursuing its larger political aim of Germanizing the Alsace with a Catholic professor.[19]

Another less publicized, but still controversial case involved the appointment of the Baltic German Theodor Schiemann as head of the Russian history institute of the University of Berlin because Emperor William II took a fancy to him as "champion of Germanness against Slavic arrogance, clairvoyant politician as well as brilliant historian and writer." Little wonder that with such recommendations Althoff was certain that Schiemann would be formally promoted to full professor "as soon as he produces a

---

[18] H. Heindorf and H. Schwabe, "Ernst Kohlschütter und die soziale Frage," *Wissenschaftliche Zeitschrift der Universität Halle* 16 (1967): 329-47; Bosse on Arons in the session of the Staatsministerium, 28 September 1894; sessions of the Ministry of State on 12 May 1897; and Bosse to his colleagues, 31 May 1898 (with the finished law and the required report to the Kaiser) in DZA Po, Rkz 2195. For the parliamentary debates, see also 2 May 1898, *AH*, vol. 418 (1898) and Andernach, *Der Einfluss der Parteien*, pp. 119-26. For Schücking, see Holle to Bülow, 15 October 1908, DZA Po, Rkz 2191. See also Ringer, *German Mandarins*, pp. 141-43.

[19] Hohenlohe to Bülow, 7 October 1901; Bülow to Hohenlohe, 12 December 1901; and Hohenlohe's reply, 27 December 1901 in DZA Po, Rkz 2191. Mommsen's manifesto in his "Universitätsunterricht und Konfession," *Münchener Neueste Nachrichten*, 15 November 1901. See also Sachse, *Althoff*, pp. 129ff.; J. E. Craig, "Mission for German Learning," pp. 578-633; and Ross, *Beleaguered Tower*, pp. 24ff. for the political context.

strictly scholarly work, which does not even have to be very long." In the meantime, he would be entrusted with the chair temporarily and paid the astounding salary of 18,800 Mk, despite the protests of the philosophical faculty.[20] A final political appointment that caused a general stir was the choice of the orthodox economist Ludwig Bernhard to counterbalance the reformist views of the Socialists of the Chair Wagner and Schmoller at Berlin, who had repeatedly (and falsely) been criticized as unreliable in the Prussian parliament by industrialists like Karl von Stumm-Halberg. This time Chancellor Bernhard von Bülow personally pressured Minister of Culture Holle: "The book of this professor, *The Polish Community in the Prussian State*, has impressed me with the fact that we possess in this young economist an excellent man whose loss would be quite regrettable for Prussia." The hint that such a professorship "could also be of political importance" in the anti-Polish policy of the government speeded Bernhard's appointment, despite the insistence of qualified experts that he was a scientific lightweight.[21] Although Lehrfreiheit was much more protected against the pressures of public opinion and interest groups than in the West, academic freedom in Imperial Germany was limited by the enlightened absolutism of the appointment process, which allowed only a certain breadth of political opinions to be represented at the universities.

CEREMONIAL SPEECHES

The political, educational, and philosophical outlook that the professors sought to convey is most evident in their ceremonial speeches to the entire academic community. Delivered at the beginning and conclusion of a rector's annual term, on the emperor's birthday, and at other special anniversaries by prominent professors as official spokesmen of the institution, these Festreden collectively reflect the academic consciousness that students were expected to absorb. Despite the celebratory nature of the occasions, famous scholars like Rudolf Virchow also spoke their mind about

[20] William II, *Ereignisse und Gestalten aus den Jahren 1878-1918* (Leipzig, 1922), pp. 165-67. "Schiemann was constantly consulted by me in rebus politicis and in regard to historical questions." Althoff to Richthoven, 23 June 1902; Studt to Bülow, 20 June 1902; Bülow to Studt, 28 June 1902 and Richthoven to Althoff, 2 July 1902 (reminding Althoff to promote him in order "not to let the Polish cause triumph"), all in DZA Po, Rkz 2185. See also F. Fischer, *Krieg der Illusionen: Deutsche Politik 1911 bis 1914* (Düsseldorf, 1969), pp. 77-82 for his Russophobia.

[21] Bülow to Holle, 2 March 1908 (inspired by National Liberal and Free Conservative support of his views on German colonization); head of the chancellery Wahnschaffe memorandum of a conversation with Councillor Elster, 29 February 1908 (who "did not at all consider it the task of a professor to be active in politics and to prophesy"); Holle to Bülow, 1 June 1908, all in DZA Po, Rkz 2191. See also Sachse, *Althoff*, pp. 194-96 and B. Stegmann, *Die Erben Bismarcks: Sammlungspolitik 1897-1918* (Berlin, 1970), pp. 274-75.

controversial issues and challenged accepted beliefs. Of the about 150 Festreden between 1870 and 1914 in Berlin and Bonn each, almost one-third explicitly touched upon political problems, while about one-fifth dealt with university questions; another fifth discussed scientific methods, and the rest presented the progress of individual fields, thereby providing self-approval for the university enterprise. Although the office usually rotated among the faculties, during the empire the election of the rector, especially at Berlin, had implications beyond university politics. Since the most vocal of the lecturers, historians, and jurists attempted to speak for the academic community as a whole, their views present some of the dominant thought patterns of the German professoriate. While individual reactions and solutions differ, certain recurring symbols reveal the shifting collective concerns and preoccupations of the faculty. "No people in the world has as much confidence in its youth as we do," Theodor Mommsen reminded his colleagues and students. "The matriculation of the German student is still a patent of nobility through which he enters into the ranks of voluntary fighters for justice, truth, and intellectual freedom. But it is also a promissory note," enjoining all to live up to this ideal.[22]

During the early 1870s university professors were intellectually preoccupied with "building a house for a great homeless people by restoring its fatherland" and founding a Second Reich. Sensing the "approaching fulfillment of our national wishes," in August 1870 Emil DuBois-Reymond held French chauvinism responsible for the war, derided the Gallic "delusion that they might, so to speak, civilize us," and extolled the coming victory of German culture. By October Rector Bruns found "the key to the riddle [of our astounding success] in a metaphorical sense here in this auditorium—in the foundation of our university" and established the often reiterated academic claim that "moral attributes and intellectual forces were decisive on French battlefields." In March 1871, Ernst Curtius professed "surprise and awe" at the accomplishment of the century-old dream of unification: "We are still like a people emerging for the first time from dark quarters into the light of day." Trying to find some overarching meaning in the rapid turn of events, the famous classicist marveled: "Never yet have we been able to call ourselves Germans with such joyous pride.

[22] Theodor Mommsen, "Über das Geschichtsstudium," *Reden und Aufsätze*, 3rd ed. (Berlin, 1912), pp. 3-16. C. Schwarz, *Reden von Rektoren der Berliner Universität 1810-1932: Eine Auswahlbibliographie* (Berlin, 1977), except for five *Rektoratsreden* of the early 1870s, which were apparently not printed. The texts were often bound together for several years and can be found in the Humboldt-Universitäts-Bibliothek or the Deutsche Staatsbibliothek in East Berlin, with a few missing copies in the Deutsche Staatsbibliothek in West Berlin. For a listing of the Bonn titles, see *Chronik der Universität für die Jahre 1875-1886*, vols. 1-11 (Bonn, 1876-86) and *Chronik der Rheinischen Friedrich-Wilhelms-Universität zu Bonn für die Rechnungsjahre 1886-1914*, vols. 12-40 (Bonn, 1887-1915). See König, "Politische Komponenten," pp. 3f., 65.

. . . Today begins the springtime of our national history.''[23] The longer Rudolf von Gneist contemplated it, the more unification seemed to vindicate ''the character of the Prussian state,'' built upon ''the duties of military service, compulsory schooling, and taxation.'' Although delighted with the success of Bismarckian Realpolitik, the majority of liberal professors, proud of the university ethos that had inspired 700 of 2,000 Berlin students to rush to the colors, hoped for a fusion of power with law and culture: ''The Prussian throne is founded all the firmer, the further it remains from any false cult of self-adulation, the more the irreconcilable Greek and Roman contrasts of royalty and senate, sovereignty and free citizenship, obedience and love merge into a harmonious whole.'' Although Theodor Mommsen paid homage to the ''beautiful death'' of the thirty-nine ''sons of our university whom the war has claimed,'' he explicitly counseled ''avoiding any even apparent abuse of our new power position'' and shunning further wars. Less aware that ''a great victory is a great danger'' and more intoxicated with German unity, many students abandoned themselves unhesitatingly to the new Prusso-German patriotism. ''The error of public opinion . . . that German culture also was victorious in that struggle,'' threatened therefore, in Nietzsche's clairvoyant prediction, ''to transform our victory into utter defeat: The subjection, yes, the extirpation of the German spirit in favor of the German Empire.''[24]

In contrast to the outpouring of reform proposals in the wake of the Napoleonic defeats, the victorious Wars of Unification led to a reaffirmation of the neohumanist tradition in higher education. Already in October 1869, DuBois-Reymond asserted that ''in the area of higher studies German institutions are superior to those of all remaining countries.'' Although many academics were less stridently arrogant, they shared satisfaction with the national and liberal outcomes of cultivation. To tackle ''the great ideal tasks of peace,'' Curtius invoked Athens to demonstrate that ''the power

---

[23] E. Curtius, *Die Tugend der Gastfreundschaft* (?) (Berlin, 1870), title somewhat unclear because the early speeches often indicate the occasion like the emperor's birthday rather than the topic. E. H. DuBois-Reymond, *Über den deutschen Krieg* (Berlin, 1870); and E. Curtius, *Die Weihe des Siegers* (Berlin, 1871). Because of his facile classicism and his intimacy with the court, E. Curtius was the favorite speaker for the emperor's birthday until 1890. See also F. Herneck, ''Emil DuBois-Reymond und die Grenzen der mechanischen Naturauffassung,'' in W. Gröber and F. Herneck, eds., *Forschen und Wirken* (Berlin, 1960), pp. 229-52. At the risk of redundancy, the Festreden need to be quoted rather than summarized, for their texture, phrasing, and imagery convey their mentality as much as does their argument.

[24] C. G. Bruns, *Hohenzollern, Preussen, Deutschland* (Berlin, 1871); R. von Gneist, *Die Eigenart des Preussischen Staats* (Berlin, 1873); E. Curtius, *Der Gruss* (Berlin, 1873); Theodor Mommsen, *Rede zur Gedächtnisfeier der Universität* (Berlin, 1875); and Nietzsche's *Unzeitgemässe Betrachtungen*, cited in Schieder, ''Kultur, Wissenschaft,'' pp. 11f. See also W. Wattenbach, *Der Kaiserbegriff in der Geschichte* (?) (Berlin, 1874). The Bonn speeches, in which the Kulturkampf looms larger, will be cited in connection with specific scholarly lectures.

of the state rests on the Bildung of its citizens." Therefore "the state should groom this noble steed, without subjecting it to service or wanting to dictate its course." Recalling Fredrick William III, Karl Weierstrass restated the central mission: "The school shall cultivate the man and the citizen." Instead of additional practical training for medical doctors, Heinrich von Bardeleben suggested "complete general cultivation" as a source of public esteem for the physician and "as a symbol of that universality . . . threatened by the fragmentation of continually spreading specialties."[25] While stressing that German universities had "saved a much greater kernel of inner freedom . . . than those in the scrupulously conservative England and the impetuously liberal France," scientists like Hermann von Helmholtz understood that "the greater their importance grew . . . the more inescapably they had to pass into the hands of the state." Though asking for even more financial support, imperial academics celebrated "the urge of free research, of incessant progress as their actual life principle" and tended to postulate the complementary nature "of state and scholarly interests." Even the fact that "the great majority of pupils seek professional training" did not disconcert the philosopher Eduard Zeller unduly because he assumed that "those practical activities demand substantively the same scholarly preparation that research requires." Recalling Immanuel Kant's dictum "They shall not learn philosophy, but to philosophize," he expressed the rhetorical consensus of imperial professors: "The ultimate purpose of all knowledge and scholarly work is the Bildung of the spirit." Instead of recognizing the "spiritual impoverishment of our nation" or acknowledging that "our higher education system is quite ill," German professors tended to interpret unification as confirmation of their ideal of patriotic cultivation through scholarship.[26]

Although some outsiders like Paul de Lagarde argued for drastic changes, most academics steadfastly refused to modernize institutions of higher education. While the famous chemist August von Hofmann was proud that "the natural sciences have grown in our universities as nowhere else in the world," he stubbornly opposed the division of the philosophical faculty into humanist and scientific segments, for he feared that further speciali-

[25] E. DuBois-Reymond, *Über Universitätseinrichtungen* (Berlin, 1869); E. Curtius, *Die öffentliche Pflege von Wissenschaft und Kunst* (Berlin, 1872); C. T. Weierstrass, *Über das Universitätswesen in Deutschland* (Berlin, 1874); H. A. Bardeleben, *Über die Bedeutung wissenschaftlicher Studien für die Ausbildung der Ärzte* (Berlin, 1877). For the institutional background, see Lenz, *Friedrich-Wilhelms-Universität*, 2: 354ff.

[26] H. von Helmholtz, *Über die akademische Freiheit der deutschen Universitäten* (Berlin, 1878); E. Zeller, *Über den wissenschaftlichen Unterricht bei den Griechen* (Berlin, 1878), and *Über akademisches Leben und Lernen* (Berlin, 1879). See also A. Bardeleben, *Über die Stiftung der Universität mit besonderem Hinblick auf die Institute der medizinischen Fakultät* (Berlin, 1877), and see A. Dillmann, *Über Theologie als Universitäts-Wissenschaft* (Berlin, 1875). P. A. de Lagarde, *Deutsche Schriften*, pp. 98-373.

zation would degenerate into more vocational training. Instead, Curtius idealized Wissenschaft as "free research" based on "craftsmanship," carried on "in inner community" with the "ethical imperative" of truth: "We are charged with representing the highest interests of mankind; through teaching and example we shall nurse the noblest drives of human nature." Similarly, the theologian Adolf Kirchhoff appealed to Luther's example in support of classical secondary education "as long as it is imperative for our national culture that anyone claiming to be truly educated consciously maintains contact with the historical life of his people." If the academic triennium was becoming too short for this task, then it had to be extended to a quadrennium.[27] Applauding Goethe for making his chief protagonist (Faust) a professor, DuBois-Reymond criticized him for extolling his pragmatism: "Students shall politicize as little as they shall teach or practice [a profession]. While it suits them well to burn for the fatherland . . . they should nevertheless eschew the parties of the day." Although believing that the university would "enrich the public life of the nation with creativity and leadership," imperial professors were vague about methods; "practical rhetoric" was hardly a sufficient preparation for politics. Celebrating Jacob Grimm for "strengthening the patriotic spirit of our scholarship," the Germanicist Wilhelm Scherer defended the humanities: "The second half of the nineteenth century is not merely a mathematic-scientific, a technical-inductive age. The liberal arts remain." Instead of responding to the technological demands of industrialization or incorporating the spirit of natural science, the German university clung to a waning scholarly-bureaucratic ethos. Although many academics realized that "the old clothes have become too tight for a body growing gigantically," most refused to restructure the imperial university: "May the cultivation of scholarship and of patriotism, which was its founding task . . . , remain its most beautiful and pure heritage."[28]

During the second decade of the empire many professors followed Bis-

---

[27] A. W. Hofmann, *Die Frage der Teilung der philosophischen Fakultät* (Berlin, 1880); E. Curtius, *Wissenschaft, Kunst und Handwerk* (Berlin, 1881); A. Kirchhoff, *Luther, die Gelehrtenschule und die klassische Philologie* (Berlin, 1883), and *Über das athenische Unterrichtswesen* (Berlin, 1884). See also K. Heinig, "Das Chemische Institut der Berliner Universität unter der Leitung von A. W. Hofmann und E. Fischer," *Forschen und Wirken*, pp. 339-57. Like DuBois-Reymond, Hofmann was a steadfast liberal who opposed the rise of anti-Semitism.

[28] E. DuBois-Reymond, *Goethe und kein Ende* (Berlin, 1882); P. Kleinert, *Vom Anteil der Universität an der Vorbildung fürs öffentliche Leben* (Berlin, 1885); W. Scherer, *Rede auf Jacob Grimm* (Berlin, 1885); and K. A. Gerhardt, *Die Entstehung der Berliner Universität und anderer Hochschulen und deren seitherige Geschichte* (Berlin, 1889). This traditionalism is also evident in the preoccupation with the institutional history of Berlin, as in H. Dernburg, *König Friedrich Wilhelm III. und Svarez* (Berlin, 1885); P. Kleinert, *Beziehungen Friedrichs des Grossen zur Stiftung der Universität Berlin* (Berlin, 1886); and J. Vahlen, *Die Gründung der Universität* (Berlin, 1887).

marck's reversal toward conservatism and abandoned liberalism in favor of some form of nationalism. "We have reached the culmination of German history. Duty and honor demand that we seek to maintain this achievement," said the jurist Georg Beseler. He counseled traditionalism: "To be sure, dangers threaten. But we shall overcome them, if along with material progress we loyally uphold and increase our ideals." German scholarship could further the "decade- , even the century-long task of internally completing" the external unification in several crucial ways: "Jurisprudence . . . must meet the challenge . . . of creating a German law for the German Reich." Heinrich Brunner was firmly convinced that "legal uniformity strengthens the feeling of national and political unity." The compilation of a new civil code (the BGB) provided the primary political task for law professors until the mid-1890s: "Securely dominating legal traditions and clearly commanding ethical, political, and economic realities, it shall become a monument of national law giving [*Rechtsbildung*]," not an abstract deduction from natural law, but an organic outgrowth of history, justifying the imperial status quo. Another important challenge was the reinterpretation of the past as a preface to Bismarckian unification and as a guarantor of "a new, largely national doctrine of politics." Even the classicist Curtius contributed to the deification of kingship as a form of government and to the glorification of its incumbents: "In the affairs of nations monarchy appears to us as a necessity of nature, as the most original, irreplaceable, and most beneficial institution of public life."[29]

The primary spokesman for the new Borussian interpretation of history was Heinrich von Treitschke. In two eloquent lectures in the second half of the 1880s he presented the new creed: "Inexorably the bright and free minds of German scholarship today turn away from the republican doctrines of the older liberal school toward positive monarchism." Celebrating the imperial constitution not as the only possible, "but, for Germany, the only suitable" arrangement, Treitschke exclaimed: "A free people under a free king—that we call Prussian freedom." He championed a marriage between royal prerogative ("the glory of war, free authority over foreign policy, and the ultimate decision in all great political questions") with popular liberty: "Completely novel among the great institutions of the Reich is the creation of a lower house, which the nation has lacked for centuries; should

---

[29] Beseler quoted by H. Dernburg, *Die Bedeutung der Rechtswissenschaft für den modernen Staat* (Berlin, 1884); H. Brunner, *Die Rechtseinheit* (Berlin, 1877); G. Beseler, *Über die Bedeutung der historischen Rechtsschule* (Berlin, 1880); E. Curtius, *Kaiser Wilhelms Friedensregiment* (Berlin, 1879), also *Die Reichsbildungen im klassischen Altertum* (Berlin, 1881); and *Der Beruf des Fürsten* (Berlin, 1882). See also P. Hinschius, *Svarez, der Schöpfer des preussischen Landrechts und der Entwurf eines Bürgerlichen Gesetzbuchs für das deutsche Reich* (Berlin, 1889).

it so desire, the new Reichstag can help determine Germany's fate." Since such emphasis on Prussian leadership and monarchical right abandoned many of the cherished goals of earlier liberalism, he reminded his students: "As from its beginning this state was the work of its princes, all liberating deeds of the last quarter century have issued forth from the crown."

A final contribution of the academics to the consolidation of the state (*innere Reichsgründung*) was the definition of national tasks for the future. Some, like Julius Weizsäcker, argued: "Putting the imperial finances on their feet is recognized as the clearest and next duty for peacetime." Others began to embrace colonialism: "If we succeed in keeping the surplus of our population together and independent in overseas settlements, then the Greeks shall be our example" as empire builders. Still others gave rhetorical support to social reform: "When the suffering of the working class, as everywhere in the world, started to threaten social peace and morality, Germany showed again that the monarchy possessed more social justice, more understanding, and more compassion for the needs of the little man than the party rule of the republics." With the accomplishment of external and, to a degree, internal unification, many academics moved from liberalism to nationalism: "It is up to us to show the world that the Germans are capable of bearing good fortune, which has always been more difficult than misfortune, that even in this century of power and wealth, they have not ceased to be the nation of idealism."[30]

For many professors the heady success of 1871 removed the necessity for political involvement and allowed them to dedicate themselves even more thoroughly to scholarship. At the same time, the internal dynamics of scientific development began, in Helmholtz's words, to favor "empirical epistemology" and "inductive method," providing "natural sciences with a firm ground on which they can seek the laws of reality." Although academics thought it "disastrous to lose sight of the eternal tasks of mankind over subordinate and practical problems," more and more Festreden in the 1880s celebrated the impressive progress of individual research fields. In the humanities Johannes Vahlen praised the philological method and demonstrated that "manifold interests of scholarship and cultivation are touched by it" in the other faculties. "University life has gained in inwardness and profundity what it has lost in public influence and outward

---

[30] Heinrich von Treitschke, *Rede gehalten zur Feier der fünfundzwanzigjährigen Regierung S.M. des Königs und Kaisers* (Berlin, 1886) and *Das politische Königtum des Anti-Machiavell* (Berlin, 1887); J. Weizsäcker, *Geschichtliche Entwicklung der Idee einer allgemeinen Reichssteuer in Deutschlands Vergangenheit* (Berlin, 1892); and E. Curtius, *Die Griechen als Meister der Colonisation* (Berlin, 1883). See also the tone of Curtius's two eulogies, *Gedächtnisrede auf S.M. Kaiser Wilhelm I.* (Berlin, 1888) and *Rede zur Gedächtnisfeier S.M. des Königs und Kaisers Friedrich* (Berlin, 1888), the first respectful and the second touching, for he had been the prince's tutor.

appearance," said the medical professor Simon Schwendener, applauding the growing withdrawal from politics. While some sought to kindle "youthful enthusiasm for scientific research," others, like the Romanicist Adolf Tobler, argued that general cultivation could only be obtained through mastery of scholarly research in a particular specialty "in order to grasp the breadth and depth of the human spirit."[31] By the early 1890s most Berlin professors had retreated from political and educational controversy, for the spirit of positivism had broken down the self-evident equation of scholarship and partisanship, of research and political teaching, which informed the work of the liberals in the 1870s and the nationalists in the 1880s. Absorbed in the "pursuit of science for its own sake," only a few echoed Wilhelm Foerster's call: "The rising seriousness of the general situation seems to entrust academe with the urgent duty to shape the fundamental judgment of student youth." When the aging progressive Virchow defined his spiritual legacy in 1892-93, he was "perplexed by the riddle of anti-Semitism; during this time of legal equality, nobody knows what it is about; and despite or perhaps because of this, it fascinates academic youth." Instead of explicitly counseling liberal values, the old rationalist advised scholarship: "What we expect and demand of you, now as before, is the free formation of a balanced, honest, and beautiful personality."[32]

In the last years before the turn of the century, the political vacuum after the fall of Bismarck and the fundamental struggle between reforming and orthodox conservatism once again forced German professors to turn their attention to politics. "What darkly clouds our sky is the domestic discord and attitude of the parties," lamented Karl Weinhold: "Unbridled self-interest and craving for pleasure, lack of respect for God and man, insane hatred against everything that exists, loud dissension, suspicion, and uncouthness are rising everywhere." Although the Kulturkampf had

[31] H. von Helmholtz, *Die Tatsachen in der Wahrnehmung* (Berlin, 1887); A. W. Hofmann, *Ein Jahrhundert chemischer Forschung unter dem Schirme der Hohenzollern* (Berlin, 1881); P. Kleinert, *Luthers Verhältnis zur Wissenschaft und ihrer Lehre* (Berlin, 1883); J. Vahlen, *Über den philologischen Sinn* (Berlin, 1886); S. Schwendener, *Über Richtungen und Ziele mikroskopisch-botanischer Forschungen* (Berlin, 1887); C. Gerhardt, *Heilkunde und Pflanzenkunde* (Berlin, 1888); and A. Tobler, *Romanische Philologie an deutschen Universitäten* (Berlin, 1890). For the rise and political motivation of positivism (which deserves more scrutiny), see F. Ringer, *German Mandarins*, pp. 296-304.

[32] A. Tobler, *Dante und vier deutsche Kaiser* (Berlin, 1891); W. Foerster, *Die Entwicklungsgeschichte der Berliner Sternwarte* (Berlin, 1892); and *Die Gründung der Berliner Universität und der Übergang aus dem philosophischen in das naturwissenschaftliche Zeitalter* (Berlin, 1893). See also W. Foerster, *Über die Stellung der Astronomie im Universitätsunterricht* (Berlin, 1891), arguing for greater openness to the Technische Hochschulen. See also K. Winter, "Rudolph Virchow," in *Forschen und Wirken*, pp. 253-66. By the first half of the 1890s political and educational lectures had been reduced to a mere trickle.

neutralized the "antinational power of ultramontanism," the new movement of socialism, with "its cosmopolitan rootlessness, wants to destroy our hard-won German state and to erect on its ruins an international community, in whose empty chaos all historical organization and moral order of the nation would have to dissolve." This internal threat created a new challenge for political cultivation: "The securest means for the preservation of our German state consists of nurturing in all our people a national consciousness together with reverence and loyalty to the imperial head of the Reich." Hence, "education for Germanness, for German feeling, thought, and will" became a central task for those professors who saw themselves as the guardians of national spirit. Instead of sinking into "practical materialism" or following "the rational ideal" of eternal peace, Otto Pfleiderer exhorted Berlin students to prepare for "the unavoidable struggle for existence" by acquiring "the virtues of a capable citizen and warrior, such as obedience, duty, honor, and bravery." Cultural Germanization might also combat the revival of minority nationalism. "Instead of using German, the foreign elements within our borders have not only turned away from it, but have started to reject all traces of it." The "political power of the national wave," which had once forced Prince Bismarck's hand, should sweep all bickering away: "Let us tend the holy fire; let us feed the flame, so that purified it rises skyward; let us pledge our strength and life so that it will never be extinguished."[33]

While many condemned socialism without informing themselves, academic economists tried to immunize their students by exploding its scientific reputation and neutralizing its political attractiveness through reforms. On the defensive because of industrialist attacks against the "Socialists of the Chair [as] handmaidens of socialism," Adolph Wagner in 1895 angrily rejected any responsibility for student radicalism: "In all main points and especially in its representatives in leading university positions, [German economics] generally contradicts the methods, results, criticisms, justifications, theorems, psychology, ethics, philosophical bases, historical analyses, and practical postulates of socialism." On the contrary, "if its teachers have any influence on their hearers and pupils at all, it counteracts the theoretical and practical thrust of Marxism." While learning from the Socialist criticism of liberalism, which exposed "the grave wounds of the economic and social body," the *Kathedersozialisten* rejected "its im-

---

[33] K. Weinhold, *Zum Gedächtnis des 18. Januar 1871* (Berlin, 1896); O. Pfleiderer, *Das deutsche Nationalbewusstsein* (Berlin, 1895) and *Die Idee des ewigen Friedens* (Berlin, 1895) ("Hence the German universities consider it their holy task to educate academic youth in true love of the fatherland"); U. Wilamowitz-Moellendorff, *Volk, Staat, Sprache* (Berlin, 1898); and M. Lenz, *Bismarck* (Berlin, 1899). In spite of its size and stridency, the literature on German nationalism is generally disappointing. See L. Snyder, *Roots of German Nationalism* (Bloomington, 1978).

measurably exaggerated and generalized'' prescriptions and developed ''a new largely social or social-political movement'' stressing societal reform derived from scholarly ''anticriticism.'' Exposing the value theory of labor as ''one great sophism,'' Berlin economists branded Marxism as ''unscientific,'' for it did not build on solid empirical research and failed to use proper methodology. In contrast to the instinctive antisocialism of the right, Wagner and his younger colleague Gustav Schmoller sought ''a mediating position between economic individualism and socialism'' in order to curb the excesses of industrialization through social policy. Because ''through acquired cultivation and social position you will become the spiritual elite of the nation,'' the former appealed to the students: ''You shall better serve our country according to your profession and ability if you recognize your duty toward those strata socially and economically below you.'' This social mission for the educated inspired Schmoller two years later to defend economics as ''a great moral science'':

The social problem stamps our age and the coming centuries with its signature. More powerfully than ever the age-old question pounds on the portals of society: How shall individual and collective interest, freedom and justice, property and work, the aristocratic position of the powerful and rich, and the democratic [place] of the masses be reconciled? As free from reactionary defense of all tradition as from rash utopian plans for change, we must soberly and scientifically seek and justify those particular reforms that continue Germany on the course of progress.[34]

The external counterpart to social reform was an increasing professorial commitment to imperialist expansion. Already in the late 1880s Treitschke had talked about the transition to ''the position of a world power'' and advocated a purposeful ''great power policy.'' During the succeeding decade reference to ''Germany's rise to a *Weltmacht*, not only politically, but also economically and culturally'' became a staple of ceremonial speeches, revealing a fundamental consensus. In 1900, Wagner presented an economic rationale for the development ''from territorial state to world power.'' Invoking spectacular population growth and the transition ''from an agrarian society to an industrial and commercial state,'' he argued:

The safeguarding of the import of foodstuffs or raw materials and of

[34] A. Wagner, *Die akademische Nationalökonomie und der Sozialismus* (Berlin, 1895); and G. Schmoller, *Wechselnde Theorien und feststehende Wahrheiten im Gebiete der Staats- und Sozialwissenschaften und die heutige Volkswirtschaftslehre* (Berlin, 1897). See Andernach, *Haltung der Parteien*, pp. 116ff. and *AH*, vol. 392, 2 March 1895 for the public attacks. See also K. D. Barkin, *The Controversy over German Industrialization, 1890-1902* (Chicago, 1970) for the general context.

the export of factory goods and—everything depends on this—the achievement and defense of favorable or at least tolerable terms of trade, such as their prices, is increasingly becoming a question of survival for us. Political constellations are beginning to change accordingly. The issue of sea power in addition to land force is growing more urgent, and great financial expenditures for the navy together with those for the land army are becoming imperative.

Even if it would be difficult to reconcile the conflicting interests of protectionist agriculture and free-trade industry in a compromise tariff, Wagner advocated a "unified and goal-oriented domestic economic and foreign trade policy. . . . We only demand for our nation the place it deserves among the peoples of this earth." He echoed Chancellor Bülow's references to "a place in the sun," sketching a fateful vision: "Perhaps the German Empire shall become the crystallization point of a new Middle and West European union of peoples and states, not by force, but by voluntary rapprochement of individual interest, economic cooperation, and alliance as a counterweight to the economically and politically overweening world powers."[35] Challenged by the economic dynamism of the new empire, its social strains and continuing political cleavages, many imperial academics therefore taught their students a triple creed of cultural nationalism, social reform, and world political imperialism.

Troubled by the growing contradiction between positivist objectivity and imperialist commitment, many scholars sought a theoretical solution which would reconcile the dictates of scholarship with the profession of values. Since this was particularly vexing to a political economist, Schmoller suggested: "This aspect especially characterizes German economics today: in close touch with the great development and tasks of our times, it undertakes research without preconceptions, or at least with fewer prejudices than before; it applies much more stringent methods and overwhelmingly relies on empirical truths." To "solve the conflict between confessional bonds and free teaching" in Protestant theology, Wilhelm Kahl stressed "the higher justification of carrying on research independent of church dogma" but acknowledged the necessity of "ethical-religious constraints by God, church, parish, and conscience" for anyone occupying a spiritual office. For his students, the liberal theologian Adolf von Harnack simply

[35] H. v. Treitschke, *Rede gehalten zur Feier*, pp. 14ff.; U. v. Wilamowitz-Moellendorff, "Neujahr Neunzehnhundert," in his *Reden* (Berlin, 1901), pp. 152-71; A. Wagner, *Vom Territorialstaat zur Weltmacht* (Berlin, 1901); H. Brunner, *Zur Erinnerung an den 22. März 1797* (Berlin, 1897); and F. von Martitz, *Der Monarchismus als Staatsform* (Berlin, 1903). See also G. Schmoller, *Das preussische Handels- und Zollgesetz vom 26. Mai 1818* (Berlin, 1898); F. v. Richthofen, *Das Meer und die Kunde vom Meer* (Berlin, 1904); and W. Marienfeld, *Wissenschaft und Schlachtflottenbau in Deutschland 1897-1906* (Frankfurt, 1957).

brushed the issue away. "The quest for truth is a service to God and you shall pursue it in this way." The most philosophical attempt to reconcile the irreconcilable was the epistemology of the Kantian revival. "One may speak with Kant about [the categorical imperative] as the a priori axiom of ethical life," Julius Kaftan urged in 1901, "in the sense that we do not lose the old strict spirit of duty that created the Prussian state." In a more probing discussion of "the ethical value of science" in 1906, he asserted flatly that cultural and moral progress were not identical: "Scholarship in and of itself is not yet something ethical." But in order to salvage a higher purpose for Wissenschaft, he went on: "Its value for morality is none other than the process of research, the conquest of the subject," which educated men to truthfulness, modesty, and persistence. Rejecting "ethical skepticism" and "modern monism," imperial professors nevertheless failed to build a solid bridge between scholarship and partisanship, only agreeing: "We want to hold onto the golden scepter of idealism in which the immortal spirit of the German university manifests itself." It is a telling comment on the political inclinations of German professors that the progressive minority (like Paulsen and Weber) by and large insisted on a strict separation of the spheres of science and politics, while the traditionalist majority (like Lenz) saw them as complementary in "Rankean objectivity."[36]

Epistemological uncertainty did not, however, keep imperial professors from speaking out about the "tasks and position of our universities" in the face of modernist challenges. In contrast to earlier decades, openminded academics like Heinrich von Waldeyer accepted the inevitability of "the continuing transformation of a number of advanced technical schools into institutions of higher learning" (such as the parity of the technical colleges) or the "widening of the circles of those who shall be admitted to our universities" (like modern graduates and women). In relation to politics, he reiterated: "Self-government requires self-discipline, and only that can form you into the men whom the fatherland needs, strong characters and free spirits, always ready to obey the demands of the commonweal to sacrifice life and limb without regret!" Since "a paper with the ominous name of maturity certificate has become the new title of nobility," Wilamowitz-Moellendorff went so far as to criticize "cultivation arrogance and hypocrisy" and extolled the "heroes in the peaceful struggle of modern

---

[36] Schmoller, *Wechselnde Theorien*, pp. 24ff.; W. Kahl, *Bekenntnisgebundenheit und Lehrfreiheit* (Berlin, 1897); A. v. Harnack, *Sokrates und die alte Kirche* (Berlin, 1901); J. Kaftan, *Kants Lehre vom kategorischen Imperativ* (Berlin, 1901), and *Der ethische Werth der Wissenschaft* (Berlin, 1906); C. Stumpf, *Vom ethischen Skeptizismus* (Berlin, 1908); B. Erdmann, *Über den modernen Monismus* (Berlin, 1914); H. Diels, *Die Scepter der Universität* (Berlin, 1905); and M. Lenz, *Freiheit und Macht im Lichte der Entwicklung unserer Universität* (Berlin, 1911). See also W. Foerster, *Wissenschaftliche Erkenntnis und sittliche Freiheit* (Berlin, 1896); and J. Kaftan, *Die Einheit des Erkennens* (Berlin, 1907).

life," such as August Borsig and Alfred Krupp. Others marvelled at "the extraordinary increase in the desire for cultivation during the last decades" and championed the popularization of higher education in the name of imperialism. Welcoming the admission of women as "a necessary consequence of our entire development" and "an act of social justice," Oskar Hertwig applauded the university extension movement, imported from England, which insisted on continuing education and "on carrying enlightenment into the broadest circles of the people" via *Volkshochschulkurse*. But he had special praise for the Berlin Institute for Oceanography (1899), which attempted "to propagate a feeling for the sea . . . for maritime commerce, communication, and sea power" and for Germany's cultural mission: "Science and general popular cultivation must partially compensate our great power position for the many intellectual advantages the other great powers have over us." In a similar vein, Hermann Diels saw new "international tasks for the university" and recommended students cultivate "connections with foreign nations and train themselves internationally out of national interest."[37]

"The general thirst for cultivation, a beautiful and great sign of the times," troubled others like Wilhelm Kahl, for "it overburdens the university" and threatened the substance of its historical purpose. In a last peacetime reflection on this theme, Max Rubner stressed defensively that "the researcher as teacher . . . is no anachronism" and that "freedom of teaching must exist" as a precondition for "the spiritual progress [which] is indissolubly intertwined with the material advance of the power position of a nation." The breathtaking growth of higher education produced a host of unanticipated problems: the expansion of knowledge and administrative tasks overburdened professors; the enrollment increase overtaxed physical facilities; the admission of modern-high-school graduates lowered academic standards; the fragmentation of fields of inquiry endangered the philosophical unity of scholarship; the rising costs of natural science research required fresh sources of finance (such as the Kaiser Wilhelm Stiftung); urbanization impaired the learning ability of students confined to slum housing; the luxurious diversions of the capital endangered youthful health unless combated by sports. . . . Nevertheless, in the full flush of Wilhelmian confidence, Rubner considered these practical difficulties surmountable, as long as the university clung to it traditional mission: "The founder of the university recognized the great thought that science is power

---

[37] W. Waldeyer, *Über Aufgaben und Stellung unserer Universitäten seit der Neugründung des deutschen Reiches* (Berlin, 1898); U. v. Wilamowitz-Moellendorff, "Neujahr 1900," pp. 152ff.; O. Hertwig, *Das Bildungsbedürfnis und seine Befriedigung durch deutsche Universitäten* (Berlin, 1905); and H. Diels, *Internationale Aufgaben der Universität* (Berlin, 1906).

and that this force is a guarantee of the strength of our nation. The German universities, and especially Berlin, have always been places of true national feeling." Although German professors understood the need for institutional adaptation, they maintained their faith in the triad of cultivation-scholarship-training despite lingering doubts that success was imperiling their soul: "Without exaggeration, it may be said that our universities have remained a jewel of our fatherland until today: this is not only recognized by us, but also acknowledged by the entire world."[38]

The same mixture of self-confidence and concern characterized professorial pronouncements on politics in the last prewar decade. Hinting after the first Morocco crisis, "we now know where we have to seek our external enemies," the Germanicist Gustav Roethe fiercely called for "a halt to the excessive greediness of the masses, whose rule would be the gravest danger for culture and freedom." Calling for a new "hero of the deed, a fighter, a knight and a creator" like Bismarck to stem "the repulsive drive toward egalitarianism," he denounced "the womanly sense which desires peace at any price" as undignified: "Science, too, knows that war is the father of all things." Similar antidemocratic and militant themes echoed through his address on the centennial of the University of Berlin. Once more he rejected "the 'freedom' that results in rule of the masses" and demanded instead German loyalty, since "the fatherland needs independent spirits as its leaders, belonging to themselves, whom the pressure of public opinion, the foulest of all tyrants, fails to sway." On the same occasion, Minister of Culture Trott zu Solz reminded students: "More directly than others this university has the duty of being an intellecutal fortress for the fatherland and of offering it an arsenal of scholarly weapons." While the liberal conservative Hans Delbrück reiterated the slogan *Waffen der Wissenschaft* in his attempt to fashion an elitist-spiritual theory of warfare, the pan-German Reinhold Seeberg praised war as "the moment of truth for national power," surmised that "racial characteristics also influence the development of spiritual life," and opined: "Only the strong harvest those happy fruits of victory."[39]

Belligerent, antidemocratic, and Social-Darwinist motifs also dominated the commemoration of the War of Liberation against Napoleon. In 1913

---

[38] W. Kahl, *Geschichtliches und Grundsätzliches aus der Gedankenwelt über Universitätsreform* (Berlin, 1909); and M. Rubner, *Unsere Ziele für die Zukunft* (Berlin, 1910). See also A. Riehl, *Fichtes Universitätsplan* (Berlin, 1910). For the concrete policy struggles, see Chapter 3 and McClelland, *State, Society and University*, pp. 289-300.

[39] G. Roethe, *Deutsches Heldentum* (Berlin, 1906); speeches of Roethe and Trott zu Solz in E. Schmidt, *Jahrhundertfeier der Königlichen Friedrich-Wilhelms-Universität zu Berlin* (Berlin, 1911); H. Delbrück, "Geist und Masse in der Geschichte," *PrJhb* 147 (1912): 192-212; and R. Seeberg, *Vom Sinn der Weltgeschichte* (Berlin, 1913). Many scholars who could not resolve the theoretical conflict between objectivity and value commitment turned to history in order to convey their attitudes indirectly.

the rightist historian Dietrich Schäfer sang a paean to German nationalism. Warning, "German Volkstum is only secure in a state," he called for "an uninterrupted and resolute gathering of all forces in order to maintain our place among the great nations with whom we want to and have to compete." Dismissing warnings against German chauvinism, he argued: "We cannot and shall not be cosmopolitans. . . . The remembrance of 1813 should be a grave warning to counter such attempts with the resolution demanded by the creeping, corroding, destruction of national power. We ought not to want to justify it with the slogan of humanity. We Germans do not need this challenge. We are humane, because we are Christians." Schäfer's volkish appeal to the universities "to work in this direction through their mere existence" reveals how far nationalist cultivation had come in the century since Humboldt. Only too few students listened to the sober critique of Rector Count Wolf von Baudissin, who rejected the argument that "the German people stand in a unique relationship to God" as "an utterly unjustified transposition of an outdated point of view to an inappropriate area." Instead of erecting a "false idol" of nationalism, he concluded in truer neohumanist spirit: "Our universities have the great task of serving the reconciliation of the national with the universal." Rarely exposed to such irenic sentiments, students were, therefore, taught the necessity and inevitability of war.[40]

The Berlin Festreden between the foundation of the Second Reich and the outbreak of the First World War suggest that German professors basically agreed on the political mission of cultivation, for they understood universities as "centers of national education." In this process academics considered their own role paramount, because "it is not the task of the students to involve themselves in politics." However, they disagreed strongly on the political content of Bildung, be it liberal, cultural, or integral nationalism; they vigorously debated educational aims and institutional arrangements, be they neohumanist, modernist, or just expansionist; and they differed emphatically on the methodological tension between scholarship and partisanship, be it as naive defenders of their unity or as critical advocates of their necessary separation. During the empire professorial ideology therefore experienced a complex and contradictory transition from a self-confident liberal, national neohumanism to an ambivalent national, social imperialism, struggling to reconcile the Humboldtian tradition with the machine and the masses while striving to provide ethical cultivation

[40] D. Schäfer, "Rede zur Erinnerung an die Erhebung der deutschen Nation im Jahre 1813," in *Aufsätze, Vorträge und Reden* 2 (Jena, 1913): 438-59; and Graf W. v. Baudissin, *Nationalismus und Universalismus* (Berlin, 1913). The tone of some of the last peacetime speeches carried directly over into wartime rhetoric. See the background chapters in K. Schwabe, *Wissenschaft und Kriegsmoral: Die Deutschen Hochschullehrer und die politischen Grundfragen des Ersten Weltkrieges* (Göttingen, 1969).

in the teeth of moral relativism. The causes of this transformation lie as much outside as inside the university. National unification, with its constitutional consequences, was clearly the dominant political event for the first decades, while the offensive-defensive adventure of Weltpolitik structured the outlook of the last years. Despite the vindication of neohumanism as the educational ideal, the challenges of industrialization and cultural modernism forced academics to concede the equality of higher technical training and the admission of modern-high-school graduates more or less voluntarily. The explosion of empirical science and the rise of positivism ruptured the self-evident unity of scholarship and moral teaching without providing new certainties. Together with the social pressures detailed earlier, these political, educational, and methodological currents gradually led to a deliberalization of the German professoriate, a turning away from the ideals of the Vormärz, and produced a leap of faith across positivist scruples toward a new nationalism that was both socially reformist and imperially expansionist. Although the institutional structure, rhetorical ethos, and even in many cases the academic vocabulary changed very little during the empire, initial professorial pride became arrogance, and occasional self-doubt grew into gnawing anxiety.[41]

SCHOLARLY LECTURES

A more specific form of political cultivation for students were the scholarly lectures in those disciplines that dealt with theoretical or practical political problems. The majority of academics regarded the "awakening, strengthening, and purifying of love for the fatherland and support for the state" in formal teaching not only as legitimate but also as necessary. Friedrich Paulsen recommended to prospective students

> courses in the area of political science [*Staatswissenschaften*], on national economics, politics, legal philosophy, general state law, constitutional and administrative law as they are offered in great variety in the philosophical and legal faculties. Often general lectures are also announced about current questions of public concern. Those dogmatic courses on state and society should be followed by the historical ones: history remains the high school of politics.[42]

Although in theology an occasional lecture on Paul's Epistle to the Romans

---

[41] For the general transformation, see J. Sheehan, *German Liberalism* (Chicago, 1978), pp. 189ff., 253, and 278. Ringer (*German Mandarins*, pp. 128ff.) assumes the outcome of the reversal and therefore does not explain it.

[42] W. Busch, "Zur Erinnerung an Wilhelm Maurenbrecher," reprint from *NBZ* (Bonn, 1893); and F. Paulsen, *Deutsche Universitäten*, pp. 455f. The informal process of political self-education of the students is analyzed in the next chapters.

and in medicine a rare course on Social Darwinism might touch upon politics, the student interested in political questions turned primarily to the legal and philosophical faculties. While the offerings on public law were clearly defined, many a *Vorlesung* on systematic (Wilhelm Dilthey), critical ("a critique of materialism"), or historical philosophy ("a history of recent philosophy in relation to the entire culture of the present"), in classics ("Plato's *Republic*") or philology ("the history of German literature from Goethe's death to the present") might spill over into politics. But since economic policy lectures (such as social policy) and contemporary history courses (post–French Revolution) addressed politics more explicitly, they present a sharper picture of political teaching than the other philosophical disciplines. In Berlin politically relevant offerings increased (except during the positivist 1890s) roughly as quickly as lectures overall (3.5 times), but in Bonn they grew more rapidly (7 times) than regular courses (2 times). Although the development of the scholarly debate in various disciplines during the empire was immensely complex, the teaching process necessarily simplified this diversity. The main thrust of political lectures in law, economics, and history therefore offers some basic clues to the transmission of attitudes to students in formal teaching.[43]

Although legal philosophy, constitutional history, and state law were somewhat neglected in examinations in favor of private law, they nevertheless helped shape the political consciousness of Germany's administrative and judicial elite, for they were required. Just beginning to be differentiated in the early 1870s into these three components, legal political lectures were dominated by the historical school of jurisprudence, which, though rejecting the Western tradition of natural law, combined an organic view of justice with a critical philological method. Many of its luminaries, like Rudolf von Gneist, were veterans of the liberal struggles of 1848 and 1862 who, while accepting political unification by the Prussian crown, nevertheless insisted upon the procedural guarantees of a Rechtsstaat against royal and Junker license. They viewed the state as "the collective will of the nation" rather than the simple outgrowth of the monarch's patrimony and defined its purpose as "welfare, culture," and "legal security," and, by implication, individual freedom. Rejecting French abstract theorizing as a negation of the rule of law and looking to the historic liberties of England, Gneist in his Berlin lectures especially advocated the estab-

---

[43] The *Verzeichnis der Vorlesungen, welche auf der Friedrich-Wilhelms-Universität zu Berlin im Sommer-Semester . . . 1871 gehalten werden* and the *Verzeichnis der Vorlesungen an der Rheinischen Friedrich-Wilhelms-Universität Bonn: Sommersemester 1871* were systematically surveyed until the summer session of 1914. Since *Vorlesungsnachschriften* (lecture notes) are only rarely available, often incomplete, and contradictory, the printed version of the lecture or, where unavailable, a closely related title (none too distant in time) and concurrent political writings were examined.

lishment of administrative courts (as citizens' protection against bureaucratic arbitrariness) and local self-government (as an indispensable school
of civic responsibility).[44] In Bonn the right-wing liberal Wilhelm Kahl, an
ardent admirer of Bismarck, emphasized the historical nature of law, which,
by transcending the imposed order of the state, became "a manifestation
of the rules of human social life." As the state therefore was not only the
creator but also the product of law, it could be measured against a conception of justice independent of the current political order.[45]

The basic thrust of the liberal historical jurists, who dominated the
teaching of legal politics in the 1870s and 1880s, was therefore a reconciliation of individual freedom with state power, of personal rights with
monarchical prerogatives. Nevertheless, after unification they generally
grew more conservative and rationalized their support of the exceptional
laws of the Kulturkampf and the anti-Socialist legislation in spite of their
continued defense of the Rechtsstaat. Turning increasingly to the compilation of existent private law for the *Bürgerliche Gesetzbuch*, they abandoned legal attempts to justify an extension of parliamentarism, especially
after the rightist reorientation of the empire in 1879. Although the first
generation of jurists during the empire presented a variety of cooperative
(Otto von Gierke), constitutional (Georg Beseler), and Catholic (Hermann
Hüffer) ideas to their students, their teaching cemented the problematic
constitutional compromise between monarchical power and popular sovereignty and provided no further democratizing impulses. Since "in great
and glorious struggles the German state has found its form and measure,"
the historical jurists of the empire were loath to threaten it by further
demands from within, even if it fell short of their own youthful expectations.[46]

Although members of the historical school continued to be active until
the First World War, the dominant scholarly methodology and thereby
also the teaching of jurisprudence shifted by the 1890s toward legal positivism. Its most influential representative, Paul Laband, strove to make

---

[44] R. v. Gneist, *Deutsches Staatsrecht* (lecture notes of A. Mange, Berlin, 1874-75) MS
collection of the HUB; and *Der Rechtsstaat und die Verwaltungsgerichte in Deutschland*,
2nd ed. (Berlin, 1879). See also E. Hahn, "Rudolf Gneist and the Prussian Rechtsstaat:
1862-78," *JMH* 49 (1977): D1361-81.

[45] W. Kahl, *Aphorismen zur Trennung von Staat und Kirche* (Berlin, 1908); and K. Achenbach,
"Recht, Staat und Kirche bei Wilhelm Kahl: Eine Darstellung seines kirchenrechtlichen und
staatsrechtlichen Werks samt einem Überblick über seine Tätigkeit im Dienste der Strafrechtsreform und sein politisches Wirken" (dissertation, Regensburg, 1972).

[46] For the rise of the historical school, see C. G. Bruns, *Zur Erinnerung an F.C. von
Savigny* (Berlin, 1879). See also O. Gierke, *Das Wesen der menschlichen Verbände* (Berlin,
1902) and *Die historische Rechtsschule* (Berlin, 1903); G. Beseler, *Über die Bedeutung der
historischen Rechtsschule* (Berlin, 1880); H. Hüffer, *Lebenserinnerungen* (Berlin, 1914),
ed. by E. Sieper; and R. v. Gneist, *Die Eigenart des Preussischen Staats* (Berlin, 1873).

law into an exact science, excluding all philosophical, political, and economic value judgments. His "juridical method" concentrated on existing positive law to the detriment of any broader notion of justice, sought to codify and explicate it and train students in applying it rather than in changing the legal order. In Bonn legal positivism was championed by Karl Bergbohm, who rejected the notions of natural law as unscientific. As not all legal quarrels were already regulated by extant positive codes, he saw his chief task as filling these gaps through precedent-oriented deduction, thereby transforming value decisions into legal technicalities.[47] A different variety of legal positivism was represented by Fritz Stier-Somlo, who opposed sociological theories as leading "straight into the Marxist and Socialist camp." Instead, he emphasized the role of force for the origin of the "ethical-political-voluntary work of art," that is, the state, and stressed "struggle [as] the meaning of life." As divergent social tendencies "must under all circumstances be educated or forced into behavior appropriate to the needs of the whole," the "exclusion of the ever present striving of subversive elements seems imperative for civilization." Because "cultivation, higher spiritual culture, economic entrepreneurship, and property are slighted in the Reichstag suffrage" and "the great untutored, unintelligent mass which is easily swayed by radical agitation is the decisive factor," he favored plural suffrage, giving additional votes to the wealthy and educated.[48]

Even if Gerhard Anschütz was the better known legal scholar, more representative of the dozen or so professors who taught state law in Berlin was Conrad Bornhak. In his textbook on *Allgemeines Staatsrecht*, he stated unequivocally: "The two axioms on which every system of natural law is built, the innate equality of every man and abstract human reason, exist only in the imagination. Without them the entire system of natural law collapses in itself." Instead, "the essence of the state cannot be constructed rationally but must be captured empirically. A dogma transcending the individual state can only be derived from a historical and comparative legal basis." Building upon the historical school, but stressing "positive legal doctrine," Bornhak sought a basis for his value judgments beyond scholarship: "For the states of the Christian world the ultimate standard can be

[47] R. Kass, "Karl Bergbohms Kritik der Naturrechtslehre des ausgehenden 19. Jahrhunderts" (dissertation, Kiel, 1972). For legal positivism, see P. v. Oertzen, *Die soziale Funktion des staatsrechtlichten Positivismus* (Frankfurt, 1974); and G. Dilcher, "Der Rechtswissenschaftliche Positivismus," in *Archiv für Rechts- und Sozialphilosophie* 61 (1975): 497-528.

[48] F. Stier-Somlo, *Der Staat als Kunstwerk und die Wirklichkeit* (Leipzig, 1908), pp. 52-63; *Politik*, 3rd ed. (Leipzig, 1916), pp. 48-143; and *Studien zum sozialen Recht, insbesondere der Reichsversicherungsordnung* (Mannheim, 1912). Although he accepted Bismarck's social measures, he opposed an extension of self-government in the imperial insurance law in order not to give the Socialists more positions and make the workers unreliable in political crises.

neither absolute human reason nor a value-free science, since both do not exist, but only Christianity.'' Such a conception of ''the state as dominion'' clearly had conservative implications. By abandoning older views of justice and screening out much of contemporary legal reality, the ''political function of the 'juridical' method . . . consisted primarily of legitimizing the newly founded doctrines of state law and of safeguarding their legal status through the elimination of any political criticism.''[49]

In the last decade before the war the climate of legal scholarship and teaching shifted again toward increased attention to specific problems of contemporary law and toward greater willingness to take a political stand. The contradiction between scholarly impartiality and political partisanship was resolved either by stressing a clear disjunction between legal and political statements or by recognizing the political implications of scholarship and accepting the consequences. While the fundamental lectures on legal philosophy and theory, on constitutional and legal history, and on state or administrative law enrolled greater numbers of students (and were taught in more concurrent sections), several new courses sprang up which tried to cope more explicitly with the demand for a juridical response to current issues. In Berlin from 1888-89 on, courses on ''Colonial Law'' (Bornhak) and later also ''Colonial Policy'' (Kobner) were added to the schedule; lectures on ''The Social Legislation of Germany'' (Dambach) and ''The Imperial Insurance Law'' (Lass) started to appear. From the mid-1890s on, various offerings on constitutional theory by Hugo Preuss began to replace Gneist's earlier commentaries on ''The Reform of the Prussian Constitution''; and the future father of the Weimar constitution eventually introduced a lecture on ''The Taxation System of the German Empire'' (1900-01). In Bonn, colonial law emerged after the turn of the century, Heinrich Pohl lectured on ''parliamentary electoral law,'' and Heinrich Lehmann spoke on ''legal questions of modern big industry, especially cartels and measures of class struggle.''[50]

Typical of the repolitization of jurisprudence was Philipp Zorn, who admitted that state law as discipline was responsible for pursuing and supporting state interests and tried to prepare his students, most notably the crown prince, for their future leadership roles. Although born in Franconia, he saw himself as ''a full and complete German on the basis of unshakable Prussian hegemony'' and understood his transfer from Kö-

[49] C. Bornhak, *Allgemeine Staatslehre*, 2nd ed. (Berlin, 1909), pp. 1-9; W. Wilhelm, *Zur juristischen Methodenlehre im 19. Jahrhundert: Die Herkunft der Methode Paul Labands aus der Privatrechtswissenschaft* (Frankfurt, 1958), p. 159. See also F. von Martitz, *Deutsches Reichs- und Landesstaatsrecht* (lecture notes of Seckel, Berlin, n.d.), MS collection of the HUB.

[50] For the new lectures, see the Berlin and Bonn *Vorlesungsverzeichnisse*, 1887ff., mentioned in note 43.

nigsberg to Bonn as a contribution toward Rhenish loyalty created by "the strict, often harsh school of Prussia's excellent administration." Rejecting public involvement after the dropping of the pilot in 1890 because of the poison of parliamentarism, he reminisced: "The empire under old Kaiser Wilhelm and his Bismarck was the best time of my life." As a member of the German delegation to the Hague peace conference, he accepted the idea of international arbitration, but maintained: "The great questions of existence among peoples and states will be decided with the sword in the future as they have in the past." He supported armament, endorsed military service in army and navy, "the grand educational institutions of the entire nation," and championed imperial expansion.[51] While legal positivism remained methodologically dominant in the last prewar years, the practical teaching of state law became repoliticized in an illiberal direction and by and large uncritically supported the internal and external policies of the empire. Only a few younger scholars groped toward a revitalized legal liberalism.[52]

In contrast to the abstractions of law, lectures on national economy, or "state, cameral, and commercial sciences" as they were known in Berlin, offered students more direct contact with practical politics. However, as an even more marginal examination subject in law and as a philosophical discipline without a corresponding professional career, economics had less of a built-in audience. Beginning with a simple bifurcation between theoretical and practical economics (the latter was the older cameralist "police science"), the field experienced an extraordinary explosion of topical offerings during the 1880s, in response to the problems of industrial society and the Habilitation of numerous eager Privatdozenten. In Berlin, A. Wagner lectured on "the social, especially the workers' question" for the first time in 1872-73, Eugen Dühring confronted the "history and present state of socialism" in 1873-74, and Privatdozent Gans mentioned "colonial policy" as subtitle of a broader course in 1882-83. By 1900 the applied courses in economic policy (Volkswirtschaftspolitik) began to dissolve into a series of specialized lectures in agrarian, commercial, financial, social,

[51] P. Zorn, Aus einem deutschen Universitätsleben (Bonn, 1927), pp. 68ff.; "Das Deutsche Reich und die internationale Schiedsgerichtsbarkeit," Internationale Wochenschrift für Wissenschaft, Kunst und Technik 4 (1910): 1499-1512, 1543-58; and Die deutsche Reichsverfassung (Leipzig, 1907). See also H. Pohl, Philipp Zorn als Forscher, Lehrer und Politiker (Tübingen, 1928).

[52] In the prewar decade several students of the liberal jurists of the early empire began to infuse the teaching of state law with more democratic (Hugo Preuss) and anti-Prussian (Carl Crome) elements, but their junior status limited their influence on the majority of students. See H. v. Planitz, ed., Die Rechtswissenschaft der Gegenwart in Selbstdarstellungen (Leipzig, 1925), pp. 73-90; G. Dilcher, "Das Gesellschaftsbild der Rechtswissenschaft und die soziale Frage," in Vondung, Bildungsbürgertum, pp. 53-66; and König, "Politische Komponenten," pp. 34-43.

and communication policy. As the older historical school of Wilhelm Roscher and others had already severely modified the unrestrained laissez-faire liberalism of the Manchesterites, the economists of the younger historical school, becoming prominent in the 1870s, continued this development toward social policy while gradually modifying political liberalism and the capitalist system.[53]

A less well-known, but nevertheless typical, transition figure was the Bonn economist Adolf Held, who considered the classical agenda of liberalism achieved and turned his anxious attention to a new enemy: socialism. In his lectures, which "especially tried to [influence] the outlook of his audience," he rejected Marx's value theory of labor and denounced socialism as "an echo of the one-sidedness of older extreme individualism." Its deification of human rights meant that "it does not want wars to quicken national feeling or military discipline and honor to divert from the pursuit of material aims." While differentiating the "harmless and implicit" socioeconomic tendency from the "dangerous" and "dominant" politically revolutionary trend, he saw socialism as useful only in attracting attention to the social question. As the most effective means to combat such subversion, he championed "socialist" (social-political) reforms: "By satisfying workers' interests we want to pull the rug out from under Social Democracy." To create a loyal middle class (staatserhaltende Mittelstand), he appealed not only to the "higher duties" of the propertied and counseled "honorable responsibility" toward the weaker but also argued that "immoral" great wealth had to be equalized through the state. Government ownership, the "voluntary introduction of a constitutional instead of an absolutist structure in the factories," and the establishment of "workingmen's associations" could help toward that goal.[54]

The emergence of social liberalism, which inspired the foundation of the Verein für Sozialpolitik in 1872, heightened the problem of relating economic scholarship to politics. In the ideological struggles of the 1870s and 1890s, the Kathedersozialisten split into three distinct camps that tried to dominate the lecture halls. The first, a small minority with support in the left wing of the liberal parties, sought to perpetuate an updated version of economic liberalism. Their brilliant leader, Lujo Brentano, "addressed

---

[53] Bleek, Kameralausbildung, pp. 288-308; Berlin and Bonn Vorlesungsverzeichnisse for the appropriate years; and J. J. Sheehan, The Career of Lujo Brentano: A Study of Liberalism and Social Reform in Imperial Germany (Chicago, 1966), pp. 58ff.

[54] A. Held, Grundriss für Vorlesungen über Nationalökonomie: Zum Gebrauche seiner Hörer verfasst (Bonn, 1876) and Sozialismus, Sozialdemokratie und Sozialpolitik (Leipzig, 1878), pp. 32-149; and Zwei Bücher zur socialen Geschichte Englands (Leipzig, 1881). As a Treitschke student and a "true liberal" in opposition to "reactionary feudalism and absolutism," he favored parliamentarization without letting the state "become a football of changing majorities."

his class as he would have political meetings, and they responded with cheers and countercheers." Criticizing the "mistakes of liberal Weltanschauung," which "led to the uncurbed domination of the economically strong," Brentano championed social reform, but without the "organized brutality" of extending Prussian bureaucracy: "I love freedom too much to see it destroyed by either Socialist or absolutist despotism." Instead of abandoning free trade and the operation of the market forces, he sought to solve the social question by devoting his "life to the struggle for the workers' right to collective bargaining" and by calling for a parliamentarization of the political structure of the empire.[55] In Prussia there were a few other liberal voices like those of Eberhard Gothein crying in the wilderness. In January 1900 he cautiously criticized the rising tide of nationalism in Bonn. Although the national idea was "a lasting part of our feelings, its excesses and distortions must be curbed, if the permanent foundations of all political life are not to be jeopardized."[56] In a similar vein, Hermann Dietzel defended economic and political liberalism as the crowning achievement of the nineteenth century. Calling for a "parliament equal to" the monarch, he championed universal suffrage in Prussia and urged greater political participation of the masses, although he emphatically rejected socialism. State policy could resolve societal tensions through stronger cooperation and self-help of the workers, who might wrest social peace from employers if their collective action were strong enough. Although Dietzel championed world trade and economic interpenetration as guarantees of peace, like Brentano he advocated a German Weltpolitik, based on a powerful battle fleet, in order to challenge British hegemony. Despite their valiant effort to modernize liberalism, these economists only communicated elements of idealized criticism to their students, for their defense of capitalism prevented comprehensive reform, while their championship of imperialism contributed to strengthening the neo-feudal forces that they detested.[57]

The centrist, bureaucratic position, which sought to reform social abuses

[55] J. Schumpeter, *A History of Economic Analysis* (New York, 1953), p. 802; L. Brentano, *Die Stellung der Studenten zu den sozialpolitischen Aufgaben der Zeit* (Munich, 1897); other quotations from Sheehan, *The Career of Lujo Brentano*, pp. 83ff. See also D. Lindenlaub, *Richtungskämpfe im Verein für Sozialpolitik* (Wiesbaden, 1967).

[56] Speech in *Kölnische Zeitung*, 10 January 1900; and M. L. Gothein, *Eberhard Gothein: Ein Lebensbild* (Stuttgart, 1931), p. 120: "My [political] activity is repugnant to the majority [of my colleagues]; it contradicts their idea of noble scholarly reserve, and hardly anyone understands that for an economist such detachment is nonsense, almost a violation of his duty." See also W. Zorn, "E. Gothein 1853-1923," in *Bonner Gelehrte: Geschichtswissenschaften* (Bonn, 1968), pp. 260-71.

[57] H. Dietzel, *Das neunzehnte Jahrhundert und das Programm des Liberalismus* (Bonn, 1900); and *Beiträge zur Geschichte des Sozialismus und des Kommunismus* (Essen, 1920). See also E. v. Beckerath, "H. Dietzel als Nationalökonom und Soziologe," in his *Lynkeus: Gestalten und Probleme aus Wirtschaft und Politik* (Tübingen, 1962), pp. 3-26; and König, "Politische Komponenten," pp. 23-34.

but idealized the Prussian system, was more widespread and influential. The conciliatory and soft-spoken Gustav von Schmoller, head of the Verein für Sozialpolitik and editor of a journal that acquired his name, presented a more indirect approach to politics: "Like the chorus in Greek tragedy, Wissenschaft should not act; rather, it should stand away from the center of the stage, guide the actors by its observations, and measure their action according to the highest ideals of the time." As champion of "historical and . . . realistic research," he was the most influential scholar of the "younger historical school," emphasizing economic development over dogmatic abstraction, advocating empirical (even statistical) source work over generalization, urging comparative study over nationalist reductionism. This methodological position implied "a critical attitude toward individualist doctrine as well as toward socialism" in order to transcend class positions "in an honest effort to keep the common good and health of nation and mankind in mind." Although unwilling to jettison "modern freedom of the individual and of property," Schmoller resolutely called for "new institutions and forms of income distribution" for "great social reforms" and worldwide economic cooperation. "The strong bureaucratic and legal mechanism" of the state, standing "above the classes," should "shed light rays of common concern" into the darkness of interest struggles in order to rectify capitalist abuses while maintaining productive momentum so that Germany could reach the higher level of culture that industrial progress made possible.[58] In terms of politics, the Berlin professor embraced "a firm hereditary monarchy" like the Hohenzollern, saw in Bismarck "the great national hero of the nineteenth century," and called "the solid, secure, national state with an orderly modern constitution and power and prestige essential." Externally he championed "a German national policy in the grand style," supported imperial expansion and the building of the battle fleet, but cautioned: "We should not and will not pursue a chauvinist world power policy." Internally he pushed for more social reform than the ministry was willing to undertake, accepted "an impartial royal bureaucratic government as given for a long time," but called for "a measured reform of the [Prussian] three-class suffrage" short of universal franchise, lest the state be engulfed by a democratic flood.[59] Al-

[58] Schmoller, "Die Wissenschaft, die Parteiprinzipien und die praktischen Ziele der deutschen Politik," *Zur Social- und Gewerbepolitik der Gegenwart* (Leipzig, 1890), pp. 183ff. and *Grundriss der Allgemeinen Volkswirtschaftslehre* (Leipzig, 1908), pp. 93ff., 442ff., 552ff.; as well as Sheehan, *Career*, pp. 67ff.

[59] Schmoller, "Vier Briefe über Bismarcks social-politische und volkswirtschaftliche Stellung und Bedeutung," in his (ed.) *Zu Bismarcks Gedächtnis* (Leipzig, 1899); "Die wirtschaftliche Zukunft Deutschlands und die Flottenvorlage," in *Zwanzig Jahre Deutscher Politik 1897-1917* (Munich, 1920), pp. 1-20; and "Die Preussische Wahlrechtsreform von 1910 auf dem Hintergrunde des Kampfes zwischen Königtum und Feudalität," ibid., pp. 63-80. See also P. Anderson, "Gustav von Schmoller," in H. U. Wehler, ed., *Deutsche Historiker* (Göttingen, 1971), 2: 39-65.

though Berlin students could learn a moderate, reformist nationalism from Schmoller, his postliberal economics provided only critiques of degree and not of kind, while his reserve toward actual involvement deepened the chasm between cultivation and politics.

The rightist "social monarchy" view, though perhaps less common, was nevertheless also popular in economics lectures at German universities. Led by the polemical and outspoken Adolph Wagner, who shouted, stamped, and shook his fist at imaginary opponents, this group of economists had fewer scruples about involvement in politics, and several joined conservative causes like the Christian Social party of Adolf Stöcker. Methodologically Wagner rejected the historical and inductive approach of Schmoller and searched for "typical regularities" deductively and statistically. The rightists abandoned lingering liberal traditions more resolutely, glorified the state more decisively, and advocated a "social monarchy" more consistently out of both altruism and self-interest. Derived from a "romantic preindustrial model based on social harmony," Wagner's "state socialism" concerned itself with the political consequences of the transformation from an agrarian to an industrial state, which threatened not only military power but also the economic self-sufficiency of the fatherland.[60]

Similarly, Max Sering championed agrarian protectionism "in order to maintain the historical basis of the state, the first source of its power, its peasant and noble estate." His Bonn colleague Theodor von der Goltz called for keeping Polish migrant workers out of East Elbia, while complaining patriarchically that rural laborers "vote against the wishes of their employers in elections. Such behavior, repeated often, must fatally poison and destroy the relationship between worker and master." Occasionally someone dared to criticize the Junkers, like Willy Wygodzinski, who claimed to speak "exclusively for the state as carrier of the common interest of all parts of the nation" in recommending a compromise between agricultural entrepreneurs and farm laborers. But in general social-conservative economists advocated reforms only to increase national power, for in the future Germany might "have to struggle for its existence against the Tamerlanes and Ghengis Khans of Mongolian industry." Hence, their lectures sought to strengthen "the spirit of discipline, of voluntary subordination, and dedication to a common task while disregarding individual interests that divide our people."[61] Practically, they added the imperative

---

[60] A. Wagner, *Theoretische Sozialökonomik oder allgemeine und theoretische Volkswirtschaftslehre* (Leipzig, 1907); and *Allgemeine Volkswirtschaftslehre* (lecture notes from the 1880s, no author), HUB manuscript collection. See also K. D. Barkin, "Conflict and Concord in Wilhelminian Social Thought," *CEH* 5 (1972): 55-71 and A. Ascher, "Professors as Propagandists: The Politics of the Katherdersozialisten," *JCEA* 23 (1963): 282-302.

[61] S. v. Frauendorfer, *Ideengeschichte der Agrarwirtschaft und Agrarpolitik im deutschen Sprachgebiet* (Bonn, 1957), vol. 1; T. v. d. Goltz, *Die ländliche Arbeiterklasse und der*

of *Mittelstandspolitik*, a policy of supporting the victims of industrialization like peasants and artisans, to the vocabulary of Conservative party politics. Although they shared much with other Socialists of the Chair, the stridency of their imperialism ("healthy national instinct") and the harshness of their authoritarianism (opposing all democratization of domestic politics) offered their students even less material for a progressive point of view. Thus economists confronted contemporary problems more courageously, but tried to adapt existing institutions rather than transform them.

As "with every year history assumes the position earlier held by philosophy in public opinion as in general cultivation," historical lectures were a final important source for political education. Although political allusions were customary even in Theodor Mommsen's courses on classical antiquity or in Dietrich Schäfer's portrayal of the medieval Holy Roman Empire, courses on contemporary history (beginning with the watershed of the French Revolution) made the most obvious attempt to politicize their audience. While the summer 1871 schedule listed only "Modern History" by Johann Gustav Droysen and "Recent History" by the legendary Leopold von Ranke, by 1891 Max Lenz taught historiography; Hans Delbrück, Prussian history; Treitschke, the French Revolution; and Theodor Schiemann, Russia after Peter the Great. By 1914 Berlin students could choose from Professor Sternfeld (German survey), Kurt Breysig (German culture, nineteenth-century Germany), Richard Schmitt (Germany 1814-1865), Schiemann (Bismarck's age), Otto Hintze (the foundation of the German Empire, constitutional history) and four other non-German offerings. Although the possibility of redefining temporal boundaries made for a great variety of titles, about a dozen areas of specialized teaching from Prussian history to contemporary themes (*Grosse Politik* by Schiemann 1901) emerged as core courses during the empire, once the 1871 boundary had been breached (Bismarck by Lenz in 1898). Since Prussian patriotism, German nationalism, and some kind of imperialism were the norm for university historians, the political dialogue between them took the form of stressing different aspects and values of this common creed. While all of them understood historical scholarship as Wissenschaft which would, like the monumental *Acta Borussica*, "extraordinarily strengthen loyalty to the state and devotion to the dynasty," they diasgreed on the manner of the political teaching. Despite the identity of their subject matter

---

Staat (Jena, 1893) and *Vorlesungen über Agrarwesen und Agrarpolitik* (Jena, 1899); W. Wygodzinski, *Agrarwesen und Agrarpolitik* (Berlin, 1912). In the last decade before the war a few younger economists like Alfred Weber began to demand reforms, while the majority, like Hermann Schumacher, championed an aggressive imperialism. See A. Weber, "Die moderne Grosstadt als soziales und kulturelles Problem," *Soziale Kultur* 26 (1906): 4-20; and H. Schumacher, "Deutschlands Interessen in China," in *Handels- und Machtpolitik*, 2nd ed. (Stuttgart, 1900), 2:75-246, edited by Schmoller, Sering, and Wagner.

and their many shared values, preoccupations and styles of historians changed sufficiently to mark them into separate scholarly generations from which students learned distinct lessons.[62]

The Borussian, or national-pedagogical, school of kleindeutsch historiography dominated historical teaching in the 1870s in Berlin and Bonn. "As certainly as the historian cannot mature without ethics, there is no morality without a definite relationship to the great earthshaking questions of religion, politics, and nationality," Heinrich von Sybel argued. "The historian who withdraws into noble neutrality will become soulless and effete without this anchor." Although building upon Leopold von Ranke's critical methods, the Prussian historians like J. G. Droysen strove for a methodology that would allow them to involve themselves in the great ideological and political struggles of their day. Progressing from facts to conditions, to the will of actors, and finally to overriding ideas, this intuitive hermeneutics of *Verstehen* allowed the scholar to discover the "ethical forces" moving history and thereby to shape political consciousness among students, to propagate his scholarly views in the general public, and to fight for his *wissenschaftliche* aims in the actual political arena.[63] Droysen sought "simultaneously to arouse and cultivate" his hearers. "Radiating and glowing," Treitschke spoke "with brilliant pathos" and emitted "a secret stream of compelling force." Wilhelm Maurenbrecher impressed William II with "the enraptured manner of his presentation, which reminded one of Treitschke."[64]

The primary didactic aim of these Prussian scholars was "the historical legitimation of the kleindeutsch national state" through a reconstruction of German history which emphasized the conscious national policy of the Hohenzollern dynasty and slighted other conflicting trends. In his chief work on Frederick the Great, Arnold Schäfer sought "to counter successfully the attacks on Prussian policy of that era," as he explained to

---

[62] Sybel to Waitz, May 1857, cited in H. Seier, "Heinrich von Sybel," *DH* 2: 24-38; *Vorlesungsverzeichnisse* Berlin and Bonn for the appropriate years; and quote from the preface of the *Acta Borussica* (Berlin, 1877), vol. 1. The literature on the historiography of the empire is complex. The periodization below is based on the political content of the lectures rather than on methodological or philosophical trends. See G. G. Iggers, *Deutsche Geschichtswissenschaft* (Munich, 1971), pp. 120-162 and König, "Politische Komponenten," pp. 7-23.

[63] H. v. Sybel, "Über den Stand der neueren deutschen Geschichtsschreibung," in *PrJhb* 1 (1858): 349-64; H. Schleier, *Sybel und Treitschke* (Berlin, 1965); W. Bussmann, "H. v. Sybel," in *Geschichtswissenschaften* (Stuttgart, 1976). See also J. Rüsen, "J. G. Droysen," *DH*, 2: 7-23.

[64] F. Meinecke, *Erlebtes, 1862-1919* (Stuttgart, 1964), pp. 57ff; L. Curtius, *Deutsche und Antike Welt* (Stuttgart, 1950), pp. 70ff.; W. Hubatsch, "Wilhelm Maurenbrecher 1838-1892," *Geschichtswissenschaften*, pp. 155-61. Opinions were divided on Treitschke's rhetoric; some students, like Paulsen, were offended by his ranting which, because of his deafness, brooked no contradiction. Paulsen, *Aus meinem Leben*, p. 157.

Bismarck. As a corollary, the "Prussian legend" had to downgrade the contribution of the liberal movement to unification and was forced to argue: "Only in close association and fusion with Prussian patriotism did the liberal spirit of our bourgeoisie have any value." Treitschke's famous dictum that "the conscious will of acting men makes history" tended to downplay cultural and social factors in contrast to personal contributions of heroes like Luther and Bismarck. The Bonn historian Maurenbrecher "idolized them with pious love and childlike simplicity; it was a heartfelt need for him to point out the lasting greatness of these two Germans to his hearers and friends at every possible opportunity."[65] Finally, the Borussian school, though initially striving for a synthesis of power with law and culture, more and more exaggerated *Machtpolitik* and stressed, like Treitschke in the most famous lecture on "the history of Germany in the nineteenth century," the primacy of foreign policy over domestic concerns. Active in the liberal parties, these Prussian historians gradually abandoned their constitutionalism and parliamentarism to consecrate the marriage of Prussia and Germany and bless Bismarck's internal policies even after his shift to the right in 1879. Not only Catholics as the ultramontane "international," but Socialists must be fought as "conscienceless agitators who undermine all foundations of social and civic order." Although for each individual scholar the transition from the opposition to propagating loyal "historical-political attitudes" differed somewhat, their collective impact on students was to fashion a pedigree for the new empire and to encourage youthful nationalism.[66]

With increasing specialization in the 1880s and greater confidence in unification, the temper of historical lectures became less political and more strictly scholarly. The rediscovery of a value-free approach led to a methodological Ranke renaissance which reinforced the historicist tradition. Thus, teaching in the 1890s became more positivist and documentary, while losing much of its sweeping rhetorical appeal to students, although professors still thought in "national" terms. The Bonn historian Alfred

---

[65] A. Schäfer to Bismarck, 1 May 1869 in J. Ansbach, *Zur Erinnerung an A.D. Schäfer* (Leipzig, 1895); idem, *Historische Aufsätze und Festreden* (Leipzig, 1873); and R. Schmidt, "A. Schäfer, 1819-1883," *Geschichtswissenschaften*, pp. 170-89. W. Maurenbrecher, *Königtum und Verfassung in Preussen* (Bonn, 1878); G. Wolf, *W. Maurenbrecher: Ein Lebens- und Schaffensbild* (Berlin, 1893); Maurenbrecher, *Gründung des deutschen Reiches 1859-1871* (Leipzig, 1892); and W. Hubatsch, "W. Maurenbrecher, 1838-1892," *Geschichtswissenschaften*, pp. 155-61.

[66] Heinrich von Treitschke, *History of Germany in the Nineteenth Century* (Chicago, 1975), selected and edited by G. G. Craig. See the ample literature listed in G. G. Iggers, "Heinrich von Treitschke," *DH*, 2: 66-80. A. Schäfer, "Norddeutsch, süddeutsch und undeutsch," in his *Historische Aufsätze*, pp. 347-63; and Schmidt, "Schäfer," p. 177. See also G. Schilfert, "Zur Neueren Geschichte an der Berliner Universität," *Wissenschaftliche Zeitschrift der Humboldt Universität zu Berlin* 9 (1959-60): 15-33 and P. E. Hübinger, *Das historische Seminar der rheinischen Friedrich-Wilhelms-Universität zu Bonn* (Bonn, 1963).

Dove typically attributed "an absolute value to each age, for itself and for us," wanted to exclude "all natural regularities" and consider only "what individually can be directly understood, felt, or experienced." While, in the constitutional conflict, he considered the crown's attempt "to maintain an independent, personally acting royalty" legitimate, Dove began to criticize the oversimplifications of the Borussian school.[67] In a similar vein, the archivist of Brandenburg-Prussia, Reinhold Koser, strove for greater objectivity, although his work and teaching were inspired "by the loyalty required of the Prussian court historian." The French Revolution had introduced universal suffrage "in contradiction to the most elementary conditions of self-government" in England, but in Prussia "the democratic wave has not yet spoilt or destroyed the feeling for justice; and legal duties, services, and rights are still in balance."[68] A lack of "rhetorical aggressiveness" actually helped Friedrich von Bezold in procuring a position at Bonn, and the less polemical atmosphere made it possible for him to muse: "Though sincerely supporting the national cause, one should not lose sight of the higher unity of everything human." Hence, Bezold could go so far as to criticize William II indirectly, admit Prussian backwardness "in the constitutional area," and explain the logic of Socialist agitation in Russia by "the unbearable pressure of an anachronistic state."[69] In Berlin the appointment of Max Lenz signaled a climate of greater objectivity and universality, although his combative temperament, his cultural Protestantism, and his support for Bismarckian colonialism provided a strong didactic undercurrent. Similarly, the rising scholar Otto Hintze rejected the explicit partisanship of Droysen, but his social and economic approach to the role of administration in state formation rested on an "axiomatic regard for the monarchical-bureaucratic state in its outward growth and internal modernization."[70] Although the neo-Rankean generation eschewed

[67] A. Dove, "Kaiser Wilhelms geschichtliche Gestalt," in his *Ausgewählte Schriften vornehmlich historischen Inhalts* (Leipzig, 1898), pp. 138-49; and "Der Wiedereintritt des nationalen Prinzips in die Weltgeschichte," ibid., pp. 1-19. See also C. A. Willemsen, "Alfred Dove, 1844-1916," in *Geschichtswissenschaften*, pp. 254-59; and Hübinger, *Seminar*, pp. 175-79.

[68] R. Koser, "Kaisergeburtstagsrede," *NBZ*, 28 January 1894; S. Skalweit, "Reinhold Koser 1852-1914," *Geschichtswissenschaften*, pp. 272-77; idem, "Das Problem von Recht und Macht und das historiographische Bild Friedrichs des Grossen," *GWU* 2 (1951): 91-106; and Hübinger, *Seminar*, pp. 182ff.

[69] F. Bezold, "Zum 18. Januar 1901," *NBZ*, 19 January 1901; idem, *Der Geist von 1813* (Bonn, 1913); and "Zur Geschichte des politischen Meuchelmords," in *Aus Mittelalter und Renaissance: Kulturgeschichtliche Studien* (Munich, 1918), pp. 271-93. See G. Beyerhaus, "F. v. Bezold," *HZ* 141 (1930): 315-26; W. Hubatsch, "F. v. Bezold, 1848-1928," *Geschichtswissenschaften*, pp. 284-92; and Hübinger, *Seminar*, pp. 190-99.

[70] M. Lenz, "Gedächtnisrede auf Bismarck," in Schmoller, *Zu Bismarcks Gedächtnis*, pp. 78ff., 110ff.; H. H. Krill, *Die Rankerenaissance: Max Lenz und Erich Marcks* (Berlin, 1962); J. L. Herkless, "Ein unerklärtes Element in der Historiographie von Max Lenz," *HZ* 222 (1976): 81-104. O. Hintze, *Die Hohenzollern und ihr Werk: Fünfhundert Jahre vaterländischer Geschichte* (Berlin, 1915); and J. Kocka, "Otto Hintze," *DH*, 3: 41-64.

explicit political indoctrination in favor of greater emphasis on accuracy and sources, its postliberal bureaucratic temper subtly reinforced conformist nationalism among the students.

During the last decade before World War I the implicit political teaching of historians once more turned into explicit political involvement and transmission of values. The external crises after 1900 and the heightening of internal tensions prodded many scholars to abandon their reserve and, like their own teachers, the Borussian school, to confront openly public questions. Unwilling to jettison exacting standards of critical scholarship, they argued, like Dietrich Schäfer: "In historical work the most scrupulous research and inspired as well as inspiring love of fatherland can go hand in hand." Or they insisted, like Max Weber, on a strict methodological separation between scientific and political statements. Although the entire dialogue took place on the right, three at least tendentially distinct groups dominated Berlin and Bonn after the turn of the century. At one extreme, the pan-German wing, led by Schäfer, rejected cultural and social history in favor of value judgments on "the development of the German state" in a self-conscious "historiography with a political bent."[71] While Theodor Schiemann in Berlin warned against the Slavic menace and called for unabashed imperialism, Justus Hashagen at Bonn criticized government policy during the first Morocco crisis for "not conducting a preventive war, which can be more moral than a belated defensive war" and drew a martial lesson from the Bosnian crisis: "It is no accident that the forceful diplomacy of the Central Powers during the annexation, which maintained its appeal to shining arms in the face of worldwide hostility, gained a complete victory against all enemies." Hence, a strong group of German historians harangued their students with appeals to a misunderstood Bismarckian Machtpolitik, championed foreign expansion or domestic repression, and "reinforced some of the most notorious and dangerous misconceptions among the educated public in Germany."[72]

More moderate in tone, though not necessarily different in ultimate aims, was a centrist group that, hearkening back to their liberal heritage, occasionally warned against the unrestrained chauvinism of their colleagues. This tendency is perhaps best typified by the military historian Hans Delbrück, who, though an outsider in the historical guild, in his influential

---

[71] D. Schäfer, *Deutsche Geschichte*, 9th ed. (Jena, 1922), 1: 6-13; and *Mein Leben* (Berlin, 1926). See also K.-G. Faber, "Realpolitik als Ideologie: Die Bedeutung des Jahres 1866 für das politische Denken Deutschlands," *HZ* 203 (1966): 1-45 and C. E. McClelland, "Berlin Historians and German Politics," *JHC* 8 (1973): 3-33.

[72] Notes 20, 94. J. Hashagen, *Weltpolitische Entwicklungsstufen* (Bonn, 1916); *Umrisse der Weltpolitik* (Leipzig, 1916), vol. 1 (1871-1907); Hübinger, *Seminar*, pp. 196f.; and Schwabe, *Wissenschaft und Kriegsmoral*, pp. 68ff. See McClelland, "Berlin Historians," p. 33, and *The German Historians and England* (Cambridge, 1971), pp. 191ff.; and W. Frauendienst, "Deutsche Weltpolitik: Zur Problematik des Wilhelminischen Reiches," *Welt als Geschichte* 25 (1959): 1-39.

Preussische Jahrbücher propagated a reform conservative program of "uniting power and culture, Prussia and Germany, national spirit but not nationalism, patriotic idealism but not chauvinism, German Volkstum as link in general humanist cultivation, state loyalty instead of partisanship." Reminiscent of the policies of Chancellor Bethmann Hollweg, such moderate rightist views nevertheless considered "military historical training" essential for general history. In Bonn, Aloys Schulte argued similarly: "The fantasies of the peace lovers are errors, noble but extremely dangerous—our nation, if it wants to maintain itself, must be martial and remain so." In other words, "our state rose by the sword and must live by the sword."[73]

Finally, among the younger scholars there were also a few who tried to move methodologically beyond the orthodoxies of historicism, be it toward a history of ideas or toward social history. Somewhat more open to liberal and reformist currents, they, however, only partially abandoned their nationalism and elitism. In his chief prewar work, which attempted to synthesize "cosmopolitanism and the national state," Friedrich Meinecke sought to communicate some of Friedrich Naumann's democratic and socially reformist imperialism to his students. Kurt Breysig, in captivating lectures, diagnosed the cultural crisis of the *fin de siècle* and suggested limited political democratization and electoral revisions.[74] United on the necessity of empire, German nationality, the primacy of Protestantism, the dangers of democracy, and the legitimacy of cultural privilege, these three groups nevertheless presented conflicting advice on how these goals were to be achieved. While the chauvinists advocated military expansion, forceful Germanization, anti-Catholic repression, open authoritarianism, or inequality, the moderates preferred an indirect strategy of cultural and economic imperialism, voluntary acculturation, religious tolerance, piecemeal concessions to parliamentarism or social policy, and the reformists wanted to go even further in specific areas. As all camps participated in Alfred von Tirpitz's naval demagoguery, until some perceptive minds like Del-

---

[73] H. Delbrück, *Krieg und Politik* (Berlin, 1919), 1: 3; A. Thimme, *H. Delbrück als Kritiker der Wilhelminischen Epoche* (Düsseldorf, 1955); and A. Hillgruber, "Hans Delbrück," *DH*, 4: 4-52. A. Schulte, lecture manuscripts on the French Revolution, the Wars of Liberation, the Vormärz, and the history of war, UB Bonn, manuscript collection, S 2789-2792; and *Die Schlacht bei Leipzig* (Bonn, 1913). See also M. Braubach, "A. Schulte—Kämpfe und Ziele," *Historisches Jahrbuch* 78 (1959): 82-109 and "A. Schulte, 1857-1941," *Geschichtswissenschaften*, pp. 299-310.

[74] F. Meinecke, *Werke* (Berlin, 1957-1969), in eight volumes, edited by H. Herzfeld and others as well as *Erlebtes 1862-1919* (Stuttgart, 1964), the combined reprint of the first two volumes of his memoirs. For recent interpretations, see R. A. Pois, *F. Meinecke and German Politics in the Twentieth Century* (Berkeley, 1972), which did not bother with the *Nachlass*, and the more balanced E. Schulin, "F. Meinecke," *DH*, 1: 39-57. See also G. Oestreich, "Die Fachhistorie und die Anfänge der sozialgeschichtlichen Forschung in Deutschland," *HZ* 208 (1969): 32-63; and B. vom Brocke, "Kurt Breysig," *DH*, 5: 95-116.

brück began to have second thoughts, they propagated a Wilhelmian consensus that enabled their students to discuss the implementation of individual policies but left them bereft of fundamental alternatives.

The political components of formal instruction in law, economics, and history during the Second Reich demonstrate a strong and continuing commitment toward influencing the political attitudes of students. Less active than in the unification decade, in the 1870s professors were still vigorously involved in public affairs and sought to reconcile the divergent imperatives of power and spirit (*Macht und Geist*) in a higher whole.[75] Although on the face of it the methodological revolution of the 1880s and 1890s toward legal positivism, economic empiricism, and apolitical historicism did reduce explicit political didacticism, lecturers continued trying to shape student values and perspectives. The repolitization of formal instruction after 1900 was facilitated by a particular notion of "national" consensus which claimed to transcend domestic partisanship and advocated active involvement in Weltpolitik in order to placate domestic strife. Thematically these lectures tended to glorify the Hohenzollern dynasty and "Prussia's German mission," while expressing academic distrust of William II's antics in comparison with the actions of his more capable predecessors. In disparagement of their liberal past, academics slighted their contribution to unification and idealized the foundation of the empire "from above." As the Reichstag had "proved incapable of suitable legislation," universal suffrage was frequently derided as "Bismarck's most fatal domestic act" and further parliamentarization of the constitution rejected out of hand.[76]

The labor movement and the Social Democratic party provoked warnings about "the brutalization of public life" and pessimistic predictions about the future of culture. Although the need for social reform was understood even by noneconomists, there was no agreement whether to industrialize further and strengthen the unions, whether to employ the state as neutral arbitrator, or whether to preserve agrarian and artisan structures through tariffs and a conscious Mittelstandspolitik. Such domestic uncertainty reinforced academic determination to support imperialist ventures abroad, be it as military aggrandizement, or as a response to business fear that "our new unity and its political and economic power will be destroyed by foreigners today rather than tomorrow," or as cultural quest "to conquer the world with intellectual weapons and stamp our national spirit upon

[75] N. Andernach, *Der Einfluss der Partien*, pp. 183, 209-12; Schwabe, *Wissenschaft*, pp. 601-603; and Hennig, *Bildungsbürgertum*, p. 354.

[76] J. Bona-Meyer, *Glück und Verdienst* (Bonn, 1887); J. Heuhäuser, *Die psychologischen Grundlagen der Entstehung und Entwicklung der staatlichen Gemeinschaft* (Bonn, 1899); Zorn, *Universitätsleben*, pp. 119f.; and *Reichsverfassung*, pp. 7ff.; M. Ritter, *Die deutsche Nation und das deutsche Kaiserreich* (Bonn, 1896); K. G. Hertling, *Erinnerungen aus meinem Leben* (Munich, 1919), 1: 270ff.; Wygodzinski, *Wandlungen*, p. 98.

it." Although explicit appeals "to keep the race pure, even in literature" were relatively rare, many courses betray conventional anti-Semitism and intolerance toward non-German minorities.[77] Instead of forming a cohesive whole or dividing into a neat orthodox versus modernist dichotomy, German professors clustered into at least three somewhat distinct groups: initially the liberals and even progressives set the tone of the university; by the 1890s the bureaucratic centrists became pre-eminent; and after the turn of the century, the hard-line imperialists, challenged by a few reformists, dominated the lecture halls. From these strains students acquired some form of nationalism, some kind of social political awareness, and some measure of enthusiasm for Weltpolitik. Thus professors like the jurist Joseph Heimberger were convinced that academic youth was ready "to forget [domestic] strife, in order to offer itself united to the Kaiser, if he should call them to defend the fatherland."[78]

POLITICAL INSTRUCTION

Although the decline of cameralism, the Kantian attack on the Aristotelian tradition, and the ideological struggle between Machiavellianism and natural law eroded politics as an independent discipline, the Politikvorlesung was the most explicit and effective form of political instruction. As courses on politics lacked a firm place in a degree-oriented curriculum, and the intellectual "definition of politics" was "quite indistinct," they reached a smaller audience than ceremonial speeches or general legal, economic, or historical lectures. But when delivered by an inspiring orator such as Friedrich Christoph Dahlmann, they could attract hearers from outside the university and exert a profound influence, because they tended to be less dry and more confessional than regular lectures. During the early years of the empire the jurist Franz von Holtzendorff distinguished three approaches: While the "historical [view] teaches the value of constitutions on the basis of past analogies," thereby recalling Aristotle, "the philosophical-legal [method] primarily seeks to elaborate the relationship to law and takes

---

[77] Ritter, *Die deutsche Nation*, pp. 18-29; Lindenlaub, *Richtungskämpfe*, pp. 196-98; G. Wolf, *D. Schäfer und H. Delbrück: Nationale Ziele der deutschen Geschichtsschreibung seit der französischen Revolution* (Gotha, 1918), p. 150; Zorn, *Reich*, col. 1500; H. Ruhle, *Über die Bedeutung der deutschen Universitäten für das Gedeihen des Vaterlands* (Bonn, 1880); A. Elter, "Das Aufleben des deutschen Nationalbewusstseins im Zeitalter des Humanismus," *NBZ*, 4 August 1895; and B. Litzmann, *Das Deutsche Drama in den literarischen Bewegungen der Gegenwart*, 3rd ed. (Hamburg, 1896), p. 214. For professorial anti-Semitism, see P. Gay, *Freud, Jews and Other Germans* (Oxford, 1978), pp. 108-31.

[78] J. Heimberger, *Was dürfen wir von einem neuen Strafgesetzbuch erwarten?* (Leipzig, 1909), p. 3. König, "Politische Komponenten," pp. 55-64. In contrast to Ringer, *Mandarins*, pp. 218ff.; Wehler, *Deutsches Kaiserreich*, p. 129; and Schilfert, "neuere Geschichte," pp. 15-33.

ethical axioms into account,'' and "the statistical-administrative [orientation] principally considers the existing numerically measurable properties of the state.'' Depending upon personnel and individual preference, politics were taught in Berlin and Bonn by lawyers, economists, and historians, in no particular order. Since in Heinrich von Sybel's view the subject could include "the sum of constitutional, ideological, and social questions considered essential for the structure of the state,'' students expected both factual details on contemporary political systems and ideological guidance in terms of a coherent theory of politics. This method of teaching politics raises a number of complex questions: What were the primary ideas on the state (its nature and constitution), on society (its conflict or harmony), and on international affairs (direct or indirect imperialism) that related the German political tradition to contemporary problems? How does the paradoxical impression of "a political spectrum that is finely nuanced" and of "a remarkable uniformity in outlook" in the university community bear on the internal erosion of liberalism? What was the effectiveness of such political education, which after the turn of the century grew into a movement for civic education (*staatsbürgerliche Erziehung*) and a campaign for world political preparation?[79]

In the early years of the empire moderate liberalism, believing its principles at last triumphant, animated the teaching of politics at German universities. At Bonn the eloquent historian Sybel sought to accommodate the liberal credo to the Bismarck phenomenon, "idealized the constitutional harmony of power, directed attention against democratic and parliamentary tendencies,'' and perpetuated a synthesis of liberal and conservative forces, identical with "national" interests.[80] In Berlin the jurist Franz von Holtzendorff, champion of prison reform, women's emancipation, and popular enlightenment, tried to purge liberalism of its doctrinaire abstractions and "continually attracted a great, enthusiastic audience of younger and older men.'' Convinced that "our present education needs a greater understanding of political questions,'' he believed, contrary to academic orthodoxy,

[79] F. von Holtzendorff, *Die Principien der Politik: Einleitung in die staatswissenschaftliche Betrachtung der Gegenwart*, 2nd ed. (Berlin, 1879), pp. 28f.; H. Seier, *Die Staatsidee Heinrich von Sybels in den Wandlungen der Reichsgründungszeit 1862-71* (Lübeck, 1961), p. 12; G. M. Schwarz, "Political Attitudes in the German Universities during the Reign of William II" (dissertation, Oxford, 1961), pp. 329ff.; M. Riedel, "Der Staatsbegriff der deutschen Geschichtsschreibung des 19. Jahrhunderts in seinem Verhältnis zur klassisch-politischen Philosophie," *Der Staat* 2 (1963): 41-63; and H. Maier, "Die Lehre der Politik an den deutschen Universitäten," in D. Oberndörfer, ed., *Wissenschaftliche Politik* (Freiburg, 1962), pp. 59-119.

[80] H. Seier, *Staatsidee*, p. 200; and "Sybels Vorlesung über Politik und die Kontinuität des 'staatsbildenden' Liberalismus," *HZ* 187 (1959): 90-112; H. Schleier, *Sybel und Treitschke: Antidemokratismus und Militarismus im historisch-politischen Denken grossbourgeoiser Geschichtsideologien* (Berlin, 1965); and König, "Politische Komponenten," pp. 8-10.

that "thoughtful consideration of public matters, observation of current affairs, and the exercise of political judgment already at a youthful age provide a healthy counterweight to the temptations of license" among students. In his lectures on "the principles of politics," he paid homage to the art of statesmanship and concentrated not on the ideal but rather "real purposes of the state," which he divided into the categories of *"national power . . . individual freedom or law and . . . social culture."* Considering Macht "the guarantee of special, individual national life," he argued typically: "The character of its neighboring states dictates the pursuit of external power more to Germany than to other confederations." Stressing the "safeguarding of free individual development within those areas not necessarily reserved for the government," Holtzendorff considered "full liberty of action" for the private personality more important than public citizenship rights of speech and assembly. Similarly, he emphasized the "legal protection of one class against rape by another" and "the maintenance of social, primarily economic, and confessional peace" above "the strengthening of public spirit as a basis of national unity" through communication, art, and scholarship. Although incorporating Anglo-French debates, this historical-legal-comparative approach reinforced the constitution of the Second Empire, which "corresponds exactly to the triple division of state purposes developed by us," rather than leading it further into a parliamentary and democratic direction. Because of its critique of "the cult of constitutional formalism," Holtzendorff's liberal synthesis furthered the dangerous idealization of duty above liberty: "Moreover, I would not know which ideal other than the state would be able to captivate our youth as permanently."[81]

More famous and effective was the historian Heinrich von Treitschke, who lectured on politics in Berlin for two decades, beginning in 1875-76. Though increasingly deaf, his tall figure, electrifying eloquence, and mixture of humor and pathos made him "a teacher who opened souls" among the hundreds of students who filled his auditorium to overflowing. "A completely new spiritual world opened itself to young people when the increasingly celebrated and beloved professor explained the nature of the Kulturstaat in his comprehensive and probing manner," a former disciple recalled in his obituary. "He became in fact the creator of new ethical standards." Accepting the call to the imperial capital in order "to counter the hubris of radical criticism with the positive power of world history,"

[81] A. Teichmann, "Franz von Holtzendorff," *ADB*, 55: 785-801; Holtzendorff, *Principien der Politik*, pp. xii f., 228-333; and Schwarz, "Political Attitudes," pp. 108ff., on the prevalent idealization of the state. Although Holtzendorff defended Count Arnim against the Iron Chancellor, befriended progressive leaders like Virchow, and was not promoted in Berlin (which he left for Munich in 1873), his political lectures aimed at reconciling liberalism with the Bismarckian Reich.

Treitschke compensated for his lack of examination privileges and seminars with the conviction: "In the end youth is everywhere the same and can be inspired." His favorite lecture "sought to recognize the basic concepts of the state by looking at the real political world, to scrutinize historically what nations have desired, created, and achieved in political life, and [to probe] the causes; thereby it shall . . . also succeed in finding some historical laws and in erecting moral imperatives."[82]

In self-conscious contrast to Leopold von Ranke, he proceeded systematically and comparatively in order to reach generalizations, which, supported encyclopedically and presented rhetorically, established a coherent political Weltanschauung. During his controversy with Schmoller over social reform, he claimed, "my actual teachers of politics were Aristotle, then the historical jurists Roscher, Dahlmann, Gneist, and Hegel's philosophy," in other words, the mainstream of moderate liberalism. Although his belligerent temper and rhetorical gifts often carried him beyond current academic opinion, Treitschke was the most influential political lecturer of the German Empire. He both reflected and helped bring about the deliberalization of the university community, signaled by his departure from the liberal Reichstag fraction in 1879 and his resignation from the editorship of the *Preussische Jahrbücher* a decade later. Edited posthumously from student transcripts of 1892-93, his laboriously prepared *Politics* lecture is a more important source for the political *Tendenzwende* of the educated middle class than his better known *History of Germany in the Nineteenth Century*. Even if a few perspicacious students like Meinecke recoiled from his increasing verbal violence, future leaders of the pan-Germans, such as Heinrich Class, Karl Peters, and Friedrich von Bernhardi, were not the only ones entranced. Literally thousands of Wilhelmine officials, teachers, and officers sat at his feet: "No historian has exerted a comparable influence on the leading stratum of the German Empire."[83]

In his politics course the self-appointed *praeceptor Germaniae* set out to revise the dominant liberal opinions of academics, which he deprecated

[82] H. von Petersdorff, "Heinrich von Treitschke," *ADB*, 55: 263-326; Treitschke to Ranke, 7 March 1874, in H. Cornicelius, ed., *Heinrich von Treitschkes Briefe* (Berlin, 1920), vol. 3, pt. 2, 384; Treitschke to Freytag, 19 December 1875, ibid., pp. 419ff. H. Cornicelius, ed., *Politik: Vorlesung gehalten an der Universität zu Berlin von Heinrich von Treitschke* (Leipzig, 1897), 1: 2f. For the methodological purpose of this investigation the fact that his *Politics* was compiled from lecture notes represents an actual advantage, for it reflects his closest students' perception of Treitschke rather than his own intent.

[83] Treitschke to Schmoller, 27 July 1874, in the *Briefe*, pp. 396f.; in contrast to Gordon A. Craig, ed., *History of Germany in the Nineteenth Century* (Chicago, 1975), pp. xii f. For a brief critical evaluation, see G. Iggers, "Heinrich von Treitschke," *DH*, 2:66-80. F. Meinecke, *Erlebtes*, pp. 90f. It is tempting to exaggerate Treitschke's influence, but since he understood himself as a political teacher and popularizer, he often formulated, albeit more sharply, general reactions of the educated and must therefore be understood as a reflection of contemporary currents as well as their source.

as "expressions of economic and social interests," by contrasting them to a realistic conception of statesmanship. As the "public force for protection and order," the state was "the independent power of the legally united people"; "power" was the principle of the state, "as faith is the principle of the church." Government, "force toward the outside and legal order to the inside," aimed at the self-preservation of the state rather than at service to the individual, even if might had to be directed toward "positive achievements for the entire spiritual and economic life of a nation" and toward a Kulturstaat. While not completely abandoning the liberal notion of a higher ethical law, Treitschke resolved the Machiavellian dilemma by postulating: If "the essence of its great personality is power, the highest moral duty of the state is to nurture its power."[84] In a clear departure from his own earlier Bildungsliberalismus, he argued: "States have not arisen out of popular sovereignty, but were created against the will of the people; the state is the self-perpetuating power of the stronger tribe." Hence, rather than with the governed, his sympathy was with the governing, who acted not from "naive selfishness" but from "a political view . . . that sees the state from the perspective of the whole." Any right of resistance against "an ethical power per se, a high treasure," was impossible.

As political parties expressed discordant social interests, Treitschke re-affirmed "the old axiom that it is the task of government to stand above parties and to find, as Bismarck has once said, the diagonal of forces between the different tendencies." Hence, the "broadest individual liberty in private life" was more important to him than formal political freedom, which he did not define as universal suffrage ("the great nonsense") or civil rights, important as they were, but rather as voluntary subjection to the greater whole. "One always returns to the same premise that personal liberty cannot be an absolute right, but is limited by the living necessity of the state itself." Instead of pressing for extension of citizenship rights, Treitschke warned against the decline of "public morality," the "general intellectual deterioration," and "greater incidence of mediocrity" resulting from excessive liberty.[85] Rejecting the doctrine of the division of power, the Prussophile historian glorified monarchy as "miraculously intelligible and natural," for it centralized power—provided, of course, the right kind

[84] Treitschke, *Politik*, 1: 1, 32ff., 68ff., 79ff., 95ff., 100f. In themselves Treitschke's political ideas are not terribly original, but rather the systematization of gradual developments in particular areas that can be traced in his political articles in the *Preussische Jahrbücher* and his correspondence. See also H.W.C. Davis, *The Poltical Thought of Heinrich von Treitschke* (Westport, Conn., 1973).

[85] Treitschke, *Politik*, 1: 113, 138f., 143f., 156f., 165, 170, 175, 182f. His contemporary evaluations were sometimes quite astute, as his warnings, during the Oriental Crisis of the late 1870s, against a world war at the side of Austria and Turkey against France and Russia, in which the Danubian monarchy would break up. Treitschke to Nöldeke, 5 July 1876, *Briefe*, 3, pt. 2, 429f.

of king exercised it. Therefore, he scorned parliamentarism, advocated limited suffrage, denounced democratic tyranny (majority rule), preferred federation over confederation, and applauded the Prussian conquest of Germany: "Not Prussia merged into Germany. This phrase which is repeated today is the exact opposite of what we can grasp with our hands: Prussia extended its own institutions to the rest of Germany."[86] In brief, though attempting to incorporate some liberal achievements (such as academic freedom!), Treitschke's conception of the state was a sustained diatribe against the democratic tradition in Central Europe. It provided not only an academic rationale for Bismarckian Realpolitik but also a passionate agenda for the future greatness of the fatherland. Explicitly subordinating liberty and culture to the imperatives of power, Treitschke's teaching hastened the erosion of political liberalism among professors and students.

While the practical reasons for his resignation from the Liberal party stemmed from Bismarck's reversal of 1879, the intellectual justification for Treitschke's abandonment of liberal ideology was his increasingly Darwinian view of society and international relations. Considering "all civil society class order," he defended the necessity of inequality with such phrases as "no culture without servants" or "millions must plow, smith, and saw so that a few thousands can research, paint, and write." Instinctively rural, Treitschke despised the degeneration of modern cities and, despite some lip service to minor social reforms, rejected academic Sozialpolitik while not even deigning seriously to polemicize against the unthinkable—socialism. Although he had to admit that "nationality is nothing fixed" and mocked the "so-called nationality principle," Treitschke was a thoroughgoing cultural nationalist who, while traveling widely abroad, prized German Kultur above all. "The concepts of nation and state have a natural tendency to coincide." Irritated by Jewish liberals, who did not follow his own drift to the right and criticized his German history in the press, he became not a racial, but a cultural anti-Semite. Calling Jews "an element of national disintegration," he demanded that they "assimilate into the people to whose state they belong."[87]

This conception of an unceasing struggle also colored his view of in-

---

[86] Treitschke, *Politik*, 2: 1ff., 52ff., 60, 162, 178f., 189ff., 249ff., 317f., 337ff. See also the critical interpretation by A. Dorpalen (*Heinrich von Treitschke* [New Haven, 1957], pp. 226-40), who perhaps overemphasizes the sterility of his thought, but correctly stresses the need to discriminate between his intent and his students' understanding.

[87] Treitschke, *Politik*, 1: 50ff., 268-98. His correspondence is full of references to the dangers of socialism and the Jews (*Briefe*, pp. 398ff., 502ff.). For a Marxist analysis, see also H. Schleier, *Sybel und Treitschke*, p. 113. His anti-Semitism will be discussed in greater detail in the next chapter. For Social Darwinism, see also W. H. Koch, *Der Sozialdarwinismus: Seine Genese und sein Einfluss auf das imperialistische Denken* (Munich, 1973).

212 · TEACHING OF POLITICS

ternational relations and made him glorify war as "politics *kat exochen*. Time and again the truth will be confirmed that only in war a people become a nation." Hence, he never doubted that war was "justified and moral, and that the idea of eternal peace is at once impossible and unethical." In the absence of a world court, war not only served as "the great litigation among nations," but promoted material progress and toughened the moral fiber of the community, if not employed frivolously. Because of European racial superiority, Treitschke also firmly believed: "It is therefore today a question of life and death for a great power to participate in the drive towards colonization." If Germany was not to be left behind in the new maritime age, it must resolve: "We want and shall take part in the domination of the world by the white race." The empire's future lay in overseas raw material or settlement colonies: "Only a fool would think that this developmental process could ever come to a halt." In between such flights of impassioned rhetoric, Treitschke also tried to dispense sagacious and well-informed political advice to correct one-sided liberal doctrinairism and counteract the naiveté of German public discourse: "I shall be content if you have learned from this lecture how many factors compose every historical event and how circumspect every political judgment has to be." But enthusiastic students like Alfred von Tirpitz only heard the overtones of robust national self-assertion and not the undertone of "humility of true scholarship." "On the whole it is a more healthy situation [than in the Vormärz] that today's youth simply believes in its fatherland and its new order instead of fighting against everything," Treitschke tried to reassure himself. But in the end his own ferocious teaching contributed in students' minds to that chauvinist "arrogance" against which he himself thought he had warned.[88]

Rejecting "the unpleasant mixture of realism and moralism" of the Borussian school, the legal positivists who took over the politics lecture in the mid-1890s at Berlin and Bonn tried to create an objective science of politics. While differing in some nuances, Ferdinand von Martitz,[89]

[88] Treitschke, *Politik*, 1: 60, 72ff., 119ff., 218ff., 233; 2: 552ff., 574f.; and Treitschke to his wife, 5 August 1881, *Briefe*, 531f. Although his own intent was to sophisticate German political judgment, his effect was in many ways the opposite. "Through his writings and lectures, he had taught thousands of young men who occupied important positions in state and society in the years before 1914 to place too high a valuation upon the use of power and to believe that their country was being denied the world position that it deserved by jealous and resentful neighbors" (Craig, *Treitschke*, p. xxviii). Little wonder that abroad his name became synonymous with Wilhelmine aggressiveness and that at home his central ideas were reprinted in brochure after brochure during wartime and the Weimar Republic.

[89] Ferdinand von Martitz, *Deutsches Reichs- und Landesstaatsrecht* (lecture notes by Seckel, Berlin, n.d.) and *Die Monarchie als Staatsform* (Berlin, 1903). Unfortunately no lecture notes could be found from his political theory course, and his limited published oeuvre also contained nothing on the subject.

who lectured on political theory, and Conrad Bornhak, who specialized in *Allgemeine Staatslehre*, offered their law students a proud consensus on the superiority of German political institutions as well as scholarship. Recognizing no authority above it, they tended to define "the state as dominion [*Herrschaft*]," which is "legally unlimited and unlimitable" and therefore "not a product of law, but a historical fact." Hence, the purpose of political organization could not be humanitarian: "Externally the state is political power and acts as such among the nations of the earth." Internally it was "primarily a source of equalizing justice between the manifold conflicting interests that fill present-day life." The reservation that "while it can legally desire everything, it can only demand what is physically and ethically possible" from its subjects, was even weaker than Treitschke's. Logically the highest form of such a state was the pure monarchy, since it represented undiluted power and stood for the interest of the whole, not the unstable French republic, which continually threatened to degenerate into democratic tyranny, or the parliamentary crypto-monarchy of England, in which the king was a mere figurehead. Having "succeeded in putting its old principle of dominion upon new foundations," the mixed form of the constitutional monarchy was a result of voluntary "constitutional self-limitation" of royal power, not of popular sovereignty. In cases of doubt, "the presumption always speaks for the free rule of the monarch." Because of the "scholarly repudiation of natural law," no individual private or public rights could limit state power, and a subject's freedom rested on royal generosity. Starting from notions of "natural social division according to property and profession into different classes" and the Hobbesian slogan of *bellum omnium contra omnes* in the economic sphere, these Prussian jurists required the state "for the compromise of social interests." They celebrated the Second Empire: "Thus, constitutional monarchy signifies the reconciliation of state and society," of the age-old contrasts of *imperium* and *libertas*.[90] Differing in style from Treitschke's fiery preaching, the dry, legalistic, and unemotional teaching of Martitz and Bornhak nevertheless reinforced Borussian self-confidence by providing a positive legal rationale for the existing semi- (or, as opponents charged, pseudo-) constitutionalism. By systematically destroying the underpinnings of liberal political theory such as Western natural law or German corporative (Gierke) thought and the neoconstitutionalism of Preuss, they legalized political thinking among students during the last two prewar decades and captured political theory for traditional ends.

Although the goal of "ennobling political attitudes" remained constant,

[90] Conrad Bornhak, *Allgemeine Staatslehre*, 2nd ed. (Berlin, 1909), pp. 9, 10, 18, 43, 82, 83, 90, and *Grundriss des deutschen Staatsrechts*, 3rd ed. (Leipzig, 1912), pp. 234, 241ff., 246, 255. See also Martitz, *Die Monarchie*, passim.

the tone of political teaching became more urgent as professors' interests moved from legal codification to contemporary problems of class struggle and imperialism around 1900. While in Bonn the Free-Conservative economist Erwin Nasse had defended the Prussian constitution and the National-Liberal Adolf Held had propagated social policy,[91] in Berlin the Privatdozent Adolph von Wenckstern rejected the value theory of labor and economic determinism on the basis of his own "national-ethical viewpoint." But he accepted "the moral challenge" of Marxism as "the first grandiose attempt to investigate the consequences of economic and social theory." Seeking limited domestic reform "to strengthen the soul of the people," Wenckstern was an optimistic advocate of Weltpolitik for gaining raw materials and markets and therefore also a naval enthusiast. "Social policy and military policy, the great achievements of the Prussian monarchy," should serve as guideposts for the future and bring about a compromise between the divergent forces of agriculture and industry. He urged the reaffirmation of the alliance of rye and steel in the tariff-fleet compromise of 1902: "A basis for unity between land and factory must be found." Although an academic lightweight, Wenckstern, a typical *Flottenprofessor*, was a persuasive spokesman for the "economic, spiritual, and political world power position of Germany." Thus, students were confronted not only with expositions of political systems but with calls for an active social imperialism.[92]

While politics officially remained within the purview of the Staatswissenschaften, historians replaced economists in this course during the last prewar decade at the University of Berlin. Lecturing on general politics, the development of political theory, and constitutional history, Otto Hintze succeeded Treitschke, but following the neo-Rankean impulse, he tried rather to present a developmental, scholarly, and documentary history of "state and society." Rejecting the Borussian legend that Prussian rulers had self-consciously worked toward German unification, on the basis of his own meticulous research he glorified "the Hohenzollerns and their accomplishment" indirectly, for "without knowing it, they created the instrument needed for the political resurgence of Germany." Celebrating "the marriage of German culture with the military-political spirit of the Prussian state," he applauded Bismarck's "Frederician spirit," which

[91] F. v. Calker, *Politik als Wissenschaft* (Strassburg, 1898); E. Nasse, *F. C. Dahlmann* (Bonn, 1885); and A. Held, *Sozialismus, Sozialdemokratie und Sozialpolitik* (Leipzig, 1878).

[92] A. v. Wenckstern, *Marx* (Leipzig, 1896), p. 265; "1806-1906," in *Staatswissenschaftliche Probleme der Gegenwart* (Berlin, 1909); and *Auf Scholle und Welle: Reden in Ost- und Westdeutschland zur Flottenvorlage 1900* (Leipzig, 1900). For the slippery concept of "social imperialism," see G. Eley, "Defining Social Imperialism: Use and Abuse of an Idea," *Social History* 4 (1976): 265-90. See also W. Marienfeld, *Wissenschaft und Schlachtflottenbau*, pp. 21ff. for a catalogue of justifications.

"recognized real power interests and pursued them with great persistence," even if he caught "a whiff of administrative Bonapartism." Hence, Hintze's teaching centered on the justification of the "heroic one-sidedness" of the Prussian *Militär- und Beamtenstaat*. Defining "the power and greatness of the state" as the main goal of politics, he called for a "national policy" to overcome disunity: "With us the contrast of tribes is aggravated by religious division, subversion of the radical parties, and a great number of foreign elements, especially in our border provinces." Although he recognized a certain democratization as the necessary consequence of universal conscription, he rejected parliamentarism because of Germany's "dangerous middle position between the strongest continental powers" and the lack of political maturity of the intransigent parties, but rather recommended "a firm, consequential, and within the limits of the possible, increased social policy." Although his methodological interest in administrative development prefigured social history, Hintze's political analysis hinged on the primacy of foreign policy, a decisive narrowing of the broader liberal vision: "The imperialist movement appears to us as the beginning of a new epoch of political balance of power. The place of the old European state system will be taken by a new world state system. . . . The struggle for such a great power position is the essence of the imperialist trend of the modern world." Contrasting irrational aggressive British imperialism with peaceful German Weltpolitik, the Hohenzollern historian sought to make Germany fit to survive "this natural selection of the nations." As a latecomer, Germany could only ask for equal access to colonies (*Gleichberechtigung*): "The meaning of German Weltpolitik is not at all a striving for world dominion, but a desire for the maintenance of the balance of power in the world state system of the future." Through his analysis of "the origin and significance of British maritime dominance," he came to the same conclusions as Wenckstern's economic reasoning: "The necessary consequence of this effort, and the obligatory precondition for its success— this cannot be repeated too often—is a strong fleet." Although he was temperamentally a moderate imperialist and domestically a reforming conservative, Hintze taught a truncated vision of politics and instilled an etatist spirit in his students.[93]

[93] Otto Hintze, *Die Hohenzollern und ihr Werk*; "Geist und Epochen der preussischen Geschichte"; "Das politische Testament Friedrich des Grossen von 1752"; "Rasse und Nationalität und ihre Bedeutung für die Geschichte"; "Imperialismus und Weltpolitik," all in *Historisch-Politische Aufsätze* (Berlin, 1908-09), 1: 5-45; 3: 3-28; 4: 144ff., 160ff.; "Staatsverfassung und Heeresverfassung," and "Die Seeherrschaft Englands, ihre Begründung und Bedeutung," both in *Deutsche Zeit- und Streitfragen* (Dresden, 1906-1907), 3: 97-140 and 4: 249-86. See G. Oestreich, "Otto Hintzes Stellung zur Politikwissenschaft und Soziologie," in *Soziologie und Geschichte* (Göttingen, 1964), pp. 10-35 and E. Köhler, *Bildungsbürgertum und nationale Politik: Eine Studie zum politischen Denken Otto Hintzes* (Bad Homburg, 1970), pp. 220-34.

In a more conservative-monarchical vein, the Russian specialist Theodor Schiemann sought to provide historical perspective "on world-political problems of the present." As a Baltic German and Treitschke pupil, this combative and influential publicist began to lecture formally on foreign policy in the mid-1900s, based on his weekly columns in the *Kreuzzeitung*. Although not speaking as freely at the university as at the war academy, he nevertheless provided much factual information about international affairs and an independent, if nationalist, point of view informed by his access to William II, Bülow, and Friedrich von Holstein. Disturbed by "the general decline of our political life" after Bismarck's fall, Schiemann set out to "awaken interest in the great problems of imperialism" and to motivate his audience "to originate or sustain a forceful governmental pursuit of German interests." Typical of much contemporary academic spirit, his political credo was simple: "With all our strength we shall support any proud, forceful, and self-confident national policy. And external power means prestige and firmness at home." Uninterested in theoretical political discussions, Schiemann subscribed to the structural transformation thesis and categorically rejected parliamentarism or social reform as manifestations of domestic weakness. "In Europe Germany has no other ambition than to secure peace on the basis of its geographic status quo as long as at all possible." But abroad grander vistas beckoned, such as "the complete improvement of our colonies, which, despite several governmental attempts, has not been accomplished due to the paralyzing apathy of the Reichstag, and the maintenance of the principle of the open door, so that we can compete on an equal footing, wherever new areas are opened to the trade of civilized nations." These aims were advanced with such harsh rhetoric that students and foreigners alike often misconstrued their real political intent. Reflecting the "deep disgruntlement of German public opinion toward British policy in the Boer War," Schiemann argued, like Tirpitz, that his goal, reconciliation with England, would only become possible "if we, as sea power, can also put a significant weight into the scales." As first full professor of Russian history in Germany and therefore as leading authority on Eastern questions, Schiemann coined the slogan of the "Russian danger" and furthered the hostility of the educated public toward the Slavs. Initially optimistic about the "widening sphere" of German influence, he maintained his verbal belligerence in the teeth of "an avalanche of hostile coalitions after 1908," though serving as translator of the Russian secret documents leaked from the London embassy.[94]

---

[94] From 1901 on Schiemann's columns in the Conservative party organ, *Neue Preussische Zeitung*, were collected and published yearly in book form as *Deutschland und die grosse Politik Anno 1901* (Berlin, 1902) until his break with the paper in 1914 over reconciliation with England. Quotations from 1: preface, 2ff., 32ff.; 2: 1ff.; 4: 4ff.; 6: 1ff.; 14: iii f. See

While he expanded the international horizon of his students, Schiemann, like Treitschke, failed to moderate political discourse, provoking hatred abroad and hubris at home.

The minority of Berlin students who felt dissatisfied with Wilhelmine smugness could turn for inspiration to an unconventional historian, Kurt Breysig, who strove "to explain the meaning of our times to aspiring youth" in more critical terms. An outsider in the professional guild with his sociocultural universalism, he successively emancipated himself from his teachers Treitschke and Schmoller and communicated "a humanly excited and exciting" search for values in his lectures on "Politics and Social Science in Ethical and Historical Perspective" after 1898-99. "Utterly opposed to the social and democratic spirit of the present, yet anything but reactionary or conservative in the conventional sense," Breysig dared to return to the central neohumanist notion of the personality and preached the "aristocracy of the individual." In contrast to the etatism of the majority of the academics, he denounced the state as "the enemy of the individual less through its pressure and overwhelming power than through its egalitarianism and collectivism" and defined "the securing of the great creative [personality] as the most essential task of good public order." Similarly, he rejected not only socialism as "threatening independence, authority, and leadership . . . through the sticky, slimy flood of the lower orders," but gradually also abandoned the university orthodoxy of social policy as debilitating to individual culture. Despite his repeated criticism of William II's personal rule in Maximilian Harden's journal, *Die Zukunft*, the post-liberal Breysig could not abide the democratic tendency because "the spiritual creativity of parliamentarism has been declining since 1848." Sensitized by Friedrich Nietzsche's flaming critique and by Stefan George's poetic quest, he saw "the mechanization of the soul in our times" as the primary danger, threatening with "uniformity, segmentation, subjection, debility, dullness, and barrenness that which ought to be our freest possession, our own self." In a curiously modern antimodernism, Breysig recognized that "the machines that hurt and squash us are in truth the great offices, states, and businesses, which turn man himself into a wheel and roll, polish, flatten, and make him uniform." While this criticism of political isms and depersonalization offered refreshing insights to "a small circle of enthusiastic students," Breysig's remedy, "a different outlook on life," the creation of a new cultivated man, remained pitifully inade-

---

also K. Meyer, *Theodor Schiemann als politischer Publizist* (Frankfurt, 1956), and, for a more critical view, K. Wernecke, *Der Wille zur Weltgeltung: Aussenpolitik und Öffentlichkeit in Deutschland am Vorabend des Ersten Weltkriegs* (Düsseldorf, 1969).

quate and revealed the dead end of a *Bildungsidealismus* which sought to ennoble politics by rejecting it.[95]

As political cultivation instilled a general sense of national loyalty without conveying much specific information or preparing for political participation, a movement for civic education (staatsbürgerliche Erziehung) emerged around the turn of the century. The granting of universal suffrage in 1867 reinforced the liberal demand for citizenship training to enable the people to use its newly won freedoms more intelligently. But "practically nothing happened in the schools to awaken interest and understanding in political and economic questions" during the first two decades of the empire. Only in April 1889, with the impending expiration of the anti-Socialist laws, did Prince Otto von Bismarck hit upon the thought "of using the different levels of schooling in order to combat the spread of Socialist and Communist ideas." He suggested that "cultivation of religiousness and love of the fatherland" could provide a

foundation for a healthy concept of the entire social and political system and convince youth that the teachings of socialism do not only contradict divine commands and Christian ethics but are impractical in reality and have pernicious consequences for the individual as well as for the whole. More than before [the school] must incorporate contemporary and recent history into instruction and prove that state power alone can protect the individual, his family, his freedom, and his rights. It must make pupils conscious of how the Prussian kings have continually tried to improve the living conditions of the workers from the legal reforms of Frederick the Great and the abolition of serfdom until today.

William II enthusiastically endorsed this suggestion and argued in the subsequent crown council that legal restrictions were not enough to preserve the loyalty of youth: "In order to grasp [subversion] at the root and stifle it in its inception one has to influence young people. Hence, the main battlefield lies in the school."[96]

---

[95] K. Breysig, *Von Gegenwart und Zukunft des deutschen Menschen* (Berlin, 1912), pp. 1-9, 36-39, 185-91, 193ff. B. vom Brocke, "Kurt Breysig," *DH*, 5: 109-13 and *Kurt Breysig: Geschichtswissenschaft zwischen Historismus und Soziologie* (Lübeck, 1971), especially pp. 133ff. As a maverick, Breysig remained *Ausserordentlicher* professor until 1923, whereas Hintze and Schiemann were promoted more quickly.

[96] A. Messer, *Das Problem der staatsbürgerlichen Erziehung historisch und systematisch behandelt* (Leipzig, 1912), a University of Strassburg prize essay. Lucanus draft, 20 April 1889 with Bismarck marginalia "a great improvement"; crown council protocol, 30 April 1889, calling for a "political-monarchical catechism" although the minister of culture countered: "Patriotism in the schools and universities is rising." The draft was published as royal decree on 1 May 1889. Crown council protocol, 10 April 1890 (discussing implementation through "patriotic-historical" and economic textbooks), all in DZA Po, Rkz 2183a. See

Although at the school conference of 1890 the Gymnasium party succeeded in limiting changes to "a more detailed treatment of modern patriotic history," the Prussian Lehrpläne of 1892 increased emphasis on civic education, and the school conference of 1900 maintained the stress on religious ethics and contemporary history. Nevertheless, the philological background of many teachers, their training in ancient and medieval history, and their reluctance to get embroiled in politics retarded the nationalization of teaching at all levels. In 1907 the Berlin theologian Harnack deplored the "bottomless ignorance" of students: "It is an unacceptable evil that pupils from a great number of Gymnasia—shall I say the majority—graduate after years of history teaching and do not even know the barest outlines of our present constitutional system and public life." The evident failure to put government directives into practice led to the December 1908 resolution of a number of leading public figures and educators: "The assembly unanimously recognizes a serious deficit in state-political education among the German people; this needs to be remedied through orderly instruction in civics at all middle and higher schools as well as at universities and through suitable teacher training." The Vereinigung zur Staatsbürgerlichen Erziehung des Deutschen Volkes carried on a vigorous campaign for patriotism and joined efforts with the Prussian government in youth work (*Jugendpflege*) and in the military youth organization Jungdeutschlandbund. The civics movement was an integral part of middle-class reformism, which was shocked by the discovery of "adolescence" and sought to fill the "great youth desert" between leaving primary school at fourteen and military service at twenty with positive social and political goals.[97]

Since the civics movement stemmed from the concerns of practicing pedagogues and educational reformers on the primary and secondary levels, the universities became involved only at a comparatively late stage. When professors joined the discussion they sought to resolve the conflict of opinion over the goals of citizenship training through "a historical-systematic treatment" and to objectify the campaign by transcending partisan differences: "Only when scientifically based legal and political knowledge of the state has been sufficiently spread can political cultivation flourish

H. J. Heydorn, "Zur Bildungsgeschichte des deutschen Imperialismus: Die Schulkonferenzen von 1890, 1900 und 1920," in his *Studien zur Sozialgeschichte und Philosophie der Bildung*, 2: 179-239.

[97] Messer, *Staatsbürgerliche Erziehung*, pp. 68ff.; A. Harnack, *Universität und Schule* (Leipzig, 1901), and *Erlass des Ministers der geistlichen, Unterrichts- und Medizinal-Angelegenheiten vom 18. Januar 1911 betreffend Jugendpflege* (Berlin, 1911), p. 37. See also A. Flitner, *Die politische Erziehung in Deutschland: Geschichte und Problematik 1750-1880* (Tübingen, 1957); K. Hornung, *Etappen politischer Pädagogik in Deutschland*, rev. ed. (Bonn, 1965); D. Hoffmann, *Politische Bildung, 1890-1933: Ein Beitrag zur Geschichte der pädagogischen Theorie* (Hanover, 1970); and J. Gillis, *Youth and History*, pp. 95-131.

in Germany." Emotional patriotism was not enough but needed to be refined through an "intellectual conception of politics" to foster responsible political action. In the complex debate about appropriate methods, advocates of *Bürgerkunde* as a special new subject were in the decided minority compared with defenders of staatsbürgerliche Erziehung as didactic principle in all subjects from history to the sciences, and civics therefore began to permeate regular offerings rather than to replace existing disciplines. Although paying lip service to Georg Kerschensteiner's preference for active character formation through experience in student self-government, most professors shrank back from the radical implications of such learning-through-doing and reasserted the necessity of cognitive skills. Convinced that "our youth is not mature enough for politics," academics rather called for "planting a national and social conscience in their hearts," in order to impart a loyal (staatserhaltende) ethos.[98]

In practical terms, universities were called upon to remedy the "complete failure" of teacher training for civics by redirecting historical studies toward more recent, domestic, constitutional, colonial, and, if possible, systematic topics. The Privatdozent Ludwig Bergsträsser pointed out: "Only if the importance of the Frankfurt parliament, the Zollverein, and of Bismarck's economic policy is portrayed as compellingly as the war of 1870 will history become fruitful for citizenship." Others demanded more legal-constitutional and economic courses and even suggested "the penetration of all instruction by the idea that an engineer's work ultimately has to be directed toward strengthening and increasing the power of the state." Those more attuned to the limitations of formal teaching pointed toward the informal influence of student corporations: "It is undeniable that these can contribute significantly to the character formation of their members, especially also as schools of citizenship virtues." Indeed, in the last half-decade before the war, the topic of staatsbürgerliche Erziehung was frequently debated in the pages of the livelier student journals, which claimed "corporate life awakens not only general social morality but also indirectly nurtures patriotism." A minority of politically conscious students responded to the call "to help in the convalescence of our public life and the struggle against disunity or discontent among the people, as well as

[98] Messer, *Staatsbürgerliche Erziehung*, part 2 (systematic); F. Stier-Somlo, "Grundsätzliches zur staatsbürgerlichen Erziehung," *Zeitschrift für Politik* 4 (1911): 544-53; C. Eckert, "Staatsbürgerliche Erziehung: Eine Rundschau," *Jahrbuch für Gesetzgebung, Verwaltung und Volkswirtschaft im Deutschen Reich* 36 (1912): 1321-63; S. Brase, "Die staatsbürgerliche Erziehung der gebildeten Jugend: Eine nationale und eine pädagogische Frage," *BBl* 23 (1910): 119-21; and essays by Dr. Blenck, Dr. Lange, and Dr. Frielinghaus in *Staatsbürgerliche Erziehung durch Schulen und Hochschulen* (Hanover, 1913), pp. 7-29; G. Kerschensteiner, *Staatsbürgerliche Erziehung der deutschen Jugend*, 4th rev. ed. (Erfurt, 1909), attracted the greatest amount of public attention through its combination of staunch patriotism and innovative pedagogy.

to participate in the spreading of political cultivation, the raising of patriotic community spirit and the strengthening of the feeling of civic responsibility.''[99]

Prussian universities began to experiment with special *Lehraufträge* in civics in the last half-decade before World War I. In Berlin the economist Ludwig Bernhard taught an introductory lecture on *Staatsbürgerkunde* for hearers of all faculties from the summer semester of 1910 on. Considering "political culture the fundamental element of national power," he sought to generate a sense of mission in his students, not in the tradition of German idealism but in the Bismarckian conviction that "the first and last thought must be the power of the fatherland." In his mind civics became a cure for "domestic fragmentation," evident in the "bureaucratization of social policy," in Socialist internationalism, and in the rise of Polish subversion in Prussia. Hence, Bernhard's aim was not to set the individual citizen free, but to indoctrinate students as obedient leaders for the future struggles of an expansionist fatherland.[100] In Bonn the jurist Fritz Stier-Somlo, charged with the same responsibility, lectured more generally on politics and sought to remedy "the lack of political-historical cultivation" among his students through a scientific politics in order to "enrich the educated with knowledge, ideas and thoughts, which will enable them to reach an independent judgment." Considering the "state a collective or an organizational unit, possessing legal personality," he sought to balance the tendencies of doctrinaire idealism and ruthless power politics in a refined *Verstandespolitik*. While in a Darwinian world state authority had to be theoretically unlimited, in practice government "bound itself through the constitution and legal system" to respect "the legal subjectivity of the individual against the state." Preferring a constitutional monarchy to other forms, Stier-Somlo advocated a graduated plural suffrage, based upon property and cultivation, and criticized the conservative parties ("outdated conceptions and institutions") as vigorously as the progressives ("old slogans without inner force") and the Socialists ("threatening the complete collapse of culture").

[99] L. Bergsträsser, "Die zur Ausbildung geeigneter Lehrkräfte erforderlichen Änderungen des Universitätsunterrichts," and W. Franz, "Rechtswissenschaftlicher und staatsbürgerlicher Unterricht und technische Hochschulen," all in *Staatsbürgerliche Erziehung*, pp. 30-45. Messer, *Staatsbürgerliche Erziehung*, pp. 101-13; K. Bahr, "Studentische Korporationen und staatsbürgerliche Erziehung," *ATZ* 30 (1913-14): 8-13; F. Roeder, "Staatsbürgerliche Volkserziehung," *AR* 12 (1910): 273f.; and R. Stahl, "Staatskunde in unserem Schulwesen," *BBl* 22 (1908): 110f. See also the "Preisausschreiben der Vereinigung für staatsbürgerliche Erziehung des deutschen Volkes," *AR* 11 (1909): 191f.

[100] Ludwig Berhard, *Die politische Kultur der Deutschen* (Berlin, 1913); *Undesirable Results of German Social Legislation* (New York, 1914); and his massive diatribe against Prussian Poles. See also C. Eckert, "Staatsbürgerliche Erziehung," p. 1321: "The academically educated must in politics march ahead of everyone, because especially in a democratic state they must provide political and social leadership." See also M. Bäcker, *Staatsbürgerlicher Gesamtunterricht* (Langensalza, 1914).

Thus, his exhortation "we must finally become a political nation" reflected the unresolved contradictions of political cultivation for the postliberal generation of academics.[101] Only an occasional outsider, like the Viennese professor of pedagogy Friedrich Wilhelm Foerster, dared criticize "the decrease in state loyalty and support" as a result of "direct instruction or patriotic propaganda" and called for a new, democratic "pedagogy of state culture" based on individual liberty instead of governmental authority.[102]

The stridency of many of its advocates indicates that the effect of civics teaching on the university level was even smaller than the already limited impact of the campaign for citizenship training on its central target, primary and secondary instruction. "The prevalent ignorance of wide circles of our nation about tasks and institutions of the state," which produced "politically unschooled and immature young students," was dispelled only for those few individuals involved in civics courses. "In political-ethical education, in the politicization of the German people, the universities of the Wilhelmian epoch, to the detriment of the entire nation, did not play the leading role that corresponded to their traditions," ruminated an advocate of political cultivation after the defeat. "Content with one-sided specialization and not recognizing emerging syntheses of knowledge as scholarly, they almost criminally neglected sociological disciplines, especially scientific politics." The absence of an academically acceptable political science was reflected in a dearth of courses, the lack of civics in any university examination (such as the *Philosophicum* for teachers), and in the dryness of texts trying to impart political information. The civics movement was also split by fundamentally divergent aims. While the Kaiser and the political right argued that "the high school of our day has no choice but to understand the national aspect of its task as its most important purpose," liberals like Friedrich Naumann, Max Weber, and Walther Rathenau looked to "political self-education" as a precondition for responsible citizenship. This conflict between authority and freedom did not disturb "the great, unshakeable tranquility of a national monarchical atmosphere" in the schools, but prevented the emergence of a scientifically and politically united teaching of citizenship. The "touching lack of po-

---

[101] F. Stier-Somlo, *Politik* (Leipzig, 1907), vol. 4. of the popular series *Wissenschaft und Bildung*, pp. 6ff., 27f., 67ff., 117ff., 155f., 161f., 165f. See also König, "Politische Komponenten," 59f., and E. Bernheim, *Staatsbürgerkunde*, 2nd ed. (Leipzig, 1919) for a typical manual. Neither Hornung (*Etappen*, 26f.) nor Hoffmann (*Politische Bildung*, 73ff.) analyzes the actual teaching of civics at the university.

[102] Fr. W. Foerster, *Staatsbürgerliche Erziehung: Prinzipienfragen politischer Ethik und politischer Pädagogik*, 2nd ed. (Leipzig, 1914) remained therefore also without lasting political or educational effect. See H. Preuss, *Das deutsche Volk und die Politik* (Jena, 1915). See also F. Wenzel, "Sicherung von Massenloyalität und Qualifikation der Arbeitskraft als Aufgabe der Volksschule," in K. Hartman, ed., *Schule und Staat im 18. und 19. Jahrhundert* (Frankfurt, 1974), pp. 323-86.

litical interest and the saddening ignorance" of German students, which foreigners pointed out repeatedly, paradoxically resulted from the very success of nationalism at the university, which removed much of the earlier urgency for involvement. The Marburg theologian Martin Rade explained in 1909: "Today the powerful seem to feel most secure about their success with the coming generation if they keep it politically in the dark as long as possible."[103]

As a result of such paternalism, the German educated elite was remarkably uninformed about conditions in other countries and about Weltpolitik. The Seminar für Orientalische Sprachen, founded in 1887 at the University of Berlin, prepared youths "for imperial service as well as private activity in the colonies" and "taught exotic languages" and "the cultures concerned, especially religion, mores and customs, geography, statistics, and recent history." The Kolonialinstitut in Hamburg (1908) imparted practical colonial skills, and the Institut für Seeverkehr und Weltwirtschaft at the University of Kiel promoted worldwide trade. But these prestigious institutions reached only a narrow circle of specialists. Impressed with the necessity of external cultural policy (*Kulturpolitik*) "in order to maintain the German position in the world in the face of new challenges," Chancellor Bethmann Hollweg favored "the full equality of colonial studies with other disciplines" in acquainting lawyers and economists "with imperial conditions" so as to "interest leading circles in Germany in that development."[104] In the spring of 1913 the budget commission of the Reichstag therefore asked the chancellor for a report "on the transformation of the Oriental Seminar into a German *Auslandschochschule.*" A year later parliament charged "the government with the improvement of foreign studies in the interest of the diplomatic and colonial service as well as trade and industry." Because "attempts to bring civi-

[103] R. H. Henning, "Staatsbürgerliche Erziehung," *AMh* 29 (1912), no. 2; P. Rühlmann, "Die deutschen Hochschulen im Dienste der politischen Erziehung," in his *Wege zur Staatsgesinnung* (Charlottenburg, 1919), p. 154; Leo, "Der nationale Gedanke in der Schule," *ABl* 22 (1908), no. 4; Hoffmann, *Politische Bildung*, p. 158; and Messer, *Staatsbürgerliche Erziehung*, pp. 104ff.: "Our German university administrations, i.e., our German states, show *no* tendencies at all to help [academic youth] in growing systematically to political maturity." For the attitude of the imperial government, see also DZA Po, Rkz 2197 and 2138.

[104] E. Sachau, *Denkschrift über das Seminar für Orientalische Sprachen an der königlichen Friedrich-Wilhelms-Universität zu Berlin von 1887 bis 1912* (Berlin, 1912); Studt to Bülow, 23 October 1901 with annual reports, DZA Po, Rkz 2193; law on the establishment of the colonial institute in Hamburg, 6 April 1908, ZStA Me, Rep 92, Schmidt-Ott, A XI, vol. 2; Diederichsen to Bethmann Hollweg, 3 June 1915 (on the Kiel institute directed by Prof. Harms) in DZA Po, Rkz 2186; Tirpitz to Bethmann, 26 March 1910, demanding the establishment of a full professorship in colonial law; Bethmann to Trott zu Solz, 14 January 1911, and Bethmann to Lamprecht, 18 January 1912, all in DZA Po, Rkz 2187. See also Jarausch, *Enigmatic Chancellor*, pp. 108-47.

lization to the Germans or to advance German culture abroad are not sufficiently supported or understood,'' Bethmann authorized the secretaries of the interior, foreign affairs, and the treasury to discuss how to advance ''cultural work abroad.'' In the 24 February 1914 session of the budget commission, Minister of Culture Trott zu Solz welcomed ''the proposal to create academic institutions that offer opportunities for the thorough study of foreign countries and encourage our students to occupy themselves with foreign organizations and work overseas more than at present.''[105]

During the last prewar years commercial and political circles were becoming aware that Germans ''more than other civilized nations are still rooted in landlocked ideas'' and began to search for ways to teach not only the rudiments of civics but also the basics of world politics. Although the idea of world political education was well received in the press, its specific form proved controversial, for it involved contradictory goals and competing institutional interests. While the director of the Seminar for Oriental Languages argued that his institute was already an Auslandshochschule and needed only ''further expansion,'' the theologian A. Harnack championed the incorporation of such training into the philosophical faculty of Berlin. In contrast, the economist Sering proposed spreading ''the advancement of general understanding of and interest in Germany's world position and its related tasks'' to every university. Similiarly, the colonial lecturer Karl Helfferich suggested using all higher educational ''institutions to give our younger generation, during their studies, the opportunity'' of acquiring foreign expertise in order to complement regular professional training. Because of ''the propagandistic nature of foreign teaching,'' Minister of Culture Trott rejected the creation of a new institution and told the Landtag that world political education would ''have to be realized in the framework of our universities, which at all times have been the foci of our national cultivation.''[106]

While the outbreak of the First World War temporarily postponed implementation, the perceived collapse of German diplomacy once again

[105] ''Denkschrift über den Ausbau des Orientalischen Seminars zu einer deutschen Auslandshochschule bzw. über den Ausbau der Auslandsstudien,'' Berlin, 1916, ZStA Me, Rep 76 Va, Sekt 1 Tit VII, No 84, vol. 1; Bethmann to the Secretaries of Interior, Foreign Affairs and Treasury, 5 August 1913; Trott zu Solz to Jagow, 27 October 1913, ZStA Me, Rep 92, Schmidt-Ott, A XI, vol. 2; Trott to the budget commission, 24 February 1917, ZStA Me, Sekt 1 Tit VII, No 84, vol. 1.

[106] H. Pohl, *Die deutsche Auslandshochschule: Eine Anregung zur Reform der diplomatischen und konsularischen Vorbildung* (Tübingen, 1913) and A. Palme, *Die deutsche Auslandshochschule und das nationen-wissenschaftliche Studium des Auslandes* (Berlin, 1914). E. Sachau, ''Seminar für orientalische Sprachen oder Auslandshochschule,'' 10 June 1913; A. Harnack memorandum, 9 September 1913; A. Sering, *Gutachten* (n.d.), all in ZStA Me, Rep 92, Schmidt-Ott, A XI, vol. 1. Trott zu Solz to the budget commission, 24 February 1914, ZStA Me, Rep 76 Va, Sekt 1 Tit VII, No 84, vol. 1 and debates in *AH*, vol. 598, 1 May 1914.

raised the issue of international studies (*Auslandsstudien*) in the summer of 1916 in the Landtag and forced the resumption of ministerial discussions. When Trott demanded 100,000 Mk for his decentralized approach, Minister of Finance August Lentze slashed personnel expenditures to one-third of the request because "a general plan has not been put forth." To save something from the red pencil, the minister of culture broadened the rationale: "The improvement of knowledge of the outside, demanded by the public, *is a task of our national education which concerns the entire academic elite*. The wartime errors of judgment make it clear that in the future every cultivated person must know something about the social-ethical development of foreign peoples." Training in practical skills had suddenly grown into a new, imperialist vision of general cultivation: "The education of such a generation is not the task of special colleges but of our broadest centers of higher learning, the universities, which train those who later occupy decisive positions in state and administration and who transmit our cultural ideals to our children." The disappointments of 1914 finally made explicit what had previously been implicit: a thoroughly politicized conception of cultivation.[107]

The novel notion of "world political training" dominated parliamentary and press discussions in the winter and spring of 1917. The brilliant *Denkschrift über die Förderung der Auslandsstudien*, written by the Prussian official Carl H. Becker, criticized the "hitherto all too one-sided literary-historical-aesthetic" cultivation of the universities and proposed redirecting attention to the challenges of the outside world:

> Political thinking must be schooled, German youth must be politicized. Not that one would want to indoctrinate it in a German party program; no, precisely through occupying it with the outside, through understanding Germany's world position and tasks, it shall be led beyond the horizon of party politics at home. Judging foreign political questions according to domestic partisan perspectives can only be overcome when a substantial political overseas education is clearly recognized and energetically pursued as a goal of our national cultural policy.

Starting from the same premise ("A world people . . . needs international

---

[107] F. Klein, "Bemerkungen über die Aufgabe der Universitäten nach dem Kriege," 28 March 1916; Antrag Hillebrand in the upper house, 5 May 1916; Trott memorandum, 24 August 1916; Lentze to Trott, 8 September 1916; Trott to Lentze, 29 November 1916; Lentze to Trott, 2 December 1916, accepting 50,000 Mk personnel costs, all in ZStA Me, Rep 76 Va, Sekt 1 Tit VII, No 84, vol. 1. For the published versions of these memoranda (and others, such as by H. Schumacher), see *Internationale Monatsschrift für Wissenschaft, Kunst und Technik* 12 (1917): entire. Previous treatments of political education have missed the crucial role of this world-political cultivation debate.

knowledge as a weapon, not only for its diplomats and traders, but as a part of its national education"), Trott zu Solz in the Prussian Landtag called for "a cultural reorientation" commensurate with "the great questions of Weltpolitik and world economy." The special aspects, such as

1. the awakening of understanding for world political activity in all circles of the population, beginning with the cultivated strata, 2. special training for imperial officials with foreign interests . . . , 3. scholarly deepening of our outside knowledge, 4. creation of a news service . . . , 5. influencing public opinion abroad . . . , 6. economic propaganda . . . , 7. cultural policy . . . expansion of overseas schools, 8. the cultivation of Germanness abroad

could best be served with a variety of measures and institutions. While Center party deputy Hess welcomed both decentralization and "what the memorandum calls the politicization of youth," the Conservative party similarly considered it "desirable to enhance the public's understanding of the outside world," and Progressive deputy Gottfried Traub celebrated the "complete education of our people" as a daring initiative. Since the National Liberals and Free Conservatives also applauded this program, only the Socialists were critical. Foreign awareness in itself was not enough unless "it leads to greater understanding between nations." By demanding a mobilization of citizens, the war forced the reluctant bureaucracy to replace the indirect instilling of patriotism through ceremonial speeches, substantive lectures, and politics courses with a direct form of "education in German national consciousness."[108]

Despite the public's enthusiasm and the Kaiser's support ("That should have been done ten years ago!"), the ideological purpose and practical effectiveness of world political education remained in doubt. The pedagogue Eduard Spranger hailed "political education in the formative sense of the word" and demanded the systematic creation of "a social conscience" and a "national consciousness" in youth. To implement his idea, Trott clustered foreign studies according to cultures and assigned responsibility for them to universities already strong in a given area. "Not foreignness as such but individual Kulturkreise shall provide measure and

[108] Foreign Office, "Denkschrift über den Ausbau des Orientalischen Seminars zu einer deutschen Auslandshochschule bzw. über den Ausbau der Auslandsstudien," 13 March 1917 session of the Reichstag; C. H. Becker, draft of 22 January 1917 and final version of 24 January, "Denkschrift über die Förderung der Auslandsstudien," for the Prussian Landtag, both in ZStA Me, Rep 76 Va, Sekt 1 Tit VII, No 84, vol. 1; speeches by Trott, Hess, Irmer, Traub, Campe, Rewoldt, and Haenisch in AH, vol. 614, 28 February to 1 March 1917. See also N. Andernach, Der Einfluss der Parteien auf das Hochschulwesen, p. 200.

direction for organizational structure."[109] Berlin therefore would be responsible for Islamic studies, while Münster could concentrate on the Christian Orient, Bonn focus on Romance countries, Kiel deal with the overseas world, Göttingen look toward Anglo-America, Greifswald work on Scandinavia, and Breslau as well as Königsberg address the Slavic East, while technical and commercial colleges were supposed to increase their general international offerings. However, small budgets for personnel (50,000 Mk) and materials (57,000 Mk) limited the effectiveness of these measures to a minority of young people. Although academics rejected the military's desire to have foreign studies "prepare the German people for a future war," the inherent contradiction between the objectivity of scholarship on non-German subjects and its nationalizing ideology was never resolved, for both goals were considered eminently compatible. Instead, heady phrases about "the dawn of a new time" created a feeling of momentous departure among politicians, professors, and officials which led to an institutional scramble for a share of the development funds. Since they could combine expansion with patriotism, "all faculties . . . with lively agreement have declared themselves ready to collaborate in the improvement of the foreign political education of our academic youth."[110] Few bothered to ask whether this abandonment of neohumanist reserve toward politics would contribute to international reconciliation or to martial imperialism.

Fearful that "the political sense is declining and many are fleeing into aestheticism or a calculating materialism," professors involved in political instruction considered it "imperative to politicize German students." When the cultivated retreated from involvement in the unification struggle into positivism, political lecturers at the universities, the civics movement, and the campaign for world-political education sought to reawaken the interest

[109] H. Groth, "Neue Bildungsideale des deutschen Volkes," *Kölnische Zeitung*, 13 February 1917; F. v. d. Leyen, "Die Erziehung zum Weltvolk," *Münchener Neueste Nachrichten*, 25 April 1917; "Die Förderung der Auslandsstudien," *Germania*, 10 February 1917; Hess, "Ein Programm," *Kölner Volkszeitung*, 23 February 1917 and numerous other articles in ZStA Me, Rep 76 Va, Sekt 1 Tit VII, No 84, vol. 1 and No 84; A. E. Spranger, "Denkschrift über die Einrichtung der Auslandsstudien an den deutschen Universitäten," 3 March 1917 with marginalia by Trott, ibid., and in No 84 C; Trott in the Landtag, *AH*, vol. 614, 28 February 1917.

[110] William II marginalia, 5 February 1917 on Valentini note of same day in response to Trott letter of 31 January 1917 (with memorandum) in ZStA Me, Rep 2.2.1, No 21406. Schulte to Trott, 26 March 1917; Trott to Lentze, 8 September 1917; Ludendorff to Chef des Nachrichtenwesens, 19 April 1918, in ZStA Me, Rep 76 Va, Sekt 1 Tit VII, No 84, vol. 1. The responses of the individual faculties are in volume 84 B of the same series. For the Bavarian measures, see P. Dirr, "Denkschrift über Förderung der Auslandsstudien an den bayerischen Hochschulen," etc. in No 84, vol. 1. Franke, "Auslandsstudien in Deutschland und der Preussische Kultusminister," *Kölnische Zeitung*, 19 February 1917. See also Bernd Zymek, *Das Ausland als Argument in der pädagogischen Reformdiskussion* (Ratingen, 1975)), pp. 113-22, for the pedagogical reaction.

of academic youth. Although the quasi-constitutionalism of the Bismarck-ian Reich required participation by responsible citizens, the content of explicit political instruction in law, history, and economics became less liberal from Holtzendorff to Bornhak, from Sybel to Schiemann, from Brentano to Bernhard. Despite their disagreements on the necessity of democratization, the continuation of social policy, and the advisability of militant imperialism, Wilhelmian professors agreed on some fundamentals that represented a remarkable academic consensus. All except Breysig extolled the power of the state, subjected the individual to its authority, and opposed further democratization of the constitution. All except Gierke saw society in a negative light as a struggle of divergent interest groups that needed to be reconciled by the government to insure its political survival, its legal order, and cultural progress. All except Foerster believed in the necessity of national power (based on monarchical control, social unity, and military force) in order to survive international competition, and justified the high adventure of Weltpolitik scientifically. Despite public concern, the effectiveness of this explicit teaching of politics hardly in-creased during the empire. Its exclusion from examinations in law or teaching and scholarly uncertainty about the subject matter, questions, and methods of Politik limited the size of student audiences, except those for dynamic lecturers like Heinrich von Treitschke. The prepolitical pater-nalism of student policy and the advice of adult academics to "study political parties, their programs, their press, their actions—not to bind yourselves to one of them before you graduate" stifled youthful enthusiasm for participatory learning. The implicit contradiction between the illiberal thrust of political instruction and the goal of awakening civic responsibility vitiated much of the propaedeutic rhetoric. Despite increasing concern with "the philistinism of our public life," foreigners as well as informed con-temporaries kept complaining about German academics' lack of political-historical cultivation: "In short, understanding for the questions and con-nections of historical development is as lacking as is a comprehensive economic-political education."[111]

ALTHOUGH containing infinite shades of opinion, the academic spectrum slowly deliberalized during the Second Empire. In order to characterize the peculiarity of German political culture, Fritz Stern has suggested the notion of "illiberalism" as a pervasive state of mind. "The political system

---

[111] Eckert, "Staatsbürgerliche Erziehung," pp. 295ff.; Anonymous, "Student und Poli-tik," *AR* 13 (1911): 81-84; F. Konen, "Student und Politik," *BBl* 23 (1909): 275-77; Stier-Somlo, *Politik*, pp. 7ff. See K. Liebknecht's complaints about "an utterly incredible naiveté about the basic clauses of our constitution" among students, *AH*, 544, 25 April 1910. See also P. v. Salvisberg, "Halbjahresbericht über das Auslandsstudienwesen auf den deutschen Hochschulen," summer 1918, IHK, CCA Scheuer.

may have formally imposed it, class antagonisms may have sharpened it, the revered army may have embodied it, the schools and universities may have taught it, but it had evolved for a long time and was part of a cultural style." No doubt "a commitment in mind and policy against any further concession to democracy," the "acceptance of a kind of civic nonage," the anxious elites' "sense of weakness," which "put a high premium on cultural pre-eminence," infected even the Socialists at home and "prescribed an aggressive stance in German policy abroad." But Peter Gay has warned that "the cherished figure of the unpolitical German is far less representative" than he is claimed to be, for "Germans were in fact strenuously political throughout the nineteenth century." Although somewhat ambiguous, the concept of illiberalism is, nevertheless, more precise than the older description of nationalism (too broad), conservatism (too narrow), authoritarianism (too psychological), or Bonapartism (too forced). The basic dictionary definition of "unworthy of a freeman" communicates the characteristic intolerance and antiliberalism of such a mentality, even if its concurrent meanings of "unschooled . . . coarse . . . vulgar" clearly do not apply to German academics of the late nineteenth century. The essential negativity of the term is its very strength, for it can include all rejections of liberalism from the volkish right through the Catholic center to the Socialist left, which were united in this one point while violently disagreeing about everything else. Moreover, such an illiberal attitude was not only confined to politics (as opposition to the liberal parties), but extended into economics (as hostility to free trade and open competition), touched on society (as disapproval of meritocracy), and pervaded even cultural life (as negation of modernism). Instead of submerging important differences of opinion or ignoring the dynamism of the reversal around 1880, with its subsequent countercurrents, the concept of illiberalism suggests a decline of academic involvement in the liberal parties and a decrease in liberality of outlook among the educated.[112]

The evidence on political instruction indicates, therefore, a gradual process of deliberalization of political culture, shifting preoccupations from the establishment of law and culture (Rechts- und Kulturstaat) to power and empire (Macht- und Weltpolitik). It would therefore be perhaps more

[112] F. Stern, "The Political Consequences of the Unpolitical German," as well as "Money, Morals and the Pillars of Society," and "Introduction" in his *The Failure of Illiberalism: Essays on the Political Culture of Modern Germany* (Chicago, 1971); and Peter Gay, "German Questions," in his *Freud, Jews and Other Germans*, pp. 3-28. See also H. A. Winkler, "Vom linken zum rechten Nationalismus: Der deutsche Liberalismus in der Krise von 1878-79," *GG* 4 (1978): 5-28; the terminological exchange between Alan Mitchell and others about "Bonapartism" in the *JMH* 49 (1977): 181-209; and for a critical and sustained reflection, Jarausch, "Illiberalism and Beyond: German History in Search of a Paradigm" (unpublished paper, Columbia, Mo., 1981).

accurate to speak of an ebbing of the liberal impulse in the 1880s, a withdrawal into the world of Wissenschaft, and a return to world political involvement in both illiberal and neoliberal ways after 1900. The apolitical stance of many academics was paradoxically political, for, though rejecting parliamentary partisanship, it supported "national" goals of completing unification at home and safeguarding the empire abroad. Similiarly, the vulgarized neo-Kantian idealism of the cultivated, which emphasized duty rather than liberty, was only partially antimodern, because there was widespread confidence in scientific and technological advance as well as satisfaction with the demonstrable spread of wealth and material progress. The self-consciousness of German professors and students at the turn of the century was therefore rather postliberal, intent on preserving such gains as academic freedom but willing to transcend liberal limitations in the march into a glorious imperialist future. Though rejecting the natural law tradition, jurists nevertheless clung to the rule of law in a positive legal order. While abandoning laissez-faire license, economists intended to complement capitalist competition with social reform. In spite of emphasizing Realpolitik and extolling the Hohenzollern dynasty, historians were not ready to abandon their idealization of German culture. The central thrust of political instruction during the empire therefore moved ideologically from liberal nationalism to nationalism, methodologically from political didactics to positivist objectivity, and substantively from social reform to imperialism, toward an increasing illiberalism modified by a renewed countercurrent of academic liberalism. While the climate of educated opinion clearly became less liberal in the last decades of the nineteenth century, the victory of illiberal mentality was never complete, for it prompted redoubled progressive efforts.

The party affiliations and public political activities of professors, which indirectly colored their teaching, reveal a similar transformation during the empire. Although unification and industrialization robbed academics of their role as primary spokesmen for middle-class interests, the stereotype of withdrawal into positive scholarship agrees neither with their self-image nor with their actions. At Bonn participation in electoral committees was heaviest in the embattled 1870s, when the Kulturkampf pitted Catholics against Protestants, but continued into the next century, even if professors lost some of their prominence in local politics. In contrast to only six identifiable faculty members campaigning for the Center party, thirty-two jurists, doctors, and historians worked for the Liberal-Conservative cartel, while one was a member of the Progressive party. Sybel could claim without fear of contradiction that the university was "a leader in our last national struggle . . . against ultramontanism," while Litzmann defended this "national" engagement as nonpartisan, since the staatserhaltende forces put "the fatherland above the party."[113] In Berlin the political coloration of the faculty was more orthodox, monarchist, and conservative, and dissenting liberals like Virchow or Mommsen increasingly found themselves in the minority compared to intellectual defenders of the throne like Treitschke and Seeberg. Formal sanctions, such as the status of professors as government officials, and informal constraints, such as the tolerated range of collegial opinions, excluded Socialists, made life difficult for democrats, and often hampered politically conscious (that is anti-Prussian) Catholics. Karl Liebknecht's recurrent complaints about the absence of Marxists among economics teachers and the causes célèbres of Arons and Michels demonstrate that Socialist convictions and a university lectern were considered incompatible. Although a few dozen intrepid "left" liberals such as J. G. Gildemeister could survive at the universities, especially when the subject matter, such as oriental studies, was removed from contemporary concerns, the stunted careers of numerous Privatdozenten like Ludwig Quidde prove that such "progressive" opinions could only be harbored in private and therefore not openly influence teaching or political activities.

Though slowly growing more diverse, the political culture of the imperial university clearly favored certain ideological commitments over others. Even if the active policy against Catholic scholars in the 1870s was eventually followed by governmental attempts to favor the minority confession in appointments in the border areas for Germanizing purposes, throughout the empire the unwritten prejudices of the majority of Prussian *Bildungsprotestanten* remained strong. Because of the continuing underrepresentation of Catholic professors, Georg von Hertling could complain: "Insurmountable obstacles, which one had to fear and face at every turn, confronted Catholic scholars in their university career."[114] The gradual ministerial cessation of anti-Jewish discrimination also fell short of numerous individual aspirations. About one dozen courageous souls among university teachers could be called pacifists; but, like the international lawyer Walther Schücking, they had to pay the price of social ostracism and professional discrimination. More typical were the 270 Flottenprofessoren (about 10 percent of all faculty members) who voluntarily and enthusiastically cam-

[113] N. Andernach, *Der Einfluss*, pp. 183f., 208-12; R. Kaiser, *Die politischen Strömungen in den Kreisen Bonn und Rheinbach 1848-1878* (Bonn, 1963); H.-J. Horn, "Die politischen Strömungen in der Stadt Bonn, in Bonn-Land und im Kreis Rheinbach von 1879-1900" (dissertation, Bonn, 1968); Litzmann, *Deutschland*, p. 345; and König, "Politische Komponenten," pp. 43-50. According to Bruch (*Wissenschaft, Politik und öffentliche Meinung*, pp. 414-23), professors did not so much withdraw from politics as concentrate on shaping public opinion through journals and the bureaucracy. Hence, he sees them as a social-conservative "governmental intelligence."

[114] McClelland, "Berlin Historians," pp. 191ff.; Ringer, *German Mandarins*, pp. 128ff.; A. Lauscher, *Die katholisch-theologische Fakultät der Rheinischen Friedrich-Wilhelms-Universität zu Bonn* (Düsseldorf, 1920), pp. 35ff.

paigned for German world power and the battle fleet around 1900, adding a note of strident imperialism to the "national" canon of cultivated politics. "During the Wilhelmian epoch, German university professors took part in daily politics in a manner which is unusual by today's standards," a young German scholar reflected after World War II. Especially lawyers, economists, historians, and theologians campaigned for "German sea power and tried to justify it in a scientifically well-nigh airtight deduction." Although most professors shunned party politics, the majority of those involved supported parties of the right and provided scholarly justification as well as practical propaganda for imperialist pressure groups like the navy and army leagues, the HKT Society, and the Alldeutsche Verband. Despite the personal, religious, and racial tolerance of F. Althoff, the structure of the academic system in the empire meant that professorial teaching by example also tended toward the right.[115]

"The greatest contribution that universities can make to public life," Friedrich Paulsen pondered in his masterly work on academe, "is that they can collectively serve as the *public conscience* of a nation regarding good and evil in domestic as well as foreign policy." This exalted view of the civic responsibility of higher education raises the question whether political cultivation at the imperial universities was adequate for the task of "representing and passing moral judgment" on public affairs. Many contemporaries, including foreigners like Matthew Arnold, were inclined to be generous: "The French university has not liberty, and the English universities have no science; the German universities have both." Other observers, like Karl Liebknecht, were not so charitable, complaining that professors provided "not objective scholarship, but science according to the will [of the elites]; Wissenschaft for their power, their purse!" Was the orthodox view that "university instructors now enjoy greater freedom than ever before" more accurate than critical strictures that ruling classes "naturally want an agrarian, bellicose, chauvinist, warmongering spirit to dominate the universities"? Strange though it may seem, both appraisals were partially correct. In comparison with times past and other centuries, German professors could, indeed, be proud that "in the actual process of instruction at the university there prevails an almost absolute liberty." On the other hand, such satisfaction largely rested on "self-deception," for the vaunted Lehr- and Lernfreiheit were circumscribed by the academics' fundamental agreement with the Bismarckian system, by a state appointment policy that weighed factors other than purely "scholarly qualifica-

[115] R. Chickering, *Imperial Germany and a World Without War*, pp. 72ff., 135ff., 176ff.; R. Marienfeld, *Wissenschaft und Schlachtflottenbau*, pp. 95-115 (42 professors in Berlin and 18 in Bonn!); and K. Liebknecht, *AH*, vol. 538, 1 May 1914. As a corrective see Brocke, "Hochschul- und Wissenschaftspolitik," pp. 80-108.

tions," and by the self-limitation of scientific "objectivity" in areas "where its subject is religious, political, or social." Paradoxically, there were infinite gradations of accepted "national" opinion, but the exclusion of the left (and of Catholics) truncated the spectrum severely and, on fundamental issues, produced "an unexpected degree of orthodoxy in academic politics." Thus, the impact of the formal curriculum on students furthered the triple division of opinion into an apolitical majority "with much patriotic enthusiasm and little knowledge," a substantial minority of imperialist "hurrah-patriots," and an even smaller group of critical citizens-to-be. Although the "first strand of 'Wissenschaft,' of the humanities, and of culture" founded the international reputation of German higher education around the turn of this century, political cultivation owed somewhat more to the second, "the 'Prussian' strand: i.e., professors as advocates of Prussian policy, interference by the state, and the Hohenzollern dynasty for purely political ends."[116]

[116] F. Paulsen, *Die deutschen Universitäten*, pp. 29ff., 329ff.; M. Arnold, *Higher Schools and Universities in Germany* (London, 1874); Liebknecht to Prussian Landtag, *AH*, vol. 538, 1 May 1914; F. Paulsen, *The German Universities*, pp. 89ff.; Schwarz, "Political Attitudes," pp. 1ff.; A. Romain, "Burschenschaft und Politik," *BBl* 23 (1909): 79ff.; and S. D. Stirk, *German Universities—Through British Eyes* (London, 1946). See also F. von der Leyen, *Deutsche Universität und deutsche Zukunft* (Jena, 1906) arguing for a new ideal: "Instead of human it is to be national education."

Five

THE HIDDEN CURRICULUM

"NEVER HAS a German Corps celebrated the beginning of a semester more solemnly and auspiciously than today in Bonn," exclaimed the Rhenania alumnus Dr. Moldenhauer, welcoming William II to his alma mater in 1891: "Your Majesty knows that the Corps seeks to educate men who shall support Your Royal Highness completely and loyally in the great and glorious work of protecting our nation externally and of bringing back internal peace." More important than formal instruction, corporate character training educated its members "in fealty to their monarch, in devotion to authority, in frank and free expression, in allegiance to the fatherland." Greeted by unending hurrahs, the Kaiser in turn praised the educational mission of student associations: "It is my firm conviction that every youth who enters a Corps receives his true direction for life through the spirit that dominates it, because it offers the best training for later manhood." As "the first Corps student in the empire," William II closed with a rousing call: "Steel your courage and self-discipline, that obedience without which our state cannot exist. I hope that in the future many officials and officers will issue from your ranks." Actives and Old Boys were elated by this imperial testimonial to the patriotic character building of the Corps. "None of us, least of all the Kaiser himself, will ever forget that inspiring moment when he turned once more at the door of the hall and the enthusiastic crowd struck up *Heil Dir im Sieger Kranz* to the martial strains of the cavalry band." Although the competing Burschenschaft found "the open partisanship of the head of the empire for a single student group somewhat distasteful," William II's gesture demonstrates the crucial significance of the hidden curriculum for the higher education of German elites. For many academics, student corporations possessed "a national importance beyond university life," because their activity emphasized the education of their members as "patriotically minded men and as well-rounded personalities."[1]

---

[1] "Hie, Kaiser Wilhelm, Hie!" *AMh* 8 (1891): 55-59; "Der SC und die deutsche Stu-

Since "voluntary associations are as characteristic for German student life as colleges are for England," their influence on academic mentality and behavior was also a constant focus of criticism.[2] "In our universities we have academic freedom without limits," Center party deputy Reichensperger complained in 1880, but "there is too little studying, too little learning." The excesses of the informal curriculum were proving detrimental to the formal. Those liberal politicians, writers, and educators who called for "a serious effort to reform student life" fastened on three major abuses. The most fundamental charge was *Verdummung*, the intellectual stultification of the student preoccupied with corporate activities: "If, in his adulthood, the Corps alumnus becomes a common philistine who lives only for his own interests and becomes a servile courtier, then it is certainly too bad that he did not at least learn something of real value," Virchow argued in the Prussian Landtag. A second basic complaint was the social exclusivity, the aristocratic caste spirit of the corporation student. "Above all he must imagine himself to be an exceptional human being and consider all [association] colors not closely related to his own inferior," a former member castigated the elitism of "the privileged of the privileged" organized in "feudal recreation clubs." The third line of criticism attacked the mindless authoritarianism of corporate organization, which, despite noble aims, fostered ritualistic apathy: "Idealism as past student generations knew it is no longer tolerated by the class state of the present; therefore, academic youth embraces a beery hurrah-patriotism, which, in hateful intolerance, beats down every dissenting opinion." Another observer commented acerbically: "These boys want to educate each other as patriotic citizens, although hardly a one has an inkling of what true patriotism means."[3] Though some criticized loafing, drinking, and duelling, many Old Boys believed: "We must accept these minor defects as the price of the advantages of freedom." More perceptive contemporaries

---

dentenschaft," *BBl* 5 (1891), no. 4; T. Ziegler, *Der deutsche Student* (Stuttgart, 1895), pp. 102-16; and R. Körner, *Das deutsche Waffenstudententum: Ein Wort an die studierende Jugend und ihre Eltern* (Leipzig, 1914). See also *Chronik der Rheinischen Friedrich-Wilhelms-Universität* 17 (1891): 81-82.

[2] F. Paulsen, *Die deutschen Universitäten* (Berlin, 1902), pp. 472ff. A corporation was "above all an excellent practice for communal life. It gives continual exercise in subordinating oneself to the whole while at the same time maintaining one's independence and prevailing against the group," thereby preparing for politics.

[3] Reichensperger to the Landtag, 13 December 1880, *AH*, vol. 286; 14 March 1882, *AH*, vol. 291; 1 February 1884, *AH*, vol. 308; and 25 February 1885, *AH*, vol. 312; Virchow, 14 March 1882, *AH*, vol. 291; Anonymous, *Couleurstudenten!?!* (Leipzig, 1890); "Die Saxo-Borussen," *Vorwärts*, 30 March 1914; K. Ludwig, "Die überlegene Kultur des deutschen Studententums," ibid., 6 July 1914; P. Freimut, *Die Bedeutung der studentischen Korporation und die wahre Aufgabe des deutschen Studenten* (Hagen, 1891). The critical literature is larger than apologetic tracts. See IHK, "Reform des Studentenlebens," F 393-422 and "Korporierte Studentenschaft," F 1540-59.

feared that student self-education trained academics "to behave as well-wound clockworks who run off correctly."[4]

This contemporary conflict of opinion about the implications of student life in the empire has largely been ignored by scholars. "These years are also somehow mentioned, but the key problems of the Wilhelmian epoch . . . are hardly addressed," wrote the Burschenschaft historian W. Klötzer, criticizing the retrospective self-approval of anniversary chronicles of local corporations: "Undoubtedly here is a gap that needs to be filled." Although more reliable, national histories of associations like the Corps also lack a critical political or social frame of reference. The only attempt at a comprehensive treatment, written by the former Freistudentenschaft leader Paul Ssymank, despite its progressive instincts and extensive documentation, provides more of a vivid narrative than a penetrating analysis of the political dynamics of student subculture.[5] The stereotype of the carousing, duel-scarred corporation member populates the pages of general works. A recent social history sums up the Anglo-American view: "Teachers at all levels and university students were strong supporters of monarchy and Empire in the years before 1914." Similarly, an East German study of Jena stresses "the national basis of student life" and "the training as subjects [Untertanen]" in contrast to national-liberal commitment in the first half of the nineteenth century. In West Germany an influential dissertation defined the "negative idol of the Wilhelmian era" as the Corps student who already in his own day "was anachronistically oriented toward the past." The prevalent cliché of the loss of political consciousness and the deflection of proscribed activism into virulent anti-Semitism reduces imperial student subculture to a prelude of the Third Reich and slights the intellectual origins of Weimar's reluctant republicans.[6] Only a few scholars have begun to

---

[4] F. Schulte's rectoral address, quoted by Reichensperger, AH, vol. 291; Gossler to Landtag, 1884f., AH, vol. 308; Reichensperger in 1885, AH, vol. 312; Wagner to Landtag in 1884, AH, vol. 308; and Anonymous, Burschen heraus! Die heutigen studentischen Korporationen und ihre Zukunft (Leipzig, 1892). See also the innumerable pamphlets under "Student und Alkohol" and "Student und Mensur" in IHK, F 2140-2366 and F 2622-96.

[5] W. Klötzer, "Zweck und Sinn studentenhistorischer Forschung," in Jahresgabe der Gesellschaft für Burschenschaftliche Geschichtsforschung (1959), pp. 5-14, BAF. See also W. Fabricius, Die deutschen Corps (Frankfurt, 1926), and G. Heer, Geschichte der deutschen Burschenschaft (Heidelberg, 1939), vol. 4. P. Ssymank, "Das deutsche Studententum von 1750 bis zur Gegenwart (1931)," in Schulze and Ssymank, Das deutsche Studententum (Munich, 1932), pp. 300-463 with completely revised chapters on the empire. J. Schwarz, "Deutsche Studenten und Politik im 19. Jahrhundert," GWU 20 (1969): 72-94 is too general. For superior examples of local associational histories, see H. Gerhardt, Hundert Jahre Bonner Corps (Bonn, 1926), and O. Oppermann, Die Burschenschaft Alemannia zu Bonn und ihre Vorläufer (Bonn, 1925), 2 vols.

[6] E. Sagarra, A Social History of Germany, 1648-1914 (New York, 1977), pp. 280-81 and G. Masur, Imperial Berlin (New York, 1970), pp. 200f. G. Steiger, Geschichte der Universität Jena 1548/58-1958 (Jena, 1958), pp. 494-97. M. Studier, "Der Corpsstudent als Idealbild der Wilhelminischen Ära: Untersuchungen zum Zeitgeist 1888 bis 1914"

follow Siegfried Kaehler's hint that student corporations "meant as much or more for the formation of the German elite in the nineteenth century as formal cultivation through academic instruction." As explanation for the flourishing of associations, the sociologist Mohammed Rassem hypothesized that the Humboldtian tradition of Lernfreiheit created "so to speak, a void in the system which needed to be filled somehow," since neohumanism simply ignored the emotional and social needs of students.[7] The obvious shortcomings of romantic celebrations or reflex condemnations suggest the need for a more thorough investigation of the inner history of academic youth. What was the social and political impact of the hidden curriculum of peer-group subculture on students in Imperial Germany?

One promising, though problematic approach to the issue of student self-cultivation is the notion of socialization. Unfortunately, the concept is often employed tautologically or in a reductionist manner, as a magic explanation of how social knowledge and cultural values are transmitted, or as a given in other theories, and thereby conceals what it purports to reveal.[8] In contrast to global sociological role studies or historical evocations of Zeitgeist,[9] socialization offers a specific focus on cognitive and noncognitive aspects of acculturation: "A broader conception would encompass all political learning, formal and informal, deliberate and unplanned, at every stage of the life cycle, including not only explicitly

---

(dissertation, Erlangen, 1965) and H. P. Bleuel and E. Klinnert, *Deutsche Studenten auf dem Weg ins Dritte Reich: Ideologien—Programme—Aktionen 1918-1935* (Gütersloh, 1967), pp. 47-48, in contrast to U. Linse, "Hochschulrevolution: Zur Ideologie und Praxis sozialistischer Studentengruppen während der deutschen Revolutionszeit 1918-19," *Archiv für Sozialgeschichte* 14 (1974): 2-114.

[7] M. Rassem, "Die problematische Stellung der Studenten im sogenannten Humboldtschen System," *Studien und Berichte der katholischen Akademie in Bayern* 44 (1968): 15-33, reviving a notion first enunciated by S. Kähler, *Wilhelm von Humboldt und der Staat*, 2nd ed. (Göttingen, 1962), pp. 228f.: "The Anglo-Saxon college system represents an attempt to integrate student social life organically into the university and to link its character-forming forces with scholarly cultivation. Humboldt, who was never really young, and was a personality determined primarily through his intellect, never felt this youthful need for society. Hence, the Humboldtian university contains a gap in this area. This void was filled by student corporations in subsequent decades." See D. Grieswelle, "Antisemitismus in deutschen Studentenverbindungen des 19. Jahrhunderts," in *Student und Hochschule im 19. Jahrhundert* (Göttingen, 1977), pp. 366-79 and H. Neuhaus, *Die Constitutionen des Corps Teutonia zu Marburg* (Marburg, 1979).

[8] P. Lundgreen considers it one of the dominant (if largely unreflected) methodological approaches to the history of education. See his "Historische Bildungsforschung," in *Historische Sozialwissenschaft* (Göttingen, 1977), pp. 96-125. Examples of slipshod usage abound. See M. Heinemann, ed., *Sozialisation und Bildungswesen in der Weimarer Republik* (Stuttgart, 1976), and O. Anweiler, *Erziehungs- und Sozialisationsprobleme in der Sowjetunion, der DDR und Polen* (Hanover, 1978), pp. 25-32, 121-22.

[9] R. H. Turner, "Role: Sociological Aspects," *IESS*, 13: 552-57; H. Schoeps, ed., *Zeitgeist im Wandel*, vol. 1, *Das Wilhelminische Zeitalter* (Stuttgart, 1967). For the equally problematic notion of "generation," see A. Spitzer, "The Historical Problem of Generations," *AHR* 78 (1973): 1353-85.

political learning but also nominally nonpolitical learning that affects political behavior, such as the learning of politically relevant social attitudes
and the acquisition of politically relevant personality characteristics.'' Eminently flexible, such a comprehensive definition needs to be narrowed in
order to grasp the formation of political attitudes among students.[10] As
primary transmission of societal norms takes place in the family, while
secondary imparting of political information occurs in elementary and high
schools, at the university public values and behavior patterns are more
likely to be reinforced and systematized into an explicit Weltanschauung
than to be totally transformed. While societal conditions (class background
and institutional structure) limit the objects of socialization, students are
at the same time self-directed subjects who choose freely among those
values made available to them. The process of socialization has a formal
component, working through the professors and the official curriculum,
as well as an informal aspect, operating through the peer group and the
''hidden curriculum'' of student subculture. The largely unconscious learning of implicit social norms through classroom behavior or student association activities complements the more conscious acquisition of information and opinion through teaching or self-study. Finally, the results of
socialization, necessarily different in every individual, nevertheless tend
to coalesce into certain group traits that determine collective behavior,
even if these remain open to choice. Thus, the concept raises some important questions about student subculture: What were the conditions of
student life affecting political learning? Which implicit and explicit processes shaped student consciousness? Which attitudes and values were cultivated in student associations?[11]

A critical but sympathetic investigation of student life requires a youth-
centered approach and comprehensive documentation. In contrast to the
direct influence of professorial instruction, the indirect impact of student
subculture is more diffuse, because of its ideological cleavages, local
variations, and rapid changes in style and content. A study of its sociopolitical characteristics must begin with the institutional framework, the
constraints of custom, and a comparison of associational goals and practices
during the 1870s. Since novel intellectual and political currents manifested

[10] F. Greenstein, ''Political Socialization,'' *IESS*, 14: 551-55 and the special issue on
socialization of the *Zeitschrift für Pädagogik*, vol. 19 (1973), especially pp. 850-55. See
also Chapter 1, note 54 and Jarausch, ''Liberal Education as Illiberal Socialization,'' pp.
610-13, 627.
[11] Greenstein, ''Socialization,'' pp. 552f.; K. Prewitt, ''Some Doubts about Political Socialization Research,'' *CER* 19 (1975): 105-14; J. Meyer, ''The Effects of Education as an
Institution,'' *American Journal of Sociology* 83 (1977): 55-77. See also R. Bendix and
G. Roth, *Scholarship and Partisanship: Essays on Max Weber* (Berkeley, 1971), pp. 109ff.;
and J. Kocka, *Sozialgeschichte: Begriff, Entwicklung, Probleme* (Göttingen, 1977).

themselves in the founding of new organizations, the investigation has to look at each major group through its own records and, from the 1880s on, through its own journals.[12] Beyond pamphlets and polemics, a statistical analysis of the relative size of different groups, a social breakdown of corporation membership, and an impressionistic tabulation of alumni careers will try to uncover some of the societal reasons for conflicting ideologies. Such a mixture of topical and chronological perspectives as well as of local and national sources might be able to resolve the contradiction between the student as "ideal of the Wilhelmian era" or as *Bürgerschreck*, as nemesis of the bourgeois. Although the forms of German student life may have been idyllic, its consequences were not. "There is no doubt that, in the end, the political ignorance and indifference of German students encouraged the government of William II in the irresponsible policies that destroyed it, deprived the Weimar Republic of support that might have saved it, and led to the naive acceptance by academic youth of totalitarianism."[13]

CORPORATE SUBCULTURE

"The most singular state of social existence to be found in the bosom of civilized Europe" was the freedom of German students, epitomized in the popular line, *Frei ist der Bursch!* In contrast to the physical and intellectual regimentation of the Gymnasium, academic youth enjoyed greater liberty in Central Europe than anywhere else in the world. Foreign visitors were amazed and domestic observers marvelled:

> This contrast [to the school] is most pronounced in the choice of subject for which a student decides; in the selection of disciplines and teachers which he hears; in the picking of a location to pursue his studies. The student is also free in the use of his time: he can work

---

[12] Despite such notable antecedents as the Zeitschrift für Deutschlands Hochschulen (1844f.) and the Deutsche Studentenzeitung (1848), permanent student journals date from the early empire, first among religious associations like Wingolf (1872ff.) and Unitas (1878ff.) and then in the 1880s by all major corporations. A 1904 survey by Krausseck estimated a circulation of around 70,000 copies altogether, divided (by 1911) into 72 organs. As the articles were often written by students or by adult Akademiker seeking to influence them, student periodicals are a more comprehensive source than corporation archives, which are preoccupied with violations of the Komment. H. Bohrmann, Strukturwandel der deutschen Studentenpresse: Studentenpolitik und Studentenzeitschriften 1848-1974 (Munich, 1975).

[13] The destruction of many student records at individual institutions like Bonn makes a combination of local case studies (Berlin and Marburg) with general Prussian (Ministry of Culture) and German (pamphlets) records imperative. Studier, "Corpsstudent," intro., and the tour de force of G. A. Craig, "Student als Bürgerschreck: German Academic Youth and Bourgeois Society, 1700-1978," John Snell Memorial Lecture, delivered at the University of North Carolina, Chapel Hill, N.C., on 22 February 1978.

or rest when he wants; he is not even forced to keep track of missed or wasted hours; he is free in the choice of his friends, free in the selection of his amusements, in short, compared to the last previous epoch of his life, he enjoys as much freedom as he could wish as a young man and as he never again encounters in later life.

Moreover, this *Lernfreiheit* in study was complemented by a surprising degree of *Lebensfreiheit* in life-style:

In all student matters that do not immediately involve the institution of higher education, the student has complete liberty; in the holding of festivities, the establishment of reading centers, the formation of corporations, the coalition of similarly structured and minded groups of different universities into cartels and associations, the student body has an entirely free hand. If someone does not want to belong to a corporation, even that is up to him; his student rights and freedoms are in no way diminished by it.

In contrast to Anglo-American collegiate paternalism, both curricular and extracurricular activities were remarkably unstructured in Germany as long as they had no political implications. But the liberal view that "a student must also, in principle, enjoy the general freedom that belongs to every citizen, every resident of the state" was "not fully agreed upon." Most professors and administrators endorsed only the intellectual liberty of "responding to reading and lectures with free criticism," not political activism. With that major exception, freshmen could look forward to an extraordinary time: "Indeed, studying is the period of the greatest and fullest freedom from external compulsion which life offers," Friedrich Paulsen enthused. "The student is utterly free to live for the task of forming himself into an independent personality." All too few youths remembered the accompanying risks: "He has the liberty to develop his character; but he has also the license to go to the dogs."[14]

Despite such theoretical unanimity, recurrent conflicts between students and authorities demonstrated that it was "actually not at all clear what academic freedom is." The public debate about "its correct meaning and true interpretation" in the Prussian Landtag from 21 to 23 February 1905 revealed two opposed conceptions, one paternalistic and the other liberal. "The notion of academic freedom is legally difficult to grasp; it is rather a historical concept, an outgrowth of tradition, which goes back to the

---

[14] W. Howitt, *Student Life in Germany* (Philadelphia, 1842); Johannes Penzler, *Der Hochschulstreit: Akademische Freiheit und Konfessionelle Verbindungen* (Leipzig, 1906), pp. 2-7; F. Paulsen, *German Universities* (New York, 1895), pp. 339ff. The literature on academic freedom is immense. See IHK, E 176-213 for some examples. See also J. M. Hart, *German Universities*, pp. 33-35, and Krause, *Burschenherrlichkeit* (Graz, 1979), pp. 56-73.

days when the center of our universities lay not in professors but in students," deputy Friedberg explained. Enraged by left-wing criticism of his mishandling of the Hochschulstreit, Friedrich Althoff argued that there were three distinct limits: "First, the limitation through the necessary correlate of freedom, self-discipline, or self-control; second, the legal provisions on student discipline," which were somewhat outdated; and third, those "corporative regulations which every member of the *civitas academica* has to impose upon himself, especially in relation to his superiors, such as administrators and professors." Though protesting his devotion to intellectual liberty, Minister of Culture Studt regretted that students had abandoned "its self-evident complement, prudent reserve." Similarly, Conservative representative Irmer supported "discipline for developing youths" because of their "lack of necessary political maturity." In contrast, liberal parliamentarians complained about the "excessive formalism" of bureaucratic practice, which smacked "of a kind of schoolboy treatment" inappropriate for German students. Following the neohumanist tradition since Schleiermacher, Progressive deputy Zwick viewed Lernfreiheit as an essential element of Bildung: "We know that this academic freedom is necessary so that our future generation, which will have to take over the direction of the state, can prepare itself in terms of scholarship and character." Going even further, his colleague Martin Peltasohn argued: "In our opinion the main issue is civil rights; academic freedom must be part of a citizen's liberty." But this was the rub. While the Ministry of Culture and the majority of "national opinion" closed its eyes on any number of social transgressions due to "youthful exuberance," political standards were much stricter. As Minister Bosse had written a decade earlier: "In my opinion it is completely incompatible with academic morality or order and the purpose of attending a university for students to engage in active and practical participation in politics and especially to agitate in political assemblies as speakers or members of the presidium."[15] In spite of rhetorical support by professors and liberals, political freedom for students remained somewhat academic.

Although students were always ready to sing: "Hurrah, hurrah, now we are free and our liberty be praised!" the practice of academic freedom

[15] Quotations from speeches by Limburg-Stirum, Althoff, Friedberg, Studt, Irmer, as well as Zwick, and Peltasohn from the 21-23 February debate of the Prussian Landtag, *AH*, vol. 474. Bosse to Steinmetz, 25 May 1894, ZStA Me, Rep 92, Althoff, AI, No 99. Daude quote from Anonymous, *Burschen Heraus! Eine Denkschrift zum Kampf um die akademische Freiheit* (Berlin, 1905). See also E. Horn, *Akademische Freiheit: Historisch-kritische Untersuchung . . .* (Berlin, 1895); Lexis to Althoff, 23 February 1905 ("the academic freedom hubub is an interesting example of an intellectual epidemic"), ZStA Me, Rep 76 Va, Sekt 1 Tit XII, No 25A, vol. 1 and ibid., Rep 92, Althoff, AI, No 15, vols. 1ff. for the context. For Schleiermacher, see also W. Hinrichs, "Geisteswissenschaftliche Sozial- und Kulturgeschichte," *IZEBF* 10 (1978): 63-102.

created innumerable problems for the university. All too often freedom *for* learning turned into freedom *from* learning. In the poetic words of Hoffmann von Fallersleben:

In all the world	It's fun to drink,
I do like best	To sing and hike.
The student's life.	It's even fun to think.
With joy it's bless't.	Joyous today, tomorrow we play,
Gaudeamus igitur	Day after once again.
Hodiem non legitur.	Always fresh, always gay:

> Juchheisa, heisa, ho, ho, ho,
> Thus lives Brother Studio.

Instead of teaching "to want to work," student life became for many an end in itself, so much so that loafing (*Bummeln*) was the vocation of more than one eternal student. When the press and the Landtag clamored too loudly about the laziness of law students, the Ministry of Culture sought to combat the abuse of *Studienfreiheit* with administrative measures. To provide orientation for incoming freshmen, Bosse suggested the establishment of "nonbinding, informative study plans" not only in law and medicine, where they were already in use, but also in theology and philology. It was less a fear of the "danger of bureaucratic interference" than the intellectual diversity of the philosophical faculty which rendered this initiative largely ineffective. Since lecture attendance could not be required, Gossler in July 1890 changed the wording of the professorial course certificate to "correct enrollment and departure" and suggested "testing industriousness and achievement" in proseminars as proof of seriousness. Because students had occasionally absented themselves for an entire semester to do their military duty, earn their keep, "pursue their pleasures, or study abroad," the ministry required the university to check on the presence of 10 percent of the student body during each semester. Such control ran counter to centuries of negligence, and students denounced this violation of their dignity as "a sign of distrust and a new attack on academic freedom." As "all proposed measures of supervision would generally remain ineffective," and faculties claimed "the university would cease to be the school of independence which it now is," Bosse eventually gave up attempts to stem the abuses of Lernfreiheit. To be a student, one had to register only for one course a semester but did not have to take it. The fear of eventual state examinations was considered enough incentive to diligence: "In the storm, the tree grows weather-hardened; in the struggle with himself and the world, a youth becomes a man."[16] Even if the "reform of academic life" was one of the favorite topics of university conversation, attempts to curb the excesses of Lebensfreiheit had equally few results. Many agreed "there has always been a great deal of drinking at German universities, but the nefariousness of alcoholism has hardly ever appeared as sharply as in our day." However, students were generally unmoved by the campaign of the Association Against the Abuse of Spirits. The Ministry of Culture primarily concentrated on the obligatory morning libation (*Frühschoppen*), which left no time for (nor interest in) lectures. But it rejected direct prohibition, and was only willing to "persuade" the offending Corps (in half the universities) "in an appropriate manner, and if necessary through suitable mediators." Time and again reformist academics challenged the custom of compulsory drinking (*Trinkzwang*) of pledges on the command of older actives, as "a self-limitation of freedom which could not be more oppressive and nefarious." But they won over only a small minority to the cause of moderation, for, as the *Vorwärts* bitingly remarked, many confused alcoholism with patriotism. "Sexual excesses of the students" were, in pretentious Wilhelmian terminology, a second "dark chapter in our cultural history." When a sensationalist piece in the *Grenzboten* charged that corporations had an "official sex evening, where it is not only permitted, but even obligatory to sin *in venere*," the problem could no longer be ignored. Although the Göttingen rector Wilamowitz considered the charge exaggerated, he acknowledged "the reputation for debauchery" of the Corps, which imitated the Officer Corps. "Without doubt frivolity and the search for pleasure have increased and appear more ugly than ever." Though willing to support such reformers as the Akademische Bund Ethos, the ministry, out of Victorian respectability, refrained from investigating the charge of a Dr. Blaschko that one-quarter of the members of the Berlin student health insurance had contracted venereal disease. Confronted with prohibition without enforcement, imperial students had no alternative but to enter a relationship (*Verhältnis*) with a shopgirl, run the health risks of using prostitutes, or sublimate their drives until a late marriage. The tightly controlled social settings (such as a chaperoned ball) which made girls of

---

[16] W. Jensinghaus, "Muluslied," and Hoffmann von Fallersleben, "Burschenlied," A. Schumacher, *Kleines Kommersbuch* (Cologne, n.d.), p. 33. Ziegler, *Der Deutsche Student* (Stuttgart, 1895), pp. 34f.; Bosse memorandum, 31 July 1892, and numerous Lehrpläne in ZStA Me, Rep 76 Va, Sekt 1 Tit VII, No 5, vols. 1-2; Gossler to rectors, 18 July 1890 and draft Althoff article for *NAZ*; Bonn student petition, 26 February 1892; Bosse decree of 21 April 1892, all in ZStA Me, Rep 92, Althoff, AI, No 84. Strassburger to Bosse, 27 March 1892 and Althoff to rectors, 16 June 1900, BUA, A16, vol. 11, and MUA 305a, Acc 1975/79, Curatorium, no. 2190. F. Paulsen, *Die deutschen Universitäten*, 373ff.

upper-class families largely inaccessible, thwarted youthful sexuality, made for an enervating tension between mind and body, and created an image of femininity, at once idealized and debased.[17]

Despite the outlawing of duelling by the Imperial Court, the ministry, headed by Old Boys of prestigious Corps, noted only the decline of real duels with satisfaction. As an alternative it welcomed the less harmful ritual duel, called *Bestimmungsmensur* (fought with protective gear until a scratch drew blood), for it allowed the controlled restoration of honor and limited possible injury. Although he disliked the "hacked-up faces of the students," F. Althoff saw "no compelling reason to begin strict supervision of student duelling through special control measures" even if a substantial chorus of international (Catholic) and domestic (left-wing) opinion considered the custom increasingly barbaric. Finally, many professors deplored "the unlimited extension of frivolous credit" to students, which "necessarily wreaked moral damage," and denounced the "excessive luxury of academic youth," which deepened "the chasm between well-to-do and poor students." Even Bosse agreed: "This phenomenon is disquieting not only for its own sake and with respect to relations within the university, but also because it is only too likely to make a lasting impression on other, less cultured groups of society." But a Bonn faculty memorandum pointed out that, according to the law of 1879, there were no legal grounds for measures against unscrupulous merchants, and the sole recourse was disciplinary action against individual students once it was too late. The ministry only sought to have the corporations discourage their members, which, given the conspicuous display of wealth by Wilhelmian nouveaux riches and court society, promised little success. Ironically, this broad conception of academic freedom, which was willing to tolerate private laziness in the name of Lernfreiheit and "drinking and whoring" in the name of Lebensfreiheit, condemned any public student involvement in politics "as criticism and subversion of existing state institutions and regulations."[18]

---

[17] C. Küster, "Zur Reform des akademischen Lebens," 2 February 1891, ZStA Me, Rep 92, Althoff, AI, No 95; Rundschreiben des Vereins gegen den Missbrauch geistiger Getränke, "An die Vorstände und Mitglieder der studentischen Vereine" (1900); ministerial "Übersicht über den Frühschoppen" (1903); Studt to Göttingen curator, replying to letter of 20 March 1902, all in ZStA Me, Rep 76 Va, Sekt 1 Tit XII, No 33; "Alkohol und Monarchenbegeisterung," *Vorwärts*, 21 July 1913. See also A. Kubatz, "Akademiker und Alkoholismus," *BuBü* 3, no. 3; T. Ziegler, *Der Kampf gegen die Unmässigkeit auf Schule und Universität* (Hildesheim, 1898), and the other voluminous literature under "Student und Alkohol," IHK, F 2622-96. Anonymous, "Zum dunklen Kapitel der Kulturgeschichte," *Grenzboten* 50 (1891): 25 June; Wilamowitz to Meier, 12 December 1891; *Satzungen des Akademischen Bund Ethos* (Berlin, 1904); "Schwarze Seiten aus dem Leben der Berliner Studentenschaft," *Reichsbote*, 9 November 1898, all in ZStA Me, Rep 76 Va, Sekt 1 Tit XII, No 31. See also Jarausch, "Students, Sex and Politics," *JCH* 17 (1982): no. 2.

[18] F. Althoff, "Das Duellwesen während des Jahres 1885," 2 December 1885 and considerable further material in ZStA Me, Rep 92, Althoff, AI, No 96; Spangenberg to Gossler,

Since after 1870 authorities contented themselves "with eliminating the pernicious excesses of corporations and with limiting the number and danger of duels as much as possible," German students were free to develop their own customs and codes. Although they were losing their distinctive estate status and academic dress, a separate "caste dialect" persisted. Influenced by medieval Latin roots, modern French imports, and by youthful deformations of adult language, a rich vocabulary defined the *Bruder Studio* in the singular or the *Kommilitonen* in the plural as superior to the *Pennäler*, still in school, the *Knoten*, already at work, or the *Philister*, graduated from the alma mater, and distinguished the corporation members from the inferior unaffiliated *Finken*, *Wilde*, or *Kamele*. Many of the special expressions described the unwritten customs (such as the *Pereat!* for a particularly disliked professor) or the written rituals (such as the drinking order of *Landesvater*) of the *Komment*, the code "legally maintaining the mores and customs in use at the university." Although originally broader, these colorful "conventions and symbols" eventually centered around the *Kneipe*, the pub, where students preferred to gather rather than in their cramped rented rooms (*Bude*), in order to eat, drink, and be merry. Elaborate rites governed the serious business of informal drinking or of celebrating a formal *Kommers*. A favorite was the *Salamander*, "a beer game in three tempi, during which the group rubs its glasses on the table, ceases on the *Senior*'s command of 'one,' empties them to the dregs at the fatal 'two,' and finally rubs them again and ceases at the order 'three.' " Although perhaps a genial antidote to the boredom of study, this alcoholic conviviality, sometimes inspiring a noble poem or a rousing song, often simply passed the time and led to intellectual stultification, called *Versumpfung*.[19]

The other focus of the Komment was the elusive estate notion of honor. "In the objective sense *Ehre* is the estimation that the individual enjoys among his peers," wrote Paulsen, seeking to grasp the code of "being an

18 March 1885; Regierungspräsident in Hanover to Gossler, 28 May 1886; Brockhoff memorandum, 19 August 1886, all in ZStA Me, Rep 76 Va, Sekt 1 Tit XII, No 32; Bosse to curators, 2 January 1891; and *Nationalzeitung Halle*, 3 August 1909 in ZStA Me, Rep 76 Va, Sekt 1 Tit XII, No 29. Bosse to Steinmetz, 25 May 1894, ZStA Me, Rep 92, Althoff, AI, No 99. See also K. Endemann, "Der deutsche Student und die sexuelle Ethik," *BuBü* 2, no. 7 and W. Fuhrmann, "Geschichte der studentischen Fechtkunst," ibid., 3, no. 8. Cf. also T. Ziegler, *Der deutsche Student*, pp. 47-101 and "Sittengeschichte der Studenten," IHK, F 2525-42 and "Student und Duell," IHK, F 2140-2366.

[19] Minister of Culture Mühler to Curator Beseler, 1 February 1870, MUA Acc 1975/79, no. 2190, specifying that only enrolled students could be corporation members, that each semester a membership roster and any change of statutes had to be communicated to the authorities, and that duels needed to be curbed. Schulze-Ssymank, *Das deutsche Studententum*, pp. 274-99, 428-51. See also C. Helfer, "Formen und Funktionen studentischen Brauchtums im 19. Jahrhundert," in Helfer-Rassem, *Student und Hochschule* (Göttingen, 1977), pp. 159-72 and "Studentensprache," and musical entries in IHK, F 2808-32, F 2892-914.

honorable Bursch,'' which seemed to forbid neither drinking, sexual promiscuity, duelling, nor making debts. Intended to refine the crudeness of earlier student behavior with an internalized code modeled on aristocratic and military conduct, academic honor meant primarily that ''the student must keep his word and show courage.'' Whether in a metaphysical sense (Fichte's ''priests of truth'') or in a more mundane meaning of not lying, honesty was generally accepted as imperative. Although ''cowardice was a devastating accusation for students,'' the definition of courage proved more problematic, for it usually did not mean an inner sense of self-worth but an externalized ''resolve to defend one's reputation, weapon in hand, if necessary.'' The shift from the physical violence of fisticuffs (*Holzkomment*) to the verbal abuse of the ''stupid boy'' (*dummer Junge*) undoubtedly represented progress of a sort. But the emergence of the Bestimmungsmensur as ''exciting sport'' cheapened the underlying concept of honor, since it was fought over trivialities as test of will and *rite de passage* into a *schlagende Verbindung* rather than for significant cause. Though honor courts (*Ehrengerichte*) tried to eliminate the worst abuses such as *pro patria Suiten* in which entire corporations duelled against each other, they could not prevent graver sabre or pistol duels. The once potent formal ostracism (*Verruf*) lost much of its meaning when applied indiscriminately to whole groups. As it often required more nerve not to fight, this ''anachronism'' tended to poison relations among students by dividing them into a *satisfaktionsfähige* elite and a dishonorable mass on the basis of their willingness to brawl and allowed many a moral weakling to brag with his unmistakable duelling scars (*Schmisse*). Even if less ''creative in the grand style'' and therefore more addicted to ''hollow form'' than their predecessors, students in the empire practiced an intricate set of verbal, alcoholic, and martial customs that filled the social gap in the neohumanist system and exerted an important influence on their shared self-consciousness as Akademiker. Tolerated by university authorities as harmless diversion, this idyllic subculture, which became increasingly irksome for the studious minority, had some typically Wilhelmian consequences: ''Admiration of wealth and luxury, stress on external appearance and conventional forms, servile and conformist fanaticism, all that now plays a role among academic youth.''[20]

The dominant form of ''voluntary educational obligation among young

[20] F. Paulsen, *Die deutschen Universitäten*, pp. 346ff.; T. Ziegler, *Der deutsche Student*, pp. 50ff., 86ff. Schulze-Ssymank, *Das deutsche Studententum*, p. 451. For literary illustrations, see also the famous *Studentenromane* by W. Bloem, *Der Krasse Fuchs* (Berlin, 1906), O. J. Bierbaum, *Stilpe* (Berlin, 1897-1904), P. Grabein, *Vivat Academia* (Berlin, 1903), and G. Samarow, *Die Saxoborussen* (Stuttgart, 1903). The view of a Heidelberg petition to the KSC ''true honor and aggressive bearing [*nassforsches Wesen*] stand in irreconcilable opposition'' was clearly a minority one. W. Fabricius, *Geschichte*, pp. 60-64.

men'' was the student association. The best known and most exclusive of the dozen or so organizations in existence in the 1870s was the Corps. "Selected friendship circles" transcending the regional Landsmannschaften, the Corps had found their identity as defenders of student tradition in their struggle with the liberal reform movements during the Vormärz and the 1848 revolution. As "a politically neutral, fraternal student association, based on a constitution . . . [and] the unconditional compulsion to duel," its principal goals were:

1. "the union of our members in sincere friendship for their entire lives";

2. "their exemplary education as honorable students without influencing their religious, scholarly or political beliefs"; and

3. their "character training as active and dutiful men."

These Corps principles aimed at the creation of a "new nobility," distinguished by "honor and friendship": "The members are to be formed into men who in every situation are capable of judging correctly what honor and propriety demand from them and always act accordingly." At the same time "the spirit of friendship shall imbue university life with a deep and serious dignity, and a lively conviviality shall contribute a beautiful color" always to be remembered. "Externally the Corps intends to protect and nurture the historical forms of student life through tight and compact organization against the dangers that arise from individualistic fragmentation and the resulting inner lawlessness." Within the student body, Corps members were to be an elite, selected according to their social standing, their willingness "to accept all duties," and the orthodoxy of their secondary education.

This character training was threefold: Though parliamentary, the Corps Convent hierarchy of officers (*Chargierte*), actives (*Corpsburschen*), pledges (*Füchse*), and guests (*Konkneipanten*) was designed "to cultivate the idea of authority." Put more bluntly: "They serve voluntarily in order to rule in the future." The *Mensur*, the ritualized and domesticated duel, was "a method of education that sharpens courage and self-control," for subjective inner self-worth forced a student "to defend his objective honor, where necessary, against attacks on his good name by risking life and limb." Every member was forced to complete at least one such trial-of-arms as *Herrenmensch* (without showing cowardice to the judges present). "All of life is a Mensur and only he who has learned to fight honorably in a student duel will also fight honorably in the duel of life." Finally, compulsive drinking (*Kneipzwang*) and demonstrative celebrations were supposed to produce "secure and polished social forms" and "a certain easy superiority" characteristic of a man born to rule. Thus, "inner worth and historical right put the Corps at the head of German students." They displayed this pre-eminence publicly at official university ceremonies and sought to maintain domination over the student body by "harshness and arrogance." Although claiming to be politically neutral and not openly proselytizing for any party, the *jeunesse dorée* of the empire made no secret of their conservative-royalist loyalties. "I Am a Prussian and You Know My Colors" was their favorite song: "Our Kaiser incorporates those ideals and attitudes that the German Corps students should cherish." Though strong youths could gain a sense of group responsibility, weak characters tended to absorb outward arrogance rather than inner tact.[21]

By establishing "the prototype of the modern duelling corporation [*Waffenverbindung*]," the Corps served as model for other student associations. "The noble spirit, the development of a painstaking concept of honor, the quick resolve to take up arms" made their members "appear as student versions of officers derived from higher circles." The Corps was the first student society to create a central national organization in 1855; the Heidelberg declaration, for instance, stipulated:

> All such associations should be recognized as Corps or their equivalent which subject themselves to the existing Komment and *Senioren Convent*, which exclude all political purposes and tendencies, which . . . cultivate student duelling, which do not accept anyone who has not been presented to and passed by the SC, and which finally have a wider association for the training of Füchse beyond the inner association and keep the pledges from participating in the decisions of the SC and the associations.

Gradually absorbing all local Corps, this Kösener S.C. Verband required "unconditional satisfaction," at least one duel, and "the obligation to fight on command [*Bestimmzettel*]" from all member organizations. Although individual chapters were proud of their autonomy, by 1884 the KSC was strong enough to launch the first major permanent student journal, called *Akademische Monatshefte*, as a "partisan organ without taking heed of parties." Gradually following South German practice, the Corps also introduced the "life principle" of continuing membership in one chapter during an entire lifetime, thereby linking active members and alumni in one common bond: "The pride and support of the German Corps are its

[21] Anonymous, "Die Bedeutung der studentischen Verbindungen in unserer Zeit," *AMh* 1 (1884-85): 259-64; "Entwurf einer Zusammenstellung der allgemeinen deutschen Corpsprinzipien," ibid., pp. 291-94, 324-27; Schulze-Ssymank, *Das deutsche Studententum*, pp. 300-301; 1910 constitution of the Marburg Corps Teutonia, in Neuhaus, *Die Konstitutionen*, pp. 24-26. H. Meyer, "An die deutschen Corpsstudenten," *AMh* 1 (1884): 1; M. Studier, "Der Corpsstudent als Idealbild der Wilhelminischen Ära," pp. 49ff.; Prof. Zorn's speech on the seventieth anniversary of the Corps Isaria, ibid. 3 (1887): 290-91. See also W. Fabricius, *Die deutschen Corps*, pp. 333ff., and the holdings of the Kösener Archiv and the entries under "Der Kösener Senioren-Convents Verband etc." in IHK, GA 47-838.

Philister, its Old Boys.'' By 1887 the Corps graduates had founded a "general association of old Corps students" as a translocal Alte Herren Verband, which through its financing of sumptuous houses and support of the journal exerted an ever greater conservative influence upon student actives.[22]

Although this example "made every society aspire to corporatism," the academic public also criticized an increasing number of Corps abuses. Professor Zorn deprecated "the overestimation of external forms." Echoing Center party strictures in the Landtag, the later Minister of Culture, Bosse, complained: "The modern students drink immensely and learn little; the elite of students, the Corps members, who especially cultivate the 'national spirit,' hardly attend any lectures; and the law students above all excel in laziness and roughness." Even the chronicler of the Corps, Wilhelm Fabricius, admitted that as "all strata of the German people were pulled along by the trend of luxury, good living, and 'ostentation,' the students did not lag behind, least of all the Corps members." While the imperial prohibition of duelling in 1883 and repeated papal encyclicals supported the public opponents of the Mensur, fencing skill degenerated into "wild brawls" as a shortcut to impressive scars. Finally, although apologists claimed a 28.85 percent increase in membership after the early 1870s, by the mid 1880s the proportion of *Corpsiers* in the student body was declining, many chapters were having difficulties surviving, and their influence on student subculture threatened to diminish. Hence, the Old Boys Zander, Hirche, and Claer, in a circular letter eventually signed by over four thousand alumni, warned: "For years Corps life has blindly steered into an abyss." Even the Iron Chancellor agreed: "I completely share the views of those gentlemen who are trying to reform corporate customs. . . . Financial debts are probably the smallest damages that a student suffers when he becomes a traveling salesman for his Corps." Hence, the reform Congress of 1881 eliminated unnecessary trips, costly duels of entire corporations against each other, and eight years later the custom of other Corps checking the validity of duels was dropped, since disagreement about the courage of the combatants led to much unnecessary fighting. Thereafter Corps students were as proud of their exalted position in society as their Alte Herren were of their esprit de corps. "If higher

---

[22] Schulze-Ssymank, *Das deutsche Studententum*, pp. 327-28; Fabricius, *Geschichte und Chronik des Kösener S.-C. Verbandes* (Marburg, 1907), pp. 13ff.; "Das litterarische Glaubensbekenntnis der Akademischen Monatshefte," *AMh* 1 (1884): 2-3; "Die Lebenscorps im Kösener S.C. Verband," ibid. 4 (1885), no. 2; "Die Idee eines 'allgemeinen Verbandes alter Corpsstudenten,' " ibid. no. 8; and "Satzungen des Verbandes alter Corpsstudenten zu Kösen," (1897) in ZStA Me, Rep 77, Tit 46, No 46, vol. 1. For further details, see also HUA, 542, 576, and 577 and the journal *Einst und Jetzt* (Würzburg, 1956), completely devoted to the history of the Corps.

authorities prefer Corps students among equally qualified applicants, they do so because they know that aside from their professional competence, they offer something else, which is chiefly taught in the Corps: character and courage, which one cannot acquire in lecture halls." Although Prussian Minister of Culture Gossler in 1884 called the Corps student "the ideal of a true German" and Minister of Interior Hans von Hammerstein in 1903 defended bureaucratic preferment, critics like the liberal burgomaster Schücking denounced "political castration by Corps patronage." Stefan Zweig put it even more bluntly: "This delight in both aggressiveness and horde servility revealed the worst and most dangerous qualities of the German spirit."[23]

More representative of the national and liberal thrust of the Bildungsbürgertum was the Burschenschaft, rivaling the Corps for the leadership of the student body. As "the most sacred legacy of the spirit of the Wars of Liberation" against Napoleon, this erstwhile protest movement had sought to purge student life of corporate anachronisms and to unify the fatherland constitutionally. But the failure of university reform and liberal unification threw the Burschenschaft into a fundamental confusion over its ideological aims and organizational structure. Progressive coalitions such as the North German Cartel of 1861 worked for "political unification on a democratic basis" and for "a democratic reform of the universities." More traditionalist corporate groupings, such as the Eisenach Convention of 1870, strove for "patriotism [prohibiting practical political activity], morality and scholarship" as well as "unconditional satisfaction." Only the 1885 statutes resolved the programmatic issues by defining the Burschenschaft as

> a corporation of like-minded, independent, and honorable German students, who have the sincere wish to spend their student days in true community and thorough pursuit of their motto: "Honor, Freedom, Fatherland!" It considers its task to educate its members as capable, free, and independently thinking and acting citizens of a unified, internally strong, and externally powerful German fatherland.

While the reference to honor indicated that the Burschenschaft also

---

[23] W. Pfitzner, "Die Corps auf den deutschen Hochschulen," *AMh* 11 (1894), no. 2; Zorn speech, note 21; "Der 'Fall Bosse,' " *AMh* 4 (1885): 192-95; Fabricius, *Geschichte*, pp. 40ff.; Ziegler, *Die deutschen Studenten*, pp. 87-101; W. Fabricius, "Die Corpsstatistik in der Presse," *AMh* 4 (1885): 324-27; Zander to Bismarck, 16 April 1881, DZA Po, Rkz 2195; Bismarck to Zander, 24 April 1881, ZStA Me, Rep 92, Althoff, AI, No 99; "Die juristischen Prüfungen und die Corpsstudenten," *AMh* 11 (1894), no. 6; Gossler on 1 February 1884, *AH*, vol. 308; Hammerstein, Traeger, Zedlitz in the Landtag, 22 January 1903, *AH*, vol. 459; Schücking, *Die Reaktion in der inneren Verwaltung Preussens*, 2nd ed. (Berlin, 1908); and S. Zweig, *Welt von Gestern* (Frankfurt, 1947).

understood itself as an elite within the student body, the double mention of force reveals the ideological shift from liberalism to nationalism. A tight corporation, it stressed a dual approach to character formation: "In regard to inner cultivation the Burschenschaft demands from it members an honorable and moral life-style, the nurturing of love for the fatherland, the upholding of the ideal of freedom, and the practice of scholarship." The accompanying instructions indicate that this meant duelling, patriotism, and academic progress, while formerly political "liberty" was narrowed to "spiritual and academic freedom." "In regard to external education the Burschenschaft demands the exercise of physical strength, maintenance of social propriety, and smart appearance." While it recognized "the equality of all honorable students" and promised to work for common concerns, it was no longer a broad reform movement, but rather a leading corporation which tried to live down its former reputation for subversiveness. Hence, the ideological thrust of patriotic training in the discussion evenings (*Kränzchen*) was explicitly German nationalist: "The cultivation of the national idea in a measured and not one-sided way shall be one of its chief tasks and its motto shall be: 'For Kaiser and Reich!' "[24]

As "schools of the national will and spirit of youth and as nurseries of character, attitude, and Weltanschauung," the Burschenschaften experienced a profound crisis during the first two decades of the Second Empire. Ideological cleavages between progressive and conservative camps over politics and the Mensur and petty organizational rivalries threatened the unity of the Eisenacher Deputierten Convent (1874), which never included more than a minority of local Burschenschaften. The competition of other associations finally forced forty-two of the warring chapters to unite in the Allgemeiner Deputierten Convent of 1881 on the lowest common denominator of "mutual respect and recognition of equality" and "unconditional satisfaction" without specifying any goals: "All other principles are the private concern of every specific Burschenschaft and the association must keep from meddling in them as well as in their constitutions." On the

---

[24] E. Voigt, 14 January 1888, quoted in "Deutsch-National," by C. Lent, *BBl* 4 (1889-90): 129-31; citations from G. Heer, *Die Burschenschaft*, 4: 16-38; *Entwurf der revidierten ADC Statuten* (Berlin, 1885), in BAF, D 20; "An unsere Leser," *BBl* 1 (1886-87): 2ff; "Die studentische Verbindung—Ein Erziehungsmittel," ibid. 1: 50ff. Although the lead poem of the *Burschenschaftliche Blätter* mentioned "liberty, its highest glory," the last strophe emphasized:

> Frisch auf, du deutsche Burschenschaft,
> An's alte Werk mit jungem Mut,
> Alldeutschlands Einigkeit und Kraft,
> Ihr weihe freudig Gut und Blut. . . .

See also Anonymous, *Burschen heraus!* pp. 7-31 ("The young people are even further to the right than the older, generally national-liberal generation."); and "Urburschenschaft, Deutsche Burschenschaft, Vereinigung alter Burschenschafter etc.," in IHK, GB 1-882.

basis of this refound national unity, the most sophisticated German student journal, the *Burschenschaftliche Blätter*, was launched in 1886-87. It aimed at "championing the cause of the Burschenschaft, as well as strengthening connections among active and former members, the Alte Herren, dispersed all over Germany." In 1891, Theobald Fischer succeeded in creating a Vereinigung alter Burschenschafter in order to "propagate and strengthen the Burschenschaft spirit among the Old Boys, cultivate relations with the young actives, and support their attempts to make our academic youth into capable men with character, for whom the love of the fatherland, of Kaiser and Reich always remains the goal. Partisanship and politics is strictly excluded from the VaB." In contrast to the apolitical Corps, the political involvement of the Burschenschaft delayed its organizational development and acceptance by imperial elites.[25]

In the Burschenschaft the corporate abuses of the Bismarckian era were compounded by an initial loss of ideological purpose. "To many it appeared that its continuation after the achievement of the great goal [of unification] made no sense," Georg Heer reminisced. "The Burschenschaft idea became hollow," for democratization of the empire was taboo for a corporation striving for respectability. "The completion of inner unification" against Catholic or Socialist subversion was much less inspiring than external unity. During the 1870s, therefore, duelling won out among its former critics: "First of all, the *Schlägermensur* is the most traditional means for settling student disputes and until today nothing better has been found." The ADC statutes justified this turn around: "Secondly it serves to keep unsuitable elements out of the Burschenschaft," underscoring an increasing elitism, for what was "undesirable" was less a matter of individual courage than of background and breeding. Finally, with the 1882 resolution that "the ADC in principle renounces any active participation in political questions," the Burschenschaft became depoliticized. Although the journal stressed time and again that "the national ideal shall be kept up and implemented everywhere," such "citizenship training" lacked conviction. In the summer of 1883 Old Boy Konrad Küster called publicly for "the elimination of the abuses that have cropped up in the course of time and the bad habits that have been adopted from the Corps and a return to the dignity of a true Burschenschafter." This ringing denunciation of

---

[25] E. Voigt, "Die akademische Jugend als vorbürgerliche Gesellschaft," *BBl* 4 (1889-90): 239-43, 303-306; Heer, *Burschenschaft*, 4: 38ff., 44-56; *Statuten des allgemeinen Deputierten Convents* (Jena, 1882) with handwritten additions, in BAF, D 20; "An unsere Leser," *BBl* 1 (1886-87): 2f. and "An unsere Leser," ibid. 4 (1889-90): 177-80; T. Fischer, "Die Vereinigung alter Burschenschafter," ibid. 5 (1890-91), no. 1 and *Verfassung des Verbandes der Deutschen Burschenschafter* (Berlin, 1894) in BAF, D 20. See also "Gesamtprotokoll über die elfte Versammlung des ADC der deutschen Burschenschaften in Eisenach, 1892," BAF, D 19a, und HUA, 546, 582, 654, and 766.

"the deplorable custom of duelling," coupled with a passionate appeal for "the cultivation of national spirit," fell on deaf ears, and thirty-two Burschenschaften forced the reformers to resign from the ADC. The constitution of the small number of *Reformburschenschaften* reveals that in their general aims the Küster purists hearkened back to the earlier, unadulterated tradition. In specific practical issues they rejected the Bestimmungsmensur (only insisting on personal satisfaction) as well as "the compulsion to immoderate drinking" and "frivolous debts." During the early decades of the empire, the Burschenschaft jettisoned the reformist and progressive aspects of its heritage and gradually became, as its enemies maintained, a "second-class Corps." Despite some lingering liberal impulses and an assertive nationalism, it made its peace with the Iron Chancellor after his resignation. Although Bismarck pointed out that he had sought to "unify the German fatherland" with different means, the Burschenschaft, and with it the educated middle class, was all too ready to heed his warning: "In this hour I want to admonish you to hold fast to what we have and to what exists—before anything better has taken its place."[26]

Deriving in spirit from the medieval *nationes*, the Landsmannschaften had even greater difficulties in establishing themselves as duelling corporations despite their long tradition. An Allgemeiner Landsmannschaftsverband was founded in 1868 by five chapters; it dispersed again in 1877, resurfaced in 1882, and went briefly under in 1897 before being reinstituted in 1898. Although "it differs from the Burschenschaft by rejecting the political principle and from the Corps by recognizing all honorable students and associations" as equals, the lack of distinctive goals evident in the motto "Honor, Friendship, Fatherland" led to repeated defections from its ranks. Stressing "as much individual freedom as possible for an honorable corporation," the Landsmannschaft demanded "unconditional satisfaction" of any insult or challenge while not prescribing any standards of moral conduct. The ideology of regionality and conviviality was to be imparted through the usual corporation methods of organization, drinking, and duelling, and in due course a rather colorless journal and an Old Boy association made their appearance. While they participated in the general

26 G. Heer, *Burschenschaft*, 4: 28ff.; *Entwurf der revidierten ADC Statuten* (Berlin, 1885), part 3 in BAF, D 20; "Gesamtprotokoll über die erste Versammlung des ADC der deutschen Burschenschaften in Eisenach vom 31. V. bis 3. VI. 1882," in BAF, D 19a; Küster speech *Jahrbuch des ADB*, 1906, pp. 6-19; *Jahresberichte des ADB* (1885-90) and *Satzungen der Burschenschaft Arminia zu Giessen* (Giessen, 1885) in BAF; "Gesamtprotokoll über die dritte Versammlung des ADC der deutschen Burschenschaften in Eisenach, 1884"; H. G. Schneider, "Der siebzigjährige Verruf zwischen Korps und Burschenschaft," *BBl* 1 (1886-87), no. 14; Puppe, "Die Adresse der Deutschen Burschenschaft an den Fürsten Bismarck," *BBl* 4 (1889-90): 33-36; Schulze-Ssymank, *Das deutsche Studententum*, pp. 356-58; and HUA, 661 and 768.

excesses of well-to-do Wilhelmian students, the Landsmannschaften struggled against a lack of profile, for they were less exclusive than the Corps and less political than the Burschenschaft. Hence, in the widespread corporatization process, they represented an intermediate stage which could be reached by a group aspiring to duelling corporation status, while some of the older chapters tried to rise into the SC or DC above it.[27]

A similar lack of ideology characterized the initial phase of the Turnerschaft, the last major schlagende Verbindung, which grew out of gymnastic clubs. In the early 1880s they split in half when the majority followed the example of Leipzig and adopted colors, duels, and full corporation paraphernalia, while the Berlin minority, which insisted on open association for any student interested in athletics, left. In 1885 the VC emerged as a duelling corporation with the inspiring motto: *Mens sana in corpore sano.* Only a faint echo of the strident nationalism of Father Jahn animated the strange combination of "the historically proven imperative of physical exercise" with the ritual of the Bestimmungsmensur. Time and again the "curious magnetic power of the Corps" transformed regional social clubs and gymnastic societies into full-fledged schlagende Verbindungen. While the Landsmannschaft practiced political restraint, but encouraged patriotism, the Turnerschaft attempted to live up to Bismarck's words: "It was no mere rhetoric when I recently said in the Reichstag that my hope rests on academic youth. . . . Cherish the national idea, without falling prey to partisanship!"[28]

The influence of the "time-honored forms of student life" was so strong that it produced a number of color-carrying (*farbentragende*) corporations that refused to duel, although their officers sported costumes and swords (*Wichs* and *Schläger*) at festive occasions.[29] Typical of this second important group of student societies was the Wingolfsbund, which, following the conservative strain of the Burschenschaft, set out "to infuse the old

[27] Gantter to Markomannia, 1 February 1870 and "Protokoll des I.L.C.-Tages, 1 March 1868," in P. Dietrich, "Die Deutsche Landsmannschaft," *Historia Academica* 3/4 (1958): 7-151. See also Max Lindemann, ed., *Handbuch der Deutschen Landmannschaft* (Hamburg, 1931), 11th ed., pp. 23-36 and idem, "Die Deutsche Landsmannschaft," in P. Grabein, ed., *Vivat Academia: 600 Jahre deutsches Hochschulleben* (Essen, 1932?), pp. 119-22. See also "Die deutsche Landsmannschaft (D.L.)," IHK, GC 1-69 and HUA, 583, 771.

[28] N. Boeder, "Der V.C. Verband der Turnerschaften auf deutschen Hochschulen," in *VA*, pp. 123-27; Vollert, "Rede gehalten am Festcommers des II. Cartellfestes zu Mühlhausen," *ATZ* 1 (1884): 5-11; "Protokoll des ordentlichen Cartelltages am 1. und 3. Juni 1884 zu Mühlhausen in Thüringen," ibid., pp. 11ff. Anonymous, *Burschen Heraus!* pp. 7ff., and Spies, "Zur Bismarckfeier," *ATZ* 1 (1884): 251-56. Schulze-Ssymank, *Das deutsche Studententum*, pp. 328f., 365f. See also "Der Vertreter Convent (V.C.)," IHK, GC 70-212 and HUA, 765.

[29] This typology seems more serviceable than P. Seiffert's distinction based exclusively on the Mensur, for it comes closer to the inner spirit of the student societies involved. *Geschichte und Entwicklung der studentischen Verbände* (Breslau, 1913), pp. 15f. is otherwise the best handbook of organizations in Imperial Germany.

student traditions with Christian spirit.'' Rejecting ''duelling, lack of moderation [in drink], and moral excesses'' such as premarital sex, the Wingolf nevertheless cultivated the positive sides of corporate life by providing ''a home, a place for exchanging thoughts, for sampling the joys of colorful academic heritage in the golden glow of youth.'' Because of the ''contempt of other students,'' Wingolfites were forced to pioneer many organizational forms, such as a national association (1852), a student journal called *Wingolfsblätter* (1872), and alumni meetings (in the 1850s). Requiring ''positive Christianity'' from its members, the Wingolf nevertheless tried to remain interconfessional (accepting Catholic students as well) and dogmatically neutral, although two-thirds of its membership was Protestant and theological. During the heyday of David F. Strauss's skepticism (in the 1870s) and Ernst Haeckel's monism (in the 1900s) the corporation was torn by fundamental debates on the ''question of belief in Jesus as son of God or God himself.'' Ultimately the irenic influence of the Old Boys prevailed, and ''all existing principles of the member chapters are recognized as justified,'' but the federation retained the right ''to judge the Christian life of a corporation.'' In the mid-1880s the axiom that ''the Wingolfs as such cannot engage in active politics'' similarly failed to resolve the conflict between implicit monarchical loyalty or explicit German nationalism. After some debate, it was agreed that ''the Christian spirit permeates all spheres of life [and] shall especially express itself in the cultivation of true German discipline and custom.'' Christian duty was redefined to imply ''the obligation of educating members as earnest, true, and honest servants of the fatherland.'' Its official condemnation of the duel created a further problem, for it meant that ''Wingolfites as such are excluded from becoming reserve officers'' and were thereby prevented from joining the imperial elite. Religious traditionalists decried the Mensur as ''merely a social imperative'' that was ''incompatible with Christian principles,'' while more modern members argued that it was neither sinful nor illegal and the federation ought to let each individual decide. In order not ''to exclude Wingolfites from 'society' and not to violate patriotic duty,'' the Wingolfsbund did tolerate duelling in exceptional cases after 1895, while not recanting its religious principles.[30] A similar color-carrying nonduelling corporation was the smaller Schwarzburgbund (ca. 1887). It

[30] G. Bartels, ''Wo stehen wir und wohin treiben wir?'' *WBl* 35 (1906): 61-64; Anonymous, *Burschen heraus!* pp. 49f.; H. Waitz, *Geschichte des Wingolfbundes* (Darmstadt, 1896), pp. 203ff.; Steinhausen, ''Wartburgfest 1880: Eine Historiographie,'' *WBl* 9 (1880): 37-40; A. Hollenberg, ''Ist die christliche Studentenverbindung Wingolf eine deutsche Studentenverbindung?'' ibid. 14 (1885), no. 4 and ditto by H. Schadla, no. 5; G. Meinhof, ''Der Wingolf und das Officierduell,'' and W. Weber, ''Princip oder Duell?'' ibid. 13 (1884): 29-32. For the further ideological evolution, see also Broisted, ''Bericht über den Chargierten-Convent zu Giessen am 17. Januar 1903,'' ibid. 32 (1903): 81-84; H. Witte, ''Denken ist leicht,'' ibid. 36 (1907): 191-93; and Prof. Waltemath, ''Neue Zeiten—Neue Aufgaben,'' ibid. 37 (1908): 89-90.

also claimed the Christian tradition of the Burschenschaft by "cultivating conviviality according to the principles of Christian morality," but it required less positive faith. These two corporations sought to combine "dashing student life" with the "quiet influence of a Christian spirit" in order to create men who would "represent religious principles in public."[31]

A Catholic counterpart to the Wingolf were the numerous corporations of the Cartell-Verband, which also carried colors without duelling and pursued religious principles. In a programmatic speech in 1863, Georg von Hertling urged Catholic youth "to develop manly character . . . according to religious-ethical principles" and to "participate in the great religious-scientific struggle of our times." Spreading quickly, Catholic student societies resolved two years later: "It is desirable for corporations and associations to separate from each other so that they can better achieve their goals." Following the motto "Religion, Scholarship, Friendship," the more elitist CV, founded in 1867, aimed at "lifting and strengthening Catholic spirit and ethical conviction . . . propagating scholarly studies" and "forming close friendships for a lifetime" in order to reinforce Catholic consciousness in a hostile Protestant or secular academic environment. Using the "beautiful, romantic, and aristocratic" forms of corporate life, the CV considered the Verbindung an effective instrument of "our religious and moral leadership" but unequivocally rejected duelling and "political tendencies." Nevertheless, the predominantly evangelical faculty at Marburg predicted "confessional struggles" which might "endanger academic discipline," set a bad example for other dangerous societies, and propagate "subversive tendencies hitherto unknown on our campus." Although using traditional corporate methods of self-education, the commitment to "faith in the dear Holy Church, loyalty to our home, and fidelity to friends" was something new. It involved not only discussion evenings but prominent participation in the mass, in holiday processions, in German *Katholikentage*, and membership in several charitable organizations like the Bonifatiusverein.[32]

[31] A. Winkler, "Der Wingolfsbund," and Prof. Gries, "Der Schwarzburgbund," in *VA*, pp. 149-54; and P. Seifert, *Studentische Verbände*, pp. 69-73, 108. F. Ulmer, *Der Schwarzburgbund und seine Verbindungen* (Rothenburg, 1912); *Verfassung des Schwarzburgbundes* (Diesdorf, n.d.); W. Kohl, ed., *Der Schwarzburgbund, sein Wollen und Wirken* (Leipzig, 1914), all in BA, ZSp 130, SB 255, 256, and 270, and correspondence as well as the protocol book of the central Verband in BA R 130, nos. 1 and 487. The last Protestant but more loosely organized (Verein) student association was the Methodist-inspired and YMCA-supported DCSV (1897). See A. Winkler, "Die Stellungnahme des Wingolfs zur DCSV," *WBl* 38 (1909): 21-33 and HUA, 772

[32] Schulze-Ssymank, *Das deutsche Studententum*, pp. 307-12, 332-34, 359-61; P. Werr, *Zur Geschichte des CV*, 2nd ed. (Berlin, 1900); Jean von Trostoff to v. Bar, 22 October 1881 with "Statuten der katholischen Studentenverbindung Rhenania" and lengthy marginal comments of the members of the Marburg University deputation in MUA, Acc 1954/16, no. 59; G. Schreiber, "Die katholischen Studentencorporationen," *WBl* 20 (1890-91): 1-2, 9-

"The task of transforming young students into loyal Catholics and at the same time into capable members of human society" nevertheless created a number of difficult problems because of the Church's doctrinal control and minority status within university and society. While the new dogmas of the Vaticanum of 1870 shook the faith of many academics, Bismarck's Kulturkampf against "the mortal enemies of German national spirit and Protestant freedom" endangered the very existence of local corporations, such as the Alsatia at Münster, which was dissolved for political reasons in 1878. Although "common defense against the outside" actually increased the number of chapters during the church struggle, the "open confession of its principles, especially of Catholicity," involved the CV in fundamental contradictions between ultramontane (Roman) allegiance and nationalistic "love of the fatherland, self-evident for Catholic students." Though continual papal support made student corporations more popular in the Catholic population, Leo XIII's letter to the German-speaking bishops in 1891 forbidding the Bestimmungsmensur as "an ugly remnant of a rough age and a strange barbarism" heightened the dislike of other student associations for the CV and led to repeated skirmishes. When the Catholic societies in Bonn refused to join in a Kaiserkommers because Bismarck was also to be toasted, the Protestant rector Camphausen dressed them down: "Your very existence is provocative. I don't understand how there can be Catholic corporations which also accept law and medicine students, who are supposed to be interested in their subjects; there are no Protestant associations either. In the interest of confessional peace I advise you to dissolve your group." The impassioned plea of Old Boy Center party deputy Felix Porsch in the Landtag that "we consider the existence of Catholic corporations not only legal but necessary!" prompted Minister of Culture Bosse to stress, "there is no doubt about their legal right of existence." But the liberals and the majority of adult academics continued to denounce ultramontane partisanship as incompatible with German nationalism. "Catholic students are to be trained as capable men who can take up the spear when our hands tire and continue the struggle for parity," the great parliamentarian Windthorst proclaimed: "I therefore make you members of the Center party faction *in petto*." Thus, equations of Catholicism with scholarship and political abstinence were less than convincing: The "sons of 'good Catholic' burghers such as lawyers, teachers, etc. are thereby to be saved from being led away from their prior training and parental beliefs by academic freedom, personal independence or the influence of professors or accidental acquaintances. Supported by the Church

11. See Dr. Grünewald, "Die katholischen Studentenverbindungen," *VA*, pp. 155-57; P. Seiffert, *Studentische Verbände*, pp. 73-76, and HUA, 794.

and recommended by priests, these corporations are designed to make students advocates or champions of Center party politics in later life."[33]

The last major category of student societies was the loose and flexible association, which was often directed to a specific purpose and varied in degree of organization from intercorporative club to quasi-corporation. Among the largest and most cohesive were the Catholic *Studentenvereine*, which organized their own Kartell-Verband in 1866 in order to "bring the life and convictions of individuals closer to the Catholic Church." Their motto of "Religion, Scholarship and Sociability" reveals that they differed little from the CV and were intent on "representing the cause of Catholicism among German students" while claiming political neutrality. Due to "the predominant materialism of modern scholarship, Catholic associations face the task of giving the Christian Weltanschauung of their members, through lectures and journals, that scholarly foundation and form that both satisfies the intellect and ennobles the soul, that safeguards against the temptations of scholarly philosophical atheism." Initially, openness to members of other groups, lack of colors, and "unpretentious, cozy, and simple" conviviality were the primary differences from the CV. But toward the end of the century the KV also "turned more and more into a student corporation" with pledges, Komment, flags, formal garb, and rapier for the Chargierte. Though less socially ambitious, the associations nevertheless experienced the same kind of enmity which, as often as not, "inspired young Catholic Germany with an energetic defiance." The profession that "we have but one policy and that is love of our closer or wider fatherland and of our Holy Church" invited the charge of "lack of national feeling," and the prohibition of duelling led to discrimination against Catholic reserve officers. Finally, "the rising opposition of the Catholic population against the ever greater arrogance of unbelief and liberalism" prompted the accusation that the KV "propagates politics, to be exact, Center party politics." Even apologists, while denying any "political tendency," had to admit "a political disposition" among their members. Hence, "protection against the withering rays of academic irreligiousness and defense against

---

[33] Neuefeind speech at "Die Cartell-Versammlung in Danzig," *Ac* 4 (1891–92): 122-24; Schreiber, "katholische Studentencorporationen," 10f.; "Satzungen und Geschäftsordnung des Cartellverbandes der katholischen deutschen Studentenverbindungen," in Werr, *Geschichte*, pp. 18-31, 65; "Das päpstliche Schreiben über den Zweikampf an die deutschen und österreichischen Bischöfe," *Ac* 4 (1891-92): 156-58; "Die Existenzberechtigung der katholischen Studenten-Corporationen," verbatim excerpt of the Landtag debates, ibid. 6 (1893-94): 345-63; Windthorst quote from Schreiber, "katholische Studentenkorporationen," pp. 10f.; Anonymous, *Burschen heraus!* pp. 49ff. See also "Unsere Aufgabe," *Ac* 5 (1892-93): 51-53; "Die Verhandlungen der 39. Generalversammlung in Mainz über die Hochschulen," ibid. 6 (1893-94): 290-93; "Das Schlägertragen im CV," ibid. 7 (1894-95), no. 5; and Gandtner to Althoff, 18 February 1893, ZStA Me, Rep 76 Va, Sekt 3 Tit XII, No 3, vol. 14.

the confusing sensuality of a bellicose and often unethical student life"
became the professed aim of the associations, but the practice was closer
to the frivolity of other groups.[34] The smaller, theological Unitas Society,
founded in 1853 and opened to others in 1887, similarly sought to advance
"morality, scholarship, and friendship." Despite recurrent conflicts, Catholic corporations and associations generally cooperated, for they all believed: "In this decisive stage of life when the entire burden of self-
determination passes onto the young man, he cannot be completely left to
himself."[35]

Even more informal were the *wissenschaftliche Vereine*, which aimed
at "scholarly discussions" in their respective fields and at providing a
modicum of "conviviality" for their members. Arising out of study or
reading groups in the 1850s and 1860s, these scholarly societies banded
together in national associations like the Arnstädter Verband Mathematischer und Naturwissenschaftlicher Vereine (1868), the Eisenacher Kartell
Akademisch-Theologischer Vereine (1874), the Weimarer Cartell-Verband
Philologischer Verbindungen (modern languages, 1879), the Naumburger
Kartell-Verband Klassisch-Philologischer Vereine (1884), the Leuchtenberg-Bund Historischer Vereine (1887), the Verband Theologischer Studentenvereine (Protestant orthodox, 1891), and the Goslarer Verband Naturwissenschaftlicher und Medizinischer Vereine (1898). They saw their
task as "providing a forum for the scholarly endeavors of their members,
furthering the exchange of opinions among them, and giving them the
opportunity of testing and defending their scientific views in open and
informed discussion." Thus, these originally intercorporative associations
excluded not only politics and religion but also scientific dogmatism and
pursued their goals through lectures and presentations and through special
libraries making new publications and important journals available. Because of their initial informality, they were looked down upon by the older
corporations and sometimes criticized by professors because they perpetuated the "narrowness of their subject" (*Fachidiotentum*). Under such

[34] H. Cardauns, *Fünfzig Jahre Kartellverband, 1863-1913: Festschrift zum goldenen Ju-
biläum des Verbandes der katholischen Studentenvereine Deutschlands* (Kempten, 1913),
especially pp. 46ff., 200ff.; "Unsere Stellung zu den katholischen Studentenverbindungen,"
AMbl 1 (1888): 54; J. Burger, "Bedeutung und Berechtigung der katholischen Studentenvereine," ibid. 2 (1889-90): 59-62; Michel, "Alamannia auf dem Württemberger Katholikentag zu Ulm," ibid. 3 (1890-91), no. 3; "Das päpstliche Schreiben über den Zweikampf
an die deutschen und österreichischen Bischöfe," ibid. 4 (1891-92): 17-20; and "Duell-
Prinzip und Reserve-Offiziere," ibid. 13 (1900-1901): 105f.; J. Schöne, "Unser Verband,
unser Verein," ibid. 4 (1891-92): 3-5, and F. J. Ortmann, "Die politische Stellung der
katholischen Studentenkorporationen," ibid., 15 (1902-03): 4-7.

[35] Seiffert, *Studentische Verbände*, pp. 76-84; A. M. Weiss, "Vom Studentenleben an
den deutschen Universitäten," *AMbl* 8 (1895-96): 91-98; Grünwald, "Katholische Studentenkorporationen," pp. 155ff.; and Schulze-Ssymank, *Das deutsche Studententum*, pp.
307-12, 332-34, 359-61.

pressures many local societies and entire national associations gradually adopted corporate forms, with some, like the Eisenacher Kartell, introducing the pledge system and the Komment but remaining as Vereine; others, like the Weimarer Cartell-Verband, became a scholarly Verbindung with colors! The Kösener Delegierten Convent of the pharmacists (who were excluded from the traditional corporations for lacking the Abitur) went even further and merged into the Turnerschaft or Landsmannschaft, thereby dissolving the entire Verband. More than others, the scholarly associations depended upon enrollments in the philosophical faculty, which was booming in the 1880s; they lost almost half of their chapters in the recession of the 1890s but recovered somewhat after the turn of the century. As "the rights of single isolated Vereine are not being sufficiently respected," in 1910 the scholarly associations coalesced into the Deutsche Wissenschafter-Verband, thereby becoming the fourth strongest student association—at least in numbers. In the last prewar years other strictly noncorporative special-interest groups, such as stenographic societies and sports clubs, also began to spring up. While they were important for the advancement of their own causes, they exerted little influence on the student body at large. The scholarly associations provided anticipatory professional training rather than "character education," for "they have neither ideology nor pronounced social purpose, but despite all cartels, life memberships, and other traits borrowed from the corporations, they are primarily directed toward studying."[36]

The "individuality of thought and freedom of action" that characterized student subculture shaped a "unique variety of the human species known as the German student." In contrast to the regimented American undergraduate, he was "a young man free to select his studies, his professors, his rooms, his hours of work, to regulate the entire course of his life, to be what his own energy and talents may make him." After the strict control of the Gymnasium, such untrammeled liberty not only made an individual desire "a brief respite," a look "around to enjoy life during the interval," or a moratorium, between school and profession, but also created a strong drive for association. Since foreigners, like James M. Hart, found "no visible sign of the university, no chapel, no huge buildings . . . no campus," students congregated in pubs and organized their conviviality around drinking. (Fraternity houses were not built until the 1880s and dormitories only after 1900.) Out of such informal "reunions, which are nothing more than

---

[36] Application of the Wissenschaftliche Vereine to the rector of the University of Berlin, August 1874, HUA, 569; W. Heilmann, "Der deutsche Wissenschafter-Verband (D.W.V.)," VA, pp. 158-60; Schulze-Ssymank, Das deutsche Studententum, pp. 329f.; Ziegler, Der deutsche Student, pp. 110ff.; Seiffert, Studentische Verbände, pp. 88-106, 108-25; Anonymous, Burschen heraus! p. 61. For different individual societies—theological, historical, etc.—see MUA 305a, Acc 1950/9, 178, 186, 199, and HUA, 527, 530, 533, etc.

social gatherings held twice a week,'' associations emerged which after 1870 became increasingly formalized, exclusive, and pretentious in their attempt to complement professorial instruction with youthful self-cultivation. Because the Corps student was their idol, student societies imitated many Corps customs, like displaying colors and wearing drinking caps (*Cerevis-Mützen*), and absorbed much of the organizational structure (the pledge system) and the arrogant tone of the Corpsiers. Corporatization transformed many a loose friendship group into an organized society (Verein). Not a few erstwhile associations, dedicated to innocuous congeniality, like the intercorporative *akademische Gesangvereine*, blossomed either into black (noncolor) corporations (Sondershäuser Verband Deutscher Sängerverbindungen, 1867) with unconditional satisfaction or even into color-carrying and duelling corporations (Deutsche Sängerschaft, 1901). Since many active members disagreed about the precise level of corporatism and were willing to defend their principles, sword in hand, this process led to an astounding fragmentation. Differing only in minor points, organizations combated one another with the exaggerated belligerence of cocks spoiling for a fight. In some cases reunification proved possible (the CV was particularly adept at swallowing rivals), and the creation of national associations, journals, and Old Boy societies sought to curb further splitting and social mutations of Vereine into Landsmannschaften or into Corps. With the establishment of several chapters at one university, corporations formed local cartels and, withdrawing from pubs into their lavish houses, increasingly lived for themselves alone, ''hardly conscious of their community with other groups any longer.''[37]

Internally, associations were characterized by a growing ritualization, elaborate *rites de passage* for probation (service as *Leibbursche*), initiation (special ceremonies), and membership (Kommerse). As ''public opinion on the continent sustains the practice, and in such matters public opinion is irresistible,'' the central ritual was the duel. It gradually differentiated into the Bestimmungsmensur, ''making student honor a matter of conventionalism and converting a final resort into an everyday pastime,'' while real Duelle were fought with heavier sabres or pistols as ''the supposed satisfaction for some gross insult.'' Although ''the general appearance of

---

[37] J. M. Hart, *German Universities* (New York, 1874), pp. 9ff., 64ff., 136ff., 287ff., and 313ff.: ''The only just way of comparing two systems is to take them at points widely apart. The idler of Germany, I am confident, has forgotten twice as much as the idler of America, the industrious student knows twice as much as the industrious undergraduate, and the future scholar of Germany is a man of whom we in America have no conception. He is a man who could not exist under our system, he would be choked by recitations and grades. What he studies, he studies with the devotion of a poet, and with the trained skill of a scientist.'' G. Kutze, ''Die deutsche Sängerschaft,'' and W. Röntze, ''Der Sondershäuser Verband deutscher Sängerverbindungen,'' in *VA*, pp. 143-48; and Seiffert, *Studentische Verbände*, pp. 48-52, 57-59.

the duellist is very comical; the pad and cravat and spectacles make them look somewhat like a pair of submarine divers in their armor," foreigners were appalled by a system that "tolerates bloodshed." Yet they preferred its manly character to the peer persecution prevalent at American colleges, "from which there is no escape." A final characteristic of imperial student life was its craving for "instant tradition," for historical legitimation of forms and goals of behavior. This tendency is apparent in the neomedievalism of illustrations in student journals and in the spring pilgrimage to a favorite castle, be it the Rudelsburg, the Wartburg, the Coburg, or some other romantic ruin, which served as symbolic center of the national association in question. Much of the neofeudal heraldry stemmed from the desire for a respectable pedigree in the newly created and nouveau riche empire, although the actual heritage was rich enough, especially in student songs: "There is a wonderful poetic vein running through them, a mingling of wit, humor, pathos, rude physical life, beautiful imagery, absurd slang. The *Commersbuch* is as chaotic, as irrepressible, as full of good and evil in glaring juxtaposition, as the student life itself." This blend of ancient remnants and modern inventions was especially evident in the compulsive ceremonialism of the Kneipe, where "you must drink with the others and not according to your own fancy," and the oratory of the Kommers: "The keynote was of course German patriotism and German unity." Since the "German boy, although well informed, grows up in comparative ignorance of the great social and political movements around him," the self-education of students tended on the whole to reinforce the formal curriculum. No doubt there were real conflicts between professors and students about the central purpose of university study, be it intellectual or social, but the inherent exclusivity of corporations and their dominance over student life strengthened academic elitism, albeit in a more martial than spiritual vein. Since "politics, in the English or American use of the word, are unknown in the German university," traditional subculture failed to modify the apolitical patriotism of cultivation. Hence, paradoxically, the very extent of academic freedom for German students contributed to their continuing political immaturity.[38]

Organizational Developments

When the over four thousand students who had fought in the Franco-Prussian War returned to their alma maters, they vigorously debated, like their predecessors of 1815, what "new contemporary form" academic life

[38] Hart, *German Universities*, pp. 64-83, 136-48, 287-313. For some of the terminology, see also T. Roszak, *The Making of a Counterculture* (New York, 1969); E. Erikson, *Childhood and Society*, 2nd ed. (New York, 1963); and P. Abrams, "Rites de Passage: The Conflict of Generations in Industrial Society," *JCH* 5 (1970): 175-90.

should take. While many sought to perpetuate corporate romanticism, critics of tradition groped for "academic progress." Echoing the reformers of the 1840s and the *Akademische Zeitung* of the 1860s, a number of pamphlets and organizations urged the "renewal of student life," reflecting the general advance of culture. The most vocal spokesman of "inner regeneration," Theodor Curti, advocated "academic equality and freedom of association among students." As "colors create a social gap" and "the mistaken concept of honor" destroyed solidarity, he rejected corporate forms as confining. Others polemicized against separate jurisdiction, "which must always nourish the estate consciousness of students," and argued: "Under no circumstances can we accept a limitation of our right of association and of the freedom of the press." In order to achieve "liberty for all without destroying individualism," these reformers founded "free student societies" in Königsberg and Marburg "as negations of corporations." In Halle and in Bonn they established a "permanent committee of noncolor students" to curb duelling through a court of honor and to pioneer labor exchanges, mutual aid funds, and so forth. Where they felt stronger, as in Freiburg (1860-64), Berlin (1868-71), and Heidelberg (1870), they convoked student councils (*Studentenausschüsse*), uniting all organizations in "representation of their interests" as long as the authorities would permit it (as in Leipzig in 1870). "Since the opponents of reform are mostly corporations," some progressives went so far as "to oppose them with Verbindungen of their own in order to prove that their benefits could be maintained without accepting their shortcomings." Because "these associations . . . will always provide a natural counterweight against conservative instincts," the entire reform movement breathed a left-liberal, *freisinnige* spirit. Nevertheless, within half a decade the impetus was spent, the Weimar Cartel of 1872 dissolved, and only an undercurrent of reformist polemics remained. Since progressives engaged in "discussions . . . but not in partisanship" and the abolition of academic justice in 1879 eliminated a major cause for complaint, students in general showed "too little interest in and understanding of the goals of the reform party." Instead of democratizing academic youth, German unification reinforced the hold of corporatism on university life. Reformers cried in vain: "Wake up German students, you sleeping beauty, you have dreamed long enough."[39]

[39] T. Curti, *Die deutsche Studentenschaft: Eine akademische Zeitstudie* (Würzburg, 1869), *Die Regeneration der deutschen Studentenschaft* (Würzburg, 1870), and *Die Reformbewegung in der deutschen Studentenschaft* (Würzburg, 1873). Anonymous, *Zur Reform des Studentenlebens: Eine Darstellung der Grundsätze und Entwicklung der freien studentischen Vereinigung zu Königsberg* (Königsberg, 1872); Max von der Porten, *Geschichte und Ziele der studentischen Reformpartei* (Heidelberg, 1870). C. F. Herrfurth, *Was ist studentische Reform?* (Jena, 1875); J. Tönnies, *Eine höchst nötige Antwort auf die höchst unnötige Frage: "Was ist studentische Reform?"* (Jena, 1875); and Anonymous, *Beiträge zur Reform des Studentenlebens und zur Veredelung des Menschengeschlechts* (Berlin, 1876). See also Schulze-Ssymank, *Das deutsche Studententum*, pp. 328f. and HUA, 550 and 639.

While the failure of the democratic movement seemed to pave the way for more radical Socialist involvement, students in Imperial Germany were ultimately politicized from another direction, the nationalist, anti-Semitic right. The crash of 1873 and the ensuing depression awakened academic interest in socialism among poor urban students, Jewish Kommilitonen, and socially conscious youths sympathetic to the plight of the proletariat. In the Berlin Mohrenclub, where students mingled with Social Democratic litterati, officials, and deputies, and in the Leipzig colloquium of Professor Birnbaum, Marxist ideas were eagerly debated. After the Prussian Ministry of Culture excluded the eccentric E. Dühring (who, among many other causes, also vaguely championed socialism) from the faculty, hundreds of students protested in the name of academic freedom "against this deplorable act of force."[40] But in early summer of 1878, when the artisan Hödel and then Dr. Nobiling tried to assassinate William I, academic youths abandoned their flirtation with Marxism or materialist atheism and rallied around altar and throne: "During the last week such a unanimous wave of patriotic enthusiasm and complete dedication swept over us that we felt ennobled in common duty to our shared fatherland despite all sadness and anger," the young Bethmann Hollweg described the awakening of his own nationalism to an intimate friend. The torchlight parade of Berlin students, the demonstrations at other universities, and the pompous address to the Kaiser were outward signs of a profound inner transformation of German youth. While the "resolute actions" of the Prussian government quickly suppressed all visible manifestations of student socialism, the general reorientation of Bismarck's domestic policy toward the right in 1879 robbed youthful liberalism of much of its adult sanction. When, in September of the same year, the demagogic court chaplain, Adolf Stöcker, publicly attacked "modern Judaism" in order "to protect our people against de-Christianization," his seductive blend of Protestant religiosity and social concern offered students an alternative, simultaneously modern and conservative.[41]

[40] Although often mentioned, this great ideological reversal of the students has yet to be explained. Report of the Berlin Police President, 13 July 1877 and student proclamation, ZStA Me, Rep 77, Tit 46 No 46, vol. 1. See Schulze-Ssymank, *Das deutsche Studententum*, pp. 334-37; I. Auer, *Von Gotha bis Wyden* (Berlin, 1901), p. 7; and Prof. Birnbaum, "Die Sozialdemokratie und die studierende Jugend," *Alma Mater* (1878), 329. For the Dühring case, see M. Lenz, *Geschichte der Königlichen Friedrich-Wilhelms-Universität*, 2: 354. See also the forthcoming dissertation by N. Schafferdt.

[41] Bethmann to Oettingen, 13 June 1878, BA, Rep 129, Oettingen, no. 30; Schulze-Ssymank, *Das deutsche Studententum*, pp. 337-38; Minister of Culture Falk circular, 14 June 1878, ZStA Me, Rep 120 BB, Sekt VII Tit 1, No 18, vol. 1; Adolf Stoecker, "Unsere Forderungen an das moderne Judentum," and "Notwehr gegen das moderne Judentum," cited by W. Frank, *Hofprediger Adolf Stoecker und die christlich-soziale Bewegung*, 2nd rev. ed. (Hamburg, 1935). For the general context, see also Hans Rosenberg, *Grosse Depression und Bismarckzeit: Wirtschaftsablauf, Gesellschaft und Politik in Mitteleuropa* (Berlin,

The decisive catalyst was an article by the most popular Berlin professor, Heinrich von Treitschke, who made "the passionate movement against Judaism" academically respectable. In November 1879 he thundered in the *Preussische Jahrbücher*, "the Jews are our misfortune," because German culture could no longer absorb increasing numbers of Eastern immigrants. Although distancing himself from the primitive agitation of popular propagandists like Wilhelm Marr, he nevertheless argued: "It is undeniable that Semites have a great share in the lying, deceit, and greed of the *Gründer* speculators [and bear] a large part of the guilt for the horrid materialism of our days, which regards work only as a job and threatens to smother the traditional pride in labor of our people." Perhaps stung by the critical reception of his German history, he ranted: "Most dangerous is the unfair preponderance of Jewry in the daily press," which threatened the very essence of German culture. Because he was aware of the great contribution of Jewish creativity, Treitschke demanded more thorough assimilation as price of emancipation: "It will probably be impossible to make the hard German heads Jewish; hence, our Jewish citizens must unreservedly decide to become German, as many, to their and our fortune, have already done." While his Berlin colleagues, led by the venerable Mommsen, decried such academic anti-Semitism, about one-quarter of all German students enthusiastically signed the virulent petition of Bernhard Förster urging a ban on further immigration and a purge of government and teaching: "German students believe they should not let the opportunity pass to express their agreement with these sentiments," the Leipzig law student Paul Dulon added to the document: "We do this, aware that the continuation of the struggle for the maintenance of our nationality will some day rest on our shoulders." While the liberal press denounced the signatories as "enemies of humanity," rightist papers applauded this "new, positive spirit": "Undoubtedly something is stirring our German youth, and as far as we see, it is the spring's awakening of a new spirit which gives us hope for a better future; the best among the cultivated are moved by this national enthusiasm." Instead of rebelling toward the left, by the second decade of the empire students, "completely reversing" their earlier commitment, began to rebel to the right in a "movement, which in strength, impetus, and fervor rivaled the early Burschenschaft."[42]

1967), who does not mention the VDSt; M. Stürmer, *Regierung und Reichstag im Bismarckstaat 1871-1880: Cäsarismus oder Parlamentarismus* (Düsseldorf, 1974); and as a summary of an immense literature, R. Rürup, "Emancipation and Crisis: The 'Jewish Question' in Germany 1850-1890," *Yearbook of the Leo Baeck Institute* 20 (1975): 13-27.

[42] H. Treitschke, "Unsere Aussichten" (originally in *PrJhb* 44 [1879]: 559-76); Forckenbeck declaration of notables (signed by seventeen Berlin professors), 12 November 1880; Treitschke, "Antwort auf eine studentische Huldigung," 19 November 1880; T. Mommsen,

During the winter semester of 1880-81 this nationalist revival crystallized into a permanent organization. In order to combat the Committee for the Struggle against Anti-Semitic Agitation among Students, nationalist partisans sought to "unite permanently all truly German students of Berlin." On 14 December the rector received the statutes of an "association of German students" (Verein Deutscher Studenten) which intended "to affirm and cultivate German national consciousness" and invited "every matriculated student of German descent, without regard to citizenship," to become a member. In the ensuing struggle against liberal professors and fellow students, the ideology of the VDSt became more Christian and complex. The associations "set as their purpose the advancement of understanding for national questions and tasks among their members as well as the clarification and strengthening of nationalism in the entire student body." Although "the Verein does not intend to take a one-sided political stand in today's public life, torn by party strife, and even less to play an independent political role," its emphasis on "preparation for later participation in politics" was stronger than in a traditional corporation: "The society intends to train its members as capable citizens, concerned with the welfare and prosperity of the German fatherland." Thus, its methods, though building on older customs, tried to be innovative. Although the national statutes "strictly forbid the societies to sport colors," the first way of propagating German ideas was "the cultivation of conviviality." The second principle derived from the Burschenschaft: "Scholarly lectures by students on topics of German history, literature, economics, and other areas in relationship to contemporary life." The third practice became the hallmark of the VDSt: "The celebration of patriotic holidays to combat lazy indifference and petty particularism." The membership criterion was gradually elaborated to include "only Christian students of German nationality matriculated in higher education in the empire," and requiring, as an anti-Semitic screen, that "its members be baptized and not hostile to Christianity in recognition of its high ethical value." As the first academic pressure group, the VDSt attempted to take "the lead in the present striving of German students toward unity in national questions as well as in student matters." By organizing nonincorporated students as well as corporation members, the Verein tried to reawaken academic youth in general:

"Auch ein Wort über unser Judentum," in W. Böhlich, ed., *Der Berliner Antisemitismusstreit* (Frankfurt, 1965); *Die studentische Petition als Annex der allgemeinen Petition betreffend die Einschränkung der jüdischen Machtstellung* (Leipzig, 1881); Hans Petersdorff, *Die Vereine Deutscher Studenten: Zwölf Jahre akademischer Kämpfe*, 3rd rev. ed. (Leipzig, 1900), pp. 7-16, and Schulze-Ssymank, *Das deutsche Studentum*, pp. 342-54. See the authoritative J. Katz, *From Prejudice to Destruction: Anti-Semitism, 1700-1933* (Cambridge, Mass., 1980), pp. 260ff., who also ignores students.

The restoration of the imperial crown has confronted our nation with great unanticipated tasks, which demand the ennobling of national consciousness, i.e., the deepening of our understanding of our duty toward the members of our own nation and the purging of any foreign influence from German life which endangers its uniqueness and values, as imperiously as the forceful assertion of our nationality toward outside powers in all areas of endeavor.

The hundreds of students who joined the VDSt at Berlin, Leipzig, Halle, and Breslau in the spring of 1881 were movitated by a confusing blend of monarchical nationalism, political anti-Semitism, and positive Christianity.[43]

Although individual professors like the Leipzig theologian Christoph Luthardt encouraged the anti-Semites, the overwhelming majority of the Berlin faculty opposed the creation of an association because they feared either for orthodoxy or for academic liberalism. University judge Schulz counselled prohibition, since name and purpose "imply that it will go beyond academic concerns and intends to discuss political topics and thereby also influence public affairs." When Rector August von Hofmann clothed his liberal opposition in legal technicalities, the students produced new statutes as rapidly as he could reject them. "Admittedly we aim at combating Jewry as an obstacle toward national development and as a denationalizing force. But we consider this not the overriding purpose, but only a means of achieving the principal goal of advancing and cultivating national consciousness." However, the Senate's clever deflection of the movement into a public Verein, registered by the police, misfired. Since continued public assemblies of opponents and proponents with such inflammatory rhetoric as "opposing Jews wherever they may appear" endangered "academic peace," authorities had to threaten both with the *consilium abeundi* to make them desist. Instead, about 350 nationalist students protested: "I consider it the right and duty of every Prussian to struggle with all his might for the strengthening of German national spirit." VDSt leader Max Lohan petitioned Puttkamer for redress: "All Christian and truly patriotic students feel gravely discriminated against" by official

[43] Rien flyer, 8 December 1880, HUA, 638; original VDSt statutes, 14 December 1880, HUA, 638; for its evolution, see also the statutes of 4 April and 24 April 1880, HUA, 619. Marburg statutes of 15 May 1886, MUA, Acc 1954/16, no. 70, together with proclamations of 1 July and 18 October 1886 and a printed copy of the "Satzungen des Kyffhäuserverbandes" dating from the last prewar years. For a detailed narrative of events, see Petersdorff, *Die Vereine*, pp. 23-51. According to the *Findbuch* for R 143 in the Bundesarchiv, the VDSt papers have apparently disappeared and only a few useful splinters survive in the BA, such as nos. 12, 14, 16, and 38. See most recently N. Schafferdt, "Bildungsbürgertum und Antisemitismus. Untersuchungen zur Sozialgeschichte, Politik und Ideologie von Studenten und Hochschullehrern im Deutschen Reich und in Österreich" (dissertation, Berlin, 1982).

university resistance. Although the reactionary minister was politically sympathetic to the nationalist cause, he could only urge yet another statute revision to conform with regulations and indicate that the program of the association itself was no reason for continued proscription. When a special Kommers for William I was prohibited, the agitators appealed to Bismarck: "Untouched by old and deplorable partisanship, academic youth enthusiastically hails its Kaiser." Heartened by such noble feelings, the Iron Chancellor complained to the minister: "From recent events at our local university I have gathered the impression that some professors fall into the same error as some students and introduce political partisanship and agitation into university life." Unwilling to curb patriotic enthusiasm, he questioned "whether it is useful to fight the conservative currents which have spread among students during the last decade." Puttkamer understood the hint and hastened to assure his irascible superior that with new statutes the VDSt would at last be permitted. At the price of greater statutory conformity with university regulations, Hofmann complied in April 1881, still convinced that the Verein intended "to participate in politics and that is intolerable."[44]

The administrative struggle over the name Verein Deutscher Studenten, or Association for the Cultivation of Germanness, grew so bitter because it involved opposing generational ideals of academic politics. While the majority of the activists considered "pronounced anti-Semitic tendencies and German nationalism" as inspiring, many professors were not willing to part with their liberal belief in emancipation and saw the movement as "a source of much nonsense and disruption." Although the Ministry of Culture initially sympathized with the liberal press, the Iron Chancellor forcefully sided with the students, whom he considered kindred spirits:

> On the basis of countless indications that I have recently received, I believe I can assume that a laudable deepening and clarification of national consciousness is taking place in our academic youth. The fantastic and hazy ideas regarding political and national questions which in earlier times dominated our universities are apparently giving

[44] Lohan to Hofmann, 16 December 1880 with long marginalia of judge Schulz, 18 December on the first statute draft; second statutes of 8 January 1881 with similar Schulz comment; protocol of Hinschius negotiations with Schubert and Lohan, 31 January 1880; excerpt of Senate protocol of 9 February 1880; protocol of session with students, 11 February 1881; Lohan to Puttkamer, 11 February 1881; Puttkamer to Berlin Senate, 18 March 1881; new statutes of 24 March 1881, all in HUA, 638. Police president report of 28 February 1881, ZStA Me, Rep 77, Tit 46 No 46, vol. 1. Berlin VDSt to Bismarck, 22 March 1881; Bismarck to Puttkamer, 27 March 1881; and Puttkamer to Bismarck, 4 April 1881; all in DZA Po, Rkz 2195. Lohan to Hofmann with Hofmann marginalia and new statutes, 28 April 1881; and Hofmann answer to Greisfwald rector inquiry, 23 June 1881, all in HUA, 619. See also Petersdorff, *Die Vereine*, pp. 23-51.

way to a clear and positive attitude. According to my opinion, a healthy national and monarchical spirit is spreading among them. The politicizing professors, who belong to that epoch against which the movement in question is reacting, are likely to do their utmost to repress the national and conservative tendencies of our student body and to further the Virchow-Mommsen direction [of left liberalism].

Because of this reversal in the attitudes of the young generation, Bismarck argued: "According to my mind the government is not only permitted, but also duty bound to oppose antimonarchical and antinational currents among professors." To undercut professorial liberalism, the chancellor was willing to foster student nationalism, even encourage academic anti-Semitism, despite his close ties to the banker Gerson Bleichröder. Such public encouragement from above ("the national spirit of the great majority of German youth guarantees that in the present struggles the enemies of Kaiser and Reich shall not prevail") gradually led professors to become more tolerant and even encourage the "laudable purposes" of the VDSt. By 1886 all four rectors who answered a Marburg inquiry about their experiences with the nationalist movement were inclined to "certify its loyalty" and blamed continuing provocations on its opponents.[45]

Reduced from an all-embracing movement to an organized Verein "around which academic life could crystallize," the VDSt celebrated the first year of its struggle at the legendary Kyffhäuser Mountain. In order to "defend German ways and customs, German loyalty and faith" against "the sinister powers of naked egotism and cosmopolitan rootlessness, demoralization and irreligiosity," six hundred students and two hundred sympathizers met on 6 August 1881 at the mythical seat of Emperor Barbarossa: "This birth anew / Today witnessed by you / As German champions bold / Leads a youthful corps / To the Kyffhäuser's fore / To guard the Parnassus of old," one "poet" rhapsodized over the pilgrimage to the ruin of the Rothenburg. Not the "night birds of atheism, internationalism, or libertinism," court chaplain Stöcker intoned, "but the eagle wings of the German-Christian idea shall soar around us—then Germany's resurrection will be complete," then the risen Kaiser would lead Germany to new

---

[45] Heinrici marginalia on Reichardt to Rector, 15 May 1886, together with comments by Bergmann and the Marburg University judge (who considered such patriotism "self-evident for every German student . . . and not needing a special society"), in MUA, Acc 1954/16, no. 70. Gossler to Curtius, 19 October and 29 December 1881, with extensive marginalia by Schulz, all in HUA, 638. Greving petition to Bismarck, 7 December 1881; and Bismarck to Gossler, 9 December 1881 in DZA Po, Rkz 2195. Negotiation of rector with Lohan, 27 January 1882 and further material in HUA, 638 and 619. Kleinert to other rectors, 20 June 1886 with answers from Königsberg, Greifswald, Breslau, and especially Berlin, 2 June 1886, MUA, Acc 1954/16, no. 70. See also F. Stern, *Gold and Iron: Bismarck, Bleichröder and the Building of the German Empire* (New York, 1977), pp. 494ff.

triumphs. Although liberal papers castigated the "ugly mixture of ambition, pseudoenthusiasm, drunkenness, and servility," participants remembered: "Our enthusiasm was never more beautiful and intense than on that day." This self-conscious imitation of the Burschenschaft's Wartburgfest of 1817 was a communal youth rite of nationalism which generated deep commitments. It led to the settling of internal feuds, the creation of a Kyffhäuser-Verband, and the publication of a *Kyffhäuser-Zeitung*, thereby completing the external organization of the new student association, which expanded quickly to North German universities. (It was initially forbidden in Bavaria.)[46]

Intent on "awakening and preserving German national ideas in our midst," the VDSt advocated a new kind of nationalism. "We admit that outside their sphere students should not agitate for a party in public assemblies" but demonstrate "their unreserved enthusiasm for the greatness of the nation and the deeds of its heroes." However, what was meant by "a strong monarchical government, a unified empire, firm social reform, and a Christian people" varied greatly among individual adherents like Dietrich Hahn (the later agrarian leader), Hellmuth von Gerlach (the erstwhile reactionary, later pacifist), Friedrich Naumann (the Christian-social pastor) and Wolfgang Heine (the Socialist). Clearly "modern, materialist Jewry" was a primary cultural enemy because of its alleged destructiveness, and a political foe because of its "antinational activity." But a strong positive current also inspired many students: "Without Christianity, no Germanness." The imperial message on social policy in November 1881 stimulated a vigorous interest in social reform, seen as applied Christianity: "Study of the social question and practice of a social conscience" complemented continuing anti-Semitism. In 1887 "the resolution of the Kyffhäuser convocation . . . made it the duty of all VDSt to concern themselves with German colonial efforts," thereby expanding domestic nationalism into imperialism, later propagated by its alumni in the Pan-German League. Although in the first decade of their existence the Associations of German Students narrowed into one society among others, they nevertheless became a most effective student party and proudly called themselves "the civil guard of the Hohenzollerns." "Deeply opposed to all parties," anti-Semites thought of themselves as a genuinely idealistic national revival movement seeking to rouse students out of sated indif-

---

[46] "Programm des alten VDSt in Berlin," *Kyffhäuser Zeitung* 1 (1881): 9; "An die deutschen Studenten!" 17 July 1881, reprinted by Petersdorff, *Die Vereine*, pp. 89f.; W. Johnsen, "Zum Kyffhäuser!" *KZ* 1 (1886): 2; A. Stöcker, "Glück auf deutsche Jugend!" ibid., *Börsenkurier*, 2 August 1881, calling the VDSt "a distorted mirror of the Burschenschaft"; Petersdorff, *Die Vereine*, pp. 86-108; Schulze-Ssymank, *Das deutsche Studentum*, pp. 345ff.; and Dr. Weber, "Der Kyffhäuserverband der Vereine Deutscher Studenten," in *VA*, pp. 164-67.

ference and urban degeneration: "The VDSt should be a steady and living protest against the individualist conception of the university, which does not primarily try to produce loyal servants of state and church as well as patriotic and faithful leaders of the people."[47]

Many other students, however, rejected such agitation as "unworthy of our traditions" and tried to rally those "united in their dislike of religious persecution, class, or race hatred." Led by the later pacifist Ludwig Quidde, one hundred and sixty-eight liberals "protested emphatically against the present attempt to draw German students into anti-Semitic agitation" which had already gained the support of four hundred Göttingen students by November 1880. Reflecting the astonishment of older academics, Quidde wrote: "Experienced politicians are surprised by the transformation that has taken place in a few decades and do not understand why the young people think so differently from themselves." Perceptively, he concluded: "If I am not mistaken, a generation of largely nationalist-chauvinist and socially inspired, moderately conservative Realpolitiker is about to emerge." When the university authorities disbanded the Committee against Anti-Semitism, on 25 June 1881, liberal students founded a Freie Wissenschaftliche Vereinigung to propagate "free scholarly spirit" in the conviction that liberty, science, and sociability were ultimately identical. "We have called it a 'free' association, because its members think freely and because they shall interact freely." The purpose of the FWV was "the advancement of general scholarly and social intercourse of Berlin students in all faculties, without distinction of faith." Hence, "every matriculated student" could, with the agreement of the presidium, become a member; but roughly half of the founders bore Jewish names, and a police report of one of the first meetings also noted: "The greatest part of the students present was of the Israelite religion." To "learn about the present political situation and activity of the country, to participate in and walk along the path of progress," the association organized "weekly assemblies which have a scholarly, business, and social part." Despite the open sympathy of the liberal professors, the authorities argued that "according to its statutes the FWV is not entitled to publish brochures with political content, and it shall not at all concern itself with political agitation" and hindered its publicity so that

[47] "Was wir wollen," *ABl* 1 (1886): 1f.; J. W., "Der Kampf gegen den Indifferentismus," ibid., pp. 39f.; Frhr. v. Zedlitz, "Die Stellung des Kyffhäuser-Verbandes zur Judenfrage," ibid. 2 (1888): 161f.; Fr. v. Schwerin, "Zur Kolonialfrage," ibid. 3 (1889): 74f.; "Unsere Aufgaben," ibid. 6 (1891): 179-81. See note 45; "Sind wir konservativ?" *ABl* 1 (1886), no. 12; Meinhold, "Über die Stellung des Kyffhäuser Verbandes zur Judenfrage," ibid. 3 (1889), no. 2, and H. von Petersdorff, "Das geistige Leibregiment der Hohenzollern," *ABl* 5 (1891), no. 9. "Among the student associations the 'German students' quickly became the most important and influential but also the most misunderstood group." Anonymous, *Burschen heraus!* pp. 53-58, and P.G.J. Pulzer, *Die Entstehung des politischen Antisemitismus in Deutschland und Österreich 1867-1914* (Gütersloh, 1966).

attendance at its assemblies was only about one-third that of the VDSt. Initial FWV branches at Breslau, Halle, Strassburg, and Leipzig withered away quickly, and only the Berlin association carried on the struggle until after the turn of the century. As a "highly necessary counterforce to the automatic condemnation of all Jews without consideration of the individual," the liberal FWV ultimately failed, because it was a double negation rather than a positive movement, it was loosely organized, and its ideas ran counter to the major currents of its generation.[48]

Exclusion from Gentile corporations and lack of success of liberal countermovements convinced Jewish youths that they "themselves should lead the fight against anti-Semitism . . . with the opportunities, means, and weapons of German students." In the winter of 1883 nine Berlin students founded an "academic association for Jewish history and literature" in order "to express their adherence to Judaism through studying its past and learning its culture." However, a scholarly approach (and membership in neutral wissenschaftliche societies concerned with medicine, law, and natural science) could at best provide a meeting place for a small number but did not solve the academic Jewish problem. More optimistic and self-assertive, twelve Breslau students gathered their Jewish friends three years later in a fraternity, called Viadrina, which spread to Berlin in 1894 (Sprevia), and led to the foundation of the Kartell-Convent in 1896:

> The KC corporations base themselves on German patriotic spirit. They have as their aim the struggle against anti-Semitism among students and the education of their members as self-conscious Jews. Aware that German Jews form a part of the nation indissolubly united through history, culture, and legal community with the German fatherland, they are always ready and able to stand up for the political and social equality of Jews. As long as they do not contradict the above, the corporations within the KC take no position on political and religious separatist tendencies within Judaism.

This unequivocal commitment to being "German students of the Jewish faith" was to be created through corporate "character building," through outduelling the nationalists "with their own weapons," and through "pos-

---

[48] Proclamation of the FWV, May 1893, in HUA, 623. L. Quidde, *Die Antisemitenagitation und die deutsche Studentenschaft*, 2nd rev. ed. (Göttingen, 1881), pp. 5f. and 12ff. H. Petersdorff, *Die Vereine*, pp. 36f; M. Spangenberg, *Der Standpunkt der FWV an der Universität Berlin zur Judenfrage und zur Wissenschaft* (Berlin, 1882); Anonymous, *Juden, Studenten und Professoren* (Leipzig, 1881). Spangenberg and Heilmann, "Statut der Freien Wissenschaftlichen Vereinigung an der Universität Berlin," 25 June 1881; police report of the meeting of 19 July 1881; DuBois-Reymond memorandum of FWV presidium, 25 November 1881 and 1912 version of the FWV statutes as well as much other material in HUA, 623. See also Schulze-Ssymank, *Das deutsche Studentum*, pp. 349-52.

itive Jewish education'' without ideological partisanship. ''Nobility and self-assurance, self-control and discipline, idealism in action, and confidence in victory of youth'' were the psychological aims of the new corporations. After initial anti-Semitic surprise at the audacity of such a program, the nationalists tried to persecute and isolate the KC students with bitter hostility. But they could prevent neither the successful challenge to the negative (cowardly) stereotype nor the leadership training vital for the self-defense of the assimilationist Jewish community.[49]

Because nationalist agitation gradually destroyed confidence in full integration, a more pessimistic group, influenced by Russian Jews, founded the Verein jüdischer Studenten an der Universität Berlin around 1900. It did not adopt the traditional corporation form but rather propagated a national Jewish program, which, after internal struggles, developed into full-fledged Zionism. The societies, united in the Bund Jüdischer Corporationen in 1902, understood themselves as

> a rallying point for all Jewish students who consciously feel themselves to be Jewish and want to participate in the development of living Judaism. It wants to educate Jewish students to active participation in Jewish life and equip them with the intellectual weapons to take positions on the scholarly, political, and social questions within Judaism. It desires the physical education of its members in order to collaborate in the physical regeneration of the Jewish people.

Although still somewhat vague, this was a far-reaching program of national separation, transcending the university. Conservative officials therefore considered such associations ''a national danger'' and predicted ''the opposition of the entire student body and endless struggles and frictions.'' Even faculty moderates who saw no legal basis for ''preventing Jews as such from forming a society'' suggested a less ''inflammatory tone'' and modification of the statutes before supporting official permission. In spite of increasing tensions between ''Germanness and Jewishness,'' the majority of Jewish students agreed to ''let us remain what we are: German Jews and Jewish Germans.'' Even though their program proved more

---

[49] L. Haas, ''K.C. Tendenz und Jugend,'' *KCBl* 4 (1914): 145-47; statutes of the Akademische Verein für jüdische Geschichte und Literatur in HUA, 649; petition by Zweig to the Berlin rector 28 February 1886 for the dissolution of the common organization of scholarly societies, because a law association ''does not want to live together with societies in one organization whose members largely belong to the Mosaic religion, whereby their own society is disadvantaged in student circles'' (HUA, 569). Statutes of the K.C. Sprevia, HUA, 723. ''Festnummer zum 25. Stiftungsfest der Viadrina in Breslau,'' *KCBl* 2 (1911): 1ff.; F. Goldmann, ''Die Religion in der jüdischen Studentenverbindung,'' ibid., 3 (1912): 8f. and F. Goldmann, ''Die Bedeutung des K.C. für das deutsche Judentum,'' ibid., pp. 2-5. See also Seiffert, *Studentische Verbände*, pp. 52f., 87f.; and Schulze-Ssymank, *Das deutsche Studententum*, pp. 352f.

farsighted in the end, Zionist associations, and a few corporations like the Berlin Hasmonaea (1902), remained smaller and less influential. Thus, Jewish student reaction betrayed the same triple division between apolitical scholarship, assertive self-defense (Centralverein), and Jewish nationalism (Zionistische Vereinigung) that was found in the adult community. Indiscriminate attacks of academic anti-Semites forced a revival of Jewish self-consciousness beyond the response of Marburg organizers to Rector Sybel: "In national regard they want to be German. To my question, what their 'Jewishness' consisted of, they gave race as a criterion, but retreated from it and admitted that they could not give a clear answer." Ironically, the nationalist agitation of the VDSt eventually contributed not to further integration but rather to a national revival of Judaism.[50]

Because during the 1880s "almost all significant intellectuals among academic youth joined the Kyffhäuservereine," the VDSt permanently altered the thrust of student politics. In many respects only a more consequential (because youthful) expression of the general deliberalization of the political climate, the KV owed this success, which far exceeded the modest number of actual members, to its novel methods of agitation. "In the VDSt we have always reminded ourselves during our festivities that the hours of celebration must give us new strength for the pursuit of our aims," the garrison chaplain, C. Rogge, reasoned during the Kommers for Field Marshall Moltke's ninetieth birthday at the Berlin Philharmonic. "Healthy forces are emerging in the army and the university." Treitschke called for their collaboration "against everything sick in national life, against all lack of discipline, baseness, and materialism, so that together they may uphold the idea of duty and patriotism." To the thundering applause of students and court society, Stöcker welcomed the political reversal: "Among the many evils of the present, one encouraging sign is that the majority of German youth now rejects the habit of arguing and criticizing, and has tired of skepticism and rootlessness; but under the impression of the great events of 1870 and the impulses emanating from them it wants to serve the German Kaiser and princes, the state and the church." Finally, a law student recognized the importance of Bismarck in a special toast: "Let us thank him as one should thank a hero, by making his ideas our own!" Although the Burschenschaft was angered by the

[50] Statutes of the Verein Jüdischer Studenten in Marburg petition to Rector Sybel, 25 October 1906 (with lengthy professorial marginalia and notes by Sybel of a conversation with the petitioning students), all in MUA, 305a, Acc 1950/9, 198; K. Löwenstein, "Deutschtum und Judentum," *KCBl* 3 (1913): 2-8; L. Holländer, "Vaterlandsrede," ibid. 4 (1914): 147-50. Statutes of the corporation Hasmonaea in HUA, 759. See also the discussion by J. Reinharz, *Fatherland or Promised Land: The Dilemma of the German Jew, 1893-1914* (Ann Arbor, 1975), pp. 30-35 and W. Habel, *Deutsch-Jüdische Geschichte am Ausgang des 19. Jahrhunderts* (Kastellaun, 1977), pp. 129-45.

pretense that "such patriotism is the exclusive preserve of the KV," and the Wingolf found its "Christian-national spirit" too secular, the Turner, scholarly associations, and Catholic corporations were only too willing to enter local electoral alliances and multiply "the galvanizing effect" of the VDSt. "Today patriotic festivals are celebrated by every student association"; nationalist articles proliferated in student journals; even the FWV began its meeting with a royal pledge; interest in colonial and social policies spread into nominally nonpolitical organizations; the expurgation of foreign words became fashionable; and military service for theologians as well as voluntary training as medics grew popular. "Germany owes the complete rejection of the fruitless doctrines of modern liberalism, which had utterly enthralled it before, to the emergence of the VDSt among academic youth." Even after the dropping of the pilot, the disgrace of the court chaplain, the retirement of the *praeceptor Germaniae*, and the dissipation of initial anti-Semitic enthusiasm, the nationalist revival "became the common property of German students" by infecting other groups: "Because of the VDSt, the overwhelming majority of German students today is monarchical. It has inspired the entire student body with the feeling that it must live and act nationalistically."[51]

During the early 1890s the impact of Social Democratic agitation, socialism of the chair, and imperial social policy shifted the attention of perceptive students to the "social question." The "ocean of suffering and misery" of the lower classes in the teeming industrial cities not only appealed to the "compassion and humanitarianism" of the academics, but also to enlightened political self-interest: "It is necessary for the educated to occupy themselves with the social problem and to support reforms if the class struggles that threaten to tear apart the nation are to be eliminated and revolution is to be avoided." The interest of the cultivated shifted from national unification to social harmony: "Each of you, theologian, doctor, lawyer, and philosopher, will be able to practice your profession better and more dutifully, the clearer you understand the present social situation, its dangers and remedies." Supported by professors like Wagner, Schmoller, and Weber, or by clergymen like F. Naumann or G. Sohm, in 1893 Berlin students formed a Sozialwissenschaftliche Studentenver-

[51] Schulze-Ssymank, *Das deutsche Studententum*, pp. 353ff.; "Moltke-Kommers des Vereins Deutscher Studenten zu Berlin," extra of *ABl* 5 (1890-91), no. 15; "Unsere guten Freunde," *BBl* 6 (1892), nos. 3-5. "Der Wingolf und die antisemitische Bewegung," *WBl* 9 (1880): 14; K. Kinzel, "Kyffhäuser," as well as "Die 'deutschen Studenten'," ibid. 10 (1881), nos. 9f., and P. Richter, "An den Wingolf," ibid., no. 13; and A. Schreiber, "Wingolf—Kyffhäuser-Verband," ibid. 18 (1888-89), no. 20. See also P. Salvisberg, "Deutsche Worte—deutsche Studenten," *AMh* 8 (1891), no. 11. "Unsere Aufgaben," *ABl* 6 (1891-92), no. 14; Petersdorff, *Die Vereine*, p. 246. See also W. Jochmann, "Struktur und Funktion des deutschen Antisemitismus," in W. E. Mosse, ed., *Juden im Wilhelminischen Deutschland 1890-1914* (Tübingen, 1976), pp. 389-477.

einigung in order "to introduce all faculties to the most important and interesting aspects of national economy and of the social movement." To "promote scholarly training for future participation in public life," these social science associations used "informal get-togethers of individual members," the "purchase of social journals, brochures, and books," as well as "inspections and tours" of industrial plants. The most important method of "awakening the interest and understanding of our Kommilitonen for the great social tasks of our time" was the public lecture by leading authorities, such as Lujo Brentano. In conformity with apolitical custom and university regulation, "the society refuses to take any stand on social-political questions and [rejects] any active participation in them." Its organization did not have "a corporate character" and allowed all interested students to join. Since the program of the Sozialwissenschaftliche Studentenvereinigung addressed the major questions of the day in an appealing mixture of "scholarship" and ethical concern, numerous students from all faculties and corporations became involved (201 in Bonn in 1896).[52]

When the reactionary Freiherr von Stumm attacked the Socialists of the Chair in the Reichstag, university authorities suddenly became suspicious of social science student associations. Out of "deference to the mood of the governing circles," the conservative Berlin rector forbade the reestablishment of the dissolved association. In 1895 the SStV had disbanded, in order not to admit all thirty-four VDSt members who wanted to reverse its philo-Semitic course "in general student affairs." Because "especially now, when social issues are the focus of controversy, it will hardly be possible to avoid dragging the related political questions into the debate," Pfleiderer remained unconvinced that "such activity cannot endanger academic discipline or public order but that it rather contributes to the future welfare of the state." He only relented and permitted readmission when his colleague A. Wagner argued eloquently that social awareness was the best vaccine against the virus of socialism. In Marburg Professor Baudissin's fears that such an organization would lead to ideological strife were allayed by Rector T. Fischer's assurance that "academic teachers should get involved" in order "to keep our students from errors which are likely if we do not participate." In Halle the local police ruling that "the association attempts to influence public affairs" led the district government to forbid the society until the rector, assuring Minister Bosse that "it

[52] E. Schultze, *Die Studentenschaft und die soziale Frage* (Göttingen, 1895), address to the SSV Berlin. Dr. Wendland speech, "Freiherr von Stumm und die Sozialwissenschaftliche Studentenvereinigung," *Berliner Tageblatt*, 12 December 1894; Mangoldt to Weinhold, 3 and 30 November 1893; *Satzungen der sozialwissenschaftlichen Studentenvereinigung zu Berlin* (Berlin, 1893), all in HUA, 720; "Satzungen der sozialwissenschaftlichen Studentenvereinigung zu Marburg," in MUA, 305a, Acc 1950/9, no. 227; L. Brentano, *Die Stellung der Studenten zu den sozialpolitischen Aufgaben der Zeit* (Munich, 1897).

represents a desirable complement to academic instruction," had the ban rescinded. Because of such intermittent persecution, the Sozialwissenschaftliche Studentenvereinigung succeeded only partially in acquainting students with social problems, in spurring them to charitable action, and in safeguarding them from socialism.[53]

Eventually the dominance of corporations led noncorporation students to mount another reformist challenge, seeking "the renewal and transformation of academic life on the basis of modern principles." In 1892 Berlin independents sought "to break the spell of medieval remnants, to oppose the excesses of corporatism, and to introduce modern ideas as well as patriotism through new institutions." Four years after the failure of this initiative, unaffiliated Leipzig students, resenting their social inferiority and lack of representation, formed a Finkenschaft association, turning the derogatory phrase "finch" into a term of honor:

> We want to give the majority of comrades who do not belong to any corporation that position in student life, that internal as well as external respect, and that valiant support of their rights which their number and importance deserve, but which have hitherto been denied. We do not oppose corporations as such, but only their predominance, and demand full equality for all students. We reject the attitude, widely prevalent outside the university, that a corporation member is superior to an independent; we are fundamentally convinced that no cap or color band can give the German student greater value and demand that personal ability be the sole yardstick of individual worth.

This "class movement" of independents spread after 1898 to Halle, Königsberg, and Berlin, where the program widened to include "common scholarly, artistic, athletic, and social activity . . . unconditional commitment to the freedom and independence of the individual," and a rejection "of politics and religious quarrels." By 1900 the idea of a "collaboration of the nonincorporated" caught on in Bonn as a "justified claim to equality and participation in public affairs" of academe, despite the determined resistance of older corporations. Five years later the "fresh

---

[53] Daude to Bosse, 13 December 1894 indicating that Pfleiderer had forbidden a lecture by the Socialist writer Ledebour on "the national idea in social-scientific perspective" and that authorities were opposed because 10 of the 26 members were thought to be Jewish; E. Schultze petition to Pfleiderer, 15 December 1895 about readmission; A. Wagner, "Die Gründe für die Genehmigung einer sozialwissenschaftlichen Studentenvereinigung," 25 November 1895, all in HUA, 720. University judge to T. Fischer, with marginalia by the Rector Baudissin and others, 6 January 1895, MUA, 305a, Acc 1950/9, no. 227. Oberpräsident to Köller, 16 March 1895 with police report of 12 March 1895; Wagner to Bosse, 3 December 1895; Bosse to Recke, 9 January 1896, etc. in ZStA Me, Rep 77, Tit 46 No 46, vol. 1. See also "Der akademisch-sozialwissenschaftliche Verein," AMh 11 (1895): 446-47; and Schulze-Ssymank, Das deutsche Studententum, p. 364.

activism and youthful enthusiasm" of the reform movement spilled over to technical and commercial colleges and to quiet provincial universities like Marburg. The aims of "creating an independent representation, free from the domination of the corporations," of "combining the great, inchoate mass of the free students," and of helping the "less fortunate" struck a sympathetic chord among the more restless and modern independents, fed up with romantic traditionalism. In May 1900 the various free-student groups coalesced into a national organization under the progressive sounding name of Deutsche Freistudentenschaft. In a fiery speech, the Leipzig alumnus Dr. Heinzig criticized the exclusivity of the universities and argued that German academics were "not healthy enough . . . not cultivated enough and . . . not artistic enough." Despite squabbling over the membership of Technische Hochschulen and over localism versus expansion, the continued growth of the free-student movement led to the foundation of a Freistudentischer Bund for alumni at Weimar in 1903. It provided the ideological and organizational backing for increasingly bitter struggles with academic authorities and rival corporations by rallying "all academics who want to collaborate in the spirit of the free-student program in reforming university life."[54]

Since the Freistudentenschaft was largely a protest movement against corporate arrogance, its goals evolved only slowly beyond the Wittenberg program, which sought "to unite the entire student body in common tasks according to the old axioms of academic freedom and self-education." Early statutes freely mingled general principles with practical provisions: "The Berlin Finkenschaft is the organization of nonincorporated students. . . . Its purpose is to offer the Finken society, intellectual stimulation, and physical education as well as the opportunity to be represented in all common student festivities according to their numbers." In different local associations, three fundamental ideas frequently recurred. The first was the demand for "a much greater degree of general cultivation than the student brings with him from high school." Such a modernized neo-

[54] Koehler, "Ist eine Organisation der Marburger freien Studentenschaft erstrebenswert?" MUA, 305a, Acc 1950/9, no. 225; E. Wachler, ed., *Die Bewegung der Unabhängigen Studentenschaft zu Berlin* (Berlin, 1892); student petition for the establishment of a student honor court, 28 January 1897, and subsequent correspondence in HUA, 729/1; proclamation of the Leipzig Finkenschaft, 1899; proclamation of the Berlin students: "Was will die Finkenschaftsbewegung?" 3 October 1899 and other material in HUA, 746; "Vorgeschichte, Gründung und Entwicklung der Bonner Freistudentenschaft," in BA R 129, no. 438; Marburg student petition to rector, 8 November 1905, MUA, 305a, Acc 1950/9, no. 225; P. Ssymank, "Die Finkenschaftstage zu Wittenberg und Berlin," *FBI* 1 (1900), no. 9 and the papers in BA R 129, no. 434/1; Harnack to Studt, 5 February 1901 as well as clippings from the *Leipziger Tageblatt* on the "Erste Congress der deutschen freien Studentschaft," 5 January 1901, in ZStA Me, Rep 76 Va, Sekt 1 Tit XII, No 34; and *Satzungen des Freistudentischen Bundes* (n.p., 1903?) in BA R 129, no. 423. See also Schulze-Ssymank, *Das deutsche Studententum*, pp. 375-81.

humanism required "economic, geographic, statistical basics, acquaintance with recent history and with the important progress of transportation, civics, knowledge of the intellectual currents of our time as well as the fundamental advances of the sciences, in short, a wealth of information that the university offers commonly and abundantly." A renewed, contemporary idealism aimed at a "steady personality" not acquired through "tutelage or the external mold of Corps training" but through "free student life and work according to one's taste." The second goal was "the principle of representation." The Freistudentenschaft was "no Verein" but "a name for the entirety of nonincorporated students . . . represented as community through a committee" constituting the presidium of the Finkenschaft. As even the benevolent Adolf von Harnack observed that only about 15 percent of the independents were actually involved, the interpretation shifted after 1905 from a personal to an interest basis. "What is that supposed to mean?" asked a pamphlet rhetorically: "Is some kind of individual being represented? He is a free student. Why should he need a representative to protect him? Only the *interests* of the whole must be represented!" The rejection of a reform Verein and the maintenance of the *Vertreterprinzip* became the ideological core of the free-student movement, because they provided the legal justification for its claim to speak for all nonorganized students who were treated as potential members (no fees, no lists) in its not always clear but progressive rhetoric.[55]

The third aim of the Freistudentenschaft was the nicely ambiguous "social principle," which spawned a complicated structure of offices and sections. Early discussions stressed personal health: "More than ever a student must compensate for one-sided intellectual work . . . ! We therefore invite him to tumble, row, fence, play soccer and tennis, or refresh body and soul in God's free world on our hikes." Collectively this principle implied "the defense of honor," which was complicated by the corporations' demand for duelling with their own weapons and by their practice of ostracizing all students who objected. While deprecating the Bestimmungsmensur as a caricature of sport, free students argued: "We must show that we are able to protect ourselves better than they," and supported the establishment of courts of honor to defend their nonduelling members.

[55] "Auszug aus dem Wittenberger Protokoll," BA R 129, no. 434/1; various program drafts and "Die Finkenschaftstage zu Wittenberg und Berlin," *FBl* 1 (1900), nos. 7 and 9; "Grundsatzungen der Berliner Finkenschaft," (1899) in HUA, 746; "Satzungen der Organisation der Bonner Finkenschaft," in G. W. Wagner, *Zehn Jahre Bonner Freistudentenschaft* (Hamborn, 1912), pp. 12f.; "Satzungen der Marburger Freien Studentenschaft," MUA, 305a, Acc 1950/9, no. 225; K. Georges, *Was wir wollen* (n.p., 1902/1903); "Der sechste deutsche Freistudententag," *FBl* 8 (1906): 91-105; F. Auer, "Das Vertreterprinzip," Berlin, 18 May 1911, BA R 129, no. 423. Remnants of the archive of the Freistudentenschaft are preserved in the West German Federal Archives under signature R 129, nos. 423ff.; see also P. Ssymank, *Dreizehn Jahre Freistudententum* (Leipzig, 1910).

After 1902 the Freistudenten also promoted "urgent social work among [needy] students" and developed a number of pioneering services, "in order to prevent the threatening proletarization of scholarship." Toward the end of the decade they also called for "the enlargement and restructuring of the student right of assembly" in order to "emancipate the young academic from his half-pupil status" and advocated "the formation of a universal, parliamentary student council." Despite this broad activism, the free-student movement strove "to observe strict neutrality toward other student groups [by] offering as well as demanding tolerance." Burned by the failure of previous progressivism, it proclaimed: "Under no circumstances does the Freie Studentenschaft take a position on religious and political matters."[56]

When this pragmatically oriented agenda seemed too mundane, the Weimar Freistudententag of 1905 commissioned Felix Behrend to work out a more philosophical program. Called *Der Freistudentische Ideenkreis*, it "identified the nonincorporated organization form with the spirit of the university itself" in compelling rhetoric: "What flows from the essence of the university is imperative for the Freistudentenschaft." However, this blending of neohumanist reformism with the claim of representation was challenged by university authorities, who rejected the Vertreterprinzip in 1910. Thus, a more radical group of self-styled "philosophical liberals" clamored for a restructuring of the Freistudentenschaft as a "cultural party" within the university by abandoning the pretense of inclusivity:

We ask the Fr.St. to undertake a ruthless struggle against all restrictions that the state still imposes on academic freedom today; we demand forceful defense of the principle of free university access for all those qualified, without consideration of economic situation, race, sex, or religion. We demand a decisive fight against those student currents that abuse the national idea to attack the freedom of scholarship. We consider the opposition to Corps students basic and . . . call for the disappearance of all associations incapable of accepting the modern spirit.

[56] *Was wir wollen*, pp. 2f.; K. Georges and others, "Die Ehre und Ihr Schutz," in "Vom vierten Weimarer Freien Studenten-Tage," *FBl* 5 (1903): 319-26; Wagner, *Bonner Freistudentenschaft*, pp. 17ff.; A. Berendsohn, "Der Weimarer Freistudententag 1914," *RHZ* 14 (1914): 49-51; P. Ssymank, "Studentische Zeitfragen," in *FBl* 8 (1906): 97ff. as well as circular by R. Speisenbecher, "An die Organisationen und Verbände," Kiel, 1909, BA R 129, no. 426; *Resolutionen und Beschlüsse des zehnten Freistudententags in Weimar* (n.p., 1910) and *Resolutionen und Beschlüsse des 11. Deutschen Freistudententages* (Egeln, 1911); *Die Tagung des Weimarer Zweckverbandes 10. u. 11. Januar 1913 in Halle a.d.S.* (Halle, 1913), point 3; "Dritter Congress der freien deutschen Studentenschaft," *Leipziger Tageblatt*, 26 May 1902, and P. Ssymank, "Der dritte Verbandstag der Deutschen Freien Studentenschaft," *FBl* 4 (1902): 215f.

After several years of heated debates, which absorbed much creative energy and threatened the survival of the organization, the Weimar Finkentag of 1913 agreed to a minimal program, formulated by the activists without, however, transforming the practice of the Freistudentenschaft. Summarizing the thinking of almost two decades, it demanded "the implementation of equality of all immatriculated students and their unification on this basis," propagated voluntary representation, advocated a reform of student discipline, self-government, and "supplementing contemporary academic instruction" with scholarly, artistic, civic, and athletic activities, economic self-help, and educational political involvement.[57]

In practicing the notion that "the finch prospers only in liberty," the organized independents showed an astounding inventiveness which, though not always successful, greatly enriched German student life. Constructed on "a democratic basis," the formal organizational structure aimed at character education through freedom rather than corporate compulsion. "The highest authority was the general assembly, which in the beginning met often, with the presidium as executive organ." This consequential parliamentarism was complemented by an advisory committee. "For separate activities such as scholarship, art and sport, sections will be formed," while "offices will be created for the accomplishment of common useful purposes." Although the lack of mandatory fees and membership lists made the Freistudentenschaft responsive to shifting currents and changing needs, it also created recurrent complaints about the "vexing indifference of the nonincorporated, affronts by the corporations, lack of money, and quarrels in the presidium based on personal vanity." The actual life of the movement took place in an ever-changing number of sections, which rose and fell according to the popularity of their subject and the talents of their organizer. Although they had to compete with the scholarly associations, the wissenschaftliche *Abteilungen* flourished by addressing instructional needs not met in the formal curriculum, such as French conversation, stenography, or, like the social science section, by inviting Reichstag members or professors to speak publicly on such topics as "The Dirigible Zeppelin"; "Trusts and Cartels"; "The State as Work of Art or Reality"; "The Social Question as Problem of Our Culture"; or "The Sexual Ques-

---

[57] F. Schulze, "Der fünfte Freistudententag zu Weimar," *FBl* 7 (1905): 605-15; F. Behrend, *Der freistudentische Ideenkreis* (Munich, 1907); W. Ohr, *Zur Erneuerung des deutschen Studententums* (Munich, 1908); Vaterrodt, "O tempora, o mores!" *RHZ* 6 (1909), no. 4; H. Schneider, "Weimar, 1912," *RHZ* 11 (1912): 25-28; E. Pischel, "Weimar 1913," *RHZ* 13 (1913): 45-47; W. Behrendsohn, "Der Weimarer Freistudententag 1914," *RHZ* 15 (1914): 49ff.; F. Löwenthal, "Zur Programmfrage," *AR* 12 (1910): 376-79; W. Ohr, "Vor dem Weimarer Tage" (n.p., n.d.) in BA R 129, no. 434/1; and the brilliant summary of the confused debate by P. Roth, "Die Entwicklung des freistudentischen Programms," *AR* 15 (1913-14), nos. 3 and 4. See also the handbill of K. Landauer and others, *Kommilitonen!* (Berlin, 1911), BA R 129, no. 425.

tion." The artistic sections prepared musical performances for the well-attended *Stiftungsfest*, while the literary Abteilung arranged readings and held amateur theatricals ranging from light farces like "The Presentation of the Law Assessor" to serious fare by Friedrich Hebbel and Henrik Ibsen. At many universities during the summer semester the sport and game sections were most popular, for they offered billiards, chess, cards, crew, fencing, hiking, soccer, and gymnastics cheaply and sometimes even excursions "in the company of ladies." Finally, in order to decrease "the mandarin ceremonialism" of academic life, social events, justified as means "of mutual education," proliferated, be it in small informal circles, in a dancing section, or even in a special Abteilung for *Karneval* in the Rhineland! Requiring neither great ideological commitment nor financial outlay, these sections provided companionship and conviviality for hundreds of students unwilling to subject themselves to corporation authority or unable to afford association expenses.[58]

More serious activity was carried on by the various offices. The most important was the labor exchange, which procured "offers of every kind of work usually done by students, such as language lessons, mathematics, stenography, music, or drawing instruction as well as applications for positions as crammer, private tutor, editor, or translator" for a nominal fee. During the summer of 1902 the Bonn office received 82 student requests and 36 job offers and succeeded in matching up between one-quarter and two-fifths, not a very large number but an essential service for an occasionally desperate student. Another institution was the *Bücheramt*, which, after abandoning an early effort at circumventing booksellers, tried to establish a used-book exchange and eventually attempted to supplement the scholarly university library and the fashionable city collection with a student library. In those urban centers (like Berlin) where slum housing was a major problem, the free-student *Wohnungsamt* performed a vital public function by posting vacancies, publicizing examples of excessive rents or substandard accommodations, and pressing for the creation of subsidized dormitories (Charlottenburg, 1903) for poor students. Equally

---

[58] Line from a Bonn free-student song: "Die Freiheit, die stets wir zu wahren gewusst, / Wir lassen die Freiheit nicht rauben. / Die Freiheit dem Zechen, der Burschenlust! / Dem Studium, dem Streben und Glauben! / Des Vaterlands Freiheit ist höchstes Panier, / Mit Leib und Seele dienen wir ihr." Wagner, *Bonner Freistudentenschaft*, pp. 2ff., 14f., 53ff., 57f. S. Nestriepke, "Demokratie und Freie Studentenschaft," *AR* 11 (1909): 89-92; "Vorgeschichte, Gründung und Entwicklung der Bonner Freistudentenschaft," p. 4. See also the statutes mentioned above in note 54 and P. Ssymank, "Berichte über die Finkenschaftsbewegung im Wintersemester 1899-1900," *FBl* 1 (1900): 59-64; idem, "Überblick über die Finkenschaftsbewegung im Sommersemester 1900," ibid. 1 (1900): 102-11; idem, "Die Finkenschaftsbewegung im Winterhalbjahr 1900-01," ibid. 1 (1901), nos. 13/4; idem, "Die Finkenschaftsbewegung im Sommerhalbjahr 1901," ibid. 1 (1901), no. 16, and so on until the summer semester 1904 in no. 49.

popular among nonmembers proved the *Auskunftsamt*, which gradually evolved out of the business office of the Freistudentenschaft and "advised students, without cost and with discretion, in academic, legal, and military matters concerning studying, matriculation, scholarships, transcripts, housing, and so on." Moreover, the free students also "gained price reductions in stores, swimming pools, and restaurants." In one of the last prewar semesters at Bonn, roughly three times as many (612) made use of student services as participated in the sections (200) or were officers (50). A final office of general importance for the nonincorporated was the ombudsman, who "offers all academics the opportunity to resolve questions of honor without duelling, through compromise or adjudication." Some even tried to extend services such as evening courses for workers, Jugendpflege, etc. beyond the university community. In contrast to the traditionalist associations, the free students also carried on an effective proselytizing propaganda with lively handbills, local newspapers like the *Berliner Hochschulzeitung* (ca. 1900) or the *Rheinische Hochschulzeitung* (1905, 1907), a national journal of opinion such as the *Akademische Rundschau*, and through public discussion evenings centered on important student questions such as the reform of academic discipline. Imitated by Catholic Freistudenten (Freiburg, 1895) or various life reformers (temperance groups, vegetarians, etc.), the democratic organization and student services, which responded to the influx of lower-middle-class masses, modernized student subculture so that even opponents admitted in 1908: "Intellectual life at German universities pulsates within the free-student associations."[59]

Despite such reformist zeal, the continued opposition of corporations and the increasing resistance of university authorities condemned the grander academic plans of the Freistudentenschaft to failure. While the Corps haughtily affected to disdain such unseemly activities, the Burschenschaft criticized the Finken as "an all too volatile element, since they lack the necessary sense of responsibility which discipline and traditions guarantee

---

[59] W. Weber, "Studentisches Arbeitsamt," proclamation 26 June 1902, reproduced in the manuscript "Chronik des studentischen Arbeitsamtes" (Bonn, 1902-08), IHK F 1780; report of the Berlin Arbeitsamt, Wintersemester 1903-1904, HUA, 746; Wagner, *Bonner Freistudentenschaft*, pp. 29ff., 41ff., 58f. Wagner to Lüttke, 31 October 1905, reporting the results of a survey of existing offices and services, BA R 129, no. 423; *Soziales Amt der Münchener Hochschulen* (Munich, n.d.); R. Walter, *Die Studentenheimfrage im Hinblick auf das Charlottenburger Ledigenheim* (Leipzig, 1909); F. Elsass, *Die studentische Wohnungsfrage in Vergangenheit und Gegenwart* (Berlin, 1914); *Bonner Freistudentenschaft*, pp. 17, 32, 35ff., 62ff. "Ergebnisse des Fragebogens des Presseamts der Deutschen Freien Studentenschaft," surveying thirteen local papers with a claimed circulation of over 20,000, BA R 129, no. 427; "Kommilitonen!" *RHZ* 1 (1905): 1; "Zu Ehren Bismarcks," *FBl* 1 (1898), no. 1, which in 1908 was renamed *Freistudentische Rundschau* and in 1912 retitled *Akademische Rundschau: Eine Zeitschrift für das gesamte Hochschulwesen und die Interessen der akademisch gebildeten Stände*. See. F. Eulenburg, "Der Student und das Volkstum," *AR* 12 (1910): 353-60; Schulze-Ssymank, *Das deutsche Studententum*, p. 418.

in old corporations.'' The VDSt decried the "excessive radicalism" of the free students, and organized Catholics stressed "the contradiction between Catholicism and free-student ideals as they now exist.'' Such resentments often surfaced in the "festival committee's refusal of seat and vote for the Finkenschaft,'' since this embryonic form of student self-government was dominated by the corporations. When the Marburg free students rejected the offer of two council places as "inequitable," the rector suspended the Freistudentenschaft because of "vagueness of its position . . . its constantly changing demands," its tendency "to appear always larger than it is," and its attempt "to denigrate academic authority.'' While the compromise of one seat for each forty students satisfied the Finken, the second issue, "the revocation of the representation principle," produced continual struggles, which escalated after 1905 and threatened the very survival of the organization.[60] Though for symbolic reasons students construed the Vertreterprinzip as essential, such legal authorities as O. Gierke argued cogently that "the German Freistudentenschaften come under the heading of student societies," for they comprised a certain limited number of students, were founded through assemblies, had officers, and thereby also "members," even if they rejected lists and dues. Only in Leipzig and Freiburg were they officially recognized "as sole legal representatives" of the independents, while in Munich, Strassburg, and Bonn they had to form a Verein, and in the other Prussian universities and Heidelberg they comprised looser Vereinigungen, halfway between. In the summer session of 1908 the Berlin free students petitioned for clarification of lecture guidelines and a revision of disciplinary provisions. Charging "they have become inappropriate," Rector Carl Stumpf, exasperated by their claim to representation, demanded future membership lists, redefinition as a Verein, and adoption of new statutes complying with the 1879 disciplinary rules. When students refused to obey, suspension followed.[61]

[60] H. B., "Vom Weimarer Freistudententage," *BBl* 20 (1906-07): 213-15; G. Kittel, "Der neue Leipziger Studentenausschuss," *ABl* 18 (1911): 252-55; L. Seifermann, "Der Katholik und die freistudentischen Ideale," *FBl* 9 (1907): 54ff. Wagner, *Bonner Freistudentenschaft*, pp. 15ff. Beerman petition to Rector Tuczek, 30 January 1908, MUA, 305a, Acc 1950/9, no. 223; Busch, *Sehr geehrter Herr Kommilitone* (Marburg, 1909); and narrative of the dispute, MUA, 305a, Acc 1950/9, no. 202. See also "Was aus einer Suspension werden kann," *FR* 10 (1908): 27f. One of the first conflicts came at the Technical University at Charlottenburg in 1905, when the rector demanded membership lists. It was resolved when the Freistudentenschaft complied but did not abandon its representation principle. See F. Schulze, "Der fünfte Freistudententag in Weimar," *FBl* 8 (1905): 605-15.

[61] O. Gierke memorandum, a detailed survey of the constitutional history of the Freistudentenschaft, 19 June 1908, and Stumpf dissolution decree, 20 June 1908, ZStA Me, Rep 76 Va, Sekt 1 Tit XII, No 34. Rector Stumpf, "Zur Geschichte der Freien Studentenschaft im Jahre 1907-1908," with numerous addenda, such as protocol of the general assembly of the Berlin Freistudentenschaft, 27 February 1908; excerpt of the Halle file on the development of the Freistudentenschaft; petition of the Berlin Ausschuss (Berninger) to Stumpf, 27 May

Outraged by these administrative demands, seven hundred free students and sympathizers protested that "inscription in lists is the first step to a Verein and therefore to perdition." When they petitioned the ministry for redress, Stumpf defended his prohibition with four reasons: First, the "claim to represent the whole without the right or duty to do so"; second, "the unmistakable opposition to university authorities, which justifies speaking of the endangering of academic discipline"; third, "the appearance of Social Democratic speakers and extremist suffragettes, as well as the discussion of sexual topics in the presence of ladies"; and finally, the "comprehensive and far-reaching attempt to modernize academic life," which implied an "inadmissible right of cogovernance." Although Socialist and progressive politicians as well as liberal papers like the *Berliner Tageblatt* were only too happy to take up the cry of "civic equality for students," the authorities prevailed.[62] In Berlin, Bonn, and Marburg free students had to abandon their claim to representation, change their statutes, and recognize paragraph 39 of the hated Vorschriften für die Studierenden: "The Berlin Freistudentenschaft is an organizational union of nonincorporated students . . . which intends to defend their general interests," which "seeks to gather them in the common task of carrying out their academic duties . . . and to train them for the fulfillment of their national obligations as citizens." Since the professors in turn accepted a name other than "Verein," the limitation of membership lists to officers, parliamentary structure, and the inclusion of representation as a goal, the Weimar Congress of 1911 revised the national statutes to recognize Freistudentenschaften with and without the representation principle. "Every officially approved, politically and religiously neutral organization of independents" as well as "every otherwise organized group of the nonincorporated" striving to represent common interests was now accepted. The free-student struggle evoked the sympathy of reformist professors and leftist deputies in the Landtag. Karl Liebknecht argued that the prohibition of handbills for "sanitary reasons" had more to do "with the mental and spiritual [than

---

1908; Stumpf to Holle, 16 June 1908 (arguing that "the rector can allow only such personalities to lecture in general student assemblies who can be expected to treat their topic scientifically and in all other respects uncontroversially"), indicating that the action was also motivated by the authorities' suspicion of the "strong radical principles" of the free students, all in HUA, 747.

[62] Protocol of the general assembly of the Berlin Freistudentenschaft, 19 June 1908, with the speech by Dr. Behrend, HUA, 747. Stumpf to Holle, 26 June 1908, with numerous *Anlagen*; "Rektorenknüppel," *Vorwärts*, 10 July 1908; "Koalitionsfreiheit der Studierenden," *Die Hilfe*, 12 July 1908, etc.; free-student petition to the ministry, 8 August 1908; "Für die staatsbürgerliche Gleichberechtigung der Studenten," *Berliner Tageblatt*, 23 July 1908, report of an assembly with speeches by Breitscheid, Heile, and Barth; Stumpf to Holle, 12 August 1908; Trott zu Solz, January 1909, upholding the rector but allowing a refoundation with modified statutes; *Berliner Tageblatt*, 16 February 1909 and *Volkszeitung*, 25 February 1909, "Die Freie Studentenschaft," all in ZStA Me, Rep 76 Va, Sekt 1 Tit XII, No 34.

the physical] health of students." But with the help of the corporations and nationalists, the authorities succeeded in stopping the progressive challenge to the teaching monopoly of the professoriate, which was threatened by the introduction of journalism courses. Fear of discontinuity domesticated the movement and limited its influence to a declining proportion of independents, rendering its representation claim indeed "preposterous."[63]

In politics the dual principle of patriotism and neutrality blunted the impact of Freistudenten education on its members and on academic youth in general. Because of the failures of the FWV and other openly liberal organizations, the earliest (Dresden) statute draft proposed "the national unification of German students" but complied with Heinzig's injunction not to descend into *Tagespolitik*: "By this we do not mean active political participation, but rather the collaboration of diverse student forces in the solution of common questions of academic cultivation and the defense of university interests." The ambivalent resolve that "they shall not promote any specific tendency but . . . propagate Germanness by word and deed" caused innumerable practical difficulties. Tolerance alone could not reconcile the inherent contradiction between an apolitical stance and a commitment to "genuine, true patriotism." The first major quarrel arose over anti-Semitism, on the issues of Jewish officers in the Freistudentenschaft and Jewish members from the Slavic East. "Anti-Semitism is spreading among free students because the Jews, not admitted into corporations, joined the Freistudentenschaft, played a leading role, and often created resentment through their behavior," Wilhelm Ohr reflected during the Weimar Freistudententag of 1903. Voicing the majority view, Guttmann counselled: "It should be harmless and uncontroversial for Jewish comrades to participate in our offices. However, equal rights do not imply equal value. In the interest of the movement and the reconciliation between the races [greater] reserve is imperative." Although anti-Semitic pressure could not revoke formal equality, many Gentile Freistudenten were uncomfortable with the "compulsory finches" (Jews had few alternatives) and wanted to keep their membership unprovocative. A second test of

[63] Ultimatum note by rector, n.d.; revised Berlin statutes of 13 February 1909; and protocol by W. Weber and H. Eicker of a general free-student assembly, 15 February 1909, etc. in HUA, 748. "Die neuen Satzungen der Bonner Freien Studentenschaft," *RHZ* 5 (1909), no. 4; "Satzungen der Marburger Freien Studentenschaft," approved 4 March 1911, MUA, 305a, Acc 1950/9, no. 202. P. Ssymank, "Das Freistudentenproblem und die Behörden," *RHZ* 9 (1911), no. 7; *Resolutionen und Beschlüsse des 11. Deutschen Freistudententages* (Weimar, 1911), reporting a decision of the Berlin rector conference of 1910 to convert all Freistudentenschaften to Vereine, BA R 129, no. 428; E. Pischerl, "Weimar 1913," *RHZ* 13 (1913), no. 3; and P. Roth, "Die Entwicklung des freistudentischen Programms," pp. 191ff.; Friedberg in the Landtag in 1908, *AH*, vol. 515, and Liebknecht on 28 March 1912, *AH*, vol. 569. See also H. Baumann, *Die Berliner Universitätsbehörde und die Freie Studentenschaft* (Berlin, 1908) with a survey of thirty-two academics and professors.

free-student neutrality came in the Catholic baiting of 1905. The bulk of the delegates of that year's Weimar congress agreed that "confessional exclusivity within academic life is an evil." But despite inflammatory rhetoric against the ultramontane danger and its incompatibility with free-student ideals, tolerance prevailed: the Freistudentenschaft opposed "all denominational corporations. It most emphatically rejects the prevalent negative manner of the struggle against these societies," such as their exclusion from student self-government. Finally, on the related question of foreign students, the Freistudentenschaft similarly deplored "damage to or discrimination against German students" while denouncing the expulsion of foreigners from Central European universities.[64]

Although "the majority of free-student officers undoubtedly hold 'liberal' convictions," this academic liberalism remained unspecified and implicit for most members. Clearly, the organizational structure was parliamentary and the tone of the rhetoric "modern," but the protosocialist radicalism surfacing now and again in Berlin assemblies was quickly condemned as "unpatriotic," and social concern was channeled into "social work." The special affinity between liberalism and the student reform movement often occurred to the Freistudenten: "Within the student body our movement represents the democratic principle. Its adherents, its true friends can be as little reactionary as conservative or ultramontanist." But after the divisive debates of the first half-decade, "the 1907 Weimar meeting resolved that the university shall not be demeaned by becoming an arena of political parties. Hence, it declares that the free-student movement . . . must implement its reforms of academic life independently of partisanship and condemns any involvement . . . in political struggles regardless of the party." In contrast to the corporations, the free students expressed their patriotism more reticently: "We have neither time nor inclination to celebrate national festivities in which the lack of positive ideas is covered up by empty rhetoric." But this admirable reserve also disguised an inability to agree on clear political principles, which made the Freistuden-

---

[64] Dr. Heinzig, "Entwurf eines Finkenschaftsprogramms," 2 May 1900, *FBl* 1 (1900), no. 7; P. Ssymank, "Die Finkenschaftstage zu Wittenberg und Berlin," pp. 85-96; W. Marks, "Ist die Freistudentenschaft national?" ibid. 8 (1906):265-68; P. Ssymank, "Der dritte Verbandstag der Deutschen Freien Studentenschaft," ibid. 1 (1902): 215-20; Ssymank speech on the question of confessional associations, in the protocol of the fifth free-student conference in BA R 129, no. 424; F. Schulze, "Der fünfte Freistudententag zu Weimar," *FBl* 1 (1905): 605-15; and P. Roth on the "Ausländerfrage," in the protocol of the eighth free-student congress, BA R 129, no. 424, as well as P. Ssymank, "Die Stellung der Freistudenten zur Ausländerfrage," *FR* 10 (1908), no. 7. The favorite slogan, which described the attitude of the movement, was "the Freistudentenschaft is neutral—or it shall cease to exist." P. Ssymank, "Freistudentenschaft und Politik," *RHZ* 1 (1906-07), no. 6 and *Studentische Zeitfragen* (Berlin, 1906). See also E. vom Bruch, "Nationale Neutralität und Freistudentenschaft," *BBl* 22 (1908): 260-63.

tenschaft only a pale shadow of the Burschenschaft. The same Weimar congress resolved: "It is eminently desirable for the individual student to acquaint himself thoroughly with all political currents and their theoretical foundations in order to acquire deeper political cultivation." In practice this meant that politicians like the Conservative Ernst von Heydebrand, the Centrist Pfeiffer, the Free Conservative O. von Zedlitz-Neukirch, and the Progressive H. Potthoff could and did address meetings sponsored by the Freistudentenschaft. But when in 1911 the Leipzig rector allowed a Socialist like Eduard Bernstein to speak to about six hundred students and three hundred guests, a major scandal ensued. Enraged by the failure of the assembly to cheer the Kaiser, the anti-Semite Ernst Henrici called a counterdemonstration in Berlin, attended by about one thousand jeering nationalists, and ranted against the "ugly prostitution" of the Leipzig free students. Ultimately the price of survival among a largely chauvinist student body was the self-limitation of the reformers to "working spiritually," which robbed their inherent liberalism of that political effectiveness which might have challenged the antiliberal consensus.[65]

In the last prewar years the "fermentation of educated youth," the generational "battle cry against the life-style of our fathers," led German students to make yet another attempt to "develop a new, genuine youth culture." Although some frightened bureaucrats warned against "the striking moral bankruptcy" of the youth movement, thousands of adolescents rebelled against the hypocrisy and decadence of their Wilhelmian elders: "A romantic longing for nature, for distance, for strangeness and adventure drove the first *Wandervögel* to their ramblings." One contemporary educator reflected: "Some opposition against school was also at work, as well as youth's need to be by itself and freely shape its own life." As this search for a simple, genuine, healthy, natural, popular, sober, and self-disciplined "youth culture" ran counter to corporate life-style, the majority of existing organizations met the youth movement with "sympathetic but sharp criticism." Though adopting some of its external manifestations,

---

[65] G. Lüttke, "Politik und akademische Bildung: Eine Erwiderung," ibid., pp. 269f.; see the minority stance in the Generalversammlung, 19 June 1908 of the Berliner Freistudentenschaft, protocol, HUA, 747 and P. Roth, "Die Entwicklung des freistudentischen Programms," *AR* 16 (1913-14), no. 4; F. Depken, *Vom modernen Geist im deutschen Studententum* (Leipzig, 1913); P. Roth, "Der Weimarer Freistudententag 1907," *FBl* 2 (1907): 302f.; W. Ohr, "Leitsätze für die akademische Gegenwart," ibid. 2 (1907), no. 5; R. Meinel, "Die Weimarer Tagung und der Leipziger Wahlaufruf," ibid., pp. 316ff.; P. Roth, "Der Bernsteinabend der Leipziger Freien Studentenschaft und die Berliner Akademikerversammlung," *FR* 12 (1910): 371-75; P. Roth speech on the national character of the free-student movement, 1 June 1909, MS in BA R 129, no. 129. See also E. Beermann, "Der politische Liberalismus und die freistudentische Bewegung," as well as S. Nestriepke, "Politik und Freistudent," *FR* 10 (1908): 217f., 235. For the left Freistudenten, see also U. Linse, "Hochschulrevolution," especially Chapter 2.

such as hiking, folk singing, and dancing, they nevertheless rejected its ideology. Some of the less ostentatious associations, like the ADB, Wingolf, and Catholic societies, even went along with sexual abstinence and alcoholic moderation. In order to express their "new way of life," some of its graduates founded the Akademische Freischar in 1907, "seeking to combine, so to speak, 'the Wandervogel spirit' with the 'free-student' ideals of self-cultivation and education." Demanding "a struggle against everything false, diseased, and unfree," the Freischar internally promoted "the free unfolding of the personality, of friendship and unforced conviviality, mutual instruction, support, and enrichment, greater understanding for the modern development of our fatherland, while excluding partisan politics, the exchange of scholarly and political views as well as the treatment of religious, artistic, and cultural questions." Externally, the ambitious program called for "the further reform of German student life through word and deed, a campaign against outdated means of character education (Mensur, Komment, duelling) and other excesses of academe, while promoting all ethical efforts toward the ennoblement of our people."[66]

These "free students in corporation form" were followed by a number of other single-issue life reformers, such as the Bund Ethos (for sexual purity), the Bund Abstinenter Studenten or the Vortrupp (for temperance). The collegiate Wandervogel at Berlin sought to sustain adolescent "love for our German homeland, its people, its nation, which is in danger of disappearing in the metropolis" and generate "a strong and happy idealism that will strengthen us for the cultural tasks of the present and the great patriotic challenges of the future." This heady but confused movement culminated in the Erster Freideutscher Jugendtag, celebrated by two to three thousand youths at the Hohe Meissner close to Kassel in 1913. As a counterdemonstration to the patriotic centennial, it was called by four student and nine youth organizations. Not so much through the conflicting speeches of adult leaders as through spontaneous togetherness, this great Wandervogelfest showed "how, voluntarily and independent of authori-

[66] L. Hammerschlag, "Vom freideutschen Jugendtag: Jahrhundertfeier auf dem Hohen Meissner 1913," *Das freie Wort* 13 (1913): 552-55; P. Natorp, "Freideutsche Jugend," *Kunstwart und Kulturwart* 27 (1913): 97-101; Anonymous, *Jugendkultur: Dokumente zur Beurteilung der "modernsten" Form "freier" Jugenderziehung* (Munich, 1914); A. Messner, *Die freideutsche Jugendbewegung* (Langensalza, 1915), 6ff.; K. Massmann, "Wir und die Zukunft: Ein vorläufiges Schlusswort zur 'freideutschen Jugendbewegung'," *ABl* 29 (1914): 31-34; "Satzungen der Freischar Berlin," approved by Kahl 22 December 1908, HUA, 809; "Satzungsentwurf der Freischar Marburg," and flyer *Die deutsche akademische Freischar* (Marburg, n.d.) with professorial comment, MUA, 305a, Acc 1950/9, nos. 189 and 632. See also W. Laqueur, *Young Germany: A History of the German Youth Movement* (New York, 1962); and H. Pross, *Jugend, Eros, Politik* (Berlin, 1964), as well as the essay by T. Nipperdey in *Gesellschaft, Kultur, Theorie* (Göttingen, 1976).

ties, our actions have produced new life-styles and forms.'' The central resolution was doctrinally ambivalent: "Free German youth intends to shape its life in self-determination, responsibility, and inner truthfulness.'' Ranging from Gustav Wyneken's internationalism to Hermann Popert's nationalism, the movement split in the spring of 1914 into a moderate and a radical wing, seeking to work within or without the existing school system, respectively. Still under the influence of the Hohe Meissner, in Berlin the Akademische Dürerbund, the Freischar, the Temperance League, and the Wandervögel founded a Freideutscher Verband in order "to cultivate and represent the common interest of the free German students.'' Although the numbers of "long hairs, short pants'' were generally small, these cult groups, together with the Freistudentenschaft, provided a potential core for an "academic action party'' fighting for "free university cultivation.'' But their ideas were ambivalent, and the Freideutsche Jugend thought it politic to withdraw its Meissen pledge: "Regardless of circumstance we stand united for this inner freedom.'' Thus, reformist optimism proved premature. Generational rebellion, especially when centered in adolescent schoolboys, was unable to resolve the contradiction between a rejection of "hurrah-patriotism'' and deep attachment to a volkish emotionalism. Although individual students played an important role in the Wandervogel, the impact of the youth movement as a whole upon university life was relatively slight.[67]

During the last half-decade before the war, mounting reform pressure produced a defensive agreement of duelling corporations to bury their differences and cooperate in the future. Prodded by the discrimination of the Officer Corps against nonduelling reservists, the Catholic Prince zu Löwenstein and the Protestant Count Erbach-Fürstenau in 1902 founded a Deutsche Antiduell Liga, which attempted "to work against the unbearable compulsion exerted by the majority.'' By the end of the decade over one hundred student groups, comprising general Christian as well as Catholic associations, the Freistudentenschaft, and the Freischar, agreed to abolish "this remnant of earlier civilization.'' By creating local councils

[67] Statutes of *Bund Ethos*, HUA, 781; statutes of *Bund abstinenter Studenten*, MUA, 305a, Acc 1950/9, no. 179; statutes of Vortrupp, ibid., no. 188; statutes of Wandervogel, ibid., no. 184; petition for admission of the Berlin Wandervogel, 29 January 1912, HUA, 824; G. Mittelstrass and C. Schneehagen, eds., *Der Freideutsche Jugendtag 1913* (Hamburg, 1913) giving the speeches; G. Wyneken, *Die neue Jugend* (Munich, 1914); H. Popert, "Freideutsche Zukunft," *Der Vortrupp* 2 (1913): 577; Messner, *Jugendbewegung*, pp. 13ff.; statutes of the Freideutsche Verband, 13 December 1913, HUA, 833; H. Kranold, *Die freie Studentenschaft in Vergangenheit, Gegenwart und Zukunft* (Munich, 1914); W. Ohr, *Vom Kampf der deutschen Jugend* (Munich, 1914); and Schulze-Ssymank, *Das deutsche Studententum*, pp. 416f. For political ambivalence and millenarian hopes, see also Quintus, *Über die deutsche akademische Freischar* (Berlin, 1913). See also the clippings on the "Freie Studenten Bewegung, 1903-1930" in the CCA, Sammlung Scheuer.

of honor they hoped to protect opponents of the duel, which between 1904 and 1914 involved 328 students among 838 combatants (not counting Bestimmungsmensuren)! Another dangerous challenge to the "foundations of the great color corporations" was the attempt of the newer, noncolor but still duelling corporations, such as the Akademische Turn-Bund, the Sondershäuser Verband, or the VDSt, to obtain equality for their weapons.[68] Hence, alumni of the four oldest corporations began to plead for cooperation: "If German duelling students do not want to lose the place they deserve according to right and tradition, then they must close ranks in defense and cease all mutual ostracism and bodily injury, these caricatures of chivalrous ideals." While stagnation in membership made the prestigious Corps ready to compromise, deliberalization made the Burschenschaft loyal enough for collaboration, organizational stability made the Landsmannschaft socially desirable, and nationalization made the Turnerschaft an acceptable partner by eliminating most traces of Jahn's populism. Led by *Corpsphilister* W. Fabricius and the Turner student Hans Neumann, a conference convened in Marburg on 15 November 1912, ostensibly to end the feuding between the four big corporations, but in fact to reassert the leadership claim of the elite over the student body as a whole. As in the Entente Cordiale, the agreement dealt with specifics such as the elimination of *Realinjurien* and the cessation of mutual proscription, but aimed at the broader principle of establishing "a local cartel at each university" which should "extend to general student interests and specific matters of duelling students." Happy to be equal to the Corps but resentful at "raising the LC and VC up" to its own level, the Burschenschaft formally limited cooperation to common corporation problems. Nevertheless, the final Marburg Agreement of July 1913 essentially forged the *Waffenring*: "This unification of the old duelling corporations should be greeted joyfully and unreservedly," the *Korpszeitung* editorialized: "It will give them strong support against the rest of the students, especially the Freistudententum . . . and also limit the influence of the confessional associations, favored by powerful interests." Corporations excluded from this "Quadruple Alliance" and critics of "this unholy color policy" recognized the significance of the agreement: "This duelling ring has not united in a defensive alliance to avoid repression and injustice; rather,

[68] "Versammlung der Zweikampfgegner," *AMh* 18 (1901-02): 231f.; "Generalversammlung der Anti-Duell-Liga," *BBl* 18 (1904-05): 9f.; "Anträge der Deutschen Anti-Duell-Liga betreffend Änderungen des Strafgesetzbuchs, der Gerichtsverfassung und der Strafprozessordnung zwecks Bekämpfung des 'Duellunwesens'," ibid. 19 (1905-06): 33f.; H. Leonhardt, "Die deutsche Anti-Duell-Liga und das Studententum," ibid. 23 (1909-10): 277f.; "Bestimmungsmensuren," *AMh* 28 (1911-12): 427f.; "Duellziffern," *Frankfurter Zeitung*, 14 March 1914. See also the clippings on "Mensur and Duell, 1875-1912," in CCA, Sammlung Scheuer.

these corporations have banded together in order to lord it over the weaker associations and to tyrannize the entire student body.'' Instead of alleviating abuses, the reform campaign rather demonstrated ''the necessity of cooperation'' to its bitter foes in order to ''defend old German student traditions against the unjustified claims of single groups, such as the Catholic associations and especially the Freistudenten.''[69]

The ideological transformation of German students after the foundation of the Second Reich was welcomed by Prince Bismarck in the Reichstag on 14 March 1885: ''I am encouraged by the direction of today's academic youth. It possesses a far more exalted conception of national life than most of us.'' The pattern of change showed a remarkable consistency in the rise of groups aspiring to a general reform of student life, their narrowing into a programmatic association like the ADB, their abandoning of ideological claims, like the Marburg Germania, or their total disappearance, like the reform party of the 1870s. Rampant corporatism spawned an unending series of efforts to overcome it, which at best registered partial success when paradoxically assuming some of its characteristics. The content of the ideological reversal was so much shaped by the Kyffhäuser-Verband that even its opponents admitted: ''The VDSt can claim the chief credit for the decade-old reputation of students for nationalism.'' If youth is, indeed, a bellwether of adult currents, showing them more clearly and radically, the ''spiritual void'' that followed the ''intoxication of victory,'' like a political hangover, provided the main impetus for replacing student liberal nationalism of the 1840s to 1860s with cultural anti-Semitism, Christian socialism, and monarchical imperialism. Novel agitation methods such as ''public lectures . . . and great patriotic festivals,'' indoctrination of members, and encouragement from above combined to turn the widespread residual patriotism of academic youth into aggressive nationalism, directed ''against the dangers of international socialism and ultramontanism.'' The dynamics of nationalism propelled it from the ''anti-Semitic-patriotic enthusiasm'' of the 1880s via the ''Christian-social ideas'' of the 1890s, to ''pure nationalism, strongly colored by racism and to a lesser extent by imperialism'' around the turn of the century. Because of its

---

[69] Prof. Trittel article on the Marburg Abkommen, *LC-Zeitung*, 15 August 1912, p. 141; ''Ein Übereinkommen der alten schlagenden Verbände an den deutschen Universitäten,'' *AMh* 29 (1912-13): 328f.; P. Wehner, ''Das Übereinkommen der schlagenden Verbände an den deutschen Universitäten,'' *BBl* 28 (1914): 293; Neumann, ''Der Zusammenschluss der vier schlagenden Verbände,'' *ATZ* 30 (1913): 32-36. Circular of the Alemannia, 11 July 1912; session of the Geschäftsführende Ausschuss of the Burschenschaft, 21 November 1913; 33rd regular DC conference, Pentecost 1914, all in BAF, II (gedruckte Rundschreiben), DB (geschäftsführender Ausschuss) and D 19b. K. Küster, ''Zweckverband gegen die Waffenringe der Bestimmung schlagenden Verbände,'' *ADB-Zeitschrift* 8 (1912): 178. See also W. Fabricius, *Chronik und Geschichte des KSCV*, p. 141; G. Heer, *Die Burschenschaft*, 4: 94-98 and Schulze-Ssymank, *Das deutsche Studententum*, pp. 418-20.

evolution from Prussian royalism to volkish pan-Germanism, the VDSt served as an ideological pressure group within the student body, spreading its message among traditional corporations, developing associations, and loose societies as well as the mass of independents. While not inventing anti-Semitism, social concern, or imperialism, the VDSt played a crucial role in the conversion of the majority of the Akademiker to the slogans of the new right.[70]

The major countermovement, the Freistudentenschaft, responded more creatively to "the problem of cultivation in the modern world." This reemergence of the latent reform tradition expressed itself in imaginative, democratic organizational forms such as the manifold sections (which could be founded and disbanded according to any imaginable interest) and diverse offices from labor exchange to *Vergünstigungsamt*. Nevertheless, its claim of offering "neutral ground, on which all conflicting opinions can meet" and its ill-fated insistence on "representing all independents" prevented it from reversing corporate authoritarianism or nationalist predominance. Its implicit liberalism did not overcome professorial obstruction or student apathy. Free students could always be accused of being nationally unreliable, "a playground for pink and dark-red elements, antinational and international forces." Its definition of patriotism, "not as that which belongs to the program of any party, but as that which serves the material welfare of the nation," made it vulnerable on the right. While student life reform foundered on the concerted resistance of the corporations and the intermittent opposition of university authorities, the political reliberalization of German students, demanded by the left wing of the Freistudentenschaft, failed because of the "political or ideological" abstinence of the movement, which did not dare to fight openly for its inherently "progressive, democratic" ideals: "Freistudent and liberal student are pretty well the same thing." Hence, organizational developments during the Second Empire directed placid academic youths into unquestioning Hohenzollern loyalty and channelled rebellious students toward the volkish right, while allowing only a minority to find subversive paths. The pervasiveness of the corporate ideal and the disproportionate influence of the VDSt transformed student consciousness and created an illiberal tradition that denied the reformist countercurrent of the Freistudentenschaft ultimate success. A student expression of the renewal of progressive currents in the

[70] K. Zuchardt, "Das VDSt-Programm und seine Wandlungen," *AR* 16 (1913-14): 261-78; "Die Bestrebungen der Vereine Deutscher Studenten," Beilage zu den *ABl* 10 (1895): 1-3; crown prince quote from "Die Reichsfeier des Vereins Deutscher Studenten zu Berlin," *ABl* 19 (1906-07): 363-67; K. Kormann, "Wandlungen im Kyffhäuser-Verband?" ibid. 25 (1910): 225f. See also G. Heer, *Marburger Studentenleben, 1527 bis 1927* (Marburg, 1927), pp. 157ff., and G. Mechow, *Berliner Studenten, 1810-1914* (Berlin, 1976), pp. 76-119.

last decades of the empire, the free students could only capture the allegiance of a minority of academic youth.[71]

SOCIETAL SETTINGS

The programs and development of German student associations become less perplexing when they are related to their structural context. Despite the ubiquitous claim that "association membership was one of the keys to society, both in the social and professional sense," the Festschriften and scholarly literature "often lack essential quantitative proof." Thus, stereotypes of "the systematic arrogance of the Corps," of shifting recruitment "from aristocracy to plutocracy," of membership "as career insurance" populate even serious works, with little attempt to check their validity. This neglect is surprising, because the corporations themselves were continually preoccupied with projecting "an image of dynamic progress" in terms of size, with bragging about the high quality of their actives, or with basking in the reflected glory of the career success of their alumni. For instance, the standard history by Paul Ssymank talks about "the strength, power, and enthusiasm" of the Vereine Deutscher Studenten instead of trying to measure their spread and analyze their societal differences from the older corporations. The difficulties posed by the incompleteness and unreliability of sources in university archives and corporation files, which tend to exaggerate membership, are compounded by disagreements about classifications, for no universal scheme of student organizations exists. Nevertheless, the importance of complementing ideological and organizational accounts by an analysis of the social dynamics necessitates an attempt to overcome these obstacles, even if it must remain tentative. Such an examination should focus on three related clichés: If the empire was "the golden age of the corporations," what was their proportion of the student body and how did it change through time and vary from one society to another? If the Corps were "the caste-like schools of the leading political strata," what was their social composition compared to other associations and to independent students? If corporations "guaranteed professional and societal success" for their alumni, how did their subjects of study, their advancement, and their political activities differ from each other and from the rest of the student body? Although such a historical sociology of student associations is fraught with numerous dangers, its rough outlines suggest

---

[71] Vaterrodt, "O tempora, o mores! Einige kritische und notwendige Betrachtungen," *RHZ* 6 (1909), no. 4; W. Schmeitzner, *Die Freistudentenschaft, eine Gefahr für unser nationales Studententum und ein nationaler Ersatz für sie* (Leipzig, 1909); W. Baum, "Der Fall Schmeitzner," *FBl* 11 (1909): 21-24. Because of its thin empirical base, G. Botztet, *Sozialer Wandel der studentischen Korporationen: Eine theoretisch-strukturelle Analyse von Kleinsystemen* (dissertation, Münster, 1971) is disappointing.

some new hypotheses about the relationship between socialization goals, organizational forms, and the nature of political involvement.[72]

According to mandatory reports to rector and senate, the size of corporate membership varied drastically among universities, between associations, and over different periods of time (table 5-1). While at the largest institutions in the Prussian capital only one-quarter of all students formally joined a society (and another 13.6 percent participated in the student library), over two-fifths of the students at the second largest Prussian university in the provincial city of Bonn enrolled in an association, and well over half of the matriculants at the Hessian center of higher learning, Marburg, followed the corporate banner. Whereas the picturesque Lahn city was dominated by duelling corporations, in the Catholic Rhineland religious societies flourished (followed by scholarly associations), and the metropolitan distractions of Brandenburg rather encouraged wissenschaftliche gatherings and alumni groups of the famous Berlin Gymnasia (which eventually turned into corporations as well).[73] Differences in the size of individual societies were also considerable. The exclusive Corps seldom enrolled more than ten members, whereas Burschenschaften and Landsmannschaften usually exceeded a dozen, and the less restrictive color corporations averaged around twenty students. Even larger were the religious associations, while the scholarly societies showed the greatest variety, ranging from a mere handful to several hundred, depending on the popularity of the subject. In contrast to the large and amorphous Freistudentenschaft, reformist groups were usually quite small. Except in time of extraordinary activity, when they grew to over a hundred, political associations attracted about twenty students, sports club membership followed not only the seasons but also the fashions of different games, and social groups were generally limited to a couple of dozen. Women's associations were usually somewhat larger. Hence, duelling and color cor-

[72] B. Oudin, *Les Corporations allemandes d'étudiants* (Paris, 1962) unfortunately analyzes post-1945 associations. Anonymous, *Burschen heraus!* pp. 12, 33, 41. "Zur Statistik der deutschen Burschenschaften," *AMh* 23 (1906-1907): 423; "Der C.V. im Jahre 1904-05," *Ac* 18 (1905): 1ff.; and W. Fabricius, "Die Corpsstatistik in der Presse," *AMh* 2 (1883): 324-27 and many other instances. Schulze-Ssymank, *Das deutsche Studententum*, pp. 342f. Hypotheses from Oudin, *Les Corporations*, p. 14; and D. Grieswelle, "Zur Soziologie der Kösener Corps, 1870-1914," in *Student und Hochschule im 19. Jahrhundert*, pp. 346-65. Typical of the lack of quantitative underpinnings is Bleuel-Klinnert, *Deutsche Studenten*, pp. 8-48.

[73] For the differences in local milieus, see G. Heer, *Marburger Studentenleben*, pp. 138ff.; F. Ortmann, "Bilder aus dem Berliner Studentenleben," *AMbl* 13 (1901-1902): 102ff., 228ff.; W. Meyer, "Berliner Studentenleben," *AMh* 3 (1886-87): 258-62; W. Piper, "Marburg," *BBl* 4 (1890): 36ff.; M. Ebeling, "Berlin," ibid. 5 (1891): 158ff., 179ff.; and Schmitz, "Bonn als Universitätsstadt," *Ac* 12 (1899-1900), no. 9. As student association figures are notoriously imprecise, the subsequent global tables represent a first effort to establish some general parameters of relative proportion.

TABLE 5-1

Local Student Organization Membership at Marburg, Berlin, and Bonn

		Marburg			Berlin		Bonn								
		1873	1893	1913	1888/9	1913/4	1887-90	1890-92	1893-95	1896-98	1899-1901	1902-1904	1905-1907	1908-11	1912-14
1. Independents	no.	281	518	546	3758.5	6855	561.4	587.7	597.5	425.1	978.5	1469.5	2146.8	2255.1	2412.4
	%	45.7	43.8	53.4	72.6	75.6	44.3	44.4	37.7	24.8	46.8	59.3	68.6	62.0	59.8
2. Duelling Corps.	no.	250	335	185	195.5	348	106.7	102.2	107.1	119.1	123.7	146.3	161.3	205	192.0
	%	40.7	28.3	18.1	3.8	3.8	8.4	7.7	6.7	6.5	5.9	5.9	5.1	5.6	4.8
3. Color-Carrying Corps.	no.	5	80	88	75	252	83	73.5	158.6	162.1	192.8	232.9	281.5	282.8	304.6
	%	0.8	6.8	8.6	1.4	2.8	6.5	5.4	10.0	8.9	9.2	9.4	9.0	7.8	7.5
4. Religious Associations	no.	21	95	82	256	205	278	303.8	433.1	737.6	544.7	387.5	243.7	414.2	533.5
	%	3.4	8.0	8.0	4.9	2.3	21.9	22.9	27.3	40.5	26.0	15.6	7.8	11.4	13.2
5. Scholarly Associations	no.	43	120	57	329	427	176	205.5	218	242.6	148	139	179	223.6	274.4
	%	7.8	10.1	5.6	6.3	4.7	13.9	14.5	13.8	13.3	7.7	5.6	5.7	6.1	6.8
6. Political Associations	no.	0	35	32	148	313	6.8	19.3	18.6	26	26.8	19.1	23	19.8	27.4
	%		3.0	3.1	2.9	3.5	0.5	1.5	1.1	1.4	1.3	0.8	0.7	0.5	0.7
7. Sports Associations	no.				129	378		8.5	15.8	14.5	54.3	56.1	62.1	71.2	114.1
	%				2.5	4.2		0.6	1.0	0.8	2.6	2.3	2.0	1.9	2.8
8. Social Associations	no.				282.5	136	56.3	24.1	35.6	65.5	23.8	27.5	31.5	7	7.8
	%				5.5	1.5	4.3	1.8	2.3	3.6	1.1	1.1	1.0	0.2	0.2
9. Reform Associations	no.	10	0	33		64						1.1	2.7	87	58.1
	(est)			(54.6)		(342.8)						(147)	(214)	(225)	(241.2)
	%	1.6		3.2		0.7						0.05	0.09	2.4	1.4
	(est)			(5.3)		(3.8)						(5.9)	(6.8)	(6.2)	(6.0)
10. Women's Associations	no.					75								72.8	110.1
	%					0.8								2.0	2.7
Corporation Members	no.	334	665	477	1415	2198	706.8	736.9	986.7	1367.4	1114.1	1009.5	984.8	1383.4	1622
Students	no.	615	1183	1023	5173.5	9026	1268.2	1334.8	1584.1	1819.5	2092.6	2479	3131.8	3638.5	4034.4

NOTE: Organizational categories 1–10 include:

Duelling Corporations: Waffenring (Corps, Burschenschaft, Landsmannschaft, Turnerschaft) except for Bonn, where the Turner were included in Farbentragende Verbindungen.

Color-Carrying Corporations: all Verbindungen (even including the *schwarze*) other than above, hence also the CV and the Wingolf.

Religious Associations: all Catholic, Protestant, and Jewish organizations based on confession or promoting religious aims, such as the KV, Unitas, ev. Bund, DCSV, Verein Jüdischer Studenten, unless they had corporate character.

Scholarly Associations: all wissenschaftliche Vereine (noncorporate), such as theological, legal, medical, and philosophical societies, including even stenographic clubs.

Political Associations: all organizations with explicit political aims such as the VDSt, FWV, Bismarckbund, Ortsgruppe des Ostmarkenvereins.

Sports Associations: all sports clubs with noncorporate structure, such as rowing, tennis, soccer, gymnastics, and other societies.

Social Associations: all societies without firm structure with largely social aims, such as the many associations of graduates of Berlin Gymnasia (before they became corporations) and the various singing societies, such as the Liedertafel, Orchestervereinigung.

Reform Associations: all student-reform groups or life-reform societies, such as the Wandervogel, Freischar, Bund Abstinenter Studenten, unless they were more tightly structured.

Women's Associations: all organizations of female students, such as the liberal Freie Vereinigung, the nationalist Frauenbund, or the Catholic *Metchild*.

The Marburg duelling corporation value for 1873 is exaggerated by the presence of the *Reformverbindungen* Hasso-Guestphalia and Germania, which, however, already in the 1870s assumed corporate character and are therefore difficult to classify. Reform association figures do not include the Freistudentenschaft, since it had no firm membership and did not send reports to the university authorities. For the smaller universities an estimate of at most 10 percent of the independents appears plausible, whereas for Berlin 5 percent would seem already large enough for the 13 sections. Estimates given in parentheses. The Bonn religious association values for the 1890s are inflated by nominal members of such societies as the Bonifatius-Verein or the Evangelische Akademische Missionsverein and the noncorporative association of Catholic students with overlapping memberships, which cannot claim to have exerted any educational influence upon students and were therefore no longer reported in this category after the turn of the century. Figure also includes a sizable proportion of the association of Catholic theologians. For the sources of table 17, see note 74.

porations dominated student life not through their size, but rather through their tight organization, impressive external appearance (*patentes Auftreten*), and quasi-official status as representatives of the student body.[74]

The fragmentary, but increasingly reliable figures indicate that the student body share of associational clusters also changed substantially during the empire. In Marburg and Bonn the degree of corporatism increased up to the late 1890s (old ones split when they reached a certain size, varying between fifteen with Corps and thirty with religious groups) before the enrollment expansion outstripped the foundation of new organizations and the rate fell, only to recover somewhat before the outbreak of the war. Since they were most reluctant to grow, the duelling corporations were almost cut in half and could rarely boast of more than 5 percent of the students of any university by 1910, which added a sense of urgency to their banding together in the Marburg Agreement. Less selective and less expensive, the farbentragende Verbindungen initially expanded to almost one-tenth of the student body, but had difficulty in keeping their older chapters from turning into a schlagende Verbindung. (Such upgrading kept the duelling corporations from contracting even further.) Similarly, the confessional associations profited from the end of the Kulturkampf and the resurgence of religious interest in the 1880s, attracting as much as one-fifth of the student body (with allowance for the Bonn exaggeration), but given the secular tone of the new century, they could not quite maintain this momentum. The scholarly associations experienced their heyday in the late 1880s, when scientific interest was at its peak, because they provided a less restricted alternative to traditional corporatism. However, the transformation of many chapters into corporations and professorial attacks on premature professionalization (*Fachsimpelei*) reduced their popularity after the turn of the century. Sports clubs proliferated rapidly after 1900 but, like the transitory social associations, often lost local chapters to corporatization and had little ideological impact upon their members. While in the overheated atmosphere of Berlin political associations could also create a momentary stir, they had difficulty in translating this excitement into memberships, and the provincial VDSt enrolled only a small fraction of students. Initial campaigns of reform groups would attract the attention

[74] "Verzeichnis der Studierenden," for 1872-73, 1893-94, and "Alphabetisches Verzeichnis der inkorporierten Studierenden," 1913-14 in MUA, 305a, Acc 1950/9, nos. 223 and 633; and "Matrikel der Philipps-Universität Marburg," MUA, ibid., vols. 730-31, 738, and 769-70. "Zusammenstellung der im Winter-Semester 1888-89 bei der Kgl. Fr. W. Universität zu Berlin bestehenden studentischen Vereine," ZStA Me, Rep 76 Va, Sekt 2 Tit XII, No 17, vol. 1, and "Verzeichnis der im Winter-Semester 1913-14 bei der Universität Berlin bestehenden akademischen Vereine," HUA, 840. The Bonn figures are culled from *Chronik der Rheinischen Friedrich-Wilhelms-Universität zu Bonn für die Rechnungsjahre 1887-1914* (Bonn, 1888-1915), vols. 13-40, item no. 6, "studentische Vereine."

of large numbers and draw several hundred to controversial lectures, but single-purpose societies like the Temperance League had difficulty in surviving, and the large Freistudentenschaft could count on hardly more than 5 to 10 percent of the independents, even if more profited from its social services. Women's groups were primarily protective societies, gaining the support of a considerable proportion of female students when these were finally admitted to higher education. Thus, during the empire the organizational structure became more diverse, less tightly controlled by the duelling fraternities, and offered students not only a number of competing and contradictory forms of character education, but also a series of innocuous activities, such as music and sports, with few ideological pretensions.[75]

The growth of individual student corporations after 1870 was no less marked, although the early figures are somewhat distorted, for they do not include any chapters not belonging to a national association (tables 5-2 and 5-3). Due to their enormous head start, the duelling corporations expanded only three times, somewhat less than the 4.4 fold increase of the student population in the half-century between 1864 and 1914. While the older Corps grew reluctantly by one-half, the newer Burschenschaft more than doubled. Thus, the continued increase of the schlagende Verbindungen derived primarily from the uneven but rapid expansion of the Landsmannschaft and the Turnerschaft. In contrast, the color-carrying corporations multiplied tenfold, led not by the doubling of the Protestant Wingolf or Schwarzburgbund, but rather by the mushrooming of the Catholic CV and the appearance of the reform Burschenschaft and Jewish corporations. Owing to the similarly rapid growth of the Catholic Vereine (KV, Unitas, and others) as well as the more limited increase of Jewish associations, the religious societies also spread like wildfire during the empire. The scholarly associations, combined eventually into the Deutsche Wissenschafter Verband, proliferated especially before 1890, while the political organizations, after the spurt of the 1880s, stagnated until the last decade before the war. Since the early gymnastic societies had become duelling corporations, the Akademischer Turnerbund and other sports clubs took longer to organize, but grew quickly around the turn of the century. Because they were mostly a transitory stage for tighter incorporation, social societies hardly increased at all, except for the Sondershäuser Verband of free glee clubs, which multiplied steadily. Beginning in 1900, reforming

[75] Above and Schulze-Ssymank, *Das deutsche Studententum*, pp. 327-420. For 1903 J. H. Bonn estimates a ratio of 1:48 between 784 corporations and about 38,000 students, indicating that almost half of the Kommilitonen were members of a bona fide student organization, which were "generally stronger in smaller universities than in the larger ones." "Statistisches über das Korporationswesen an den deutschen Universitäten im S.S. 1903," *AMbl* 16 (1904-05): 97-98.

TABLE 5-2

Number of National Student Organization Chapters

	1864	1866	1868	1870	1872	1874	1876	1878	1880	1882	1884	1886	1888	1890	1892	1894	1896	1898	1900	1902	1904	1906	1908	1910	1912	1913	1914 Un	1914 TH	1914 For	1914 Total
1. Korps	65	67	66	69	66	68	72	82	82	84	83	81	81	80	80	78	79	85	87	88	86	91	93	93	96	97	93		4	97
Burschft.	25	18	17	14	15	21	22	25	28	41	39	46	42	45	49	47	50	58	59	60	61	62	64	65	65	66	65	1		66
Landsmsch.			5	6	9	11	14	9	10	9	13	21	26	25	30	34	34	14	22	28	26	37	41	49	52	51	51			51
Turnersch.					3	5	6	9	10	12	15	19	20	18	20	21	26	31	29	36	41	44	50	50	56	57	46		11	57
DUELLING	90													168													255	12	4	271
2. ADB																														
Wingolf	11	12	12	13	14	15	14	13	13	13	15	15	15	15	15	15	15	15	17	19	21	23	23	25	27	28	18	9		27
Schwarzb.															4	5	5	7	4	10	12	18	23	21	22	22	19	3		22
[?]											6	6	9	4	7	6	6	7	7	7	8	9	9	10	11	11	11			11
Cath. Vbd.	4	5	5	5	7	8	8	9	11	11	16	16	17	18	21	21	22	26	32	38	43	55	66	71	79	80	48	14	20	82
Jüd. KC																	5	5	5	4	5	9	10	10	10	10	8	2		10
K.Zion. V.																						x	3	5	5	5	5			5
WCC Säng.																	21	14	8	8	16	14	19	19	21	17	10	4		14
RKV														4	4	5	5	7	7	7	7	7	6	6	4	4	4			4
REC																						7	8	8	8	9	9			9
COLOR CORP.	15													51													132	32	20	184
3. Cath. Ver.	2	5	6	6	8	12	16	18	19	21	21	21	22	22	23	25	27	27	31	34	41	46	45	47	51	51	34	16	1	51
Unitas		2	2	2	2	2	3	3	3	3	3	3	3	3	3	3	4	4	5	9	10	12	15	16	17	20	18		1	19
Oth. Cath.											2	2	2	2	3	4	5	5	6	7	7	7	7	9	10	10	10			10
B. Jüd. Cor.																4	4	5	6	5	6	8	8	9	11	10	9	1		10
B. Jüd. Ak.																						x				7	7			7
DCSV																		x									20	7		27
Leucht.																								3	3	4	4			4
RELIGIOUS	2													27													102	24	2	128
4. VDSt										9	11	14	15	15	17	17	18	21	21	23	24	25	28	29	29	29	20	8		28
FWV																						3	3	3	3	3				3

Bismarck.																					x			9	3		12
Freibund																					x				—		7
Dt.Völk.S.																						x		—	—		14
POLITICAL												15												53	11		**64**
	3	6	8	9	9	12	13	15	15	17	18	17	14	14	13	16	19	22	24	26	29	30	33	34		1	
5. Arnst.V.													14	14	13	16	21	21	18	18	18	18	18	18	18		19
Eisen.K.			7		10	11	12	13	14	14	15	15	15	15	15	14	12	12	13	13	7	7	6	6	14	12	14
Weimar.						8		9	11	10	14	13	13	12	13	13	12	11	12	11	11	9	9	9	10		10
Landw.V.									7	6	7	8	8	8	8	8	8	8	8	8	7	7	7	8	8		8
Naumb.V.									6	5	8	11	13	13	12	13	12	11	11	12	13	11	13	13	15		15
Leucht.B.											6	8	8	8	8	9	7	7	10	9	9	9	9	8	7		7
Leipzg.V.													9	9	9	9	9	8	9	11	11	11	11	11	11		11
Gosl.V.													7	7	9	8	8	8	9	9	10	8	8	11	10	9	9
(DWV)																							(x	(x	70	3	73)
Gablsb.																2	2	4	8			9	9	8	8		8
Sten.S.																			4			6	6	7	8		6
Arnst.C.																						7	8	7	8		9
V.Lit.V.																						8	8	8	8		8
SCHOLARLY												72													124		**124**
6. ATB		5	5				11	12	14	16	19	22	24	26	29	30	33	34	39	39					25	12	1	38
ARB															7	7	6	6	7	7						12		7
ASB																	x	x	x							12	—	43
SPORT ASSOCIATIONS												12													75	12	1	**88**
7. Sondh.	4	5	7	10	10	6	9	10	12	14	13	13	15	15	16	17	17	20	21	21	21	21	21	21	19	2		21
Sieb.S.											x												3			2	4	7
SOCIAL ASSOCIATIONS												14													21	2	5	**28**
8. Fr.St.																			4			33	33		16	18		34
F.V.Kat.S.																						7			9		1	10
Babs.St.																		x				16	16	16	15	1		16
Kabst.V.																		x				18	18	18	5	12	1	18

TABLE 5-2 (cont.)

	1864	1866	1868	1870	1872	1874	1876	1878	1880	1882	1884	1886	1888	1890	1892	1894	1896	1898	1900	1902	1904	1906	1908	1910	1912	1913	1914 Un	TH	For	Total
Freisch.																								x	8					8
Int.St.V.																									7					7
REFORM ASSOCIATIONS																											60	31	2	93
9. VStV																						x			19		20			20
DCVSF																						x			17		14	3		17
KKatSV																										4	6		3	6
WOMEN'S ASSOCIATIONS																											40	3		43
10. Weinh.S.	12	10	10	11	13	19	24	23	19	19				14	20	25	24	28	29	33	34	40	41	44	46	45		46		46
Rud.SC											7	8	8	8	9	10	11	12	15	13	14	12	12	13	21	26	11	15		26
Rüdsh.V.																	19	19	21	25	28	33	34	34	34	34	2	33		35
ALC Mksb.																					5	6	8	10	12	9	2	8		10
Teutob.																							3		4	4		4		4
(total)	12													22													15	106		121
Münd.VC																					7	9	9	8	7	5		5		5
Rothn.B.																	10	11	11	11	11	12	12	11	7	7		7		7
Aklng.V.																			9	9	10	10	10	9	8	8		8		8
OTHER HOCHSCHULEN																												15		15

NOTE: Table 5-2 includes all national student organizations typical of student life, but not branches of national adult voluntary societies. The subdivisions are the same as in table 5-1, except that there are no independents and that heading (10) includes corporations at other institutions of higher learning, since there was some overlap into universities and vice versa. Organizations not included are, for instance, the academic missionary societies, the Bonifatius Society, the association of German clinicians, and the association for German workingmen's courses. The table understates the early local existence of corporations, since it includes them only from the point of founding a national association. Moreover it contains a number of organizations for which the date of establishment (marked by an x) and the number of affiliates in 1914 are known, but not their intervening numerical development. For the abbreviations of some of the smaller societies (such as RKV, REC, etc.), see the sources for the table in note 76, especially Seiffert, *Studentische Verbände*.

TABLE 5-3

Distribution of Student Organizations in 1914

	Universities		Other Institutions		Abroad	Total	
	No.	Percent	No.	Percent		No.	Percent
1. Duelling	288	31.9	127	49.2	4	419	35.0
2. Corporations	114	12.6	28	10.8	20	162	13.5
3. Religious	102	11.3	24	9.3	2	128	10.7
4. Scholarly	124	13.7	15	5.8		139	11.6
5. Political	53	5.9	11	4.3		64	5.3
6. Sport	75	8.3	12	4.6	1	88	7.4
7. Social	21	2.3	2	.8	5	28	2.4
8. Reform	60	6.6	31	12.0	2	93	7.8
9. Women	40	4.4	3	1.2		43	3.6
10. Other	26	2.9	5	1.9		31	2.6
TOTALS	903		258		34	1195	

NOTE: This table presents a summary and percentage comparison of the last four columns of table 5-2.

associations sprang up everywhere, but failed to leave organizational records or membership statistics, so one can only guess at their increased importance in the last prewar years. Similarly, the various women's groups were too new a feature of the academic scene to establish firm traditions before 1914. The association structure of the technical and other colleges was overwhelmingly dominated by the duelling corporations (Corps and Burschenschaft equivalents), and only the Turner, the Catholic corporations, the VDSt, and the Freistudentenschaft integrated their chapters into the regular university organizations.[76] During the last prewar years, the schlagende Verbände constituted roughly one-third of the approximately nine hundred local groups, followed by the scholarly associations, the color corporations, and religious societies. While the sports clubs were making inroads, the reformist organizations, political clubs, and women's Vereine hovered above one-twentieth of the total chapters.

Although rudimentary and somewhat contradictory (since some include

[76] "Die studentischen Verbände und ihre Entwicklung," *AMh* 31 (1913): 314f.; "Statistische Übersicht über den Stand der studentischen Korporationsverbände auf den Hochschulen deutscher Zunge am 1. Januar 1914," ibid. 32 (1914): 582f.; and P. Seiffert, *Studentische Verbände*, pp. 16-125. The last includes time series for all major organizations until 1912 and was used as a supplement. Its figures diverged only slightly from those in *AMh*. See also Fr. Sellentin, "Das Anwachsen der katholischen Studentenverbindungen und seine Ursachen," ibid. 29 (1913): 632f.

all student members, others count only the current number of actives), membership figures between 1903 and 1913 confirm the general outlines of the above distribution (table 5-4). While the Burschenschaft overtook the Corps, both were in turn outstripped by the Catholic corporations (CV) (which, however, also included many Technische Hochschulen and Austrian members) as largest student organizations (with over 4,000). They were closely followed by the Landsmannschaft, gymnastic societies, and Catholic associations (KV) with above 2,000, while the Turnerschaft, VDSt, and Sondershäuser Verband attracted over 1,000 students each. The rank order of 1908 is virtually identical with the 1913 sequence of organizations, except that the corporations (because of the CV) have a few more members and the scholarly associations somewhat fewer, while a 10 percent estimate of independent students puts the Freistudentenschaft into third place overall, with between 2,500 and 3,000 followers. Thus, the national figures substantiate the local impression of the continued but lessening predominance of duelling corporations, challenged by the rise of a host of scholarly associations, color corporations, and religious societies before 1900 and a welter of political, reformist, and women's groups during the last decade of peace. Although they are even more impressionistic, the two estimates of the associations' alumni suggest that the predominance of the Corps rested not so much on its small *activitas* as on its overwhelming Alte Herren numbers. Thus, duelling corporations had well over two-fifths of all former members, and those groups whose growth had been most recent had a proportionately smaller share. With the introduction of the Lebensprinzip, tradition in the form of the Old Boys became an important asset which guaranteed financial support and organizational continuity as well as prestige for ancient but not very large groups, like the Wingolf or the Sondershäuser Verband.[77]

If "entering a corporation became a sort of worldly obligation, inseparable from higher studies," the structural composition of German student associations should reflect "the ambition of all levels of society to follow

[77] J. H. Bonn, "Statistisches über das Korporationswesen an den deutschen Universitäten im S.S. 1903," *AMBl* 16 (1902-03): 97f.; "Die Verbände an den 46 Hochschulen," *BBl* 21 (1907): 99; "Vergleichende Tabelle," *WBl* 28 (1909): 253; Dr. Wulsten, "Die Leibesübungen in der deutschen Burschenschaft," *BuBü* 4, no. 4, 11f.; W. Kessler, "Graphische Darstellung der Entwicklung von 17 Vereinen Deutscher Studenten," *ABl* 27 (1913): 180; Fr. Beyhoff, "Der wachsende CV," *Ac* 26 (1913): 19; Dr. Moll, "Der Aktiven-Bestand des Kösener SC und der Deutschen Burschenschaft im Vergleich zur Zahl der Studierenden seit 15 Jahren," *AMh* 30 (1913), no. 19; "Aktivenbestand der grösseren studentischen Verbände im Winter-Semester 1913-14," ibid. 31 (1914): 142; and "Der Mitgliederbestand des Kyffhäuser-Verbandes der Vereine Deutscher Studenten," *ABl* 29 (1914), no. 6. For a roughly similar breakdown, see K. Rolf, "Die akademischen Verbindungen im Reiche," *RHZ* 1 (1905): 9-11. Of the chapters, 13.5 percent had their own houses, especially the SC and the DC.

the illustrious example of the crown prince.'' The survival of corporation membership lists at the University of Marburg, submitted to the rector each semester, makes it possible to test the accuracy of such impressions through a case study of 2,821 students during three sample years: 1873, 1893, and 1913. A comparison of independent and corporation students reveals a number of demographic patterns that differentiate them and distinguish kinds of associations from one another (table 5-5). While the independents' median age was well over twenty-two years, members of duelling corporations (except for the Landsmannschaft, which contained many pharmacists who were first apprenticed in business) were almost one and a half years younger. Other association students were around twenty-one, but members of scholarly societies (the loosest organizations) approached the independent average. Since many of them went directly from high school to their provincial university, corporation members and Catholics were most often from Prussia, while the Corps, Turner, and Sänger also recruited from Germany as a whole. Whereas Corpsiers, Burschenschafter, and members of social corporations, Wingolfites, and scholars tended to come more often from Hesse than unaffiliated students, the VDSt also contained many Berliners, and Catholic association students hailed primarily from Westphalia and the Rhineland. In general, duelling corporation actives were more rural (the Corpsiers from small towns, the Büchsiers and Landsmannschafter from villages), Sänger and Catholics were much more urban than the rest, and student reformers, gymnasts, and new Burschenschafter came from a greater variety of milieus. Whereas about one-third of the independents had moved between birth and matriculation, the Corps, Landsmannschafter, and Catholics were more stable. In contrast, reformers, scholars, and Protestant corporation members were more mobile than the average. Although there were 17.3 percent Catholics among the Marburg independents, almost half of all organized Catholics belonged to their own confessional associations, while only one-tenth ignored the papal injunction against duelling and joined a Corps or Burschenschaft. All other organizations were overwhelmingly Protestant. As Marburg had no Jewish fraternities, 59 of 64 Jews of the sample were unaffiliated, indicating that traditional student subculture was virtually closed to Jews well before World War I. While only three-fifths of the independents were schooled in the Gymnasium, over four-fifths of the duelling corporation members had been trained there (and about two-thirds of the Catholics), whereas reformers, social club members, scholars, and politicians had graduated from the less prestigious Realgymnasium or Oberrealschule. Except for the Landsmannschafter (many of whom were pharmacists admitted without the coveted Abitur) and, to a lesser degree, scholars and reformers, all organization members were more likely than

TABLE 5-4

Membership in National Student Organizations

	Actives				Alumni	
	1903	1907	1911	1913	1903	1908
1. Corps	2,665	2,864	3,000	2,907	40,000	30,100
Burschft	2,260	2,735	3,600	3,280	10,000	11,000
Landsmnsch.	185	1,239	1,700	2,052	2,700	3,560
Turnersch.	900	1,073	1,700	1,630		3,556
DUELLING	6,910 = 39.8%	7,911 = 34%	10,000 = 36.8%	9,869	52,700	48,216 = 43.8%
2. Wingolf	700	612	600	692	5,300	4,120
Schwarzbg.	480	583	600	719	2,100	2,000
CV	2,183	2,213	3,300	4,171	3,897	5,436
Sängersch.		1,426	1,500			5,400
KC		251	200			300
ADB		711		885	630	711
COLOR CORP.	3,363 = 22.3%	5,796 = 25.2%	6,700 = 24.6%	6,467	11,297	17,967 = 16.3%
3. KV	1,649	1,722	2,000	2,003	4,939	5,152
Unitas	360	506	500	655	1,100	1,121
DCSV			200			
BJC		310				257
RELIGIOUS	2,009 = 13.3%	2,538 = 11%	2,700 = 9.9%	2,658	6,039	6,530 = 5.9%

	1903	1907	1911	1913		
4. DWV SCHOLARLY	590 = 3.9%	2,387 = 10.1%	2,800 = 10.4%		1,085	14,051 = 12.7%
5. VDSt POLITICAL	990 = 6.5%	1,176 = 5.1%	1,250 = 4.6%	1,440 / 1,511	2,545	2,861 = 2.5%
6. ATB ARB	1,137	1,250 / 240	1,450 / 200 + 800dsb	2,023	3,064	3,120 / 323
SPORTS ASSOCIATIONS	1,137 = 7.5%	1,490 = 6.5%	2,450 = 9.0%	2,023	3,064	3,443 = 3.1%
7. Sonderh.	880	1,100	1,300		4,300	6,000
SOCIAL ASSOCIATIONS	= 5.8%	= 4.8%	= 4.8%			= 5.4%
8. OTHER ASSOCIATIONS	124 = .8%	2,002 = 8.7%	2,000 = 7.4%	1,351	200	11,411 = 10.4%
	15,103 +4,000 (miss.) 19,000 of 36,547 stud. = 52%	24,400 −1,400 (TH) 23,000 of 44,338 stud. = 51.9%	29,200 −2,000 (TH) 27,100 of 54,456 stud. = 50%	23,879 +4,776 (miss.) 28,655 of 57,705 stud. = 49.6%		110,179

NOTE: For the categories, see table 5-1. The 1903 and 1913 student data are incomplete and the totals have been adjusted according to contemporary estimates. The 1907 and 1911 student data include also technical college students in some corporations which have been eliminated in the percentage calculations of the totals. Percentages in the table refer to all known corporation members at a given date. The alumni figures, which are more unreliable, are from the same source as the membership counts in note 77.

TABLE 5-5
Demographic Characteristics of Marburg Student Organizations

	Median age	Origin (in percent)				Religion (in percent)			Schooling (in percent)				Fresh-man	Percent Male
		In-state	Provin-cial	Urban	Mobile	Catholic	Protestant	Jewish	Gymn.	Realgymn.	Oreal.	Abitur		
Unaffiliated (1345)	22.22	75.8	38.4	36.9	33.8	17.3	77.5	4.4	59.8	17.9	14.3	86.6	47.4	96.4
1. Corps (250)	20.81	77.6	53.1	31.6	23.2	11.6	87.2	.4	90.5	8.4	1.1	96.8	68.0	100
2. Bschaft. (250)	20.71	82.8	47.8	26.4	32.8	11.6	86.8	.4	77.7	16.5	5.0	96.0	75.6	100
3. Landsms. (146)	23.72	89.7	35.9	26.1	19.2	9.7	90.3		81.8	15.9		43.0	80.1	100
4. Turner (124)	20.47	78.2	40.2	41.9	35.5	3.2	95.2		60.9	21.9	17.2	95.1	63.7	100
5. Refburs. (29)	20.40	89.7	42.3	41.3	26.6	3.4	93.2	3.4	50.0	30.0	20.0	92.9	58.6	100
6. Sänger. (100)	21.06	83.0	33.7	48.0	37.0	9.0	91.0		59.6	28.8	11.5	94.8	53.0	100
7. Social (44)	20.94	86.4	63.2	17.5	25.0		97.7		36.8	21.1	42.1	97.7	65.9	100
8. Wingolf (90)	21.11	87.8	46.8	31.0	39.9	2.2	97.8		69.7	21.2	6.1	98.7	50.0	100

9. Catholic (108)	20.93	95.4	8.7	44.4	19.4	94.4	4.6	.9	64.3	25.0	10.7	97.2	45.4	99.1
10. Scholar (225)	22.20	82.7	46.2	35.9	40.4	8.1	91.4		42.6	29.5	23.0	81.7	68.0	100
11. Political (67)	20.53	92.5	9.7	31.4	32.8	4.5	95.5		56.3	34.4	9.4	97.0	52.2	100
12. Reform (43)	21.44	69.8	40.0	41.9	44.2	11.6	86.0	2.1	36.7	46.7	16.7	83.3	48.8	55.8

NOTE: Burschenschaft includes the Germania, which joined the DC after 1900. Landsmannschaft includes the Hasso-Guestphalia, which joined the LC after 1900. Turnerschaft includes two academic sports clubs (ATV) and is therefore not completely made up of duelling corporations. Sängerschaft includes also the Akademische Musikverein, which was not a corporation but rather a society. The Catholic religious associations include chapters of both associations and corporations. Reform associations do not include the Germania and Hasso-Guestphalia, since those members who made up the intercorporative *Akademische Verein* were analyzed separately in the text. Political societies include both the VDSt and the Richard Wagner Verein. The above classification, which in general follows the previous scheme but modifies it in details, was necessitated by the tyranny of small numbers in several of the categories and by the analytical desire to contrast related organizations like the Protestant Wingolf and the various Catholic religious groups. For the sources of tables 5-5 to 5-8, see note 78.

the unaffiliated to have finished secondary schooling with a proper certificate. Though slightly more than half of the independent students had previously enrolled in another university, 70 percent of the members of duelling or color-carrying corporations and of scholarly societies were freshmen, in contrast to Catholics and reformers, who ranged further afield. Finally, corporate subculture in Imperial Germany was totally male, except for an occasional reformist group, forcing female students to found their own Vereine Studierender Frauen. Despite local distortions, these demographic data reveal significant distinctions between members of duelling corporations, heterogeneous associations, and independents in general.[78]

A look at the social structure of Marburg students confirms this picture, but also suggests the need to modify some preconceptions (table 5-6). Because this Hessian university possessed an educated middle-class reputation, only 41 noblemen (1.5 percent) attended during the sample years, three of whom were members of the Corps. The impression of its aristocratic nature thus rests on a handful of the most exclusive chapters, such as the Bonn Borussia, the Göttingen Saxonia, and the Heidelberg Saxo-Borussia, which were more than half noble and included a number of princes. In the other ninety or so affiliates, neofeudalism was an aspiration rather than a birthright. In Marburg the Corpsiers were only slightly more agricultural than the independents and otherwise closely followed the general pattern of less than one-tenth industrial sons, one-fifth commercial children, and well over one-half governmental offspring. In terms of economic functions, the Burschenschaft was also no haven for plutocrats, containing slightly fewer commercial sons and more bureaucratic children, while the Landsmannschaft was a bit more industrial than the average, and the Reformburschenschaft almost three-quarters governmental in composition. Only Sängerschaft (one-fourth commercial), social association members (one-third commercial), and Catholics (more agrarian, industrial, and commercial) substantiate the thesis of the increasingly bourgeois character of student subculture. In contrast, the Protestant Wingolf, scholarly societies (largely composed of members of the philosophical faculty), and reformers recruited from more traditional bureaucratic groups. An attempt to establish the proportion of elite membership within different organi-

[78] Oudin (*Les Corporations*, 97f.) compares only the Old Boys of the CV and the Miltenberger Ring of black duelling corporations. As student organizational records have perished in Bonn and Berlin, Marburg membership lists offered a welcome alternative. The amount of labor required to trace corporation students in the matriculation records made the taking of three time slices rather than a more sophisticated sampling technique necessary. Because of the problem of empty cells, the above discussion deals with the overall pattern rather than with the dynamic developments between the three cross sections. See also G. Heer, *Marburger Studentenleben*, pp. 138ff. and H. Neuhaus, *Die Konstitutionen des Corps Teutonia*, pp. 43-86 for reasons for classifying the forty-three Marburg corporations.

zations also yields surprising results. Only the Corps and the reformers contained more members of both the economic or administrative ruling class, while the Burschenschaft approximated the unaffiliated average of one-tenth and one-sixth, respectively. The Landsmannschaft and the Catholic students also recruited more heavily from leading business circles, but other association members were more plebeian. Thus, Marburg corporation members were not necessarily superior to the rest of the Kommilitonen and differed substantially among themselves.[79]

In social class categories, the Corps drew two-thirds of its members from the upper middle class (in contrast to about one-half of the independents), and the Burschenschaft (bureaucratic) and Landsmannschaft (bourgeois) were also more exclusive than the unaffiliated. All other organizations recruited more from the lower middle class, except for the reformers, who interestingly enough duplicated the duelling corporation pattern, but with more emphasis on Besitz. The Reformburschenschaft attracted over half its members from the new middle class, while Sänger and social societies showed greater balance. The Protestant Wingolf stemmed over one-third each from higher as well as lower officials, while Catholic religious associations drew largely from the bourgeoisie (one-fifth), the old (one-third), and new (one-fifth) middle class. Only the Landsmannschaft and the scholarly societies (because of the pharmacists) enrolled more free professionals than the average. The VDSt membership seems to have been spread fairly evenly across class lines and does not substantiate a lower-middle-class hypothesis of protofascism. Sons of clerics (29), tradesmen (23), doctors (17), and farmers (15) appear to have been more numerous among the Corpsiers than children of lawyers or professors (13 each), industrialists (12), landed proprietors or businessmen (11 each). In the Burschenschaft there were many offspring of pastors (23) and teachers (20), but also considerable numbers from trading (19), farming (13), and professorial families (10). In the Landsmannschaft, actives from small business (18) and pharmacists' homes (17) were most frequent, while the Turner drew primarily from nonacademic teachers (24) and petty traders (19), as did the Sänger (15 and 15, respectively). Whereas the Wingolf recruited from clergymen (28) and lower teachers (19), Catholic associations drew upon small businessmen (15), industrialists (9), innkeepers (9), and postal clerks (9). Scholarly societies enrolled a broad spectrum of teachers' (31), traders' (21), pastors' (20), apothecaries' (17), artisans' (17), and lower state officials' sons (17). While volkish students stemmed

[79] The above results confirm and amplify the hypotheses of J. D. Cobb, "Vormärz Bonn Student Organizations: Variety and Homogeneity," (MA thesis, University of Missouri, 1973) which investigated the Bonn Corps, Burschenschaft, and radicals during the 1840s. See also K. H. Jarausch, "The Sources of German Student Unrest," pp. 533-69.

TABLE 5-6
Social Structure of Marburg Student Associations

	Nobles	Economic Sector (in percent)					Elite (in percent)					Social Class (in percent)		
		Agri-culture	In-dustry	Com-merce	Govern-ment	No Profes-sion	Eco-nomic	Bureau-cratic	High Official	Free Profes-sional	Bour-geois	Old Middle Class	New Middle Class	Lower Class
Unaffiliated (1345)	32	9.3	9.0	20.1	57.3	4.3	11.7	19.3	27.2	9.0	15.6	25.1	22.8	.3
1. Corps (250)	3	11.6	8.4	19.3	57.4	3.2	17.6	21.2	33.7	11.2	21.7	19.7	13.7	
2. Bschaft. (250)	1	10.0	9.6	16.5	59.8	4.0	10.4	15.2	33.3	7.2	14.1	25.3	20.1	
3. Landsms. (146)	1	8.2	13.7	15.8	58.2	3.4	13.0	8.2	17.1	15.8	17.1	22.6	27.4	
4. Turner (124)		8.9	9.7	20.2	56.5	3.2	8.9	11.3	20.2	8.1	12.1	29.0	30.6	
5. Refburs. (29)		3.4	10.3	13.8	72.4		3.4	6.9	13.8	3.4	6.9	24.2	51.7	
6. Sänger. (100)		7.0	10.0	24.0	54.0	5.0	8.0	14.0	26.0	4.0	15.0	30.0	25.0	1.0
7. Social (44)		15.9	4.5	31.8	45.5	2.4	6.8	9.1	22.7	2.3	9.1	27.3	24.0	

Group														
8. Wingolf (90)		5.6	6.7	11.1	75.6	1.1	5.6	8.9	32.1	6.7	7.8	11.1	34.4	
9. Catholic (108)		13.0	14.8	24.1	44.4	3.7	22.2	9.3	12.0	11.1	20.4	34.2	22.2	
10. Scholar (225)	2	4.4	12.0	11.6	69.3	1.8	6.7	11.6	22.7	14.2	7.1	21.8	33.3	.9
11. Political (67)		7.5	10.4	16.4	55.2	9.0	6.0	10.4	26.9	6.0	16.4	25.4	25.4	
12. Reform (43) (women)	2	4.7	9.3	16.3	62.8	7.0	14.0	23.3	27.9	4.7	25.6	11.6	30.2	

NOTE: If one were to include the Germania and Hasso-Guestphalia among the Reform Associations (N = 137), their profile would be more Instate (86.7%), Provincial (56.2%), Mobile (68.6%), Gymnasium-trained (65.7%), Freshmen (70.0)%, Male (86.1%), Agrarian (8.0%), Governmental (75.9%), High Official (38.3%), Free Professional (9.4%), and New Middle Class (31.2%), thereby resembling the duelling corporations more closely, from which (DC and LC) these figures would have to be subtracted.

from church (11) and school (8) families, student reformers followed the same bipolar pattern (21 and 16) with the addition of 9 professors. Although some groups largely follow the general distribution among independents (tradesmen 11.7, teachers 9.4, and pastors 7 percent) and show little social identity, other organizations (like the Corps, Burschenschaft, Catholics, etc.) reveal stronger affinities with social strata which distinguish them from each other.[80]

What hypothesis does the above evidence suggest about the social basis of German student corporations? As Marburg just approached 2,000 students by 1914 and ranked sixth among ten Prussian universities, its students were less Prussian, provincial, widely travelled, or aristocratic but more rural, immobile, Protestant, modernly trained, and female than those at Bonn (table 5-7). Because Hessian students derived more from bureaucratic backgrounds, were less connected to modern industrial professions, and also more likely to be recruited from the governmental elite, from higher officials, and the lower bureaucracy, more pursued Protestant theology, medicine, and philosophy than law. While this traditional academic pattern accounts for the high degree of corporatism at the Lahn and for the Protestant and bureaucratic character of most associations, the demographic and social structure of Marburg students is nevertheless close enough to the general German distribution to suggest several conclusions that transcend Hessian provincialism. Some impressions from memoirs and student journals turn out to be correct. Because actives concentrated on rushing incoming freshmen (*keilen*) rather than older transfer students, corporation members were younger, more Prussian, and generally also more provincial than the rest. In terms of elite membership and upper-middle-class background, the charge of exclusivity is largely accurate for the Corps and other duelling corporations (except for the Turner, which contained too many sports club members). Their arrogance toward other association students derived from their orthodox backgrounds (they recruited more from small towns and Gymnasia) in contrast to the urban, modern educated, and socially inferior Reformburschen, Sänger, social club, scholarly association, or political society members. However, other preconceptions need to be revised. Contrary to expectations, independent students were not as a whole inferior to organization members, but rather fit neatly

[80] If one isolates the 118 corporation officers (*Chargierte* down to *Schrift-* or *Kassenwart*), which is possible for 1873 and 1893, one finds that the presidents are over a year older than the actives and that *Ehrenbeamte* in general are a third of a year older than the rest. They are less Hessian, but more smalltownish, more immobile, more agrarian and industrial, and less bureaucratic, hence more old middle class, more upperclassmen with previous university attendance elsewhere, less Gymnasium trained, more Abiturienten, and more medical students. But aside from their academic seniority, they represent no discernible economic, social, or religious elite.

TABLE 5-7
Student Body Structure of Bonn and Marburg
(percentage)

	Bonn (1840s, 1865–1914)	Marburg (1873–1913)
1. Median Age	21.870 years	21.693 years
2. Origin		
Prussia	86.4	79.9
province	64.5	39.6
village	27.4	33.7
large city	21.2	12.4
immobile	61.2	67.7
3. Religion		
Catholic	52.5	15.9
Protestant	43.3	82.1
Jewish	3.5	2.3
4. Schooling		
Gymnasium	82.0	63.3
Realgymnasium	8.0	20.1
Oberreals.	3.8	12.3
Abitur	83.3	87.5
freshmen	46.9	56.5
5. Sex		
female	1.7	2.4
6. Estate		
noble	3.64	1.45
7. Economic Sector		
agriculture	13.8	9.0
industry	15.1	9.7
commerce	22.3	18.8
government	42.6	58.5
no profession	6.1	3.8
8. Elite Status		
business	14.8	11.4
bureaucratic	14.8	16.2
9. Social Class		
high official	19.2	26.6
free professional	8.3	9.3
bourgeois	24.4	15.2
old middle class	31.4	24.6
new middle class	15.9	24.1
lower class	.7	.2

TABLE 5-7 (cont)

	Bonn (1840s, 1865–1914)	Marburg (1873–1913)
10. Studies		
Protestant theology	6.2	14.0
Catholic theology	9.3	
law	33.5	19.9
medicine	13.0	26.2
philosophy	24.0	29.4
other philosophy	8.7	10.0
cameralia	1.0	.4

between the privileged duelling corporations (sometimes also the Wingolf, Catholic associations, and reformers) and the rest of the association members. Thus, for most indicators the cleavage in Marburg was rather within the corporate group. It is therefore inaccurate to view the bulk of the unaffiliated students as underprivileged in a socioeconomic sense. They were simply content with looser friendship groups or, after 1900, with the informal Abteilungen of the Freistudentenschaft. While some the *jeunesse dorée* flocked into duelling corporations, many of the lesser corporations and associations were filled by nontraditional (more urban) or less acceptable (nonelite) students from the lower middle class who sought to compensate for their shortcomings by joining a prestigious club. Finally, those minorities visibly disqualified from membership even in the second-choice groups, such as Catholics, Jews, and females, in defiant self-defense founded societies and in some cases even corporations of their own. If the fundamental thrust of the Marburg pattern holds for other universities, corporation membership in Imperial Germany was therefore motivated both by a sense of exclusive superiority and by a desire to compensate for social inferiority.[81]

Similar distinctions between duelling corporations, independents, and other associations characterize relationships between society membership and subject of study (table 5-8). The choice of faculty is only an imperfect indication of future careers, since some students switched fields, and the level of success within a given pursuit cannot be predicted. Nevertheless, the area of study depends not only on individual aptitude but also on social aspirations. In terms of demographic attributes, Marburg theological stu-

[81] For the source of the Bonn data in table 5-7, see Chapter 3. For institutional development of Marburg, see W. Heinemeyer, T. Klein, and H. Seier, eds., *Academia Marburgiensis: Beiträge zur Geschichte der Philipps-Universität Marburg* (Marburg, 1977), vol. 1. See also H. Tompert, *Lebensformen und Denkweisen der akademischen Welt*, pp. 50-58.

dents were average in age and origin, more heavily Hessian and rural, most classically educated, largely freshmen, and exclusively male. In social respects they were almost totally non-noble, the most bureaucratic but second least elitist, and more stemmed from high and lower officials than any others. Since they loved to join, their share was disproportionately high in eight of the twelve organizations analyzed. While they constituted almost two-fifths of the Wingolf (making it in effect a Protestant pre-professional association), theological students were even more numerous among the scholarly societies and the Burschenschaft owing to scientific interest and earlier tradition. Only reformers, Corps, and Landsmannschaft showed disdain for the cloth. In contrast, law students were the youngest, second most Prussian as well as least provincial, most urban, Catholic, and Jewish, second most classically trained, had most Abiturienten as well as most upper classmen, and were equally exclusively male. At the same time they were the most noble, most commercial, and somewhat agrarian, unquestionably most elitist (two-fifths!), and also most upper-middle-class faculty (over 60 percent). Hence, it is not surprising that they flocked primarily into the old duelling corporations like Corps and Burschenschaft, which comprised almost one-quarter of law students. Although newcomers like the social groups and Sänger tried to follow this example, only among Catholic associations and political societies could they also be found in considerable numbers. Contrary to expectation, independents were also somewhat more frequent, indicating that not all future lawyers felt compelled to join an organization that, like the Landsmannschaft, the scholarly societies, the reform groups, or the Wingolf, offered not enough prestige, corporate conviviality, or social protection. Each in its own way, the theological and law faculty show a close connection between the status of a field of study and the reputation of the student association its future practitioners were likely to join.[82]

On a somewhat less extreme level, medical students repeated the legal pattern, albeit with minor modifications, such as greater gregariousness. Because of the length of their study, they were the second oldest, cos-

[82] The demographic profile of the faculties is:

	Age	Prussian %	Hessian %	Rural %	Immobile %	Gymnasium %	Abitur %	Freshman %	Female %
Theology	21.533	80.2	60.8	63.2	59.4	87.2	93.3	57.9	
Law	20.946	84.9	31.9	40.6	62.8	76.7	100	46.1	
Medicine	21.880	80.2	32.6	50.3	75.6	70.2	98.6	51.1	10.3
Academic Philosophy	21.472	75.2	44.6	39.2	68.4	45.5	85.7	58.4	85.3
Practical Philosophy	24.244	83.6	30.6	50.9	65.5	40.9	21.6	82.6	2.9
Other		73.3	45.4	18.8	28.8	22.2	97.1	81.2	1.5

TABLE 5-8
Fields of Study of Marburg Student Associations

		Protestant Theology	Law	Medicine	Philosophy (academic)	Philosophy (practical)	Other	Number	Average percent of col.
Unaffiliated	% row	12.1	21.5	24.5	34.2	7.1	0.6	1345	47.7
	% col.	41.4	51.4	44.6	55.4	34.2	50.0		
1. Corps	% row	6.0	27.6	44.8	19.2	2.4		250	8.9
	% col.	3.8	12.3	15.2	5.8	2.1			
2. Bursch.	% row	15.6	24.8	32.4	23.6	3.2	0.4	250	8.9
	% col.	9.9	11.0	11.0	7.1	2.8	6.2		
3. Landsman.	% row	13.0	4.1	17.1	13.7	52.1		146	5.2
	% col.	4.8	1.1	3.4	2.4	27.2			
4. Turners.	% row	17.7	16.9	27.4	32.3	4.0	1.6	124	4.4
	% col.	5.6	3.7	4.6	4.8	1.8	12.5		
5. Refburs.	% row	17.2	20.7	20.7	34.5	6.9		29	1.0
	% col.	1.3	1.1	0.8	1.2	0.7			
6. Sängers.	% row	23.0	22.0	18.0	31.0	6.0		100	3.5
	% col.	5.8	3.9	2.4	3.7	2.1			
7. Social	% row	29.5	25.0	22.7	28.3	4.5		44	1.6
	% col.	3.3	2.0	1.4	1.0	0.7			

								Number	%
8. Wingolf	% row	37.8	13.3	18.9	30.0			90	3.2
	% col.	8.6	2.1	2.3	3.3				
9. Catholics	% row		35.2	46.3	11.1	6.5	0.9	108	3.8
	% col.		6.8	6.8	1.4	2.5	6.2		
10. Scholars	% row	20.9	1.8	15.1	31.6	30.2	0.4	225	8.0
	% col.	11.9	0.7	4.6	8.6	24.2	6.2		
11. Politic.	% row	14.9	29.9	23.9	22.4	6.0	3.0	67	2.4
	% col.	2.5	3.6	2.2	1.8	1.4	12.5		
12. Reforms.	% row	9.3	4.7	14.0	67.4	2.3	2.3	43	1.5
	% col.	2.0	0.4	0.8	3.5	0.4	6.2		
Number		394	562	738	830	281	16	2821	
Average	percent of row	14.0	19.9	26.2	29.4	10.0	0.6		

NOTE: Because of its heterogeneity the philosophical faculty was divided analytically into academic (philology, philosophy, mathematics, natural sciences) and practical (pharmacy, dentistry, agriculture) sectors. The entries under "Other" represent a smattering of cameralist studies and a few other specialties not regularly taught. In 1914 the distribution of German VDSt students was: theology, 20.9%; law, 24.6%; medicine, 25.6%; and philosophy, 28.9%.

mopolitan, relatively rural and immobile, most Catholic (since not dependent upon government employment), third most classically trained, had the second most Abiturienten as well as transfers from other universities and included an occasional female student. In social attributes they were the second most noble as well as elitist, drawn from all sectors of the economy, and especially recruited from the old middle class and the free professions (practicing physicians). Hence, medical students preferred the old duelling corporations and the Turner (with over 30 percent). Exceeding even their interest in law, almost half of the organized Catholic students were in medicine. But because of the expense of medical training, eight of the twelve Marburg organizations had fewer future doctors than their one-quarter share of the student body as a whole would lead one to expect. In demographic characteristics, academic philosophy was somewhat further down the scale, since it was second youngest, least Prussian, but still provincial, second most urban, fairly stable, but overwhelmingly Protestant group of students with predominantly modern secondary training and fewer high-school diplomas, and most women students. Although some noblemen strayed into it, fewer members of the elite chose the humanities or sciences, while industrial as well as commercial parents encouraged them; the new lower middle class especially (and somewhat less so the old lower middle class) favored this area. Thus, the most exclusive duelling corporations had proportionally fewer philosophy students, in contrast to the less prestigious Turner, Reformburschen, Sänger, and social associations. Not interested in the instant traditionalism of the older corporations, they opted for the reform of student life and were somewhat reluctant to join organizations altogether. In almost all measurable respects the practical philosophical subjects had the lowest academic status. Largely comprised of pharmacists, these students were the oldest (half over twenty-four), second most Prussian, least Hessian, second most rural, third most Catholic, most modern trained, fewest high-school graduates (almost four-fifths not), most freshmen, and also most male. Overwhelmingly non-noble, they were the least elitist, most industrial and free professional (apothecaries), as well as the most lower-middle-class group. Nevertheless, they were zealous joiners, where they could get in. Certainly they were not in the Corps or Burschenschaft or, for that matter, in most other corporations. Over one-quarter of them entered the Landsmannschaft (one of which had grown out of a Pharmazeutisch-Naturwissenschaftlicher Verein), and slightly fewer gravitated into the scholarly associations. These preferences among the four faculties demonstrate the close affinity of the old duelling corporations for legal and medical studies (and the Catholic preference for nongovernmental careers) as well as the association of the Wingolf, scholarly societies, and other less exclusive groups with theology and philosophy. The Reformburschenschaft, Turnerschaft, and VDSt attracted a more varied membership, and the Marburg Landsmannschaft constituted a peculiar case.[83]

"Wherever we may look, in every field of human endeavor, where not only bloodless theory but decisiveness and character count," the *Akademische Monatshefte* reflected with satisfaction, "the Corps and the duelling corporations that most resemble it rightly occupy a significant place among the leading figures of the nation beyond their actual numbers." Appalled by the professional success of the Corpsiers, the *Vorwärts* nevertheless concurred: "Whoever has the pope as a cousin or a minister as a fraternity brother will succeed, regardless of his lack of brains. Since the Corps Saxo-Borussia fills its ranks from our ruling caste, the Corps ribbon results in the fatal inbreeding of our official hierarchy." Long accepted without question, "this morass of corporate nepotism" is clearly evident in the subsequent careers of the student association alumni, but in a somewhat less conspiratorial way than is often assumed. Although the incompleteness and unreliability of the evidence hampers comparisons, fragmentary data suggest the following profiles (table 5-9). While the overall proportion of nobles had sunk to 8 percent in the Corps by the turn of the century, Prussian, Badensian, Mecklenburgian, and other princes joined only these most exclusive corporations and as reigning monarchs maintained a benevolent interest in them. Although Corps membership was often exaggerated as requirement for political success ("among the five imperial chancellors Bismarck was the only one"), it was also true that "in the rest of the ministries one old Corpsier often followed another." The Prussian Ministry of Interior, the Ministry of Culture, the Provincial Presidencies, the Imperial Chancellery, and the Berlin Police Presidency seemed largely to be owned by former Corps brethren. "Naturally the old Corps students are most strongly represented in the general Prussian administration and diplomacy," an Old Boy gloated: "It is probably not exaggeration

[83] The social characteristics of the faculties (all figures in percent) are:

	Noble	Agrn.	Indstrl.	Com.	Gov.	No Prof.	Bus. Elite	Gov. Elite	High Off.	Free Prof.	Bourg.	Old Mid. Class	New Mid. Class	Lower Class
Theology	.5	8.7	6.4	10.2	73.1	1.5	5.1	12.7	37.6	2.8	8.2	17.6	33.8	
Law	3.0	11.2	7.1	21.9	54.1	5.5	15.3	26.5	32.4	7.3	21.5	22.6	16.2	
Medicine	1.2	12.0	9.7	18.6	55.5	3.8	17.5	15.3	23.0	13.7	15.2	27.6	20.1	.3
Academic Philosophy	1.0	5.5	11.8	21.1	57.3	3.9	7.7	14.6	24.8	5.3	14.6	25.9	28.7	.5
Practical Philosophy	1.4	7.5	12.1	16.7	59.8	3.9	8.2	8.2	15.3	22.4	13.2	24.9	23.8	.4
Other		6.2	31.2	37.5	25.0		8.3	8.3	6.2	6.2	25.0	43.7	18.8	

TABLE 5-9

Careers of Alumni of Student Associations

		High Officials						Free Professionals				Businessmen		
		State	Justice	Church	Medicine	Education	Military	Lawyer	Doctor	Apothecary	Engineer	Landed	Industry	Commerce
1. Corps	no.	872	699	116	353	462	130	331	612	105	113	257	178	63
(4,291)	%	20.3	16.3	2.7	8.2	10.8	3.0	7.7	14.3	2.5	2.6	6.0	4.1	1.5
2. Bursch.	no.	1,015	1,932	1,060	351	1,798	56	904	2,438	145	472	96	397	202
(11,074)	%	9.2	17.4	9.6	3.2	16.2	.5	8.2	22.0	1.3	4.3	.9	3.6	1.8
3. Turner.	no.	184	472	252	54	521	13	109	780	450	278	25	232	73
(3,466)	%	5.3	13.6	7.3	1.6	15.0	.4	3.1	22.5	13.0	8.0	.7	6.7	2.1
4. VDSt	no.	227	632	754	53	740	59	283	362	144	55		145	103
(3,542)	%	6.4	17.9	21.4	1.5	21.0	1.7	5.2	10.3	4.1	1.6		4.0	3.2
5. CV	no.	283	76.7	814		284		94.3	333	41	34	25		27
(2,012)	%	14.0	3.8	40.4		14.1		4.7	16.5	2.0	1.7	1.2		1.2
6. KV	no.	435	118	1,208		479		144	727		201		103	
(3,415)	%	12.7	3.5	35.4		14.0		4.2	21.2		3.0		3.0	

NOTE: Corps figures are based on Grieswelle's compilation for the 1870s to 1880s. Burschenschaft data are for 1912. Turner members represent the Old Boys of 1906 and before, but include a few hundred TH graduates. VDSt distributions are based on the 1914 membership with the exclusion of the technical, veterinary, mining, agricultural, and forestry college graduates. CV and KV entries are based on an 1896 comparison of Alte Herren of Catholic corporations and associations.

A 1913 juxtaposition shows a ratio of 96:82 high government officials, 23:53 judicial officials, 89:87 professors and academic teachers, 33:22 officers, and 126:82 noblemen out of virtually identical totals of 6,500 respectively. The 1896 CV State, Justice, and Law figure is prorated according to the KV distribution, since the ratios in 1913 of 476 to 210 versus 494 to 233 between state and judicial officials are virtually identical. For the sources of table 5-9, see note 84.

to assert that about half of all district presidents and a great portion of all Landräte are Alte Herren of German Corps.'' Although among "the present Catholic clergy there are hardly any more former members" and "among the high Protestant divines an Old Corps student is pretty well an exception,'' in "the Reichstag and Landtag Old Boys have always been strongly represented,'' many mayors were former Corpsiers, and "numerous great landowners belong to the KSC.'' Moreover, Corps alumni tended to reach higher levels of office than their other competitors. On protest from industrial and commercial circles, the *Akademische Monatshefte* added that such notable entrepreneurs as Friedrich Bayer, Georg von Caro, Joseph Neven Du Mont, Richard von Vopelius, Gustav von Mallinckrodt, Ernst von Borsig, Ernst Poensgen, Emil Hoesch, and the Krupp consort Tilo von Wilmowski also belonged. As the editor of the *Burschenschaftliche Blätter* enviously remarked, the top governmental and economic positions in Prussia and somewhat less so in South Germany were at the beck and call of "ample means, close aristocratic relations, and laudable Corps connections."[84]

Similarly, "the Burschenschaft has, at all times, been able to count outstanding representatives of state and nation as its own.'' Although not quite admitted into the central core of power because of their erstwhile revolutionary origins, Burschenschafter "were considered acceptable material as ministers of finance, justice, and other posts and were active in the rest of Germany as presidents and leading administrative officials.'' But they were only half as numerous in higher government offices as Corpsiers and concentrated rather on "justice, scholarship, and the fine arts" as well as on medicine and the Protestant church. In contrast, the duelling Turnerschaft was only rarely found in high office, the judiciary, or the clergy, but preferred medical practice and the ownership or running of pharmacies as well as the technical professions, consequently occupying an inferior position within the elite. To this duelling corporation pattern the graduates who were in the political Vereine Deutscher Studenten form an instructive contrast, for, though more numerous in the court system

---

[84] "An Ihren Früchten sollt ihr sie erkennen," *AMh* 20 (1903-04): 1-4; "Die Saxo-Borussen," *Vorwärts*, 30 March 1914; H. Nieders, "Corpsstudenten als 'Machthaber.' Deutsche Korpsstudenten in Vergangenheit und Gegenwart," *AMh* 28 (1911): 1-9, 86-89; H. Böttger, "Die Corpsstudentische preussische Verwaltung," *BBl* 17 (1903-04): 33f. For the sources of table 5-9, see D. Grieswelle, "Zur Soziologie der Kösener Corps 1870-1914," in *Student und Hochschule*, pp. 346-65; Petzold, "Die Berufe der alten Burschenschafter," *BBl* 17 (1902-03): 29-33 and ibid. 27 (1912-13): 15-17, 32-33, 63-64; R. Grundmann, "Berufstatistik der nicht mehr studierenden Turnerschafter S.-S. 1906," *ATZ* 23 (1906-1907): 326-27; W. Rumstieg, "Eine Berufstatistik des K.V.," *ABl* 29 (1914): 198-99; Anonymous, *Die katholischen Studentenkorporationen: Bedeutung und Aufgaben derselben in der Gegenwart* (Frankfurt, 1897), pp. 243-45; and O. Fecht, "C.V. und K.V. Einige statistische Hinweise," *Ac* 27 (1914): 18ff. Wherever possible the last prewar compilation was used.

than any other group, their primary careers were the propagandistic callings of the ministry and teaching, through which they could effectively propagate their ideology. Because the organizational differences between Catholic corporations and associations were not that great, the former, which grew more slowly at the beginning, lagged behind the latter in high bureaucrats, but were socially more ambitious, as their greater number of aristocrats and officers testifies. Nevertheless, in contrast to more Protestant groups, both contained an astounding proportion of Catholic priests (between one-third and two-fifths!), a sizable number of doctors or apothecaries, and a considerable proportion of state officials (in South German governments). Owing to the nature of Catholic elites, they were increasingly underrepresented among academic teachers, lawyers, and judicial officials.

As there is no career data on independent students, one can only speculate that the reasons for the presumably greater professional success of corporation alumni included but transcended "the pervasive system of preferment." The *Deutsche Soziale Blätter* reasoned: "Every unbiased observer must conclude that either Corps education enables alumni to become good officials or that only such personalities turn to the Corps who have the talents to insure productive work as administrators. Presumably both is the case." Hence, superior social background, reinforced by corporation training and connections, accounted for unusual overall advancement, especially in an organization appropriate for an individual field, like the Wingolf for the Protestant ministry. The consequences of such corporatist "leadership" for state and society were a remarkable perpetuation of elites, modified by some competition based on knowledge or ability. "Special representative qualities, tact, vision, energy, self-assurance in official and social appearance" could be acquired at home, but if necessary also learned in a student association. The cost of this system was heavy, for it often exacted a personal price in time, money, and conformity, not to mention envy and frustration at rebuffs. Corporatism also tended to fragment elites severely, directing Corpsiers to Prussian administration, Büchsiers into the judiciary, Turner into medicine, VDSter into teaching, and Catholics into their own priesthood. The corporations were indeed "highly important organizations for church and state" in reinforcing respective segments rather than the whole. Even a National Liberal like H. Böttger complained: "Since the Prussian governmental machine is built on a somewhat one-sided system, it runs the danger of stalling in complicated political situations, of not doing justice to important cultural tasks, and of unreasonably preferring inbred circles more thoroughly and consistently than is good for the entire body politic."[85]

[85] "Corpsstudenten als Machthaber," p. 9; "Korpsstudentische preussische Verwaltung,"

The distribution of Reichstag members drawn from student corporations between 1906 and 1912 indicates connections between the makeup of associations and the political proclivities of their members in a more specific way (table 5-10). While about half of the deputies had received some higher education, fully two-fifths of those who had attended a university were alumni of student associations, and over 70 percent of these had belonged to a duelling corporation! Though their share declined gradually, the Corps still produced the most representatives, while in the Socialist landslide the Burschenschaft lost its second place to the Catholic corporations and associations. Although Corps apologists continually claimed, "the frequent accusation of political one-sidedness ought to be splendidly refuted" by their distribution over the entire political spectrum, there is no doubt that about half of their deputies preferred various varieties of conservatism (including Guelphs), and that an occasional maverick among Progressives or Socialists served as salon radical rather than as an indicator of their central ideological tendency. Hence, the liberal press correctly called "the Corps mainstays of conservatism." In contrast, the erstwhile liberal Burschenschaft showed no hardline Conservatives and clustered among National Liberals and Progressives. Landsmannschaft and Turnerschaft were about evenly distributed between right and left, but the Reformburschenschaft clearly gravitated toward radicalism (as did the Jewish KC), while the other (often duelling) corporations preferred bourgeois respectability. Catholic societies appeared exclusively in the Center party (and its Alsatian allies), while scholarly association alumni tended toward the left, as did graduates of the Freie Wissenschaftliche Vereinigung. Typically, the VDSt Old Boys were to be found on the right. Since academics from similar backgrounds could choose between Corps or Burschenschaft, Wingolf or VDSt, KC or Zionism, these political affinities between certain organizations and parties suggest that by attracting particular kinds of youths, student associations did have a generalized ideological impact upon their members according to their self-image and goals. One contemporary commentator therefore concluded: "Bismarck's observation about the division of parties analogous to the separation of student associations is

p. 34; Güldner, "Zur A-H Liste 1899," *ABl* 13 (1900): 300f.; P. Blunk, "Statistische Übersicht über die Berufs- bezw. Fakultätsverhältnisse der Mitglieder des K.V. am 1. Januar 1908," ibid. 23 (1910): 94f. *Soziale Blätter* and *Hamburger Nachrichten*, quoted in "An ihren Früchten," *AMh* 20 (1903-04): 3f., claiming five Burschenschafter as Prussian ministers and twelve as district presidents. *Die katholischen Studentenkorporationen*, pp. 246ff.; and Böttger, "Korpsstudentische preussische Verwaltung," p. 34. Hence, neither the stereotype of universal preferment, such as J. C. G. Röhl, "Higher Civil Servants in Germany 1890 to 1900," *JCH* 2 (1967): 107, nor the denial of protection by Henning, *Bildungsbürgertum der preussischen Westprovinzen*, pp. 375f. is entirely correct.

TABLE 5-10

Corporation Members in the Reichstag, 1903–12

		Conservatives	Free Conservatives	Other Conservatives	National Liberals	Center Party	Progressives	Social Democrats	Minorities	TOTAL 1903	TOTAL 1907	TOTAL 1912
1. Corps	1903	11	2	2	5	6	1		5	32	26	25
	1907	14		2	4	4		1	1			
	1912	7	3	1	5	5	1	1	2			
2. Buschft.	1903		2	2	2	2	5			13	12	6
	1907		2		2	2	6					
	1912				5		1					
3. Landsm.	1907		1							1	1	3
	1912			1			1	1				
4. Turn.	1907		1	1	1		1	1		4	5	5
	1912		1	1			2	1				
5. RefB.	1907			1	1		1	1		3	4	3
	1912						1	2				
6. CatVb.	1903					13				13	11	9
	1907					11						
	1912					9						
7. JüdVb.	1912						1					1
8. OthVb.	1907	2			3		3			8	8	8
	1912	1		1	4				(2)			
9. CatVe.	1907					5				x	5	9
	1912					9						

	1	2	3	4	5	6	7	8	Total	
10. Unit. 1907						2	x	2	5	
1912							5	4	1	
11. Schol. 1907						2	4	7	4	
1912										
12. VDSt 1907					3	1	1	1		
1912								1		
1912						2	2	2		
13. FWV 1912								2		
Deputies in 1912 no.	45	13	11	43	90	42	110	33	397	
%	11.3	3.3	2.7	10.8	22.7	9.6	25.0	7.5 (10 other)		
Academics no.	24	7	5	28	60	25	24	22(+6)	201	83
%	53.3	53.8	45.5	62.2	66.7	59.5	21.8	66.7	50.6	
Corporation Members no.	9	6	4	15	26	7	7	7	89	81
%	37.5	85.7	80.0	53.6	43.3	28.0	29.0	31.8	40.3	

NOTE: The 1903 information is too incomplete to be distributed over the entire table. The figure of 13 comprises not only the CV but also the KV and Unitas (x). The numbers in parentheses are for *Fraktionslose*. In 1907 and 1912 one of the Progressive and Socialist Minorities include Poles, Alsatians, and a few Guelphs. The deputies under "(4) Turn." was a member of the nonduelling ATB. For the source of table 5-10, see note 86.

[generally] accurate, only not all members of the same corporation enter the same party."[86]

Taken together, the size, social structure, and professional success of student corporations reveal a pattern of informal preferment and discrimination, which, though never insurmountable for an exceptional individual, influenced not only social standing but also political commitment of academics. Through controlling its numbers the Corps represented the most exclusive group, rivalled by the Burschenschaft and imitated but not reached by the lesser duelling corporations. Since the schlagende Verbindungen were generally superior to color-carrying corporations and these to associations, be they scholarly, convivial, sporting, or political, it appears that the degree of social elitism corresponded generally to the level of corporatism within an organization, thereby supporting contemporary claims. To survive in such a subculture, minorities like Catholics, Jews, and women had little choice but to form associations of their own. To the hilarity of all but its intended founder, there was even briefly talk of a Catholic Corps in 1900, despite the express opposition of the Church. However, the independents were only socially ostracized (if Marburg is typical in this regard), not sociologically inferior, and rhetorical aspersions on the depressed state of the Finken are self-serving exaggerations of either the Corps or the Freistudentenschaft, albeit for opposite ends.

In contrast, it is difficult to present any firm conclusion about the social bases of recurrent student, university, or political reform attempts, because the organizations were self-consciously loose and either perished quickly or were forced by university administrators to comply with disciplinary rules that pushed them again into a corporatist mold. If the pattern of the Bonn or Heidelberg progressives of the 1840s and the Marburg reformers of the 1870s holds for a later period as well, one might speculate that they were an intellectual counterelite, drawn from philosophy and theology rather than from the professional faculties and recruited from academic or teacher families rather than from the commercial-industrial upper or lower middle class. On the other extreme, the nationalists of the VDSt flourished in Protestant church and school circles and not in the traditional elites, even if they came only slightly more from the lower middle class than the rest. Ultimately, perceptive observers in the press and the 1903 Landtag

---

[86] "Corpsstudenten im Reichstag," *AMh* 23 (1906), no. 12; F. Schäfer, "Reichstagsabgeordnete als Korporationsstudenten," *Ac* 25 (1912): 76-79; K. Massmann, "Alte Herren studentischer Verbände im neuen Reichstage," *ABl* 26 (1912): 378; and "Korpsstudenten im Reichstage," *AMh* 29 (1912), no. 3; "Burschenschafter im Deutschen Reichstag," *BBl* 3 (1888-89): 137f. For the 1907 figures, see A. Blaustein, *Der Student in der politischen Entwicklung Deutschlands seit den Freiheitskriegen* (Munich, 1909), 24ff.; and H. Böttger, "Die Korps und die Politik," *BBl* 18 (1904): 54-58. R. Däumler, "Die Burschenschafter im Reichstag von 1912," *BBl* 26 (1912-13): 9f.; and J. Schmidt, "Zur Kritik des Begriffs Partei," *PrJhb* 42 (1878).

debate realized that the Prussian state's "reliance upon a pronounced class and status consciousness" made the Corps' favoritism in the narrower sense and the duelling corporations' preferment in the broader sense, "something Chinese which harms the people and hinders the modern state in fulfilling its difficult tasks."[87]

IN ASSESSING the impact of the hidden curriculum, the methodological problems posed by the socialization approach are formidable. Its shortcomings—superficiality, imprecision, and tautology—are all too obvious to the historian. However, student novels and academic memoirs indicate that the participants in the educational process thought they were engaged in a meaningful attempt to shape attitudes through formal Bildung or informal *Korporationserziehung*. The tension between uniformity and diversity lessens if the discussion clearly focuses on the group rather than on the individual. Although exceptional persons time and again transcend the patterns of their peers, the outlines of the collectivity must be known in order to establish their distinctiveness. Even if the interaction of differences in university climate, personal background, corporation membership, and field of study created an incredible variety of student styles, certain shared traits nevertheless made them identify with each other and set them apart from other social groups. Precision and documentation, particularly difficult for the largely mute independents and academic proletarians, can be improved through the use of quantitative methods and cumulative citation. By submerging individual differences, the measurement of collective attributes and the layering of opinion can reveal central tendencies of structures and mentalities as long as they do not vanish into nominalist abstractions. Finally, a comparison between programmatic statements and actual student behavior can help assess the impact of student self-education both on campus and after graduation. The introduction of the Lebensprinzip by the corporations created a lifelong bond which for a considerable proportion of Alte Herren perpetuated some influence of their university environment through the association journal, attendance at reunions, and the like. Instead of serving as an answer, the concept of

[87] H. Wurm, "Katholische Corps," *Ac* 14 (1901): 205-21; "The newly founded corporation wants to achieve equality through imitating the Corps with small membership, social appearance, representation and clothing, and by possibly adopting the name of Catholic Corps." Most Catholic organs treated the news as a "bad joke" and rejected this attempt at assimilation as excessive. Böttger, "Die Korps und die Politik," pp. 57f. and discussion of the law on the qualification for higher administrative service, *AH* vols. 459-60. See the derision of the *AMh* about "these female Corps," in "Catholic Corps," ibid. 19 (1901), no. 7. See also Cobb, "Vormärz Bonn Student Organizations," pp. 40ff., and Jarausch, "Sources of German Student Unrest," pp. 533f.

socialization, viewed as a way of approaching the sociopolitical aspects of formal and informal education, can help sharpen the question.[88]

In Central Europe informal education through corporate student subculture was particularly important, for the neohumanist tradition appealed more to the mind than to the heart. "We professors have hardly any direct educational influence upon you at all," Theobald Ziegler addressed his class: "You are left alone, cut off from the rest of civil society, and therefore have to educate yourself." As a formal response to this freedom and the lack of housing, dining, or recreational facilities, student associations proliferated. According to Paulsen, self-education of the youthful peer groups was their primary raison d'être, if not always in a positive sense. "After the regimented Gymnasium years a youth needs social support, contact with the like-minded, a friendship circle, which sustains and directs him, protecting him against loneliness and also against excesses of youthful libertinage and freedom." Character formation was so effective because, unlike formal education, it was "not imposed from above on passive recipients but it proceeds quietly and almost imperceptibly in intimate groups." Youthful self-education involved three key institutions. The center of conviviality was the Kneipe, the pub, which provided a place for drinking, carousing, and making new friends. Festival orators were fond of repeating: "During the clanging of cups and the singing of songs, during nature hikes and with shining swords, we grow beyond ourselves and truly sing, 'Weit geht das Herz mir auf zu neuem Lebenslauf!' " More demanding was the code of honor, expressed in "the often criticized duelling practice of the color corporations." As late as 1912 the Burschenschaft justified the Bestimmungsmensur as an essential school of character: "By putting young people on their own resources . . . by strengthening discipline . . . by reaffirming respect for an opponent . . . the duel, as long as it is honest, is an incomparable educational tool and creates friendships that last until death." The Mensur was also a crucial instrument of social selection: "Without exclusivity—no corporation." Finally, in an intellectual sense Korporationserziehung revolved around the Kränzchen, the lecture and discussion evening which perpetuated corporation lore, allowed scholarly debates, and provided political training. How effective was corporate self-education? "By entrusting himself to a color corporation the student subjects himself to a freely chosen authority; he gives up his unlimited liberty and accepts the permanent supervision

[88] Notes 10 and 11. A. Astin, "Impact of College on Students," Encyclopedia of Education (New York, 1971), 2: 221-27; comment by John E. Craig on the problem of socialization at the Social Science History Association meeting in Ann Arbor, October 1977; and Jarausch, "Liberal Education as Illiberal Socialization," p. 627. For a list of Wilhelmian professorial memoirs, see H. Tompert, Lebensformen, p. 112, and for student reminiscences, see Mechow, Berliner Studenten, pp. 90-94, 110-15.

of his comrades and the no less strict control of the public.'' Nevertheless, reality fell considerably short of such comprehensive goals. While recurrent complaints in student journals about the lack of serious dedication indicate that conscious character training left much to be desired, unconscious absorption of peer patterns was nevertheless substantial. In shared convictions, in social bearing, and in cultural style, the hidden curriculum left its mark.[89]

On balance, corporate character building reinforced those strains of formal instruction and of adult politics that tended toward academic illiberalism. Many movements propagated the renewal of student subculture (the progressives, the ADB, and the Freistudentenschaft), advocated the reform of academic life-style (the Freischar and associated youth groups), and championed political liberalism (the ALV, the Akademische Freibund) or socialism (during the 1890s). But these leftist impulses lost their hold on the majority of students during the 1870s and afterward formed an important, but rarely dominant countertradition. One overriding reason for this ideological reversal of academic youths was the primacy of corporatism. A product of the humanist neglect of student life, a reflection of the cleavages of society, and a response to the dislocation of rapid modernization (emergence of the mass university), this tradition created a wealth of groups, self-preoccupied and often anti-intellectual. Although liberal theorists heralded the rise of voluntary associations as a democratizing force, the proliferation of student societies prevented common action, created numerous rivalries, and established a status hierarchy that locked academic youth into premodern customs, substituting Lebensfreiheit for political liberty. When confronted with a choice between activism or pranks, authorities almost invariably encouraged the drinking and duelling romanticized as *Alte Burschenherrlichkeit*. Since their unquestioning patriotism promised future loyalty, the very diversity of organizations, ranging from tight duelling corporations all the way to loose social clubs, supported the existing system by offering choices that threatened neither state nor university. Given the prominence of their Old Boys, the ostentatiousness of their houses, and the persuasiveness of their journals, the traditional corporations exerted a gravitational pull on newly founded organizations which made many, like the VC gymnasts, adopt their prestigious forms in order to be accepted on equal terms. Because the newer duelling and other associations could not match the social superiority of the older corporations, they tended to emulate either the reserved patriotism of the Corps, the

[89] T. Ziegler, *Der deutsche Student*, pp. 104f.; F. Paulsen, *Die deutschen Universitäten*, pp. 472ff.; H. Böttger, ''Rückblick und Ausblick,'' in his *Handbuch für den Deutschen Burschenschafter* (Berlin, 1912), pp. 304ff.; and Lorentzen in ''Die Reichsfeier des Vereins deutscher Studenten zu Berlin,'' *ABl* 19 (1905): 363-67.

active nationalism of the Burschenschaft, or the loud-mouthed indoctrination of the VDSt. The enticing prospect of a bureaucratic career also hardly put a premium on training members for critical citizenship. Despite their purported differences of aims and method, most student organizations were internally authoritarian, socially exclusive (at least in aspiration), and politically nationalist. Though challenging corporate predominance time and again, the reformist countercurrents (whose leadership represented a counterelite) never quite succeeded in breaking this mold. Looking back sadly across two lost world wars, the classicist Ludwig Curtius pondered: "The German university accomplished excellent things in the training of scholars, but it failed in its task of intellectually educating the nation."[90]

[90] L. Curtius, *Deutsche und Antike Welt*, p. 330. See also C. E. McClelland, *State, Society and University in Germany*, pp. 274, 314-21.

Six

THE POLITICS OF ACADEMIC YOUTH

"ONLY IGNORANCE will depreciate the students' organizations of Germany as outlived and useless institutions better honored by extinction than preservation," the historian William H. Dawson explained to British readers: "Viewed from their best sides, the associations appeal to the poetry, the sentiment, the highest and manliest feelings in young natures" by providing "the close society of others similarly circumstanced," by invoking old and "glorious traditions," and by creating a strong "personal tie" between lifelong friends. Foreign observers of the "rollicking freedom of the Corps student's life" were not much troubled about its "shady side," such as "the too serious spirit in which they are taken" or the bloody Mensur, to which they attributed "a distinct disciplinary and moral value" in fostering courage and manliness. Instead, Anglo-American visitors worried about the political conformity engendered by corporatism: "No one can accuse German students of lack of patriotism or of insusceptibility to hero worship." Admitting "I am an admirer of Germany and her Emperor, with a distinct love of discipline and a bias in favor of military training," the journalist Price Collier wrote in 1913: "But I am bound to say I found this pounding in of patriotism on every side distinctly nauseating." Although recent unification, the threat of socialism, and the exposed position of the empire could excuse a preoccupation with national self-consciousness, it often appeared excessive: "The German lion is a fine, big fellow now, with fangs and teeth, and claws as serviceable as need be, and it only makes him appear undignified to be forever looking at himself in the looking-glass." About the quality of scientific instruction, there rarely was a critical word: "It may be dull reading to tell the tale of damned professordom, but it is to Germany that we must all go to school in these matters." Instead, outside commentators worried that "her superior mental training" had deleterious political consequences: "That she has not made the [educated] independent and ready to grapple with new situations, and strange peoples, and swift emergencies, their own past and present history shows."

The contrast of scholarly excellence or freedom of student life with such cultured illiberality raises the question: How did social setting, formal teaching, and informal self-cultivation structure the politics of academic youth?[1]

In methodological terms the debate about students' political involvement has implicitly or explicitly centered on the paradigm of social control. Initially conceived as a functionalist sociological notion to explain "the way in which the major social values are established and maintained," this concept stresses solidarity among small groups and legitimacy in larger society and defines the role of educational institutions as both transmission belts of norms and gatekeepers of the professions.[2] Critical pedagogical historians have used the idea of "social control of educational institutions" to explain the "radical turning of cultivation and learning processes away from enlightenment towards systematic and conscious service in the class struggles of mature capitalism." In order to demonstrate the perversion of schooling into "a vehicle of control and repression," these revisionists have pointed to measures like "systematic prohibition of liberating communication," avoidance strategies, such as "depoliticization of cultivation," special class divisions "according to school types," the "integration of the adolescent into the religious value system," the "militarization of schools," and the inner metamorphosis of neohumanism from liberal beginnings to imperialist ends.[3] Though argued with ethical pathos, the social control thesis has been attacked for its tendency "to fuse the past with the present," its habit of assuming functions rather than documenting them, and its simplification of the conflicts and ambiguities of the past. Hence, revisionists of revisionism deplore its conspiratorial air, which tends "to reify the 'controllers' to the point that they become either a homogenous elite or are indistinguishable from society as a whole . . . and to assume that institutions are imposed by that elite or that society upon passive, malleable subjects." Because some of these weaknesses are inherent in the concept itself, one might be tempted to jettison the entire notion, had not Central European governments from Prince Metternich on sought to

---

[1] W. H. Dawson, *Germany and the Germans* (London, 1914), 1: 183-253; P. Collier, *Germany and the Germans from an American Point of View* (London, 1913), pp. 275-334; and K. H. Jarausch, "The Universities: An American View," forthcoming in J. Dukes, ed., *Wilhelmian Germany* (Berkeley, 1983).

[2] T. Parsons, *Social Structure and Personality* (New York, 1964) and C. K. Watson, *Social Control* (London, 1975).

[3] H. Titze, *Die Politisierung der Erziehung: Untersuchungen über die soziale und politische Funktion der Erziehung von der Aufklärung bis zum Hochkapitalismus* (Frankfurt, 1973), especially introduction and pp. 251ff.; C. J. Karier, P. Violas, and J. Spring, introduction to *Roots of Crisis: American Education in the Twentieth Century* (Chicago, 1973), and the essays by Karier, "Business Values and the Educational State," pp. 6-29, and Spring, "Education as a Form of Social Control," pp. 30-39, in the same volume.

foster "patriotic education" and to curb activism or dissent. Instead of debating the usefulness of social control theory in general, it seems more profitable to investigate in particular how German student politics were dictated by adult authorities and how they were controlled by academic youth itself.[4]

As much political learning took place in campus politics, an analysis of its ideological content and manner of interaction has to focus on the interplay between general setting, specific movements, and emergent institutions. Because student politics in Imperial Germany have hardly been investigated, the extant literature does not offer much guidance.[5] The social control hypothesis, however, suggests the utility of a closer look at the legal constraints and the normative formulations about the relationship between students and politics which provided the framework for youthful actions. The criticism of foreign observers indicates the need for greater scrutiny of the ideological content of the campus struggles beginning in the 1880s in order to distinguish the pattern, reasons, and results of the new nationalism. Finally, the contemporary controversy about the role of student self-government hints at the advisability of more sustained attention to the tortuous and self-contradictory evolution of representative institutions of academic youth and of probing the contradictions between their procedural liberalism and their illiberal substantive use. On the one hand, William II continued to extoll corporatism: "As in the Middle Ages manly strength and courage were steeled by the practice of jousting in tournaments, so the spirit and habits acquired from membership in a Corps furnish us with that degree of fortitude necessary to us when we go out into the world, and which will last as long as there are German universities." On the other hand, the Socialist *Vorwärts* deprecated youthful efforts at participation and emancipation: "The sad descendants of the revolutionary German students [of 1848] justly deserve their lack of rights." But despite adult indifference or annoyance, a vigorous student politics emerged during the empire which, though much less known, was at least as important for

---

[4] B. Franklin, "Education for Social Control," *HEQ* 14 (1974): 131-36; F. M. Hammack, "Rethinking Revisionism," ibid. 16 (1976): 53-61; R. Fox, "Beyond 'Social Control': Institutions and Disorder in Bourgeois Society," ibid., 203-207.; D. K. Cohen and B. H. Rosenberg, "Functions and Fantasies: Understanding Schools in Capitalist America," ibid. 17 (1977): 113-37 and P. Lundgreen, "Historische Bildungsforschung," *Historische Sozialwissenschaft* (Göttingen, 1977), pp. 96-106.

[5] Typical of these shortcomings is the deductive sociologese of G. Bartol, *Ideologie und studentischer Protest. Untersuchungen zur Entstehung deutscher Studentenbewegungen im 19. und 20. Jahrhundert* (Munich, 1978). The massiveness and dispersal of documentation dictates a mixed exemplary and narrative approach. As the University of Berlin was the most politicized institution, the analysis will focus on its struggles and draw in other Hochschulen whenever conflicts spread beyond the German capital.

the political self-education of academic youth as the hidden curriculum of corporatism.[6]

CONSTRAINTS ON ACTIVISM

While the Prussian government set few positive goals for youth's political participation, the Ministry of Culture used student law and regulations to eliminate negative political influences. As a relic of the medieval corporate structure of the university, students (in the decree of 1819) enjoyed special academic jurisdiction, setting them apart as a separate estate from bourgeois society and imposing a stricter social and political discipline than on working youths. This tradition furnished the legal basis for Metternich's repression of the subversive Burschenschaft as well as for the de facto toleration of student social excesses (drinking, duelling, etc.) by the university authorities, more sympathetic to upper-middle-class life-style rebellion than to seditious activism. One of the central demands of progressive agitation during the 1840s and a keystone of student and professorial reform proposals during the 1848 revolution, the abolition of academic justice became an irritant for subsequent ministries which, though ruthlessly suppressing unrest, gradually groped toward ending this legal anomaly.[7] The Prussian acquisition of the universities of Göttingen, Marburg, and Kiel during 1866 made a uniform set of student rules imperative and led to the inclusion of the principle "academic justice is abolished" in the Mühler draft of the Prussian school law of 1869. "In regard to the students, the disciplinary power of the university offices remains in force." Aside from "actual academic violations that concern estate and profession of the students and their relations toward their superiors," most of the transgressions that fell under its scope involved duelling. Ironically, the only section of the ill-fated *Unterrichtsgesetz* to become law under Minister Falk were the provisions dealing with students, since the imperial *Gerichtsverfassungsgesetz* of 1877 abolished separate academic jurisdiction and therefore required a "reform of the legal and disciplinary situations of the students . . . through a special law." As one of the last liberal measures of the founding of the empire, the Prussian Ministry of State in November 1878 endorsed "elim-

---

[6] William II in May 1891, quoted by Dawson, *Germany*, p. 247. Article on the establishment of a Berlin student council in the *Vorwärts*, 15 July 1914, clipping in ZStA Me, Rep 76 Va, Sekt 2 Tit XII, No 26, vol. 1. See also K. E. Pollmann, "Das politische Verhalten der Studenten im deutschen Kaiserreich," *Mitteilungen der technischen Universität Braunschweig*, 14 (1979): 21-25.

[7] K. H. Jarausch, "The Sources of German Student Unrest," *University in Society* (Princeton, 1974) 2: 533ff.; R. Müth, *Studentische Emanzipation und staatliche Repression: Die politische Bewegung der Tübinger Studenten im Vormärz* (Tübingen, 1977), pp. 47-224; and W. König, *Universitätsreform in Bayern in den Revolutionsjahren 1848-49* (Munich, 1980).

inating the exceptional status" of students and charged the university "with maintaining order, morality, and honor among students and with interceding against the excesses of academic life preventively or repressively without unsuitable reduction in academic freedom."[8]

The fifteen-paragraph draft that Falk submitted to the Prussian Landtag in January 1879 breathed a spirit of legal modernization and bureaucratic control. The first provision "abolished the previously anomalous position of the student in regard to material law," thereby "subjecting him to the power of the police like any other citizen" and eliminating all ancient credit regulations. The following sections left "the disciplinary authority of the university untouched," emphasized that "all student actions should correspond to the purpose for which they attend the university," while adding detailed stipulations about the locus of disciplinary powers, the severity and manner of punishment, the possibility of appeal, and so on. In the justice commission of the upper house, Professor Beseler only warned that "one ought not to deceive oneself about the effectiveness of academic discipline. It might negatively prevent abuses or impose retribution, while it could not positively force industriousness and morality." But few changes were suggested, for the deputies saw the students as "future bearers of morality, patriotic attitudes, and scholarship among the nation" and as keepers "of idealism in our national life." In contrast, the more liberal lower house exposed the political and social limitations of the bill. Progressive deputy Paul Langerhans rejected the second part of paragraph 2, regulating "associations and assemblies" in order to "maintain order, custom and honor among students." Since many were already twenty-one years old, this clause appeared "an infringement of such rights as attendance at political assemblies, which belong to them according to general law." The leading constitutional lawyer and old liberal Gneist answered typically: "Disciplinary concern for the honor of student life has largely arisen because of unchecked association, especially due to participation in Social Democratic Vereine." Other academic spokesmen, like the famous classicist Theodor Mommsen, called the university "an educational institution above all," and the Prussian historian Sybel went so far as to argue that "in a broader and higher sense students are still pupils," recalling the Vormärz, "when our students in great numbers enthusiastically cultivated political associations" without much benefit to the fa-

---

[8] Halle curator to Raumer, 31 August 1857; Beseler to Raumer, 2 November 1862; Wildenow to Mühler, 20 February 1866; de la Croix note of 31 October 1866; Falk to Horn, 13 January 1873, all in ZStA Me, Rep 76 Va, Sekt 1 Tit XII, No 22, vol. 1; Mühler draft in BUA, C 12; Falk to Ministry of State, 12 October 1878 with draft law and motives, ZStA Me, Rep 92, Falk, No 10; debate of Prussian Ministry of State, 20 November 1878, ZStA Me, 2.2.1., No 21404. See also Falk to Prussian curators, 1 June 1876, and the answer of the Marburg curator, MUA Acc 1975/9, no. 2031.

therland: "As long as I have had any influence on our students . . . I have always said to them: 'For the present you are here to learn, to prepare yourself through scholarship for later political activity. Therefore, don't fritter away your learning time in political associations, which produce nothing but immature things anyway.' " This academic endorsement of "the right and the duty to control the political life of students" drew a caustic reply from the old Bismarck opponent Eduard Lasker: "The students are being denied rights that cannot be taken away from any journeyman!"⁹

The continuation of the debate in the lower house demonstrated that behind its seemingly innocuous language the student bill contained social prejudices as well. The two-week incarceration in a special, romantically hallowed university gaol (*Karzer*) was, according to Progressive objections, "incompatible with Imperial German law." But Conservative defenders called it "the last vestige of the honor status of the students." Once again Gneist exposed the elitist basis of the arguments for the continuation of this symbolic anomaly: "Ask yourself, can one justify punishing a [slight] transgression in a manner that locks a young man from a good family up with the dirtiest class of prisoners, who cannot be segregated in the mass institutions of the teeming cities?" On the basis of rose-colored student recollections, the Catholic leader Windthorst sought to belittle the issue as "excessive egalitarianism," but Mommsen replied angrily: "We, at least, want no privileges; if you put them in, I must, as far as I know our mood, say: you are forcing privileges on us which we reject." Another controversial issue was the question of relegation, of expulsion from the university. Because it was the most severe punishment, Liberal deputy Albert Hänel wanted to restrict it to students who "had been found guilty of those crimes that result from a dishonorable spirit." In contrast, Privy Councillor Göppert, speaking for the Ministry of Culture, argued: "This punishment intends to purify the scholarly profession in time." Some "dishonest elements" might not be legally liable, but nevertheless be so objectionable that they needed to be excluded from academe. When the left wanted students to maintain their academic rights while being tried in civil court, the right warned against violating the solidarity (*Corpsgeist*) of German youth: "If a student is so disreputable that he is being inves-

⁹ "Entwurf eines Gesetzes betreffend die Rechtsverhältnisse der Studierenden und die Disziplin auf den Landes-Universitäten, der Akademie zu Münster und dem Lyzeum Hosianum in Braunsberg," *HH*, Anlagen 1878-79, pp. 79-86. "Bericht der Justizkommission über den Entwurf eines Gesetzes. . . ." ibid., pp. 150-56, for Beseler quote: "If one wanted to go further in this direction, one would endanger the essence of German universities, whose value for national cultivation is inestimable, especially at a time when material interests are pressing forward everywhere." Debates in the upper house are in *HH*, 6 February 1879, pp. 77-85, while the lower house discussions are in *AH*, 19 February 1879, pp. 1500-1512.

tigated because of a crime for which his civil rights can be revoked, should he, during this proceeding, which sometimes takes months, sit on the same bench with his comrades? What would happen then! What excesses would arise!'' Despite some misgivings, the government accepted eliminating any reference to associations and assemblies, for ''it does not change anything in the present situation,'' swallowed a more explicit mention of the Karzer than it had intended, and tolerated the modifications regarding relegations so that the bill could become law on 21 February 1879.[10]

This disciplinary law reveals the fundamental ambivalence of bureaucratic, professorial, and parliamentary attitudes toward social and political control of students. On the one hand, the corporatist legacy of separate legal status was offensive to liberal opinion. On the other hand, the experience with student radicalism in the first half of the nineteenth century led to governmental fears about subversive instruction and to strict limitation of student political activity. The implementation of the reform in the *Vorschriften für die Studierenden*, promulgated by the new Minister of Culture, Puttkamer, recognized the change in legal position, but sought to reinforce academic discipline with two separate lists of violations (paragraphs 25 and 26), totaling fourteen counts, for which punishment could be imposed. While many particulars, such as ''lack of obedience to official orders,'' stated necessary institutional safeguards, others, like ''actions that violate custom and order of academic life'' or ''behavior that contradicts the purposes of university attendance,'' were so vague as to allow administrators to use them virtually at will against whatever they considered deviant conduct. In particular, the concluding section (paragraphs 38-44) concerning ''associations and assemblies'' severely limited student freedom by ''authorizing the disciplinary officials to forbid associations temporarily or permanently, if their existence endangers academic discipline.'' Perceptive students were not slow to realize that these regulations went beyond institutional needs for self-preservation and sought to curb undesirable social and political dissent. ''As long as we applaud, we are the healthy core of the nation . . . if we criticize, we are once again immature [*grüne Jungen*],'' one pamphlet complained, attacking the ''regrettable confusion of patriotic-national enthusiasm with agitatory partisanship.'' Another saw the purpose of the rules ''as keeping students, if possible, away from public life and struggles about contemporary questions'' and

[10] *AH*, 20 February 1879, pp. 1514-19 and *HH*, 21 February 1879, pp. 263-64; ''Zusammenstellung der Beschlüsse der Justizkommission über den Gesetzentwurf . . .'' *HH, Anlagen 1878/9*, pp. 155-58. Session of the Prussian Ministry of State, 27 May 1879 (Falk explaining the changes), ZStA Me, 2.2.1, No 21404; Falk to the curators of the Prussian universities, 8 July 1879, ZStA Me, Rep 92, Falk, No 10. See also BUA, Kuratorium, F 1.

resented this attitude as paternalistic tutelage.[11] Ironically, the fulfillment of the old progressive demand for abolishing university justice led to a reinstitution of ideological conformity through academic discipline.

Although gratified that the spirit of the majority of students "is very healthy and patriotic," the Prussian government became increasingly preoccupied with "the danger of rising Social Democratic agitation for our state, nation, culture, and mentality." Fearing that subversion would "penetrate those strata called upon to maintain and advance the foundations of our civilization," Minister Falk, even before the anti-Socialist law, called upon university authorities to watch vigilantly and report on Socialist associations, student membership in nonacademic Vereine, and participation in Communist propaganda. By the mid-1880s this campaign to safeguard "the perpetuation of sound patriotic and moral attitudes" among students led to a series of indictments in Breslau, where the district attorney arraigned thirty-eight suspected Socialists, among them the students H. Lutz (mathematics) and J. Markuse (medicine). Although academic youths were a small minority among the largely artisan (20) and working-class (11) activists, their organizational role in forming a secret association, circulating the forbidden *Sozialdemokrat* and other writings, or raising money was not unimportant. More specifically, they were charged with having maintained an intellectual circle "aiming entirely at the advancement of tendencies seeking to overthrow the existing political and social order." As a result of this plot, Minister of Culture Gossler called for closer cooperation between judicial and police authorities and demanded that "the universities also immediately take all measures for the elimination of the discovered abuses." Despite a broad scholarly and social definition of academic freedom, the application of the disciplinary code of 1879 set strict limits upon political subversion.[12]

Even before criminal conviction, Socialist students faced disciplinary

---

[11] Minister Puttkamer, *Vorschriften für die Studierenden der Landesuniversitäten, der Akademie zu Münster und des Lyzeum Hosianum zu Braunsberg vom 1. Oktober 1879* (Berlin, 1879); "Instruktion zu den Vorschriften," 1 October 1879, in ZStA Me, Rep 76 Va, Sekt 1 Tit II, No 22, vol. 2. The explanatory instruction stressed the abolition of debt regulations, the incompleteness of the list of transgressions, and the illegality of duels; copy also in MUA, 1965/9, no. 2091; M. Münsterberg, *Studentenpflicht und Studentenrecht* (Leipzig, 1884) and H. Maier, " Das studentische Vereins- und Versammlungsrecht," *Das Freie Wort* 8 (1908): 653-56. See also H. Maach, *Grundlagen des studentischen Disziplinarrechts* (Freiburg, 1956), pp. 63-76; and N. Andernach, *Der Einfluss der Parteien auf das Hochschulwesen in Preussen, 1848-1918* (Göttingen, 1972), pp. 71-73.

[12] Oberpräsident Hanover to Maybach, 24 June 1878, and Falk to Prussian rectors, 14 June 1878, ZStA Me, Rep 120 BB, Sekt VII, 1, No 18, vol. 1. Friedberg to Gossler, 9 April 1877; Gossler to Friedberg, 9 May 1887; memorandum by Breslau district attorney, 27 May 1887; "Anklageschrift des ersten Staatsanwalts zu Breslau," 22 August 1887, all in ZStA Me, Rep 76 Va, Sekt 1 Tit II, No 27, vol. 1. For the general background, see also V. Lidtke, *The Outlawed Party: Social Democracy in Germany, 1878-1890* (Princeton, 1966).

action by university authorities. In Königsberg, "Raphael Friedberg and
. . . Johannes Weiss were found guilty of illegal propagation of Socialist
tendencies and were therefore punished for one year with exclusion from
their studies because of violating academic order and custom and because
of behavior conflicting with the purpose of university attendance." With
a prostitute testifying against them, they were accused of seeking close
connections with a local Socialist leader, cobbler Godan, of attending
Socialist assemblies (where there had been talk of exterminating the propertied one-fifth of society!), of possessing radical literature, and of per-
forming electioneering services. Such active "support for Social Democratic tendencies is completely incompatible with the order and morality
of academic life . . . and must be designated as quite unacceptable for
students." The "extraordinary gravity and great danger" of this case led
the Ministry of Culture to renew its appeal "for increased vigilance in
keeping the poisonous influences of socialism from our students, whose
loyal and patriotic sentiments deserve every recognition." When the lapse
of the anti-Socialist law reduced governmental weapons to disciplinary
actions alone, universities, especially in the East, shifted to petty harassment instead. At the same time, increasing nationality tensions in the
Second Reich drew attention to "serious political concerns" about Polish
students, led to the "dissolution of existing Polish associations," and
brought about prohibitions against joining them in the future.[13] Although
at the height of the anti-Socialist hysteria universities preferred to fight
sedition with intellectual weapons, the Prussian state insisted less subtly
on proscribing Socialist and Polish nationalist ideas as legally incompatible
with cultivation.

In countless articles, university speeches, Landtag discussions, and ministerial memoranda on the theme of *Student und Politik*, a consensus on
how students ought to relate to politics gradually evolved in Imperial
Germany. Because of the national and constitutional activism of the Burschenschaft before 1871, literature on how to study unanimously advised:
"Practical politics is a task for men and not for youths." Theobald Ziegler
echoed: "Today, when our policies must above all strive to conserve . . .
active participation of students in political life is undesirable." Instead of

[13] Zorn and V. D. Trenck, "Erkenntnis in der Disziplinarsache wider 1. den Studierenden
der Medizin Raphael Friedberg und 2. den Studierenden der Medizin Johannes Weiss";
Lucanus to Prussian curators, 19 August 1887; von Giesel to Erlangen Senate, 21 September
1887, all in UA Erlangen, III, no. 1463. See also the subsequent correspondence in ZStA
Me, Rep 76 Va, Sekt 1 Tit XII, No 27, vols. 1-3; Gossler to Prussian curators, 1 June 1886,
MUA 305a, Acc 1950/9, no. 664, and Studt to Prussian rectors, 20 December 1901, expelling
two Polish students "because they agitated for the founding and participated in the running
of a Polish workers' association, dedicated to the consolidation of Polishness in the German
provinces and to the struggle against Germanness." See H. K. Rosenthal, *German and Pole:
National Conflict and Modern Myth* (Gainesville, 1976).

activism, adult educators counselled "the study of politics and political life" in every possible way in order "to acquire a political conviction." Arnold Ruge put the matter thus: "Indeed, it seems most advisable that a student limit himself to learning and observing, in order to draw conclusions as a mature man in a secure position." Only with a firm political Welt-anschauung could the Akademiker assume the leadership role for which he was destined. Since whoever "dedicates himself to the pursuit of truth cannot be a partisan," a student "ought not to be sworn to one party. The spiritual imprisonment that partisanship demands conflicts with academic freedom, which above all means liberty to examine, to doubt, and to see with one's own eyes." Because many academics "considered the present inchoate party system a misfortune—too many and too small factions are fighting each other with hatred," they emphatically opposed student (and association) identification with political parties. "Scholarship is nonpar-tisan, for it is free of prejudice; the same reason that forbids a lecturer to propagandize from his lectern, prohibits a student as student from binding himself to a party." The injunction "to stand above parties" did not, however, mean a rejection of "true and warm patriotism." Put more bluntly, although academic youth was supposed to learn rather than act, "a German student of today cannot be anything other than *national*, re-gardless of which party currently controls government." Despite claims of political neutrality (as future members of the "common estate"), the instilling of "a spirit of most sincere and active patriotism" was the essential task of political cultivation. Instead of educating students polit-ically through self-government and gradual participation in public affairs, Imperial German academics generally preferred nationalist acclamation tempered at best with appeals to the "social mission" of "bridging the chasm between the people and the cultivated."[14]

Within this prevailing nonpolitical politics a minority advocated not outright participation but greater student involvement in political education. Deploring widespread "indifference," the student press repeatedly criti-cized: "If there is an estate today which keeps aloof from the interest struggle of political and economic parties, it is the students in their en-tirety." As "he will be called upon to play a leading role in life, it is even more important for the student to be active in politics." Because apathy

[14] F. Malvus, *Das heutige Studium und das Studiertenproletariat* (Berlin, 1899), pp. 24ff.; F. Paulsen, *Die deutschen Universitäten und das Universitätsstudium* (Berlin, 1902), pp. 452-65; T. Ziegler, *Der deutsche Student* (Stuttgart, 1895), pp. 116-30; A. Ruge, *Kritische Betrachtungen und Darstellungen des Deutschen Studentenlebens in seinen Grundzügen* (Tübingen, 1906), pp. 87-90. See also H. Flach, *Der deutsche Student der Gegenwart* (Berlin, 1887): "We presuppose as self-evident, that every German student must be nationalist and firmly support Kaiser and Reich"; and Anonymous, *Briefe eines Vaters an seinen Sohn* (Breslau, 1895), pp. 102f.

and privatism endangered the presumptive leadership of the academics, a number of pamphlets answered the question: "Shall the student concern himself with politics?" affirmatively. Although but a faint echo of the Vormärz, Burschenschaft publications reiterated as "their most noble principle: to make their members into capable citizens who are willing to collaborate with all their might in the fulfillment of patriotic tasks." Similarly, the Vereine Deutscher Studenten tried to rouse German students from their comfortable lethargy: "To champion this kind of politics, to be active in politics, especially national ones, in order to learn with the conscious aim of being useful to the fatherland, that is a high and beautiful task for German students, which is truly worth the effort of the best!"[15] Although Corps, Turnerschaft, and especially Catholic student associations initially disclaimed "so-called political involvement," after 1900 they increasingly promoted active political education of their members. "Teaching the great questions of the nation, attending political and economic lectures wherever they may come from, practicing public speaking and political dialectics in the narrow sense of the word" were generally the means with which the interested academics proceeded to educate the future citizen. Ranging from pan-Germans to Socialists, the political minority championed a more active form of political education within its own circle, but nevertheless agreed: "What German students, in contrast to their Austrian, Romance, and Slavic peers, shall not and cannot do is to involve themselves in partisan politics, to create their own political organizations, and to associate politically for pursuing and achieving certain political aims." To transcend "current politics, such as race arrogance and hatred, partisanship and class struggle," the activists strove for "a really great student politics" on an ideological and cultural plane.[16]

Another aspect of the framework for political cultivation was the privileged military service of students, which cemented militarism ideologically and socially. "A great number of you are helped to acquire a patriotic attitude and a state consciousness," Theobald Ziegler lectured, "by the

[15] The number of articles on "students and politics" is so great that one can offer only some exemplary citations: J. W., "Der Kampf gegen den Indifferentismus," *ABl* 1 (1886): 39-40; A. Marbach, "Die Politik unter den Studenten und die Berliner Lesehallenwahl," *SA* 2 (1896): 344-47; W. Heile, "Student und Politik," *ABl* 20 (1905): 185-87; A. Goetz, *Soll sich der Student mit der Politik beschäftigen?* (Berlin, 1901); "Die nationale Aufgabe der Burschenschaft," *BBl* 1 (1886-87): 50-52. See also J. Quandt, "Die deutschen Studenten und die Politik," *ABl* 1 (1886), no. 2.

[16] Dr. Porsch, "Die angebliche politische Betätigung des Cartellverbands," *Ac* 21 (1908): 185-87; Gerstenhauer, "Ein Programm," *ATZ* 11 (1894-95): 442ff.; H. Böttger, "Politisches aus dem Studententum," *BBl* 25 (1910-11): 225f.; Dr. von Blume, "Der Student und die Politik," *AR* 13 (1911): 177-82; H. Schrömbgens, "Student und Politik," *AMbl* 25 (1913): 55-59, 83-86; J. Koch, "Die Corps und die Politik," *AMh* 23 (1906-1907): 365ff.; F. W. Foerster, *Student und Politik* (Berlin, 1901).

fact that you can and often really do serve your one volunteer year" in the military. This Einjährige Freiwilligen privilege not only shortened the two-year term but also made it possible for students to discharge their military obligation by entering a regiment in a university town, while enrolling for one or two courses and retaining their student status (and financial aid) for fulfilling examination requirements. Despite these advantages, only a small number (5.13 percent in 1886-87 and 1.50 percent in 1911-12) served while at the university, whereas about one-quarter (decreasing to one-eighth) had already completed their tour of duty, while two-thirds (to three-quarters) had yet to decide. Because the initially perfunctory (half-day) training became more demanding during the empire and led to "a shortening and disturbance of studies," reform-minded professors suggested that "the military service year shall not be counted toward the triennium and that public academic benefices be terminated." Moreover, there were numerous tensions between officers and students, centering on the social preferment and outward polish of the former and the intellectual superiority and inner grace of the latter, only occasionally bridged in the hospitality of an exclusive Corps. Although "that military spirit and tone that lets a young lawyer or teacher put his reserve lieutenant title first on his calling card, as if he were something higher and better than a civilian, even a minister," offended academic sensibilities, this privilege was not abolished for social and ideological reasons. According to Friedrich Paulsen, "in the past century the army has become the second great educational institution for our people, next to the school. Aside from instilling a number of elementary and important virtues, such as order and cleanliness, punctuality and discipline, it fills all sons of our people, even those coming from the lowest circles, with national self-consciousness and personal dignity, by making them into armed men, into links of that power that decides the fate of nations." Despite initial grumbling, "as soon as the young man has passed his officer examination and has later become a reserve officer, a fundamental reversal in the mutual distaste takes place," turning it into pride and comradeship. Many a former volunteer mused, "it is surprising how the uniform changes one's politics" and marvelled about "the reserve of reliable support for state policy" created by such service.[17]

To foreign observers like André François-Poncet the legal and atti-

---

[17] T. Ziegler, Der deutsche Student, pp. 123-30; PrSt, 102: 67ff.; and ibid., 236: 126ff.; M. Kähler, Die Universitäten und das öffentliche Leben (Leipzig, 1891), pp. 31ff.; F. Paulsen, Die deutschen Universitäten (Berlin, 1902), 470f.; F. Malvus, Das heutige Studium, pp. 35-41; M. Messerschmidt, "Schulpolitik des Militärs," in Bildungspolitik in Preussen (Stuttgart, 1980), pp. 242-255 and F. Paulsen, Aus meinem Leben: Jugenderinnerungen (Jena, 1909), pp. 157ff. See also ZStA Me, Rep 76 Va, Sekt 1 Tit XII, No 6, vol. 1, and MUA 305a, Acc 1950/9, no. 341. University towns actively competed for attractive cavalry regiments.

tudinal constraints on student politics looked like successful social control: "To begin with, one must consider university youth as a caste," a sort of aristocracy, set off from the general population by deference. Moreover, "their model is the officer. The student copies the lieutenant," and though he cannot rival the military, he insists on following immediately behind in esteem. "In solidarity with the officers, the learned estate similarly identifies with government," because the state provides both good pay and honorific rewards. Hence, the sharp-tongued Frenchman concluded: "The fatherland is their whole ideal, their entire politics." Instead of being free, the imperial student was a product of the *"most conservative institution in Germany."* Although exaggerated to persuade the French public to accept three-year military service in the face of *le péril allemand*, this unflattering picture nevertheless contains some grains of truth. While social exclusivity was not nearly as great as François-Poncet made out, the rivalry of students and Officer Corps more often led to imitation of barracks manners and militarization of spirit than to pacifist rejection. For the state and the public the goal of political cultivation was the patriotic official, above parties, although its actual content, be it liberal reformist in the Stein tradition or reactionary capricious in the Manteuffel mold, remained undefined. Undoubtedly, Socialists and Polish nationalists were excluded from organizing students for their cause, and Catholics and democrats were hardly encouraged; but within these legal limits a rich and varied student subculture flourished which did not merely instill passive obedience to the status quo. Undeniably this conception of Student und Politik encouraged apathy and patriotic acclamation, or as a Socialist critic put it: "Only on special occasions does the student body break into nationalist hurrahs, which then again often leads to quarrels, since every group claims it shouted the loudest." However, a strong minority argued for a more active student role in political self-education, and the ideological affinities of organized student groups spanned the entire spectrum from crypto-Socialist to pan-Germans.[18] Although the framework of campus politics skewed learning in a nationalist direction, German universities provided enough diversity of opinion for meaningful individual choice.

VARIETIES OF NATIONALISM

The character of student politics in the empire was therefore more complex and competitive than stereotypes suggest. In contrast to earlier activism, a turn-of-the-century visitor marveled at *l'espèce d'atonie politique* of

---

[18] André François-Poncet, *Ce que pense la jeunesse allemande* (Paris, 1913), pp. 39-50, and A. Marbach, "Die Politik und die Berliner Lesehallenwahl," *SA* 2 (1896): 344ff. See also R. Chickering, *Imperial Germany and a World Without War* (Princeton, 1975), pp. 165-81.

German students: "Their ignorance is touching and their indifference sad. Sleep envelops their immature heads." Native observers explained this apathy by "their preoccupation with the varieties of corporate life and the struggles of the individual associations against each other as well as through their greater isolation from the outside and their more pronounced caste formation" than abroad. Others argued that this impression was misleading, since every "great and new intellectual idea" profoundly affected students as a group: "The ideal of German freedom and unity created the Burschenschaft; the newer nationalism, the VDSt; social concern, the sozialwissenschaftliche student societies; individualism, self-cultivation, and tolerance principles, the Freistudentenschaft and its successor. [Hence] conservative or anti-Semitic, clerical, liberal, and socialist currents have flowed through the students." This diversity of opinion raises the question: To what degree were students politically active at all? Although after 1870 authorities no longer automatically repressed such involvement, they encouraged participation as acclamatory patriotism rather than as criticism of student life, academic instruction, or governmental policy; youthful agitation was bureaucratically curbed whenever it attracted the unfavorable notice of the press or the Ministry of Culture. Nevertheless, a minority of students, regardless of persuasion, continually tried to stretch the limits of academic discipline and to create institutions that would facilitate their collective political expression, such as councils, elections, and newspapers. This contradiction poses the additional problem: What were the actual processes of student politics which served "as preparation for future political campaigns and parliamentary activity"? "Until the year 1871 the careerist was provincial, afterwards he became national; at the beginning of the nineties he turned a bit pan-German and social; and today in all cultural questions, he is instinctively conservative and self-evidently 'national.' " The free-student leader W. Ohr criticized these successive metamorphoses as "German, all too German." This observation suggests a final query: What was the ideological content of student politics, how did it evolve, and what effect did it have upon the student body at large?[19]

Even during quiet periods German campuses experienced more political conflict than has often been assumed. In the 1860s foreign and domestic observers agreed: "The students, Catholic no less than Protestant, are liberals." However, "after the war of 1870 began the forceful pursuit of currents hostile to liberalism, because of the rapidity of economic devel-

[19] J. Huret, *En Allemagne: Rhin et Westphalie* (Paris, 1907), pp. 426f.; Blaustein, *Der Student in der politischen Entwicklung* (Munich, 1909), pp. 5ff., and W. Ohr, *Zur Erneuerung des deutschen Studententums* (Munich, 1908). See also Schulze-Ssymank, *Das deutsche Studententum* (Munich, 1932), pp. 448f.: "In an age when Germans slowly became a political people, politics could not be kept away from students completely. But in general academic youth was not involved in actual party politics."

opment, the rule of material interests, and the erosion of liberalism, whose formal and negative tasks seemed accomplished.'' The slackening of political interest after victorious unification, the rapid rise of Catholic associations during the Kulturkampf, and the flirtation of unorthodox spirits with socialism led to a gradual abandoning of that instinctive youthful commitment to freedom that previously had struck commentators as typical. Another reason for this reversal was the ineffectiveness of progressive activism, which limited itself to restructuring student life. ''The reform party of the late 1860s and early 1870s had no aims beyond the student body, but aggressively campaigned against the conservatives within it and therefore was treated accordingly by university authorities, especially in Berlin.'' Not only self-limitation in goals and bureaucratic hostility, but also ephemeral organization contributed to the failure of ''the rebirth of German student spirit.'' The progressive slogan, ''Let's rally around common purposes at individual institutions; let's create councils [*Ausschüsse*], permanent student committees,'' sparked a half-dozen councils, which, however, ''nowhere showed a great deal of life, and disappeared again after a short time.'' Either the traditional corporations subverted their reformist aims from within, or the authorities closed them down from without, as in Berlin in early 1870.[20]

These defeats led to the establishment of ''closed reform associations which eventually succumbed to corporatism'' and the ''independent continuation'' of such services as the Akademische Lesehalle. This reading room was designed ''to make the outstanding novelties of scholarly, belletristic, and political literature available to its members,'' especially in periodical form. As it met a widespread need for informal Bildung, ''its importance for the education of students into citizens can hardly be exaggerated.'' Permitted in the German capital in July 1870, the Lesehalle flourished because it dared to subscribe to radical papers such as the *Berliner Freie Presse*, the *Leipziger Vorwärts*, or the *Hamburg-Altonaer Volksblatt*. Although the student directorate in 1878 ''explicitly refutes [the charge] that any Socialist or Social Democratic tendencies are propagated by it,'' the university senate tightened censorship and tolerated its continuation only as long as most controversial papers were removed. Since for ceremonial purposes authorities needed some organ that represented students as a whole, in February 1880 a majority of six hundred free association, scholarly society, and Burschenschaft members petitioned for

<hr />

[20] Blaustein, *Der Student in der politischen Entwicklung* (Munich, 1909), pp. 12ff. J. M. Hart, *German Universities* (New York, 1874), p. 295. T. Curti, *Die Reformbewegung in der deutschen Studentenschaft*, pp. 10ff.; M.v.d. Porten, *Geschichte und Ziele der studentischen Reformpartei*; Schulze-Ssymank, *Das deutsche Studententum*, pp. 327-29. See also notes 39-40 of Chapter 5.

"permanent representation in the form of a council of fifteen, elected by the students." While the student reformers wanted true self-government charged with "representing the interests of the student body of the University of Berlin" and competent to call assemblies "as often as necessary," Rector Beseler intended to keep firm control on the number of meetings and purpose of deliberations. Eventually he was willing to "recognize it, provided the rector can retract his permission at any time and that it only be allowed to prepare and direct festivities or public parades . . . but on the other hand more extensive powers not be granted." Nevertheless, during the first decade of the empire, the liberal student tradition was in full retreat: "The time when students were political conspirators had gone by; the time when they may take part in the liberal discussion of political questions of the day has not yet arrived." But the reform movement left a significant legacy of institutions, like student councils and libraries, that became central in the revival of student politics in the next decennium.[21]

The rise of a new nationalism in the early 1880s, orchestrated by the Vereine Deutscher Studenten, repoliticized German students with a vengeance. On 3 March 1881 eighty VDSt members and sympathizers packed an extraordinary general assembly of the Berlin Lesehalle which was supposed to discuss the establishment of a debating club, overrode the agenda, and "demanded the replacement of the directorate as it did not sufficiently stand up to the curatorium, proceeded in a partisan manner, and so on." Because the rector was the liberal Hofmann and other such progressive luminaries as Virchow and Mommsen were members of the board, the leftist directory simply walked out and was reinstated by the authorities. When, in a raucous student meeting on 23 May, the liberals rammed through a slate of ten new directorate members, it was the turn of the anti-Semites to complain to the rector, who voided the election for procedural reasons but permitted "the former directory to continue to conduct business until the next general assembly." In the fall semester of 1881 the right was better prepared, raised the membership from 506 to 837, and brought along another 250 students to elect a nationalist directorate. But it was again not recognized by the liberal faculty, which revised the statutes to require longer membership, since "student partisanship in the Lesehalle

---

[21] Blaustein, *Der Student in der politischen Entwicklung*, p. 13. Student petition for the continuation of the Lesehalle, 19 July 1870; Senate protocol of 20 July 1870; Statuten der akademischen Lesehalle, 10 September 1870; notes on the interrogation of the law student Passow, 22 June 1878; Senate resolution of 3 July 1878 and revised statutes of 15 July 1880, all in HUA, 553. Note by Beseler, 17 February 1880; report of the warden about a student assembly, 29 February 1880; Beseler note of 8 March 1880; statutes of the student committee with marginalia by rector; Beseler changes, 8 June 1880; official permission, 9 July 1880, all in HUA, 602. J. M. Hart, *German Universities*, p. 294.

is incompatible with an institution supported largely by university funds.'' When the VDSt leader complained to Minister of Culture Gossler about such illegal favoritism and the predominance of "specifically Jewish Berlinese elements," the president of the directory, J. Grossman, argued: "There is not the slightest cause for the supposition that the ALH is being used by any side as its exclusive domain." Instead, it had occupied a "position of strict neutrality." The ideological struggle between left and right came to a head in a general assembly in January 1882. Despite a long and personally bitter attack by Theodor Greving (VDSt), the eloquent Max Spangenberg (FWV) prevailed with his motion to ratify the constitutional violations of the provisional directory and to accept its financial report by a vote of 436 to 370. In the spring semester of the same year, new statutes were accepted by 260 to 56, and another directory was elected by acclamation. By counterorganizing in the Freie Wissenschaftliche Vereinigung and by using faculty support, campus liberals succeeded in beating back the initial onslaught of the nationalists, because the Lesehalle attracted the more bookish and intellectual students to whom they could appeal.[22]

In the general *Studentenausschuss*, the anti-Semitic movement was more successful from the beginning. Because of the support of the Sänger, free associations, Catholic associations, Wingolf, and the nationalist part of the scholarly societies, the right swept the first council election 550 to 102 and captured all four faculty seats in May 1882. As victor, the VDSt quickly changed the statutes to provide a guaranteed seat for its allies and for itself, and in the showdown of January 1882, the VDSt and its corporate partners won a resounding triumph of 570 to 340 votes. Only occasionally did liberals like Spangenberg or Ascher carry the philosophical or medical faculties. But the rector opposed "extending the competence of the student council and granting it a quasi-official status" as a VDSt attempt "to legalize its domination over the student body." In response to this ideological polarization, the disinterested majority founded a centrist party, standing for "friendly association, concord and peace," when the ATV, the Landsmannschaft, singing groups, and scholarly societies defected from the rightist camp. Although the FWV tactically supported this apolitical alternative, it was defeated 597 to 584 in the December election, and the

---

[22] Albrecht and others to the curatorium, 3 March 1881; Hofmann negotiation with Greving and others, forcing their resignation; Grossmann report on the general assembly of 23 May 1881; directory of the ALH, 1 December 1881; curatorium to directory, 2 December 1881; draft of new statutes with university judge Schulz's comments of 15 December 1881; Grossmann to rector, 10 January 1882, rebutting the Greving petition; protocol of general assembly in the Tonhalle, 11 January 1882; protocol of the general assembly of 17 May 1882, all in HUA, 553. See also Petersdorff, *Zwölf Jahre akademischer Kämpfe* (Leipzig, 1900), pp. 45ff. and Schulze-Ssymank, *Das deutsche Studententum*, pp. 351-54. Other Lesehallen, especially in Leipzig, were also contested electorally, but there the nationalists were even more successful.

nationalists reigned supreme until the winter semester of 1887-88. In order not to yield "control to an association which, under the harmless flag 'German' and 'national,' sails in reactionary waters," several adult liberals and "a considerable number of truly liberal students" founded an Aka- demisch-Liberale Verein to "advance political liberalism among stu- dents." Police permission, however, did not suffice, for Rector Heinrich Dernburg argued: "It would neither correspond to the interests of the university nor to those of the students or their parents nor to those of the state, if political clubs could freely be formed among students" by poli- ticians who circumvented academic discipline. Although Gossler finally yielded to the protests, the ALV never became an effective counterweight to the VDSt because it failed to attract more than fifty members. By the mid-1880s, the Berlin campus was highly politicized, with the left con- trolling the Lesehalle and the right entrenched in the Studentenausschuss. Instead of Gemütlichkeit, rowdy student assemblies debated and passed resolutions; glossy flyers called for "opening the ALH to the entire student body" or demanded "breaking [nationalist] terrorism during the coming council elections"; ponderous pamphlets discussed "the Jewish question in scholarship"; well-organized election campaigns used all manner of rhetoric, obstruction, and intimidation; if these were unsuccessful, casuistic appeals to university authorities or the Ministry of Culture tried to reverse the verdict of the polls.[23]

Political strife between liberals and nationalists grew so heated in the second half of the 1880s that, given the duelling tradition, it claimed several lives. In late December 1884 a VDSt council member, Richard Holzapfel, accused a representative of the FWV, Alfred Oehlke, who had just beaten him for the philosophical faculty seat by four votes, of having falsely tendered his word of honor. Outraged, Oehlke demanded satisfaction and fatally shot Holzapfel on 15 February. Incensed both by the duel and its deadly outcome, the press demanded retribution; the victorious liberal was

[23] Police reports of general student assembly, 5 March 1881; Hofmann negotiations with the vacation committee, 15 August and letter to the council of 16 August, 1881; proposal for statutory revision, 19 July 1881; protest against the October election, 17 November 1881; rulings of Rector Curtius, 3 December 1881; Wölbling to Kirchhoff, 24 January 1884 with judge Schulz marginalia; text of new statutes 7 February 1884, all in HUA, 602. Quotes from the apolitical alliance in Petersdorff, *VDSt*, 154ff. Dernburg note, 24 November 1884; flyer of the Akademisch-Liberale Verein, signed by Hopf; statutes of the ALV; police president to rector, 24 November 1884; Dernburg to Madai, 15 December 1884; *Berliner Volkszeitung* article, 21 December 1884; Dernburg to Gossler, 9 April 1885; Gossler to Dernburg, 6 December 1885; report of 4 July 1886 (48 of 115 members), all in HUA, 668. See also Achenbach to Puttkamer, 13 January 1885; police president to Puttkamer, 8 December 1885 reporting on deliberations "about how academic youth which of late has become more strongly conservative might return to the flag of liberalism"; and Puttkamer to Gossler, 6 August 1885, all in ZStA Me, Rep 77, Tit 46, No 46, vol. 1. Flyers in HUA, 602. For pamphlets, see IHK, "Student und Judentum," F 1504-24.

sentenced to five years of fortress imprisonment, and the Berlin rector decided: "In the interest of maintaining peace among students, regular assemblies for council elections can no longer be permitted." Instead, he restructured the Ausschuss statutes so that "elections are to be held by faculties, discussions about candidates will not take place," and all at-large representatives were transformed into faculty delegates. After much wrangling, Dernburg got both the VDSt and the FWV permanent seats so that he could mediate between the fronts and "on the one hand, strengthen the position of the council and, on the other hand, significantly improve the control of university authorities." As a result of all the publicity, the nationalists recaptured the Ausschuss and even conquered the medical faculty. Since, after the abolition of general election meetings, "the agitation centered entirely on the Lesehalle" Rector Kleinert, in the fall of 1885, introduced a new list system with one representative per 100 votes cast. Under this procedure the heated campaign led to the first VDSt victory, with 431 to 410 votes, and after one more liberal triumph in the following year, the nationalists dominated the Lesehalle until 1894. The popular liberal Spangenberg could only shake his head in disgust: "What shall become of the seed thereby sown in muddled heads?" However, the VDSt grip on the council weakened in the fall of 1888 when the ATV and its allies once again deserted the nationalist coalition, since they considered it "undignified to use the sublime concept of fatherland as a propaganda tool" and "failed to understand how one could drag the highly important issue of self-government . . . into politics, with which it has nothing to do." As a result, the Turners and liberals together polled 1,055 votes, the VDSt was held to 677, only capturing all theological and half of the law seats, and the corporations came in last with 317. In the ensuing council session the Jewish medical student Hugo Blum of the FWV exclaimed: "Yes, gentlemen, you have, I assert, no other principle than the persecution of the Jews" and went on to say: "It is a shame that an association like the VDSt, whose sole raison d'être is its anti-Semitic tendency, can exist at our university." Livid with rage, the nationalist Otto Eichler picked up the gauntlet. On 11 December 1888 Blum was shot and paid for his convictions with his life. Because of the clamor of the appalled press, the VDSt ringleaders were expelled, Eichler sentenced to two years in the fortress, and the council suspended. Ideological intransigence, coupled with the duelling tradition, had destroyed the very organization it was designed to capture.[24]

[24] *Berliner Zeitung*, 16 February 1885; Göppert note, 11 March 1885; Dernburg to Gossler, 14 August 1885; *Statuten des Ausschusses der Königlichen Friedrich-Wilhelms-Universität* (Berlin, 1885), all in ZStA Me, Rep 76 Va, Sekt 2 Tit XII, No 1, vol. 1. Dernburg note,

The nationalist faction ultimately triumphed for a number of complex reasons. Certainly Bismarck's continued support and the old emperor's benevolent "recognition of the patriotic movement that animates academic youth" helped. With 115 members in 1892 compared to only 34 of the FWV, the VDSt had a more powerful organizational base. Rightist students also proved adept at coalition politics, usually winning the support of the VC gymnasts, the ATV, the organization of the Berlin Gymnasium alumni, the Wingolf, and for a long time also of Catholic groups, while sometimes gaining the toleration of the duelling corporations. The VDSt was so successful at the polls because it usually put up only two to three of the nine rightist candidates itself, leaving the rest of the seats for its allies, and ruled council and Lesehalle indirectly. Moreover, the slogan "Nationalism above color" proved more potent than liberal appeals for tolerance, since these could be denounced as "social democratic, antinational, and anti-Christian," whereas patriotism always claimed to be above politics. Once in power, the nationalists "pursued their political goals" so unscrupulously that Rector Paul Hinschius complained about the "terrorism" of the illiberal party, which was aided and abetted by the "indifference of the majority of the students," who did not participate in elections but passively preferred the rightist coalition over the vaguely subversive left.[25] Because the council attempted to gain "the status of an unofficial academic authority alongside constitutionally existing offices and became a playground on which contending student parties . . . have struggled to dominate the entire student body," attempts by rectors Hinschius, Foerster, and Virchow between 1889 and 1895 to resuscitate the Ausschuss with more restrictive electoral systems (like written lists) foundered on student opposition to such "a bureaucratic instrument."[26] As the ministry as well

---

[24] April 1885; Ausschuss to rector, 25 April 1885; Kleinert to Breslau rector, 25 January 1886, all in HUA, 602. Kleinert to Curatorium, 24 December 1885, and 12 January 1886; report on the first list election of the ALH, 27 January 1886; protocol of the joint session of the directory and the curators, 1 January 1888, all in HUA, 553. Petersdorff, *VDSt*, pp. 193ff. ATV and allies handbill, December 1888; VDSt and allied corporations flyer; *National Zeitung*, 10 January 1889; *Deutsches Tageblatt*, 15 December 1888; Gerhardt to Gossler, 20 December 1888, all in ZStA Me, Rep 76 Va, Sekt 2 Tit XII, No 16, vol. 1. Election protocol, winter semester 1888-89; council to rector, 13 December 1888; petition for return of the student word of honor, 14 January 1889 and Gerhardt note of negotiation with council members, 21 January 1889, in HUA, 602. See also Schulze-Ssymank, *Das deutsche Studententum*, pp. 353-54.

[25] Gossler to Berlin rector, 14 March 1887, HUA, 602. VDSt flyer, December 1888, ZStA Me, Rep 76 Va, Sekt 2 Tit XII, No 16, vol. 1. Student council to rector, 25 April 1885, HUA, 602. Hinschius to Gossler, 20 November 1889, HUA 603. For the contradictory attitudes of the VDSt and the duelling corporations toward elections and the student council in general, see "Für studentische Ausschüsse," *ABl* 3 (1888), no. 6; M. Ebeling, "Berlin," *BBl* 5 (1890-91): 158ff.; and W. Meyer, "Berliner Studentenleben," *AMh* 3 (1886): 258f.

[26] Daude note, 3 February 1889; excerpt of Senate protocol, 14 May 1889; *Revidierte Satzungen des Ausschusses der Studenten der königlichen Friedrich-Wilhelms-Universität*

as the faculty agreed that "situated at the center of national politics, the Berlin university more than any other institution . . . should protect its students from the excitement of election campaigns," the propagandistic excesses of the ideological struggles led to the formal proscription of student politics and thereby robbed the liberals of their chance to reverse the victory of the right.[27]

The most important consequence of the triumph of the VDSt was the spread of its social, cultural, and political anti-Semitism throughout the student body and its gradual diffusion among the entire Bildungsbürgertum. After the 1819 exclusion of Jews from the Burschenschaft was rescinded in 1830 and even the Corps accepted Jewish members in the 1850s, "anti-Semitic tendencies were brought onto the campus through the Vereine Deutscher Studenten, because their lifeblood is anti-Semitism." Although the famous paragraph 34 of the Kösen Statutes prohibited "influencing their religious, scholarly, and political direction," Corps students in fact were proud: "Together with the officers we are perhaps the strongest prophets of Germanic aspirations, and in this sense we mold our members' attitudes toward the highest questions of life." Because local autonomy made a formal KSC resolution impossible, "after 1880 the Corps excluded Jews" and thereby practiced social anti-Semitism without any change of constitution.[28] The more politicized Burschenschaft abandoned yesterday's

---

(Berlin, 1889); "Die akademische Freiheit—ein dehnbarer Begriff," *Das Volk*, 14 November 1889; Hinschius to Gossler, 20 November 1889; Hinschius to Leipzig rector, 7 February 1890, all in HUA, 603. Gerhardt to Gossler, 1 March 1889; Gossler answer, 17 May 1889; Althoff note on *Deutsches Tageblatt*, 14 September 1889: "One could wait and see what the students want, since one could get along without a council"; Gossler to Hinschius, 9 December 1889, all in ZStA Me, Rep 76 Va, Sekt 2 Tit XII, No 16, vol. 1 as well as the statutes of other councils in Göttingen, Bonn, Greifswald, Freiburg, Heidelberg, and Strassburg which varied between festival committees (Bonn) and student self-government.

[27] C. Supprian petition for the reestablishment of the council with list of petitioning associations, 1 January 1892; Foerster to Bosse, 25 February 1892; Bosse to Foerster, 6 May 1892; newspaper clipping, "Eine überaus lebhafte Studentenversammlung," n.p., 1892; student representatives to Foerster, 17 May 1892; Foerster public notice, 28 June 1892; Foerster to Bosse, 20 August 1892; Virchow to Bosse, 17 November 1892; Bosse answer, 30 November 1892; flyer of nationalist students, 18 November 1892; Wacher to Virchow, 18 November 1892 (with over 400 signatures), all in HUA, 603. Weyrauch note, 5 November 1892; Schmidt memorandum, 19 November 1892 and Virchow to Bosse, 30 December 1892, all in ZStA Me, Rep 76 Va, Sekt 2 Tit XII, No 16, vol. 1. See also "Leipziger Studentenausschuss," *AMh* 5 (1888): 367f., a petition of the duelling corporations against the council, since there was little need for it, earlier attempts had failed, a council would "provoke disunity and strife," the role of the traditional corporations would be diminished, and so on.

[28] Dr. Dietz, "Zur Berichtigung," *BBl* 7 (1892-93): 276f.; C. Bürger, *Antisemiten-Spiegel: Der Antisemitismus im Lichte des Christentums, des Rechtes und der Wissenschaft* (Berlin and Frankfurt, 1911), pp. 168ff.; Schmidt, "Das Programm des Kösener S.C.," *AMh* 30 (1913), no. 10; see also "Corpsstudenten, Juden und getaufte Juden," *AMh* 20 (1903), no. 3: "My advice would be that a man . . . who has some pride should not become a Corps student as matters are today." See also M. Studier, "Der Corpsstudent," pp. 158ff. Despite the importance of the topic, only the short article by D. Grieswelle, "Antisemitismus in

liberalism for "today's nationalism" only after severe internal struggles, for many alumni viewed the rise of anti-Semitism among the actives as "a betrayal of its own history." While the *Burschenschaftliche Blätter* remained studiously neutral in the 1880s and rejected all official discussion of the subject, by 1891-92 the journal opened its pages "equally to enemies and friends of the Jews," thereby precipitating a journalistic controversy that raged for the next five years. Although "the naked fact [is] that the actives as well as a number of younger and older alumni consider the struggle against Jewry a national task for the Burschenschaft," the Eisenach DC initially rejected any official action, hoping that "in the course of a few years a purification process will have taken place peacefully" through the action of local chapters. In the fall of 1892-93 the Heidelberg professor Osthoff precipitated further debate with a well-meaning defense of tolerance, which was supported by many letters to the editor. But the majority of students considered "the battle against this materially and ethically dangerous Semitism truly Christian, German, and noble," and an extraordinary delegation convention in December 1892 voted 27 to 12 (with four abstentions) to require the publication of religious affiliation in future membership rosters.[29]

Although in the summer of 1893 only two Jews remained in the Strassburg Germania, which had merely seven members, the polemics continued in the Burschenschaft. Liberal alumni like Dr. E. Dietz appealed to the emancipatory tradition, while committed students invoked a German-national mission: "The German Burschenschaft has the duty to participate in the campaign against the national dangers of Jewish influence and Jewish superiority." The gradual victory of anti-Semitic practice was not enough for youthful hotheads who demanded the adoption of the principle of "German Volkstum." A bitter debate at the May 1896 Eisenach convention led to the resolution: "The active Burschenschaften have no Jewish members at present as well as during the recent past. In light of these facts, the ADC expects that in the future the Burschenschaften will unanimously reject Jewish students." Although Gleiwitz alumni deplored "such intolerance, which is neither German nor Christian but a travesty of the hallowed principles of the Burschenschaft," and about 800 of over 6,000 Alte Herren

---

deutschen Studentenverbindungen des 19. Jahrhunderts," in *Student und Hochschule*, pp. 366-79, attempts an analysis.

[29] An excellent summary is by B. Weil, *Juden in der deutschen Burschenschaft* (Strassburg, 1905), p. 34; "Unsere guten Freunde," *BBl* 6 (1891-92), no. 4: "They demand at least that the Burschenschaft, through gradual exclusion of Jewish pledges, reassume the Christian-German standpoint of the old Burschenschaft"; Osthoff speeches, *BBl* 7 (1892-93), no. 8 and nos. 10-12 for the further discussion: "Despite all their attempts the Jews remain a foreign branch on the German stem." Vote of the Ausserordentliche DC Versammlung, 15-19 December 1892, BAF D 19b. There is no evidence that the proportion of Jewish members in the corporations was rising rapidly before their exclusion.

signed a protest petition, active student members persevered in open anti-Semitism. "A student association that accepts Jews undercuts its prestige among the anti-Semitically minded academic youth of today." While the Landsmannschaft formally excluded Jews in 1894, the sports (ATV) and the majority of scholarly organizations did not admit any Jews informally. Neither were they welcome in the Protestant Wingolf or Schwarzburgbund, nor, in fact, in the various Catholic societies. At the price of being denounced as *verjudet*, only the Reformburschenschaft, the Finkenschaft, and some other minor societies maintained their openness and accepted pledges "irrespective of racial or religious prejudices or political opinion." Within one and one-half decades academic youth had moved from assimilationist liberalism to exclusivist illiberalism.[30]

Anti-Semitism conquered the majority of German students so swiftly and completely because of its superior organization and the ideological appeal of antiliberalism. "Kick the Jews out of German corporations!" was an effective slogan for the VDSt and its allies, because in the academic climate of the 1880s no organization could afford to be less than nationalistic. In contrast to liberal claims that Jews "want to assimilate with the nation and be nothing but German," romantic nationalists argued: "If German means 'volkish,' i.e., deriving from a unified people, then the patriotic Burschenschaft should not accept any student belonging to a foreign race, neither a Latin southerner, nor a Slavic Russian, nor a Semite." Moreover, in politics "Jewish liberalism is the sworn enemy of Christianity" and, even worse, "has prepared the way for socialism; Jews are founders and leaders of this party; Jews donate immense sums to its coffers." Although philo-Semitic liberals time and again ridiculed the danger that 600,000 citizens could pose to a mighty empire of over 40,000,000 inhabitants, enlightened appeals to "humanity" could not succeed against an agitation that played on emotions. Some Jewish members "were excellent fellows and all of them improve with German education, but they are just not German and can never become so either."[31] Cultural anti-

[30] E. Dietz, "Der neue Leitplan der BBl und unsere Stellung zu demselben," *BBl* 8 (1893-94): 37-41; and "Declaration of the Burschenschaft Germania at Jena," ibid. 11 (1896-97): 174-86. Regular deputy convention at Eisenach, 5-8 May 1895; 27-31 May 1896, in BAF, D 19a. Weil, *Juden in der Burschenschaft*, pp. 56ff. Dr. Kleinschmidt, "Zur Judenfrage," as well as "Erwiderung der alten Herren zu Basel," *BBl* 11 (1896-97): 188f. "Jahresberichte des ADB, 1889-90," BAF; and C. Bürger, "Der Antisemitismus in der Studentenschaft," pp. 168-81. The culmination of the debate in the *Burschenschaftliche Blätter* occurred in a series of retrospective articles on "Warum ist die deutsche Burschenschaft antisemitisch geworden?" in nos. 6-11 of vol. 11 (1896-97).

[31] K. Müller, *Das Judentum in der deutschen Studentenschaft* (Leipzig, 1891); Dr. Blau, "Erwiderung auf die 'Eingesandt' in no. 11 der BBl über 'Burschenschaft und Antisemitismus,'" *BBl* 7 (1892-93): 271f; "Erklärung der Burschenschaft Germania zu Jena," ibid. 11 (1896-97): 174ff.; F. Jaeckel, "Zweiter offener Brief an Herrn Professor Dr. Osthoff, Heidelberg," ibid. 7 (1892-93): 277-81; F. Lange, "Aus der Täglichem Rundschau vom 4.

Semites claimed: "Where Jewry takes hold, the dignity of idealism is trampled into the dust, and without idealism every estate and vocation threatens to decay." Christianity was imperiled as well. Although some political and cultural fear of "the enemies within" was no doubt genuine, lesser motives also played their part. "Some Jews have, in recent times, devoted themselves to study and have brought to bear the same energy and perseverance that characterizes them in general. That arouses the envy of those who do not possess these qualities to the same degree and naturally lag behind." Hence, there is an unmistakable undertone of professional rivalry with Jewish academics in the nationalist polemics. Finally, all attempts at reasoning foundered on the rock of racism: "I would want to exclude an adherent of the Jewish religion as little as a Catholic . . . if only he were determined to feel German. But that he cannot do. The bonds of Jewish blood awaken as soon as Jews are at issue." Argumentation proved fruitless, for "modern anti-Semitism is not a religious controversy but a racial struggle," and an inwardly turned xenophobia fastened on imagined enemies of the Reich, in the same vein as on other minorities. The effect of this volkish nationalism was fateful. Not only did it "isolate Jews within the German student body," undermine the defensive assimilation of the KC, and hasten the emergence of an opposed nationalism in the Kartell Zionistischer Korporationen; it also infected the majority of student organizations with anti-Semitism, which, though not always equally prominent, permeated the "intellectual atmosphere" and became "the air we breathe." In 1910, Dr. Karl Kormann could write with satisfaction in the VDSt journal: "Today the idea of social anti-Semitism has become the common property of all academic circles."[32]

During the 1890s the cultured elite was, however, equally preoccupied with the spread of socialism. Many academics warned: "Social Democracy finds more and more adherents among students," albeit "less as a logical consequence of its theories than from sympathy with the suppressed, ex-

---

März 1893," ibid. 7 (1892-93), 281f. Anonymous, *Juden, Studenten, Professoren* (Leipzig, 1881); O. H. Jaeger, *Unsere Korpsburschen, Börsenjuden und Semitenburner* (Hanover, 1892); *Unsere Stellung zum Judentum: Reden gehalten von Mitgliedern des Kyffhäuserverbandes* (Berlin, 1903).

[32] Müller, *Das Judentum*; "Aus den Burschenschaften," *BBl* 8 (1893-94): 138-39; F. Meinecke, "Eine Schlussbetrachtung," ibid. pp. 158f.; H. Wagner, "Weitere Bemerkungen," ibid. 7 (1892-93): 274-76; Jaeckel, "Zweiter offener Brief," ibid., p. 281; "Erklärung der Burschenschaft Germania," ibid. 11 (1896-97): 181f.; Anonymous, *Die Juden in Deutschland* (Berlin, 1911); Ein alter Breslauer Burschenschafter, "Kurz vor Toresschluss," *BBl* 7 (1892-93): 273ff.; E. Rosenberg, "Vom Burschenschafter zum K.Z. Ver," in *Der Zionistische Student* (Berlin, n.d.), pp. 1-12; C. Bürger, "Der Antisemitismus," pp. 173ff.; H. G. Schneider, "Die Burschenschaft und Ihre Zeitschrift," *BBl* 12 (1897-98): 282f.; K. Kormann, "Wandlungen im Kyffhäuser-Verband?" *ABl* 25 (1910): 225f. See also E. Hamburger, *Der Antisemitismus und die deutsche Studentenschaft* (Leipzig, 1891) versus C. Müller, *Unwesen auf deutschen Hochschulen* (Leipzig, 1894).

ploited, destitute, and disinherited and especially because of horrid student poverty, which troubles all universities, most notably Berlin." Although police persecution lessened with the expiration of the anti-Socialist law, radical students could not organize openly or "participate in proletarian organizations" owing to the restrictions of academic discipline, which could be circumvented only through social science student associations. On 24 December 1893, the *Vorwärts* grudgingly published the declaration of an unspecified number of Berlin, Freiburg, Münster, Marburg, and Kiel students to the International Socialist Student Congress at Geneva: "We believe that the intellectual proletariat plays an important role in the Socialist movement, on the one hand as teacher and illuminator of the people in social and scientific matters, on the other hand as developer of Socialist theories, corresponding to the general progress of scholarship." When the Socialist academics Dr. Lux and Dr. Zadek tried to report on the proceedings to 3,000 workers and students in February 1894 they were jeered by nationalist students belonging primarily to the VDSt. Stressing the common interests of the "workers of the hand and the brain" Lux stated "the propagandistic task for students is to gain ever more adherents for the idea of Socialism." Similarly Zadek exclaimed: "A well-known Berlin professor has called students the bodyguard of the Hohenzollern; strive rather to become the avant-garde of socialism!" Stung by Georg Ledebour's charge that "today's nationalist students are pawns of the rulers and have lost sight of the people," rightist activists protested vehemently and called another assembly two days later. Denouncing the Jewish leadership of the Socialists, the two thousand present passed a nearly unanimous resolution: "This academic convocation . . . declares, in opposition to recent attempts to carry the teaching of socialism into student ranks, that it is full of social spirit and love for its less fortunate brethren, but that it now as before rejects the subversion of rootless Social Democracy with unshakable resolve." While the Corps feared the politicization of the student body, even such quietist groups as the Wingolf rallied to protest against the inroads of socialism.[33]

Since about sixty Berlin students and a handful at other universities had demonstrated interest in Marxism, in January 1895 leftist alumni launched

[33] A. Dippe, *Sozialismus und Philosophie auf den deutschen Universitäten* (Leipzig, 1895); E. Feuchtwanger, *Sozialistische Gesinnung und soziales Elend auf den deutschen Hochschulen* (Leipzig, 1895); note in *Der Vorwärts*, 24 December 1893; "Burschenschaft und Sozialdemokratie," *BBl* 8 (1893-94): 202-208; "Studentenschaft und Sozialdemokratie," ibid., pp. 315-20; Dr. Wendland, "Die Studentenschaft und die Sozialdemokratie," *ABl* 8 (1894): 289-93; and G. Schreiber, "Die Sozialdemokratie und die deutsche Studentenschaft," *WBl* 23 (1894): 97ff. The subject of students and socialism in Imperial Germany deserves further exploration, since Schulze-Ssymank (*Das deutsche Studententum*, p. 364) ignores it for the 1890s, and Blaustein (*Der Student in der politischen Entwicklung*, pp. 18f.) is too cursory.

a new journal, *Der Sozialistische Akademiker*, designed "to win capable students for socialism." Invoking the radical democratic tradition of the first half of the nineteenth century, this student paper appealed to self-interest ("the academic sinks ever further into the proletariat") and to "the power of logic, which inevitably leads all freedom-loving spirits to socialism" in order to "protest against the arrogant superiority of the cultivated world." Although Eduard Bernstein was none too sanguine that "the mass of students, instead of following the ultra patriotic-reactionary fronde or of spearheading anti-Semitic know-nothingism, will join the radical opposition," Wolfgang Heine lectured to over three thousand students on "Social Democracy and the Student Strata" on 25 May 1897. Defending himself against charges of internationalism, antimonarchism, and revolutionism, he called for "a struggle against despotism, capitalism, and bureaucracy and a defense of intellectual freedom under the banner of socialism." In contrast, the conservative student Paul Baecker loudly proclaimed: "German students are the dike on which the Socialist tide shall break!" Because "the university allows German-national, Christian-social, and anti-Semitic politics, only socialism is forbidden," the grand old leader of the SPD, August Bebel, addressed students a year later on "Academics and Socialism." In order to "demonstrate the immense one-sidedness of those institutions that greatly influence the entire development of our public life," he presented the core of the Socialist message and concluded with an appeal to something higher than the fatherland: "One can believe in benefiting humanity, and that is the most beautiful ideal that we treasure and that I advise you to follow." Despite such eloquent and well-publicized speeches, "merely a few attempt to understand socialism" and "only individuals learn to value or defend it." Hence the first congress of German Socialist academics in October 1895 wisely refused to found a special organization.[34]

Part of the reason socialism failed to attract a large student following was the nature of its ideological message. Although unsure whether academics should play a special role within the movement as "teachers and leaders of the masses," most Socialist intellectuals sought to reach students through dire predictions of the eventual disappearance of the cultivated as

---

[34] "Was Wir Wollen," *Der Sozialistische Akademiker* 1 (1895): 1-7; E. Bernstein, "Der Sozialismus und die Studenten, einst und jetzt," ibid., pp. 8-11; K. Sohlich, "Studentenschaft und Sozialdemokratie," *ABl* 12 (1897): 53ff.; "Die Sozialdemokratie und die Schichten der Studierten," *BBl* 11 (1896-97): 268-77; A. Bebel, *Akademiker und Sozialismus* (Berlin, 1898); K., "Die Berliner Studentenschaft und die Sozialdemokratie," *ATZ* 14 (1897): 163ff.; "Der erste Kongress deutscher sozialistischer Akademiker," *SA* 1 (1895): 393f. For the hostility of the party, see Dr. -t-, "Das gebildete Proletariat und die Sozialdemokratie," *SA* 1 (1895): 162-64: "The present dominant dislike for academics goes decidedly too far." See also H. Weber, *Geschichte des VDSt zu Berlin* (Berlin, 1912), pp. 43-49, 183-90.

petite bourgeoisie between the grindstones of capital and labor. Because numerous rebuffs had taught them that "the lower-middle-class origins of these people prevent their unprejudiced judgment of their own existence," Socialist academics concentrated "on those educated proletarians who have personally experienced being a worker" and on the material needs of a growing academic proletariat. "Above all, discontent with its own position must ultimately lead the academic estate to socialism." Whether as free professionals or state officials, university graduates, "in the struggle for existence, appear either as dependent wage-slaves with more or less capital of cultivation or as representatives of independent enterprise." Because of this contradictory class position, a second set of more political appeals was directed toward the instinctive liberality of academics: "The honest friend of the people cannot but add a certain concrete solidarity and material concern for his fellow man to his devotion to political liberty and academic or spiritual freedom; and putting aside all scruples, this inevitably leads every consequential man to social democracy, whether he agrees with all points of the Socialist program or not." Dramatized by Prussian bureaucratic (lex Arons, Ignaz Jastrow case, Delbrück incident) or industrial authoritarianism (Stumm's campaign against the Socialists of the Chair), this reasoning reached at least some students: "Not material conditions, which prepare the way through the proletarianization of a part of the academics, but rather their ideological proclivities, their feeling for freedom and truth, and knowledge gained from the study of historical development form the foundation." Subsidiary themes therefore stressed the scientific nature of Marxist Weltanschauung and the humanitarian spirit of the movement to attract those few idealists who "come to us for the sake of justice."[35]

Socialism also gained little ground among German students because of the continued hostility of the authorities. Not only did they do their best to make Socialist lectures impossible, but they repeatedly dissolved social science associations when they smacked too much of radicalism and persecuted individual students who openly advocated socialism or were caught distributing Socialist tracts in the Lesehalle. But repression alone did not

[35] G. Zepler, "Zweites Armeecorps vor!" *SA* 1 (1895): 231f.; "Das gebildete Proletariat und die Sozialdemokratie," ibid., pp. 139-43; Berthold, "Sozialistisches Studententum," ibid., pp. 137f.; Ddf, "Die soziale Lage des Akademikers," ibid., pp. 233-36, 254-57; Sk., "Das Kleinbürgertum und seine Beziehungen zur 'Intelligenz'," ibid., pp. 85-90; F. Haupt, "Die Stellung unserer Privatdozenten," SA 2 (1896): 24ff.; "Der erste Kongress deutscher sozialistischer Akademiker," ibid. 1 (1895): 392ff.; S. Katzenstein, "Die Akademiker in der Sozialdemokratie," ibid. 2 (1896): 729-36. See also "Unser Antrag zum Breslauer Parteitage," and "Zu unserm ersten Kampfesjahr," ibid. 1 (1895): 349-50, 465-67. In 1897 the journal was continued as a special supplement of *Die Neue Zeit*, indicating that the party had abandoned all hope of creating a Socialist student movement and that students henceforth participated as individuals.

suffice, for the early Burschenschaft as well as contemporary Russian radicals weathered it quite successfully. More important was the manifest disinterest of the proletarian party, which, owing to its conviction that "We think not what we want but what we must," never trusted "the illusions or the caste spirit of students" and believed: "As Socialists, academics have more to learn from workers than they can teach them in their field of study." Finally, students themselves, though socially concerned, were not Socialists, because their class position removed them from working-class life and their entire education and outlook militated against leftist commitment. Moreover, "the Burschenschaft as eternal opponent of Socialist internationalism" and the VDSt did their best to immunize their comrades against the Socialist virus through propagating charitable reform. "Social Democracy strives for political power, for working-class domination. Therefore, it seeks to destroy the present state and contemporary society. It is clearly antinational, antimonarchist, and reserves the right to decide on the defense of the fatherland in each individual case, i.e., if we are attacked by Russia." Similarly, professors emphasized that socialism was "ethical materialism, in contrast to the ethical idealism" of their own teaching, and added that "its scientific basis has been outdated for fifty years." Finally, anti-Semitic agitators in student assemblies predicted that "in the prosaic Socialist state of the future all scholarly freedom will cease" and attacked their opponents as "Social Democratic Asiatics" collaborating with international Jewry, "since socialism means the decline of the German people." Though intellectually poorer than the arguments of the left, these nationalist criticisms nevertheless swayed the majority of students.[36]

Instead, concerned students were systematically deflected into the study of social problems or into charitable actions. With William II's ostensible blessing, academics in the early 1890s began to exhort the younger generation "to participate in the life of the people as in earlier centuries" and to "bridge the dangerous chasm that yawns between the cultivated and the masses." Monarchist, statist, or neoliberal Socialists of the Chair agreed

---

[36] H. Böttger, "Burschenschaft und Politik," *BBl* 12 (1897-98): 206ff.; "Die Sozialdemokratie und die Studentenschaft," ibid. 15 (1900-01): 149ff.; "Burschenschaft und Sozialdemokratie," ibid. 21 (1906-07): 223ff.; S. B., "Burschenschaft, Sozialdemokratie und Ultramontanismus," ibid. 22 (1907-08): 58ff.; "Die Studentenschaft und die Sozialdemokratie," *ABl* 7 (1893), no. 24; K. Sohlich, "Studentenschaft und Sozialdemokratie," ibid. 12 (1897): 53ff.; as well as the tenor of advice by T. Ziegler, *Der deutsche Student*, pp. 131f.; and F. Paulsen, *Die deutschen Universitäten*, pp. 315ff. For the continued harassment of social science student associations, see Bosse to Berlin rector, 26 June 1899, asking "that in future cases the admission of Socialist speakers to lectures in the association must be resolutely opposed," ZStA Me, Rep 76 Va, Sekt 2 Tit XII, No 17, vol. 2. Part of the reason for the rejection of socialism was also its feminist stance; see Clara Zetkin, *Der Student und das Weib* (Berlin, 1899) and E. Schultze, *Die Studentenschaft und die soziale Frage* (Göttingen, 1895).

on the importance of raising students' social consciousness through "the means of scholarly research." Realizing that evangelism or church charity no longer sufficed, Protestant divines like Friedrich Naumann or Friedrich Siegmund-Schulze, active in the Evangelisch-Sozialer Kongress, called upon academic youth to give new meaning to the term "brotherhood of man" and to reach out to the working class with "practical help." Not content with "training for social objectivity," the Volksverein für das Katholische Deutschland began to propagate "social study circles among students" in order to "introduce the young man to practical charity work, because the love of one's neighbor, rooted in living faith, is the best foundation for such commitment." Clergymen were motivated by the realization that "Social Democracy is the sharpest opponent of Christianity" and by the ideal of harmony: "Only through a reconciliation of class interests can a healthy political life be achieved."[37] In their journals student organizations quickly echoed these appeals, even if they seem not to have moved the unconcerned majority, which regarded them as pious wishes rather than as actual commands. When the initial anti-Semitic excitement had worn off, nationalists argued that "the VDSt should throw itself upon the social question with all its might," and debated social problems in its discussion evenings. Similarly, Hugo Böttger demanded that the Burschenschafter "become aware of social developments and sophisticate his judgment" through economic lectures, factory inspections, and pamphlets. Old Boys of the Wingolf argued that "new times [posed] novel tasks" and that students had a "social duty" that required "shedding academic arrogance" and "serving the people" in some practical capacity. Frightened by increasing Socialist electoral success, Catholic student associations also asked themselves, "What can we do?" Under the influence of the indefatigable Carl Sonnenschein and the Sekretariat sozialer Studentenarbeit in Mönchen-Gladbach, they answered: Work toward "a Christian, humane, idealist, and social spirit."[38]

[37] M. Kriele, *Soziale Arbeit* (Leipzig, 1894); F. Naumann, *Der Student im Verkehr mit den verschiedenen Volkskreisen* (Göttingen, 1895); J. Siegmund-Schultze, *Aus der sozialen Studentenarbeit* (Berlin, 1912); Volksverein für das katholische Deutschland, *Soziale Konferenzen und Studienzirkel* (Mönchen-Gladbach, 1907); O. Gerlach, *Die rechte Stellung der Studenten zur Tagespolitik und zur sozialen Frage* (Königsberg, 1901). This topic was one of the favorites of academic pamphleteers.

[38] "Unsere Aufgaben" *ABl* 6 (1891): 179ff.; O. Dibelius, "Die Mitarbeit der Studentenschaft an der Volksbildung," ibid. 17 (1902): 69ff.; Dr. Kormann, "National- und Sozialpolitik," ibid. 22 (1907): 185f.; Hugo Böttger, "Die rechte Stellung des Studenten zur Politik und zur sozialen Frage," *BBl* 15 (1900-01): 247ff.; G. A. Fritze, "Wirtschafts- und sozialpolitische Fragen, ein Arbeitsfeld für den deutschen Burschenschafter," ibid. 17 (1902-03): 10ff.; Prof. Waltemath, "Neue Zeiten—neue Aufgaben," *WBl* 37 (1908): 89f.; Dr. Vogt, "Die soziale Pflicht des Studenten," ibid. 38 (1909): 256f.; Nuss, "Was können wir tun?" *Ac* 24 (1912): 406f.; C. Sonnenschein, *Kann der moderne Student sozial arbeiten?* (Mönchen-Gladbach, 1908) and *Die sozialstudentische Bewegung* (Mönchen-Gladbach, 1910), pp. 32f.

The most effective implementation of the "social-student" ideal were the workingmen's courses (*Arbeiterunterrichtskurse*) started by the Freistudentenschaft. "Our enterprise has set itself the goal of raising the educational level of Berlin workers . . . through free elementary instruction," bringing together the student's intellectual expertise and the worker's desire for enlightenment. A second "prominent motive is bridging the gap between cultivated and uncultured, so strongly apparent in our day. The courses intend to awaken and strengthen the sense of social responsibility among those who are called upon to become the spiritual leaders of the nation." As student equivalent to the professorial *Volkshochschulkurse* (the German version of the university extension movement), these worker's courses were designed "to let students and workers gain understanding for each other and for a higher goal, the welfare of the entire nation." On the basis of "strict confessional and political neutrality," the Arbeiterunterrichtskurse aimed "only at elementary instruction" in order to create "a small island of peace in the middle of the class struggle" so that worker and student could develop "a friendly, trusting relationship" with each other. Of the 450 classes at 25 institutions (including technical colleges), 136 taught German and 33 writing, 120 offered introductory and 39 higher mathematics, 27 instructed in white-collar skills such as bookkeeping, 25 in stenography, while 21 and 20 provided French and English, respectively. Within a decade the movement, supported locally by the VDSt, the Burschenschaft, and the Wingolf and sponsored by concerned professors, reached about 11,000 workers and involved 660 male as well as 80 female students as staff, considerable numbers for a voluntary youth effort with no state support. While some traditionalists balked at the implicit liberalism of the idea ("the courses are progressive, otherwise they would not exist"), Socialists, though willing to accept instruction, detected the political wolf beneath the sheepskin of neutrality: "Their goal is to influence the participants in an anti-Socialist . . . spirit." The effect of these and other academic efforts on the workers was slight, since even supporters admitted: "Few practical results were achieved." For the students involved, "social work" provided an expiation of guilt, a form of applied religious conscience, and a strengthened belief in "social peace, reconciliation between different classes."[39]

[39] W. Wagner, *Der Student im Dienste der Volksbildung* (Berlin, 1902); "Aufruf an die Studierenden der Universität zu Berlin" (Berlin, n.d.), HUA, 749; session of the Prussian Ministry of State, 22 January 1898, DZA Po, Rkz 2184; H. F. Kitzing, *Student und Arbeiter* (Leipzig, 1910); B. Kiesewetter, *Student und Arbeiter* (Dresden, 1909); R. Kahn, *Die akademischen Arbeiterunterrichtskurse Deutschlands* (Gautzsch, 1912); *Lehrbuch für den deutschen Unterricht* (Berlin, 1908); Heidelberger Freistudentenschaft, *Satzungen der Studentischen Unterrichtskurse für Arbeiter und Arbeiterrinnen* (Heidelberg, 1908); A. Philippi, *Der Student und die soziale Frage* (Munich, 1896); A. Wilhelm, "Die studentischen Arbeiterun-

During the middle of the 1890s, nationalist associations shifted their attention from socialism to imperialism. In the Burschenschaft "the majority of the actives gradually turned away from liberal views toward conservative [ideas], insofar as one can talk at all about political attitude," Georg Heer remembered, reflecting on the emergence of "modern nationalism." The *Burschenschaftliche Blätter* proclaimed: "Instead of great power position, world power—that is the new goal of German nationalism!" and in 1891 it urged its chapters to play a "leading role" in the foundation of the Pan-German League (ADV). Tired of apolitical corporatism, the editor Gustav Heinrich Schneider proposed new guidelines in 1893, encouraging "German language and customs" in order to make his journal "a battleground for burning national issues." As some Old Boys squeamishly "protested against dragging the Burschenschaft movement into politics," the 1894 Eisenach conference stressed that "in patriotic training as in every regard" the actives were "primarily learners." But it also emphasized the necessity of struggling against "inner enemies" through greater "national" indoctrination of pledges. After several years of internal debates about the advisability of an organizational commitment, the ADC resolved in 1897 to "join the Pan-German League as a group," thereby demonstrating the "victorious power of the *alldeutsche* idea." During the next several years the Burschenschaft (which had supported the Schulverein already in 1888) also joined the Ostmarkenverein, the Colonial League, the North Schleswig Society, and the Navy League (until 1901), indoctrinating not only its actives in their imperialist ideology but also opening the pages of its respected journal to all manner of nationalist propaganda. The new editor, Hugo Böttger, appointed in 1898, promised to "struggle against un-Germanness wherever it appears and to collaborate in the great pan-German tasks at home and across the sea." For instance, he published such rabid diatribes as Rudolf Rabe's series on "The Education of the Germans to National Egotism."[40] In order "to influence German students

terrichtskurse Deutschlands," *Die Neue Zeit* 30 (1912): 1019ff.; and P. Dienstag, *Soziale Tendenzen im deutschen Studentenleben* (Munich, 1909). See also F. Eulenburg, "Der Student und das Volkstum," *FBl* 12 (1910): 353-60, and H. Weber, *Geschichte des VDSt*, pp. 5-13.

[40] G. Heer, *Die Burschenschaft*, 4: 62-72; C. Lent, "Deutsch National," *BBl* 4 (1890): 129ff.; Dr. Piper, "Eine Aufgabe der deutschen Burschenschaft," ibid. 5 (1891): 18f. H. G. Schneider, "An unsere Leser," ibid. 7 (1892-93), no. 12; "Die Vereinigung alter Burschenschafter Hannovers an die Schriftleitung" and "Antwort der Schriftleitung," ibid. 8 (1893-94): 13ff.; "Aus den Burschenschaften," ibid., pp. 138ff.; *Sitzungsberichte der a.o. Versammlung des allgemeinen Deputierten Convents* (Eisenach, 1894), pp. 20ff.; "Vom Alldeutschen Verbande," *BBl* 9 (1894-95): 169-73; "Alldeutsche Bewegung," ibid. 11 (1896-97): 208-17; H. G. Schneider, "Die deutsche Burschenschaft und ihre Zeitschrift," ibid. 12 (1897-98): 277-95; H. Böttger, "An die Leser!" ibid., pp. 1-2; R. Rabe, "Die Erziehung der Deutschen zum nationalen Egoismus," ibid. 14 (1899-1900): 91ff., 118ff., 140ff., 169ff.; A. R., "Will Deutschland die Ostmarken behaupten oder nicht?" ibid. 15 (1900-01):

so that the academic citizen regains his appropriate share of public life,'' he founded a *Burschenschaftliche Bücherei*, a pamphlet library that propagated imperialism, antisocialism, militarism, protection of the Mittelstand, the strengthening of Germanness, social harmony, financial reform, domestic colonization, air travel, emigration control, sport, minor student reforms, and a strong foreign policy.[41]

Not to be outdone, the VDSt abandoned its Christian-social preoccupations, turned first to strictly national education, and then resumed the colonial propaganda of the late 1880s: "We want a German world power and a German world policy.'' In 1894 the Berlin chapter demonstratively celebrated the imperial pioneer Karl Peters: "In earlier years we had more of a cabinet policy; now we need more of an economic policy. Germany shall carry its head high among the nations, that is our goal.'' Reversing its previous effort to stay aloof from Austrian nationalities' struggles, many chapters attended the 1897 Congress of the Pan-German League. In this "alldeutsche spirit,'' they rejected Count Caspar Badeni's anti-German language policy and resolved to send one member per every twenty-five actives to study one semester in Prague to prevent the oldest German university from becoming completely Czech. Closer to home, the Berlin VDSt enthusiastically joined the anti-Polish Ostmarkenverein in order to fight "for propagation of Germanness'' in Prussia's Eastern provinces and pressure the government into taking a stronger anti-Slavic stand. Toward the turn of the century the *Akademische Blätter* began to proclaim: "We need a forceful overseas and naval policy for demographic and national philosophical reasons,'' and the VDSt, *in corpore*, joined the Naval League, telegraphing Admiral Tirpitz: "With joyous enthusiasm national academic youth greets the decision to create a maritime force for our nation which commands respect.'' Thus, with the opening of the twentieth century, VDSt and Burschenschaft rivaled each other as centers of imperialist self-education of German students.[42]

This "sort of spiritual rebirth'' of academic youth centered around two

231f.; Pfister, "Vaterlandsarbeit,'' ibid., pp. 36-38; H. Böttger, "Die nationale Wirksamkeit der deutschen Burschenschaft,'' ibid., 17 (1902-03): 253-56.

[41] H. Böttger, "Ein Wort auf den Weg,'' *BuBü* (Berlin, 1901), 1: i-x. Altogether thirty-three issues appeared, presenting in lively and popular form arguments championing nationalist and imperialist commitment, but also revealing some lingering traces of liberalism in the openness to such questions as housing reform, workers' educational aspirations, international arbitration, revision of student association law, and so forth.

[42] O. Hötzsch, "Der deutsche Weltmachtgedanke,'' *ABl* 18 (1903): 17f. (written for the third edition of the VDSt *Taschenbuch* in contrast to the second, which declared: "We want neither particularism nor pan-Germanism; we want a united Reich''); H. Weber, *Geschichte des VDSt*, pp. 54ff., 169ff., 197ff., 218ff.; K. Sohlich, "Alldeutsche Pfingsten,'' *ABl* 12 (1897): 70ff.; and O. Eichler, "Deutsche Flottenpolitik,'' ibid. 12 (1898), no. 2. See also P. Baecker, "Gobineaus Rassenbuch,'' ibid. 14 (1899), no. 4; and O. Hötzsch, "Zum III. Jahrzehnt der Kyffhäuserbewegung,'' ibid. 16 (1901), no. 8.

slogans, deutschnational and Weltpolitik. Frustrated with the knee-jerk hurrah-patriotism of "the drinking and card-playing loafer without intellectual ambition" and "the unprincipled climber whose ideal is the exact reproduction of the dominant views of the ruling classes," the new nationalists wanted to "eliminate the lack of idealism among academic youth." One of the most spectacular (and least known) examples is the transformation of the duelling gymnasts (VC of the ATVs) from apolitical patriotism to pan-German activism in 1894-95. In a series of controversial articles in the *Akademische Turnerzeitung*, the law student Max Gerstenhauer proposed as "a program" for the Turner: "Let's join the national movement!" Invoking Father Jahn, he pointed out: "Our attitude toward the national principle is solely determined by our gymnastic tradition." Typically, he considered this "the exact opposite of current partisan politics, for national activity is directed outward" toward such problems as "the survival of the Germans outside the Reich" and toward "the exclusion of Jews, i.e., negative anti-Semitism." This impassioned plea for "a national commitment of the VC" frightened some of its alumni, who disliked politicizing the placid Turnerschaft, but many actives hailed it as "a fresh, new breeze . . . which makes the heart of a true patriot . . . swell and quicken." Although formal membership in the ADV was voted down, since the VC was "not yet ripe for a total commitment in the national struggle," the Turner journal's editor, Martin Beltz, wrote a series of propagandistic articles on pan-Germanism abroad and "national tasks" at home as "a short survey of the current state of the national movement and the entire nationalist system." Continual appeals for "a national education of individuals and the propagation of nationalism" as well as for "the organization of nationally minded students in nationalist associations" soon led to the triumph of this imperialist nationalism in the Turnerschaft. The VC began to rival the VDSt and Burschenschaft in organizing local student chapters of the ADV and in promoting pan-German ideas among the Catholic groups and the Wingolf as well as the independents.[43]

German national spirit triumphed among the three corporations and eventually among the majority of the indifferent for a variety of reasons. The post-Bismarckian generation discovered that "the empire is not a

[43] M. Gerstenhauer, "Ein Programm," *ATZ* 11 (1894-95), issues 13-15, especially pp. 442ff. and 477ff. in contrast to the tenor of "Rede gehalten am Festcommers des II. Cartellturnfests zu Mühlhausen von Vollert, Bergassessor," ibid. 1 (1884): 5ff.; J. Schlecht, "Unsere Stellung zur nationalen Bewegung" and P. Opitz, "Hic Rodus, his salta!" ibid. 11 (1894-95): 600ff.; M. Beltz, "Zum Semester-Anfang," ibid. 12 (1895-96): 37ff.; C. C., "Zur Klärung," pp. 177ff.; M. Beltz, "Alldeutsches," pp. 209ff., 245ff., 280ff., 317ff. Beltz added a new lead category to the journal, called *Vaterländisches*, 353ff. and 389ff. See H. G. John, *Politik und Turnen: Die deutsche Turnerschaft als nationale Bewegung im deutschen Kaiserreich* (Ahrensburg, 1976), pp. 73ff.

German national state; 1870 was not the end, but the beginning of German unification,'' for 20 million Germans were still outside of the Reich: ''Our people are split into one main and at least four completely separate parts that do not help one another but confront each other as enemies.'' In a very real sense the resurgence of nationalism among German students was a continuation of the Burschenschaft tradition, seeking to transcend Bismarck's Kleindeutschland in a Wilhelmian Grossdeutschland. An equally important theme was the necessary advance toward ''national world policy'' and toward ''enlarging ethnic territory'' in order to stop the hemorrhage of emigration by directing settlers to German colonies and insuring markets and raw materials for industry. Although not necessarily ahead of the adult trend, students more enthusiastically than philistine academics embraced the Weltmacht message of their Flottenprofessoren: ''Among the educated it is primarily youth, and especially the students, to which the ADV appeals.'' Finally, during an age that viewed itself as epigonic, ''the modern national idea'' met the youthful need for ''dedication to great goals, thirst for idealism'' and desire for commitment. Ironically, liberalism, democratic radicalism, or socialism appeared as ideologies of the past, whereas imperialist nationalism somehow embraced the future. The victory of deutschnationale Weltpolitik led to a sometimes ludicrous ''race'' among corporations in which each sought to outdo the other in displays of patriotic fervor and aggressive nationalism. ''The Turnerschaft will strengthen its influence on the student body and acquire the sympathy and respect of the cultivated circles that provide our pledges, less through corporate activity than through taking a public stand and participating in the development of the academic world by addressing relevant questions and current ideas.'' In contrast to the instinctive patriotism of the Corps, the new nationalism of the VDSt, DC, and VC was volkish (anti-Semitic, anti-Socialist, and largely antidemocratic) and imperialist. ''To strengthen and spread the yearning for Germany's unification and colonial expansion,'' it was willing to challenge old taboos: ''Thus, students will become involved in politics, will cultivate themselves nationalistically!''[44]

[44] M. Beltz, ''Alldeutsches,'' *ATZ* 12 (1895): 245ff., 281ff.; O. Kleinrath, ''Die Ziele und Aufgaben des Alldeutschen Verbandes,'' ibid. 14 (1897): 35ff.; ''Deutsche Flottenpolitik,'' *ABl* 13 (1898): 37f.; M. Gerstenhauer, ''Über die Klage, dass der deutschen Jugend der Idealismus fehle,'' *ATZ* 12 (1895): 461ff., 498ff., 536ff.; and Anonymous, *Deutschnational: Ein Weckruf an Deutschlands Studentenschaft zur 25-jährigen Jubelfeier der Reichsgründung* (Lepzig, 1896). The rich literature on the national pressure groups tends to slight students, although many of their leaders were at one time nationalist activists who then attempted to use academic youths for the propagation of their ideas. See H. Class, *Wider den Strom* (Leipzig, 1932), pp. 12ff., and G. Eley, *Reshaping the German Right* (New Haven, 1980).

STUDENT SELF-GOVERNMENT

In 1904-05 nationalist intolerance and a growing desire for student representation combined in a preposterous and pathetic series of events known as the *Hochschulstreit*. The rapid growth of Catholic associations (amounting to about 100 in 1905 with around 4,000 members, approximating one-fifth of all organized students) led to "the envy and jealousy of other corporations." Endemic tensions erupted in the winter of 1903 at the University of Jena when the newly founded CV corporation Sigambria had the audacity to adopt colors. On Ash Wednesday forty Corps students staged a mock procession, preaching as bishops and monks to the heretic Johann Huss, inviting bystanders to confession, and denigrating Catholic rites. In protest against even the mild punishment of these "educated boors," the VDSt called a student assembly, featuring the notorious ex-Jesuit, Count Paul von Hoensbroech, in order to combat "the antinational spirit of this artificial ultramontane creature," Sigambria. "The Jena student body considers it a serious undertaking, violating the essence of student tradition, and a grave assault on German sensibilities that color-carrying confessional corporations are formed on German soil." The Protestant senate, led by the theologian Otfried Nippold, agreed: "Student associations that pursue principally religious goals, as well as statutorily only accept members of one denomination, *shall not carry colors*."[45] This spark soon ignited the technical college at Hanover, where there were even fewer Catholics, but new equality with the university made students intent on proving their parity through patriotism. Without provocation, two petitions suddenly appeared on the agenda of the 24 June 1904 student assembly, the first "demanding from the rector and senate the suspension of the existing confessional corporations," the second suggesting "the exclusion of denominational associations as such from the student council." One week later the VDSt leader, Wilhelm Heile, denounced Catholic associations as "nurseries of antinational spirit" that produced ultramontane Center party adherents. Over the protests of a Catholic spokesman, who warned against "the brutal rape of the minority," the overwhelming majority of the thousand students present petitioned the sympathetic rector for the prohibition of confessional corporations. Impotent, Catholic journals fumed that "justice is on our side" and rejected "the accusation of

---

[45] H. Wurm, "Die katholische Studentenschaft im 19. Jahrhundert," *Ac* 13 (1901): 357-60; E. Sch., "Die Existenzberechtigung der katholischen Studentenkorporationen," *AMbl* 17 (1904): 229-32; J. Giessler, "Angriffe auf die katholischen Studentenkorporationen," *Ac* 17 (1904): 169-72; *Erklärung des Verhaltens der Bonner Studentenschaft* (Bonn, 1890); Rottenburg to Bosse, 17 November 1897, in ZStA Me, Rep 76 Va, Sekt 3 Tit XII, No 3, vol. 14; P. Stitz, *Der akademische Kulturkampf* (Munich, 1960), pp. 15ff.; M. Steinmetz, *Jena*, p. 497; and Schulze-Ssymank, *Das deutsche Studententum*, pp. 381-98.

national unreliability as so ridiculous and calumnious that we do not have to refute it!''[46]

The rapid spread of the agitation to the Charlottenburg and other Technische Hochschulen made "the term 'new Kulturkampf' appear truer every day,'' for neither Protestant nor Jewish associations were attacked. Despite the dampening efforts of the Aachen, Darmstadt, and Karlsruhe administrations and the advice of student moderates to use spiritual means, the agitation resumed in the fall semester. This time the blaze was fanned not by the Evangelische Bund but rather by the nationality conflict in Austria. When a German painter was bayoneted in student clashes over the establishment of an Italian law faculty at Innsbruck, the VDSt proposed a sympathy telegram: "With pride and joyous satisfaction the Hanover students have heard of your manly defense of German interests. We congratulate you and wish you great success as vanguard of the nationalities' struggle.'' During the same meeting the council renewed its petition to exclude Catholic associations from its ranks and justified it by an elaborate memorandum, "To German Students: On Confessional Corporations.'' Calling them a "continual danger,'' the Hanoverian nationalists argued, "academic freedom is the right to form a personal conviction in all questions'' and can "therefore not recognize the legitimacy of groups who oppose this point of view, for their principles contradict the essence of being a student.'' In Berlin, this demonstration caused consternation because of its diplomatic repercussions in Vienna and Rome, even if the rumor that "the Triple Alliance is shaking dangerously'' was probably unfounded. Hence, ministerial director Althoff called Rector G. Barkhausen and two council members to give them a tongue-lashing about meddling in foreign policy and overstepping the bounds of their authority, and reprimanded the professors for privately supporting the agitation. But administrative strictures were no longer enough to stem the tide. On 22 November the Charlottenburg student Freiherr von Buttlar contrasted international, anticultural ultramontanism with "Germanic-Protestant national feeling'' and called for a campaign against local and national Catholic corporations: "Their existence threatens academic life and the entire culture of the German people.'' The dire "consequences'' of prejudice against which Center party leader Porsch had warned at the Katholikentag were

---

[46] Stitz, *Akademischer Kulturkampf*, pp. 25ff.; W. Otte, "Zur Frage der konfessionellen Verbindungen auf den deutschen Hochschulen,'' *BBl* 18 (1904): 184-86; text of petition of 30 June in J. Penzler, *Der Hochschulstreit: Akademische Freiheit und Konfessionelle Verbindungen*, 2nd ed. (Leipzig, 1906), pp. 71ff. (for the answer of Barkhausen to the students that the senate would get in touch with other universities); and articles by E. Sch. and J. Giessler, above, note 45. See also Victor, *Akademische Freiheit in der Zwangsjacke* (Berlin, 1905); P. Baecker, *Die Kämpfe um die akademische Freiheit einst und jetzt* (Prenzlau, 1905).

becoming a frightening reality. An unprecedented organizational and ideological struggle for control of German student life and student councils had begun.[47]

The alternately lenient and heavy-handed efforts of the Prussian Ministry of Culture and of the local rectors to uphold tolerance through administrative edict turned the conflict into a clash over academic freedom. In early December Professor Barkhausen rejected the council request, "for there is no reason to proceed against existing corporations which have not violated discipline," and warned the leaders of the agitation: "Drawing outside circles into questions involving university regulations . . . is inadmissible and forbidden." All actions to the contrary would be punished. Instead of silencing the nationalists, a "serious reprimand" by the ministry for the Innsbruck telegram provided a pretext for a new student assembly on 13 January 1905: "The prohibition [of communication] is not only an unheard of and unwarranted interference in student rights but actually a brutal suppression of academic freedom, which should not be tolerated by students under any circumstances." With the approval of the Catholic groups, the council drafted a new petition asking, in the name of endangered akademische Freiheit, that "the injunction be lifted and the threat of punishment" withdrawn. Since "an agitation transcending the bounds of the institution is directed against the existing order," the rector refused to comply. In order to head off an explosion, the ministry sent three officials, led by Geheimrat Naumann, "who instructed the students that, according to tradition, councils are an organ of mediation between rector and student body for executing the orders of academic authorities," for instance in the preparation of festivities. "This conception of duties without rights did not meet with the approval of the deputies, who argued that the council had hitherto not at all been considered an instrument for the procurement of missing clothes-hangers or for the organization of torchlight parades but rather a representative of common interests for the implementation of student decisions, so to speak a student parliament." This democratic view provoked the strict Berlin university judge to retort angrily: "What you understand as academic freedom would lead to general anarchy." When

---

[47] Stitz, *Akademischer Kulturkampf*, pp. 28ff.; H. Weber, *Geschichte des VDSt*, pp. 261ff.; Penzler, *Hochschulstreit*, pp. 13ff., 72ff. (for the "Denkschrift der Hannoverschen Studentenschaft an die Studenten Deutschlands über die konfessionellen Verbindungen"); Schulze-Ssymank, *Das deutsche Studententum*, pp. 384f.; Sachse, *Althoff* (Berlin, 1928), pp. 158ff.; P. Freiherr von Buttlar, *Frei ist der Bursch!* (Berlin, 1905); speech of Dr. Porsch in "Vom Regensburger Katholikentage," *Ac* 17 (1904): 196-201; and "Von der Hetze," ibid., pp. 293-96 for the text of the Charlottenburg memorandum of 13 December 1904, which argued that "confessional corporations hinder free scholarly research" and "stand in closest connection with a political party and obligate their members to its views." See also Sapper, "Unsere Aufgabe im Kampf gegen die konfessionellen Verbindungen," *WBl* 35 (1905), no. 5.

contradicted, he fumed: "Academic freedom is a concept that we do not know at all, but which you have invented for yourself!" Whether the agitators misconstrued this untimely phrase to gain revenge for Judge Daude's authoritarianism matters little. Since it appeared in character with Prussian practice, it was widely accepted when reported in the *Hannoversche Courier* and spread like wildfire through the entire educated public. The threat of repression gained further credence with the rector's terse announcement on the bulletin board: "I hereby inform the students of the Technische Hochschule at Hanover that today I have dissolved the student council by a declaration to its three representatives." The student dispute was escalating into a political scandal.[48]

Although the government tried to ridicule the official gaffe in the *NAZ*, the perceived danger to academic freedom made the movement spill over to regular universities. Appealing to akademische Freiheit as "the fundamental principle of all academic life," a Marburg student assembly on 31 January rousingly reaffirmed "the untrammelled right of free speech, of free action based on German spirit, and of unfettered and independent exchange of ideas." Because it ignored the divisive issue of Catholic corporations, this "unanimous protest" against bureaucratic authoritarianism found an extraordinary echo at Dresden, Aachen, Bonn, Danzig, Darmstadt, Halle, Heidelberg, Jena, Kiel, and Munich as well as Karlsruhe. In Hanover 928 students signed a new petition complaining about the complete breakdown of communication between professors and students: "Mutual trust has disappeared from our college, a factor essential for its flowering." In Charlottenburg a meeting of 2,000 academics heatedly debated the Hanoverian events and argued: "The technical colleges have yet to prove that they are equal to the universities . . . by protecting academic freedom." Denouncing "the actions of the Ministry of Culture as a violation of academic freedom," the assembly demanded the reaffirmation of this principle and the council's right of free communication with other universities. On 17 February the public campaign culminated in a meeting at a Berlin brewery attended by 3,000 academics, who vigorously discussed the contradiction between "paying lip service to academic freedom while calling for police measures against comrades of different con-

[48] Barkhausen to council, 1 December 1904; protocol of conference with student leaders, 5 December 1904; Wentzel to council, 3 January 1905; Hanover student petition, 13 January 1905; Barkhausen to council, 14 January 1905, all in Penzler, *Hochschulstreit*, pp. 78-84. Reports of the *Hannoversche Courier* of assembly of 17 January and Naumann mission of 21 January as well as subsequent student meetings in "Hochschulstreitigkeiten," *Ac* 17 (1905): 325-35. Barkhausen notice at the *schwarze Brett*, 21 January 1905, Penzler, *Hochschulstreit*, pp. 85. See also Stitz, *Akademischer Kulturkampf*, pp. 36ff. and Schulze-Ssymank, *Das deutsche Studententum*, pp. 385ff. For a sampling of press reaction, see *Ac* 17 (1905): 328-35.

viction." The tortuous resolution combined a ringing affirmation of the right of free speech with a clear denunciation of "tendencies inimical to state and country which have no right to exist at the universities, because they are not only scholarly but also national institutions." The conference of technical college representatives at Eisenach a day later followed the same dual course. Gradually some observers began to notice the danger of using academic liberty for illiberal ends. H. Böttger still ranted, "this proves how far we have descended into Jesuitry," and he condemned ministerial support for tolerance as "a new act of subservience to the Center party." But the free-student leader W. Ohr mused: "The saddest and most incomprehensible feature of this entire muddle is the fact that the students themselves, especially the so-called liberals, are assassinating their right of association."[49]

The contest between students and authorities gradually turned from a debate over academic freedom into a struggle for power over the university. To forestall the closing of the college, Althoff and Naumann sought to reassure Hanover student leaders that the government would approve "their right to organize and communicate freely" if they apolized for their "serious official insult to academic authorities." Although they were willing to comply, in a stormy assembly of 1,400 students Wilhelm Heile and Gustav Zimmerman got so carried away with their rhetoric that they revealed the rector's initial support of the anti-Catholic agitation. In private he had admitted indiscreetly: "They are the greatest cancer of our universities." Stung by this breach of confidence, Barkhausen did not respond to the moderate tone of the resolution for reinstatement of the council but began disciplinary proceedings to expel the agitators. At the same time in Marburg, Daude's mediation eliminated some of the disputed points, but the student assembly, instead of composing a letter of contrition to Minister Studt, reasserted its liberal principles:

> Together with all German comrades, Marburg students are united in the conviction that every free academic citizen has the right to a governmental hearing for justified complaints and demands at any time. . . . Equally, Marburg students consider it the right of a free

[49] *NAZ*, 1 February 1905; resolution of the Marburg student council, 31 January 1905 and sympathetic resolutions in Bonn and Göttingen 7 and 9 February, ZStA Me, Rep 76 Va, Sekt 1 Tit XII, No 25A, vol. 1; Hanover student petition to rector, 2 February 1905; H. Seck to Studt, 1 February 1905; resolution of academic assembly in Berlin, 17 February 1905; resolution of the Association of Technical Colleges, 18 February 1905, all in Penzler, *Hochschulstreit*, pp. 86ff., 108ff. H. Böttger, "Akademische Freiheit in Preussen," *BBl* 19 (1905): 199-202; and W. Ohr, "Ein Wort über akademische Freiheit," *FBl* 7 (1905): 539-43. See also "Hochschulstreitigkeiten," *Ac* 17 (1905): 329ff.; H. Paalzow, "Die akademische Freiheit der Studenten," *Deutsche Rundschau* 31 (1905), no. 7; and Anonymous, *Burschen heraus! Eine Denkschrift zum Kampf um die akademische Freiheit* (Berlin, 1905).

citizen, founded on the Prussian constitution, to express his opinions openly in the press. . . . Similarly, Marburg students unanimously declare that academic citizens, meeting in their councils, have the unquestioned right to communicate with each other about general student questions, as long as state laws do not contain limiting provisions.[50]

This "most courageous demonstration of a Prussian student body toward the ministry" developed a coherent rationale for resisting bureaucratic absolutism, however well intentioned. In order to head off the formation of a progressive academic movement, William II telegraphed to Hanover, "You have no reason to be concerned about the protection of *true* academic freedom *correctly understood*," and Althoff invited the Hanover and Charlottenburg leaders for a personal consultation on 13 February. In a "long and relaxed discussion" in the Weinstube Rüdesheimer, the wily chief of the Prussian university section, before whom professors trembled, amiably suggested, between toasts of Rhine wine, that he would lift all prohibitions if the students would only cease persecuting Catholic corporations. But treating the dispute as a mere misunderstanding fundamentally misjudged the ideological commitment of the youthful activists. His conciliatory conclusion, "I see, gentlemen, that we are completely agreed," evoked the devastating reply: "Yes, your excellency, in all but the essential points!"[51]

Although in Marburg ministerial concessions on the right of petition, press publication, and communication quickly restored peace, in Hanover the conflict culminated in a student strike, which led to a passionate Landtag debate about the "Althoff system." When on 19 February ringleader Wilhelm Heile was unanimously expelled from the college, one thousand students celebrated him as "a real hero" in a festive procession (*Komitat*)

---

[50] "Die Unterredung im 'Rüdesheimer' am 13. Februar 1905," Paalzow memorandum on the background and course of the ill-fated discussion, ZStA Me, Rep 92, AI, No 15, vol. 1. Althoff protocol of Hanover negotiations, 4 February 1905 with marginal comments in the ministry, indicating that neither the right of petition nor of publication were ever contested, ZStA Me, Rep 76 Va, Sekt 1 Tit XII, No 25A, vol. 1. Cf. Stitz, *Akademischer Kulturkampf*, pp. 43ff. and the local documents in MUA, 305a, Acc 1950/9, no. 641.

[51] Schulze-Ssymank, *Des deutsche Studententum*, p. 389; Studt to Hanover students, 12 February 1905; "Die Unterredung im 'Rüdesheimer'," pp. 10f., ZStA Me, Rep 92, AI, No 15, vol. 1. For other reports of the conversation, see also Anonymous, *Burschen heraus!*; Buttlar, *Frei ist der Bursch!*; the statements of Baeckmann and Buttlar in the assembly of 17 February; and deputy Jaenecke's summary in the Landtag debates, *AH*, vol. 474, 23 February. See also Sachse, *Althoff*, pp. 160ff. The press reaction was overwhelmingly hostile. The *Vorwärts* called the affair "a stupid drinking joke." The *Deutsche Zeitung* of 25 February saw it as defeat for Althoff. The *Münchener Neueste Nachrichten* on 28 May criticized his methods. The *Welt am Montag* ridiculed "Althoff als Studentenvater." Paul Liman in the *Leipziger Neueste Nachrichten* was most savage on 6 May: "Wenn Herr Althoff heimwärts zieht."

to the railroad station, singing the traditional tune: *"Bemooster Bursche zieh ich aus."* The following day all academic activity ceased, and in thirty streetcar wagons the Hanover nationalists left the city for neighboring Hildesheim, where Heile counselled courage: "This is a great struggle which does not concern the university alone, but a spiritual war which Germany has been forced to wage for the last two thousand years, a conflict between empire and popery." Two days later in the Landtag, a National Liberal member ridiculed Althoff's previous assurance in the Budget Committee that peace was on its way: "Today discord is stronger than ever." Angered, the Ministerialdirektor replied: "In enthusiasm for academic freedom, gentlemen, we are second to none, least of all to deputy Friedberg." This insult to one of their leaders infuriated the parliamentarians. Goaded by the left, they began to vent years of frustration over Althoff's high-handed administrative methods and accused the ministry of "servility to the Center party." Deeply wounded by the charge of authoritarianism, the embattled head of the university section replied that the Innsbruck telegram was irregular, and confessional corporations were "no blessing," but there was no question of their right to exist: "Only you must not let your freedom turn into unfreedom for others." He went on to read the amused and agitated house an object lesson on academic freedom. Admitting that the disciplinary law of 1879 "no longer completely suits our times," he sarcastically suggested that "the educational administration has much more liberal views" than liberal professors like Mommsen and Sybel. "You are struggling against something that does not exist at all"—methodical repression. Although personal apologies to Friedberg could not silence "the cry of German conscience against ultramontanism," Studt's pacification policy eventually prevailed over "the elemental movement." In Hanover a "peace commission" of professors and students worked out a compromise, restoring the council in exchange for an apology to the rector. In Charlottenburg the authorities lifted all prohibitions in return for a promise that in the future the question of confessional corporations would be settled in a manner "that shall not disturb or endanger academic order and peace in any way." Finally, William II reassured the educated public by saying to the director of the Berlin Technische Hochschule: "I don't understand at all how our students can fear an abridgement of academic freedom in a country whose sovereign was a student and who sent his sons to university. There is not the slightest cause for such concerns."[52]

[52] Declaration of Marburg students, 14 February 1905, and Studt response on 18 February 1905, ZStA Me, Rep 76 Va, Sekt 1 Tit XII, No 25A, vol. 1. Barkhausen announcement, 19 February 1905, Penzler, *Hochschulstreit*, pp. 115f.; Heile speech in "Die Hetze gegen die katholischen Korporationen und die akademische Freiheit," *AMbl* 17 (1905): 121-27; Friedberg and others in the Prussian lower house, 21 and 23 February 1905, *AH*, vol. 474; Launhardt announcement, 27 February 1907; William II to Miethe, 1 March 1905, ZStA

In order to exploit their "victory," thirty-one delegations of student representatives at Eisenach during Easter 1905 "organized all councils into an association so that future attacks will founder on its solid structure." Nineteen Corps of the technical colleges, eighteen Burschenschaften, twelve Turnerschaften, five regular SCs, five Landsmannschaften, four Sänger-schaften, four VDSts, twenty other associations, two Wingolfs, and seven Finkenschaften "succeeded, for the first time, in getting German students to take common action and disregard all special interests." The chief result of this anti-Catholic conference was "the Verband Deutscher Hochschulen, [which] intends to represent and propagate general student and national interests" that were defined as apolitical in principle. In the stormy discussion, the corporation representatives personally censured Althoff and Daude and demanded the rights of student assembly, free communication, and student councils. After lengthy debates about the degree of anti-Catholicism, the newly founded Verband agreed to a convoluted resolution condemning bureaucratic infringements on academic freedom. But it also called "confessional separation . . . a serious national danger" and recommended the nonrecognition of denominational corporations, "considering their dissolution emphatically desirable." In contrast to his earlier sympathy, William II reprimanded the agitators in a telegram: "I trust that our students will always strive to uphold German intellectual freedom out of respect for the convictions of their opponents." Enunciated during the second VdH meeting at Weimar in May 1905, the basic nationalist program was ambiguous and self-contradictory. It was easy to talk about "a bulwark of true academic freedom and a defense of general national interests," but the specification of these principles remained difficult. Few could quarrel with defining student years as a time of preparation for "(1) acquiring the knowledge necessary for a later profession and (2) forming the character through self-education into a spiritually and morally free personality." But if the "unification of German students" was the goal, then the exclusion of Catholic corporations seemed illogical, even if the VdH retreated to recommending it in theory rather than requiring it in practice.[53]

To forestall the elimination of all Catholic associations from student

Me, Rep 92, AI, No 14, vol. 1. See also B. vom Brocke, "Hochschul- und Wissenschafts-politik in Preussen und im Deutschen Kaiserreich 1882-1907: Das 'System Althoff' " in *Bildungspolitik*, pp. 9-118.

[53] *Sitzungsberichte der Tagungen des Verbandes deutscher Hochschulen* (Bonn, 1905), pp. 9-40; William II to VdH, 15 March 1905, ZStA Me, Rep 2.2.1, No 21405; "Der Eisenacher Studententag," *BBl* 19 (1905): 3-8; "Nach dem Kampfe um die akademische Freiheit," ibid., pp. 31ff.; and C. Bornhak, "Der Ministerialerlass vom 16. März, 1905 nach Rechtmässigkeit und Zweckmässigkeit," arguing that it was both, ZStA Me, Rep 92, AI, No 16a. "Die Hetze gegen die katholischen Korporationen u. die akademische Freiheit," *AMbl* 17 (1905): 121-27; "Sitzungsbericht des 1. Verbandstages deutscher Hochschulen zu Weimar am 10.-11. Mai 1905," in *Sitzungsberichte*, pp. 41-72; Stitz, *Akademischer Kulturkampf*, pp. 68-71.

councils, the Ministry of Culture ordered that any change in statutes or the foundation of new councils would temporarily have to be approved by Berlin. Since university authorities felt slighted by the direct intervention of government commissars, a conference of rectors at Halle demanded that "negotiations with the student body be conducted only by academic authorities" and "student councils not be regulated generally." Especially in those Protestant universities where the professors were sympathetic to the nationalists, as in Göttingen, the ad hoc ministerial decree caused a faculty uproar about academic freedom. As "at present students deeply mistrust the Ministry of Education," the senate argued, "it is imperative that no new fuel be added to the agitation." Urging that "the current relationship of mutual trust between the senate and the student council not be disturbed," the Göttingen professors asked that "the remnants of traditional self-government not be atrophied" by central decisions determined by "nonacademic considerations of a highly political nature." Since the Marburg and Greifswald faculties sent similar protests to Berlin, the ministry retreated in the *NAZ*, stressing the "thoroughly provisional character" of the measure. The decisive Conference of Rectors 16-19 May 1905 at Berlin debated with curiously reversed fronts. Prodded by Althoff, the Prussian Ministry of Culture suggested a general solution of the council issue to insure uniformity of treatment and to guarantee tolerance, which, if one can believe the internal drafts, was more liberal toward nonincorporated students and the right of petition and communication than most existing regulations. But because of the unanimous resistance of Prussian universities to any solution imposed from above, which would only fan the flames anew, the meeting resolved "not to pass general regulations." Yielding in form, Minister Studt remained firm in substance: "From the negotiations of our conference I have gained the sincere confidence that in the question of student councils, academic authorities will succeed in maintaining order and peace without general rulings, protect the equality of confessional associations or societies against all infringements, and also meet the justified wishes of the nonincorporated students."[54]

[54] Stitz, *Akademischer Kulturkampf*, pp. 60-68. Ehrenburg to Studt, 7 April 1905 with Studt answer of 21 April, stressing the authority founded in the state's "right of supervision" and expressing his "decided displeasure"; Marburg rector to Studt, 20 April 1905 with angry marginalia, all in ZStA Me, Rep 76 Va, Sekt 1 Tit XII, No 25A, vol. 1; *NAZ*, 22 April; petition of Greifswald faculty, 3 May 1905; resolution of the Halle Conference of Rectors, delivered on 10 May 1905, in Penzler, *Hochschulstreit*, pp. 166ff.; Paalzow, "Denkschrift über die Ausschüsse der Studierenden an den Universitäten," and "Allgemeine Gesichtspunkte" as well as "Entwurf einer königlichen Verordnung für die Landesuniversitäten," in ZStA Me, Rep 76 Va, Sekt 1 Tit XII, No 25A, vol. 2; "Ergebnisse der Rektorenkonferenz, 16.-19. Mai," and "Protokoll der Rektorenkonferenz, 16. Mai 1905," all in ZStA Me, Rep 92, AI, No 29. See also Althoff's "Entwurf II" for a general council statute, ibid., No 15, vol. 1, and P. Baecker, "Zum Entscheidungskampf um die studentische Freiheit," *ABl* 20 (1905): 33-37.

Although "during the past semester excitement at German universities ran higher than in many a decade," the first national student association was a resounding failure. Student organizations reacted in three broad ways to the ideological contradictions of the VdH. Seeking to regain its ancient leadership, the Burschenschaft expected "individual chapters to work for VdH aims and make it their duty to fight the confessional corporations." Similarly, the Reformburschenschaft, the Burschenschaft and Corps of the technical colleges, the Landsmannschaft, the philological associations, and the academic Turner association, and somewhat less (limited to legal means) the duelling gymnasts (VC) campaigned against the "ultramontane danger." The university Corps, while struggling against Catholics "with all means at their disposal," disdained endorsing the VdH, and the VDSt, the spiritual father of much of the agitation, also declined to take a collective position, although many locals were heavily involved. While sympathizing with the aims of the movement, the duelling and nonduelling glee clubs preferred spiritual means.[55] Somewhat confused, the Protestant Wingolf as well as the Schwarzburgbund applauded the unification of students, but rejected the repression of Catholics. The Jewish associations argued: "Rarely has a struggle been carried on with more self-deception than this one." After a passionate debate about whether the "free-student standpoint mitigates in favor of tolerance," the majority of the Freistudentenschaft also came out for neutrality. Only Catholic associations were unalterably opposed, "demanding academic freedom for confessional corporations and therefore their equality with the others, especially in the councils representing the common interest of the students." Since about 364 chapters favored the agitation, while 172 were somewhat sympathetic but technically neutral, and 145 were adamantly hostile (with another 310 unaccounted for), the VdH could hardly claim to represent a united student body.[56]

[55] *Sitzungsberichte des ordentlichen Burschenschaftstags* 24-26 (1905-07) for the resolution and annual surveys of the movement, as well as P. Prion, "Die Berechtigung des Kampfes gegen die katholischen Korporationen," *BBl* 20 (1905-06): 149ff.; W. Fabricius, "Corps, Ausschüsse und Studentenverband," *AMh* 22 (1905), no. 2; resolution of the SC, 12 May 1905, ZStA Me, Rep 76 Va, Sekt 1 Tit XII, No 25A, vol. 2; O. Hoetzsch, "Der Kyfferhäuserverband und die konfessionellen Studentenverbindungen," versus P. Baecker, "Der Kampf um die akademische Freiheit," *ABl* 19 (1904-05), nos. 11 and 21. See also Penzler, *Hochschulstreit*, pp. 60ff. for the views of the smaller organizations.

[56] Sapper, "Unsere Aufgabe im Kampf gegen die Konfessionellen Verbindungen," *WBl* 35 (1905-06), no. 5; P. Ssymank, "Der fünfte Freistudententag zu Weimar," *FBl* 7 (1905): 608ff.; transcript of the debates in "Protokoll des Verbandstags 1905," BA R 129, no. 424; "Abwehrkundgebungen katholischer Korporationen," *Ac* 18 (1905-06): 138ff.; resolution of representatives of Catholic student associations, 3 May 1905, Penzler, *Hochschulstreit*, p. 189; calculation based on the tabulation of association size by the Prussian Ministry of Culture, spring 1905, ZStA Me, Rep 76 Va, Sekt 1 Tit XII, No 25A, vol. 1. See also Schulze-Ssymank, *Das deutsche Studententum*, pp. 396ff. In Berlin 82 organizations with 1,029 members belonged to the projected Studentenverband, whereas 28 organizations with 615 members did not belong (like the 122 member VDSt) or were opposed (like the

Finally, the movement foundered on the resistance of the authorities, who were willing to recognize student councils without Catholics only as Studentenverband, rather than under "the misleading name 'Ausschuss'," which implied representation of all collegians. In Charlottenburg this ruling led to further altercations when the rector refused to recognize the new council "because it creates the impression that it is not an association but student government." Despite the foundation of a journal, *Die Deutsche Hochschule*, more and more associations and universities withdrew from the VdH when it failed to become an impartial student association, and it dissolved in 1908. "Since the Verband could neither [persecute Catholics nor be truly representative] it was incapable of living in the long run."[57]

The causes of this "struggle under a false flag against Catholic corporations in the name of academic freedom" were complex. The central reason was confessional cleavage. The Protestant majority equated religious liberalism with akademische Freiheit and resented a minority whose commitment to scholarly objectivity was suspect: "Catholic student societies reject the principle of the freedom of scholarship, just as the Church does." The influx of thousands of Catholic students whose agrarian, commercial, and industrial backgrounds threatened the social cohesion of the Bildungsbürgertum raised fears that Protestant universities would be subverted from within by ultramontanism and Center party politics: "The integrity of our student life demands that these corporations of unfreedom be considered academic weeds." The Prussian government's attempt to impose peace from above aroused the hostility of liberal professors, the left parties, and a considerable segment of the press against "such violations of academic freedom . . . typical of a system that endangers the high mission of German universities." Although local authorities "took many a regrettable and hasty step that poured oil on the fire rather than on the waves," the ministry's "premature intervention" produced a temporary closing of ranks between students and professors against "the Althoff system," while the rights of Catholic corporations were conveniently

---

six Catholic groups with 193 members and six Jewish ones with 140 members), Daude to rector, 4 January 1906 (with survey and statutes), HUA, 795.

[57] Tilmann votum about the legality of the Hanover Studentenverband, 26 April 1905, ZStA Me, Rep 92, AI, No 15, vol. 1; memoranda on student councils, 8 March 1905, ibid., No 16a; Barkhausen to Studt, 27 March, with statutes of Hanover Verband and subsequent emendations, and general memorandum on councils of 15 May 1905, ibid., No 20. "Zur Aufklärung!" Charlottenburg student flyer, fall 1905; Studt note of 20 September 1905; Ssymank to Althoff, 1 November 1905; Studt to rector of TH Berlin, 22 November 1905, etc., ibid., No 19. For the abortive Berlin University negotiations to establish a similar Studentenverband, see the papers in HUA, 795. For the gradual dissolution of the VdH, see the correspondence of the *Vorort*, 1905, and the *Protokolle der Verbandstage Deutscher Hochschulen*, 1906-08, in IHK, F 1583 in folio. Although implicitly anti-Semitic, the VdH never quite took a formal stand on the issue.

ignored. Another factor was the ambivalent nature of the "nationalistic spirit ruling the universities." Sparked by fears of the empire's disruption by "enemies from within," the agitation was part of the Wilhelmian "anti"movements directed against visible minorities like Jews, Socialists, and members of other nationalities. Elements of liberalism inspired the anticlericalism of the campaign, which fastened on Catholic obscurantism and separatism. At the same time, the movement contained a heavy dose of xenophobia, for the Technische Hochschulen directed many resolutions against foreign students "to keep outsiders from overrunning our colleges." Finally, on many a campus the "envy of the duelling corporations for the growing number of nonduelling" associations played an important role, for the Catholic societies were increasing so rapidly that they endangered the dominance of the Corps. "In Germany so far one can hardly say that students are very committed to freedom," the *Vorwärts* ridiculed. "Hence, one cannot expect the Socialist press to take this grotesque freedom struggle of our Corps and beer students too seriously."[58]

The consequences of this confused national liberal wave in student politics were nonetheless considerable, albeit largely negative. If numbers of chapters and actives are any indication of vitality, Catholic associations emerged stronger than ever, gaining about 30 of the former and 1,200 of the latter to become the third (CV) and fourth (KV) largest student groups between 1903 and 1908. At the same time, chauvinist pressure from without led them to nationalize within. In the spring of 1907 the Tübingen Guestphalia, Alamannia, and Cheruskia publicly declared that "their patriotic spirit is not influenced by ultramontanism," criticized "the nonparticipation of Catholic corporations in national festivities," and rejected Center party politics at the annual Catholic congresses. Because Tübingen corporations unanimously vouched for their national reliability, the VdH was forced to "admit even councils with such confessional corporations whose national spirit is guaranteed." To conform with practice, the CV added a commitment to patriotism (*Vaterlandsliebe*) to its principles during the Würzburg meeting of 1907. When the VdH began to crumble, some of its backers, weaned on the anti-Catholicism of the Evangelische Bund, founded "a free, intercorporative, and interconfessional society of German students" called Der Akademische Bismarckbund. "Through cultivation

---

[58] E. Schönfelder, "Grundfragen des Schwarzburgbundes," *SBl* (1906), nos. 3-4; Penzler, *Hochschulstreit*, pp. 40-70; Stitz, *Akademischer Kulturkampf*, pp. 45, 108ff.; *Deutsche Zeitung*, 21 February 1905; *Protokoll des dritten Verbandstags, 2.-23. Juni 1907*, pp. 23ff.; "Die bedrohte 'akademische Freiheit'," *Vorwärts*, 3 February 1905. See also H. Cardauns, *Mehr Licht! Zur Verständigung im Kampfe gegen die konfessionellen Studentenkorporationen* (Cologne, 1905). As he more than anyone else became the focus of public criticism, Althoff was personally "gravely disappointed, because his honest intentions were grossly misunderstood and distorted," which hastened his retirement (Sachse, *Althoff*, pp. 163f.).

of German-national attitudes and mores as well as through a regular journal, lectures, flyers, and broadsides, it wants to enable its members to fulfill their national duty against ultramontanism." Although the venerable Sybel sympathized with this "purified but decided nationalism," he wondered about its methods: "A group that only polemicizes cannot have an educational effect and is therefore not truly collegiate." After an initial stir, the Bismarckbund never managed to create more than twelve local chapters, and the Catholic publicist Cardauns correctly concluded in 1913: "The academic Kulturkampf has been a complete fiasco." Finally, the persecution of Catholic associations vitiated the progressive impulse in the struggle against bureaucratic paternalism. Ironically, by perpetrating intolerance, "the new active spirit of academic youth" destroyed the very instrument of its potential emancipation, effective national student self-government. Already in September 1905 Althoff had reported to Minister Studt: "The student movement has proven inept and is internally broken."[59]

Despite the collapse of the national movement, the campaign for "public legal representation of the entire student body" continued on a local level. Resuming the illustrious Burschenschaft tradition of the Vormärz, pressure for self-government also grew out of "the trend of all professional classes to organize themselves which dominates current social and legal life." While progressive reformers had long urged "the unification of all groups," the actual implementation in festival committees, let alone legitimate councils, foundered time and again on corporate jealousy, bureaucratic paternalism, and youthful impatience. The oldest continually successful council was the Heidelberg Studentenausschuss, founded in 1886 with "the task of regulating common concerns and representing the interests of the students" to academic administration and the public at large. The Heidelberg experiment overcame subsequent crises, for the council was compulsory (with 2 Mk dues per semester), was composed of twenty-two association representatives and eight elected independent students, limited its activities to "external interests" such as running the Lesehalle, and "only rarely saw fit to take a position on general questions of the day." In contrast, the ideologically charged climate of Prussia and administrative heavy-

[59] Stitz, *Akademischer Kulturkampf*, pp. 110-19; *Protokoll des dritten Vertretertags vom 20. bis 23. Juni 1907*, pp. 18ff.; J. Basten, "Die Tübinger Erklärung in ihren Folgen," *Ac* 20 (1907): 80-83; "Der VdH und die katholischen Korporationen," ibid., no. 4; Sybel votum, 29 January 1907, and notes for a "Referat über den akademischen Bismarckbund" for the nonofficial conference of Prussian rectors, Halle, 11 March 1907, MUA, 305a, Acc 1950/9, Nos 176 and 181; Seiffert, *Studentische Verbände*, p. 115; H. Cardauns, *Fünfzig Jahre Kartellverband*, pp. 210-40; Blaustein, *Der Student*, pp. 21ff.; Bornhak memorandum, ZStA Me, Rep 92, AI, No 16a; Schulze-Ssymank, *Das deutsche Studententum*, p. 398; and Althoff to Studt, 2 September 1905, ZStA Me, Rep 92, Studt, Nos 13 and 14. For a Catholic counterargument, see G. Freiherr von Hertling, *Akademische Freiheit* (n.p., 1908).

handedness quickly doomed the 1898 Halle council, which introduced the term Allgemeiner Studentenausschuss, thereafter the notorious AStA.[60] While the struggle over academic freedom in 1904-05 resulted in new nonconfessional organizations in Breslau and Jena, the concomitant academic Kulturkampf reduced six Ausschüsse by excluding Catholics, heightened the splits between confessional groupings at Bonn, Freiburg, and Würzburg, and left only four councils at Giessen, Heidelberg, Marburg, and Tübingen unscathed (table 6-1).[61] To provide "a leading idea, a more precise definition of purpose and functions, and a legitimacy based on real elections," the Freistudentenschaft endorsed "the formation of obligatory parliamentary student councils" at its 1906 Weimar meeting. As the Studentenverbände of the VdH were only "a false union" while the authorities blocked the representation principle of free students, the council movement toward "a uniform constitution" provided new hope for progressive students. "On a small scale the Ausschuss must fulfill the same task as does the Reichstag on a larger plane for the entire people." However, the resistance of traditional student groups forced the Freistudentenschaft to resolve in 1910 that the general council be composed of "two groups, the corporations and the unincorporated," with representatives of the former designated by their organizations and only the latter elected proportionally. Although it was a partial retreat from the hopes for "a new kind of democratically inspired academic culture," this bicameral system had the advantage of appealing to the corporations as well. Hence, "constitutionalism . . . liberation, [and] self-government" became general goals of German student organizations during the last half decade before the war.[62]

Such a "home rule" AStA program was first realized in the Leipzig

[60] Bornhak memorandum and Paalzow memorandum, ZStA Me, Rep 92, AI, No 16a or No 29. E. David, *Zweck und Mittel einer einheitlichen Organisation der deutschen Studentenschaft* (Berlin, 1888); R. Sperling, *Der Ausschuss der Heidelberger Studentenschaft* (Heidelberg, 1911); *Satzungen des Ausschusses der Heidelberger Studentenschaft* (Heidelberg, 1913); and *Satzungen des allgemeinen Studentenausschusses zu Halle a.S.* (Halle, 1898). See also Friedebach, "Der Studentenschafts-Ausschuss und die katholischen Corporationen an der Universität Freiburg i.Br.," *Ac* 14 (1901-02): 121-25; and Schulze-Ssymank, *Das deutsche Studentum*, pp. 423f., a very rudimentary summary.

[61] For the sources of table 6-1 see *Sitzungsberichte der Tagungen des VdH*, pp. 3ff., 41ff.; *Protokolle der Verbandstage Deutscher Hochschulen*, 1906, pp. 9ff., and 1907, pp. 9ff.; and *Sitzungs-Berichte des ordentlichen Burschenschaftstags*, 1906, pp. 67ff., and 1907, pp. 56ff. See also the reports of the Bonn, Breslau, Göttingen, Greifswald, Halle, Kiel, Königsberg, Marburg, and Münster rectors, February 1905, in ZStA Me, Rep 76 Va, Sekt 1 Tit XII, No 25A, vol. 1, and summary by Schmaltz of the non-Prussian developments, 27 October 1905, ibid., Rep 92, AI, No 19.

[62] E. Horn, *Akademische Freiheit* (Berlin, 1905), appendix on student councils, pp. 106-17; P. Ssymank, "Die Notwendigkeit allgemeiner Studentenausschüsse," *Comenius Blätter* 13 (1905), no. 5; P. Ssymank, "Der sechste deutsche Freistudententag," *FBl* 8 (1906): 91ff., especially the resolution of Leipzig alumni; *Resolutionen und Beschlüsse des zehnten*

council of 1911. As "corporations were willing to assure the independents just representation," while the "nonincorporated made the significant concession of sacrificing their free-student organization and thereby their independence," the negotiations sponsored by the liberal Rector Lamprecht eventually produced a bicameral system acceptable to both sides. The complicated structure was composed of a corporation council A (made up of the subgroups of the old duelling corporations, the new duelling corporations, the color corporations, and the associations) and of a nonincorporated council B (elected by each of fifty independents) whose delegates formed the managing presidium. Completely separate, the corporate and independent halves could act alone, if necessary, but were directed toward cooperation by a 400 Mk limitation on their individual budgets. Their competence included outside representation, support of indigent students, supervision of diverse offices, the right of petition and of advice on consultation, the advancement of sport, the sponsorship of educational travel, and official communications with the student body. Since membership in one or the other section was compulsory and a .50 Mk per semester contribution was levied by the bursar, the council had a firm financial base. Although it cemented "the rupture within the student body," this dual system treated both sides with "full equality" and, by excluding politics and questions of honor, provided "a barrier against the appearance of excessive radicalism." In Breslau, owing to the smaller number of independents, the 1912 council constitution favored the corporations, but thereby avoided an unnatural division within the student body.

The last major victory of student self-government came in Berlin, where negotiations, begun with the 1913 jubilee, succeeded a year later in resolving the question of foreign students, the distribution of votes among associations, and the classification of inactives from other campuses. Under the aegis of Rector Max Planck, the senate on 22 July 1914 announced, "the authorities see no further obstacles to the constitution of the council," but World War I interrupted the process. To represent students, support the poor, assist war victims, administer student finances, advise the authorities, and create a war aid commission, a council of thirty-four members nevertheless came into being in December. The corporations were represented by the KSC, LC, VC, DC, RSC, ATV, DWV, VDSt, KJC, Sondershäuser Verband, KV, Freischar, Dt.-Akad. Frauenbund, ADB, V.f. Natwiss., Wingolf, and one Sängerschaft, while independent delegates were provided by the Deutschvölkische (2), the Deutsch-Christliche (2), the Catholics (3), the Freideutsche (3), the Freistudentenschaft (6), and

---

Freistudententages in Weimar (16. bis 19. Mai 1910), BA R 129, no. 425; as well as E. Knoll and A. Schwab, *Allgemeine Studentenausschüsse: Ein Programm* (Cöthen, 1912).

TABLE 6-1
Student Councils at German Universities

	Before 1905	1905 to 1907	After 1907
1. Berlin	1869-71, 1880-88	VdH attempt	general council 1914
2. Bonn	common festival committee broken up in 1894, Corps vs. Catholics	Corps, VdH presidium, Catholics continued	1911 unification into council
3. Breslau	1882-89 general council	nonconfessional corporation organization, VdH delegate	general council 1912
4. Erlangen	festival committee	general council, VdH delegates split into Catholic council, VdH council and Freistud.	
5. Freiburg	general council	joined VdH with Catholics on waiver	eventually reunified
6. Giessen	general council with Catholics	VdH Studentenverband	left VdH 1907
7. Göttingen	general council	VdH Studentenverband	
8. Greifswald	corporation council		
9. Halle	1895–1903 general council	VdH council, neutrals like Wingolf, FrSt. & 2 Cath. corporations	
10. Heidelberg	1885 general council	unsuccessful exclusion of Catholic corporations, VdH member on waiver	continued
11. Jena	none	1906 VdH Studentenverband	
12. Kiel	general council	1906 VdH Studentenverband	

13. Königsberg	none	delegate to VdH	general council refounded 1911
14. Leipzig	general council	delegates to VdH	
15. Marburg	1888 general council	no attempt to exclude Catholic corporations, VdH on waiver	continued (some difficulties)
16. Munich	none	VdH delegates	
17. Münster	Catholic and liberal council	corporation council of Catholic and nonconfessional, latter VdH membs.	
18. Rostock	corporation council	no Catholics to exclude	
19. Strassburg	festival committee	VdH organization vs. Catholic council	general council 1907ff
20. Tübingen	general council	split DC vs. SC, VdH member on waiver	1907 general council with Catholic corporations
21. Würzburg	duelling Corps.	Catholic corporations vs. Corps, VdH delegate	

NOTE: This table illustrates the gradual development of student councils out of corporation committees, the impact of the Studentenverband movement, and the emergence of student self-government in the last prewar years. The paucity of information after 1907 makes the listing after that date less complete. For the sources of this table, see note 61.

one female student. Though continuing the emancipatory tradition of 1848, these councils were also a tenuous compromise with the corporate traditions of German student life.[63]

To combat the implicit liberalism of the council movement, the nationalist corporations stepped up the political indoctrination of their members as well as their general propaganda in the student body. Somewhat more willing "to adapt to the demands of the times" than rival groups, the Burschenschaft emphasized liberal imperialism in "the training of its actives as politically thinking men." Although its "progressive" heritage was but a faint memory, the DC earnestly groped for "a modern Burschenschaft Weltanschauung" which "combined love of freedom with patriotism, which does not exclude modern trends but . . . confronts them more clearly and critically than before." After long internal debates, H. Böttger (Young Liberal deputy) changed the editorial policy of his *Burschenschaftliche Blätter* to downplay organization news and historical essays in order "to interest and orient students about the social and economic questions" of the present. Handbooks, discussion evenings, and articles sought to overcome the proverbial inertia: "The Burschenschaft presupposes as axiomatic the patriotism of a warrior in every German; but he still needs to be trained in national idealism, which inspires him to serve his fatherland with head and heart, with his knowledge and professional ability and to participate in the political life of the state."[64]

Limited to one chapter per campus, the VDSt turned inward but sought to maintain its general influence by controlling the Lesehalle, sponsoring public political discussions, and holding national celebrations. When liberal actives in 1905-06 wanted to follow alumnus Friedrich Naumann's democratic national socialism, conservative Old Boys and the Berlin Verein

[63] "AStA Programm," as well as G. Hericht, "Rückschau und Ausblick," and "Satzungen des allgemeinen Studenten-Ausschusses der Universität Leipzig," *AR* 13 (1911): 352-64; G. Kittel, "Der neue Leipziger Studentenausschuss," *ABl* 21 (1911): 253-55; "Der neue Breslauer Studentenausschuss," ibid. 22 (1912): 158ff; Ausschuss der Kgl. Friedrich-Wilhelms-Universität zu Berlin, *Semesterbericht WS 1914-15 bis WS 1915-16* (Berlin, 1916), pp. 3-18; and F. Behrend, *Student und Studentenschaft: Sozialpädagogische Betrachtungen über akademische Lehrfreiheit* (Leipzig, 1913), pp. 6-38. See H. Husmann, "Die Einigungsverhandlungen in der Bonner Studentenschaft," *Ac* 20 (1907-1908): 299ff.; Dr. Daude, "Geschichte des Studentenausschusses der Universität Berlin," spring 1905, ZStA Me, Rep 92, AI, No 16a; documents ibid., Rep 76 Va, Sekt 2 Tit XII, No 16, vol. 2 as well as statutes of the Berlin student council, approved 22 July 1914, and Planck to Trott, 28 July 1914, in HUA, 840.

[64] R. Friedemann, "Die deutsche Burschenschaft des XX. Jahrhunderts," *BBl* 18 (1903-04): 6-9; "Bericht der Commission zur Regelung der Angelegenheit der Burschenschaftlichen Blätter," *Sitzungsberichte des 25. ordentlichen Burschenschaftstages, 1906*, pp. 15-20; H. Böttger, "Unser Ziel," *BBl* 22 (1907-08): 54-56; R. Friedemann, "Politik und deutsche Burschenschaft," ibid. 24 (1909-10): 50-52. See also the programmatic articles in H. Böttger, ed., *Jahrbuch der Deutschen Burschenschaft* (Berlin, 1903) published annually thereafter, and Heer, *Burschenschaft*, 4: 92-94.

balked, forcing the controversial pastor to resign because he had dared to endorse a Socialist candidate in a Reichstag election. A split was narrowly averted through a compromise resolution that defined the VDSt purpose as "advancing national understanding and activity among its members, as well as clarifying and strengthening national consciousness in the entire student body." In practice this meant an unstable social imperialism: "National and social policy . . . are not opposites, but rather siblings, expressions of one and the same idea, means to the same end. Their aim is the strength and stability of our state." This amalgam of expansionism and social concern satisfied the needs of the Alte Herren for national power and of the younger members for political modernity. In the winter semester 1913-14, 20 percent of about 200 lectures, speeches, and discussions in the Kyffhäuser-Verband dealt with nationalist themes, 18 percent provided cultural entertainment, 13.4 percent propagated imperialist goals, and 12.9 percent addressed social reform. Less troubled by ideological controversy, the duelling Turnerschaft championed a pan-German imperialism focused on an aggressive foreign policy: German military might "must be so considerable that the other great powers are forced to take it into account so that we cannot be pressed to the wall and left out when great political changes occur." During the height of the Balkan Wars, the *Akademische Turnerzeitung* indicated a direction for future expansion: "The only way which is still half open is the Southeast."[65]

In the last prewar years nationalist rhetoric also spread to formerly nonpolitical associations and led to the foundation of new extremist groups. To retain "their leading position" in the student body, the Corps abandoned their "national indifference" and joined patriotic societies such as the Navy League and the Ostmarkenverein. Since "new times demand new measures," the *Akademische Monatshefte* urged "demonstrative participation in national causes" such as a student counterdemonstration to the Socialist party conference in Jena. Although the majority of the Alte Herren insisted on reserve, many actives reasoned that "purely national questions are not party issues." Thus, they could safely get involved in "colonial and naval problems and the ancient defensive struggle against the westward movement of the Slavs." Similarly, Catholic corporations and associations inched closer to nationalist teaching, if only to take the wind out of their

<hr />

[65] H. Weber, *Geschichte des VDSt zu Berlin*, pp. 292ff.; "Die ausserordentliche Verbandstagung," *ABl* 21 (1906-07), no. 20; Dr. Kormann, "National- und Sozialpolitik," ibid. 22 (1907-08): 185ff.; "Verehrte Bundesbrüder!" supplement to *ABl* 26 (1910-11), no. 4; "Das Vortragswesen des K.-V. im Wintersemester 1913-14," ibid. 29 (1913-14): 75-76. For the VC, see R. Schmaltz, "Akademische Freiheit und Vaterlandsliebe," *ATZ* 23 (1906): 513-15, 539-41; E. Baumgart, "Vom deutschen Michel," ibid. 26 (1909): 453ff.; W. Bertram, "Der Machtgedanke in der preussischen Politik," ibid. 30 (1913): 1-3; and "Der Balkan-Krieg und die deutsche Ausdehnung," ibid., pp. 190-93.

critics' sails. Moreover, the foundation of the Deutsche Wissenschafter Verband in 1910 combined scholarly societies into a large (81 chapters) national organization which did not want to be outdone in patriotism. The majority of organized students was indoctrinated in conscious nationalism, shading into various forms of imperialism, although the increasing stridency of the appeals indicates that results continued to fall short of ideological expectations.[66] Prewar rightist trends among German students culminated in the creation of the Deutsch-Völkische Studentenverband in 1909. As a "loose association of corporate and independent students," this most radical of nationalist organizations purported "to cultivate and propagate Germanness at the universities and to give its members the opportunity of deepening their nationalist convictions through scholarship." Under Austrian influence and propelled by imperialists such as Adolf Bartels and Georg von Liebert, the DVSt wanted to revive VDSt racism by "combatting the foreign and Jewish influence at the universities, in so far as it is obnoxious." Its volkish propaganda, pioneering many of the Nazi themes of a decade later, was hailed by the *Staatsbürger-Zeitung* in Weimar style as an "academic and national rebirth." Although this rightist sect with its fourteen chapters captured only a small proportion of the entire student body, its agitation injected an ominous crudity into student politics, for it was no longer willing (as in the VDSt-FWV struggles) even to abide by academic forms.[67]

Despite the dogma that students "should avoid partisanship at the university," a modern student politics gradually evolved during the Second Empire. For that minority of young academics who wanted "to work for the fatherland . . . to [act out] their convictions or to become known publicly," the stereotype of the apolitical German is misleading. Certainly in small, traditional institutions like Rostock there was little activity, but

[66] J. Koch, "Die Corps und die Politik," *AMh* 23 (1906-07); 365ff.; "Corps und Ostmarkenverein," ibid., p. 423; Dr. Loesener, "Burschen heraus! Ein deutsches Wort an alle Aktive," ibid. 25 (1908), no. 9; "Über die studentische Gegendemonstration zum Sozialdemokratischen Parteitag," ibid. 28 (1911), no. 11; B. Thurn, "Die Zukunft der Corps," ibid., no. 14 as well as Schmidt, "Modernisierung," no. 17. See also Studier, "Corpsstudent," pp. 133ff.; and "Die Corps und die nationale Bewegung," *BBl* 23 (1909): 184ff. For the other groups, see also Schulze-Ssymank, *Das deutsche Studententum*, pp. 404-21 and the prewar issues of *Academia* and *Akademische Monatsblätter*. The Landsmannschaft was largely nonideological but patriotic, according to its own chronicler, Dietrich, *Deutsche Landsmannschaft*, pp. 66ff.

[67] *Satzungen des Deutsch-Völkischen Studenten-Verbandes* (Berlin, 1909); flyer of a lecture by Liebert on "Weltbürgertum oder Deutschtum," 8 November 1912; "Satzungen des Deutsch-Völkischen Studentenverbandes" approved 1 November 1912; *Statzungen des Deutschen Studentenverbandes Leipzig* (n.d.), and other material in HUA, 814. P. Seiffert, *Studentische Verbände*, p. 118; C. Bürger, "Der Antisemitismus in der Studentenschaft," *KCBl* 2 (1911): 205, calls the DVStV program "the most fanatical racial anti-Semitism" in the empire. In contrast, VDSt anti-Semitism had abated considerably, even if it was also reaffirmed in 1911.

in the middling universities like Marburg or Göttingen, major events like the Hochschulstreit could and did arouse passions for a while. In the largest metropolitan centers like Berlin (and to a lesser extent Leipzig or Munich), groups continually contested for ideological dominance on campus. "The Lesehalle election is a part of the great spiritual struggle of our time, a part of the conflict between Jewry and Germanness, between individualism and socialism, between patriotism and cosmopolitanism." The successive conflicts between student reformers and corporations in the 1870s, between the anti-Semitic VDSt and the liberal FWV in the 1880s, the nationalist DC or VC and the Socialists during the 1890s, the anti-Catholic VdH and the tolerant Freistudentenschaft in the 1900s, and the corporate tradition-alists and the youth movement rebels during the 1910s produced an arsenal of techniques characteristic of student politics. Internally, associations emphasized the "correct national and political education" of members through discussion evenings, reports on current questions, or alumni pre-sentations as a complement to formal scholarly training. On the campus, activists concentrated on "energetic propaganda for our cause" through "flyers, getting out the vote," and holding meetings on controversial topics such as anti-Semitism, usually sponsored by adult alumni. In the general public, student politicians sought to gain notoriety through resolutions, such as the Leipzig council vote in favor of "quicker expansion and greater strengthening of our navy than foreseen in the law," and through patriotic manifestations. The Burschenschaft attracted attention with its campaign to erect Bismarck memorial columns, designed by Wilhelm Kries in neo-German primitivism, which provided a physical focus for patriotic cele-brations in about 150 towns.[68] Although the institutions of student politics were still subject to administrative suspension, journals proved influential and durable, councils reemerged after dissolution, service offices (such as the Lesehalle) survived as centers of student life, and even the abortive national association returned in equally controversial form during the Wei-mar Republic. While their efforts were unevenly distributed, ideologically polarized, and often transitory, interested students nevertheless succeeded in politicizing campus life with a diversity that reflected the inner cleavages of the Second Empire.

[68] K. Sperling, "Der Student und die Politik," *ATZ* 14 (1896-97): 544ff.; R. Grützmacher, "Betrachtungen zur Berliner Lesehallenwahl," *WBl* 26 (1897): 17f. and "Zur Berliner Lesehallenwahl," ibid., pp. 153-54; "Eine studentische Kundgebung für die Flotte," *BBl* 20 (1905-06): 151f.; "Die Denkmalsweihe der deutschen Burschenschaft in Eisenach, 21.-23. Mai," ibid. 16 (1902): 110-25. See also "Kommilitonen," flyer of the nationalist coalition (ATV, Ascania, Catholic Suevia, VDSt, Verb. ak. Gymnasialvereine, Wingolf) for the 1886 Berlin Lesehalle election; "Eine Versammlung des akademisch 'liberalen' Vereins," *Deutsches Tageblatt*, 31 May 1886; and report of the *Deutsche Zeitung* of 5 December 1886 on a library polling assembly, BA R 143, no. 38.

A chief result of such "civic education and preparation for political maturity" through student politics was the "national" cluster of convictions that characterized German academics as a group. While Arthur Blaustein hailed the foundation of the Deutsch-Akademische Freibund in 1907 as evidence "that a more liberal current has reemerged among students," such "conscious, active . . . neoliberalism" was hardly typical. During the election of 1907 the majority rather followed the call to arms of the Studentenverband of the University of Kiel and campaigned "against Center party socialism," since "our national honor is in jeopardy and . . . the fatherland must be defended." Because "Socialists and clericals dance on tables and chairs in Mother Germania's house," the *Burschenschaftliche Blätter* encouraged the mobilization of "national reserves" at Königsberg, Berlin, Leipzig, Jena, Erlangen, and Kiel for the ideal academic ticket, the Bülow bloc. As long as students favored a national cause, adults "could not see a disadvantage in it" but rather encouraged such activity as "doing one's patriotic duty," but progressive, clerical, or Socialist participation, as in 1912, was rejected as immature "partisanship." The cumulative effect of such gradual politicization of German universities was the transformation of instinctive patriotism into self-conscious modern nationalism. Although the degree of involvement and particular accent differed widely among individuals, the student majority was unquestioningly monarchist, anti-Semitic, anti-Socialist, and imperialist. As it was not seen as political, but rather as self-evidently patriotic, this shared nationalism provided the common political ground among hostile academic camps, be they conservative or progressive, Catholic or Protestant, Prussian or Bavarian. Contemporaries perceived the condition but misconstrued the reasons: "Youth is in favor of freedom everywhere; only here it has partly turned against it, not, as is claimed, because Bismarck broke its back, for on the contrary he stiffened it, but rather because it is offended by the behavior of the majority of liberal newspapers." Instead of admitting his own departure from the Burschenschaft tradition, Böttger blamed the spread of anti-Semitism on the Jews: "I accuse the so-called liberal press of having made our youth illiberal."[69]

"MORE THAN ever before we need men" for our time, William II defined the political goals of cultivation during the matriculation of the crown prince at the University of Bonn on 24 April 1901. "Now everyone in

---

[69] Blaustein, *Der Student*, pp. 22f.; P. Baecker, "Zur Reichstagswahl," *ABl* 21 (1907): 338f.; H. Böttger, "Die Reichstagswahlen und die Studenten," *BBl* 21 (1906-07), 232f.; Dr. Porsch, "Die angebliche politische Betätigung des Cartellverbandes," *Ac* 21 (1908): 186ff.; "Student und Politik," *AR* 13 (1911): 81-84; H. Böttger, "Reichstagswahlen 1912," *BBl* 26 (1912): 256-57; and "Burschenschaft and freisinnige Presse," ibid. 16 (1902): 168f.

Germany, in our nation, is called to work together for our future. We are here to prepare for it, not to pursue one-sided partisan interests but to continue what has begun, with courage, joy, and strength.'' In contrast, Karl Liebknecht feared that German universities were becoming "boot camps" (*Drillanstalten*) for the "Junker-capitalist materialism of our day," seen "not as politics, but as patriotism." However, neither the Kaiser's confidence in nor the radical's critique of academic social control was entirely accurate. "Liberating communication" was no longer suppressed in the crude manner of Metternich, but rather hindered through student discipline, which denied rights of association and assembly to Socialist and non-German subversives. Avoidance strategies limited learning not overtly but screened out critical influences (through selecting professors) and militated against drawing political conclusions from scholarly discourse (through stressing the disjunction between thought and action). Class division according to faculties and institutional types was strong enough to channel lower-middle-class youths into less prestigious tracks, but Latin no longer served as an absolute barrier. With the decline of the theological faculty the religious value system was important only for a shrinking minority, while the majority absorbed a secular cultivation idealism. The militarization of the universities surfaced in the pomp and rhetoric of festivals, the duelling corporations, and the privilege of one-year military service, but was rudimentary compared to the later paramilitary training of the Third Reich. Neohumanism did transform itself ideologically enough to embrace imperialism, but the dilution of its cultural liberalism robbed it of much of its compelling force. The freedom of student life meant that social control operated, if at all, indirectly, by skewing the gamut of student politics administratively to the right. Equally important was the self-imposition of anti-Semitic, anti-Socialist, or pro-imperialist nationalism by the politically active minority of academic youth. Thus, the emancipatory movement toward student self-government was often deflected into an intolerant direction and modernized the methods but not the goals of activism.[70]

Not surprisingly, student politics on the whole reinforced the ideological reversal of academic youths. The internal reasons for the triumph of the new nationalism over liberal currents were organizational, administrative, intellectual, and social. Rightist pressure-group politics, pioneered by the VDSt and adopted by the Burschenschaft and Turnerschaft, were more

---

[70] "Immatrikulation S.K.u.K. Hoheit des Kronprinzen des deutschen Reichs und von Preussen am 24. April 1901," *Chronik der Rheinischen Friedrich-Wilhelms-Universität zu Bonn* 26 (1900-01): 95ff.; and "Der Kaiser in der Rostocker Universität," *ATZ* 30 (1913): 270; Liebknecht in the Prussian Landtag, 1 May 1909, *AH*, vol. 528, and 4 April 1913, *AH*, vol. 569. See also Titze, *Die Politisierung der Erziehung*, 251ff. and above, notes 2-4.

effective than leftist agitational methods. Since they could never embrace all students, the Kyffhäuser associations sought to transform existing groups and independents into ardent nationalists through flyers, assemblies, festivities, and use of the student councils. While anti-Semitic propaganda only intermittently disturbed their romantic customs, many corporations could not afford to be outdone in demonstrative nationalism. In contrast, liberals were usually content to associate loosely and lacked cohesion, stability, and permanence, always in danger of fragmenting during disputes (like the Bonn free-students after 1900), or of returning to the corporate mold (like the reform Burschenschaft after the 1880s). Moreover, the aspiration of representing the entire student body in a quasi-official legal capacity, voiced first by the Finkenschaft and taken up by the council movement, provoked the resistance of the corporations and the authorities, who saw such attempts as an illicit infringement on their own prerogatives. Rightist agitation could always claim to be "patriotic," and authorities were generally inclined to tolerate nationalism as "unpolitical," whereas liberal propaganda was often forbidden as "divisive" violation of academic discipline. As the basic impulse was a critique of the shortcomings of student life and imperial politics, the intellectual thrust of the progressive movement was negative, directed against abuses and bigotry rather than toward a positive inspiring goal. The inherent conflict between academic reform and general political involvement was never resolved, while studious impartiality blunted the wider message. When they awoke to the threat to their dominance, duelling corporations buried the hatchet and systematically cooperated with each other and sometimes also with the VDSt to defeat progressive initiatives. Finally, the established corporate as well as the new nationalist elite succeeded in suggesting that the reformers were largely recruited from Jews, academic proletarians, and other outsiders, whose cosmopolitanism was somehow socially un-German, despite the fact that the dissenting leadership was largely a cultivated counterelite.[71]

The external reasons for the deliberalization of student politics stemmed largely from political, ideological, and generational developments outside the university. Ironically, the very triumph of political liberalism, which made the Rechts- and Kulturstaat after 1871 appear freer than any previous

[71] See, for instance, the justification for the foundation of an *Internationale studentische Vereinigung*, inspired by Norman Angell: "We live at present in a time when national consciousness is rightly furthered and strengthened. Hence, it will also be a self-evident task of the I.St.V. to make foreigners aware of this new German spirit, which was often missing earlier. But at the same time, there are the beginnings of international discussion on diverse questions of mutual understanding. . . . While energetically emphasizing the national, the I.St.V. believes it can call a *corda fratres* to members of other nations; international cultural tasks exist on which we want to work together." Muuss to Traeger, 3 November 1913, MUA, 305a, Acc 1950/9, no. 192.

state in German history, removed the older reform agenda from academic concern. In many ways the students' rejection of liberalism during the 1880s was only a more thorough and rapid version of the reorientation of the entire middle class in the wake of the Iron Chancellor's domestic reversal of 1878-79. While some progressive luminaries like Mommsen and Virchow continued to cling to their beliefs, the most effective academic teachers were nationalists like Treitschke, who sought to transcend earlier liberal achievements with a new imperial program. Building on prior indoctrination in middle-class families and secondary schools, nationalist ideology exerted a powerful pull on German academics. While unification seemed to have achieved its central aim, the new nationalism of the 1880s insisted on the completion of that process at home by eliminating discordant elements such as Catholics and abroad by bringing another 20 million Germans *heim ins Reich*. Modern nationalism proved eminently flexible, accommodating such different nuances as conservative (Corps), national liberal (Burschenschaft), volkish (VDSt), pan-German (Turnerschaft), Protestant (Wingolf, Schwarzburgbund), and, paradoxically, even Catholic (CV, KV, Unitas) strains. Because it provided every academic group with its own national mission, it proved an ideal integration ideology. Finally, the paternalist ambivalence of adults toward youthful political involvement also militated in favor of rightist commitment. On the one hand, professors argued that "political discussions of young people during their university study carry unrest among the students" and "the premature commitment to a certain party line takes away the desire for objective work." On the other hand, academics considered "patriotic learning" essential for the future leadership role of the Gebildete and prided themselves on the firm national spirit of the young generation. But only a minority regarded it a "patriotic duty" for students "to acquaint themselves in an unprejudiced and scholarly manner with politics," and even fewer supported the acquisition of practical political experience through student self-government with genuine responsibility and authority. The combination of these internal and external reasons led youth to rebel to the right and to associate modernity with chauvinism rather than to seek release for their generational resentment on the left. But the liberal countertradition did not fail entirely, for it created significant student institutions (like councils) and served as vital training ground for many *Vernunftrepublikaner* and some Social Democrats of Weimar.[72]

[72] "Student und Politik," *Deutsches Lehrer-Blatt*, 11 November 1910; "Hansabund and Studentenschaft," *National-Zeitung*, 4 December 1911; "Student und Politik," *Berliner Tageblatt*, 7 February 1911, and other clippings in ZStA Me, Rep 76 Va, Sekt 1 Tit XII, No 35. The liberal countertradition is usually slighted in the literature. Even Ssymank in the 1932 edition of *Das deutsche Studentum* moves away from his erstwhile free-student sympathies toward nationalism. See also Bleuel and Klinnert, *Deutsche Studenten*, pp. 47f., and Sheehan, *German Liberalism*, pp. 181-283, who ignores students during the empire.

The national enthusiasm that had been growing everywhere in the West culminated in Central Europe in the celebrations of 1913: "In this extraordinary year waves of patriotic fervor sweep powerfully through the German states, and commemorations are more numerous than ever." During the summer the festivities honored the Kaiser: "At the head of our united empire stands the person of our illustrious ruler, William II, a worthy representative of the imperial crown, experienced and successfully proven in the quarter-century of his richly blessed reign." In the fall students from all over Germany and Austria converged on Leipzig to commemorate the centennial of the Wars of Liberation against Napoleon. Behind hundreds of fluttering banners, thousands of Chargierte, in colorful uniforms, rode or marched toward the memorial to the gay tune of military bands. Tens of thousands of onlookers applauded. Even the weather cooperated. "A sunny, cloudless sky covers the autumnal land. Out of the blue haze the immense monument begins to emerge. Soon we stand at its feet, overwhelmed by the impressions of this manifestation of German power." Loud hurrahs announced the arrival of the beloved emperor, accompanied by the Saxon king and the Austrian crown prince. "It is a great, unforgettable moment. Reverently our flags dip, the swords gleam, and a hundred thousand voices cheer!" In the evening of 18 October, Kommerse of the forty-eight student groups attempted to define the meaning of the symbolic celebration. For the speaker of the Catholic CV, "this proves that the spirit of German students is the same as a hundred years ago, that today one of their best qualities is love of the fatherland and of freedom" from foreign oppression. Another orator ridiculed the charge of Catholic unreliability and reaffirmed: "Great Germany, we firmly cling to thee." Arguing that organizational diversity was the strength of student life, he concluded: "When the fatherland calls to arms, it will become clear that we have marched separately but can fight together." Ironically, the unquestioning national loyalty formally taught by professors and informally perpetuated in student corporations and campus politics contributed to the very conflict it claimed to prevent.[73]

[73] O. Hintze's jubilee speech, reprinted in the *Hohenzollern Jahrbuch*, 1913, pp. 78-95; "Jahrhundertfeier des CV in Leipzig," *AC* 36 (1913-14): 390-98. For a comparative reflection on the illiberalism of students outside of Germany, see Chapter 7, below.

Seven

FOR KAISER AND REICH

WHILE the scholarly quest for Wissenschaft and the idyllic pursuit of romance continued, an undercurrent of unease began to permeate academic consciousness in the years before 1914. Growing numbers of articles on foreign policy in student journals and increasing references in ceremonial speeches to international dangers generated a widespread but vague sense of foreboding. Although a few professors and youths desperately sought to preserve peace through the international student movement, the overwhelming majority of the educated confronted the coming catastrophe with an unblinking self-assurance, vocalized by F. Lüdtke in the *Burschenschaftliche Blätter*:

> Thunderheads gather in East and West,
> Flames flash through the darkening weather.
> But we shall cling together
> As Germans, we shall stand fast.
>
> If ever the Slav should raise his hand,
> If ever the Frank should vengeance find,
> If ever envious thoughts should blind
> Our false brethren from English land—
>
> A sea of hatred pounds on our shore!
> We silently sharpen our blade
> And yet think undismayed:
> The more enemies—the greater the honor.
>
> God gave us Germans also a fist,
> Not to threaten but to strike.
> Let them see, if ever they like,
> How it feels when we hit!

Germans and Austrians as brothers call,
May the storm now rage in the sky:
We fear only God on high
But nothing else at all.

The pervasiveness of such cultural nationalism in the prewar years raises three final questions: What was the response of the universities to the First World War? What were the social and ideological causes of this academic illiberalism? What were the long-term consequences of such structures and mentalities of the educated?[1]

STUDENTS AT WAR

"What our enemies have prepared for decades has finally arrived—the great European war for the annihilation of Germany and its Austrian ally." During the growing tension of July 1914 many a student wondered: "Am I ready, as I have often vowed in word and song? Am I willing to lay down my life for my people and my country?" While a few hesitated, most were swept along by a powerful wave of enthusiasm:

Give me arms, lead me to the field.
Make me a hero, a shining shield
For my land, my people, my Germany.
Join the struggle toward victory.

When Serbia's rejection of the Austrian ultimatum became known, "politically agitated students . . . gravely paraded with patriotic hymns" to the imperial palace in Berlin and the rector's house in Bonn. Heartened, professors cheered on academic youth in the spirit of 1813: "As once the nations rallied around their rulers to overthrow the giant who threatened civilization and freedom . . . so we today struggle fundamentally for culture, for Western ethical values against the greed of the Slavic race, which now believes it can thrust us, its erstwhile masters, aside." The students' rush to the colors proved the success of national cultivation: "The joyous enthusiasm, the serious dedication, and the courageous enlistments show that Germany was right to educate its sons in the noblest civic consciousness—unconditional sacrifice for state, fatherland, emperor, and king." Student corporations saw their patriotic training vindicated: "Now that the hour has come when that seed must grow and bear fruit which our organization planted in many young hearts and carried into other circles

---

[1] F. Lüdtke, "Neunzehnhundertdreizehn," *BBl* 27 (1912-13): 259. W. A. Berendsohn, "Die internationale Studentenbewegung und die deutsche Studentenschaft," *AR* 2 (1913-14), no. 10; and MUA, 305a, Acc. 1950/9, no. 192.

of the nation in long decades of quiet work." Among various groups, explanations for the conflict differed. Catholics considered the war a defensive struggle "for the protection and glory of our fatherland." Corps members saw its purpose as "freeing our nation from the encirclement of our foes and gaining new respect for its name in the entire world." Volkish nationalists went even further: "We know it is a matter of survival for the German people. Moreover, the entire future of Germanity is at stake." All over Europe the onset of battle unified students and adult academics in the resolve: "Forward with God, forward for emperor and country!"[2]

The ghastly reality of mechanized warfare soon dampened this "incredible" fervor. "Dawn comes. A yell, first on the right, then everywhere, on the whole front—the signal to attack . . . ! Relieved, we climb out of the trenches, form ranks. Now decision is near," a survivor recalled the German attempt to break through to the Channel coast in October 1914: "Hurrah . . . ! Bullets hail upon us. Machine guns and infantry fire. Grenades howl above us, roar and burst. . . . Again we are in a swarm of missiles. Rushing, men sink and fall. Some quietly, some with a cry. Our cheers are soon silenced, smothered by iron. Our rows are mowed down." And yet the spirit of these veritable "children's regiments," hastily assembled from students and other volunteers, would not break. "In the most horrible hours of the battle, when death leads entire columns away and the Flemish canals run red with blood, when impotent despair creeps through the corpse-strewn meadows—a singing rises, which makes dying eyes sparkle and relentlessly drives the living forward, which sounds above the battle and lifts the doomed crowds beyond reason: *Deutschland, Deutschland, über alles, über alles in der Welt. . . .*" This legend of Langemarck, created by a military report trying to cover up the misuse of reserves, celebrated the self-sacrifice of the flower of academic youth, who attacked, in parade-ground order, superior Anglo-French defensive positions in front of Ypres.

About 16,000 of the between 40,000 (1914) and 58,000 (1918) student soldiers gave their lives, tens of thousands of others paid with their limbs for their unquestioning nationalism. In the first intoxicating weeks many intended "to charge like [Field Marshal] Blücher" and "to stand firm in

---

[2] "Der Krieg," *AMh* 31 (1914), no. 8; "Liebe Bundesbrüder!" *ABl* 29 (1914): 3; L. R. poem, "Es gilt!" *Ac* 27 (1914): 205; Landsberg and Schulte, "Die Universität Bonn im ersten Kriegsjahre," *Chronik* 40 (1914): 3-8; Dr. Weiss, "Vorort Cheruskia-Münster," *Ac* 27 (1914): 205-206; "Der Krieg," *AMh* 31 (1914): 237ff.; O. Hoetzsch, "Zum Sedanstag 1914" *ABl* 29 (1914): 174-78. See also the send-off by A. Wagner, W. Kahl, General v. Liebert, D. Schäfer and G. Roethe, "Geleitworte," ibid., pp. 4-9 as well as R. Seeberg, "Unsere Jugend!" and Field Marshal v. d. Goltz, "An die V. D. Ster," ibid., pp. 172f. See also Schulze-Ssymank, *Das deutsche Studententum* (Munich, 1932), pp. 452f. While the following few pages cannot do justice to the impact of the war on academic youth, they intend to sketch the development of the previously treated topics until the end of the empire, since there is no systematic secondary literature.

this Mensur without batting an eyelash'' in order to defend "parents, siblings, my dear home, everything I have treasured. Poetry, art, philosophy, culture are the purpose of the struggle.'' But disillusionment was rapid and complete: "With what joy and eagerness I went into the fight, which appeared as a glorious opportunity to live to the fullest. With what disappointment I sit here, terror in my heart!'' In political terms, a minority considered the war "so terrible, inhuman, senseless, outdated, and in every way detrimental, that I have firmly resolved, when I come back, to do everything in my power in order to render something like this impossible in the future.'' Though sobered, the majority nevertheless clung to the vision of victory, purified by their dedication: "I want to fight and perhaps also die for my belief in a beautiful, great, ennobled Germany, purged of baseness and egotism, with faith and honor restored to their old rights.'' Resentful toward the easy life of the home front and frustrated by the elusiveness of victory, many despaired in the Kaiser as well as in the entire system of the Second Empire. While in the short run the *Fronterlebnis* contributed to Socialist and democratic unrest, in the long run "Langemarck was the birth hour of volkish Germany, of National Socialism.''[3]

For those university members who remained behind, the war years were also a trying time. Although total higher education enrollment increased from about 79,000 to 84,600, most of the growth was fictitious, for "the majority of our Kommiltonen is now serving at the front.'' In Prussia the number of students actually present was cut in third (from 29,781 to 10,035) between 1913-14 and 1917-18, before it recovered somewhat (17,653) in 1918-19 and finally surpassed prewar levels (38,050) in 1919-20. At Bonn an average of about three-fourths of all regular students were on leave at the front or at home for auxiliary service. The structure of the student body altered drastically: "Disabled veterans, those unfit for duty, temporarily furloughed, eighteen-year-olds not yet drafted, women and auditors, priests and monks'' formed most of the audience. As the number of female students grew somewhat, women made up over one-third of all Prussian students by 1917-18 but, with the return of peace, decreased to one-tenth. In the short run the war almost brought regular instruction to a standstill. In the

---

[3] W. Dreysse, *Langemarck 1914: Der heldische Opfergang der Deutschen Jugend* (Minden, 1930), pp. 11, 62ff., 68ff., 96f. (with a watercolor by A. Hitler); G. Kaufmann, *Langemarck: Das Opfer der Jugend an allen Fronten* (Stuttgart, 1938), pp. 103-14; figures from Schulze-Ssymank, *Das deutsche Studententum*, pp. 453f.; Ph. Witkop, *Kriegsbriefe gefallener Studenten* (Munich, 1928) a selection from 20,000 letters, pp. 8, 11, 15, 18, 21, passim; P. Grabein, "Der Student im Weltkriege," *VA*, pp. 236-46. For a military account, see W. Beumelburg, *Langemarck* (Berlin, 1938). Weimar academics drew the lesson that "the unrest of the youthful blood shed drives us, the living, to complete the Reich" (J. M. Wehner, *Langemarck: Ein Vermächtnis* [Munich, 1932], pp. 3-9). For the astounding unanimity of support for the war among the educated of Europe, see R. N. Stromberg, "Redemption by War: The Intellectuals and 1914," *Midwest Quarterly* 20 (1979): 211-27.

long run, however, it accelerated the enrollment expansion and social opening of the previous decade.[4]

Wartime also intensified nationalism in instruction, which more and more permeated ostensibly apolitical subjects. As "most of us can only offer our intellectual power," professors sought to provide a spiritual rationale "so that precious blood has not been shed in vain." The "national regeneration of the great war and the touching experience of national community" were welcomed well-nigh unanimously, for "the war, like a cleansing storm after oppressive days, has blown away everything that clouded the inner unity of our people." Many academics abandoned the ideal of value-free scholarship: "We shall continue our courses. . . . But the ideas of the war shall animate our teaching." Jettisoning its political neutrality, the Rheinische Friedrich-Wilhelms-Universität awarded honorary doctorates to G. Krupp von Bohlen und Halbach for constructing the "fabulous and monstrous 42 cm mortars" as well as to Rudolf Havenstein for his contribution to the war effort as director of the Imperial Bank. Although moderates who signed the Delbrück counterpetition cautioned, "we shall not be so un-German as to imitate the chauvinism of our enemies," the majority of the politicized faculty supported the pan-German Schäfer petition in favor of annexationist war aims. Even in case of a compromise peace, nationalists like Albrecht Penck insisted on "balancing necessary losses with corresponding gains, on keeping of our conquests what is necessary as living space for our people, and on obtaining colonial possessions large and rich enough to supply us with scarce tropical raw materials." In countless public lectures, pamphlets, and literary greetings to the students at the front, academics sought to strengthen morale: "May benign providence protect you in the suffering and horror of battle, may your brave courage bring glorious success to your work, may an honorable peace reunite you with us in new scholarly endeavors and shared academic life after a splendid victory!"[5]

[4] Totals from Schulze-Ssymank, *Das deutsche Studentum*, p. 453; Prussian figures from *Statistisches Jahrbuch für den Freistaat Preussen* 19 (1923): 303-307; Bonn calculations from the introductory compilations of vols. 40-44 of the *Chronik*. 40-44 of the *Chronik*; quote from Anschütz and Landsberg, "Die Universität Bonn im zweiten Kriegsjahre," 41: 1-9. See also G. Steiger, *Geschichte der Universität Jena* (Jena, 1958), pp. 509-12. Since the Bonn Matrikel only discriminates between those enrolled and those actually in attendance during the later war years (and even then the accuracy varies), it proved impossible to analyze the composition of the student body prosopographically. See also the excellent introductory chapters in J. Schwarz, *Studenten in der Weimarer Republik: Die deutsche Studentenschaft in der Zeit von 1918 bis 1923 und ihre Stellung zur Politik* (Berlin, 1971).

[5] Landsberg and Schulte in *Chronik* 40: 7; M. Planck, "Bericht des abtretenden Rektors über das Amtsjahr 1913-14," in *Rektoratswechsel an der Friedrich-Wilhelms-Universität* (Berlin, 1914); E. Landsberg, *Die Verdrängung des Rheinischen Fremdrechts* (Bonn, 1914), p. 21; C. H. Becker, *Das türkische Bildungsproblem* (Bonn, 1916), p. 5; U. Wilcken, *Über Werden und Vergehen der Universalreiche* (Bonn, 1915), p. 5; T. Kipp, "Kriegsaufgaben

The impact of the war on student subculture was equally drastic. With the two-thirds reduction in attendance, many organizations had to suspend activities and faced extinction, especially if, like the Freistudentenschaft, they could not rely upon a group of dedicated and generous alumni. In Bonn the number of active associations fell from 72 in 1914 to an average of 22.9 in the next four years, while membership dwindled from 1,720 (without free students) to 223.1 in the same period, and the corporate proportion of the student body dropped from about two-fifths to one-seventh. Since about six of the organizations and around 144 of the members were female, women dominated corporate subculture, and only the strongest Corps, Burschenschaften, and Catholic associations carried on in a much chastened (no duelling) manner. Instead, "conscious that in the hour of need all their strength belongs to the fatherland," many students worked for local welfare institutions, while several corporations "dedicated their houses, otherwise intended for joyous conviviality, to patriotic purposes." Led by the "burning eagerness" of several professors, some patriotic students founded a Wehrbund "to propagate the necessity and importance of military preparation for academic youth" through paramilitary instruction. Medical students participated in the "Bonn hospital train," supported financially by the local citizenry, which "gained an excellent reputation in bringing aid and comfort to countless wounded" on their way home from the front. Displacing such long-awaited celebrations as the centennial of the Burschenschaft in 1915, the imperatives of the fighting created new student needs which called for greater faculty and student collaboration. The "terrible situation of student prisoners" led to the creation of a Deutscher Studentendienst 1914 "in order to supply them with intellectual nourishment, especially scholarly literature." The special sufferings of "war-injured academics" prompted the founding of an Akademischer Hilfsbund which sought to help reintegrate invalid veterans into university life with advice and financial support. Aside from easing certain high-school examination requirements (*Notabitur*) and awarding posthumous doctorates, university authorities also "suggested establishing a war kitchen for university members, because of the difficulties of student nu-

---

der Rechtswissenschaft," *Rektoratswechsel*, pp. 19-51; BUA, phil. Fak., Ehrenpromotionen Havenstein, Krupp und Rausenberger; U. v. Wilamowitz-Moellendorff, *Von der Universität Erreichtes und Erhofftes* (Berlin, 1916); A. Penck, *Über politische Grenzen* (Berlin, 1917); Anschütz, "Liebe Kommilitonen!" in *Ostergruss der Rheinischen Friedrich-Wilhelms-Universität zu Bonn an ihre Angehörigen im Felde* (Bonn, 1916), p. 5; and R. Seeberg, *Politik und Moral* (Berlin, 1918): "The only firm point of political orientation remains the life of one's own nation." See also *Deutsche Weihnacht, Erste Liebesgabe deutscher Hochschüler* (Kassel, 1914), and many subsequent uplifting tracts under "Liebesgaben für deutsche Hochschüler," IHK, F 867-918. See also König, "Politische Komponenten," pp. 50-55; Ringer, *German Mandarins* (Cambridge, Mass., 1969), pp. 180-99; and K. Schwabe, *Wissenschaft und Kriegsmoral* (Göttingen, 1969), entire.

trition in restaurants,'' anticipating the later *Mensa*. Since ''all of you comrades are equally loyal to our fatherland,'' organizational rivalries and political disputes were largely suspended between 1914 and 1918. Nevertheless, the initial unanimity of ''the ideas of 1914'' evaporated in the carnage at the front and the hunger at home. Those who did not withdraw into privatism either gravitated with the left wing of the Freistudentenschaft toward democratic reform and political socialism or, with the right wing of the nationalists, they joined the protofascist Reichsverband Deutschvölkischer Akademiker (1917) as well as the student chapters of the annexationist Deutsche Vaterlandspartei (1918) in the intention of ''unifying the German people in a forceful will to victory.'' Although the war forced painful adaptations, the enthusiastic response to its outbreak, the dogged self-sacrifice of students, the patriotic rhetoric of professors, and the organizational self-help of academic youth demonstrated the strength of the national commitment of the university, which harkened back to the Fichtean tradition: ''Not victory or death, but victory at any price.''[6]

Sources of Illiberalism

How did the social and ideological transformation of educated youth during the empire produce such nationalist dedication among students and academics? Although the previous chapters suggest several partial answers, the specificity of most concepts linking society, polity, and university, such as economic development, educational opportunity, social control, and generational rebellion, renders a comprehensive explanation difficult. The broader new social histories focusing on sociopolitical developments, the ''qualification of labor,'' the structure and mentality paradigm, or on quantitative model building have yet to produce a grand synthesis of higher learning, social matrix, and political behavior. The absence of an integrative theory dictates an inductive historical rather than a deductive functional approach, which looks at the interplay of five crucial factors without predetermining their relative importance or the quality of their interaction.

---

[6] General account in Schulze-Ssymank, *Das deutsche Studententum*, pp. 456-63; Bonn calculations from heading ''5. Studentische Vereine,'' in *Chronik*, vols. 40-44; Landsberg and Schulte, ''Die Universität Bonn im ersten Kriegsjahr,'' *Chronik* 40: 7; A. Brinkmann to rector, 6 January 1915 and other material on the Wehrbund in BUA, A50, 16, vol. 1; F. Heer, *Geschichte der deutschen Burschenschaft* (Heidelberg, 1939), 4: 98ff.; for the Deutscher Studenten-Dienst 1914, see BUA, MF 1502; for the Akademischer Hilfsbund, see 14 March 1915 session of the executive committee of the Burschenschaft, BAF, DB, Geschäftsführender Ausschuss 1913-18, III; Ribbert and Anschütz, ''Die Universität Bonn im vierten Kriegsjahre,'' *Chronik* 43: 1-10; Witkop, *Kriegsbriefe*, p. 19; Linse, ''Hochschulrevolution,'' chapter 3; ''Ortsgruppe der deutschen Vaterlandspartei,'' MUA, 305a, Acc 1950/9, no. 203. See also the numerous pamphlets under ''Student und Krieg'' in IHK, F 765-814; and the material in ZStA Me, Rep 76 Va, Sekt 1 Tit I, No 36.

Instead of a tight model, such a tentative framework centering on enrollment growth, demographic and social structure, educational policy and
political instruction, as well as on corporate subculture and student politics,
treats the university not merely as a dependent variable of changes in
society and polity but rather as an intermediate factor with sufficient weight
of its own to affect them in turn. Since higher education represents only
a relatively short four years of an academic's life, such a *modus procendi*
allows for the formative importance of primary or secondary education
and of later professional experience, while maintaining the significance of
the social selection and political socialization taking place at that critical
transition from youthful adolescence to early adulthood.[7] Seeking to present
the full range of the contradictory past and to develop a coherent interpretation from within the quantitative and qualitative evidence, such an
approach raises a series of specific questions about the relationship between
social transformation and ideological reversal: What was the general developmental pattern? How did various subgroups differ? Which traits were
shared by academic youths? What were the internal as well as the external
reasons for these characteristics? How did structures and mentalities affect
each other? What were the social, cultural, and political implications of
such cultivation? How did the imperial legacy influence the behavior and
outlook of students and academics after 1918?

Although they coalesced into self-conscious generations only during the
anti-Semitic 1880s and youth-oriented 1900s, students in Imperial Germany
developed in a series of cohorts, each with a distinctive consciousness.
During the liberal 1870s, rising numbers in every faculty but Catholic
theology meant increasing opportunities for all strata, while professorial
and student satisfaction with unification as the vindication of cultural superiority contributed to the triumph of corporatism over academic reform.
In the nationalist 1880s, the continued expansion of the medical and,
initially, the theological and philosophical fields threatened professional
unemployment, and the influx of the lower middle classes produced defensive fears of the dilution of cultivation through the masses. Hence, the
deliberalization of teaching, led by the Borussian historians but echoed in
other areas, facilitated the nationalization of the students by the propaganda
of the VDSt. Throughout the social-imperialist 1890s, the enrollment stagnation of the philosophical, theological, and medical faculties reversed

---

[7] L. Krieger, "German History—In the Grand Manner," *AHR* 84 (1979): 1007-17;
P. Lundgreen, "Steigen die Bildungsanforderungen bei technischem Fortschritt? Zwei un-
terschiedliche Untersuchungen zum Verhältnis von Qualifikation und Arbeitsplatzstruktur,"
GG 3 (1977): 273ff.; J. A. Henretta, "Social History as Lived and Written," *AHR* 84 (1979):
1293-1333; J. Kousser, "The Agenda for 'Social Science History', " *SSH* 1 (1977): 383-
91; and G. Iggers, *New Directions in European Historiography* (Middletown, 1975). See
also Rolf Reichardt, "Histoire des Mentalités," *IASL* 3 (1978): 130-66.

much of the petit bourgeois influx and produced a plutocratic student body, dominated by the new commercial-industrial elite. While positivist retreat from commitment among professors abetted the culmination of corporate romanticism among the students, the emergence of an academic proletariat threatened to spread socialism to the universities, which was combated both by the reformist teaching of the Kathedersozialisten and by the beginnings of naval imperialism. One important dimension of the evolution of academic consciousness is therefore the pendulum-like swing of discourse from cohort to cohort superimposed upon the tension of adult and youth generations.

During the reformist 1900s, the resumption of numerical growth in the legal and philosophical fields once again created an optimistic institutional climate, since most social groups found opportunities for study, even the Kleinbürgertum, with its burgeoning white-collar sector. While academics vigorously championed Weltpolitik, progressive professors were willing to concede the admission of modern-high-school graduates and women, and the self-assertively youthful Freistudentschaft struggled for a corresponding modernization of student life. In the ambivalent half-decade before the First World War, the renewal of medical and Protestant theological expansion as well as the arrival of more Catholic and heterogeneously prepared students, most of them recruited from the lower middle class, fragmented the social homogeneity of the university by dividing it into elite, middle, and lower layers. These increasing social tensions were not resolved by the professoriate, at odds with itself over political and academic reform, while the unclear challenge of the youth movement, the corporate counterattack against the free students, and the emergence of the volkish fringe further disunited the student body. During periods of uncomplicated enrollment growth and expanding opportunities for mobility (1870s, 1900s), professorial attitudes therefore tended to be optimistic and flexible, whereas student consciousness was likely to be reformist or liberal. In times of excessive expansion and real or anticipated academic unemployment (1880s, 1890s, 1910s), the social struggle for higher education became more severe, faculty opinion grew traditional and defensive, while student attitudes turned more nationalist, imperialist, or volkish.[8]

While figures such as the braggart (*Renommist*) had existed earlier, the enrollment explosion of the empire created new types and divided the student body into several political camps. In social terms, the arrogant

[8] Hence the pattern of development is more complex than E. Tannenbaum, *1900: The Generation Before the War* (Garden City, 1976) or R. Wohl, *The Generation of 1914* (Cambridge, 1979) make out. For the concurrent deliberalization of Austrian culture and politics, see C. E. Schorske, *Fin-de-Siècle Vienna: Politics and Culture* (New York, 1980). These swings of academic mood are also more than cyclical, for in a spiral fashion they build upon previous attitudes and move forward through time.

Stutzer continued as fashionable *Gigerl*, whereas the ordinary Bruder Studio made up the comfortable middle stratum, well above the poor *Hungerstudent* struggling as an academic proletarian. In intellectual respects, the small coterie of disciples of scholarship contrasted with the large numbers of *Brotstudenten*, intent on acquiring professionally useful skills as rapidly as possible, and the ever-popular *Bummler*, enjoying the freedom of student life without corresponding scientific or careerist ambition. Organizationally the proud *Corpsstudent* or active of a duelling corporation aspired to leadership of the student body, while the member of a less exalted association still attempted to lord it over a lowly independent "finch" or "camel."

In a multitude of combinations these types dominated student politics, which, though somewhat discontinuous in specific organizations, demonstrated a remarkable constancy of basic tendencies: First, a minority of sometimes poor, scholarly, and loosely affiliated students sought to continue the liberal and democratic impulses of the Vormärz at the university as well as in general politics. The progressive countertradition manifested itself in the campus reformers of the 1870s, the Freie Wissenschaftliche Vereinigung and the Akademisch-Liberaler Verein of the 1880s, the Socialist students and the Sozialwissenschaftliche Studentenvereinigungen of the 1890s, the Freistudentenschaft and the council movement of the 1900s, and the life reformers (Akademische Freischar) of the youth movement in the 1910s. Second, a substantial number of fashionable and comfortable careerists or loafers within or without corporations remained apolitical-patriotic, content with the joys of student life and, to the continual frustration of the committed, well-nigh oblivious to any larger responsibilities. This unconcerned majority of academic youth relished its carefree existence, implicitly trusted the imperial government and, out of monarchical or regional loyalty, supported the status quo at home and expansion abroad. Finally, a further large segment of elite or middling students of all different academic persuasions, but usually organized in corporations or associations, became active in nationalist and imperialist causes, be it somewhat more liberally, conservatively, or anti-Semitically. This politically dominant strain extended from the Vereine Deutscher Studenten of the 1880s to the anti-Catholic Verband Deutscher Hochschulen and the Akademischer Bismarckbund of the 1900s to the proto-Fascist fringe of the Deutschvölkischer Studentenverband of the 1910s. Containing the various shadings of German nationalism, these circles provided the recruiting ground for the propagandists of Weltpolitik, German Kulturmission, and annexationist war aims, that is, the spokesmen for the majority of the adult political elite. Competing outside influences and internal structures of student life therefore created surprising diversity, which offered considerable individual choice. While the struggle between these tendencies led to a "progressive politicization of the student body, based upon ideology," the liberals lost their campus leadership, which they had enjoyed until the 1870s, to the indifferents and the new nationalists, despite all valiant efforts to the contrary.[9]

Across these differences, students in Imperial Germany shared certain fundamental reflexes that made them recognizable to others and established their common self-image as "academics." Although not found equally in each individual, three characteristics predominate. First, basic to all was an idealization of cultivation which considered allgemeine Menschenbildung as a supreme value, irrespective of any concrete content. Its initial emancipatory optimism was, however, undercut by the reactionary and bureaucratic implementation of neohumanism after 1819, the failure of the Revolution of 1848, and the social disruption in the wake of industrialization. Increasing scholarly specialization and mass influx into higher education led to a philosophical erosion and an externalization of the Humboldtian legacy, which expressed itself in an esthetic withdrawal from the present into a cultured inner world or in a reduction of the classical heritage into a specific form of elite discourse (Latin phrases). Hence, rightist students saw no contradiction between their intolerant racism and their protestations of academic freedom. Second, equally important, was the widespread elitist (bildungsaristokratisch) consciousness of the educated, which set academics apart from the industrial-commercial bourgeoisie and lifted them above the petit bourgeois and working masses, thereby creating an important noneconomic status barrier within society. On the top, the higher Bildungsbürgertum sought to fuse with the nobility and the propertied into an imperial elite, the notorious triad of birth, wealth, and education. In the middle, the comfortable cultivated formed the bulk of the professions and the upper bureaucracy and thereby the core of the staatserhaltende circles, proud of their superior culture in contrast to mere Besitz. On the bottom, the less fortunate academics (in backgrounds or careers) attempted to separate themselves from the lower middle class and proletariat through pronounced educational arrogance, thereby compensating for the disparity between their social prestige and humble income. This instinctive elitism complicated the students' understanding of the consequences of modernization and predisposed them to solving the "social question" through charity and reconciliation. Finally, similarly pervasive was a disdain for politics, which rejected the descent from ideal heights into the depths of interest struggles and limited involvement to private,

[9] Schulze-Ssymank, Das deutsche Studententum, p. 492. Delineating student types was one of the favorite pastimes of German academics. See also the lavishly illustrated and nostalgic Krause, O Alte Burschenherrlichkeit (Graz, 1979), pp. 133-59.

professional, or local concerns. The cliché *politisch Lied, garstig Lied* illustrates a profound lack of interest as well as a refusal to sully the abstract superiority of one's ideas by compromise. At the same time, the reflex patriotism of academics gradually evolved toward a modern nationalism, an unconditional loyalty to the ruling dynasty, an unquestioning glorification of the heroic figure of Bismarck, an elemental fear of social revolution, and an enthusiastic support of power and world politics. This strange ambivalence made students largely incapable of confronting the structural problems or criticizing the expansionist designs of the empire and thereby rendered their leadership claim problematic. Together these three traits coalesced into a widespread academic illiberalism which molded students for scholarship, professional careers, and citizenship into conformist patterns, thus deflecting pressures for change away from state and society toward Wissenschaft and personal development. In Imperial Germany, Humboldt's concept of Bildung as liberation of the individual personality, which implied not only cultural but also social and political emancipation, was only intermittently and limitedly a living force.[10]

The cultural reasons for the great reversal from academic liberalism to illiberalism during the Second Reich are complex. "The term Bildung belongs to the favorite slogans of the present and if that alone counted, we would have to call our age 'cultivated.' Unfortunately it does not at all deserve this name." Ironically, the very progress of science and the spread of professional training meant that "the value of scholarship for general education has become less and less, its relevance for the whole man and his higher life has diminished, and the strictness of its method threatens to lead to apprenticeship and shallow routine." While advancing the frontiers of research, the "continually increasing specialization of individual subjects and the growing dryness of philological scholarship" broke up the philosophical unity of knowledge and destroyed the formative value of classicism. Nietzsche was not alone in complaining: "Most philologists lack the ennobling general view of the ancients, for they stand too close to the painting and only analyze the oil pigment instead of admiring, and even more, enjoying the grand and bold features of the entire picture." The erosion of the moral-scientific synthesis of cultural liberalism therefore diminished the authority of academics as teachers. "The growth of careerism" within the university, moreover, routinized lecturing and reduced contacts between faculty and students: "The rela-

---

[10] K. H. Jarausch, "Liberal Education as Illiberal Socialization," *JMH* 50 (1978): 624. For a definition of this central but somewhat ambiguous concept, see "Illiberalism and Beyond: German History in Search of a Paradigm," entire. In many ways the crucial problem is not what the university did, but rather what it failed to do, since cultivation rarely reversed the generalized illiberality of bourgeois mentality in Imperial Germany.

tionship is usually not as close as one would like.'"[11] As professors provided less and less "unified training of the young in an ennobling, grand, and clear Weltanschauung," students were "thrown back upon their own resources." However, corporate self-education, preoccupied with character and social behavior, could not compensate for deficiencies in formal Bildung, for it often pursued the opposite values: "That new-German tendency toward Junker bravado leads to brusqueness toward those below, to sycophancy toward those above, and to arrogance toward the outside as well as to a coarsening of feelings toward the inside." Although this stultification applied only to a minority, the fundamental ambivalence of student intentions hampered cultivation: "Only a few penetrate into the antechambers of scholarship; others are impressed by an outstanding teacher for their entire career. But the majority loyally remembers only the images of student life, the sufferings and joys outside the classroom." There was little interest in intellectual developments among "the great number of students, [who] only want to acquire information for the state examination while avoiding 'all unnecessary knowledge'." Thus, student self-education was hardly any more liberal than cultivation through scholarship.[12]

The "ideal influence of university studies diminished in the last decades" because "the entire direction of scholarship and life of our time has raised not the banner of speculation but of empiricism, not of idealism but of realism." This shift in intellectual climate created the "fundamental error" that "cultivation equals knowledge," which underestimated the "ethical component" and "the concept of decorum as well as . . . the aesthetic aspect" of what it meant to be educated. Attempts to popularize cultivation necessarily led to "a devaluation of the older cultural values, especially of ancient languages and of philosophy, since they did not appear relevant to the special needs of the industrial and commercial circles of our society." The "tendency of our times toward the merely practical, toward so-called Americanism" and the exaggeration of the "importance of modern scientific training" led many academics to warn: "Woe to us if realistic education should win and the national spirit descend more and more into shallow materialism!" Defined as a loss of idealism, the emergence of modernism corroded the neohumanist synthesis of morality and scholarship

[11] A. Langguth, "Bilanz der akademischen Bildung," *BuBü,* 1: 304; A. Harnack, *Geschichte der königlichen Preussischen Akademie der Wissenschaften zu Berlin* (Berlin, 1900), p. 791; Langguth, "Bilanz," pp. 28, 41, 26f., 39f. L. Burchardt, "Science Policy in Imperial Germany," *HSR* 13 (1980): 26-32. The discussion of the causes of the reversal summarizes the conclusions of the previous chapters.

[12] Langguth, "Bilanz," p. 49; *Zeitschrift für höheres Unterrichtswesen,* 1887, no. 36; Langguth, "Bilanz," pp. 36, 41, 38, 41. "The influence of student years might perhaps be compared with that of a moderate intoxication, from which one quickly awakens to become completely reasonable again."

without putting another compelling and generally accepted ethos of humanism into its place. "Despite the explosion of knowledge, there is a widespread dissatisfaction with the condition of cultivation, which ultimately also involves our universities as highest educational institutions." One perspicacious observer pondered: "Our nation's progress toward greatness and power . . . would be a dangerous risk, if through the decline of idealism, we should lose our inner moral stability, if we were to lack youthful men who, strong in enthusiasm and capable of sacrifice, could withstand the blandishments of the day." Although liberals generally applauded specialization, realism, empiricism, and scientism as progressive, the concomitant narrowness, materialism, positivism, and ahumaneness ironically rendered the process and ethos of liberal education less liberal.[13]

The social dynamics of the rise of illiberalism are equally complicated because "transitory status as a student is no link in the societal chain" but rather a developmental stage with its own unstable society. Although it initially bolstered the self-confidence of a growing academic stratum, the enrollment expansion eventually hastened deliberalization when it produced an excess of educated men: "It is clear that these great masses of graduates cannot be used up by the modern state, [and] that must become a real danger for our culture." The "immeasurable sum of suffering and resentment pent up in such proletarian hearts" led either toward socialism, since "out of desperation they throw themselves into the wide-open arms of that movement which promises them an existence in dignity," or toward "practical materialism, which more and more weakens . . . spiritual values." The partial opening of the imperial universities made for some increase in social mobility for minorities and the Kleinbürgertum, as well as women. However, this restructuring of the student body was more a result of co-optation of aggressive lower-middle-class elements than of a genuine democratization and led to a broadening of the lower academic professions (teaching, preaching) while leaving the higher pursuits (law, medicine) largely a preserve of traditional academic, noble, and wealthy elites. The psychological price of admission generally was ideological and behavioral conformity. "The exclusive, the standesgemässe students group themselves around a principle that has not grown on academic soil and without regard for personal ability or intellectual dignity divides their comrades into first-class and second-class students," one contemporary criticized:

---

[13] Langguth, "Bilanz," pp. 42, 5f., 8f., 12, 64, 10, 64. Not that Langguth is particularly profound, but the very mediocrity of his assessment reflects the prevailing cultural attitudes after the turn of the century better than more trenchant analyses. See also the essays by K. Kupisch on theologians, F. Kreppel on teachers, and A. Voigt on lawyers in H. Schoeps, *Das Wilhelminische Zeitalter* (Stuttgart, 1967), pp. 40-59 and 199-234, as well as R. Pascal, *From Naturalism to Expressionism* (London, 1973) for some of the illiberal implications of modernism.

"And according to what criteria? On the basis of the quality of clothes, of their genealogy, or of their father's moneybags." Intent on "connection and protection," the student elite groomed itself for a brilliant official or private career, the comfortable middle group toed the line to achieve at least moderate bureaucratic or professional success, while "the careworn proletariat" conformed in order to insure financial survival. Moreover, the professionalization of academics' careers hardened the entitlement system and fostered a search for statist security rather than a faith in the virtues of free occupational competition. Many observers complained: "The dominant circles which talk big in the casinos or ballrooms, the *jeunesse dorée* with the well-turned mustache and the dashing appearance, are incredibly superficial and betray a blasé mentality of the worst kind, which runs counter to any inwardness, any serious intellectual concerns."[14]

In many ways, the attitudes of academic youth reflected the social transformation of the middle class. Perspicacious contemporaries like Friedrich Paulsen understood that in the first decades of the century, when the Bürgertum struggled for equality, it was deeply committed to political liberalism. But after reaching many of its national, constitutional, economic, and cultural goals with the *Reichsgründung*, the educated middle class, feeling threatened by the thirst for cultivation of the lower middle and lower classes, turned politically defensive, made its peace with the existing order, and reduced its prior role as "carrier of national consciousness and political progress" to the former alone. "Feudalism and plutocracy" made considerable inroads into "the students' spiritual estate, which contrasts with mere acquisitive estates." The amalgamation of educated leaders with the nobility and propertied into a cultured-aristocratic-wealthy elite largely turned the spokesmen of the Bildungsbürgertum from critics of the existing sociopolitical order into defenders. For the middling cultivated in state office or the free professions, their self-image as backbone of the state, their dynastic loyalty, and their aversion to political struggles balanced an instinctive liberal individualism with a sense of national responsibility. Among poor academics seeking to stave off descent into the working class, ambition of achieving a secure place in the middle class put a premium on proving cultural superiority and patriotism in contrast to the uncultured and internationalist masses. The change of sociopolitical fronts robbed the Bildungsbürgertum of some of its public authority: "Other social strata have assumed political leadership which is now so much the task of practical professions that 'professorial wisdom' has be-

---

[14] H. Kienzl, "Der standesgemässe Student," *Die Hilfe* 18 (1912), no. 17; Langguth, "Bilanz," pp. 15-23, 54. See also K. H. Jarausch, "Frequenz und Struktur," *Bildungspolitik* (Stuttgart, 1980), pp. 146-49, and H. Titze, "Enrollment Expansion and Academic Overcrowding," in *Transformation of Higher Learning* (1982).

come a derogatory term, while students are not mentioned at all any longer." In an attempt to recapture their former prominence, those academics still involved in politics sought to become the propagandists of all manner of nationalist pressure groups. Despite deep fears of radicalization due to academic unemployment, the expansion of the cultivated stratum within society and its internal differentiation shifted its primary allegiance from liberalism to nationalism, be it exclusive, statist, or social.[15]

The political outcome of liberal education was largely illiberal because critical attitudes toward state and society were rarely reinforced through professorial teaching or through corporate character building. In many middle-class families the earlier liberal tradition lingered. Primary-school teachers, frustrated in their aspirations to professional equality with Gymnasium Oberlehrer, continued to vote for leftist parties. The staff of the modern secondary schools, piqued by the resistance of classical philologists to educational reform, was also receptive to some progressive ideas. The discovery of adolescence by artists and literati made naturalist and expressionist forms of youthful rebellion accessible. The survival of left-wing liberalism and the spectacular growth of Social Democracy suggested political alternatives. Finally, the youth revolt of the Wandervogel against the rigidity of the school system and the duplicity of adult Wilhelmian mores offered life-style alternatives, some of which carried political overtones. However, on the whole university teaching turned these liberalizing tendencies into uncritical directions. Less because of Prussian limitations on academic freedom via appointment policy than through self-censorship, faculties in their ceremonial speeches, academic lectures, and courses on politics imparted a credo summed up by the moderate historian Otto Hintze at the University of Berlin in 1913: "The twenty-five years of Emperor William II's reign, on which we look back today, have passed without great crises of defeat or victory for our fatherland; and we have reason to praise this dispensation of providence with a glad heart, since we need peace to complete what our fathers have wrought." In foreign policy he vocalized academic consensus by supporting imperialism, navalism, and "the securing of our equality with other powers in the new world state system." Domestically, Hintze argued for "the idea of social justice" as "internal complement to the notion of world power" and pleaded for cautious reform: "A firm, consistent, and, wherever possible, increased social policy is and remains a necessary complement to the otherwise all

---

[15] F. Paulsen, *Geschichte des gelehrten Unterrichts* (Berlin, 1921), 2: 573, 686. Kienzel, "standesgemässer Student"; Langguth, "Bilanz," p. 55; and K. H. Jarausch, "The Social Transformation of the University," *JSH* 12 (1979): 628-31. Although the movement of the universities after 1879 paralleled the shift of bourgeois society from liberalism, higher education is more than simply a dependent factor but rather an intermediary variable that needs to be analyzed in its own right.

too rigid system of our monarchical, military, and bureaucratic state.'' Students and academics had a mission to counteract divisiveness: "I hope that when you go out into life one day, you will have learned from the development of our fatherland that the party is not the most important thing, but above all the welfare of our country and our people."[16]

Reinforced by the general political tone of the Second Reich, the dominant strain of student politics also directed academic youth toward nationalism. Despite a long and vigorous tradition of reform, a counterculture of student dissent failed to form. Since repression proved largely ineffective during the Vormärz, the intermittent harassment of university authorities and the police persecution of Socialist students cannot have been solely responsible. Rather, the dominance of corporatism in student subculture militated against liberalism, for its ideals of self-education, training practices, and social customs were curiously collectivist, despite their youthful flaunting of authority. The organizational superiority of the VDSt and the Burschenschaft over the various reform groups was also striking, because the latter's penchant for individualism hampered effective common action, although they created innovative institutions like councils and libraries. Much of this turn to the right was only a student expression of the wider *Tendenzwende* of the German middle class. Satisfaction with the achievement of unification, with economic progress, and cultural advancement was shared by youthful academics. The spread of corporatism and the rise of the new nationalism of the VDSt paralleled Bismarck's repudiation of liberalism: "As long as German students cherish the idea of unity [*den Reichsgedanken*], nothing will be amiss, and I shall rest in peace when my hour comes." The visible progress of the "military-bureaucratic empire" made the liberal heritage of the midcentury appear obsolete to many academic youths who sought a different combination of "individualism, nationalism, and idealism." Although students did not act independently of adult politics, they responded to the reversal more rapidly and thoroughly than their elders and subsequently perpetuated nationalism in their own self-education across all the innumerable organizational differences and ideological shadings of student life. Hugo Böttger's appraisal in 1910 was not far off the mark:

What characterizes German students today is a firm national conviction which does not lead to chauvinist rowdyism, but to a serious desire

---

[16] Jarausch, "Liberal Education," p. 616; O. Hintze, "Rede, gehalten zur Feier der fünfundzwanzigjährigen Regierung seiner Majestät des Kaisers und Königs Wilhelm II," *Hohenzollern Jahrbuch*, 1913, pp. 78-95. See also K. Wegner, "Linksliberalismus im wilhelminischen Deutschland und in der Weimarer Republik," *GG* 4 (1978): 120-37. In some respects students therefore reflected the self-mobilization of the new German right. G. Eley, "The Wilhelmine Right: How it Changed," *Society and Politics* (London, 1978), pp. 112ff.

to understand the far-flung challenges of the fatherland and to develop men capable of meeting them. Hence, all of the corporations show a vivid interest in world economic and colonial issues, in civic education, in learning about the problems of the empire and the member states. Combined with this is an unshakable loyalty to monarchy and dynasty and the confidence that governmental institutions have hitherto done their duty in reconciling class struggles and that the undermining of state authority through socialism must be resolutely opposed as a threat to the empire and to the entirety of higher culture.[17]

The implications of such academic illiberalism for German culture, society, and politics were considerable. Some scholars have argued that the "partial modernization" of cultivation created "special tensions which were not resolved," whereas others have stressed "education as tradition" which "perpetuated outlooks that were more or less explicitly at variance with its time." Part of this perplexity about the relationship between cultivation and change derives from the internal contradiction within the neohumanist concept of Bildung. While an individualist emphasis on the "improvement of our inner selves" carried an emancipatory thrust against the restrictions of estate society, the "salvation of the soul as final aim" spiritualized the development of the free personality. By midcentury cultivation had become a kind of secular substitute for religion; it transferred the focus of reform from social conditions to individual self-perfection and exerted a conservative influence disguised by progressive rhetoric. When specialization and positivism undermined idealism, technology and modern secondary training undercut classicism, the influx of the masses threatened elitism, and cultural modernism challenged tradition, many academics abandoned their liberal optimism and viewed the modern age with deep-seated ambivalence. Though the Gebildete applauded "the enormous scientific advances," the spread of material progress to the lower orders, and "the rise of Germany to world power," they worried about the deculturing influences of industrialization, the rise of the masses, and the yellow press.

Attitudes toward the emerging metropolis are a case in point. Whereas many right-wing critics echoed the antiurbanism of Wilhelm von Riehl by stressing the demographic dangers, the moral degeneration (criminality), the cultural degradation, and the political disintegration of the big city, others criticized urban problems with a view to improving them. But an

---

[17] K. Ahlborn, *Studentische Reform* (Göttingen, n.d.), in CCA Scheuer; H. Böttger, "Die Studenten und die Sozialdemokratie," *BBl* 25 (1910), no. 8; Bismarck quote from speech of Herbert Bismarck at his father's funeral, in H. Weber, *Geschichte des VDSt*, pp. 191-96. For the general reversal of the middle class, see H. A. Winkler, *Liberalismus und Antiliberalismus: Studien zur politischen Sozialgeschichte des 19. und 20. Jahrhunderts* (Göttingen, 1979); and W. J. Mommsen, "Der deutsche Liberalismus zwischen 'klassenloser Bürgergesellschaft' und 'Organisiertem Kapitalismus'," *GG* 4 (1978): 77-90.

equally vocal group of academics, intellectuals, and professionals praised the liberating forces of the *Grosstadt* as cultural center, economic hub, communication link, and welfare haven in an outpouring of progressive civic pride. Instead of a simple dichotomy or a partial adaptation, the relationship between cultivation and modernity therefore reveals a whole gamut of responses from volkish antimodernism to Socialist futurism with the majority of academics somewhere between these extremes, sharing pride as well as anxiety. Some characteristics of Bildung, such as stress on scholarship (science), individual responsibility and professional skill, contributed to the rationalization and bureaucratization of society, while the Greco-Roman content of neohumanism, its emotional ties to an agrarian age and its classical aestheticism, made it less appropriate for the technological demands of the new industrial age. Since much of its liberal anti-aristocratic thrust shifted after 1870 toward an illiberal fear of the masses, cultivation remained the middle-class educational ideology par excellence, although it failed to find a compelling modern form for its individualism.[18]

The chief social consequence of the transformation of higher learning was the perpetuation of the noneconomic character of the German Bürgertum. "The key confusion . . . between middle class and capitalism" led to consistent underestimation of the importance of cultivation as societal divide, and the preoccupation with bureaucratization and the emergence of the white-collar managers or employees ignored the crucial role of professionalization for the bourgeoisie. During the nineteenth century a number of academic occupations became modern professions that owed much of their theoretical knowledge, practical skill, general cultivation, and collective ethos to shared university study and the state credentialling based upon it. A series of increasingly stringent state examinations after 1740 forced clergymen and lawyers to demonstrate scholarly competence, mastery of specific skills, and a modicum of Allgemeinbildung, a pattern followed also by medical doctors, university professors, and Gymnasium teachers. In the empire a number of "new" professions, such as modern-high-school teachers, engineers, architects, chemists, and economists, lobbied for including their training in the university course, and for official certification with degrees insuring both occupational monopoly and social

---

[18] D. Rüschemeyer, "Modernisierung und die Gebildeten im kaiserlichen Deutschland," *KZfSS, Sonderheft 16* (1973), pp. 515-29; F. K. Ringer, *Education and Society in Modern Europe* (Bloomington, 1979), pp. 6ff., 18ff.; W. H. Bruford, *The German Tradition of Self-Cultivation* (New York, 1975); U. V. Wilamowitz-Moellendorff, "Neujahr 1900," *Reden* (Berlin, 1901), pp. 152-71; A. Lees, "Critics of Urban Society in Germany, 1854-1914," *Journal of the History of Ideas* 40 (1979): 61-83, and "The Civic Pride of the German Middle Classes, 1890-1933," paper delivered at the AHA meeting, New York, December 1979. Though not preventing technical or industrial progress, academic illiberalism rendered the political and social adjustment to "modernization" more difficult.

prestige. Although their claim to recognition rested on persuading the public (and the state) of the significance of their fiduciary service, Central European professionals treated their Bildung as Besitz, their cultivation as property, turning scholarly concern into special interest. Because their prosperity depended upon control of the market, which had been freed of restraints on competition in the 1860s, professional organizations increasingly shifted their concern from meritocratic openness to guildlike exclusivity. As the very term *Berufsstand* implies, German professions represented an uneasy compromise between liberal aspirations (among the free practitioners) and etatist desires for security. Like the commercial-industrial circles, the professions wanted an economy free enough to provide *carrières ouvertes aux talents*, but also regulated enough to safeguard them against the vicissitudes of the business cycle or an excess of university graduates. Hence, bourgeois definitions need to be broadened to recognize the importance of the Akademiker entrenched in government, the free professions, and even in some parts of industry and commerce through an entitlement system that assigned occupational rank according to educational achievement.[19]

The political effect of the professionalization of cultivation was the ambivalent politicization of the educated, which reflects the contradictory character of the German Empire. Echoing contemporary dissidents, critics charge that the university was one of the key "integration mechanisms" that perpetuated "social structure and societal power relationships" by "manipulative use of nationalism," while the corporations "imbued bourgeois sons with a neofeudal code of honor and behavior" and provided bureaucratic patronage. Traditionalists counter such negative functionalism: "The worst example is perhaps the educational system, because here only possibilities of authoritarian and nationalist indoctrination are emphasized in such a way that the concurrent possibilities for cultural emancipation, which liberal education necessarily created, are completely lost." The new evidence of this study indicates that both sides are only partially correct. While the university was an institution of the elite and the middle class, and thereby perpetuated the upper layers of society, it also allowed for an increasing ascent from the lower middle class and thereby broadened

---

[19] P. Stearns, "The Middle Class: Towards a Precise Definition," *CSSH* 21 (1979): 377-96, and L. O'Boyle, "The Classless Society: Comment on Stearns," ibid., pp. 397-413; J. Gillis, *The Prussian Bureaucracy in Crisis* (Stanford, 1971), and J. Kocka, *Unternehmensverwaltung und Angestelltenschaft am Beispiel Siemens 1847 bis 1914* (Stuttgart, 1969); R. G. von Westphalen, *Akademisches Privileg und demokratischer Staat* (Stuttgart, 1979), pp. 90-132; and C. E. McClelland, "Professionalization and Higher Education in Germany, 1860-1930," *Transformation of Higher Learning* (1982). See U. Haltern, "Entwicklungsprobleme der bürgerlichen Gesellschaft," *GG* 5 (1979): 274-92; and P. Lundgreen, "German Technical Associations Between Science, Industry, and the State, 1860-1914," *HSR* 13 (1980): 3-15.

its base. Whereas the Ministry of Culture saw the training of obedient bureaucrats as an essential function of higher education, and most professors considered it their duty to instill patriotism through scholarship, the differing definitions of national loyalty provided a spectrum of opinion, truncated on the left, which also offered substantial ideological variety. Although student self-education was dominated by anti-intellectual corporatism or influenced by nationalist agitation, there was a considerable countercurrent of reformism, which again offered some individual choice. Not as instruments of reaction but as an arena of conflict between old versus new students, progressive versus conservative faculty members, reformist versus nationalist associations, academics were gradually politicized in those "national" causes like Weltpolitik which were defined as apolitical. Paradoxically, Imperial German universities were both less than centers of scientific objectivity and more than training grounds for imperialist cadres. They were no longer repressive enough, as during the Carlsbad Decrees, to foster student radicalism, but despite the abolition of special jurisdiction in 1879, they were not yet free enough to imbue the majority of students with a spirit of liberty. The transition from elite to mass, from Bildung to Ausbildung, from apathy to involvement created among academic youths the same unresolved tension between freedom and order that characterized adult bourgeois politics.[20]

Foreign observers were keenly aware of the contradiction between the world leadership of German scholars and the illiberalism of German students. Though he deplored that "the city in which Fichte and Hegel lectured has become a commercial center as well as a focus of Realpolitik," the American professor C. A. Armstrong nevertheless concluded, "the German universities constitute a principal bulwark of ideal culture in our age" against the onslaught of materialism. In spite of the astounding growth of the student body, "German scholarship makes an abiding impression of depth, thoroughness, of far-reaching extent. The standards of achievement have not been lowered or altered into conformity to the 'practical' tendencies of the age. Inquiry, research, discovery, retain their central position in the scheme of university life." Although French journalists were generally less well-disposed toward la jeunesse allemande, Eduard Delage

[20] H. U. Wehler, *Das Deutsche Kaiserreich 1871-1918* (Göttingen, 1973), pp. 122-31; T. Nipperdey, "Wehlers 'Kaiserreich'," *GG* 1 (1975): 539-60; H.-G. Zmarzlik, "Das Kaiserreich in neuer Sicht?" *HZ* 222 (1976): 105-26; V. Berghahn, "Der Bericht der Preussischen Oberrechnungskammer," *GG* 2 (1976): 125-36; H. U. Wehler, "Kritik und kritische Antikritik," *HZ* 225 (1977): 347ff.; G. Eley, "Die 'Kehrites und das Kaiserreich," *GG* 4 (1978): 91-107; H.-J. Puhle, "Zur Legende von der 'Kehrschen Schule'," ibid., pp. 108-19; and T. Nipperdey, "Organisierter Kapitalismus, Verbände und die Krise des Kaiserreichs," ibid. 5 (1979): 418-33. See also F. Meyer, *Schule der Untertanen* (Hamburg, 1976), pp. 253ff.; V. Berghahn, "Politik und Gesellschaft im Wilhelminischen Deutschland," *NPL* 24 (1979): 164-95; and Blackbourn-Eley, *Mythen*, pp. 54-58, 123-29.

distinguished "early signs of the transformation" of the corporations: "Survivals of heroic times, they claim to conserve the heritage of glory and idealism. But their animating spirit has long fled. The form alone persists," for "more than the religion of the color, more than the grand recollection of the defense of the fatherland, it is the hope of a career which pushes many young Germans towards the Corps and the Burschenschaft." Attempting to do justice to the modernizing currents of the Freistudentenschaft, to the Munich bohème, and to the widespread interest in French culture, the Parisian writer pondered: "This is another Germany which prepares itself, more free and humane, as Goethe would have liked." But he hastened to add: "Will it ever replace that Gemany of today?" which was still characterized by "a narrow and aggressive patriotism." The outbreak of the war answered this question unequivocally. While A. von Harnack appealed to the common "spirit of deep religious and moral civilization" to bind Germany and America more closely together, British scholars warned that "the poison of Treitschke's teaching" created "a new barbarism" which posed "a menace to the freedom and civilization of Europe." Instead of scholarly objectivity or idealist Kultur, Russian, French, and English intellectuals suddenly discovered "the academic garrison of Germany," which preached a "cult of war and gospel of hate." Destroying the old romantic Germany of story and song, this expansionist "Prussianism" appeared not as justified patriotism but as dangerous nationalism: "German thought, German virtue, German culture must now be all as proudly and consciously German as the German army, and, like that, must be organized for victory." Sharpened by a feeling of betrayal, this polemical oversimplification of former friends nevertheless underlines the unanimity with which students and academics subordinated freedom of scholarship to the survival of their fatherland.[21]

Since professors and students in other belligerent nations also rallied around their flags, was the degree and manner of academic illiberalism unique to Germany? Because the educated shared much educational protectionism, social elitism, ritualistic classicism, as well as apolitical nationalism across frontiers, they abandoned liberalism on the continent and also liberality elsewhere. Often unduly overlooked, the most useful *tertium*

---

[21] C. A. Armstrong, "German Culture and the Universities," *Educational Review* 45 (1913): 325-38; E. Delage, "La Jeunesse universitaire en Allemagne," *Revue de Paris* 6 (1913): 610-26; A. Harnack, "Germany and the Present War," *Educational Review* 47, (1914): 325-31; W. H. C. Davis, "German University Teaching and the War," ibid., pp. 341-46; J. H. Morgan, "The Academic Garrison of Germany," ibid., pp. 347-52; "Did Nietzsche Cause the War?" ibid., pp. 353-57; "France," ibid., pp. 358-62; "Germany," ibid., pp. 363-67; and N. M. Butler, "The Great War and its Lessons," ibid., pp. 368-74. See also Jarausch, "The Universities: An American View," in *Wilhelmian Germany*.

comparationis is Austria. While the radicalism of the Viennese student legion in the 1848 revolution was perhaps even more politically important than the progressivism of German academic youth, administrative repression postponed the foundation of corporations until the Schiller centennial of 1859, when they sprang forth in a largely liberal, Burschenschaft vein. During the Wars of Unification, students in Vienna divided into grossdeutsch (Austrian) and kleindeutsch (Prussian) camps, a division that hardened over the years when the former (the Corps) supported the Hapsburg monarchy, while the latter deserted adult liberalism, flirted with anti-Semitism, and clamored for volkish unification with the Bismarckian Reich. With the rise of national consciousness in the non-German provinces of the empire, student life fragmented into a series of heated and often deadly nationalities' struggles between Germans, Slavs (Czechs), Magyars, and Italians, which culminated around the turn of the century. At the same time, the deutschnationale (and gradually all duelling) student groups excluded Jews on racial grounds (since they could not be true nationalists) and provoked anti-Semitic clashes, unparalleled in intensity after the Zionists fought back with their fists. Finally, the liberal minority also struggled against the clericalism of the majority and sought to ostracize Catholic student groups in an Austrian version of the Kulturkampf. Hence, on the Danube the German pattern was rehearsed in a more virulent, intolerant, and physically violent form, which was often imitated in the North. To a lesser degree, French and Italian students followed the same reversal from left to right, since a considerable group abandoned proverbial democratic and Socialist radicalism around the turn of the century and embraced rightist, monarchist, and even anti-Semitic (or proto-Fascist) causes.[22] However, outside of the continent there are fewer similarities. If British dons were imperialist and anti-industrial, why did they temper their snobbism with a dash of parliamentarism? If American students were rebellious and racist, why did they reject ideological polarization until the 1930s? If in Russia repressive educational policy tried to create an obedient student body, why then did a "school of dissent" foster a revolutionary tradition? The comparative perspective suggests that all Western countries shared some degree of academic illiberalism around the turn of the century but that only those that most closely approximated the German cultural, social,

[22] K. H. Jarausch, "Student Movements," *American Academic Encyclopedia* (New York, 1980); Schulze-Ssymank, *Das deutsche Studententum*, pp. 423-26; F. Gall, *Alma Mater Rudolphina 1365-1965: Die Wiener Universität und ihre Studenten* (Vienna, 1965), pp. 176-88; J. McGrath, "Student Radicalism in Vienna," *JCH* 2 (1967): 183-201; and the less than reliable L. Feuer, *The Conflict of Generations*, pp. 54ff., 88ff., 264ff., 318ff., as well as A. Esler, *Bombs, Beards and Barricades*. See also P. Stock, "Students versus the University in Pre-World War Paris," *French Historical Studies* 7 (1971): 93ff.

and political structure produced cultivated nationalism in an equally virulent form.[23]

ACADEMIC CONTINUITIES

Finally, the question of the lasting impact of university study on academics after 1918 raises the difficult issue of historical continuity. Whereas Western historians tend to stress militarism and Prussianism, Marxist scholars generally indict some kind of capitalist culprits. Typical of the more eloquent critics of the "continuity of error" is Fritz Fischer, who asserts flatly: "School, university, and church, especially the Protestant *Landeskirchen* in the Lutheran tradition with their close association of throne and altar, sanctioned this order. The core of the morality formed by them was obedience." Imbued with authoritarianism, "the Conservative or National Liberal supporters of the state preserved the memory of the rise of the empire and of their social position through the war and carried the continuity of a domestically defensive and externally expansive policy through 1930 and 1933 to 1939, thereby connecting the First to the Second World War in the consciousness of German hegemony." Against this claim of a continuity of structures, goals, and methods, Thomas Nipperdey has protested vigorously that fascism was a general European phenomenon, that capitalism did not lead to such warlike consequences elsewhere, that hypotheses hearkening back to Tacitus lack concreteness, and that "there is naturally also a countercontinuity, a continuity of the democratic, of the liberal movement." Instead, he suggests that "political culture, political behavior, and mentalities" created "collective values and dispositions" such as antiliberalism, anti-Semitism, and anti-Marxism which allowed Hitler and National Socialism "to link to these continuities and yet to transcend them." As "continuity is in truth a plurality of continuities . . . and the participants relate in different ways and degrees to them," he concludes that the past is more than prehistory. These contradictions about the contribution of cultivation to the "German catastrophe" suggest several concluding reflections: How did the imperial legacy affect the political attitude and involvement of students after 1918? What role did professors trained in the Wilhelmian period play in the Weimar Republic and the Third Reich? How did university graduates in the bureaucracy and the professions col-

[23] A. J. Engel, "Political Education in Oxford, 1823-1914," paper delivered at the Social Science Association meeting, Ann Arbor, 1977; literature cited in the provocative J. McLachlan, "The American College in the Nineteenth Century: Toward a Reappraisal," *Teachers College Record* 80 (1978): 287-306; and D. R. Brower, *Training the Nihilists: Education and Radicalism in Tsarist Russia* (Ithaca, 1975).

lectively react to the crises of defeat, inflation, consolidation, depression, and the rise of Nazism?[24]

Among students there was a remarkable but selective continuation of imperial patterns, aggravated by the tumultuous birth of the Weimar Republic. With the return of the veterans, enrollment swelled to 120,000 in 1919 and peaked at 50 percent over the 1914 figure in 1923, thus perpetuating prewar expansion. At the same time the galloping inflation and the economic crisis of the salaried middle classes depressed between one-half and three-quarters of academic youths below the subsistence minimum, and the minority of Wilhelmian Hungerstudenten became a majority. The contraction of career possibilities for university graduates caused by the shrinkage of bureaucracy, the loss of colonies, and the retrenchment of business produced a much larger academic proletariat than in the 1880s. However, the students met this heightening of prewar problems with a courageous spirit of self-help through individual work (almost half were Werkstudenten) and through collective aid (Wirtschaftshilfe), which built on the pioneering efforts of the Freistudentenschaft. After initial wavering between radical enthusiasm for the revolution (and participation in workers' and soliders' councils) or monarchical defense of law and order (in the student free corps), the veteran generation at least tolerated the republican government, while a progressive minority struggled for positive integration into the new state. The greatest achievement of this new solidarity was the creation of the Deutsche Studentenschaft, a formally recognized student self-government uniting local councils (AStAs) into one national association for which reformers had struggled for three-quarters of a century. However, after the symbolic humiliation of Versailles, nationalist instincts reasserted themselves over democratic currents and the longing for community (Volksgemeinschaft), bridging the gap between students and workers, produced a sharp turn to the right. Rejecting the neutrality of the DSt, the growing volkish movement, in the tradition of the chauvinist VdH of 1905, founded a propagandist Hochschul-Ring which was both grossdeutsch (including Austrians) and anti-Semitic. Hence, the "great possibilities" of a revolutionary and parliamentary rebirth passed with the graduation of the veterans, and despite the efforts of republican, Socialist, and Catholic groups, German students, having outgrown Wilhelmian monarchism, embraced the volkish idea of the former rightist fringe as credo of the future. Although the ideological impact of the First World War and

---

[24] F. Fischer, "Der Stellenwert des Ersten Weltkriegs in der Kontinuitätsproblematik der deutschen Geschichte," *HZ* 229 (1979): 25-53; T. Nipperdey, "1933 und die Kontinuität der deutschen Geschichte," ibid. 227 (1978): 86-111; and the literature cited in K. H. Jarausch, "From Second to Third Reich: The Problem of Continuity in German Foreign Policy," *CEH* 12 (1979): 68-82. For a not untypical individual example, see H. Lange, "Julius Curtius: Aspekte einer Politikerbiographie" (dissertation, Kiel, 1970).

the national shame of the defeat had much to do with the squandering of this progressive opportunity, the social legacy (elitist aspirations versus proletarian reality) and political traditions (both nationalist and volkish) of the empire contributed significantly to this reversion to a new form of the past.[25]

For professors and bureaucrats, elements of personal and ideological continuity from the imperial university similarly complicated the adjustment to the Weimar Republic. Since the new state appeared as "rescue anchor" in the revolutionary chaos, university teachers in loyalty declarations "resolutely supported the new political order from which they expected the firm and united leadership of a free people." But with the dictated peace the old conflict between annexationists and moderates erupted anew in the summer of 1919, when the former circulated a deutschnationale "Declaration of Professors [Opposing] the Extradition" of William II, signed by 300 monarchists, typical of the older generation. After the abortive Kapp Putsch, a group of progressive instructors sponsored a "Statement of Professors Loyal to the Constitution," which declared its allegiance to Weimar "without reservations and hesitations." The Wilhelmian political spectrum reemerged, although somewhat shifted to the left. A few dozen Socialists and several hundred democrats constituted a small minority among the German faculty. The great majority of academics in the early twenties were "politically indifferent" and belonged to the "party of those without party," but the self-styled spokesmen of the professoriate were outspokenly antidemocratic, and a few joined the volkish right. Typically, those professors indifferent or opposed to the republic used the legacy of academic freedom to resist the democratizing efforts of the Weimar coalition. Although more directly dependent upon political parties, the structure and outlook of the largest group of graduates, higher public officials, also showed a considerable degree of continuity with the empire. "Even the most conservative bureaucrats accept the new facts and remain in office, rule, speak, and act completely in the old style," Ernst Troeltsch observed in 1919. Since only about 10 percent of the higher political officials voluntarily resigned, the efforts of the Weimar government to purge administration made more headway at the top than on the bottom, and only after the appointment of Carl Severing did public service slowly begin to reflect the new regime. Hence, public officials divided themselves into a minority of republicans, a passively tolerant majority

---

[25] J. Schwarz, *Studenten in der Weimarer Republik*, especially pp. 415ff.; T. Nipperdey, "Die deutsche Studentenschaft in den ersten Jahren der Weimarer Republik," in H. Grimm, ed., *Kulturverwaltung der Zwanziger Jahre* (Stuttgart, 1961), pp. 19-38; M. Franze, *Die Erlanger Studentenschaft 1918-1945* (Würzburg, 1972), pp. 19-94; and W. Kreutzberger, *Studenten und Politik 1918-1933: Der Fall Freiburg im Breisgau* (Göttingen, 1972), pp. 75-143. By reducing the developments of the empire to "background," these studies do not sufficiently appreciate the degree of continuity.

with "a peculiarly split understanding of duty," which discriminated between allegiance to the state and reservations about the constitution, and a considerable group of conservatives. Like lawyers and doctors, Gymnasium teachers were skeptical of the republic and only traditionally discontented groups such as public-school teachers mustered more enthusiasm for the national liberalism of the DVP. The reaction of adult academics to the political upheavals and socioeconomic problems of the Weimar Republic was therefore largely conditioned by the values acquired in home, school, and university during the empire.[26]

During the consolidation of the republic between 1924 and 1929, the improving economy and stabilizing polity began to overshadow the legacy of illiberalism. Student enrollment receded toward prewar levels (under 100,000), easing the unemployment crisis and restoring the Wilhelmian recruitment pattern (with over two-fifths drawn from the educated or propertied middle class, about one-third from the new middle class, and one-quarter from the old middle class). In the less turbulent campus atmosphere, corporate life reasserted its former dominance, including over one-half of the students at middling universities (in contrast to large urban institutions) with the duelling corporations maintaining their earlier 40 percent share and Catholic groups plateauing at less than one-third. During this Indian summer of corporatism, the ideological struggle between the prorepublican minority, the conservative middle (Corps, Catholic, and Protestant corporations), the nationalist propagandists (Burschenschaft, LC, and VC), and the volkish extremists (VDSt and National Socialist Student League) kept academic youth polarized, sometimes against its own will. The radical nationalists' capture of the national student association in 1924 led to a clash with the democratic Prussian Minister of Culture Carl Becker, who in 1927 withdrew official recognition and financial support from the DSt, because it departed from German citizenship requirements by including Austrians but excluding Jews.[27] For professors, the relaxation of initial Weimar tensions meant a return to research and teaching, albeit under

[26] H. P. Bleuel, *Deutschlands Bekenner* (Bern, 1968), pp. 94-124 (somewhat oversimplifying); F. K. Ringer, *German Mandarins*, pp. 200ff.; H. Döring, "Deutsche Professoren zwischen Kaiserreich und Drittem Reich," *NPL* 19 (1974): 340-52 and *Der Weimarer Kreis: Studien zum politischen Bewusstsein verfassungstreuer Hochschullehrer in der Weimarer Republik* (Meisenheim, 1974), pp. 57-76; W. Runge, *Politik und Beamtentum im Parteienstaat* (Stuttgart, 1965), pp. 16ff., 100ff.; and R. Bölling, *Volksschullehrer und Politik: Der Deutsche Lehrerverein* (Göttingen, 1978). Obviously these concluding reflections cannot do justice to the full complexity of Weimar developments, but they are intended to add some concreteness to the rather general debate about continuity and higher education.

[27] Franze, *Erlanger Studentenschaft*, pp. 85-102; W. Zorn, "Die politische Entwicklung des deutschen Studententums 1918-1931," in *Darstellungen und Quellen zur Geschichte der deutschen Einheitsbewegung im 19. und 20. Jahrhundert* (Heidelberg, 1965), 5: 223-307; and M. S. Steinberg, *Sabers and Brown Shirts: The German Students' Path Towards National Socialism, 1918-1935* (Chicago, 1977), pp. 21-71 with somewhat questionable figures. See also Kreutzberger, *Student und Politik*, pp. 145-80.

somewhat reduced circumstances. Organized into the Hochschulverband, universities proved quite resistant to the modest reforms in self-government and instruction proposed by C. H. Becker. While pacifist and Socialist academics remained a tiny minority, the Weimarer Kreis of moderate Vernunftrepublikaner gained some ground (representing about 169 sympathizers); but the stronger nationalist (DNVP) circles (with as many as 416 supporters) continued to propagate rightist causes. "The broad mass" of the educated in the middle "leans instinctively toward the right, does not love today's state, while not exactly despising it, and tries to justify the cool relationship through eager criticism of its shortcomings." Lectures during "Constitution Day" at Marburg indicate that professors clung to the leadership claim of the university, propagated academic "neutrality," and gradually began to live with the new system in spite of inner resentment. This limited national-liberal resurgence and a much smaller involvement in the volkish fringe set adult academics in university, government, and free professions apart from the students. Sparked by the progressive countertradition, the partial consolidation of the prorepublican or at least statist forces during normalization found its limits for the older generation in the traditions that academics had absorbed in the Second Reich.[28]

The students' embrace of National Socialism during the crisis of the republic demonstrates both the persistence of imperial nationalism and its transcendence by the new volkish right. As a result of the Great Depression enrollments once again mushroomed to over 133,000 by 1930-31, drawing even more new-middle-class (37 percent), old-middle-class (22 percent), and working-class (2 percent) students into the universities, contributing to a swelling mass of unemployed academics (estimated at about 40,000 by 1933). Since the Weimar government showed little sympathy for the renewed hunger, lack of housing, and health problems of educated youth and counselled redoubled dedication to Wissenschaft in the face of a struggle for survival, German students were plunged into a profound crisis of consciousness. Is it simple coincidence that the National Socialist Student League suddenly sprang into life during the second half of the twenties with a radical German-Socialist program, calling for immediate physical and psychological relief? Under the respectable leadership of Baldur von Schirach the NSDStB appealed to the traditional corporations, who either

---

[28] Note 27 and Döring, *Weimarer Kreis*, pp. 124ff.; H. Seier, "Radikalisierung und Reform als Probleme der Universität Marburg 1918-1933," in W. Heinemeyer, ed., *Academia Marburgensis: Beiträge zur Geschichte der Philipps-Universität Marburg* (Marburg, 1977), pp. 303-54; and, more superficially, W. Laqueur, *Weimar: A Cultural History*, pp. 183-223. See also K. Düwell, "Staat und Wissenschaft in der Weimarer Epoche," *HZ, Beiheft 1* (1971): 31-74; and P. Forman, "The *Naturforscherversammlung* in Nauheim, September 1920: An Introduction to Scientific Life in the Weimar Republic" (unpublished paper, Washington, 1980).

joined as individuals or entered electoral alliances, which led to the capture of the AStAs at Erlangen and Greifswald during 1929-30.[29] As a result of snowballing student council victories, the Nazi Student League won the chairmanship of the DSt at the Fourteenth Deutsche Studententag in 1931, thereby symbolically "conquering the Hochschulen" two years before the political *Machtergreifung*. Was this "landmark of German history" primarily due to novel factors or an older legacy? Hitler's rhetorical appeals to generational resentment could build upon a tradition of rightist rebellion since the empire. The agitation and intimidation of the NSDStB "counterfraternity" improved on earlier VDSt methods, and the ideology of the new fascism exaggerated the older national socialism in an uncompromising cult of violence, learned in the steel-storms (*Stahlgewitter*) of the Great War. Equally important was the renewal and surpassing of the triple social crisis of the Second Reich with its institutional overcrowding, influx of the masses, and academic unemployment, which increased the tension between elitist aspirations and proletarianized reality. Finally, in its postwar volkish form, the imperial nationalist heritage was too powerful for republican or Catholic countercurrents. Hence, the Nazi victory in the student body represented the culmination of older problems and attitudes, exacerbated by Weimar circumstances, which at the same time transformed them into something new and more potent. Ironically, in 1935 the NSDStB swallowed those nationalist fraternities that had helped them to power and propagandistically completed their hold upon all German students, although their domination was sometimes more verbal than real.[30]

"Since most university teachers generally lived according to the values prevailing before 1914," the connection between the rise of the Nazis and the German professoriate is more indirect. Although many instructors were developing democratic loyalty, the crisis years around 1930 reinforced

---

[29] *Deutsche Hochschulstatistik*, 1928-1933, edited by the Hochschulverwaltungen; M. Kater, *Studentenschaft und Rechtsradikalismus in Deutschland, 1918-1933* (Hamburg, 1975), pp. 43ff.; and "Der NS-Studentenbund von 1926 bis 1928," *VJHfZG* 22 (1974): 148-90; A. Faust, *Der nationalsozialistische Deutsche Studentenbund: Studenten und Nationalsozialismus in der Weimarer Republik* (Düsseldorf, 1973), 2: 17ff., 121ff.; P. Spitznagel, "Studentenschaft und Nationalsozialismus in Würzburg, 1927-1933," (DGfH paper, Würzburg, 1975); M. Franze, *Erlanger Studentenschaft*, pp. 101-74; and W. Kotschnig, *Unemployment in the Learned Professions* (London, 1937).

[30] R. Koshar, "Two 'Nazisms': The Social Context of Nazi Mobilization in Marburg and Tübingen," *Social History* 7 (1982): 27-42; P. Loewenberg, "The Psychohistorical Origins of the Nazi Youth Cohort," *AHR* 75 (1971): 1457-1502; and P. Merkl, *Political Violence under the Swastika* (Princeton, 1975); Steinberg, *Sabers and Brown Shirts*, pp. 104-21; Kater, *Studentenschaft und Rechtsradikalismus*, pp. 197-205; Faust, *NSDStB*, 2: 136ff.; and G. Giles, "Der NS Studentenbund und der Geist der studentischen Korporationen" (DGfH paper, Würzburg, 1975). For the contribution of professorial teaching, see also Kreutzberger, *Studenten*, pp. 176-80. Figures from H. Kaelble, "Social Mobility in Germany, 1900-1960," *JMH* 50 (1978): 439-61.

academic preferences for an authoritarian strengthening of the constitution in a bureaucratic-military-clerical direction short of Nazism. Among the established professors, at best a dozen were open Hitler partisans, while the younger group of beginning scholars was more sympathetic to his promises. Nevertheless, the responsibility of the German professoriate lies not in active pro-Nazi involvement but rather in ideological congruity (anti-Semitism, nationalism, militarism) with some of the party's aims and in undermining the republic by supporting a neoconservative alternative. Although disagreeing with the brutal methods of the NSDStB, many adult academics welcomed the national revolution in the somewhat myopic hope that the Third Reich would reaffirm the virtues of the Second and thereby restore professors to their former leadership of public opinion. "Hearken German people! This is the time, in the morning dew of the Third Reich, when the thousand-year-old tree of German longing is bearing fruit which must be harvested," the Erlangen rector welcomed students to the fall semester of 1933: "In our deepest need, a national hero has arisen. Let us rally around him and throw off everything un-German, especially divisiveness, then victory shall be ours." The educated officials showed a similar mixture of traditionalist self-deception and ideological sympathy, which underestimated the irrational and antibureaucratic dynamism of the Hitler movement. Because republican retrenchment measures threatened social degradation, many bureaucrats abandoned their apolitical etatism and a considerable number joined the party before 1933, when bourgeois alternatives collapsed. Despite some suspicion of the plebeian radicalism of the SA, Nazi promises of the "restoration of professional public service" were persuasive because of resentment against the instrumentalization of the bureaucracy in contrast to an idealized recollection of the cultivated notable system of the empire. Especially the younger generation responded to volkish appeals to self-interest, for the Nazis resolutely cut enrollment in higher education and, by purging government service of Jews and leftists, solved the crisis of the academic professionals by restoring demand. Although Wilhelmian traditions immunized some university graduates, many adult academics silenced their doubts about uncouth Storm Trooper methods in order to share in the feeling of regeneration of the national revolution.[31]

---

[31] U. D. Adam, *Hochschule und Nationalsozialismus: Die Universität Tübingen im Dritten Reich* (Tübingen, 1977), pp. 6ff.; Seier, "Radikalisierung und Reform," pp. 338f.; Bleuel, *Deutschlands Bekenner*, pp. 225f.; Döring, *Weimarer Kreis*, pp. 255ff.; Franze, *Erlanger Studentenschaft*, pp. 175f.; Ringer, *German Mandarins*, pp. 435ff.; H. Mommsen, *Beamtentum im Dritten Reich* (Stuttgart, 1966), pp. 20ff.; L. Jones, " 'The Dying Middle': Weimar Germany and the Fragmentation of Bourgeois Politics," *CEH* 5 (1972): 23-54; and the essays in M. Heinemann, ed., *Erziehung und Schulung im Dritten Reich* (Stuttgart, 1980), vol. 2.

ALTHOUGH National Socialism "cannot credibly be seen as the outcome of some autonomous evolution of the inherent weakness of German culture," the example of students, society, and politics suggests that the German problem had an important academic dimension. "There is a conception of liberty that holds that a man can be free only where an experimental attitude to knowledge, the competition of social forces, and liberal political institutions are combined," Dahrendorf argued in his brilliant self-indictment. "This conception has never really gained a hold in Germany. Why not? That is the German question." One does not need to share his exaggerated esteem for Anglo-American liberality in order to ask: Did cultivation contribute to inequality, an avoidance of conflict, the cartelization of elites and to privatism? Or was it its victim? In his authoritative comparison of American, English, and Central European universities, Abraham Flexner could still write in 1930: "Of the countries dealt with in this volume, Germany has in theory and in practice come nearest to giving higher education its due position." Half a generation later Fredric Lilge was forced to ponder "the reasons for the catastrophe of German intellectual culture" and denounced the political "failure of the German university" as "the abuse of learning." After the collapse, German traditionalists, clinging to the "old Humboldtian ideal of free, manifold, and self-acquired . . . Bildung," blamed the uncultured Nazi hordes. But progressives decried "the failure of critical spirit" and concluded: "Through their attitude during the Weimar Republic, German professors became the midwives of the Third Reich."[32] On balance, students, by voting for the NSDStB (about half of the ballots in at least half of the universities), must bear the most direct responsibility for succumbing to the appeals of National Socialism. Professors have to share a more indirect blame for failing to embrace the republic and for perpetuating antidemocratic thought in the younger generation. Academics in official or professional careers similarly deserted the republic during its critical years and looked at least to a neoconservative authoritarian alternative before the younger ones especially flocked to Hitler's cause. The political failure of the cultivated was clearly no better or worse than the shortsightedness of business or military elites, but the claim of educated leadership renders it particularly galling. Much of this disgrace of the Bildungsbürgertum resulted from the cultural, social, economic, and political upheavals of the Great War and the tumultuous 1920s. Falling back on

---

[32] D. Calleo, *The German Problem Reconsidered: Germany and the World Order, 1870 to the Present* (Cambridge, 1978), pp. 123-59; R. Dahrendorf, *Society and Democracy in Germany*, pp. 3-16; R. Ulich, ed., *Abraham Flexner's Universities: American, English, German* (New York, 1967), pp. 271-318; Frederic Lilge, *The Abuse of Learning* (New York, 1948); G. Ritter, *Die Krisis des deutschen Universitätswesens* (Tübingen, 1960), pp. 9ff.; Bleuel, *Deutschlands Bekenner*, pp. 7f.; and Krause, *Burschenherrlichkeit*, pp. 178-83.

those ritualized, elitist, and nationalist values they had received in the imperial university, many Gebildete forged ahead into a more modern and contradictory National Socialism. Almost no professors, a few students, and somewhat more officials were propelled by their neohumanist ethos into the resistance.[33]

World-renowned for their scholarship and professional training, Imperial German universities functioned, in Karl Jaspers's phrase, only imperfectly as "the intellectual conscience of their era." In Wilhelmian terms, neo-humanist liberal education was a modest success in providing a passing acquaintance with the classics, an awareness of social responsibility, and an intense patriotism. But in a larger, more critical sense, Bildung failed to prepare the educated for the challenge of cultural modernity, class warfare, and political democratization. Hence, German academics gravitated to illiberalism not merely because of contemporary pressures, but also because of the erosion and transformation of the Humboldtian legacy. Although not free of ambiguities and institutionalized restrictively, the reform heritage of allgemeine Menschenbildung contained critical, egalitarian, and liberal imperatives. In principle, the Humboldtian challenge to "consider Wissenschaft as something not yet entirely grasped and never to be completely found but to be searched for unceasingly" recognized no limitations on the pursuit of pure truth. "The advancement of that development of human powers, equally necessary for all estates," contained a fundamental commitment to educational equality, "since man is only a good artisan, merchant, soldier, and businessman if, without regard for his specific profession, he is a good, decent, and, according to his calling, enlightened human being and citizen." Moreover, the stress on "loneliness and freedom [as] the dominant principles" of pure scholarship as well as repeated references to "liberality" and warnings to the state that "matters would go infinitely better without it" indicate a deep belief in human liberty in the political as well as the spiritual realm. But by the late nineteenth century this cultivation liberalism had eroded into positivism, elitism, and illiberalism, and the connection between science, professional training, and cultivation had broken down, so university study no longer provided an ethical compass for action. In a postliberal age, the

[33] E. Y. Hartshorne, *The German Universities and National Socialism* (Cambridge, 1937), pp. 165-74: "And least forgivable of all, they have submerged all the fine, free play of the human intellect under the dull, stupefying vapor of ideological conformity." M. Heidegger, *Die Selbstbehauptung der deutschen Universität* (Breslau, 1933); E. Krieck, *Die Erneuerung der deutschen Universität* (Marburg, 1933); essays by H. Kuhn, W. Kunkel, O. Roegele, and F. Leist, in *Die deutsche Universität im Dritten Reich* (Munich, 1966); and P. Hoffmann, *Widerstand, Staatsstreich, Attentat*, 3rd ed. (Munich, 1979), pp. 27, 41. See also M. Kater, "Die nationalsozialistische Machtergreifung an den deutschen Hochschulen," in H. J. Vogel, ed., *Die Freiheit des Anderen* (Baden-Baden, 1981), pp. 49-75.

necessary link between cultural, social, and political liberty and academic freedom was no longer clearly understood. As a particularly compelling formulation of the general Western conception of liberal education, the original neohumanist ideal of cultivation provides an inspiring example of the creative tension between personal and public emancipation.[34] But the Imperial German experience cautions that the humaneness of humanism in higher education should not be taken for granted, that equality in the pursuit of knowledge can insidiously justify privilege, and that the relationship beween liberal education and freedom needs to be rethought by every generation.

[34] Karl Jaspers, *The Idea of the University* (Boston, 1959), p. 121; Wilhelm von Humboldt, "Über die innere und äussere Organisation der höheren wissenschaftlichen Anstalten in Berlin," in B. Gebhardt, ed., *Wilhelm von Humboldts Gesammelte Schriften* (Berlin, 1903), 10: 250-60, as well as "Bericht der Sektion des Kultus und Unterrichts," ibid., pp. 199-224. See Paul R. Sweet, *Wilhelm von Humboldt* (Columbus, Ohio, 1978-80), 2 vols. For contemporary support of the normative impact of schooling see also H. H. Hyman and C. R. Wright, *Education's Lasting Influence on Values* (Chicago, 1979), pp. 60-67.

A Note on Sources

BECAUSE of the prolificacy of German academics, documentation on students in the Second Empire is abundant. As in turn-of-the-century photographs, some areas are, however, overexposed, while others remain shadowy and obscure. The Second World War destroyed many depositories and fragmented others. Moreover, the transient nature of student life inhibited consistent record keeping, thereby biasing written remains in favor of adult university authorities or stable youthful organizations. Hence, the majority of students at any given time is likely to remain mute. The key problem is, therefore, analytical control over the partial dearth and partial excess of material.

One often neglected but crucial unpublished source is the archive of the Imperial Chancellery in Potsdam (now partially available on microfilm in Coblenz). Although cultural affairs were technically none of the imperial government's business, the most important political issues nevertheless involved the chancellor. Hence, the volumes on general education policy, on the reforms of 1890 and 1900, on university questions, and on professors offer interesting insights into the philosophy and actions of Bismarck and his successors.

More immediately obvious as documentation are the papers of the Prussian Ministry of Culture (in the Merseburg Archives), since for reasons of cohesion this study is limited to the largest state of the empire. Although the ministry usually let individual institutions handle their own student affairs, issues of general policy were decided in Berlin, and particularly important local crises also attracted the attention of the central bureaucracy. The holdings are rich for rules and regulations, for criteria for admission, for academic standards, for student social mores, for student organizations, for political clashes, and for particular institutions like Berlin and Bonn. The perspective of these administrative orders, discussions, letters, and newspaper clippings is, however, from the top down, and students are treated as policy objects rather than as subjects in their own right. The extensive papers of Friedrich Althoff and the smaller Nachlässe of Bosse, Falk, Schmidt-Ott, and Studt round out the official picture and contribute a personal note to government proceedings. The reports of the sessions of the Prussian cabinet (Ministry of State protocols) illuminate the process of formal decision making, while the files of the Civil Cabinet record the Kaiser's personal initiatives and reactions to ministerial proposals.

Considerably closer to students is the material in the university archives, some of which are important and active depositories, while others, as neglected stepchildren of university libraries, are disorganized and largely inaccessible. The bombing of the Second World War unfortunately destroyed all but one excellent set of student organizational records at the Humboldt-Universität in East Berlin. Documentary survival was somewhat better, but still spotty, at the Rheinische Friedrich-Wilhelms-Universität at Bonn. The handwritten matriculation register (in two versions) is an important source for the social composition of the student body. The remains of the *Rektorat* offer clues to faculty opinion (in the senate protocols), local implementation of rules and regulations, and other academic matters. The papers of the university curator contain correspondence with Berlin and the professoriate, for he was supposed to mediate, and the few faculty records reflect corporate self-government. The documents of the archive of the Philipps-Universität Marburg, housed in the Hessische Staatsarchiv, are similarly broad and incomplete. However, they do provide another matriculation register with semester reports of student associations (which form the basis of the sociology of corporations), an interesting set of organization files, and some other evidence on general university policy toward academic youth. Some splinters from Erlangen, Giessen, and Göttingen were also consulted. On the whole, university archives present the professorial point of view rather than student concerns (since those were not deemed important enough to be preserved unless they came into conflict with authorities), but the close local interaction with their clientele made faculties often more responsive than the central administration.

Most directly relevant were the records of student corporations, unfortunately still largely in private hands, which renders access difficult. The somewhat disorganized core of the Freistudentenschaft papers is in the Federal Archives in Coblenz among the files of the Deutsche Studentenschaft. The Bundesarchiv also holds a fragment of the VDSt papers (which largely perished in World War II) and of the Schwarzburgbund archives. The branch office of the Federal Archives in Frankfurt contains the central records of the Deutsche Burschenschaft as well as a few papers of its ADB reform offshoot. Most useful were the protocols of the annual Eisenach conventions (especially for the spread of anti-Semitism), the alterations in statutes, the business correspondence of the presidium, and a full set of the *Burschenschaftliche Bücherei*. Because of their disappointing preoccupation with quarrels between chapters, evaluations of the Mensur, questions of form and precedence, the Corps archives in Würzburg (in the IHK) were only consulted for the newspaper clipping collection of the student historian Oskar Scheuer. In general, the interpretational value of these corporation archives was somewhat lower than expected.

To a considerable degree, the lacunae in the archival material were filled by an equally massive but uneven set of published sources. The present home of the *Hochschulkunde* and *Studentengeschichte* collection (started during the Weimar Republic by Paul Ssymank at the Georg-August-Universität Göttingen) is the Institut für Hochschulkunde at the Universität Würzburg, which is a veritable treasure trove of material on university history. Its *Bestände der Bibliothek* (published irregularly but continually) is a catalogue of its holdings, subdivided into background literature (A), academic journals (B), general university matters (C), individual institutions of higher learning (D), and problems, reforms, or studies (E). Particularly valuable are the headings in general history (F), which begin in the Middle Ages, go up to the present, and cover almost every imaginable topic from student letters through self-government and moral behavior in pamphlets, broadsides, brochures, tracts, books, and monographs. Similarly useful is the final division on student associations (G) which, beginning with Studentische Orden, has presently progressed to the Deutsche Sängerschaft, although the collection also includes materials on groups or societies not yet catalogued. As many of these ephemeral writings were produced by students themselves, their liveliness and disagreement compensate for the opaqueness of national corporation records, although here, too, the selection is weighted heavily in favor of continuing corporations and against loosely organized reform groups or unaffiliated individuals.

Much of what is missing in the IHK can be found in the collections of university libraries. Since in the empire it was the central depository for *Universitätsschriften*, the Bibliothek der Humboldt-Universität in East Berlin still has the best holdings of contemporary writings on university affairs and on student pamphlets. Moreover, the HUB has an almost complete set of Festreden delivered in the nineteenth century and unbroken runs of the *Universitäts-Chronik* (reporting since 1887 on its officers, faculty, employees, students, degrees, donations, scholarships, institutes, ministerial directives, and festivities), of the *Vorlesungsverzeichnis* (listing professors with their lectures for all faculties), and of the official *Personalverzeichnis* (indicating both faculty and students in residence). Similar, but regionally slightly different, collections of student titles are in the Giessen University library and in the library of the Bonn University archive. Although the old catalogue of the Deutsche Staatsbibliothek still presents the most impressive listing of university literature, wartime destruction and postwar division have left only about one-tenth of the material unscathed in East Berlin and a considerably larger (partly uncatalogued and by no means complete) portion in West Berlin.

Among those printed records most widely available, the journals of the student associations (hardly any of which seem to survive in North American libraries) are the most important. Although financially supported and thereby controlled by adult alumni, most of them were edited by youthful academics, and students contributed a considerable proportion of the articles. Since the actives protested vociferously in letters to the editor and on occasion forced the resignation of adult *Herausgeber*, these publications can be assumed to reflect the feelings of at least part of the organized students reasonably accurately. Widely varying in quality and interest between mere newsletters and polished journals, these *Zeitschriften* also molded student opinion with their editorial line. Although it is impossible to cover all the individual organs (and some like the Landsmannschaft *L. C. Zeitung* were simply too uninteresting), it is important to include as much of the full range of views as possible. The *Academia* (CV), *Akademische Blätter* (VDSt), *Akademische Monatshefte* (KSC), *Akademische Monatsblätter* (KV), *Akademische Turner Zeitung* (VC), *Burschenschaftliche Blätter* (DC), *Finkenblätter* (Freistudentenschaft with varying successors such as the *Akademische Rundschau*), *K. C. Blätter* (Jewish), *Rheinische Hochschul-Zeitung* (Bonn-Cologne-Aachen Freistudentenschaft), *Sozialistische Akademiker* and *Wingolfsblätter* are the leading journals of the major associations, which might also be complemented by P. Salvisberg's *Hochschulnachrichten* (more or less neutral). Significant for the quantitative discussion of the transformation of higher learning are also the statistical series of various governments, especially of the empire (for the *Volkszählungen* of 1882, 1895, and 1907) and the *Preussische Statistik*'s volumes on universities, 102-236. Finally, the best source for public views on student questions are the stenographic reports of the debates of the Prussian lower house (Landtag) during the discussion of the budget of the Ministry of Culture in March of each year or on the occasion of particularly startling disturbances (volumes 274-614).

As a full bibliographical listing of all primary and secondary literature would require a short volume of its own, this note can only conclude by pointing to some of the basic bibliographies in the field. Still fundamental for contemporary literature is the authoritative compilation by W. Erman and E. Horn, *Bibliographie der deutschen Universitäten* (Leipzig, 1904-05, reprinted in Hildesheim, 1960), 3 vols., and continued by O. E. Ebert and O. Scheuer, *Bibliographisches Jahrbuch für deutsches Hochschulwesen* (Vienna, 1912). Newer works are discussed by L. Petry in "Deutsche Forschungen nach dem Zweiten Weltkrieg zur Geschichte der Universitäten," *Vierteljahrschrift für Sozial- und Wirtschaftsgeschichte* 46 (1959): 145-203; G. Steiger and M. Straube, "Forschungen und Publikationen seit 1945 zur Geschichte der deutschen Universitäten und

Hochschulen auf dem Territorium der DDR," *Zeitschrift für Geschichtswissenschaft* (Sonderheft 1960), pp. 563-99, updated by W. Fläschendräger and M. Straube, *Die Entwicklung der Universitäten, Hochschulen und Akademien* . . . (Berlin, 1970); E. Hassinger, ed., *Bibliographie zur Universitätsgeschichte: Verzeichnis der im Gebiet der Bundesrepublik Deutschland 1945-1971 veröffentlichten Literatur* (Munich, 1975); and J. M. Fletcher, ed., *The History of European Universities* (Leeds, 1978), vols. 1ff. on work in progress. Because standard references like the Dahlmann-Waitz or the Gebhardt are not particularly instructive, the reader might also want to consult John C. Fout, *German History and Civilization 1806-1914: A Bibliography of Scholarly Periodical Literature* (Metuchen, N.J., 1974); H.-U. Wehler, *Bibliographie zur modernen deutschen Sozialgeschichte* (Göttingen, 1976); or H. Aubin and W. Zorn, eds., *Handbuch der deutschen Wirtschafts- und Sozialgeschichte* (Stuttgart, 1976), vol. 2. The most comprehensive introduction to the older student writings is still the "Schrifttum zum zweiten Teil" section of F. Schulze and P. Ssymank, *Das deutsche Studententum von den ältesten Zeiten bis zur Gegenwart* (Munich, 1932), while the current scholarly literature is cited throughout the footnotes of the present volume.

Index

Aachen, 368, 370

Abitur, 30, 85; high school graduate (*Abiturient*), 35, 36, 38, 41, 74, 91, 104, 108, 320; requirement of, 62, 72, 75, 135, 139, 141, 144, 147, 154; symbolic value of, 76, 88, 185; modern high schools, 100-09; female high schools, 110-13; during wartime (*Notabitur*), 398. *See also* admissions

Academia, 64, 429

academic discipline, 267, 276, 338, 350; campaign for reform of, 283, 336-41; *Vorschriften für die Studierenden*, 285, 338-39; persecution of socialist students, 340-41, 357, 359-60, 389; use against Catholic baiting, 369-78. *See also* academic justice

academic freedom, 7, 49, 161, 162, 177, 186, 211, 230, 425; of living, 19, 235, 240; of learning and teaching, 20, 169-70, 237, 239; limitations on, 170, 171, 173-74, 241, 408; practice of, 170-72, 232-33, 244, 418; debate about, 240-41, 372-73; student protests about, 264, 280; anti-Catholic struggle over, 369-78. *See also* student freedom

academic justice, 263; use as discipline, 267, 276, 284; abolition of separate jurisdiction, 336-39. *See also* academic discipline

academic proletariat, v, 20, 24, 33n, 57, 60, 69-70, 159, 358-59, 390, 402, 406, 417

academic standards, 51, 67, 76, 129, 148

academic unemployment, 54, 57, 63, 77, 420, 421

ADB, 252-53, 289, 292, 306, 326, 331, 381, 427. *See also* Reformburschenschaft

ADC, *see* DC

admissions, 29-30, 51, 68, 134, 185; of modern high school graduates, 36-37, 48, 63, 100-09; of women, 37-38, 48, 102, 110-13; of foreigners, 66-67. *See also Abitur*

agriculture, 116-18, 119, 151

agronomy, 47, 57, 150

Akademiker, 82-83, 103, 181, 400-04; elitism of, v, 6, 8, 20, 33, 43, 78-79, 131, 212, 262, 403; political reversal of, vi, 12, 188, 358-59, 400-04; leadership role, 5, 8, 115-16, 343; national mission, 6, 7, 8, 69, 160, 187, 388, 404, 409; collective mentality, 17, 19, 238, 246; stratification of, 42-43, 72, 78-79, 133, 157-59, 403; ambivalence about modernity, 77, 103, 410-12; self-recruitment of, 79, 80, 119, 151, 155; deliberalization of, 209, 292-93, 400-04; international education of, 225-28. *See also Bildungsbürgertum*; graduates of the university

Akademische Blätter, 364, 429

Akademische Freischar, 289, 402

Akademische Gesangvereine, 261

Akademische Lesehalle, 347-52, 359, 379, 384, 387

Akademische Monatsblätter, 429

Akademische Monatshefte, 102, 323, 385, 429

Akademischer Bismarkbund, 279, 302, 378, 379, 402

Akademischer Bund Ethos, 243

Akademischer Dürerbund, 290

Akademischer Freibund, 331

Akademischer Hilfsbund, 398

Akademischer Turnerbund (ATB), 291, 299, 302, 307, 327

Akademischer Turnverein (ATV), 349, 351, 352, 365, 381

Akademische Rundschau, 283, 429
Akademische Turnerzeitung, 365, 385, 429
Akademische Zeitung, 263
Akademisch-Liberaler Verein, 331, 350, 402
Alldeutsche Blätter, 51, 292
Alldeutscher Verband (ADV), 65, 235, 365, 366. *See also* Pan-German League
Allgemeiner Landsmannschaftsverband, 253
Allgemeiner Studentenausschuss (AStA), 380, 421. *See also* student councils
Alte Herren, 249, 252, 304, 322, 323, 329, 385. *See also* Old Boys
Altenstein, Hans von Stein zu, 165
Althoff, Friedrich, 33, 40, 41, 57, 173, 232, 244, 426; political views, 66, 368, 371-74; secondary school reform, 108, 112, 113; Althoff system, 171, 341, 373, 387. *See also* Ministry of Culture
Anderson, C. Arnold, 26
Anschütz, Gerhard, 192
anti-Polish policy, 173-74, 221
anti-Semitism, 5, 6, 67, 69, 100, 181, 206, 236, 346, 358, 415, 417; cultural, 211, 265, 292; among students, 264, 265, 267-68, 270, 351-56; among adults, 265, 353-56; resistance to, 266, 271-74, 276, 286, 351; racist, 360, 365, 386. *See also* Verein Deutscher Studenten
Armstrong, C. A., 413
Arnim-Züsedom, Karl von, 66
Arnold, Matthew, 232
Arnstädter Verband Mathematischer und Naturwissenschaftlicher Vereine, 259, 302
Arons, Leo, 172, 173. *See also* lex Arons
Ascher, liberal student, 349
Assessoren, 62, 142. *See also* law faculty; lawyers
Association Against the Abuse of Spirits, 243. *See also* Bund Abstinenter Studenten
Aubin, Hermann, 430
Auguste Victoria, Empress, 113
Auslandshochschule, 223, 224
Austrian students, 368, 415, 417, 419

Baden, 119, 130
Badeni, Caspar, 364

Baecker, Paul, 358
Bardeleben, Heinrich von, 177
Barkhausen, G., 368, 369, 371
Bartels, Adolf, 386
Baudissin, Wolf von, 188, 276
Bayer, Friedrich, 323
Bebel, August, 358
Becker, Carl H., 225, 419, 420
Behrend, Felix, 280
Bell, Johannes, 64
Beltz, Martin, 365
Bergbohm, Karl, 192
Bergsträsser, Ludwig, 220
Berlin, 264, 274, 321, 362; Seminar for Oriental Languages, 223, 234; Technische Hochschule, 373, 378. *See also* Berlin University; Charlottenburg
Berliner Freie Presse, 347
Berliner Hochschulzeitung, 283
Berliner Tageblatt, 285
Berlin University, v, 18, 66, 67, 106, 111, 160, 164, 165, 172-75, 186, 188, 224, 243, 337, 394, 408; enrollment, 12, 23, 30, 31; social origin of students, 87, 93, 122, 123; political activity, 176, 181-83, 187, 202, 203, 217, 284, 285, 287-88, 296, 350-51, 370; nationalism, 187, 289, 368; political education, 188, 190, 194, 197-99, 207, 208, 212, 214, 221, 227; historical teaching, 200, 219; student organizations, 273-77, 296-98, 305, 353, 364, 375, 382, 387; academic freedom, 368, 369; sources on, 426-28
Bernhard, Ludwig, 174, 221, 228
Bernhardi, Friedrich von, 209
Bernheim, Ernst, 68
Bernstein, Eduard, 258, 288
Beseler, Georg, 179, 191, 337, 348
Beseler, Hans von, 112
Bestimmungsmensur, 244, 246-47, 249, 253-55, 261-62, 279, 289, 291, 330, 333, 396. *See also* duelling
Bethmann Hollweg, Theobald von, vi, 159, 204, 223, 224, 264
Bezold, Friedrich von, 202
Bildung, 9, 19-20, 51, 102, 164, 177, 181, 217-18, 337, 403, 410; arrogance of, 20, 43, 120, 187; erosion of, 24, 51, 404-05; social conception of, 78, 83, 99, 133, 411; vindication by victory, 160; political mission of, 161, 162-63, 166,

188-89, 225-28; tension with professional training, 165; apolitical tone of, 165, 262, 345; freedom necessary for, 241; modernization of, 278-79; wartime brutalization, 414; political failure of, 423-25. *See also* liberal education; neohumanism

Bildungsbürgertum, 8, 20, 69, 86, 87, 311-12; as stratum, 81-82, 88, 121-22, 129, 131, 187, 411-12; neohumanist ideology, 83-84, 158; self-recruitment of, 86-87, 122, 124, 127, 130, 135, 143, 146, 149, 150; influence of, 89, 158, 161, 408; fields of study, 151; reversal of, 158-59, 353-56, 377, 400-04; internal differentiation, 158-59, 401, 403, 407; ambivalence toward Nazis, 422. *See also Akademiker*

Bildungsroman, 9

Birnbaum, professor, 264

Bismarck, Otto von, vi, 32, 46, 58-61, 171, 187, 194, 199, 201, 220, 268, 274, 292, 338, 352, 366, 404, 426; cult of, 3-6, 387; unification and nationalism, 6, 20, 21, 167, 179, 182, 192, 207, 214, 257; conservatism, 178, 181, 218, 264, 269; power politics, 203, 232; universal suffrage, 205; *Realpolitik*, 210, 211; and student corporations, 249, 253, 254, 321, 325, 388

Blaschko, Dr., 243

Blaustein, Arthur, 388

Bleichröder, Gerson, 269

Blücher, Field Marshal von, 395

Blum, Hugo, 351

Bohlen und Halbach, G. Krupp von, 397

Bonifatiusverein, 256, 297, 302

Bonn University, 3, 18, 67, 106, 116, 164, 194, 227, 234, 244, 394, 396-98; enrollment in, 23, 24, 35-37, 56, 90-94, 113; social origin of students, 93-96, 101, 115, 117, 122-28, 137-41, 143, 145-46, 149-50, 152, 314-15; nationalism, 116, 196, 198; political activity, 175, 214, 230, 285; political education, 190-95, 200-04, 207, 212, 221, 388; student organizations, 257, 263, 276, 283, 284, 295-98, 328, 370, 380, 382, 390; sources on, 426-28

Bornhak, Conrad, 192, 193, 213, 228

Borsig, August, 186

Bosse, Robert, 112, 172, 241, 242, 244, 249, 257, 276, 426

Böttger, Hugo, 324, 361, 363, 370, 384, 388, 409

Bourdieu, Pierre, 81

Brandenburg, 202, 295

Brentano, Lujo von, 21, 195, 196, 228, 276

Breslau University, 113, 227, 267, 272, 340, 380-82

Breysig, Kurt, 199, 204, 217, 228

Brotstudenten, 402, 405

Bruch, A., 3

Brunner, Heinrich, 179

Bruns, Carl, 160, 175

Bülow, Bernhard von, 65, 113, 174, 184, 216, 388

Bund Abstinenter Studenten, 243, 289, 290, 297, 299

Bundesarchiv, 427

Bundesrat, 112

Bund Jüdischer Corporationen (BJC), 273-74, 302, 306. *See also* Jews

Bünger, Richard, 62

bureaucracy, 30, 40-46, 71, 73; demand for academics, 40, 45, 48, 56, 74; composition of, 89, 126; based on higher education, 116-18, 119, 126, 155, 157; training for, 142-43, 155; attitudes toward, 196-98; and student corporations, 310-12, 320-24; authoritarianism of, 114, 359, 370, 371; political ambivalence of, 418-19, 422-23. *See also* Prussia, government

Bürgerschule, 59, 69, 84, 100

Bürgertum, 403, 407, 409, 411-12; *Spiessbürgertum*, 84, 126, 130; *Besitzbürgertum*, 86, 87, 122, 123-24, 126, 128, 130, 151, 167-68, 311-12, 409; *Kleinbürgertum*, 86, 87, 123-24, 151, 311-12, 401, 406. *See also Bildungsbürgertum*

Burschenschaft, 3, 5, 7, 10, 11, 12, 234, 236, 256, 265, 266, 270, 274, 283, 288, 291, 297, 299, 300, 303-06, 330, 332, 336, 374, 387, 388-91, 398, 409, 414-15, 419; erstwhile liberalism, 250, 346; organization (ADC), 251-52; corporatization, 252; reform discussion, 252-53; demographic pattern, 308-10; social structure, 310-14; study preferences,

Burschenschaft (*cont.*)
317-30; careers of, 322-24; Reichstag members of, 325-28; repoliticization, 343, 384; exclusion of Jewish members, 353-55; tradition of, 356, 379; opposition to socialism, 360-61; imperialism, 363-66; and Catholic baiting, 376; view of inpending war, 393-94. *See also* ADB
Burschenschaftliche Blätter, 252, 323, 354, 363, 384, 388, 393, 429
Burschenschaftliche Bücherei, 364, 429
Busz, Dr., 67
Buttlar, Freiherr von, 368

Cambridge, 41
Cardauns, H., 379
Carlsbad Decrees, 171, 413
Caro, Georg von, 323
Cartell Verband (CV), 261, 297, 299, 301, 304, 391; Catholic corporation, 256; hostility of Protestants, 256-57, 367-78; Center Party allegiance, 257-58, 343; demography of, 308-10; social structure of, 311-14; field of study, 317, 320; alumni careers, 324; Reichstag members of, 325-28; exclusion of Jews, 355; nationalization of, 378, 392. *See also* Catholic students
Catholics, 96; underrepresentation among academics, 96, 173, 231; campaign for equality, 98-99; academic hostility toward, 201, 230-31; dogmatic problems, 257, 377. *See also* Cartell Verband; Catholic students; Kartell Verband
Catholic students, 6, 84-85; underrepresentation, 96-98, 345; corporations, 256-58, 305; associations, 258-59, 305, 309, 367, 378; demography, 308-10; social structure, 310-16; field of study, 319-20; social activism, 361-62; campaign of Protestant students against, 373-76; nationalization of, 378, 386, 395. *See also* Cartell Verband; Kartell Verband; Unitas
Center party, 226, 235, 249, 257, 258, 325, 367, 368, 371, 373, 377, 378, 388
ceremonial speeches (*Festreden*), 164, 428; as expressions of academic mentality, 174-75; content of, 176-88; analysis of, 188-89

Charlottenburg, 368, 370, 372, 373, 377. *See also* Berlin, Technische Hochschule
chemists, 42, 53, 57, 119
Chicago, World Exhibition of 1893, 78
Christian Social party, 198
civic education, 165, 207; emergence of movement, 218-19; involvement of universities, 219-22; *Bürgerkunde*, 220, 221; effect on students, 222-23, 227
Civil Code (BGB), 47, 141, 179, 191
Claer, Old Boy, 249
Class, Heinrich, 209
clergy: Catholic, 42, 46, 96, 139-40; Protestant, 42, 46, 54, 62, 135-36; number of, 64, 68, 71; propensity to study, 119. *See also* theological faculty
Coblenz, 426, 427
Coburg, 262
Collier, Price, 333
Cologne, 96
Colonial League, 363
commerce, 116-18, 119, 126-27, 151
commercial academies, 32
Conrad, Johannes, 29, 33, 35, 40, 41, 43, 44, 46, 47, 53, 64, 100, 108, 126, 143, 145
conservatism, 179, 181, 264, 391, 409
Conservative party, 226, 241, 338, 420
Corps, 5, 11, 41, 155, 234-46, 252-54, 261, 279-80, 283, 291, 294-300, 303-06, 329, 331, 335, 374, 378, 382-83, 391, 398, 414-15, 419, 427; duelling code, 247; elitism, 247; political neutrality, 247; character training, 247-48; *Senioren Convent* (SC), 248; reform of, 249; life principle, 249, 304; career patronage, 250, 294, 321-24; demography, 308-10; social structure, 311-14; study preferences, 317-20; political influence, 321, 343; Reichstag members of, 325-28; exclusion of Jews, 353; opposition to socialism, 357; politicization, 366, 385, 395; dominance of, 402
Curti, Thoedor, 263
Curtius, Ernst, 175, 176, 178, 179
Curtius, Ludwig, 332

Dahlmann, Friedrich Christoph, 206, 209, 430
Dahrendorf, Ralf, 80, 156, 423

Dambach, jurist, 193
Danzig, 370
Darmstadt, Technische Hochschule, 368, 370
Darwin, Charles, 170, 211. *See also* Social Darwinism
Daude, Paul, 370, 371, 374
Dawson, William H., 333
DC, 254, 354, 381, 383, 384, 387. *See also* Burschenschaft (ADC)
DCSV, 297, 306, 381
Delage, Eduard, 413
Delbrück, Hans, 187, 199, 203, 204, 359, 397
demographic structure of student body, 84-85, 90-113; Protestant theology, 137; Catholic theology, 139; law, 143; medicine, 145-46; philosophy, 149, 150; corporations, 305-10; Marburg students, 314-16; faculties of study, 317-20. *See also* student age; student geographic origin; student religion; student secondary education; student sex
Denkschrift über die Förderung der Auslandsstudien, 225
dentistry, 47, 150
depression, 30; *Grosse Depression* (1873-96), 44, 73; Great Depression (1929), 31, 420
Dernburg, Heinrich, 350, 351
Dertz, law student, 4
Deutsch-Akademischer Freibund, 388
Deutsche Hochschule, 377
Deutscher Studentendienst 1914, 398
Deutscher Wissenschafter Verband (DWV), 260, 307, 381. *See also* scholarly associations
Deutsche Soziale Blätter, 324
Deutsche Staatsbibliothek, 428
Deutsche Studentenschaft, 417, 419, 421
Deutsche Vaterlandspartei, 399
Deutsche-Völkischer Studentenverband, 381, 386, 402
Diels, Hermann, 186
Dieterici, Wilhelm, 27, 29
Dietz, E., 354
Dietzel, Hermann, 196
Dilthey, Wilhelm, 196
doctors, 42; victory over surgeons, 47, 82, 144; surplus of, 53, 56, 62, 71; associa-tion of, 63, 89; opposition to modern high school graduates, 104; opposition to women, 113; propensity to study, 119; rivalry with lawyers, 145. *See also* professions
Dove, Alfred, 201, 202
Dresden, 370
drinking, 235, 243, 246, 249, 262; rites, 4-5, 245, 262, 268, 274, 392; compul-sion of, 243, 245, 247, 253; rejection of, 243, 255, 284, 289, 290. *See also* Bund Abstinenter Studenten
Droysen, Johann Gustav, 199, 200, 202
Dubois-Reymond, Emil, 160, 175, 176, 178
Dubrowski, Dimitri, 66
duelling, 235, 244, 246, 247, 251, 254; rejection of, 244, 253, 255-57, 279, 290; social discrimination, 252; ritualiza-tion of, 261-62; *Waffenring* and Marburg Agreement, 291-92, 298; test of charac-ter, 330; political duels, 350-51. *See also Bestimmungsmensur*
duelling corporations, 235-36, 245, 247-54, 298, 331, 335, 346; demography of, 308-10; social structure of, 310-14; fields of study, 316-21; Reichstag mem-bers, 325-28. *See also* student corpora-tions
Dühring, Eugen, 194, 264
Duisberg, Carl, 28
Dulon, Paul, 265
Du Mont, Joseph Neven, 323
Durkheim, Emile, 217

Ecole, Normale, 6
economic growth, 399; enrollment expan-sion, 16, 40, 42-43, 44-45, 48, 73; changes in academic recruitment, 119, 123, 128
economic sectors, 114, 116-20; rise of service sector, 129; Protestant theologi-ans, 137; Catholic theologians, 140; law students, 143; medical students, 146; philosophy students, 149, 150; changes in, 155-56; student corporations, 310-14; faculties of study, 317, 320. *See also* agriculture; bureaucracy; commerce; in-dustry
educational inequality, v, 17, 81, 90-91;

educational inequality (*cont.*)
neohumanist egalitarianism, 9, 78, 83, 424; of working-class offspring, 80, 86, 133; of rural children, 80, 93-95; of Catholics, 80, 95-99; of women, 80, 109-13; shift from formal to informal discrimination, 156-57. *See also* social mobility
educational mobilization, 16, 32, 48-49, 70, 72-73, 76. *See also* enrollment growth
educational opportunity, 80, 91, 115, 129-31, 156, 280
educational protectionism, 30, 63, 65, 66, 406
Eichler, Otto, 351
Einjährige Freiwillige, 88, 344. *See also* student military service
Eisenach, 371, 374
Eisenacher Deputierten Convent, 250, 251, 354, 363
Eisenacher Kartell Akademisch-Theologischer Vereine, 259, 260, 302
elite, 86, 315-16; fusion into imperial ruling class, 133, 144, 146, 158, 403; background of corporations, 311, 314, 317, 320; of student reformers, 328
enrollment growth, 12, 16, 18, 23, 27, 30-31, 39, 63, 74, 123, 127, 417, 420; consequences of, 24, 25, 61-62, 186; causes of, 24, 28-30, 33-49, 417, 420; contraction of, 25, 27, 30, 34, 396, 419, 422; of secondary schools, 35-37; in different faculties, 46-48; per age cohort, 75-76; and social mobility, 128-30; and deliberalization, 401, 405
entitlements, 10, 25, 34, 63, 84, 134, 151, 153-55, 157, 407, 412
Erbach-Fürstenau, Count, 290
Erlangen University, 388, 421, 422, 427
Ernst Moritz Arndt Gymnasium, vi
Eulenberg, Franz, 34, 38, 125, 131
Evangelischer Akademischer Missionsverein, 299
Evangelischer Bund, 297, 368, 378
Evangelisch-Sozialer Kongress, 361

Fabricius, Wilhelm, 249, 291
Falk, Adalbert, 36, 104, 106, 110, 166, 337, 340, 426

Fallersleben, Hoffman von, 242
Farbentragende Verbindungen, 297. *See also* student organizations
fees, 30, 40, 61, 66
Fichte, Johann Gottlieb, 84, 161, 399, 413
financial aid, 40-41, 60-61, 131
Finken, 277, 278, 283, 284, 374. *See also* Freistudentenschaft
Finkenblätter, 429
First World War, 12, 31, 224, 393; student reaction to, 394, 396, 397; professorial support for, 394, 397; death of volunteers, 395; front experience, 396; political impact, 396, 399, 421; effect on student subculture, 398-99
Fischer, Fritz, 416
Fischer, Theobald, 252, 276
Fläschendräger, W., 430
Fletcher, John M., 430
Flexner, Abraham, 423
Flottenprofessoren, 214, 231
Foerster, Friedrich Wilhelm, 222, 228
Foerster, Wilhelm, 181, 352
Fontane, Theodor, 158
foreign students, 38, 51, 64-67, 91, 93, 287, 381
forestry, 47
Förster, Bernhard, 265
Fout, John C., 430
François-Ponçet, André, 344, 345
Franconia, 193
Frankfurt, 11, 220, 427
Frauenbund, 297, 381. *See also* women
Frederick the Great, 161, 200, 218
Frederick William III, 83, 165, 177
Free Conservatives, 226
Freiburg University, 263, 284, 357, 380, 382
Freideutscher Jugendtag, 289
Freideutscher Verband, 290
Freie Vereinigung, 297. *See also* women
Freie Wissenschaftliche Vereinigung (FWV), 266, 271-72, 275, 286, 297, 325-28, 349-51, 352, 355, 387, 402. *See also* student politics
Freischar, 289, 290, 297, 302, 331, 381. *See also* Akademische Freischar
Freistudentenschaft, 51, 66, 92, 236, 295, 297, 399, 302-04, 363, 374, 387, 401-02, 414, 417, 427, 429; organization of, 277-78, 281; goals, 278-79, 280, 282,

356; reform of cultivation, 279, 280, 293, 331; representation principle, 279, 280, 284-86, 293, 390; social activism, 279, 280, 287; political neutrality, 280, 285, 286, 288, 293; implicit liberalism, 280, 281, 286-87, 293; sections, 281-82, 293; offices, 282-83; hostility of corporations, 283-84, 292; and Catholics, 287, 376; influence of, 290; vulnerability on right, 293; social composition of, 316, 328-29; campaign for self-government, 380; wartime activities, 398-99. See also student reformers
Freistudentischer Bund, 278, 381
Friedberg, Raphael, 341
Friedberg, Robert, 58, 241, 373

Gans, economist, 194
Gay, Peter, 229
Gebildete, 8, 53; arrogance of, 43, 82-83, 84, 129; levels of, 88; leadership role, 391; disdain for politics, 403-04; ambivalence toward the city, 410-12; politicization, 412; attitude toward Weimar, 420; political failure of, 423-25. See also Akademiker; Bildungsbürgertum
Gelehrtenstand, 82, 104
generational rebellion, 15, 391, 399, 400-01, 421
George, Stefan, 217
Gerber, minister, 61, 106
Gerhardt, Carl, 103, 172
Gerlach, Hellmuth von, 270
German problem, vi, 229-30, 416-17, 423-25
Gerstenhauer, Max Robert, 365
Gewerbeschule, 37
Gierke, Otto von, 228, 284
Giessen University, 380, 382, 427, 428
Gildemeister, J. G., 231
Gneist, Rudolf von, 141, 176, 190, 193, 209, 338
Godan, cobbler, 341
Goethe, Johann Wolfgang von, 178, 190, 414
Göppert, councillor, 338
Goslarer Verband Naturwissenschaftlicher und Medizinischer Vereine, 259, 302
Gossler, Gustav von, 37, 53, 54, 58, 60, 70, 171, 242, 250, 340, 350

Gothein, Eberhard, 19, 196
Göttingen University, 4, 5, 11, 86, 87, 105, 227, 243, 310, 336, 375, 382, 387, 427, 428
graduates of the university, 70, 89; deficit of, 30, 62, 64; demand for, 34, 40, 45-46, 54-57, 62; career choices, 134-51, 312-14. See also Gebildete
Greifswald University, 106, 227, 375, 382, 421
Grenzboten, 243
Greving, Theodor, 349
Grimm, Jacob, 178
Grossman, J., 349
Gruber, Hugo, 42
Guttmann, free-student, 286
Gymnasium, 29, 34-35, 59-60; classical training, 8, 43; university monopoly, 30, 34, 60, 63, 85, 108, 134, 178; enrollment in, 38-39, 51, 59; as comprehensive school, 70, 83; social composition of, 78, 85, 86, 101-02; struggle to defend prerogatives, 100-09; political ignorance of pupils, 219; regimentation of, 239, 260. See also Abitur

Habilitation, 167, 168, 194
Haeckel, Ernst, 255
Hague peace conference, 194
Hahn, Dietrich, 270
Halle University, 33, 67, 103, 112, 172, 263, 267, 272, 276, 370, 380, 382
Hamburg, 4, 223
Hamburg-Altonaer Volksblatt, 347
Hammerstein, Hans von, 250
Hänel, Albert, 338
Hannoverscher Courier, 370
Hanover Technische Hochschule, 368, 370-73
Harden, Maximilian, 217
Harnack, Adolf von, 24, 184, 219, 224, 279, 414
Hart, James Morgan, 260
Hashagen, Justus, 203
Havenstein, Rudolf, 397
Hebbel, Friedrich, 282
Heer, Georg, 252, 363
Hegel, Georg Friedrich Wilhelm, 161, 209, 413
Heidelberg University, 86, 263, 284, 328,

Heidelberg University (*cont.*)
354, 370, 380, 382; declaration, 248;
Saxo-Borussia, 310; Studentenausschuss,
379
Heile, Wilhelm, 367, 371-73
Heimberger, Joseph, 206
Heine, Wolfgang, 270, 358
Heinzig, Dr., 278
Held, Adolf, 195, 214
Helfferich, Karl, 224
Helmholtz, Hermann von, 170, 177, 180
Henrici, Ernst, 288
Hertling, Georg Freiherr von, 96, 231, 256
Hertwig, Oskar, 186
Hess, Joseph, 226
Hessisches Staatsarchiv, 427
Heuss, Theodor, 20
Heydebrand und der Lase, Ernst von, 288
higher education, 26, 27, 30-32, 423; rela-
tive autonomy, 73; inclusiveness, 75-76,
80; segmentation, 91, 100-09; progres-
siveness, 114; reform of, 177-78, 185-
86; as intermediary factor, 400. *See also*
technical universities; university
Hildesheim, 373
Hinschius, Paul, 252
Hintze, Otto, 45, 199, 202, 214, 215, 408
Hirche, Old Boy, 249
history: Prussian school, 179-80, 200-01,
212, 214, 400; lectures, 199; hermeneutics, 200; Ranke renaissance, 201-03; repoliticization, 204-05
history of education, 13, 14-15, 18, 53,
79, 236, 399-400
Hitler, Adolf, vi, 416, 421, 422
HKT Society, 232. *See also* Ostmarkenverein
Hoche, Alfred, 20
Hochschulnachrichten, 429
Hochschulstreit, 100, 241, 287, 387; origin, 367-68; spread, 368-69; academic
freedom, 369-71; mediation by the ministry, 371-72; Landtag debate on, 372-
73; national student government, 374-75;
conference of rectors, 375; reasons for
agitation, 377-78; consequences of, 378-
79. *See also* Catholic students
Hochschulverband, 421
Hödel, assassin, 264
Hoensbroech, Paul von, 367

Hoesch, Emil, 323
Hoffmann, Johannes G., 29, 44
Hoffmann, Walter G., 44, 45
Hofmann, August W. von, 177, 267, 268
Hohe Meissner, 290
Hohenlohe-Langenburg, Alexander von,
173
Hohenzollerns, 5, 200, 205, 214, 215,
230, 233, 270, 357
Holle, minister, 113, 174
Holstein, Friedrich von, 216
Holtzendorff, Franz von, 206-08, 228
Holzapfel, Richard, 350
Horn, E., 429
Hüffer, Hermann, 191
Humboldt, Wilhelm von, 9, 15, 30, 36,
78, 83, 84, 102, 161, 188; reforms of,
v, 9, 30, 78, 83; liberalism of, 161,
403; gap in system, 237, 246, 330; ero-
sion of legacy, 404, 424. *See also Bil-
dung*; liberal education; neohumanism
Humboldt-Universität, 427, 428. *See also*
Berlin University
Huss, Johann, 367

Ibsen, Henrik, 282
illiberalism, 12, 21, 194, 334; concept,
228-29; political instruction, 229-30;
Verein Deutscher Studenten, 274-75;
corporate character training, 331-32,
352; Catholic baiting, 371-78; sources
of, 388, 404-10; pattern of, 399-404;
consequences of, 410-14; comparative
perspective on, 414-16; continuity of,
416-25. *See also* liberalism; nationalism
immaturi, 56, 91
Imperial Bank, 397
imperialism, 183-84, 196, 199, 231-32,
408; navalism, 204, 205-06, 214; in political teaching, 208, 212, 215-16, 223-
24; among students, 270, 363-65, 366;
liberal, 384; pan-German, 385; social,
395, 400-01; wartime, 397. *See also*
Alldeutscher Verband; *Flottenprofessoren*
industry, 116-18, 119, 126-27, 151
Innsbruck University, 368
institutes, 47, 49, 50, 186
Institut für Hochschulkunde in Würzburg,
19, 428

international education, 186, 207, 223-27. *See also* imperialism; political education
international student movement, 303, 392
Irmer, deputy, 241

Jahn, Friedrich Ludwig, 254, 291, 365
Jaspers, Karl, 424
Jastrow, Ignaz, 359
Jena University, 236, 370, 380, 382, 385, 388
Jencks, Christopher, 17
Jews, 64-65; structure of German students, 96-100; discrimination against, 231, 350, 378, 390; student associations, 272-74, 305, 356; Reichstag members, 325-28; Gentile attitudes toward, 355, 356, 360. *See also* anti-Semitism; Bund Jüdischer Corporationen; Kartell Convent
journalism, 42, 286
Jungdeutschlandbund, 219

Kaehler, Siegfried, 237
Kaelble, Harmut, 80
Kaftan, Julius, 185
Kahl, Wilhelm, 50, 184, 186, 191
Kaiser Wilhelm Stiftung, 50, 186. *See also* institutes
Kanitz, Hans von, 58
Kant, Immanuel, 177, 185, 206
Karier, Clarence, 17
Karlsruhe Technische Hochschule, 368, 370
Kartell Convent (KC), 272-73, 301, 356, 376, 381; *KC Blätter*, 429. *See also* Jews
Kartell Verband (KV), 297, 299, 301, 304, 306, 322; organization of, 258; Catholic ideology, 258-59; demography, 308-10; social structure, 311-14; study preferences of, 317-20; alumni careers, 324; Reichstag members of, 325-28; expansion of, 347; exclusion of Jews, 355; persecution of, 367-78. *See also* Cartell Verband; *Hochschulstreit*
Kartell Zionistischer Korporationen, 274, 301, 306
Kassel, 289
Kempener, Max, 69
Kerschensteiner, Georg, 220

Kiel University, 223, 227, 336, 357, 370, 382, 388
Kirchhoff, Adolf, 178
Kleinert, Hugo, 99
Klötzer, W., 236
Kobner, jurist, 193
Kocka, Jürgen, 80
Kohlschütter, Ernst, 172, 173
Königsberg University, 106, 110, 193, 227, 263, 341, 383, 388
Kormann, Karl, 356
Kösener S. C. Verband (KSC), 248, 254, 260, 322, 323, 325, 327, 353, 374, 381, 391. *See also* Corps
Koser, Reinhold, 202
Kotzebue, August Friedrich von, v
Kries, Wilhelm, 387
Krupp, Alfred, 186
Kultur, 89, 230; cultural mission, 65, 186, 223-24, 402; *Kulturstaat*, 161-62, 176, 208, 210, 390; victory over France, 161, 175
Kulturkampf, 6, 46, 55, 98, 181, 191, 230, 287, 298, 347; academic, 368-78, 380, 415
Küster, Konrad, 252, 253
Kyffhäuser-Verband, 270, 385. *See also* Verein Deutscher Studenten

Laband, Paul, 191
Lagarde, Paul de, 177
Lamprecht, Karl, 50, 381
Landrat, 42, 323
Landsmannschaft, 260, 261, 291, 297, 299, 300, 304, 306, 321, 349, 374, 376, 381, 419, 429; tradition, 247; organization, 253; lack of ideology, 254; demography of, 308-10; social structure, 310-14; study preferences of, 317, 320; Reichstag members of, 325-28; exclusion of Jews, 355
Landtag, 47, 51, 53, 61, 66, 67, 78, 108, 341; debate on overcrowding, 58, 64, 76; on secondary education, 106; on female study, 110-13; reform of legal training, 142; on Socialists, 173-74; on world political education, 224-25; on Corps abuses, 235, 242, 249; on academic freedom, 240-41; on Catholic associations, 257; on free students, 285-

Landtag (*cont.*)
86; members from student corporations, 323, 325-28; on academic discipline, 337-39; on Althoff system, 372-73
Lange, Helene, 111
Langemarck, 395
Langerhans, Paul, 337
Lasker, Eduard, 338
Lass, jurist, 193
Lavisse, Ernest, 6
law faculty, 27, 31, 46-47, 48, 56, 62; social composition, 87, 142-43; Latin requirement, 108-09; legal training, 140-42; legal nationalism, 179; political lectures, 190-95; rejection of natural law, 191-92, 213, 230; student corporations, 317. *See also* lawyers
lawyers, 42, 53, 56, 62, 64, 68, 104-07, 142-44
lectures, 40, 242; legal, 164, 189-90, 190-93; economical, 164, 189-90, 194-99; historical, 166, 189-90, 199-205; political, 164, 206-18, 227; implications of, 189, 205-06. *See also* history; political science
Ledebour, Georg, 357
Lehmann, Heinrich, 193
Lehmann, Rudolf, 133
Lehrplan, 59, 107, 219
Leibniz, Gottfried Wilhelm, 76
Leipziger Vorwärts, 347
Leipzig University, 34, 50, 254, 265, 278, 288, 387, 392; enrollment, 31, 61; student origins, 93, 122, 123, 125; student groups, 263, 267, 272, 277, 284, 381, 383; politics, 264, 388
Lentz, August, 225
Lenz, Max, 125, 185, 199, 202
Leo XIII, Pope, 257
Leuchtenberg-Bund Historischer Vereine, 259, 302
lex Arons, 167, 172-73, 359
Lexis, Wilhelm, 54-57, 62, 63, 112
liberal education, vii, 9, 10, 43, 176-77, 425; erosion of, 12, 51, 76, 404-05; teacher training, 147-48; political impact, 163-64, 188-89; in civics, 218-23; in international education, 225-28; illiberal outcome of, 405, 408-09, 424. *See also* Bildung; neohumanism
liberalism, 11, 70, 182, 355, 371-76, 377,

400; *Bildungsliberalismus*, vii, 9, 10, 11, 89, 165-66, 242, 267, 408; desertion of, 7, 12, 178-79, 180, 198, 201, 209-18, 221, 228-33, 250-52, 292-93, 348-49; in scholarship, 190-91, 194, 195-96; postliberalism, 198, 203, 222, 230; neoliberalism, 204, 230, 388, 420; as minority student tradition, 272, 287-88, 402; reasons for failure of, 389-90, 404-05, 414-16, 423-25
Liebert, Georg von, 386
Liebknecht, Karl, 66, 76, 78, 116, 231, 232, 285, 389
Lilge, Fredric, 423
Litzmann, Berthold, 230
Lohan, Max, 267
Löwenstein, Prince zu, 290
Luthardt, Christoph, 267
Luther, Martin, 99, 164, 178, 201
Lutz, H., 340
Lützow free corps, 7
Lux, Dr., 357
Lyzeum, 101, 109, 110, 113

Mallinckrodt, Gustav von, 323
mandarins, 8, 157, 282, 329
Marburg University, 19, 223, 256, 336; political activity, 106, 269, 285, 370-72, 375, 380, 386, 420; student organizations, 263, 274, 276, 278, 284, 293, 295-98, 305, 308, 311, 312, 318, 320-21, 328, 357, 383; social structure of, 310, 314-16; sources on, 427
Markuse, J., 340
Marr, Wilhelm, 265
Martitz, Ferdinand von, 212, 213
Marxism, 116, 182, 183, 192, 195, 214, 231, 264, 357, 359, 416. *See also* Socialism
Massow, Julius von, 135
matriculation, 36-37, 90n, 112-13, 175, 242; registers, 18, 90, 114, 427. *See also* admissions
Maurenbrecher, Wilhelm, 200, 201
medical faculty, 27, 31, 47, 48, 56, 62; social composition of, 87, 146; admission of modern high school graduates, 107-08; admission of women, 110-13; training in, 144-45; demography of, 145-46; student corporations, 317, 320. *See also* doctors

Medizinalrat, see doctors

Meinecke, Friedrich, 7, 19, 204

Meinhof, Ulrike, v

Merseburg Archives, 426

Metchild, 297. *See also* women

Metternich, Clemens von, 10, 30, 334, 389

Michels, Robert, 161

Ministry of Culture, 18, 39-40, 243, 244, 249, 250, 257, 419, 426; policy toward overcrowding, 58-61, 63-64, 70, 74-75; policy toward foreign students, 65-67; policy toward school reform, 106-09, 110-13; policy toward political education, 162-64, 171-74, 218-28; policy toward student politics, 228, 240-41, 336-39, 349-51; policy toward socialism, 264, 340-41; policy toward student organizations, 267-68, 276-78, 285, 321; policy toward religious student struggles, 369-78. *See also* Prussia

Miquel, Johannes von, 63, 108

Mittelstand, 4, 70, 86, 124; old, 122, 123, 125-26, 130; new, 122, 123, 125-26, 129, 130; policy to strengthen, 130, 195, 199, 205; underrepresentation, 133, 168; arrival of, 156; student corporations, 311-12. *See also Bürgertum*

mittlere Reife, 72, 88, 150

modernization, 8, 14, 16, 25-26, 410; and enrollment expansion, 40, 48-49, 72-74; and transformation of student origins, 114-34; of higher education, 177-78

Moldenhauer, Dr., 234

Moltke, Helmuth von, 274

Mommsen, Theodor, 24, 76, 173, 175, 176, 199, 231, 265, 269, 337

Mönchen-Gladbach, 361

Mönckeberg, burgomaster, 4

Mühler, Heinrich von, 36, 106, 110, 166

Müller, Detlev K., 25, 52

Münchener Allgemeine Zeitung, 57

Munich University, 31, 284, 370, 381, 387, 414

Münster University, 67, 144, 227, 257, 357, 381

Napoleon, 7, 27, 128, 165, 176, 187, 215, 250, 292

Nasse, Erwin, 214

nationalism, vi, 4-7, 12, 21, 69, 176, 179, 188, 203, 392, 408, 421; academic, 162, 180, 187, 211, 288, 393-94, 400; shift from liberal to conservative, 188, 230, 292, 391, 400; critique of, 188, 196, 271-72, 280; in teaching, 203, 218-23, 219-28; among student corporations, 234-36, 268-69, 321-22, 342, 345, 348-49, 363-66, 367-73, 374-75, 402; anti-Semitic, 264-66, 270-71, 272-73; Nazi appeal, 423-24. *See also* liberalism

National Liberals, 58, 214, 226, 324, 338, 384, 419

National Socialism, v, 12, 396, 416, 420-24

National Socialist Student League (NSDStB), v, 419-23

Nationalzeitung, 54

Naumann, Friedrich, 204, 222, 270, 275, 361, 384

Naumann, Geheimrat, 369, 371

Naumburger Kartell-Verband Klassisch-Philologischer Vereine, 259, 302

Navy League, 363, 364, 385

neoconservatism, v, 12, 422, 423

neohumanism, v, 20, 48, 73, 82, 84, 160, 165-66, 241, 403; classicism, 9, 84, 89; hold on secondary education, 35, 102-03, 107-09; reaffirmation of, 176-77, 188-89, 217-18; modernization of, 278, 405-06; metamorphosis of, 334, 389, 410, 424-25. *See also Bildung*; liberal education

neo-Kantians, 185, 230

Neumann, Hans, 291

Nietzsche, Friedrich, 160, 176, 217, 404

Nipperdey, Thomas, 163, 416

Nippold, Otfried, 367

Nobiling, Karl Eduard, 264

nobility, 85, 86, 87, 120-21, 143, 310, 321

Norddeutsche Allgemeine Zeitung (NAZ), 53, 60, 112, 370, 375

North Schleswig Society, 363

NSDStB, *see* National Socialist Student League

Oberlehrer, see teachers

Oberrealschule, 36-37, 59, 60, 101-09. *See also* secondary education

Oehlke, Alfred, 350

Ohr, Wilhelm, 286, 346, 371

Old Boys, 19, 234, 235, 244, 249, 253, 255, 257, 261, 304, 321, 323, 331, 361, 363, 384, 385. *See also* Alte Herren
Old Heidelberg, 19
Ordinarius, 50, 169. *See also* professors
Osten-Warnitz, Count von, 67
Osthoff, professor, 354
Ostmarkenverein, 297, 363, 385. *See also* HKT Society
overcrowding, v, 24, 30, 32-33, 46-47, 50-72; effect of, 61-62, 63, 107, 110, 406, 410, 421. *See also* academic proletariat
Oxford, 41

Paasche, Herrmann, 68
pacifists, 172-73, 188, 204, 231, 392
Pan-German League, 203, 270, 363, 364. *See also* Alldeutscher Verband
Parsons, Talcott, 16
Paulsen, Friedrich, 13, 43, 78, 133, 185, 240, 245, 330; on social transformation, 116, 158, 407; political views, 170, 189, 232, 344
Peltasohn, Martin, 241
Penck, Albrecht, 397
Peters, Karl, 209, 364
Petersilie, Albert, 33, 129
Petry, Ludwig, 429
Pfleiderer, Otto, 182, 276, 288
pharmacy, 47, 150, 320
philosophical faculty, 27, 30, 31, 47, 48, 56-57; component subjects, 36, 57, 62, 103; social composition, 87, 148-50; admission of modern high school graduates, 106-09; curriculum of, 146-47, 177-78, 222; and student corporations, 320-21
Planck, Max, 66, 381
Poensgen, Ernst, 323
Pohl, Heinrich, 193
Polish students, 65, 341, 345
political culture, 17, 163-64, 221, 231
political education, 17, 20-21, 162-65, 167, 182, 391; patriotic indoctrination, 165-66, 188, 334, 391; in scholarly lectures, 205-06; in political lectures, 206-18; in civics, 219-22; in international education, 223-28; deliberalization of, 228, 232-33, 408-09, 413; effectiveness of, 228, 394; by students themselves, 342-

43, 384-86. *See also* lectures; student politics
political science, 206-07; moderate liberalism, 207-08; deliberalization of, 208-12; science of politics, 212-13; historical politics, 214-18. *See also* state
Politische Wochenschrift, 32
Popert, Hermann, 290
population increase, 34, 48, 73, 93-94, 127-28
Porsch, Felix, 257, 368
Posadowsky-Wehner, Arthur von, 112
positivism, 181, 185-86, 189, 227, 401; legal, 191-93; economic, 197; historical, 201, 205; political, 212-13
Potsdam, 426
Potthoff, Hans, 288
Prague University, 131, 364
Preuss, Hugo, 193
Preussische Jahrbücher, 62, 204, 209, 265
Princeton University, 6
Privatdozent, 50, 168, 169, 172, 194. *See also* professors
professions, 8, 72, 73, 82, 89, 134-35, 144, 152, 411-12; training, 10, 20, 51, 135, 139, 141, 177, 260, 298, 413; examinations, 20, 82, 134; economic situation of, 29, 42, 45, 62, 68, 70-72; opening of, 109, 113; generic, 121, 124, 126; hierarchy, 121, 126, 133-34, 154, 412; political impact, 407, 420, 422. *See also* Akademiker; Bildungsbürgertum
professors, 49, 50, 67-68, 163-64, 169, 333; social origin, 79, 167-68, 231; and educational reform, 106, 113, 176-77, 185-86; patriotism, 170, 173, 182, 228, 230; deliberalization of, 189, 232, 260; political spectrum, 206, 230-31, 233, 418, 420; lingering liberalism, 268, 348; paternalism toward students, 391; support of war, 397; and Nazi seizure of power, 421, 423
progress, 11, 172. *See also* student reformers
Progressive party, 5, 226, 230, 241, 325, 327
Progymnasium, 59. *See also* Gymnasium
proletariat, 41, 86, 122, 123, 126, 133, 151, 168. *See also* academic proletariat; student poverty
Protestants, 84-85, 96-99, 100, 377

Prussia, 42, 66, 214; government, 8, 17, 58, 70, 75, 130, 148, 172, 173, 219, 264, 265, 324, 340, 377; reforms of, 9, 10, 78, 83, 176; cabinet (Ministry of State), 59, 63, 66, 107-09, 111-13, 172, 336-39, 413, 426-27; army, 107, 120; constitution, 214, 372; Ministry of Interior, 250, 321. See also Hohenzollerns; Ministry of Culture
Prussian Code (ALR), 8, 82
Puttkamer, Robert Victor von, 74, 267, 268, 339

qualification crisis, 25, 52, 69-70. See also overcrowding
Quidde, Ludwig, 231, 271

Rabe, Rudolf, 363
Radbruch, Gustav, 21
Rade, Martin, 223
radicalism, 53-54, 69, 77, 172, 406. See also student activism
Ranke, Leopold von, 199-202, 209, 214
Rassem, Mohammed, 237
Rathenau, Walter, v, 222
Realgymnasium, 36, 38-39, 58, 100; struggle for university admission, 59, 60, 103-09; social composition, 102. See also secondary education
Realpolitik, 176, 211, 230, 271, 413. See also Bismarck, Otto von
Realschule, 36. See also Oberrealschule
Reformburschenschaft, 311, 312, 314, 318, 320, 321, 325, 376. See also ADB
Reichensperger, Peter Franz, 235
Reichstag, vi, 5, 110, 142, 172, 180, 193, 209, 216, 223, 254, 276, 281, 292, 323, 380, 385; members from student corporations, 325-28
Reichsverband Deutsch-Völkischer Akademiker, 399
reserve officer ideal, 243, 290, 344, 345
Rheinbaben, Georg von, 112
Rheinische Hochschulzeitung, 283, 429
Rhenania, 234
Rhineland, 93, 94, 137, 139
Richard Wagner Verein, 309
Riehl, Wilhem von, 410
Rienhardt, Albert, 125, 127
Riezler, Kurt, vi
Ringer, Fritz, 80

Roethe, Gustav, 49, 187
Rogge, Christian, 274
Roscher, Wilhelm, 195, 209
Rostock University, 383, 386
Rothenburg, 269
Rubner, Max, 186
Rudelsburg, 262
Rüdesheimer affair, 372
Ruge, Arnold, 342
Ruppel, Wilhelm, 101
Russian students, 64-67

Salvisberg, Paul von, 429
Samassa, Paul, 65
Sand, Karl, v
Sängerschaft, 261, 305, 306, 349, 374, 381, 428; demography of, 308-10; social structure of, 311-14; study preferences of, 317-20. See also Sondershäuser Verband
Saxo-Borussia, 321. See also Corps
Schäfer, Arnold, 200
Schäfer, Dietrich, 199, 203, 397
Scherer, Wilhelm, 178
Scheuer, Oskar, 428
Schieder, Theodor, 162
Schiemann, Theodor, 173, 199, 203, 216, 217, 228
Schiller, Friedrich von, 415
Schirach, Baldur von, 420
Schleiermacher, Friedrich, 241
Schmidt-Ott, Friedrich, 426
Schmitt, Richard, 199
Schmoller, Gustav von, 122, 130, 174, 183, 184, 197, 198, 209, 217, 275
Schneider, Gustav Heinrich, 363
scholarly associations, 129, 159-60, 381; demography of, 308-10; social structure of, 311-14; study preferences of, 317-20; Reichstag members of, 326; patriotic indoctrination, 386. See also Deutscher Wissenschafter Verband
Schöneberg Gymnasium, 59
Schönfliess, A., 62
school conferences: of 1890, 37, 60, 70, 107, 219; of 1900, 36, 63, 70, 108-09, 219. See also secondary education
school law, 166, 336
Schrader, Wilhelm, 172
Schücking, Walter, 173, 231, 250
Schulte, Aloys, 204

Schulz, judge, 267

Schulze, Friedrich, 430

Schwarzburgbund, 255-56, 299, 300, 306, 355, 376, 391, 427

Schwendener, Simon, 181

secondary education, 34-37, 68, 91; enrollment in, 35-37, 61-62; reform of, 70, 74, 100-09

Seeberg, Reinhold, 187, 231

Sekretariat sozialer Studentenarbeit, 361

seminar, 49, 135, 147

seminaries, 31, 46, 135, 139

Sering, Max, 198, 224

Severing, Carl, 418

Siegmund-Schulze, Friedrich, 361

social control, 17, 334-35, 345, 389, 399

Social Darwinism, 188, 190, 211-12, 221

Social Democratic party, 5, 172, 195, 226, 229, 264, 325, 327, 341, 358, 360, 361, 385, 391, 396, 415. See also Marxism; Socialism

Socialism, 21, 123, 170, 172, 191, 201, 356, 385, 396, 415; academic hostility toward, 182, 205, 217, 378; criticized as unscientific, 183, 195-99; Christian Socialism, 292, 361; combatted by civics, 318-19; excluded from the university, 337, 340-41, 345; identified with Jews, 357; disinterest in students, 360, 362. See also Social Democratic party

Socialists of the Chair, 174, 276, 359, 360-62; immunization through reform, 182-83, 275, 401; liberals, 195-96; centrists, 196-98; social monarchists, 198-99. See also Verein für Sozialpolitik

socialist students, 6, 264, 331, 347, 401; persecution of, 340-41, 356-57; reasons for failure of, 358-60. See also Socialism

socialization, 17, 237-38, 329-30

social mobility, v, 52, 80, 155-56; through education, vii, 48, 129, 412-13; in various university faculties, 138, 140, 146, 149, 150; through cooperation, 406. See also educational opportunity

social origins (of students), 12, 17, 18, 79-80, 85-86, 126-34, 396; in terms of power, 115-16; in terms of class, 116-20; in terms of status, 120-34; of various professions, 137, 140, 144, 146, 149, 150; of Marburg students, 310, 314,

317; comparison of Marburg and Bonn patterns, 315-16; of faculties of study, 317, 320; of postwar students, 417, 419, 420

social question, 20, 281; academic reformism, 180, 195, 230, 275, 342, 408-09; social policy movement, 183, 195-99, 214; in political teaching, 208, 211-12, 213; student social activism, 275-77, 361-62. See also Socialists of the Chair

Sohm, Gustav, 275

Sondershäuser Verband, 291, 299, 304, 307, 381. See also Sängerschaft

Sonnenschein, Carl, 361

sources, 18-19, 426-30. See also matriculation

Sozialistischer Akademiker, 358, 429

Sozialwissenschaftliche Studentenvereinigung, 275-77, 357, 359, 402

Spahn, Martin, 173

Spangenberg, Max, 349-51

Spranger, Eduard von, 84, 165, 226

Ssymank, Paul, 13, 236, 294, 428, 430

Staatsbürger-Zeitung, 386

state, 51, 74, 83-84, 176, 215; ideal of Rechtsstaat, 89, 162, 176, 177, 190, 191, 201, 208, 392; rule of culture, 161-62, 176, 208, 210, 390; legal conception of, 191-95, 213; economic conception of, 196-99; historical conception of, 200-05, 215; political teaching about, 208, 210, 214-15, 216, 221-22. See also political science

state examinations, 10, 134; in theology, 135, 139; in law, 142; in medicine, 144-45; in philosophy, 145, 150; entitlement effect, 154-55, 242, 411

Statistical Bureau (of Prussia), 33-34, 54, 90, 116

Steiger, Günter, 429

Stein, Freiherr vom, 345

Stern, Fritz, 228

Sternfeld, professor, 199

Stier-Somlo, Fritz, 192, 221

Stöcker, Adolph, 5, 198, 264, 274

Stone, Lawrence, 16

Strassburg University, 5, 106, 166, 173, 272, 284, 384

stratification matrix, 81, 114-16, 120, 121-26

Straube, M., 429, 430

Strauss, David F., 255
student activism, v, 13, 15, 21, 65, 182, 264-65, 399. *See also* student politics
student age, 84, 90, 91-93; in various faculties, 137, 139, 143, 145, 149, 150; of corporation members, 305, 314. *See also* demographic structure of student body
student corporations, 51, 220-21, 237, 283, 414; character training, 17, 234, 247, 251, 331, 405; alumni of, 89, 249, 304, 324, 329; criticism of, 235-36, 245; dominance of corporatism, 261-62, 292, 293, 298, 331, 335, 346, 400-01, 409; patronage preferment, 294-95, 324, 328-29, 414; membership figures, 296-97, 298-99, 300-03, 304, 307-08; demography, 305, 308-10, 314; social origin, 314-16; fields of study, 316-21; Reichstag members, 325-28; political indoctrination, 333, 387, 392, 394; anti-Semitism, 353-56, 390; imperialism, 363-65, 366; Catholic baiting, 367-78; national organization of, 374, 376-78; postwar reemergence of, 419; collaboration with Nazis, 421; records, 427. *See also* Burschenschaft; Corps
student councils, v, 263, 280, 284, 335, 346, 347-48; Berlin struggle, 349-53; Catholic corporations, 368-77; emergence of student self-government, 379-84, 387; postwar struggle over, 417, 419; capture by Nazis, 421. *See also* Deutsche Studentenschaft; Verband Deutscher Hochschulen
student customs (*Komment*), 245, 246, 248, 258, 260, 289; *Kommers*, 4-5, 245, 262, 268, 274, 392; dialect, 245; songs, 262; *Kneipe*, 262, 330; *Kränzchen*, 330, 385, 387; *Karzer*, 338, 339. *See also* drinking; duelling
student debts, 244, 246, 253, 337
Studentenroman, 19
Studentenverband, 377, 380, 382-83, 388. *See also* Verband Deutscher Hochschulen
student experience, 19-21, 51-52, 132
student freedom, 19, 51, 239-41, 242-44, 260-61, 330, 333; lack of political freedom, 331, 337-39, 345, 369-72, 374-75, 381-84, 388, 389. *See also* students and politics

student geographic origin, 84-85, 90, 93-95, 98; in various faculties, 137, 139, 143, 145, 149, 150; of corporation members, 305, 314
student honor code, 245-46, 330; honor court, 246, 263, 279, 292; *satisfaktions fähig*, 246, 248, 251, 253; social discrimination, 249, 252, 338. *See also* duelling
student housing, 260, 261, 282
Studentische Orden, 430
student journals, 19, 239, 248, 252, 253, 255, 261, 283, 329, 331, 358, 361, 363, 377, 429
student loafing, 52, 131, 235, 242, 249, 402
student luxury, 132, 244, 249
student military service, 91, 242, 343-44, 345, 381
student organizations, 239, 294; corporatization, 237, 246, 260-62, 330; duelling, 246-54, 261; color carrying, 254-58, 261, 263; associations, 258-60, 261; size, 298-304; demography, 308-10; social composition, 310-14; fields of study, 316-21; nationalism of, 321-22, 333; regulation of, 337-40. *See also* student corporations
student politics, 17, 19, 335, 343, 346; impact of Verein Deutscher Studenten on, 274-75; emergence of modern, 335-36, 386-87; university control over, 338-40, 353; deliberalization of, 346-47, 390-91, 403; nationalist triumph in, 352, 389-90, 392, 409-10; anti-Catholic struggle, 367-78; divisions in, 400-03. *See also* students and politics
student poverty, 68, 129, 131-32, 357
student reformers, 11, 250, 263, 347, 401, 409; structure of, 309, 313, 319. *See also* Freistudentenschaft
student religion, 84, 91, 95-99; of various faculties, 143, 145-46, 149, 150; of corporation members, 305, 314
students and politics, 21, 170, 220, 225-28, 335, 341-43; ignorance of, 221-23, 228, 346; proscription of, 240, 241, 337-38, 339, 342-43; reversal to the right, 265, 335; nationalism of, 342, 345, 346, 389, 402
student secondary education, 84, 100-09;

student secondary education (*cont.*)
of various faculties, 137, 140, 143, 146, 149, 150; of corporation members, 305, 314
student sex, 91, 109-13, 243-44, 246, 255, 281, 289; of various faculties, 137, 143, 146, 149, 150; and student corporations, 289, 310, 316
students in other countries, 21, 414-16
student subculture, 12, 17, 19, 234, 236, 238, 239-40, 388; social structure of, 131-32, 406-07; traditional, 247-60, 331-32; modern, 277-83; reform of, 289, 292; turn to the right, 293, 356, 360, 366, 367-78; impact of war on, 398-99; illiberalism of, 413-14. *See also* student corporations; student organizations
student types, 401-02
Studt, Konrad von, 63, 66, 104, 112, 241, 371, 375, 379, 426
study: length, 38, 91; costs, 40, 41, 60-61; purpose, 132
Stumm-Halberg, Karl F. von, 174, 276
Stumpf, Carl, 284
Sybel, Heinrich von, 200, 207, 228, 230, 274, 337

Tacitus, 416
teachers, 42, 68-69; Gymnasium *Oberlehrer*, 42, 82, 408; demand for, 47, 53, 57, 62, 63; *Hilfslehrer*, 57, 58, 64; female, 113; propensity to study, 119; certification of, 147-48; demography, 149; social origin, 149-50; civics training, 222
technical universities, 32, 100, 120, 278; enrollment, 44, 48, 64; equality of, 74, 185; student organizations, 303, 304; anti-Catholic agitation, 367-78
theological faculty, 87, 108-09, 316-17; Catholic, 27, 31, 46, 48, 55, 139-40; Protestant, 27, 31, 46, 48, 55, 62, 135-38. *See also* clergy
Tirpitz, Alfred von, 204, 212, 216, 364
Tobler, Adolf, 181
Traub, Gottfried, 226
Treitschke, Heinrich von, 7, 20, 179, 199-201, 216, 217, 228, 231; Bismarck cult, 5, 265, 391; great power policy, 183; lectures on politics, 208-14

Troeltsch, Ernst, 418
Trott zu Solz, August von, 64, 67, 75, 187, 244-46
Tübingen University, 122, 123, 125, 147, 378, 380, 383
Turnerschaft (VC), 260, 275, 291, 297, 299, 300, 303-06, 322, 351-52, 374, 376, 381, 387, 389, 391, 419; organization, 254, 331; demography, 308-10; social structure, 311-14; field of study, 317-21; alumni careers, 323-24; Reichstag members of, 325-28; nationalization of, 343, 365-66, 385

Unitas, 259, 297, 299, 300, 306, 327, 391. *See also* Cartell Verband; Kartell Verband
Universität des Saarlandes, vi
Universitäts-Chronik, 428
university, 10, 16, 23, 28, 31, 32, 49, 50, 186-87; world renown of German, 7, 10, 23, 50, 187, 413; reform of, 11, 105-09, 112-13, 185, 186; social transformation of, 12, 24, 49, 72, 86, 134-55, 156, 401; curriculum of, 18, 135, 139, 141, 145, 147, 150, 190-232, 242; statistics on, 33, 54; state control over, 44, 161, 165-66, 171, 334; nationalist teaching, 219-22, 223, 331, 336, 378, 416-21; as public conscience, 232, 423-25; politicization of, 388, 390, 397, 408-09, 412-13; wartime adjustments, 396-99. *See also Bildung; Wissenschaft*

Vahlen, Johannes, 180
Vatican Council of 1870, 96
Verband Deutscher Hochschulen (VdH), 374-78, 382-83, 417. *See also* student councils
Verband Studierender Frauen Deutschlands, 113. *See also* women
Verband Theologischer Studentenvereine, 259
Verein Deutscher Studenten (VDSt), 4, 5, 65, 100, 258, 276, 284, 291, 294, 297, 298, 300, 303-05, 307, 319, 321-22, 348-50, 352, 365, 368, 374, 381, 387, 389, 391, 400, 402, 419; new nationalism, 266-67, 270-71, 332, 346, 364, 366, 384-85, 395; innovative methods,

266, 274, 390, 409, 420; anti-Semitism, 266-67, 270, 353-56; Christianity, 266-67; struggle for recognition, 267-69; Kyffhäuser celebration, 269-70; anti-Socialist reformism, 270, 357-58, 360, 361-62; impact on student politics, 274-75, 292-93, 343, 351; demography, 308-10; social composition, 311, 328; alumni careers, 323-24; Reichstag members, 325-28; anti-Catholicism, 367, 376. *See also* Kyffhäuser Verband

Verein für Sozialpolitik, 195, 197. *See also* Socialists of the Chair

Vereinigung zur Staatsbürgerlichen Erziehung des Deutsche Volkes, 219

Verein Jüdischer Studenten, 297

Vernunftrepublikaner, 420

Viadrina, 272

Vienna, 223, 368, 415

Virchow, Rudolf, 102, 112, 172, 174, 181, 231, 269, 352, 391

Volkshochschulkurse, 186, 362

Volksverein für das Katholische Deutschland, 361

Vopelius, Richard von, 323

Vorlesungsverzeichnis, 428

Vortrupp, 289

Vorwärts, 335, 357, 378, 379, 402

Wagner, Adolph, 23, 24, 182-84, 194, 198, 275, 276

Waldeyer, Heinrich von, 185

Wandervogel, 288-90, 297, 408

Wartburg, 262

Weber, Max, 79, 114, 115, 121, 153, 171, 185, 203, 222, 275

Wehrbund, 398

Weierstrass, Karl, 177

Weimar, 278, 418, 420; Freistudententag, 280, 281, 285, 286, 287, 288, 380; meetings of Verband Deutscher Hochschulen, 374; students, 417, 419, 420-22, 423

Weimarer Cartell-Verband Philologischer Verbindungen, 259, 260, 302

Weinhold, Karl, 181

Weiss, Johannes, 341

Weizsäcker, Julius, 180

Wenckstern, Adolph von, 214, 215

white-collar employees, 45, 126

Wilamowitz-Moellendorff, Ulrich von, 49, 107, 185, 243

William I, Kaiser, 4, 164, 194, 264, 268

William II, Kaiser, 4, 60, 107-09, 164, 173, 202, 205, 206, 216-18, 222, 226, 234, 239, 248, 288, 335, 360, 372-74, 388, 389, 392, 396, 408, 418

Wilmowski, Tilo von, 323

Wilson, Woodrow, 6

Windelband, Wilhelm, 5

Windthorst, Ludwig, 58, 257

Wingolf, 275, 297, 299, 300, 304, 306, 316, 319, 320, 324, 325, 349, 365, 374, 381, 391; organization and ideology, 255; demography, 308-10; social composition, 310-14; Protestant theological coloration, 317, 355, 376; anti-Socialist reformism, 357, 361-62

Wingolfsblätter, 255, 429

Wissenschaft, 9, 10, 16, 20, 177-78, 393, 404, 420, 424; world renown, 7, 77, 413, 424; rise of big science, 24, 76, 180-81; specialization of research, 50, 51, 76; loss of educational impact, 76, 160, 404; Protestant theology, 135; Catholic theology, 138-39; jurisprudence, 141; medicine, 144; philosophy, 147; problem of objectivity, 184-85, 193, 197, 203, 230, 232, 397; nationalism of, 187, 232, 233, 397. *See also* university

Wissenschafter Verband, 299. *See also* Deutscher Wissenschafter Verband

Wittenberg, 278

women, 39, 85, 109, 110, 396, 398; university admission, 24, 37-38, 64, 74, 109-13, 186; social composition of, 109; secondary training, 109-10, 112-13; associations of, 299, 302-03, 316, 381. *See also* student sex

workingmen's courses, 362

work-study, 40, 132, 417

Württemberg, 122, 127

Würzburg University, 19, 380, 383, 427

Wygodinski, Willy, 198

Wyneken, Gustav, 290

youth, 15, 92, 226, 330; moratorium, 19, 260; *Jugendpflege*, 219, 283; discovery of adolescence, 219, 408; youth move-

youth (*cont.*)
    ment, 288-89, 290; rightist rebellion,
    391. *See also* generational rebellion;
    Wandervogel

Zacher, professor, 103
Zadek, Dr., 357
Zander, Old Boy, 249
Zedlitz-Neukirch, Oktavio von, 64, 288

Zeller, Eduard, 177
Zentraluntersuchungskommission, 171
Ziegler, Theobald, 21, 131, 330, 341, 343
Zimmerman, Gustav, 371
Zorn, Philipp, 23, 24, 193, 249
Zorn, Wolfgang, 430
Die Zukunft, 217
Zweig, Stefan, 250
Zwick, deputy, 241

Library of Congress Cataloging in Publication Data

Jarausch, Konrad Hugo.
Students, society, and politics in imperial Germany.

Includes bibliographical references and index.
1. Education, Higher—Germany—History—19th
century. 2. Students—Germany—Political activity
—History—19th century. I. Title.
LA727.J36   378'.1981'0943   81-47926
ISBN 0-691-05345-6   AACR2
ISBN 0-691-10131-0 (pbk.)